Why You Need This New Edition

This fourth and newest edition of *Communication: Principles for a Lifetime* does more than present you with communication theories, principles, and skills to learn for a course. Beyond that, it aims to help you apply what you've learned in your life outside of the classroom and college. The authors have dedicated themselves to helping students understand the relationships among the concepts, skills, theories, and contexts of communication by framing their discussions around these five fundamental communication principles:

1. Be **aware** of your communication with yourself and others.
2. Effectively use and interpret **verbal** messages.
3. Effectively use and interpret **nonverbal** messages.
4. **Listen** and **respond** thoughtfully to others.
5. Appropriately **adapt** messages to others.

The previous three editions of *Communication: Principles for a Lifetime* have given countless students the tools needed to become more competent, confident communicators. The fourth edition is no exception, and it reflects the latest research and trends in the field. Following are some features of the fourth edition of *Communication: Principles for a Lifetime:*

- New **Assessing Your Knowledge** and **Assessing Your Skill** self-tests and assessment activities are included at the end of every chapter. These new assessment measures will help you master chapter material and enhance your communication skills.

- New and **expanded coverage of technology** and communication throughout the text looks at the ways technology influences our communication with others.

- New and updated web resources are included at the end of every chapter.

- A new emphasis on ethical communication includes expanded coverage in Chapter 6 and a newly revised interactive ethics feature, "**Ethics and Communication**," which challenges you to consider scenarios involving ethical issues and answer questions that reveal your own ethical views.

- An updated and revised feature in the Presentational Speaking section, "**Developing Your Presentation Step by Step**," illustrates one student's path through the steps in speech creation and delivery.

- Thoroughly updated research and content keeps you up to date on the latest information in the field.

PEARSON

Communication
Principles for a Lifetime

Steven A. Beebe
Susan J. Beebe
Diana K. Ivy

FOURTH CUSTOM EDITION
FOR EASTERN KENTUCKY UNIVERSITY

Taken from:

Communication: Principles for a Lifetime, Fourth Edition
by Steven A. Beebe, Susan J. Beebe, and Diana K. Ivy

Custom Publishing

New York   Boston   San Francisco
London   Toronto   Sydney   Tokyo   Singapore   Madrid
Mexico City   Munich   Paris   Cape Town   Hong Kong   Montreal

Cover Image: Courtesy of Photodisc/Getty Images.

Taken from:

Communication: Principles for a Lifetime, Fourth Edition
by Steven A. Beebe, Susan J. Beebe, and Diana K. Ivy
Copyright © 2010, 2007, 2004, 2001 by Pearson Education, Inc.
Published by Allyn & Bacon
Boston, Massachusetts 02116

Copyright © 2009, 2008, 2007, 2006 by Pearson Custom Publishing
All rights reserved.

Permission in writing must be obtained from the publisher before any part of this work may be reproduced or transmitted in any form or by any means, electronic or mechanical, including photocopying and recording, or by any information storage or retrieval system.

All trademarks, service marks, registered trademarks, and registered service marks are the property of their respective owners and are used herein for identification purposes only.

Printed in the United States of America

10 9 8 7 6 5 4 3 2 1

2009560095

LM

**Pearson
Custom Publishing**
is a division of

PEARSON

www.pearsonhighered.com

ISBN 10: 0-558-32143-7
ISBN 13: 978-0-558-32143-7

The Communication Studies Program at EKU

You are enrolled in a course offered by one of the most dynamic academic programs on the Eastern Kentucky University campus! The Communication Studies program offers a wide and interesting variety of courses that give students the opportunity to develop their professional knowledge and skills in such things as public speaking, interpersonal communication, conflict management and mediation, corporate communication training and development, interviewing, and organizational communication.

In the last few years, the number of EKU students who have declared a major in Communication Studies (CMS) *has nearly quadrupled*…and for many good reasons! Ask any CMS major and they will tell you that the CMS program is designed to prepare students to enter a broad spectrum of careers, including corporate communication, human services, sales and marketing, law and politics, seminary, human services, communication consulting, and higher education/research….just to name a few.

The Communication Studies program is driven by excellent, award-winning faculty. Full-time faculty currently includes: Dr. Amy Thieme, Dr. Karen Rudick, Dr. Jayne Violette, Dr. Angela Cooke-Jackson, Mr. John Strada, and Dr. Jennifer Fairchild, each of whom offers unique academic strengths to the program such that CMS majors and minors are well-rounded in their experiences, perspectives, and skills.

Upon completion of this class, we invite you to explore the CMS program further by taking more of our courses. Currently, the following courses are offered in the CMS program:

CMS 200 Interpersonal Communication
CMS 205 Advocacy and Opposition
CMS 210 Public Speaking
CMS 250 Interviewing
CMS 300 Business & Professional Speaking
CMS 305 Research Design in Comm. Studies
CMS 310 Small Group Communication
CMS 320 Persuasion
CMS 325 Conflict Management
CMS 349 Co-op Experiences
CMS 350 Organizational Communication
CMS 353 Health Communication

CMS 375 Intercultural Communication
CMS 400 Communication and Gender
CMS 410 Communication Theory
CMS 420 Negotiation
CMS 450 Mediation
CMS 485 Communication Training & Development
CMS 490 Special Topics in Communication
    i.e. Political Communication
       Family Communication
         Computer Mediated Communication
CMS 495 Communication, Leadership, & Change
CMS 499 Independent Study

You can major or minor in Communication Studies. If interested, contact any of the faculty above for information or visit our departmental website at http://www.communication.eku.edu/.

We have high expectations for you as a CMS student. You will work hard and we are here to help you succeed!

CSSA

The Communication Studies Student Association is an official National Communication Association (NCA) student club dedicated to the continued professional and personal development of EKU's Communication Studies students. This organization is student-led, with students taking the primary responsibility for the creation, planning and implementation both social and professional events designed to promote out of class learning, networking and other communication-related business skills. Join us!

Contact Mr. John Strada (John.Strada@eku.edu) or Dr. Amy Thieme (Amy.Thieme@eku.edu) for more information.

THE DEPARTMENT OF COMMUNICATION AT EASTERN KENTUCKY UNIVERSITY

In addition to the Communication Studies major and minor, the Department of Communication offers EKU students three other majors – Journalism (JOU), Public Relations (PUB), and Broadcasting & Electronic Media (BEM) – led by world-class faculty who are recognized in their chosen fields for excellence in teaching, research, and professional service.

EKU's Journalism program has a strong tradition of educating outstanding professionals in the field. Journalism majors receive the theoretical, ethical, and practical background essential to mastering the ever-increasing demands of today's rapidly changing, media-hungry environment. Students work hard writing and reporting stories to develop an understanding of modern journalism and why it matters. The journalism faculty provides students with hands-on experience, writing for The Eastern Progress, a nationally-acclaimed student newspaper. Journalism students also gain the knowledge and experience necessary to work for newspapers, magazines, and web-based outlets. A wide variety of opportunities exist for journalism students through internships, co-ops, and other student organizations. For more information about the Journalism major or minor contact Dr. Elizabeth Hansen at Liz.Hansen@eku.edu or call her at 622-1488.

The Public Relations program at EKU is designed to teach students how the success or failure of professional organizations depends on the experts who manage the communications and public relations activities of those organizations. Public Relations students master the skills necessary to manage the speed-of-light communications flow of the information age, employing skills necessary to craft messages for worldwide audiences of newspapers, magazines, television, radio, and the Internet. For more information about the Public Relations major or minor contact Dr. Mike Hesse at Mike.Hesse@eku.edu or call him at 622-1085.

Taught by faculty with exceptional professional insight, EKU students who major or minor in Broadcast and Electronic Media pursue careers at television, cable outlets, networks, video production houses, corporations, and government agencies at various levels. There are three options under this major: news, general, and film techniques. Career options for BEM majors include duties as producers, video editors, audio technicians, videographers, directors, account executives, general managers, reporters, and on-air talent. The BEM program offers state-of-the-art digital video and audio labs, digital cameras, and computer writing stations for students who are ready to gain a wide variety of skills in the mass communication field. For more information about the Broadcast and Electronic Media major or minor, contact Dr. John Fitch at John.Fitch@eku.edu or call him at 622-6769.

This CMS Course:
One Key to Developing "Informed, Creative, Critical Thinkers Who Communicate Effectively"

This CMS course has been deemed by the General Education Committee at Eastern Kentucky University as an *essential* part of your higher education. This course is one of the few that is required of all Eastern Kentucky University undergraduate students and for this reason, I'd like to take this opportunity to introduce you to this course by explaining what we, the faculty, see as its significance to you (personally and professionally) and how this course is related to the theme of the "Quality Enhancement Plan" (or QEP) of EKU.

The QEP theme states that "<u>EKU will develop informed, critical and creative thinkers who communicate effectively</u>". In this course, you will certainly become more informed about human communication processes, theories, and skills and how these relate to your personal and professional success. You will certainly also learn more about what it means to be a critical and creative thinker and gain experience in developing these kinds of higher-order thinking skills. Finally, through the information and thinking skills you gain through this course, you will develop your public communication skills.

Students sometimes question why we chose to customize this textbook. We offer this customized textbook to enhance the connections between the content of this course and the specialized goals set forth by the Quality Enhancement Plan theme as well as the unique qualities of the Eastern Kentucky University student community. You will find in the beginning section of this textbook, for example, documents such as the syllabus, rubrics that will help you interpret what it means to be a competent communicator and critical thinker, evaluation and "how-to" forms, sample/model assignments, and enhanced information about organizing public speeches, critical listening, and speaking dialects. These extra documents have been included as a direct result of course assessments from past semesters indicating that students at EKU have additional interest and/or need to focus on these areas of communication education.

We are excited about your participation in a CMS course this semester! It is our collective goal that you ultimately view this course as a rich and essential part of your success...as a person, as a professional, and as a deep learner.

I invite you to contact me personally with questions, comments, or suggestions about this course at any time during the semester!

Dr. Jayne L. Violette, Associate Professor
Basic Course Director
Communication Studies Program, Eastern Kentucky University
Jayne.Violette@eku.edu

First assignment in this course...

READ THE FOLLOWING ESSAY and BE PREPARED TO DISCUSS sometime during the first week of class:

Critical Thinking and Communication

As students of human communication this semester, you will discover the relationship between being a competent communicator and thinking critically. Being an effective communicator means that you develop and use "other-oriented" messages – messages tailored to meet the social goals within a certain context or situation (i.e., public speaking, interpersonal relationships, problem-solving groups).

The concept of "critical thinking" is commonly found in textbooks and in syllabi across campus, but do you really know what your professors mean when they say that they want you to "think critically"? Here is some help to frame your thinking about the concept:

Dr. Gerald Nosich, professor, author, and noted authority on critical thinking from Buffalo State College and the University of New Orleans, claims that in order for students to develop their critical thinking skills, two conditions are necessary: (1) the thinking has to be reflective (that is, you have to think about your thinking) and (2) the reflective thinking must meet high standards. The readings, assignments, and activities you engage in for this course will require that these conditions are met **because in order to be an effective (other-oriented) communicator, you must use good reasoning both as you design your messages** *and* **as you analyze the messages from others.**

Drawing from The Miniature Guide to Critical Thinking: Concepts and Tools, by Drs. Richard Paul and Linda Elder (2008)*, the **Elements of Reasoning** involve:

1. Establishing PURPOSE (intent of article, speech, essay, conversation, etc.)
2. Identifying the QUESTION or ISSUE at hand (deciding what the author or speaker had in mind when he she said this, wrote this)
3. Gathering INFORMATION relevant to the issue (what facts, data the speaker or author is using to support his/her ideas)
4. Identifying the important CONCEPTS related to the issue (what are the most important ideas that author or speaker is communicating)
5. Asking yourself from what POINT OF VIEW (frame of reference) is the author/speaker taking and how is he/she "seeing" it
6. Identifying ASSUMPTIONS (usually unstated) that might be present (what is author/speaker taking for granted, what are *you* taking for granted as you read/listen)
7. Asking yourself what IMPLICATIONS and CONSEQUENCES might exist if you hold that position (what consequences might follow if people accept or ignore the author or speaker's line of reasoning)
8. Drawing accurate CONCLUSIONS about the issue

These scholars also suggest that there are universal **Intellectual Standards** which you and your CMS instructor should apply to ensure quality critical thinking. The application of these standards should serve as the guide for your reasoning about human communication and **will serve as the basis for how your instructor will evaluate your work in this course!** The Intellectual Standards include:

1. CLARITY – If what is being communicated is not clear, it is not possible to evaluate its accuracy or relevancy. Clarity is demonstrated in both *what* is said and *how* it is said.
2. ACCURACY – Is what is being communicated really true? What evidence is offered to support accuracy? Remember that something can be clear, but not accurate.
3. PRECISION – Does what is being communicated offer details for specificity?
4. RELEVANCE – Is what is being communicated *connected* to the question or issue at hand (or audience)?
5. DEPTH – Is that which is being communicated discussed superficially or show a lack of understanding of the complexities of the issue or question at hand?
6. BREADTH – Does that which is being communicated acknowledge different ways of looking at the issue or question at hand?
7. LOGIC – Does the message make sense? How do elements of the message follow each other?
8. FAIRNESS - Does the message reflect all relevant viewpoints in good faith? Is there any distortion of the information that might demonstrate an unwillingness to examine the question or issue at hand in a balanced way?

Writing and speaking assignments that are not clear, unorganized, use inappropriate or inaccurate language, offer inconsistent, misleading, misquoted, superficial information, and/or are not "connected" to their audiences (self-serving) ***do not*** demonstrate much, if any, critical thinking.

Consider one of the major assignments of this course – the informative speech. Your instructor will ask you to choose a topic, analyze your audience, conduct in-depth research about that topic, organize your research into a formal preparation outline, rehearse your speech, deliver your speech to an audience extemporaneously using a set of speaking notes to keep you on track, and engage in self-evaluation of your speech to

identify relative strengths and areas needing improvement. Think about and then discuss with the instructor of your course at what points in this process you will be using the above-mentioned Elements of Reasoning and Intellectual Standards to complete this assignment.

To understand the application of critical thinking to communication activities better, also ask your instructor to show you where on your class Blackboard site and/or MySpeechLab site you can go for further illustration of the relationships between effective communication and critical thinking. These types of excellent resources, among others, are available through your instructor!

It is not just in developing speeches and listening to speeches that you will be engaged in critical thinking in this course. We encourage you to engage in more discussion with your instructor this first week of class (and throughout the semester) about the interesting and important relationships between critical thinking and effective communication….for the purpose of exploring, evaluating, expanding, and then expressing related ideas this course will generate in you. Then as you become more involved in these kinds of processes – in *all* of your courses at EKU – the more likely you are to reflect the goal of the stated EKU Quality Enhancement Plan (QEP) theme: to become "an informed, critical and creative thinker who communicates effectively".

* Note that <u>The Miniature Guide to Critical Thinking</u> is also a required "textbook" for this course! Your instructor will ask you to read it early in the semester. It is a very small booklet, but *do not underestimate its importance* in this course! You will want to keep it readily available for reference throughout this course.

Possible discussion starters:

After reading this short essay and "The Miniature Guide", have your ideas about critical thinking changed? Why or why not? If so, how?

How do you think the emphasis on critical thinking in this course might impact how this course will be taught and your role in this course?

How would you describe your "ideal learning experience" as a student taking CMS 100? What might the role of critical thinking be as you anticipate your ideal experience?

Essential Intellectual Traits

As a framework for your expectations in this course, we'd like to encourage you to embrace the following Intellectual Traits deemed essential for free, creative, and critical thinking. Refer to pp. 14 – 15 in your blue "Miniature Guide" for further explanation and examples.

Consider how often (if ever) you've been invited to think and talk about these important intellectual traits in your higher education. The instructors of this course also invite you to hold us accountable to demonstrate these same traits, as we attempt to model these qualities in our classrooms. Enactment of these traits by *both* students *and* faculty, we believe, results in the best possible learning environment for this CMS course!

Intellectual Humility vs. Intellectual Arrogance

Intellectual Courage vs. Intellectual Cowardice

Intellectual Empathy vs. Intellectual Narrow-mindedness

Intellectual Autonomy vs. Intellectual Conformity

Intellectual Integrity vs. Intellectual Hypocrisy

Intellectual Perseverance vs. Intellectual Laziness

Confidence in Reasoning vs. Distrust of Reasoning and Evidence

Fair-mindedness vs. Intellectual Unfairness

CMS 100
Introduction to Human Communication

Instructor:
Office:
Office Hours:
Phone:
Email:

CATALOG COURSE DESCRIPTION: "An introduction to the study of human communication. Overview of major topics in contemporary theories of intrapersonal, interpersonal, small group, and public communication. Practice in the development of these areas."

Stated more conceptually, this course is designed to help you learn the logic of human communication by exploring the foundational concepts and theories of human communication in critical and creative ways. The primary goals of this course are to help you come to think and communicate competently by working through communication challenges common to successful living. To reach these goals, your instructor for this course will foster, in the words of Francis Bacon (1605) "a desire to seek, patience to doubt, fondness to meditate, slowness to assert, readiness to consider, carefulness to dispose and set in order, and a hatred for every kind of imposture" related to basic human communication activity. Simply put, the core of this course involves development of communication knowledge and skills, using critical and creative thinking processes.

STUDENT LEARNING OBJECTIVES: Through critical and creative thinking processes, you should be able to demonstrate all of the following by the end of the semester:

1. Identify and define foundational theories, components, and concepts related to effective human communication, including communication competency, self-concept and perception processes, language, non-verbal communication, listening, and cultural/contextual influences.

2. Discuss the relationship between self-understanding (self-concept, self-esteem, and perception) and effective communication.

3. Integrate gained interpersonal communication knowledge and skills to enhance personal and professional lives.

4. Develop competent verbal and nonverbal communication skills related to informative public speaking.

5. Analyze small group communication processes and demonstrate effective small group problem-solving skills.

6. Demonstrate effective comprehensive and critical listening skills.

7. Explore contextual and cultural differences in human communication processes, leading to appropriate message construction and adaptation.

8. Value the role of communication in personal and professional lives.

GENERAL EDUCATION and QE GOALS: These course objectives align with goals set forth by the General Education curriculum and the Quality Enhancement (QE) theme at Eastern Kentucky University. More specifically, this course is designed to help you communicate effectively by applying skills in reading, writing, speaking, and listening and through appropriate use of information technology, to use appropriate methods of critical thinking to examine issues and to identify solutions, and to integrate knowledge that will deepen your understanding of, and will inform your own choices about, issues of personal and public importance. Also, in direct alignment with the QE theme, this course is designed to help you become "an informed, critical and creative thinker who can communicate effectively".

To realize these objectives, CMS 100 centers around **four units of instruction** including, (1) Foundations of Communication, (2) Interpersonal Communication, (3) Small Group Communication and (4) Public Speaking. Activities and assessments of these units (participation in in-class or online discussions and activities, exams, and presentations) will serve as assessment of the course objectives.

REQUIRED MATERIALS:

Beebe, S. A., Beebe, S. J. & Ivey, D. K. (2008). *Communication: Principles for a Lifetime* (customized edition). Boston, MA: Allyn & Bacon/Pearson Education.

Paul, R. & Elder, L. (2008). *The Miniature Guide to Critical Thinking: Concepts and Tools*. The Foundation for Critical Thinking. NOTE: This is a very small blue booklet available at the on campus bookstore.

NOTE: It is important that you purchase an UNUSED customized version of the Beebe, Beebe & Ivey textbook that is designed specifically for EKU students! It is available at area bookstores, but check at the on-campus bookstore first. This special edition allows EKU students access to an online support product called MySpeechLab and other course-related documents. Your instructor may be making assignments related to the MySpeechLab technology.

Two or more DVD-Rs to use to record your speeches. Your instructor will give you specifics on exactly what and how many to purchase.

You also need an active EKU email account that you check on a regular basis. Your instructor *may* also utilize **Blackboard** technology in this course to help communicate assignments, promote discussion, and/or disseminate additional information relative to your learning. Your instructor will provide more specific direction about Blackboard if necessary.

CLASSROOM POLICIES:

Attendance: Your regular attendance is imperative to the successful completion of this course. We will be covering a great deal of material during each class period, so students who make it a goal not to miss any classes will gain the most. Acknowledging, however, the fact that illness, and other legitimate reasons for missing class do arise, the following policies are, therefore, extended:

You can miss FOUR HOURS of class without penalty to your grade. Absences beyond these hourly limits will result in a reduction PER ABSENCE from your final point total. **It is entirely possible that you may fail this class due to excessive absences.** Your instructor will define what the term "excessive absences" means and will provide other specific guidelines for your particular class. **For most CMS faculty, missing more than 20% of the total class meetings is grounds for failure of this course.**

If you must miss class, please know that **you** are responsible for all of the material covered in class that day. Deadlines for assignments can be renegotiated *only* if your absence is a university approved absence. (Proper documentation for the absence is required and will be collected.)

Tardiness: Attendance is taken each day in this class. Please don't be late for class! If you've arrived late to class after attendance has been taken, **you will be considered absent unless you talk to your instructor immediately after class**. It is **your** responsibility to do this – not the instructor's. Your tardiness will be recorded. Every three times you are late is equal to one absence!

Assignments/Due Dates: You are expected to turn in written work on time, take exams when scheduled, and COMMAND ADHERENCE to the schedules related to graded presentations! You should never be surprised as to when any assignment is due or exams given, as your instructor will make such announcements well in advance to the due dates.

Unless otherwise specified by your instructor, failure to complete any major assignment (any assignment worth 25 points or more) will result in failure of this course, regardless of the number of points you have accumulated.

For written work (outlines, evaluations, etc.): Two letter grades can be deducted for the first day a written assignment is late, plus one letter grade for each subsequent day the assignment is late. A "day" is defined as the next day…not the next class period.

For exams: Make-up exams will only be given if a student provides an official "university-approved" excuse PRIOR to the exam or other documented medical reasons. **No other reasons will be considered, so please do not ask**. Please note that make-up exams **are often more difficult** that the original exam. Avoid make-up exams if you can!

For speeches: Students who miss class the day they are scheduled to present ("no-shows") will receive a failing grade for that assignment…NO EXCEPTIONS! Only students who present a written, university-approved excuse PRIOR to a scheduled speech or group presentation will be given another opportunity.

Unless otherwise specified, **all work you turn in to your instructor should be typed**, representing your best effort for that assignment. Because your instructor has high expectations for you in this class, extra-credit assignments are seldom, if ever, offered.

Your instructor expects your work to be your own. **Copying, borrowing, plagiarizing (using another's materials without proper documentation), or in any way representing others' work as your own is a serious academic offense and may result in a failing grade for the course, and can result in expulsion from the university**. If you are not sure about plagiarism, please consult with your instructor before you turn in the assignment. Please refer to the rules, regulations, and penalties for academic misconduct in your Student Handbook.

Students with Disabilities: If you are registered with the Office of Services for Individuals with Disabilities, please obtain your accommodation letters from the OSID and present them to the course instructor to discuss any academic accommodations you need. If you believe you need accommodation and are not registered with the OSID, please contact the Office in the Student Services Building Room 361 by email at disserv@eku.edu or by telephone at (859) 622-2933 V/TDD. Upon individual request, this syllabus can be made available in an alternative format.

Respect for Others: The foundation of effective communication is being "other-oriented." Please turn off cell phones, pagers, beepers, other electronic devices when in class. Avoid bringing small children to our class. The use of tobacco products is prohibited in this class. Please avoid racist, sexist, or other negative unethical language that may make others in our classroom community uncomfortable.

ASSIGNMENTS AND GRADING: You will experience a wide variety of interesting learning assignments and activities in this course. Grades will be determined on specific set criteria and on a 90 – 100% scale.

1. **EXAMS and/or QUIZZES**: (200 points total) Cognitive learning will be assessed primarily through a combination of exams and/or quizzes. Your instructor will explain what you can expect on the exams/quizzes in terms of format and content.

2. **INFORMATIVE SPEECHES AND FORMAL OUTLINES**: (100 points total for the speeches + 25 points for each formal outline): One of the most powerful experiences you will encounter in this course is learning how to articulate yourself well publicly. You will have **two** opportunities to develop and extemporaneously deliver informative speeches to your classmates. (NOTE: You will *not* have the opportunity to develop and deliver persuasive speeches in this course.) Generally speaking, you will choose your own topics for your informative speeches (subject to instructor approval), conduct in-depth research about that topic, organize your information by developing a formal preparation outline, practice your speeches with speaking notes, and then deliver your speeches extemporaneously. More specific criteria for each speaking assignment will be provided in written format by your instructor. Your instructor reserves the right to weight each speech as he/she desires, the total for both speeches not to exceed 100 points.

3. **UNIT ASSIGNMENTS**: (100 points total) You will be required to participate in a wide and interesting variety of written assignments related to critical self-reflection, observation and/or application of knowledge and skills representing the four foundational units of this course. The purpose of these assignments is to help develop your interpersonal, public, and small-group communication knowledge and competence by challenging your critical and creative thinking skills. These assignments are often in the form of short papers or essays, requiring appropriate academic writing style. Unit assignments may also involve activities in MySpeechLab or through online discussion forums. The nature of these assignments is determined specifically by your instructor, per the needs and interests of the class participants. Assessment of these assignments will be based on specific "Intellectual Standards", to be explained by your instructor at the onset of this course.

GRADING SUMMARY: (90 = 100% scale)

Exams/Quizzes	200 points
Informative Speeches (2)	100 points
Speech Outlines (2 @ 25 points each)	50 points
Unit Assignment(s)	100 points
TOTAL POSSIBLE POINTS	450 points

GRADING PROFILES *:

The Grade of F – F-level work fails to display an understanding of the basic nature of human communication, and in any case does not display the critical thinking or communication skills and abilities which are at the heart of this course. The work at the end of the course is as vague, imprecise, unreasoned, and unskilled as it was in the beginning. There is little evidence that the student is genuinely engaged in the task of taking charge of his or her thinking as it relates to communication competency. Many assignments appear to have been done without putting significant effort into thinking through them. Evidence exists that the student is not analyzing communication situations clearly, not formulating communication information accurately, not distinguishing relevant from irrelevant information, not able to identify key questions or issues pertaining to communication competence, not able to identify assumptions or concepts about communication, not able to identify or analyze different/competing points of view, not reasoning carefully from clearly stated premises, and is not recognizing implications about communication practices in various contexts. The student's work does not display discernable reasoning or problem-solving skills related to human communication.

The Grade of D - D-level work shows only a minimal understanding of what communication competence is, along with the development of some, but very little, critical thinking skills or abilities. D work at the end of the course shows that the student only occasionally demonstrates communication knowledge and skills. Most assignments are poorly done. There is little evidence that the student is "reasoning through" communication situations or assignments. Often the students seems to be only going through the motions of the assignments, carrying out the form of the assignment without reaching the essence of the intended learning objective. D work rarely shows any effort to take charge of ideas, assumptions, inferences, and intellectual processes. In general, D-level thinking lacks discipline and clarity. In D-level work, the student rarely analyzes communication issues clearly or precisely, almost never formulates communication knowledge accurately, rarely distinguishes the relevant from the irrelevant, rarely recognizes key questionable assumptions made about communication, almost never clarifies key communication concepts effectively, frequently fails to use communication language in keeping with establish professional usage, only rarely identifies competing communication points of view, almost never reasons carefully from clearly stated premises, or recognizes important implications or consequences of communication acts. D-level work does not show good reasoning about communication and frequently displays poor reasoning and problem-solving skills.

The Grade of C – C-level work illustrates some but inconsistent achievement in grasping what human communication competence is, along with the development of modest communication thinking skills or abilities. C-level work at the end of the course, it is true, shows some emerging communication knowledge and skills, but also pronounced weaknesses as well. Although some assignments are done reasonably well, others are poorly done or are at best, mediocre. There are more than occasional lapses in reasoning. Only on occasion does C-level work display a mind taking charge of its own ideas, assumptions, inferences, and intellectual processes. Only occasionally does C-level work display intellectual discipline and clarity. The C-level student only occasionally

analyzes communication issues clearly and precisely, formulates communication information accurately, distinguishes the relevant from the irrelevant, recognizes key questionable assumptions, clarifies key communication concepts effectively, uses communication language in keeping with established professional usage, identifies relevant competing points of view about communication, reasons carefully from clearly stated premises, or recognizes important communication implications and consequences. On the whole, C-level work shows only modest development in communication knowledge and skills and demonstrates inconsistent reasoning abilities.

The Grade of B – B-level work represents demonstrable achievement in grasping what communication competence is, along with the clear demonstration of a range of specific communication-related thinking skills or abilities. B-level work at the end of the course is, on the whole, clear, precise, and well-reasoned, though with occasional lapses into weak reasoning. On the whole, communication terms and distinctions are used effectively. The work demonstrates a mind beginning to take charge of its own ideas, assumptions, inferences, and intellectual processes. The student often analyzes communication issues clearly and precisely, often formulates communication information accurately, usually distinguishes the relevant from the irrelevant, often recognizes key questionable assumptions about communication, usually clarifies key communication concepts effectively, typically uses communication language in keeping with professional usage, frequently identifies relevant competing points of view about human communication, and shows a general tendency to reason carefully from clearly states premises, as well as noticeable sensitivity to important implications and consequences within human communication activity and contexts. B-level work displays good reasoning and problem-solving skills related to human communication.

The Grade of A – A-level work demonstrates real achievement in grasping what communication competence is, along with clear development of a range of specific communication-related thinking skills and abilities. The work at the end of the course is, on the whole, clear, precise, and well-reasoned, though with occasional lapses into weak reasoning. In A-level work, communication terms and distinctions are used effectively. The work demonstrates a mind clearly taking charge of its own ideas, assumptions, inferences, and intellectual processes. The A-level student usually analyzes communication issues clearly and precisely, usually formulates communication information accurately, usually distinguishes the relevant from the irrelevant, usually recognizes key questionable assumptions about human communication, usually clarifies key communication concepts effectively, typically uses communication language in keeping with established professional usage, usually identifies relevant competing points of view about communication, and shows a general tendency to reason carefully from clearly stated premises, as well as noticeable sensitivity to important implications and consequences within human communication activity and contexts. A-level work displays excellent communication reasoning and problem-solving skills. An A student's work is consistently at a high level of intellectual excellence.

* Note that the articulation of these Grade Profiles is based on Linda Elder's (1999) publication entitled _Critical Thinking: Basic Theory and Instructional Structures_. Students enrolled in this course should use these grade profiles in conjunction with the EKU Communication Competence rubic(s) when discussing course or assignment grades with your instructor.

Please note that the instructor of this course reserves the right to make adjustments in the assignments and format of this class at any time during the course. Such adjustments will _only_ be made to enhance the course and/or meet the unique learning needs of the students who are enrolled.

CMS 100
Introduction to Human Communication
ONLINE CLASSES ONLY

Instructor:
Office:
Phone:
Email:

Please note that the instructor of this course reserves the right to make adjustments in the assignments and format of this online class at any time during the course. Such adjustments will *only* be made to enhance the course and/or meet the unique learning needs of the students who are enrolled.

CATALOG COURSE DESCRIPTION: "An introduction to the study of human communication. Overview of major topics in contemporary theories of intrapersonal, interpersonal, small group, and public communication. Practice in the development of these areas."

Stated more conceptually, this course is designed to help you learn the logic of human communication by exploring the foundational concepts and theories of human communication in critical and creative ways in an online teaching and learning environment. The primary goals of this course are to help you come to think and communicate competently by working through communication challenges common to successful living. To reach these goals, your instructor for this course will foster, in the words of Francis Bacon (1605) "a desire to seek, patience to doubt, fondness to meditate, slowness to assert, readiness to consider, carefulness to dispose and set in order, and a hatred for every kind of imposture" related to basic human communication activity. Simply put, the core of this course involves development of communication knowledge and skills, using critical and creative thinking processes.

STUDENT LEARNING OBJECTIVES: Through critical and creative thinking processes, you should be able to demonstrate all of the following by the end of the semester:

1. Identify and define foundational theories, components, and concepts related to effective human communication, including communication competency, self-concept and perception processes, language, non-verbal communication, listening, and cultural/contextual influences.

2. Discuss the relationship between self-understanding (self-concept, self-esteem, and perception) and effective communication.

3. Integrate gained interpersonal communication knowledge and skills to enhance personal and professional lives.

4. Develop competent verbal and nonverbal communication skills related to informative public speaking.

5. Analyze small group communication processes and demonstrate effective small group problem-solving skills.

6. Demonstrate effective comprehensive and critical listening skills.

7. Explore contextual and cultural differences in human communication processes, leading to appropriate message construction and adaptation.

8. Value the role of communication in personal and professional lives.

GENERAL EDUCATION and QE GOALS: These course objectives align with goals set forth by the General Education curriculum and the Quality Enhancement (QE) theme at Eastern Kentucky University. More specifically, this course is designed to help you communicate effectively by applying skills in reading, writing, speaking, and

listening and through appropriate use of information technology, to use appropriate methods of critical thinking to examine issues and to identify solutions, and to integrate knowledge that will deepen your understanding of, and will inform your own choices about, issues of personal and public importance. Also, in direct alignment with the QE theme, this course is designed to help you become "an informed, critical and creative thinker who can communicate effectively".

To realize these objectives, CMS 100 centers around **four units of instruction including**, (1) Foundations of Communication, (2) Interpersonal Communication, (3) Small Group Communication and (4) Public Speaking. Activities and assessments of these units (participation in in-class or online discussions and activities, exams, and presentations) will serve as assessment of the course objectives.

REQUIRED MATERIALS:

Beebe, S. A., Beebe, S. J. & Ivey, D. K. (2008). *Communication: Principles for a Lifetime* (customized edition). Boston, MA: Allyn & Bacon/Pearson Education.

Paul, R. & Elder, L. (2008). *The Miniature Guide to Critical Thinking: Concepts and Tools*. The Foundation for Critical Thinking. NOTE: This is a very small blue booklet available at the on campus bookstore.

NOTE: It is important that you purchase an UNUSED customized version of the Beebe, Beebe & Ivey textbook that is designed specifically for EKU students! It is available at area bookstores, but check at the on-campus bookstore first. This special edition allows EKU students access to an online support product called MySpeechLab and other course-related documents. Your instructor may be making assignments related to the MySpeechLab technology.

Two or more DVD-Rs to use to record your speeches. Your instructor will give you specifics on exactly what and how many to purchase.

An active **EKU** email account that you check on a regular basis. Your instructor will utilize MySpeechLab (MSL) and/or Blackboard (Bb) technology in this course to communicate assignments, promote discussion, and/or disseminate additional information relative to your learning. Your instructor will provide specific directions about using MSL and Blackboard on or before the first day of class.

REQUIRED TECHNOLOGY and SKILLS:
This course requires that you have DAILY access to a computer with up-to-date software and technology that allows you to easily send and receive email and view streamed video. Ideally, you should have access to high-speed internet as well. Students should also have a good, reliable printer.

Students enrolled in this course must also be able to:

1. Successfully submit attachments to email (Word or rtf documents only, unless otherwise specified by your instructor.)
2. *Quickly* learn to use MSL and/or Bb technology
3. Participate in online discussion boards, as assigned by your instructor
4. Take online exams via Bb
5. KEEP back-up copies of EVERYTHING on your hard drive in the event that your instructor would ask you to resubmit a document or submit a document in hard-copy format.

POLICIES:
Due dates and times will be clearly articulated by your instructor ahead of time. No late work is accepted, unless official university-approved excuse is submitted prior to due date. The instructor reserves the right to re-negotiate new due dates, under special circumstances; penalties for negotiated due dates may be incurred.

Assignments: All major assignments are designed for you to integrate gained knowledge from this course. They are important not only for learning assessment to take place, but to reinforce long-term retention and understanding of human communication processes and skills. Therefore, YOU MUST COMPLETE ALL ASSIGNMENTS in order

to receive a passing grade for this course. **Failure to complete any major assignment will result in failure of this course**.

Your instructor expects your work to be your own. **Copying, borrowing, plagiarizing (using another's materials without proper documentation), or in any way representing others' work as your own is a serious academic offense and may result in a failing grade for the course, and can result in expulsion from the university**. If you are not sure about plagiarism, please consult with your instructor before you turn in the assignment. Please refer to the rules, regulations, and penalties for academic misconduct in your Student Handbook.

Netiquette: The foundation of effective communication is being "other-oriented." It is important that everyone has mutual respect for one another in interactions related to this course. Online discussions and emails should be free of racist, sexist, or other unethical language that might make your instructor and others in the online learning community uncomfortable. Refrain from using online discussion boards for anything other than course-related exchanges. **Netiquette should also be extended to your instructor!**

For speeches: Every student enrolled in CMS 100 will deliver two informative speeches, the criteria and format of which will be determined by the instructor of your class. Some students enrolled in the online CMS 100 course are required to deliver their speeches in person, on campus. Under these circumstances, students who miss class the day they are scheduled to present ("no-shows") will receive a failing grade for that assignment. Only students who present a written, university-approved excuse PRIOR to a scheduled speech or presentation will be given another opportunity.

Other students will submit their speeches by sending in tapes. Under these circumstances, tapes must be post-marked by a specific due date (determined by your instructor), audience members must also be shown on the tape, and outlines must be included with the tape. Failure to send tapes and outlines in by post-marked date will result in a failing grade for that assignment. It is a good idea to send these tapes and outlines in through registered mail! Again, your instructor will provide the specific requirements for acceptable forms of video-recording.

PLEASE BE SURE YOU KNOW what the specific expectations of your instructor are for this online class! Additional requirements may also be articulated by your instructor on the Web Course descriptions posted within the EKU Online Learning page (http://www.eku.edu/onlinelearning/courses/)

Students with Disabilities: If you are registered with the Office of Services for Individuals with Disabilities, please obtain your accommodation letters from the OSID and present them to the course instructor to discuss any academic accommodations you need. If you believe you need accommodation and are not registered with the OSID, please contact the Office in the Student Services Building Room 361 by email at disserv@eku.edu or by telephone at (859) 622-2933 V/TDD. Upon individual request, this syllabus can be made available in an alternative format.

ASSIGNMENTS AND GRADING: You will experience a wide variety of learning assignments and activities in this course. Grades will be determined on specific set criteria and on a 90 – 100% scale.

1. **EXAMS and QUIZZES**: (200 points total) Cognitive learning will be assessed primarily through a combination of online exams and/or quizzes. Specific criteria for these assignments will be provided by your instructor.

2. **INFORMATIVE SPEECHES AND FORMAL OUTLINES**: (100 points total for the speeches + 25 points for each formal outline) One of the most powerful experiences you will encounter in this course is learning how to articulate yourself well publicly. You will have **two** opportunities to develop and extemporaneously deliver informative speeches. (NOTE: You will *not* have the opportunity to develop and deliver persuasive speeches in this course.) Generally speaking, you will choose your own topics for your informative speeches (subject to instructor approval), conduct in-depth research about that topic, organize your information by developing a formal preparation outline, practice your speeches with speaking notes, and then deliver your speeches extemporaneously to an audience. More specific criteria for each speaking assignment will be provided in written format by your instructor. Your instructor reserves the right to weight each speech as he/she desires, the total for both speeches not to exceed 100 points.
See notes about speech delivery format under the "Policies" section of this syllabus.

3. **UNIT ASSIGNMENTS**: (100 points total) You will be required to participate in a wide and interesting variety of written assignments related to self-reflection, observation and/or application of knowledge and skills related to the four units of instruction identified earlier in this document. The purpose of these assignments is to help develop your interpersonal, public, and small-group communication knowledge and competence. These assignments are often in the form of short papers or essays, requiring appropriate academic writing style. Unit assignments may also involve activities in MySpeechLab, Blackboard or through online discussion forums. The nature of these assignments is determined specifically by your instructor, per the needs and interests of the class participants.

4. **ONLINE DISCUSSION GROUPS**: (100 points total) You will participate in online discussions (via Bb or MSL) that will require that you answer specific questions from your instructor, related to information from your textbook. You should also expect to respond to others in your group in these discussions. Your instructor will inform you as to how often you will need to participate in these groups.

GRADING SUMMARY: (90 = 100% scale)

Exams/Quizzes	200 points
Informative Speeches	100 points
Speech Outlines	50 points
Unit Assignment(s)	100 points
Discussion Groups	100 points

TOTAL POSSIBLE POINTS 550 points (90 – 100% grading scale)

STUDENT REGISTRATION & LOGIN
MySpeechLab

Before You Begin
To register for MySpeechLab you will need:

- Your **school's zip code**:_____40475_____
- A MySpeechLab **student access code** (packaged with your new text or available for purchase at www.myspeechlab.com).
- A valid email address.

Registration
1. Enter **http://www.myspeechlab.com** in your Web Browser.
2. Click **Students** under "First-time users."
3. Select **MySpeechLab**
4. Click **"I already have an access code."** (Note: If you need to buy access online, click that link and simply follow those prompts to register.)
5. Read the License Agreement and Privacy Policy and click **"I Accept."**
6. Select **"No, I am a New User"** and type in your **Access Code** in the fields provided.
7. Enter your School's Zip Code, select your **Country** and click **Next**.
8. Enter your **Name** and **Email** and select **Your School**.
9. Create your **Login Name** and **Password**, answer the **Security Question** and click **Next**.

If successful, you will receive a **Confirmation Screen** with your information (this screen was also emailed to you).

Logging In
1. Enter **http://www.myspeechlab.com** in your Web Browser.
2. Under "Returning Users" click **MySpeechLab.**
3. Enter the **Login Name** and **Password** you created and click **"Log In."**
4. Select the **book** for your course. You now have access to the resources in MySpeechLab!

NOTE: If any time you forget your login name or password, simply click the "Forgot Login? link on the login page and we will email it to you.

We wish you success in your course!

myspeechlab
Where students learn to communicate with confidence

MySpeechLab is your gateway to the multimedia and online resources for your course.

Here's how it will help you:

www.myspeechlab.com

Want to SEE the concepts you read about?

Your MySpeechLab e-book contains icons linking to interactive features for each subject area.

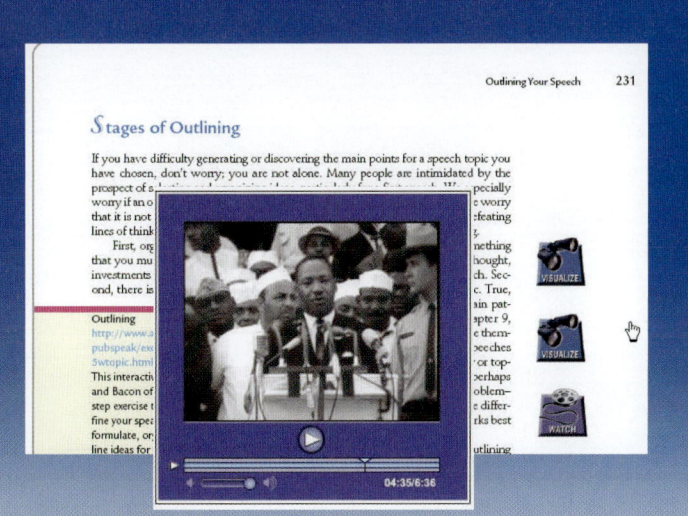

Professional and student speeches offer prime examples of what's discussed in the text.

www.myspeechlab.com

Wondering where to begin writing speeches?

The speech prep tools in MySpeechLab offer step-by-step research help and outlining wizards to get started.

Complete research help, _plus_, access to credible sources.

Outlining tools for different speech-types.

myspeechlab

www.myspeechlab.com

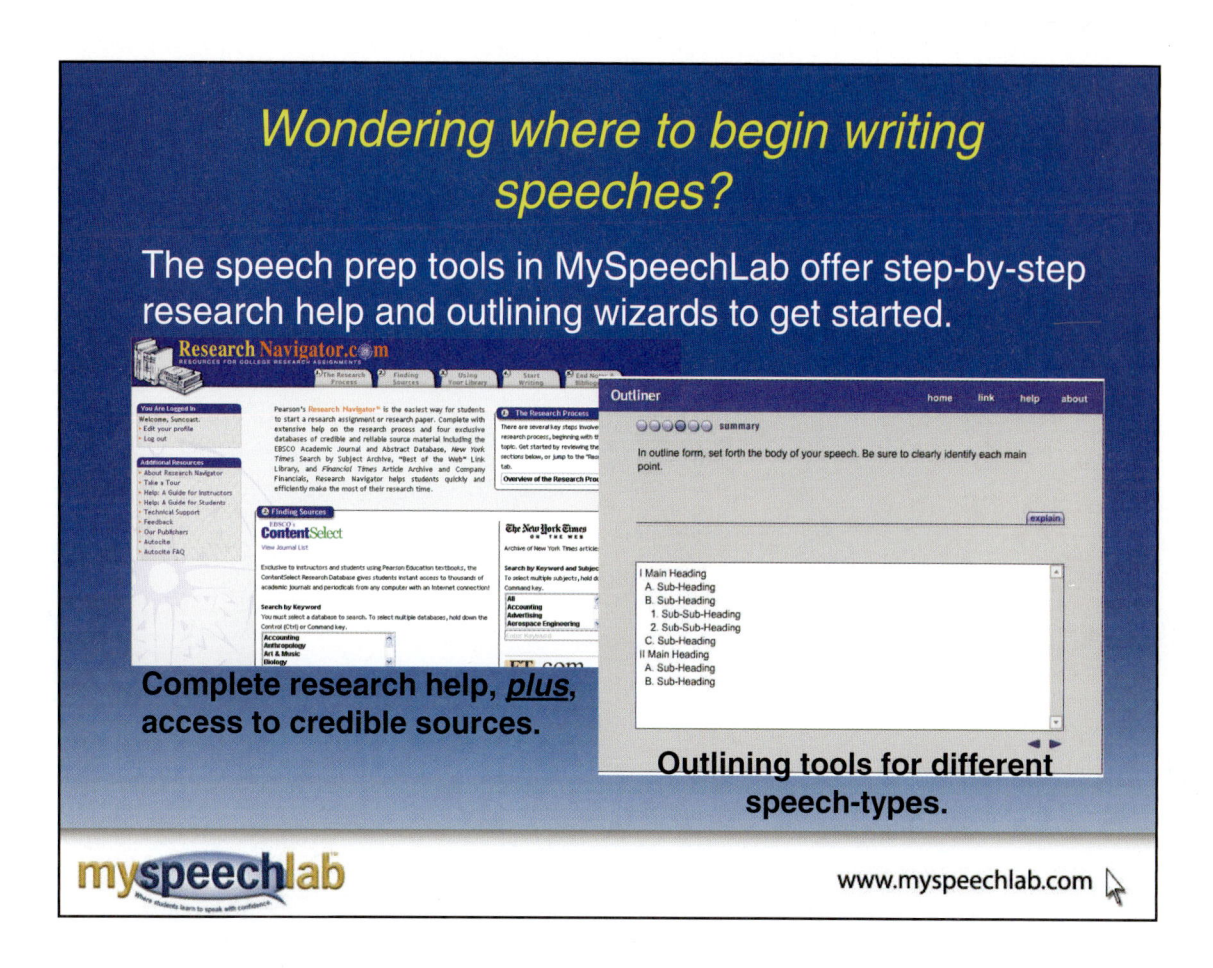

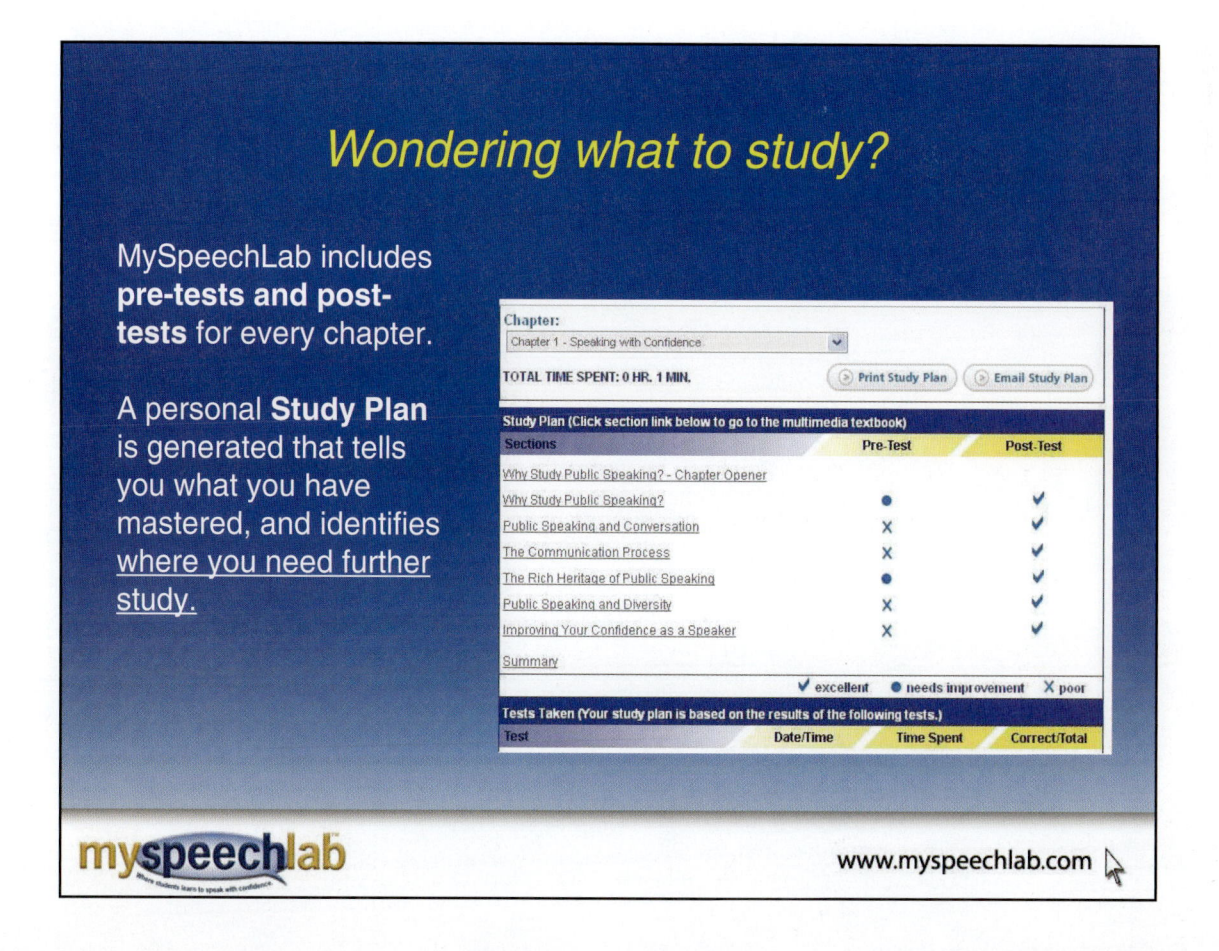

Wondering what to study?

MySpeechLab includes **pre-tests and post-tests** for every chapter.

A personal **Study Plan** is generated that tells you what you have mastered, and identifies where you need further study.

myspeechlab

www.myspeechlab.com

Additional activities & resources will help you make the grade!

www.myspeechlab.com

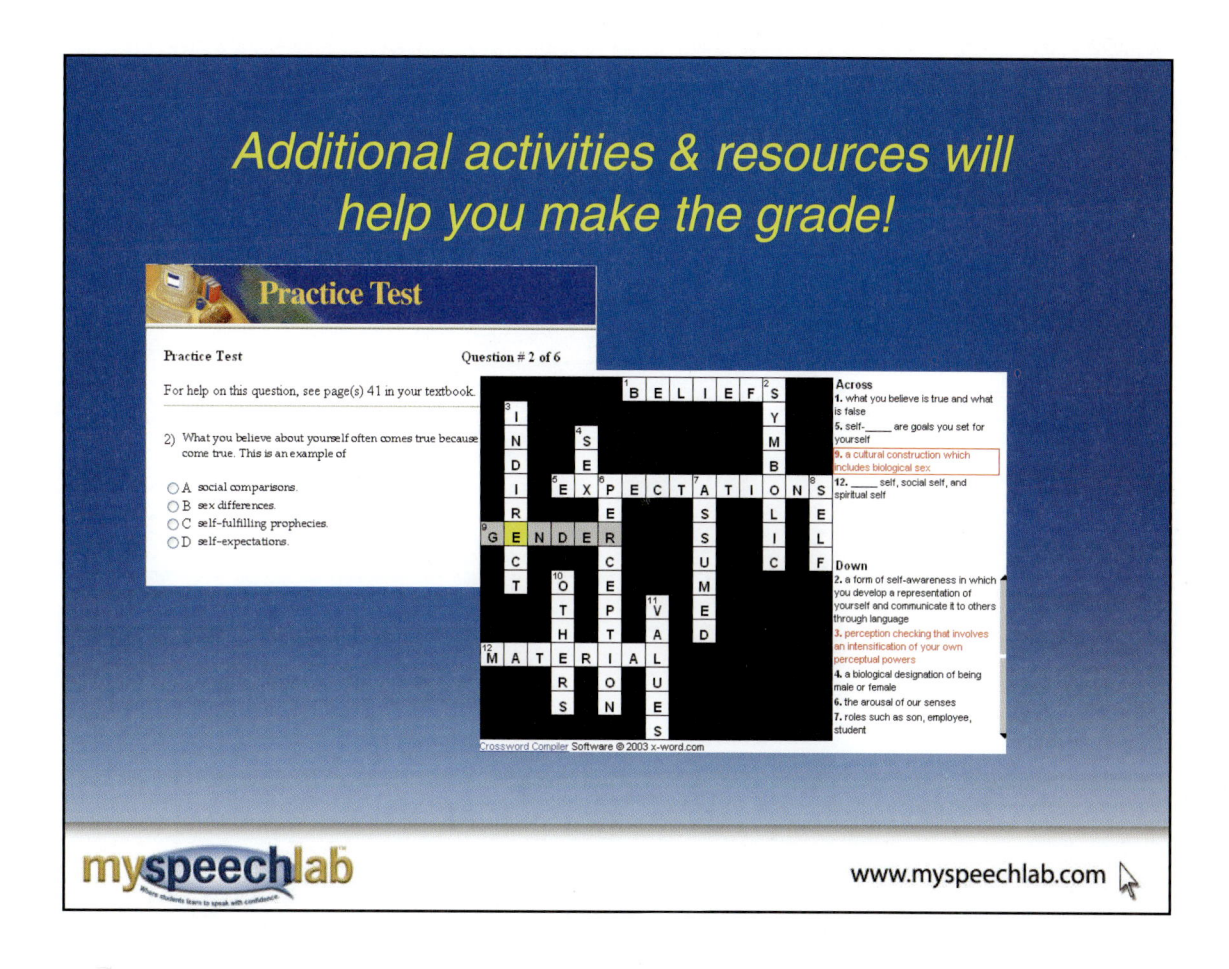

MySpeechLab Student Registration

- Go to: www.myspeechlab.com

- Click "**Students**" under "First-time users"

www.myspeechlab.com

MySpeechLab Student Registration

- Click **MySpeechLab**
  - If you already have an access code, click "**I already have an access code**"
  - If you need to buy access online, click "**I need to buy access.**" *Note: You will then follow those prompts to complete the purchase and registration process all at once.*

www.myspeechlab.com

MySpeechLab Student Registration

- Read the License Agreement & Privacy Policy and click "**I Accept**"

www.myspeechlab.com

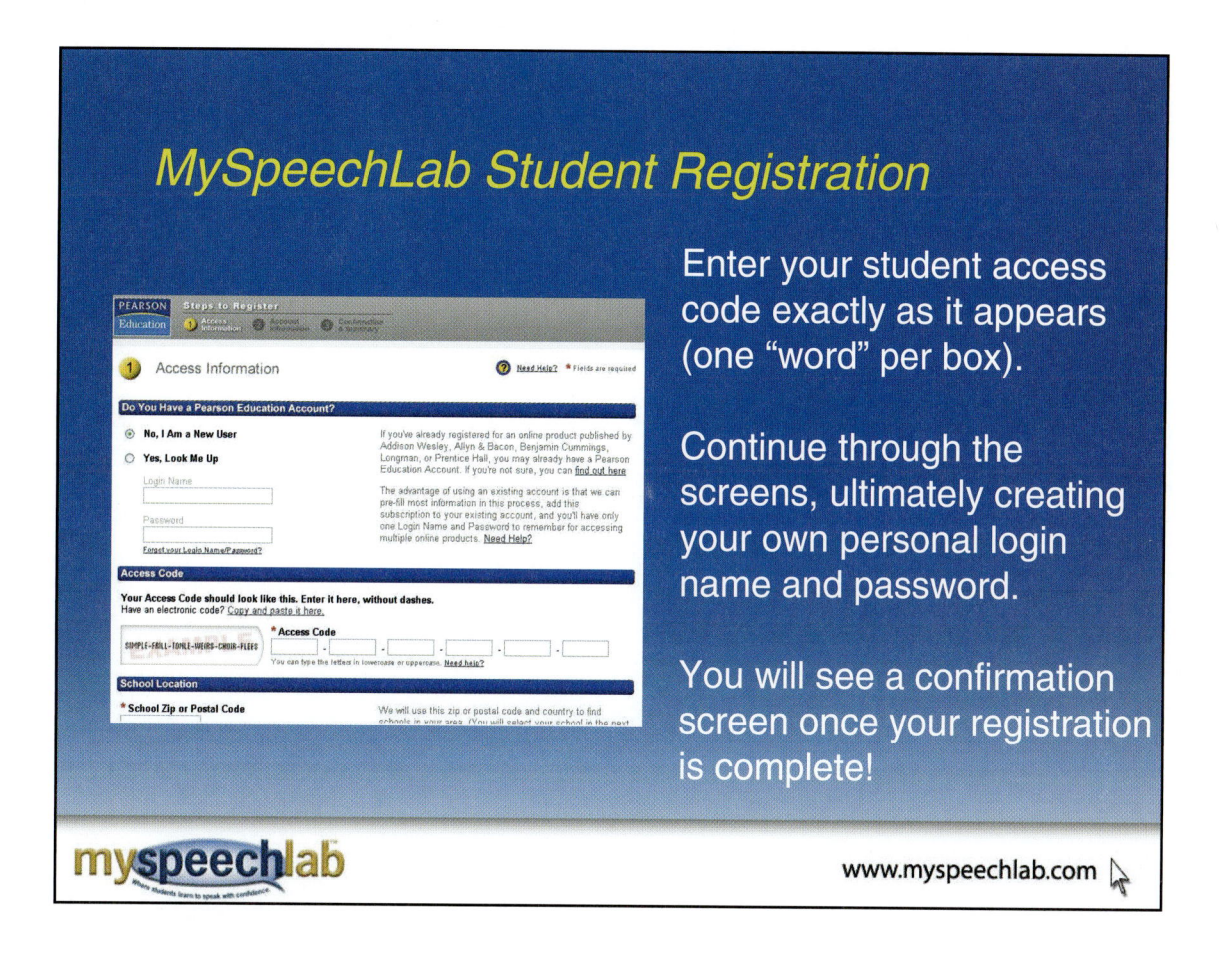

MySpeechLab Student Registration

Enter your student access code exactly as it appears (one "word" per box).

Continue through the screens, ultimately creating your own personal login name and password.

You will see a confirmation screen once your registration is complete!

myspeechlab

www.myspeechlab.com

Logging in to your course

- Go to: www.myspeechlab.com

- Click "**MySpeechLab**" under "Returning users."

- Simply enter the personal login name & password you created.

myspeechlab

www.myspeechlab.com

Congratulations!

You are now ready to take advantage of your book-specific resources!

Need help?

- Click the "**Help**" tab at www.myspeechlab.com

- Visit **http://247.ablongman.com** for online "Chat" or to email a problem to technical support.

www.myspeechlab.com

Make the grade!
www.myspeechlab.com

myspeechlab
Where students learn to communicate with confidence

www.myspeechlab.com

THE COMPETENT SPEAKER FORM for EKU STUDENTS

Speaker: _____   Topic _____

Key: 1 = BEGINNING   2 = DEVELOPING   3 = COMPETENT   4 = ACCOMPLISHED

Message Structure

_____ **Introduction**
Attention Getter? Established Credibility?
PURPOSE of speech CLEAR?
Audience RELEVANCY?
Main points of speech previewed through Thesis Statement?

_____ **Main Points/Body**
Main points CLEAR?
LOGICAL Organization?
CLEAR/Proper Transitions Used?

_____ **Conclusion**
Signal to End? Restated Thesis?
Restate of/Summary of main points?
Closing Thought/Closed with Impact?

Message Content

_____ **Supporting Materials**
RELEVANT? Sufficient? PRECISE?
BREADTH of sources offered? (facts/stats, narrative, examples, etc.)
Enough information offered, demonstrating DEPTH of topic?

_____ **Outside Sources**
Credible? FAIR? SIGNIFICANT?
Sources accurately cited during speech?

_____ **Visual Aids**
Reinforced Message? Distracting in any way?
Well constructed/Professional/Artistic Merit?

Physical Delivery:

_____ **Audience Awareness**
Eye Contact/Connection?
Drew audience into speech? Made information RELEVANT?

_____ **Body Movement**
Posture? Gestures?
Movement? Visual Aid Use (if applicable)?

_____ **Voice**
Volume? Rate? Tone?
Pitch? Quality?
Clear articulation? Correct pronunciations?

_____ **Expressiveness**
Facial Expressions? Vocal Variety?
Energy/Enthusiasm?

_____ **Fluency**
Flow of Delivery?
Extemporaneous?

_____ **Overall Impact**
PURPOSE fulfilled? Effective Q & A? Overall Effectiveness?

Overall Rating (circle one):   Accomplished   Competent   Developing   Beginning
                                          4   3.5   3   2.5   2   1.5   1

GRADE:

PREPARATION AND SPEAKING OUTLINE PRINCIPLES

For the Preparation Outline:

These are the 9 criteria you are expected to follow when constructing your formal preparation outline. The preparation outline represents the "mule work" necessary for effective public speaking; you should not expect to complete a formal preparation outline the night before it is due! Taking the time to research and organize your message adequately will enable you to be IN CONTROL of your presentation at all times!

1. Articulate your purpose by including a heading at the top of your outline consisting of: TOPIC, GENERAL PURPOSE, SPECIFIC PURPOSE, and THESIS STATEMENT (central idea that previews main points of presentation).

2. Separate and label the parts of your presentation: INTRODUCTION, BODY, CONCLUSION

    a. functions of effective intro include…

    b. functions of effective conclusion include…

3. Utilize the principles of COORDINATION and SUBORDINATION. Use the standard alpha-numeric outlining format. No bullets or manuscripts!

4. Articulate EACH MAIN POINT as a SINGLE FULL SENTENCE. Sub and sub-sub-points may also be in full sentences (this is optional). NO PARAGRAPHS of information in your formal outline!

5. Parenthetically, INDICATE YOUR SOURCES within the structure of the outline. Indicate what sources you are bringing in at what points in the presentation.

6. Demonstrate the DEPTH of your content.

7. Write in (word-for-word) your TRANSITION STATEMENTS between each part of your presentation and between each main point.

8. TITLE your presentation creatively!

9. ATTACH (this means staple!) and ANNOTATED BIBLIOGRAPHY to your formal outline. All sources that you list must also be found cited in the outline as well!

For the Speaking Outline:

After you complete your formal preparation outline, you can begin constructing your speaking notes. It is best not to use your preparation outline as your speaking notes because in doing so, you are likely to be too dependent on your outline as you speak. **The goal for extemporaneous delivery is to be so familiar with your material, you can present your message by using a limited number of note cards (or a single sheet of paper) to cue yourself on the key points of the presentation.**

Speaking notes, therefore, should be a skeletal representation of the formal outline. Your speaking notes should follow the same general organization of your preparation outline, but with key phrases instead of full sentences.

The best way to develop your speaking notes is by beginning your rehearsal process with your full formal preparation outline. After practicing your speech 5 or 6 times using the preparation outline, you will discover that you won't need to look at the notes quite so much…that certain key points and phrases will "jump out" at you to kick off the next thought you want to convey. These key points will serve as the basis of your speaking notes.

Your goal is to develop a set of notes that you can simply glance down at to keep you on track and in control of your message. Feel free to write yourself brief delivery notes on your speaking outline (EX: "Breathe!" "Pause here." "Louder!") as well as the specific source citations you will need to make as an ethical communicator.

SAMPLE FORMAL PREPARATION OUTLINE

The following outline demonstrates the 9 criteria for a formal preparation outline. After you develop your own preparation outline, come back to this page and make a comparison. How does yours measure up?

Burn, Baby, Burn: The Phenomena of Spontaneous Human Combustion

Topic: Spontaneous Human Combustion
General Purpose: To inform
Specific Purpose: At the end of my presentation, my audience will be able to explain the theoretical causes of spontaneous human combustion and reflect on cases of this phenomena from around the world.
Thesis (Preview of Main Points): Today I would like to first, define the unusual phenomena known as spontaneous human combustion, second, provide theories about how and why it happens, and finally, illustrate this unusual phenomenon by giving you examples of case studies of actual occurrences.

INTRODUCTION:

    What would you think if, one day while sitting in biology class, the person sitting next to you calmly taking notes suddenly burst into flames for no apparent reason? Even odder, while that person rapidly disintegrated into mere ashes, the pencil he was holding, the notebook he was writing upon, and the desk in which he once sat were completely unscathed by the flames. This phenomena, known as "spontaneous human combustion" or simply "SHC" by alternative scientists, represents one of the most unusual natural occurrences in human existence. While I have never witnessed this phenomena firsthand (and I doubt any of you have either), my fascination with spontaneous human combustion grew out of a book I read while in junior high, introduced to me by Mr. Fields, my 8th grade science teacher. The book, "De Incendiis Corporis Humani Spontaneis," penned by French scientist Jonas Dupont in 1673, brings to light this strange subject and challenges us even today to consider the mystery of spontaneous human combustion as one of many unusual human experiences not yet fully understood by modern scientists.

    As college students, we are challenged by our professors to think critically about the world around us. As such, today I'd like for you to rise to this challenge by learning more about spontaneous human combustion as I, in the next six minutes, first explain what, exactly spontaneous human combustion is, second, provide theories about how and why it happens, and finally, illustrate this unusual phenomena by giving you examples of case studies of actual occurrences.

(Transition: Let's begin by examining the defining the qualities of spontaneous human combustion…)

BODY:

I. Alternative scientist James Smithton claims that spontaneous human combustion occurs when the human body catches fire as a result of heat generated by internal chemical actions. (www.crystallinks.com).

    A. Chemical reactions potentially caused by a number of factors (The Skeptic's Dictionary)
        1. Body fat
        2. Presence of flammable liquids (i.e. alcohol)
        3. Poor diet
        4. Digestive failures
        5. Electrical fields in the body

    B. Body is severely burned (Haslam, p. 25)
        1. more than normal fire, usually torso is most severe
        2. extremities often untouched
        3. objects around body often untouched by fire
        4. greasy residue on ceiling and walls
        5. temperatures estimated as high as 3,000 degrees F

    C. References to this phenomena found throughout history (www.crystalinks.com)
        1. Bible (God's punishment)
        2. DuPont's recorded cases
        3. Charles Dickens' (Bleak House)
        4. Modern records (police and fire records)

(Transition: Now that we know a bit about what spontaneous human combustion is and the alleged historical references to this phenomena, let's look more closely at the theories of how, exactly, SHC might occur…)

II. There are several theories about SHC, but two are most prominent.

    A. Body Fat Theory (www.skeptic.com)
        1. "flammable" body fat caused by poor diet
        2. flammable body fat caused by alcohol consumption
        3. presence of methane with fat

    B. Electrical Fields Theory (Arnold)
        1. Short circuits in body's electrical fields
        2. Atomic chain reactions
        3. Build up of human gasses

(Transition: As preposterous as these theories may sound to you, there have been several interesting documentations of SHC...)

    III.   Cases of SHC are peppered through history (Nickell; Arnold; DuPont)

        A. The case of Jean Lucille Safin
        B. The case of Helen Conway
        C. The case of Nicole Millet
        D. The case of Grace Pett
        E. More recently, the cases of Mary Reeser and Dr. Irving Bentley
        F. In some cases, photos are available of the remains

(Transition: These stories, whether you believe them or not, are a fascinating way to end my presentation today and offer us a glimpse into the world of alternative thinking...)

CONCLUSION:

Today I summarized the basic knowledge alternative scientists have gathered related to spontaneous human combustion by explaining the definition, theories, and examples of this phenomena. The next time you are sitting in biology class, I'd like you to think about my presentation today and who knows? When the person sitting next to you suddenly implodes, you'll be able to provide a reasonable explanation. Are there any questions?

References (Annotated)

You should document all of the sources you used in your research here. You may use APA or MLA styles, but be accurate and consistent in how you do it.

Annotations should follow each source citation. Annotations are simply 2 – 3 sentence descriptions of the source and how, specifically, you used that source as support for your speech.

EXAMPLE:

Nickell, J. T. (2004). Explaining the unexplainable: 20th century cases of spontaneous human combustion. Duluth, MN: Alternative Press.

This recent text offers a complete history of cases of SHC in the 20th century from around the world. Detailed explanations of each significant case are included, along with photographs (when available) of the SHC victims. This source also provided me with information about the most recent theories that are prevalent related to SHC.

Regional Dialects and Public Speaking

A question that many EKU students who are studying communication often ask is "What should I do with my accent?" The CMS faculty contends that **there is no such thing as a "bad" accent** and it is important to remember this! At the same time, we acknowledge the communication research which suggests that people with southern dialects are often **perceived** as being less credible or somehow less competent than their northern, mid-western, and/or western counterparts. As such, your CMS instructor will not suggest to you that you need to rid yourself of your dialect, but rather that in raising your awareness about how your dialect might impact your audience's perceptions of you and your message, you may want to make adjustments for the sake of clarity or to reduce potential distractions from the message that your dialect may cause.

It is also important to note that there is a difference between dialect and poor grammar or poor articulation. **Your southern dialect is to be culturally valued**, but having a southern dialect does not give you license to use double negatives, neglect subject-verb agreement, mispronounce words, "mush" words together, or drop endings from words. These are entirely different issues that every public speaker should avoid!

Jo Sprague and Douglas Stuart (2003) offer the following suggestions for speakers who have "broad" dialects so that you can be better understood and appreciated by your audiences:

1. Take the time to develop a strong introduction to allow your audience to adjust to your manner of speaking (your patterns and pronunciations).
2. Speak just a little more slowly and distinctly than you do in conversation.
3. Be alert to feedback from your audience as you speak. If you see confused faces, repeat your ideas more slowly and/or adjust your word choices appropriately.
4. Be alert to amused faces as well. Acknowledge that you may sound different, but point their attention to the *message* that you are bringing to them and the commonalities between your ideas and those of your audience.
5. Don't drop your endings (especially "ings") as this will make you sound much less credible and professional. Push your words to the front part of your mouth to maximize the articulation of the word and increase your clarity.
6. Practice your speech ahead of time with someone who is representative of your audience and who can give you constructive feedback on what words or sounds might be confusing.

We encourage you to engage in a lively discussion about dialect in class (or online) for additional insights, ideas, and suggestions about how to handle your dialect in public speaking situations. We also suggest that you think about perceptions (or misperceptions) you yourself might have as an audience member, listening to someone who sounds different from you!

Brief Contents

UNIT I   Principles of Communication

Chapter 1	Foundations of Human Communication	1
Chapter 2	Self-Awareness and Communication	31
Chapter 3	Understanding Verbal Messages	59
Chapter 4	Understanding Nonverbal Messages	85
Chapter 5	Listening and Responding	113
Chapter 6	Adapting to Others: Diversity and Communication	141

UNIT II   Interpersonal Communication

| Chapter 7 | Understanding Interpersonal Communication | 173 |
| Chapter 8 | Enhancing Relationships | 201 |

UNIT III   Communicating in Groups and Teams

| Chapter 9 | Understanding Group and Team Performance | 231 |
| Chapter 10 | Enhancing Group and Team Performance | 259 |

UNIT IV   Presentational Speaking

Chapter 11	Developing Your Presentation	293
Chapter 12	Organizing and Outlining Your Presentation	327
Chapter 13	Delivering Your Presentation	349
Chapter 14	Speaking to Inform	377
Appendix B	Sample Speeches for Discussion and Evaluation	448

Contents

Preface xvi

UNIT I Principles of Communication

Chapter 1 Foundations of Human Communication 1

Why Study Communication? 2
- To Improve Your Employability 3
- To Improve Your Relationships 3
- To Improve Your Health 4

Communication Defined 5
- Communication Is About Making Sense 6
- Communication Is About Sharing Sense 6
- Communication Is About Creating Meaning 6
- Communication Is About Verbal and Nonverbal Messages 6

Communication Competence 7
- The Message Should Be Understood 7
- The Message Should Achieve Its Intended Effect 7
- The Message Should Be Ethical 8

Communication Models 9
- ■ **Communication and Ethics:** What Are the Sources of Your Ethical Views? 10
- Communication as Action: Message Transfer 10
- Communication as Interaction: Message Exchange 12
- Communication as Transaction: Message Creation 13
- Mediated Communication 13

Communication Characteristics 16
- Communication Is Inescapable 16
- Communication Is Irreversible 17
- Communication Is Complicated 17
- Communication Emphasizes Content and Relationships 18
- Communication Is Governed by Rules 18

Communication Principles for a Lifetime 18
- Principle One: Be Aware of Your Communication with Yourself and Others 19
- Principle Two: Effectively Use and Interpret Verbal Messages 20
- Principle Three: Effectively Use and Interpret Nonverbal Messages 20
- Principle Four: Listen and Respond Thoughtfully to Others 21
- Principle Five: Appropriately Adapt Messages to Others 22

Communicating with Others: Three Contexts 22
- Interpersonal Communication 23
- Group Communication 23
- ■ **Communication and Diversity:** Principles for a Lifetime: Principles for All Cultures? 24
- Presentational Communication 25

Principles for a Lifetime: Enhancing Your Skills 26

Summary 27

Assessing Your Knowledge 27

Assessing Your Skill 28

Web Resources to Improve Your Knowledge and Skill 29

Chapter 2 Self-Awareness and Communication 31

Self-Awareness: How Well Do You Know Yourself? 32

Self-Concept: Who Are You? 34
- Self-Concept Components 34
- One or Many Selves? 35
- ■ **Communication and Diversity:** Self-Concept from East and West 35
- How the Self-Concept Develops 37

Self-Esteem: What Is Your Value? 40
- Gender 40

Social Comparisons 41
Self-Expectations 42
■ **Communication and Technology:** Searching for One's Self Online 43
Self-Fulfilling Prophecy 43

Communication and the Enhancement of Self-Esteem 44
Engage in Positive Self-Talk 44
Visualize 45
Reframe 45
■ **Communication and Ethics:** Can You Have Too Much Self-Esteem? 46
Develop Honest Relationships 47
Surround Yourself with Positive People 47
Lose Your Baggage 48

The Perception Process 48
Stage One: Attention and Selection 49
Stage Two: Organization 50
Stage Three: Interpretation 51

When Perceptions Vary 51

Communication and the Enhancement of Perceptual Accuracy 53
Increase Your Awareness 53
Avoid Stereotypes 53
Check Your Perceptions 54

Principles for a Lifetime: Enhancing Your Skills 55

Summary 55

Assessing Your Knowledge 56

Assessing Your Skill 57

Web Resources to Improve Your Knowledge and Skill 57

Chapter 3 Understanding Verbal Messages 59

Why Focus on Language? 61

The Nature of Language 62
People Use Words as Symbols 62
People Attach Meanings to Words 63
People Create Denotative and Connotative Meanings for Words 63
People Convey Concrete and Abstract Meanings Through Words 63
■ **Communication and Technology:** Computer Terms: Denotation and Connotation 64
Meanings Are Culture Bound 65
Meanings Are Context Bound 65

The Power of Words 65
■ **Communication and Diversity:** Code-Switching as Linguistic Flexibility 66
The Power to Create and Label Experience 66
The Power to Affect Thoughts and Actions 67
The Power to Shape and Reflect Culture 68
The Power to Make and Break Relationships 68

Confronting Bias in Language 69
Biased Language: Race, Ethnicity, Nationality, and Religion 69
Biased Language: Gender and Sexual Orientation 72
Biased Language: Age, Class, and Ability 74
■ **Communication and Ethics:** "That's So Gay!" 75

Using Words to Establish Supportive Relationships 76
Describe Your Own Feelings Rather Than Evaluate Others 77
Solve Problems Rather Than Control Others 77
Be Genuine Rather Than Manipulative 78
Empathize Rather Than Remain Detached from Others 78
Be Flexible Rather Than Rigid Toward Others 78
Present Yourself as Equal Rather Than Superior 78
Avoid Gunny-Sacking 79

Principles for a Lifetime: Enhancing Your Skills 80

Summary 81

Assessing Your Knowledge 81

Assessing Your Skill 82

Web Resources to Improve Your Knowledge and Skill 83

Chapter 4 Understanding Nonverbal Messages 85

Why Focus on Nonverbal Communication? 85
Nonverbal Messages Communicate Feelings and Attitudes 87
Nonverbal Messages Are More Believable Than Verbal Ones 88
■ **Communication and Technology:** Computer-Mediated Communication: Conveying Emotions 88
Nonverbal Messages Are Critical to Successful Relationships 89
Nonverbal Messages Serve Multiple Functions 89

The Nature of Nonverbal Communication 91
The Culture-Bound Nature of Nonverbal Communication 91
The Rule-Governed Nature of Nonverbal Communication 92
The Ambiguous Nature of Nonverbal Communication 93
The Continuous Nature of Nonverbal Communication 93
The Nonlinguistic Nature of Nonverbal Communication 93
The Multichanneled Nature of Nonverbal Communication 94

Codes of Nonverbal Communication 94
Appearance 95
Body Movement, Gestures, and Posture 95
■ **Communication and Ethics:** Lie Detectors 98
Eye Contact 98
Facial Expressions 99

Touch 100
- **Communication and Diversity:** Cultural Meanings of Silence 100
  The Voice 101
  Physical Environment, Space, and Territory 102

How to Interpret Nonverbal Cues More Accurately 105
  Immediacy 106
  Arousal 106
  Dominance 107

Principles for a Lifetime: Enhancing Your Skills 108

Summary 108

Assessing Your Knowledge 109

Assessing Your Skill 110

Web Resources to Improve Your Knowledge and Skill 111

Chapter 5 Listening and Responding 113

The Importance of Listening and Responding Skills 114

How We Listen 115
  Selecting 115
  Attending 115
- **Communication and Technology:** Listening When No One Is Home 116
  Understanding 116
  Remembering 116
  Responding 117

Listening Styles 117
  People-Oriented Listening 118
  Action-Oriented Listening 118
  Content-Oriented Listening 118
  Time-Oriented Listening 119

Listening Barriers 119
- **Communication and Diversity:** East and West Listening Styles 120
  Self Barriers 121
  Information-Processing Barriers 123
  Context Barriers 124

Improving Your Listening Skills 125
  Stop: Turn Off Competing Messages 126
  Look: Listen with Your Eyes 127
  Listen: Understand Both Details and Major Ideas 128
- **Communication and Diversity:** Who Are Better Listeners: Men or Women? 128

Responding Skills 131
  Be Descriptive 131
  Be Timely 132
  Be Brief 132
  Be Useful 132

Responding with Empathy 132
  Understand Your Partner's Feelings 133
  Ask Appropriate Questions 133
  Paraphrase Message Content 133
  Paraphrase Emotions 134
- **Communication and Ethics:** Expressing Honest Social Support to Others 135

Principles for a Lifetime: Enhancing Your Skills 136

Summary 137

Assessing Your Knowledge 138

Assessing Your Skill 139

Web Resources to Improve Your Knowledge and Skill 139

Chapter 6 Adapting to Others: Diversity and Communication 141

Understanding Diversity 143
  Gender 143
  Sexual Orientation 145
  Ethnicity 146
  Age 146

Ethically Adapt Your Communication to Others 148

Culture and Communication 148
- **Communication and Diversity:** Diversity Almanac 149
  Defining Culture 150
- **Communication and Technology:** Adapting to Cultural Differences When Communicating Electronically 151
  Cultural Contexts 151
  Cultural Values 152

Barriers to Bridging Differences and Adapting to Others 157
  Assuming Superiority 157
  Assuming Similarity 158
  Assuming Differences 158
- **Communication and Ethics:** Stereotyping Others 160
  Stereotyping and Prejudice 160

Adapting to Others Who Are Different from You 161
  Seek Information 162
  Ask Questions and Listen 163
  Tolerate Ambiguity 163
  Develop Mindfulness 164
  Become Other-Oriented 164
  Adapt to Others 166

Principles for a Lifetime: Enhancing Your Skills 168

Summary 168

Assessing Your Knowledge 169

Assessing Your Skill 170

Web Resources to Improve Your Knowledge and Skill 171

UNIT II Interpersonal Communication

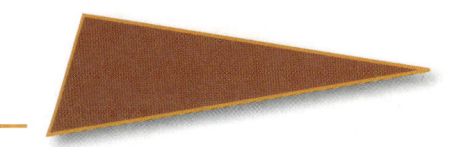

Chapter 7 Understanding Interpersonal Communication 173

What Is Interpersonal Communication? 174
- Interpersonal Communication Involves Quality 175
- Interpersonal Communication Involves Mutual Influence 175
- Interpersonal Communication Helps Manage Relationships 175

Initiating Relationships 176
- Interpersonal Attraction: Why We Like Whom We Like 177
- ■ **Communication and Diversity:** Thinking Outside the Race 179
- Communicating Our Attraction 180
- Getting That First Conversation Going 182

Maintaining Relationships 187
- Self-Disclosure: Revealing Yourself to Others 187
- ■ **Communication and Technology:** "High Tech" Self-Disclosure 189
- Two Models of Self-Disclosure 191
- Expressing Emotions 193
- ■ **Communication and Ethics:** PostSecret 194

Principles for a Lifetime: Enhancing Your Skills 195

Summary 196

Assessing Your Knowledge 197

Assessing Your Skill 198

Web Resources to Improve Your Knowledge and Skill 199

Chapter 8 Enhancing Relationships 201

The Importance of Friendship 202
- Communication Principles for a Lifetime: Enhancing Friendships 204

The Importance of Family 204
- Communication Principles for a Lifetime: Enhancing Family Relationships 204

The Importance of Colleagues 205
- Communication Principles for a Lifetime: Enhancing Workplace Relationships 205

Stages of Relationship Development 206
- Relational Escalation 207
- Relational De-Escalation 208
- ■ **Communication and Ethics:** How Easy Should a Breakup Be? 210
- ■ **Communication and Technology:** Cheating in Cyberspace 211

Tensions in Relationships: The Dialectical Perspective 211
- Integration–Separation: Autonomy versus Connection 212
- Stability–Change: Predictability versus Novelty 213
- Expression–Privacy: Openness versus Closedness 213

Managing Interpersonal Conflict 214
- A World of Conflict 214
- Types of Conflict 214
- ■ **Communication and Diversity:** Conflict and Culture 217
- How Conflict Functions in Relationships 217
- Styles of Managing Conflict 220
- Conflict Management Skills 221

Principles for a Lifetime: Enhancing Your Skills 225

Summary 227

Assessing Your Knowledge 227

Assessing Your Skill 228

Web Resources to Improve Your Knowledge and Skill 229

UNIT III Communicating in Groups and Teams

Chapter 9 Understanding Group and Team Performance 231

Groups and Teams Defined 232
- Communicating in Small Groups 233
- Communicating in Teams 234
- When Not To Collaborate in Groups and Teams 236

Understanding Types of Groups and Teams 237
- Primary Groups 237
- Study Groups 237
- ■ **Communication and Ethics:** Ethically Achieving a Team Goal 237
- Therapy Groups 238
- Problem-Solving Groups 238
- ■ **Communication and Technology:** Does Virtual Group Communication Improve Decision Making? 238
- Focus Groups 238
- Social Groups 239

Understanding Group and Team Dynamics 239
- Roles 239
- Rules 241
- Norms 241
- Status 244
- Power 245
- Cohesiveness 246
- Communication Interaction Patterns 247

Understanding Phases of Group and Team Development 249
- Orientation 249
- Conflict 249
- Emergence 250
- Reinforcement 250
- The Process Nature of Group Phases 251
- ■ **Communication and Diversity:** The Impact of Individualism and Collectivism on Groups and Teams 252
- How Real Groups and Teams Interact in Organizations 252

Principles for a Lifetime: Enhancing Your Skills 253

Summary 254

Assessing Your Knowledge 255

Assessing Your Skill 256

Web Resources to Improve Your Knowledge and Skill 257

Chapter 10 Enhancing Group and Team Performance 259

What Effective Group Members Do 260
- Identify and Implement Key Functions to Achieve Results 261
- Identify a Clear, Elevating Goal 261
- Develop a Results-Driven Structure 262
- Gather and Use Information Effectively 262
- Develop Options 262
- Evaluate Ideas 263
- Develop Sensitivity Toward Others 263

Structuring Group and Team Problem Solving 264
- Step 1: Identify and Define the Problem 266
- Step 2: Analyze the Problem 267
- Step 3: Generate Creative Solutions 268
- Step 4: Select the Best Solution 270
- ■ **Communication and Ethics:** Managing Conflict in Groups and Teams 272
- Step 5: Take Action 273

Enhancing Group and Team Leadership 273
- Trait Approach 274
- Functional Approach 274
- Styles Approach 275
- Situational Approach 277
- Transformational Leadership 277

Enhancing Group and Team Meetings 279
- ■ **Communication and Diversity:** Differences in the Use of Time in Groups and Teams 280
- Manage Meeting Structure 281
- Manage Meeting Interaction 283
- ■ **Communication and Technology:** Participating in Virtual Meetings 286

Principles for a Lifetime: Enhancing Your Skills 286

Summary 287

Assessing Your Knowledge 288

Assessing Your Skill 289

Web Resources to Improve Your Knowledge and Skill 289

UNIT IV Presentational Speaking

Chapter 11 Developing Your Presentation 293

An Overview of the Presentational Speaking Process 295
- **Developing Your Presentation Step by Step:** Consider Your Audience 296

Understanding Speaker Anxiety 296

Managing Speaker Anxiety 297
- Know How to Develop a Presentation 298
- Be Prepared 298
- Focus on Your Audience 298
- Focus on Your Message 299
- Give Yourself a Mental Pep Talk 299
- Use Deep-Breathing Techniques 299
- Take Advantage of Opportunities to Speak 299
- Seek Professional Help 299

Selecting and Narrowing Your Topic 300
- Who Is the Audience? 300
- What Is the Occasion? 300
- What Are My Interests and Experiences? 300
- Conducting Silent Brainstorming 301
- Scanning Web Directories and Web Pages 302
- Listening and Reading for Topic Ideas 302
- **Developing Your Presentation Step by Step:** Selecting and Narrowing Your Topic 302

Identifying Your Purpose 303
- General Purpose 304
- Specific Purpose 304
- **Developing Your Presentation Step by Step:** Identifying Your Purpose 304

Developing Your Central Idea 305
- An Audience-Centered Idea 306
- A Single Topic 306
- A Complete Declarative Sentence 306
- Direct, Specific Language 307
- **Developing Your Presentation Step by Step:** Developing Your Central Idea 307

Generating Main Ideas 307
- Does the Central Idea Have *Logical Divisions*? 308
- Can You Think of Several *Reasons* the Central Idea Is True? 308
- Can You Support the Central Idea with a Series of *Steps* or a *Chronological Sequence*? 308
- **Developing Your Presentation Step by Step:** Generating Your Main Ideas 309

Gathering Supporting Material 310
- Sources of Supporting Material 310
- **Communication and Technology:** A New Kind of Search Engine 311
- **Communication and Ethics:** A Question of Speechwriting 314
- **Developing Your Presentation Step by Step:** Gathering Supporting Material 315
- Types of Supporting Material 315
- **Communication and Diversity:** Adapting to Diverse Audiences 318
- Acknowledgment of Supporting Material 320

Principles for a Lifetime: Enhancing Your Skills 321

Summary 322

Assessing Your Knowledge 323

Assessing Your Skill 324

Web Resources to Improve Your Knowledge and Skill 325

Chapter 12 Organizing and Outlining Your Presentation 327

Organizing Your Main Ideas 328
- Organizing Ideas Topically 329
- Organizing Ideas Chronologically 329
- Organizing Ideas Spatially 329
- Organizing Ideas to Show Cause and Effect 330
- Organizing Ideas by Problem and Solution 330

Organizing Your Supporting Material 330
- **Communication and Diversity:** Acknowledging Cultural Differences in Organizing Messages 332

Organizing Your Presentation for the Ears of Others 333
- Previews 333
- Verbal and Nonverbal Transitions 333
- **Communication and Ethics:** The Ethics of Primacy and Recency 333
- Summaries 334

Introducing and Concluding Your Presentation 335
- Introductions 335
- Conclusions 337

Outlining Your Presentation 339
- Preparation Outline 339
- **Communication and Technology:** Using Outlining Software 340
- Sample Preparation Outline 341
- Speaking Notes 343

Principles for a Lifetime: Enhancing Your Skills 345

Summary 345

Assessing Your Knowledge 346

Assessing Your Skill 347

Web Resources to Improve Your Knowledge and Skill 347

Chapter 13 Delivering Your Presentation 349

Methods of Delivery 350
   Manuscript Speaking 350
   Memorized Speaking 351
   Impromptu Speaking 351
   Extemporaneous Speaking 352

Effective Verbal Delivery 353
   Using Words Well 353
   Crafting Memorable Word Structures 354

Effective Nonverbal Delivery 357
   Eye Contact 357
   Physical Delivery 357
   Facial Expression 359
■ **Communication and Diversity:** The Academic Quarter 359
   Vocal Delivery 360
■ **Developing Your Presentation Step by Step:** Rehearsing Your Presentation 361
   Appearance 361

Effective Presentation Aids 362
■ **Communication and Technology:** Rehearsing on Videotape 363
   Types of Presentation Aids 363
   Guidelines for Preparing Presentation Aids 367
■ **Communication and Ethics:** Profanity in an Audio Presentation Aid 368
   Guidelines for Using Presentation Aids 368

Some Final Tips for Rehearsing and Delivering Your Presentation 370
■ **Developing Your Presentation Step by Step:** Delivering Your Presentation 371

Principles for a Lifetime: Enhancing Your Skills 372

Summary 373

Assessing Your Knowledge 374

Assessing Your Skill 375

Web Resources to Improve Your Knowledge and Skill 375

Chapter 14 Speaking to Inform 377

Types of Informative Presentations 378
   Presentations About Objects 378
■ **Communication and Ethics:** Confidential or Potentially Dangerous Information 379
   Presentations About Procedures 379
   Presentations About People 380
   Presentations About Events 380
   Presentations About Ideas 381

Strategies for Organizing Your Informative Presentation 381
   Organizing Presentations About Objects 381
   Organizing Presentations About Procedures 381
   Organizing Presentations About People 382
   Organizing Presentations About Events 382
   Organizing Presentations About Ideas 382

Strategies for Making Your Informative Presentation Clear 383
   Simplify Ideas 384
   Pace Your Information Flow 384
   Relate New Information to Old 384

Strategies for Making Your Informative Presentation Interesting 385
   Relate to Your Listeners' Interests 385
■ **Communication and Diversity:** Using an Interpreter 386
   Use Attention-Catching Supporting Material 386
   Establish a Motive for Your Audience to Listen to You 387
   Use Word Pictures 388
   Create Interesting Presentation Aids 388
■ **Communication and Technology:** Using an Electronic Thesaurus 389
   Use Humor 389

Strategies for Making Your Informative Presentation Memorable 390
   Build in Redundancy 390
   Use Adult Learning Principles 390
   Reinforce Key Ideas Verbally 390
   Reinforce Key Ideas Nonverbally 391
   Sample Informative Presentation 392

Principles for a Lifetime: Enhancing Your Skills 393

Summary 394

Assessing Your Knowledge 395

Assessing Your Skill 396

Web Resources to Improve Your Knowledge and Skill 397

Appendix B Sample Speeches for Discussion and Evaluation 448
Informative Speech: Advertising and Reptilian Codes 448
   by Mary Kate Raffetto
Persuasive Speech 450
   by Amy Solomito

Endnotes 452

Practice Test Answer Key 475

Index 476

Boxed Features

Communication and Ethics

Chapter 1	What Are the Sources of Your Ethical Views? 10		Chapter 10	Managing Conflict in Groups and Teams 272
Chapter 2	Can You Have Too Much Self-Esteem? 46		Chapter 11	A Question of Speechwriting 314
Chapter 3	"That's So Gay!" 75		Chapter 12	The Ethics of Primacy and Recency 333
Chapter 4	Lie Detectors 98		Chapter 13	Profanity in an Audio Presentation Aid 368
Chapter 5	Expressing Honest Social Support to Others 135		Chapter 14	Confidential or Potentially Dangerous Information 379
Chapter 6	Stereotyping Others 160			
Chapter 7	PostSecret 194			
Chapter 8	How Easy Should a Breakup Be? 210			
Chapter 9	Ethically Achieving a Team Goal 237			

Communication and Diversity

Chapter 1	Principles for a Lifetime: Principles for All Cultures? 24		Chapter 9	The Impact of Individualism and Collectivism on Groups and Teams 252
Chapter 2	Self-Concept from East and West 35		Chapter 10	Differences in the Use of Time in Groups and Teams 280
Chapter 3	Code-Switching as Linguistic Flexibility 66		Chapter 11	Adapting to Diverse Audiences 318
Chapter 4	Cultural Meanings of Silence 100		Chapter 12	Acknowledging Cultural Differences in Organizing Messages 332
Chapter 5	East and West Listening Styles 120 Who Are Better Listeners: Men or Women? 128		Chapter 13	The Academic Quarter 359
Chapter 6	Diversity Almanac 149		Chapter 14	Using an Interpreter 386
Chapter 7	Thinking Outside the Race 179			
Chapter 8	Conflict and Culture 217			

Communication and Technology

Chapter 2	Searching for One's Self Online 43
Chapter 3	Computer Terms: Denotation and Connotation 64
Chapter 4	Computer-Mediated Communication: Conveying Emotions 88
Chapter 5	Listening When No One Is Home 116
Chapter 6	Adapting to Cultural Differences When Communicating Electronically 151
Chapter 7	"High Tech" Self-Disclosure 189
Chapter 8	Cheating in Cyberspace 211
Chapter 9	Does Virtual Group Communication Improve Decision Making? 238
Chapter 10	Participating in Virtual Meetings 286
Chapter 11	A New Kind of Search Engine 311
Chapter 12	Using Outlining Software 340
Chapter 13	Rehearsing on Videotape 363
Chapter 14	Using an Electronic Thesaurus 389

DEVELOPING YOUR PRESENTATION Step by Step

Chapter 11	Consider Your Audience 296
	Selecting and Narrowing Your Topic 302
	Identifying Your Purpose 304
	Developing Your Central Idea 307
	Generating Your Main Ideas 309
	Gathering Supporting Material 316
Chapter 13	Rehearsing Your Presentation 361
	Delivering Your Presentation 371

Preface

Communication is essential for life. The purpose of this book is to document this claim by presenting fundamental principles of human communication that enhance the quality of our communication with others as well as the quality of our own lives. Most students who read this book will take only one course in communication during their entire college career. Because communication is an essential element of living, we want students to remember essential communication principles and skills for the rest of their lives. In our fourth edition of *Communication: Principles for a Lifetime*, our goal remains the same as in the first edition: to provide a cogent presentation of what is essential about human communication by organizing the study of communication around five fundamental communication principles that are inherent in the process of communicating with others. We want students to view this course on communication as a vital, life-enriching one that will help them enhance their communication with others—not just as another course in a string of curricular requirements. To remember and apply these essential communication principles, we believe students need a digest of classic and contemporary research and practice that will help them with both the mundane and the magnificent, the everyday and the ever-important communication experiences that constitute the fabric of their lives.

The Challenge of Teaching a Fundamentals of Communication Course

The problem with many introduction to communication courses is there is often too much of a good thing. An introductory course covers a vast terrain of communication concepts, principles, and skills. The barrage of ideas, contexts, and theories can leave students and instructors feeling overwhelmed by a seemingly unrelated hodgepodge of information. Besides learning about several theories of communication, students are also presented with what may appear to them to be miniature courses in interpersonal communication, group communication, and public speaking. In addition to developing a conceptual understanding of human communication, students are expected to master a long list of communication skills, including group problem-solving skills, listening and paraphrasing skills, conflict management skills, and public speaking skills for both informative and persuasive presentations. How to interview others is also a skill commonly presented in an introductory communication course. At the end of a typical hybrid or introductory communication fundamentals course, both students and instructors have made a breathless dash through an astounding amount of information and number of skills; students may not, however, have an appreciation of either the superstructure of human communication or the foundation on which it is based. They may end up viewing communication as a fragmented area of study that includes a bushel basket full of concepts and applications, but have little understanding of what is truly fundamental about how we make sense out of the world and share that sense with others.

Our Solution: An Integrated Approach to Communication Principles and Skills

To help students remember and integrate essential communication principles, we've organized the study of human communication around five fundamental communication principles. Organizing seminal communication content using these five principles is helpful not only for students but also for instructors. The principles can provide the common threads that stitch together the plethora of ideas and information typically presented in an introductory communication course. Rather than an unrelated crazy quilt of ideas and skills, we want students to see a unified fabric of common principles that they will remember long after the course is over. The principles provide a framework for understanding the importance of communication in our lives. No, we don't claim that everything you need to know about communication is embedded in our five communication principles. These principles do, however, synthesize essential research and wisdom about communication. They are designed to help students in an introductory communication course see the "big picture" of the role and importance of communication, both as they sit in the classroom and as they live their lives.

The communication principles we highlight should look familiar—they are included in some way in most introductory communication texts. However, they are not often used as a scaffolding to provide coherence to the entire course. In most texts, communication principles are typically presented in the first third of the book and then abandoned, as material about interpersonal, group, and public communication is presented. We don't use a "hit-and-run" approach. Instead, using examples and illustrations to which students can relate, we carefully discuss each principle early in the book. Throughout the latter two-thirds of the book we gently remind students of how these principles relate to interpersonal relationships, group and team discussions, and public presentations. We cover classic communication content but organize it around five principles so the information has coherence. What are the five fundamental principles?

Principle One: Be aware of your communication with yourself and others.
Principle Two: Effectively use and interpret verbal messages.
Principle Three: Effectively use and interpret nonverbal messages.
Principle Four: Listen and respond thoughtfully to others.
Principle Five: Appropriately adapt messages to others.

A subtext for these five principles is the importance of communicating ethically with others. Throughout the book we invite students to consider the ethical implications of how they communicate with others, through the use of probes and questions. As we discuss in Chapter 1, we believe that in order to be effective, a communication message must achieve three goals: It must be understood, it must achieve its intended effect, and it must be ethical. Our five communication principles for a lifetime are designed to help students achieve these three goals.

Our pentagon model illustrates the relationships among the five communication principles that are the over-arching structure of the book. As a principle is being introduced or discussed, the appropriate part of the model is highlighted.

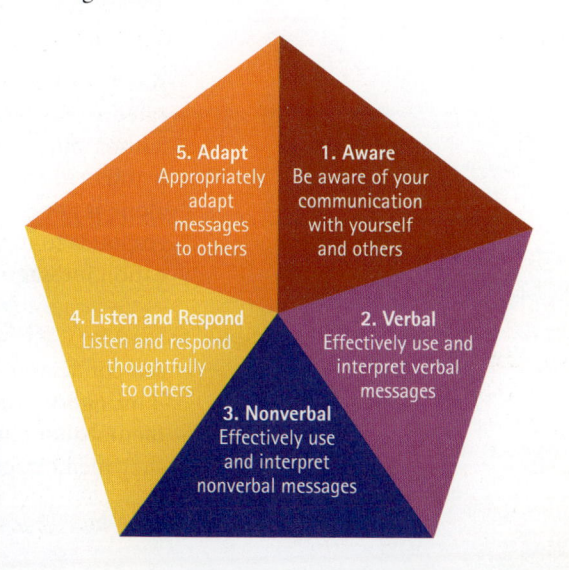

But in addition to identifying five communication principles, we want to show students how these principles relate to the classic communication contexts of interpersonal communication, group and team communication, and presentational speaking. We link the five communication principles with specific content by using a margin icon to indicate that a discussion in the text of a skill, concept, or idea is related to one or more of the five communication principles. The icons, described in Chapter 1 and illustrated on the following page, first appear in the margin in Chapter 7, "Understanding Interpersonal Communication," which is the first context chapter of the book. The icons help students see the many applications our five communication principles have to their lives as they read about interpersonal communication, group and team communication, and presentational speaking.

Overview of the Book

The book retains the overall structure of the three previous editions and is organized into four units. Unit I introduces the five principles (Chapter 1), and then each principle is explained in a separate chapter (Chapters 2 through 6). Each communication principle is discussed and illustrated to help students see its value and centrality in their lives. Chapter 2 discusses the principle of being self aware. Chapter 3 focuses on using and interpreting verbal messages, and Chapter 4 focuses on using and interpreting nonverbal messages. Chapter 5 includes a discussion of the interrelated processes of listening and responding, giving special attention to the importance of being other-oriented and empathic. The final principle, appropriately adapting to others, is presented in Chapter 6; we use this principle to illustrate the importance of adapting one's behavior to culture and gender differences among people.

Unit II applies the five communication principles to interpersonal relationships. Unlike many treatments of interpersonal communication, our discussion links the concepts and strategies for understanding interpersonal communication with our five Communication Principles for a Lifetime. Chapter 7 presents information to help students better understand the nature and function of communication in relationships. Chapter 8 identifies strategies that can enhance the quality of interpersonal relationships with others.

Unit III discusses how the five communication principles can help us understand and enhance communication in small groups and teams. Chapter 9 explains how groups and teams work. We offer practical strategies for collaboratively solving problems, leading groups and teams, and running and participating in meetings in Chapter 10.

Our final unit, Unit IV, presents classic content to help students design and deliver a speech, referring to contemporary research and using the latest tools of technology. Based on our popular audience-centered approach to developing a presentation, we emphasize the importance of adapting to listeners while also being an ethically vigilant communicator. Chapters 11 through 14 offer information and tips for developing presentation ideas, organizing and outlining presentations, delivering a presentation (including using presentational and multimedia aids), crafting effective informative presentations, and developing ethical persuasive messages.

We conclude the book with an appendix designed to supplement our instruction about communication fundamentals. Appendix B includes examples of recent presentations to illustrate what effective, well-planned presentations look like.

Our Partnership with Students to Help Them Learn

A textbook is essentially a "distance learning" tool. As we write the book, we are separated from the learner by both time and space. To help lessen the distance between author and reader, we've incorporated a variety of learning resources and pedagogical features to engage students in the learning process. As we note in the text, information alone is not communication. Communication occurs when the receiver of information responds to it. Our special features help turn information into a responsive communication message that has an effect on students' lives.

Principles Model and Icon
Our pentagon model and margin icons help students see connections between the various communication concepts and skills we present. Throughout the book we provide an integrated framework to reinforce what's fundamental about human communication. Long after students may have forgotten the lists they memorized for an exam, we want them to remember the five fundamental princi-

ples we highlight throughout the book. Remembering the principles can also help them remember strategies and concepts to enhance their interpersonal relationships, improve group and team meetings, and design and deliver effective presentations.

Chapter End Summary of Principles for a Lifetime In addition to using the margin icons to highlight material in the text related to one or more communication principles, we conclude each chapter with a summary of the chapter content organized around the communication principles. Our chapter summaries at the ends of the first six chapters distill essential information about the specific communication principle presented in the chapter. Starting in Chapter 7, we review and summarize the chapter content using all five communication principles for a lifetime as a framework. Miniature versions of our principles icons appear with headings to highlight the five fundamental principles. The purpose of this chapter-end feature is to help students synthesize the material related to the context discussed (e.g., interpersonal communication) and the five principles that undergird the descriptive and prescriptive information presented in the chapter. This feature will help students connect the variety of ideas and skills with the five communication principles.

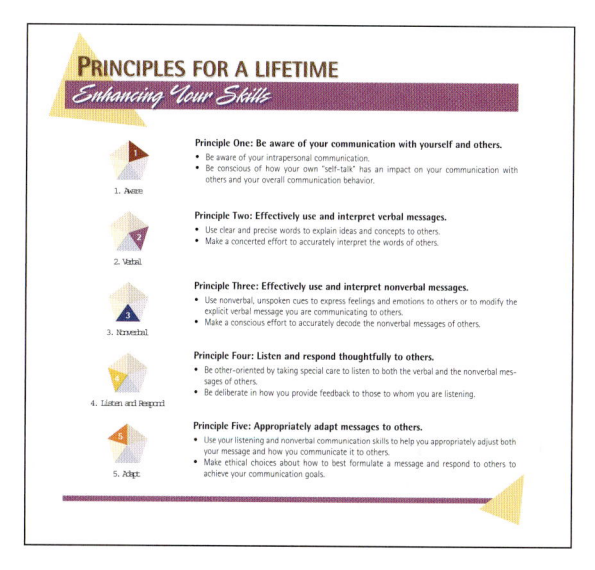

Communication and Ethics To help students consider the ethical dimensions of human communication, in each chapter we provide a special boxed feature called Communication and Ethics. In this edition, as in the third edition, we present a case study and then pose ethical questions for students to consider. We ask students to ponder how they would respond to a specific ethical dilemma. The questions we pose are designed to be thought-provoking, to spark insightful class discussion, or to be used in combination with a journal assignment or other learning method to help students see connections between ethics and communication.

Communication and Technology Because of the importance of technology in our lives, in each chapter we include special material about technology and communication to help students become sensitive to the sometimes mind-boggling impact of new technology on our communication with others. We also discuss the importance and role of technology in several chapters throughout the book. The prevalence of technology in students' lives offers powerful teachable moments to help students learn and apply communication principles.

Communication and Diversity Each chapter includes a Communication and Diversity feature designed to help students see the importance of diversity in their lives. Yet we don't relegate discussions of diversity only to a boxed feature. Because we believe diversity is such an important communication topic in contemporary society, we discuss diversity in the text, not only in relation to our fifth principle of communication (appropriately adapt messages to others) in Chapter 6, but throughout the book.

Comprehensive Pedagogical Learning Tools To help students master the material, we've built in a wealth of study aids:

- Learning objectives provide a compass to help students know where they are headed.
- Chapter outlines preview key concepts.
- Concise and highly praised Recap boxes distill essential content.

- Key terms in boldface with marginal glossary help students master essential terms.
- Chapter-end narrative summaries of each chapter.
- Chapter-end summaries of the five communication principles.
- Chapter-end questions for review and discussion keyed to the five communication principles.
- New chapter-end self-tests and assessment activities.
- Skill assessment activities and collaborative learning exercises.
- Chapter-end web site information gives students a wealth of ideas and applications available on the Internet.

New to the Fourth Edition

Reviewers, instructors, and our students have given us feedback about the three previous editions. This feedback has helped us make the fourth edition the best possible teaching and learning resource. We listened and responded (Principle Four) to their suggestions. In *every* chapter we have included the following:

- A new chapter-end feature, "Assessing Your Knowledge," provides discussion questions keyed to the five Communication Principles for a Lifetime and also presents a test (with answers provided at the back of the book) so that students can quickly assess their mastery of key chapter content.
- A new chapter-end feature, "Assessing Your Skill," offers self-tests and skill assessment tools, many of which can be used either for individual analysis or for collaborative learning class activities.
- New, redesigned margin icons better integrate these fundamental principles and their relationships to all communication contexts.
- Significantly updated and expanded research incorporates the latest research findings about human communication principles and skills.
- New, contemporary examples and illustrations to which students can relate.
- New cartoons and other illustrations to amplify the content of our message.
- Revised and expanded "Communication and Diversity" features as well as discussions of new applications of research about diversity throughout the book.
- Revised and expanded "Communication and Technology" features include an expanded discussion of the role of online communication in relationships.
- "On the Web" features at the end of each chapter help students easily find a host of new and interesting information, activities, and self-tests.
- Revised chapter-end Principles for a Lifetime summaries in Chapters 7 through 14.
- Revised and expanded "Developing Your Speech Step by Step" features in the presentational speaking chapters walk students through the process of designing and delivering a speech.
- Two new speeches in Appendix B.

We've made many other specific changes to chapter content throughout the book. Here's a brief list of selected major revisions, changes, and additions that we've made to specific chapters:

Chapter 1: Foundations of Human Communication

- Newly expanded discussion of mediated communication and of how the Internet, text messages, and e-mail continue to change the way we interact with others.
- New coverage of how the attributes of effective communication apply to both sender and receiver.
- New references to health communication and organizational communication.

Chapter 2: Self-Awareness and Communication

- Expanded discussion of self-concept development and social networking web sites such as MySpace and Facebook.

- New information on symbolic self-awareness.
- New emphasis on diverse cultural views of self-concept.
- New discussion of the relationship between self-concept clarity, loneliness, and online communication.
- New discussion of self-esteem and college student narcissism.
- Enhanced treatment of perception, including information on coping with divergent perceptions.

Chapter 3: Understanding Verbal Messages

- New examples of text messaging as a unique form of verbal communication.
- New information on computer terms that illustrate denotation and connotation.
- New discussion of language and diversity, in the form of code-switching and linguistic flexibility.
- Enhanced explanation of the role of context in message transmission, with reference to media coverage of the 2008 presidential election.
- New discussion of racial language and self-descriptors stemming from census data.
- New treatment of ethics and communication, specifically the use of homophobic and heterosexist language.

Chapter 4: Understanding Nonverbal Messages

- Updated treatment of nonverbal cues of emotion and computer-mediated communication.
- Increased emphasis on nonverbal communication and cultural diversity.
- Enhanced discussion of nonverbal codes.
- New application of territoriality to computer-mediated communication.

Chapter 5: Listening and Responding

- New discussion of listening in the twenty-first century and the expanded importance of asynchronous listening, such as listening to voice mail and other recorded messages.
- New discussion of the relationship between listening skills and marital satisfaction.
- Expanded discussion of listening styles.
- New discussion of research that documents the corrosive effects of interrupting others instead of listening calmly and attentively.
- New research that documents skills and strategies for being more attentive and focused when tuning in to the messages of others.
- New material about meta-messages and the importance of being aware of the meta-message when listening to others.
- New discussion of tips and skills for providing ethical social support to others.

Chapter 6: Adapting to Others: Diversity and Communication

- Expanded discussion of diversity including age, social class, ethnicity, sexual orientation, and other factors that make us different from one another.
- New and expanded discussion of the attributes of intercultural communication competence and a new six-stage model of the stages of intercultural communication competence.
- New discussion of an ethnorelative cultural perspective and intercultural communication competence.
- New discussion of time orientation as a cultural value.

Chapter 7: Understanding Interpersonal Communication

- New discussion of race and friendship.
- Enhanced discussion of the benefits of social networking web sites in the development of friendship.

- New research on the enduring effects of first conversations on relationship development.
- New information on alternatives to dating, with an emphasis on initial interactions.
- New research on sex differences and complimenting.
- New section on motivations for self-disclosure and how self-disclosure operates online, including a discussion of the need for retaining privacy online.
- New discussion of ethics and keeping secrets.

Chapter 8: Enhancing Relationships

- Revised treatment of communication ethics in relation to breakup techniques.
- New section on relationship tensions, or the dialectical perspective.
- New discussion of how people explain or account for conflict in their relationships
- Expanded information on types of conflict.
- New information on self-silencing as a reaction to aggressive communication.

Chapter 9: Understanding Group and Team Performance

- Revised discussion of when not to collaborate in teams.
- Expanded discussion of strategies for collaborating in virtual teams and groups, including a description of the advantages and disadvantages of collaborating virtually.
- New discussion of bona fide groups and teams, which describes how real teams operate in business and professional contexts.

Chapter 10: Enhancing Group and Team Performance

- New discussion of the latest research on transformational leadership.
- New information about leadership in computer-mediated settings and a list of the best practices for leading a virtual team.
- New tips and strategies for making the most of mediated meetings.

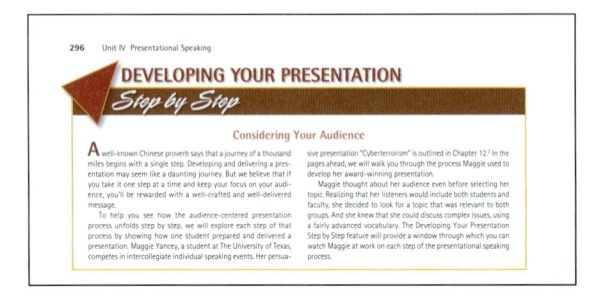

Chapter 11: Developing Your Presentation

- New discussion of why Wikipedia is not a reliable academic source.
- Updated examples, including a new student speech for the Developing Your Presentation Step by Step feature.
- New research regarding recommendations for managing speech anxiety.
- Clarified applications of specific purpose statement and central idea.
- More explicit links between ways to generate main ideas and ways to organize a presentation.
- New discussion of vertical search engines.
- Updated discussion of full-text databases.
- Personal Report of Communication Apprehension (PRCA-24) in the chapter-end "Assessing Your Skill" feature.

Chapter 12: Organizing and Outlining Your Presentation

- Re-ordering of organizational strategies to reflect the frequency with which topical organizational patterns are used.
- More explicit links between ways to organize a presentation and ways to generate main ideas, including an expanded Recap box.
- Updated examples from both student presentations and some of the most acclaimed presentations of the day—for example, Randy Pausch's "Last Lecture" and Barack Obama's speech on racism.
- Section on delivery outline shortened and retitled "Speaking Notes."

Chapter 13: Delivering Your Presentation

- Coverage of new research that suggests an explicit link between language style and engaging delivery.
- Integration into chapter text of material on technology and presentational communication (formerly in an appendix).
- Updated discussion of contemporary audio and video presentation aids, including MP3 files and streaming video.

Chapter 14: Speaking to Inform

- Streamlined and clarified discussion of using word pictures.
- Sample informative presentation integrated into chapter text via a new explicit introduction.
- New "Checklist for an Effective Informative Presentation" provided in end-of-chapter "Assessing Your Skill" feature.

Appendix B: Sample Speeches for Discussion and Evaluation

- New sample informative and persuasive speeches.

Our Partnership with Instructors

As authors, we view our job as providing resources that instructors can use to bring communication principles and skills to life. A textbook is only one tool to help teachers teach and learners learn. As part of our partnership with instructors to facilitate learning, we offer an array of print and electronic resources to help teachers do what they do best: teach.

In addition to the vast array of learning resources we've built into the text, we offer a dazzling package of additional resources to help instructors generate both intellectual and emotional connections with their students.

Supplements for the Instructor

Print Resources **Instructor's Resource Manual**, by Travis L. Russ, Fordham University. For each chapter in the text, the *Instructor's Resource Manual* provides Chapter-at-a-Glance grids that link text objectives to the manual's content as well as to other supplements. Additionally, each chapter includes outlines, discussion and journal questions, classroom activities and assignments, and Internet suggestions. Free on request to adopters; available in print and electronically through the Pearson Instructor's Resource Center (http://www.pearsonhighered.com/irc).

Test Bank. The *Test Bank* contains multiple-choice, true/false, and essay questions for each chapter. More than 1,200 questions are referenced by text chapter and page number.

A Guide for New Teachers of Introduction to Communication, 4/e. This instructor's guide is designed to help new teachers effectively teach an introductory communication course. The guide covers topics such as choosing a text, structuring your course, effectively using group work, dealing with classroom challenges, and giving feedback and includes a number of sample materials in the appendix.

Electronic Resources

MyCommunicationLab. MyCommunicationLab is a place where students learn to communicate with confidence! As an interactive and instructive online solution designed to be used as a supplement to a traditional lecture course or administered as a completely online course, MyCommunicationLab combines multimedia, video, communication activities, research support, tests and quizzes to make teaching and learning more relevant and enjoyable. Students benefit from a wealth of video clips that include student and professional speeches, small group scenarios, and interpersonal interactions—some with running commentary and critical questions, and all geared to helping students learn to communicate with confidence. Available at http://www.mycommunicationlab.com (access code required).

MyTest Computerized Test Bank. The test questions in the print *Test Bank* are also available electronically through our new, web-based, computerized testing system, MyTest. The user-friendly interface enables instructors to view, edit, and add questions, transfer questions to tests, and print tests from any computer with Internet access. Available at http://www.pearsonmytest.com (access code required).

PowerPoint Presentation Package, by Renee Brokaw, University of North Carolina, Charlotte. This text-specific package consists of a collection of lecture outlines and graphic images keyed to every chapter in the text. Available for download at Pearson's Instructor's Resource Center (www.pearsonhighered.com/irc; access code required).

Allyn & Bacon Communication Digital Media Archive, Version 3.0, available on CD-ROM, offers more than 200 still images, video excerpts, and PowerPoint slides that can be used to enliven classroom presentations.

VideoWorkshop for Introduction to Communication, Version 2.0 (www.ablongman.com/videoworkshop), by Kathryn Dindia, University of Wisconsin. *VideoWorkshop for Introduction to Communication* enables you to bring video into your course for maximized learning. This total teaching and learning system includes quality video footage on an easy-to-use CD-ROM, plus a *Student Learning Guide* and an *Instructor's Teaching Guide*. The result? A program that brings textbook concepts to life with ease and helps students understand, analyze, and apply the objectives of the course.

Video Resources

Textbook adopters may choose appropriate video material from Pearson Allyn & Bacon's Communication Video Libraries (some restrictions apply). Please contact your Pearson Allyn & Bacon representative for details and a complete list of videos and their contents from which to choose those that would be most useful in your class.

Pearson A&B Interpersonal Communication Video Library. Each of the videos features a variety of scenarios that illustrate interpersonal concepts and relationships. Videos address topics such as nonverbal communication, perception, conflict, and listening.

Pearson A&B Small Group Communication Video Library. This small group communication video collection presents video case studies of groups working in diverse contexts and highlights key concepts of communication, including group problem solving, leadership roles, diversity, power, conflict, virtual group communication, and more.

Pearson A&B Public Speaking Video Library. Pearson Allyn & Bacon's Public Speaking Video Library contains a range of different types of speeches delivered on a multitude of topics, allowing you to choose the speeches best suited for your students. Samples from most of our public speaking videos are available on www.mycoursetoolbox.com.

A&B Contemporary Classic Speeches DVD. This exciting supplement includes over 120 minutes of video footage in an easy-to-use DVD format. Each speech is accompanied by a biographical and historical summary that helps students understand the context and motivation behind it.

Supplements for the Student

Print Resources   **Study Cards for Introduction to Communication.** Colorful, affordable, and packed with useful information, Pearson's Study Cards make studying easier, more efficient, and more enjoyable. Course information is distilled down to the basics, helping you quickly master the fundamentals, review a subject for understanding, or prepare for an exam. Because they're laminated for durability, you can keep these Study Cards for years to come and pull them out whenever you need a quick review.

Speech Preparation Workbook, by Jennifer Dreyer and Gregory H. Patton, of San Diego State University. This workbook takes students through the stages of speech creation—from audience analysis to writing the speech—and includes guidelines, tips, and easy-to-fill-in pages.

Preparing Visual Aids for Presentations, 5/e, by Dan Cavanaugh. This brief booklet provides a host of ideas for using today's multimedia tools to improve presentations, including suggestions for how to plan a presentation, guidelines for designing visual aids and storyboarding, and a walkthrough that shows how to prepare a visual display using PowerPoint.

Public Speaking in the Multicultural Environment, 2/e, by Devorah Lieberman of Portland State University. This two-chapter essay focuses on speaking and listening to a culturally diverse audience and emphasizes preparation, delivery, and how speeches are perceived.

Multicultural Activities Workbook, by Marlene C. Cohen and Susan L. Richardson, both of Prince George's Community College, Maryland. This workbook is filled with hands-on activities with a multicultural focus—such as checklists, surveys, and writing assignments.

The Speech Outline: Outlining to Plan, Organize, and Deliver a Speech: Activities and Exercises, by Reeze L. Hanson and Sharon Condon, of Haskell Indian Nations University. This brief workbook includes activities, exercises, and answers to help students develop and master the critical skill of outlining.

Electronic Resources   **Introduction to Communication Study Site**, accessed at www.abintrocomm.com. This web site includes links to sites with speeches in text, audio, and video formats, as well as links to other valuable web sites. The site also contains flashcards and a fully expanded set of practice tests covering all major topics.

Speech Writer's Workshop CD-ROM, Version 2.0. This exciting public speaking software includes a *Speech Handbook* with tips for researching and preparing speeches; a *Speech Workshop*, which guides students step-by-step through the speech writing process; a *Topics Dictionary*, which gives students hundreds of ideas for speeches; and the *Documentor* citation database, which helps students format bibliographic entries in either MLA or APA style.

VideoLab CD-ROM. This interactive study tool for students can be used independently or in class. It provides digital video of student speeches that can be viewed in conjunction with corresponding outlines, manuscripts, notecards, and instructor critiques. A series of drills to help students analyze content and delivery follows each speech.

VideoWorkshop for Introduction to Communication, Version 2.0, by Kathryn Dindia, University of Wisconsin. *Video Workshop for Introduction to Communication* enables you to bring video into your course for maximized learning. This total teaching and learning system includes quality video footage on an easy-to-use CD-ROM, plus a *Student Learning Guide* and an *Instructor's Teaching Guide*. The result? A program that brings textbook concepts to life with ease and helps students understand, analyze, and apply the objectives of the course.

Acknowledgments

Although our three names appear on the cover as authors of the book you are holding in your hands, in reality hundreds of people have been instrumental in making this book possible. Communication scholars who have dedicated their lives to researching the importance of communication principles, theories, and skills provide the fuel for this book. We thank each author we reference in our voluminous endnotes for the research conclusions that bring us to our contemporary understanding of communication principles. We thank our students who have trusted us to be their guides in a study of human communication. They continue to enrich our lives with their enthusiasm and curiosity. They have inspired us to be more creative by their honest quizzical looks and challenged us to go beyond "textbook" answers with their thought-provoking questions.

We are most appreciative of the outstanding editorial support we continue to receive from our colleagues and friends at Allyn & Bacon. We thank Joe Opiela for helping us keep this project moving forward when we wondered if the world needed another communication book. Karon Bowers, Allyn & Bacon Editor-in-Chief, has continued to provide valued support and encouragement. Our thoughtful and talented development editor, Kristen LeFevre, helped us polish and prune our words. Karen Black, Diana Ivy's sister, who provided permissions research, was again a true blessing to us in providing skilled assistance with important details and administrative support. We acknowledge and appreciate the ideas and suggestions from Mark Redmond, a valued friend, gifted teacher, and skilled writer at Iowa State University. His co-authorship with us on *Interpersonal Communication: Relating to Others* significantly influenced our ideas about communication, especially interpersonal communication.

We are grateful to the many educators who read the manuscript and both encouraged and challenged us. We thank the following people for drawing on their teaching skill, expertise, and vast experience to make this a much better book:

Reviewers of the First Edition: Michael Bruner, University of North Texas; Diana O. Cassagrande, West Chester University; Dan B. Curtis, Central Missouri State University; Terrence A. Doyle, Northern Virginia Community College; Julia F. Fennell, Community College of Allegheny County, South Campus; Phil Hoke, The University of Texas at San Antonio; Stephen Hunt, Illinois State University; Carol L. Hunter, Brookdale Community College; Dorothy W. Ige, Indiana University Northwest; A. Elizabeth Lindsey, The New Mexico State University; Robert E. Mild, Jr., Fairmont State College; Timothy P. Mottet, Texas State University–San Marcos; Alfred G. Mueller II, Pennsylvania State University, Mont Alto Campus; Kay Neal, University of Wisconsin–Oshkosh; Kathleen Perri, Valencia Community College; Beth M. Waggenspack, Virginia Tech University; Gretchen Aggert Weber, Horry-Georgetown Technical College; Kathy Werking, Eastern Kentucky University; Andrew F. Wood, San Jose State University

Reviewers of the Second Edition: Lawrence Albert, Morehead State University; Leonard Assante, Volunteer State Community College; Dennis Dufer, St. Louis Community College; Annette Folwell, University of Idaho; Mike Hemphill, University of Arkansas at Little Rock; Teri Higginbotham, University of Central Arkansas; Lawrence Hugenberg, Youngstown State University; Timothy P. Mottet, Texas State University–San Marcos; Penny O'Connor, University of Northern Iowa; Evelyn Plummer, Seton Hall University; Charlotte C. Toguchi, Kapi'olani Community College; Debra Sue Wyatt, South Texas Community College

Reviewers of the Third Edition: Dom Bongiorni, Kingwood College; Jo Anne Bryant, Troy University; Cherie Cannon, Miami–Dade College; Thomas Green, Cape

Fear Community College; Gretchen Harries, Austin Community College; Xin-An Lu, Shippensburg University of Pennsylvania; Sara L. Nalley, Columbia College; Kristi Schaller, University of Hawaii; David Shuhy, Salisbury University; John Tapia, Missouri Western State College

Reviewers of the Fourth Edition:

Ellen B. Bremen, Highline Community College
Patricia A. Cutspec, East Tennessee State University
Edgar D. Johnson III, Augusta State University
Peter S. Lee, California State University, Fullerton
Kelly Aikin Petcus, Austin Community College
Natalia Rybas, Bowling Green State University
Sarah Stout, Kellogg Community College

We have each been influenced by colleagues, friends, and teachers who have offered support and inspiration for this project. Happily, colleagues, friends, and teachers are virtually indistinguishable for us. We are each blessed with people with whom we work who offer strong support.

Steve and Sue thank their colleagues at Texas State University–San Marcos for their insights and ideas that helped shape key concepts in this book. Cathy Fleuriet and Tom Burkholder, who served as basic course directors at Texas State, influenced our work. Tim Mottet, also a former basic course director at Texas State, is a valued, inspirational friend and colleague who is always there to listen and freely share his ideas and experience. Marian Houser, the current basic course director at Texas State, is a wonderful friend and provides important insight and support. Richard Cheatham, Dean of the College of Fine Arts and Communication, continues to provide enthusiastic encouragement for this project. Dr. Kosta Tovstiadi, University of Oklahoma, provided skilled research assistance to help us draw upon the most contemporary interpersonal communication research. Michael Hennessy and Patricia Margerison are Texas State English faculty who have been especially supportive of Sue's work. Finally, Steve thanks his skilled and dedicated administrative support team at Texas State. Administrative assistant Sue Hall, who continues to be Steve's right hand, is a cherished friend and colleague. Manuscript typist Sondra Howe and technical support expert Bob Hanna are two additional staff members who provide exceptional support and assistance for this project and many others. Meredith Clayton offered tremendous support and assistance in manuscript preparation.

Ivy is grateful to her students, colleagues, and friends at Texas A&M University–Corpus Christi, for their patience and unwavering support for her involvement in this book project. In particular, Kelly Quintanilla, Chair Don Luna, and Dean Richard Gigliotti constantly reaffirmed the value of a well-written, carefully crafted book—one that speaks to students' lives. Their support of Ivy's research efforts, along with constant "fueling" from her wonderful students, has made this project a real joy. Ivy's deepest thanks also go to Steve and Sue Beebe for their generosity in bringing her into this project, and for their extraordinary friendship.

Finally we express our appreciation to our families. Ivy thanks her ever-supportive family, parents Herschel and Carol Ivy, sister Karen Black (who supplied the permissions research and constant encouragement), and nephew and niece Brian and Sumitra Black. They have been constant and generous with their praise for her writing accomplishments. Ivy is especially grateful to her father, Herschel Ivy, for lovingly offering many lessons about living the highly ethical life.

Sue and Steve especially thank their parents, Herb and Jane Dye and Russell and Muriel Beebe, who taught them much about communication and ethics that truly are principles for a lifetime. They also thank their sons, Mark and Matthew Beebe, for teaching them life lessons about giving and receiving love that will remain with them forever.

Steven A. Beebe and Susan J. Beebe, *San Marcos, Texas*

Diana K. Ivy, *Corpus Christi, Texas*

Unit One

Principles of Communication

Diana Ong, "Dialog A." © Diana Ong/Superstock, Inc.

Good communication is as stimulating as black coffee and just as hard to sleep after.

Anne Morrow Lindbergh

Chapter 1

Foundations of Human Communication

Chapter Outline

- Why Study Communication?
- Communication Defined
- Communication Competence
- Communication Models
- Communication Characteristics
- Communication Principles for a Lifetime
- Communicating with Others: Three Contexts
- Summary

Chapter Objectives

After studying this chapter, you should be able to

1. Define communication and explain why it is an important course of study.
2. Describe three criteria that can be used to determine whether communication is competent.
3. Compare and contrast communication as action, interaction, and transaction.
4. Identify five characteristics of communication.
5. List and explain five fundamental principles of communication.
6. Define and describe communication in interpersonal, group, and presentational communication contexts.

Communication is essential for life. Communicating is a fundamental aspect of being human. Even if you live in isolation from other people, you talk to yourself through your thoughts. Like life-sustaining breath, communication is ever-present in our lives. Understanding and improving how we communicate with others is a basic life skill.

Human communication is inescapable. Consider the number of times you have purposefully communicated with someone today, as you worked, ate, studied, shopped, or went about your daily duties. Most people spend between 80 and 90% of their waking hours communicating with others.[1] It is through the process of communication that we convey who we are, both to ourselves and to others; it is our primary tool for making our way in the world.

This book presents fundamental principles that undergird all aspects of communicating with others when both sending and receiving messages. In the course of our study of human communication, we will discuss a myriad of skills, ideas, concepts, and contexts. To help you stitch together the barrage of ideas and information, we will organize our study around five fundamental communication principles. Together, these five Principles for a Lifetime will provide a framework for our discussion of the importance and pervasiveness of human communication.

Principle One:	Be aware of your communication with yourself and others.
Principle Two:	Effectively use and interpret verbal messages.
Principle Three:	Effectively use and interpret nonverbal messages.
Principle Four:	Listen and respond thoughtfully to others.
Principle Five:	Appropriately adapt messages to others.

These five principles distill decades of research as well as the wisdom of those who have taught communication during the past century. We don't claim that everything you need to know about communication is covered by these five principles. They do, however, summarize considerable knowledge about the communication process and what constitutes effective and ethical communication.

Before we elaborate on the five fundamental communication principles, it is important to provide some background for our study of communication. The purpose of this first chapter is to provide that background. We will discuss why it is important to study communication, define communication, examine various models of or perspectives on communication, and identify characteristics of human communication. Having offered this prelude, we then discuss the five foundational principles of human communication that we will use throughout the book to help you organize the concepts, skills, and ideas we present in our discussion of interpersonal, group, and presentational speaking situations.

Why Study Communication?

Why are you here? No, we don't mean "Why do you exist?" or "Why do you live where you do?" What we mean is "Why are you taking a college course about communication?" Perhaps the short answer is "It's required." Or maybe your advisor, parent, or friend encouraged you to take the course. If it is a required course, what's the rationale for that requirement? And required or not, what can a systematic study of human communication do for you?

Communication touches every aspect of our lives. To be able to express yourself to other people is a basic requirement for living in a modern society. From a practical standpoint, most of you will make your living with your minds rather than your hands.[2] Even if you do physical labor, you will need communication skills to work with others. When you study communication, you are developing leadership skills. "The art of communication," says author Daniel Quinn, "is the language of leadership."[3]

Although the value of being a competent communicator is virtually undisputed, there is evidence that many people struggle to express themselves clearly or to accurately understand messages from others. One study estimated that one-fifth of the students in the United States were not successful with even elementary communication tasks; in addition, more than 60 percent of the students could not give clear oral directions for someone else to follow.[4] When leaders in major corporations were asked to specify the most important skills for workers to have, 80 percent said listening was the most important work skill; 78 percent identified interpersonal communication skill as the next most important. However, the same leaders said only 28 percent of their employees had good listening skills and only 27 percent possessed effective interpersonal communication skills.[5] In support of these leaders' observations, another national study found that adults listen with 25 percent accuracy.[6] In addition to lacking communication skills, there is also evidence that the majority of adults are fearful of speaking in public; about 20 percent of the population is acutely apprehensive of presentational speaking.[7]

Aren't some people just born to be better communicators than others? If so, why should you work to develop your communication skill? Just as some people have more innate musical talent than others, there is evidence that some people may have an inborn biological ability to communicate with others.[8] This does not mean you should not work to develop your communication ability. Throughout the book, we will offer ample evidence that if you work to improve your skill, you will be rewarded by enjoying the benefits of enhanced communication competence. What are these benefits? Read on.

To Improve Your Employability

Regardless of your specific job description, the essence of what you do when working at any job is to communicate; you talk, listen, relate, read, and write, whatever your job title. People who can communicate effectively with others are in high demand. As noted by John H. McConnell, CEO of Worthington Industries, "Take all the speech and communication courses you can because the world turns on communication."[9] McConnell's advice is supported by research as well as by personal observations.

Based on a survey of personnel managers—those people who are in charge of hiring you for a job—here's a ranking of the top factors in obtaining employment right after college:[10]

1. Oral communication (speaking) skills
2. Written communication skills
3. Listening ability
4. Enthusiasm
5. Technical competence
6. Work experience
7. Appearance
8. Poise
9. Resume
10. Part-time or summer work experience

We're sure you know why we cited this survey. Communication skills were the number one factor; note that listening ability was also highly valued. And this isn't the only survey that reaches the same conclusion; several other research studies have shown that communication skills are the most sought-after skills in the workplace.[11]

To Improve Your Relationships

We don't choose our biological families, but we do choose our friends. For unmarried people, developing friendships and falling in love are the top-rated sources of satisfaction and happiness in life.[12] Conversely, losing a relationship is among life's most stressful events. Most people between the ages of 19 and 24 report that they have had from five to six romantic relationships and have been "in love" once or twice.[13] Understanding the role and function of communication can help unravel some of the mysteries of human relationships. At the heart of a good relationship is good communication.[14]

Oral communication is valued by employers as the top skill an employee should master. How can you make a concerted effort to use clear and precise words, and to accurately interpret the words of others while you are at work—either now or in the future?

Virginia Satir, a pioneer in family enrichment, described family communication as "the largest single factor determining the kinds of relationships [we make] with others."[15] Learning principles and skills of communication can give us insight into why we relate to other family members as we do. Our early communication with our parents had a profound effect on our self-concept and self-worth. According to Satir, people are "made" in families. Our communication with family members has shaped how we interact with others today.

Many of us will spend as much or more time interacting with people in our places of work as we do at home. And although we choose our friends and lovers, we don't always have the same flexibility in choosing those with whom or for whom we work. Increasing our understanding of the role and importance of human communication with our colleagues can help us better manage stress on the job as well as enhance our work success.

To Improve Your Health

Life is stressful. Research has clearly documented that the lack or loss of close relationships can lead to ill health and even death. Having a social support system—good friends and supportive family members—seems to make a difference in our overall

When we are young, we develop much of our "self-talk"—a concept that has significant impact on our communication with others throughout our lives. In what ways has your early communication with your family members shaped your own communication behaviors?

health and quality of life. Good friends and intimate relationships with others help us manage stress and contribute to both physical and emotional health. For example, physicians have noted that patients who are widowed or divorced experience more medical problems, such as heart disease, cancer, pneumonia, and diabetes, than do married people.[16] Grief-stricken spouses are more likely than others to die prematurely, especially around the time of the departed spouse's birthday or near their wedding anniversary.[17] Terminally ill patients with a limited number of friends or social support die sooner than those with stronger ties.[18] Without companions and close friends, our opportunities for intimacy and stress-managing communication are diminished. Studying how to enrich the quality of our communication with others can make life more enjoyable and enhance our overall well-being.

So again, we ask the question: Why are you here? We think the evidence is clear: People who are effective communicators are more likely to get the jobs they want; have better quality relationships with friends, family, and colleagues; and even enjoy a healthier quality of life.

Communication Defined

Communication is one of those words that seem so basic you may wonder why they need to be formally defined. Yet scholars who devote their lives to studying communication don't always agree on its definition. One research team counted more than 126 published definitions.[19]

In its broadest sense, **communication** is the process of acting on information.[20] Someone does or says something, and others think or do something in response to the action or the words as they understand them.

Communication is not unique to humans. It is possible, for example, for you to act on information from your dog Martin. Martin barks; you feed him. Your canine friend can also act on information from you. If you say to Martin, "Do you want a treat?" and he enthusiastically barks in response, there's no doubt that you and your pet have communicated with each other. Although researchers study communication between species as well as communication systems used by particular animal species, these fields of study are beyond the scope of this book. The focus of our study is human communication: people communicating with other people.

communication
The process of acting on information.

To refine our definition of communication, we can say that **human communication** *is the process of making sense out of the world and sharing that sense with others by creating meaning through the use of verbal and nonverbal messages.*[21] Let's look at the key components of this definition.

Communication Is About Making Sense

We make sense out of what we experience when we begin to interpret what we see, hear, touch, smell, and taste with sensations, feelings, thoughts, and words. Identifying patterns and structure in what we experience is a key part of making sense out of what happens to us. Although we often think that "making sense out of something" means rationally and logically interpreting what we experience, we also make sense through intuition, feelings, and emotions.[22]

Communication Is About Sharing Sense

We share what we experience by expressing to others and to ourselves what we experience. We typically use words to express our thoughts, but we also use music, art, clothing, and a whole host of other means to convey what we are thinking and feeling to others.

Communication Is About Creating Meaning

It's more appropriate to say that meaning is *created* through communication rather than sent or transmitted. To say that we send or transmit messages is to imply that what we send is what is received. In human communication, however, what is expressed by one person is rarely interpreted by another person precisely as intended. In reality, meaning is *co-created* by both the speaker and the listener. By this we mean that all individuals who are involved in the communication process shape how a message is understood by drawing on their own experiences while attempting to make sense of the message. Meaning is created in the heart and mind of both the message source and the message receiver, based on such things as the characteristics of the message, the situation, and the perceptions and background of the communicators.

Communication Is About Verbal and Nonverbal Messages

One way we communicate is by using words that trigger meaning in others symbolically. **Symbols** are words, sounds, gestures, or visual images that represent thoughts, concepts, objects, or experiences. The words on this page are symbols that you use to derive meaning that makes sense to you.

Not all symbols are verbal; some are nonverbal. You use gestures, posture, facial expression, tone of voice, clothing, and jewelry to express ideas, attitudes, and feelings. Nonverbal messages primarily communicate emotions—our likes and dislikes, whether we're interested or uninterested, and our feelings of power or lack of power.

Some scholars assert that *all* human behavior is really communication. When you cross your arms while listening to your friend describe her day, she may conclude that you're not interested in what she's talking about. But it could just be that you're cold. While all human expression has the potential to communicate a message (someone may act or respond to the information they receive from you), this does not mean you *intentionally* are expressing an idea or emotion. Presenting information to others does not mean communication has occurred: Information is not communication. "But I told you what to do!" "It's there in the memo. Why didn't you do what I asked?" "It's in the syllabus." These exasperated communicators assumed that if they sent a message, someone would receive it. However, communication does not operate in a simple, linear, what-you-send-is-what-is-received process. People don't always accurately interpret the messages we express—and this unprofound observation has profound implications.

Because of the ever-present potential for misunderstanding, communication should be *other-oriented*—it should acknowledge the perspective of others, not just the creator

---

human communication
The process of making sense out of the world and sharing that sense with others by creating meaning through verbal and nonverbal messages.

symbol
A word, sound, gesture, or visual image that represents a thought, concept, object, or experience.

of the message. Communication that does not consider the needs, background, and culture of the receiver is more likely to be misunderstood. We'll emphasize the importance of considering others or considering your audience throughout the book. Knowing something about the experiences of the person or persons you're speaking to can help you communicate more effectively and appropriately.

Communication Competence

What does it mean to communicate competently? Does it mean that you are able to present a well-delivered speech? Or that you are able to carry on a brilliant conversation with someone? Is the fact that you are usually asked to chair a committee meeting because you are so organized evidence of your communication competence? Being a competent communicator is more than just being well liked, glib, able to give polished presentations, or able to interact smoothly with individual people or in groups and teams. Although it is difficult to identify core criteria that define competent communication in all situations, we think certain goals of communication serve as measures of competence regardless of the setting. We suggest the following three criteria:[23]

- The message should be understood as the communicator intended it to be understood.
- The message should achieve the communicator's intended effect.
- The message should be ethical.

These three criteria for competence apply equally whether you're the sender or the receiver of a message. You have a responsibility not only to express ideas so that they will be understood, but also to listen carefully to accurately interpret the message. When speaking to someone, you typically want to achieve a goal (even if it's just experiencing the joy of connecting with another human being). When listening, your corollary task is to ponder what the speaker is attempting to accomplish. Finally, a speaker should send messages that are ethical—truthful, honest, and nonmanipulative. Ethical listeners are sensitive to and tolerant of diversity; they listen critically, clarifying expectations and providing appropriate responses to the speaker.

The Message Should Be Understood

A primary goal of any effective communication transaction is to develop a common understanding of the message from both the sender's and the receiver's perspectives. You'll note how the words *common* and *communication* resemble each other. We acknowledge the challenge of communicating with others; differences in culture, language, experience, gender, education, and background all are sources of misunderstanding. One of the aims of the principles we discuss in this book is to create clarity of expression and a common understanding.

Message clarity is missing in the following headlines, which have appeared in local U.S. newspapers:

> Panda Mating Fails: Veterinarian Takes Over
> Drunks Get Nine Months in Violin Case
> Include Your Children When Baking Cookies
> Police Begin Campaign to Run Down Jaywalkers
> Local High School Dropouts Cut in Half

Meanings are fragile, and messages can be misunderstood. An effective message is one that the receiver understands.

The Message Should Achieve Its Intended Effect

When you communicate intentionally with others, it is for a specific purpose: to achieve a goal or to accomplish something. Because different purposes require different strate-

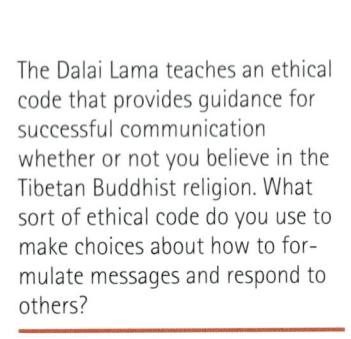

The Dalai Lama teaches an ethical code that provides guidance for successful communication whether or not you believe in the Tibetan Buddhist religion. What sort of ethical code do you use to make choices about how to formulate messages and respond to others?

gies for success, being aware of your purpose can enhance the probability of your achieving it.

Typical goals of speaking in public are to inform, to persuade, or to entertain. In small groups, we often communicate to solve problems and make decisions. In our interpersonal relationships, we interact to build trust, develop intimacy, or just enjoy someone's company. Thus, another criterion for judging the effectiveness of communication is whether the intent of the message is achieved.

Whether you are attempting to close a sale, get a date, give directions to the mall, or tell a joke, you should consider your goal. The purpose of our communication with others is not always to give or receive something tangible. Sometimes it is simply to make human contact, to establish a relationship, or just to be with someone. But one way to assess whether your communication was effective, regardless of the purpose, is to determine whether the outcome you sought is the outcome you got.

The Message Should Be Ethical

Communication can be used to achieve good or bad objectives. A message that is understood and achieves its intended effect but that manipulates listeners, unfairly restricts their choices, or uses false information may be effective, but it is not appropriate or ethical. **Ethics** are the beliefs, values, and moral principles by which we determine what is right or wrong. Ethics and ethical behavior have long been considered critical components of human behavior in a given culture.

Philosophers have debated for centuries whether there is such a thing as a universal moral and ethical code.[24] British author and scholar C. S. Lewis suggests that there is a universal ethical code that serves as the basis for interpreting the "goodness" or "badness" of human behavior; evidence for such a code can be found, says Lewis, in the teachings of cultures throughout the world and through time.[25] In their book *Communication Ethics and Universal Values*, communication scholars Clifford Christians and Michael Traber make the following claim: "Every culture depends for its existence on norms that order human relationships and social institutions."[26] What are these universal norms—these beliefs and behaviors that describe what is normal, appropriate, or inappropriate? Christians and Traber suggest there are three universal cultural norms: (1) the value of truth, (2) respect for another person's dignity, and (3) the expectation that innocent people should not suffer harm.[27]

Scholars and philosophers who suggest that a universal code of ethics exists do not claim that people in all cultures always behave in ways that are true to universal standards. Proponents of a universal ethical code do suggest that a universal moral code is the ideal basis for evaluating right and wrong behavior, including communication behavior.

ethics
The beliefs, values, and moral principles by which we determine what is right or wrong.

All religions of the world have a moral code that provides guidance for how people should treat others.[28] The Ten Commandments serve as ethical guidelines for those who adhere to Judeo-Christian ethical principles. In Christianity, the Golden Rule—"Do unto others what you would have others do unto you"—is a fundamental value. Buddhism teaches a similar value: "One should seek for others the happiness one desires for oneself." Hinduism asks adherents to live by the precept "Do nothing to others which would cause pain if done to you." Judaism teaches, "What is hateful to you, do not do to others." Islam suggests, "No one of you is a believer until he desires for his brother that which he desires for himself." The underlying ethic of how to treat others can clearly be seen across most of the world's religions.[29]

Our purpose is not to prescribe a specific religious or philosophical ethical code, but rather to suggest that humans from a variety of cultures and traditions have sought to develop ethical principles that guide their interactions with others.

Philosophy and religion are not the only realms that focus on ethical behavior. Most professions, such as medicine, law, and journalism, have explicit codes of ethics that identify appropriate and inappropriate behavior. The National Communication Association has developed a Credo for Communication Ethics to emphasize the importance of being an ethical communicator:

> Ethical communication is fundamental to responsible thinking, decision making, and the development of relationships and communities within and across contexts, cultures, channels, and media. Moreover, ethical communication enhances human worth and dignity by fostering truthfulness, fairness, responsibility, personal integrity, and respect for self and others.[30]

Echoing the wisdom offered by others, we suggest that competent communication is grounded in an other-oriented ethical perspective that is fundamental to all human interactions.

For most people, being ethical means being sensitive to others' needs, giving people choices rather than forcing them to behave in a certain way, keeping private information others wish to remain private, not intentionally decreasing others' feelings of self-worth, and being honest in presenting information. Unethical communication does just the opposite: It forces views on others and demeans their integrity.

Being honest is a key element of ethical communication. If you knowingly withhold key information, lie, or distort the truth, then you are not communicating ethically or effectively. For example, after Paul missed the test in his communication class, he mournfully told his professor that his grandmother had died and he had to attend the funeral. Paul's professor allowed him to make up the test. Paul's professor understood the message, so Paul achieved the effect he wanted. Paul's grandmother, however, is alive and well. According to our criteria for effective communication, Paul's dishonesty made his communication inappropriate and unethical.

Throughout the book, we will offer opportunities for you to examine ethical issues in a feature called Communication and Ethics.

Communication Models

Communication researchers have spent a considerable amount of time trying to understand precisely how communication takes place. In the course of their study, they have developed visual models that graphically illustrate the communication process.

By reviewing the development of communication models, you can see how our understanding of communication has evolved over the past century. Early models viewed communication as a transfer or exchange of information, but this view evolved to include a more interactive, give-and-take approach. Researchers' understanding then progressed even further to today's view that communication is a process in which meaning is co-created simultaneously among people. The three models of the communication process that we show here begin with the simplest and oldest perspective and then move to more contemporary models.

Communication and Ethics

What Are the Sources of Your Ethical Views?

Many people think that success means achieving what they want to achieve. Success is often equated with acquiring money, power, position, and influence. But when communicating with others, we've suggested, we achieve success if the communication message is understood as intended, achieves its intended effect, and satisfies a third criterion: It is ethical. Success is based not only on the communication outcome, but also on the methods and approaches used to communicate. If you lie, knowingly withhold key information, or use force to achieve your communication goals, then your message has not been successful, even if you are understood perfectly and you get what you want.

The question of who gets to decide what constitutes ethical behavior is one that arises often. Ethics are the beliefs, values, and moral principles by which we determine what is right or wrong. But where do your ethical beliefs, values, and principles come from? What are the sources of your sense of what is right and wrong?

Use the checklist below to identify the key sources of your ethical views.

INSTRUCTIONS: First, rate the influence of each factor listed below on a scale from 1 (a minor influence on your ethical beliefs and practices) to 5 (a major influence on your ethical beliefs and practices).

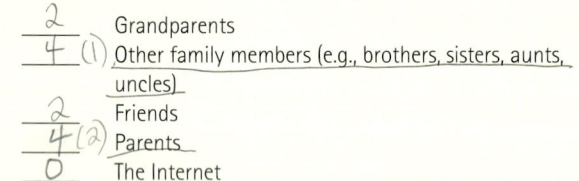

- _2_ Grandparents
- _4 (1)_ Other family members (e.g., brothers, sisters, aunts, uncles)
- _2_ Friends
- _4 (2)_ Parents
- _0_ The Internet
- _0_ Government officials and public figures
- _2_ Laws and the legal system
- _2_ Music
- _1_ Works of art
- _3_ Sacred and inspired writing (e.g., the Bible)
- _3_ Religious beliefs
- _1_ Clergy and religious leaders
- _1_ Fiction and poetry
- _4_ TV and radio
- ___ Newspapers and magazines
- _4 (3)_ Teachers
- _?_ Other sources

After you have rated the sources of influence, circle the sources of ethical influence that you rated the highest. (Perhaps you rated several sources a 5.) Of those items you circled, rank-order the top three. Assign a rank of 1 to the most important ethical influence, 2 to the second most important, and 3 to the third most important.

- What connection can you make between the top sources of ethical influence in your life and the way you communicate with others?
- Can you think of specific ways in which the sources of your ethical beliefs and practices have directly influenced your communication with others?

Often we are unaware of the underpinnings of our ethical beliefs. This activity invites you to consciously examine the link between the sources of your perceptions of what is right and wrong and your communication behavior toward others.

Communication as Action: Message Transfer

"Did you get my message?" This simple sentence summarizes the communication-as-action approach to human communication. In this model, communication takes place when a message is sent and received. Period. Communication is a way of transferring meaning from sender to receiver. In 1948, Harold Lasswell described the process as follows:

> Who (sender)
> Says what (message)
> In what channel
> To whom (receiver)
> With what effect[31]

Figure 1.1 shows a simplified representation of the communication process developed by communication pioneers Claude Shannon and Warren Weaver, who viewed communication as a linear input/output process consisting of a source, a message, a channel, a receiver, and noise. Today, although researchers view the process as more complex, they still define most of the key components in this model in basically the same way that Shannon and Weaver did.

source
The originator of a thought or emotion, who puts it into a code that can be understood by a receiver.

Source The **source** of communication is the originator of a thought or an emotion. As the developer of that thought or emotion, the source puts a message into a code

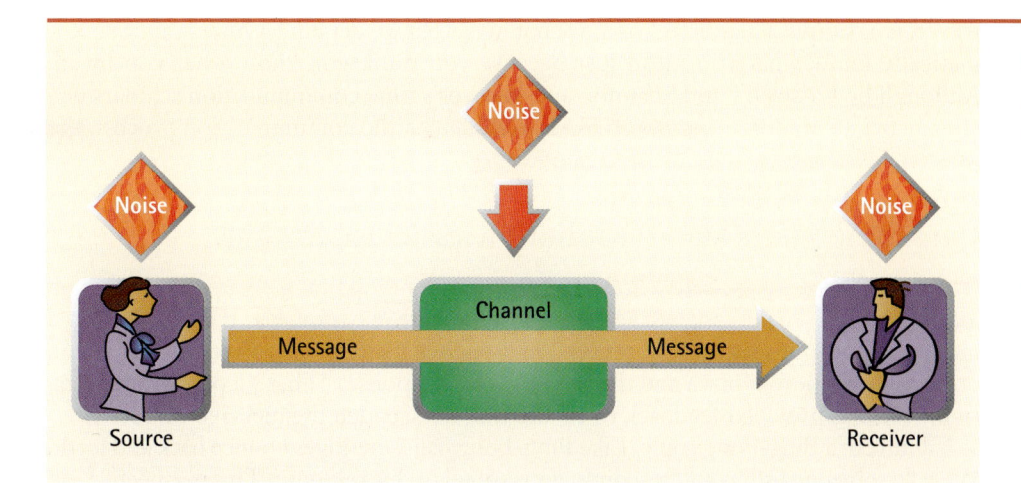

Figure 1.1
A Model of Communication as Action

Source: From *The Mathematical Theory of Communication.* Copyright 1949, 1998 by the Board of Trustees of the University of Illinois. Used with permission of the authors and University of Illinois Press.

that can be understood by a receiver. Translating ideas, feelings, and thoughts into a code is called **encoding**. Vocalizing a word, gesturing, and establishing eye contact are means of encoding our thoughts into a message that can be decoded by someone. **Decoding**, the opposite process of encoding, occurs when the words or unspoken signals are interpreted by the receiver.

Receiver The **receiver** is the person who decodes the signal and attempts to make sense of what the source encoded. Think of a TV station as a source broadcasting to a receiver (your TV) that picks up the station's signal. In human communication, however, there is something between the source and the receiver: We filter messages through past experiences, attitudes, beliefs, values, prejudices, and biases.

Message **Messages** are the written, spoken, and unspoken elements of communication to which we assign meaning. You can send a message intentionally (talking to a friend before class) or unintentionally (falling asleep during class); verbally ("Hi. What's up?"), nonverbally (a smile and a handshake), or in written form (this book); or through any number of electronic channels.

Channel A message is communicated from sender to receiver via some pathway called a **channel**. With today's technological advances, we receive messages from a variety of channels. With your phone, the Internet, or a fax transmission, the communication channel may be a telephone line. Cell phones use a wireless channel. Ultimately, communication channels correspond to your senses. When you call your mother on the telephone, the message is conveyed via an electronic channel that activates auditory cues. When you talk with your mother face to face, the channels are many. You see her: the visual channel. You hear her: the auditory channel. You may smell her perfume: the olfactory channel. You may hug her: the tactile channel.

Noise **Noise** is interference. Noise keeps a message from being understood and achieving its intended effect. Without noise, all of our messages would be communicated with considerable accuracy. But noise is always present. It can be literal—the obnoxious roar of a gas-powered lawn mower—or it can be psychological, such as competing thoughts, worries, and feelings that capture our attention. Instead of concentrating on your teacher's lecture, you may start thinking about the chores you need to finish before the end of the day. Whichever kind it is, noise gets in the way of the message and may even distort it. Communicating accurate messages involves minimizing both literal and psychological noise.

It may appear that scholars have neatly identified the components of communication, such as source, message, channel, receiver, and noise, and can prescribe precisely what is needed to make communication effective. While the communication-as-action approach is simple and straightforward, it has a key flaw: Human communication rarely,

encoding
The process of translating ideas, feelings, and thoughts into a code.

decoding
The process of interpreting ideas, feelings, and thoughts that have been translated into a code.

receiver
The person who decodes a message and attempts to make sense of what the source has encoded.

message
Written, spoken, and unspoken elements of communication to which people assign meaning.

channel
The pathway through which messages are sent.

noise
Interference, either literal or psychological, that hinders the accurate encoding or decoding of a message.

if ever, is as simple a matter as "what we put in is what we get out." Others cannot automatically know what you mean just because you think you know what you mean. Although by Lasswell's and Shannon and Weaver's time communication scholars had already begun identifying an array of key elements in the communication process, the action approach overlooked their complexity.

Communication as Interaction: Message Exchange

The communication-as-interaction perspective uses the same elements as the action model but adds two new ones: feedback and context. **Feedback** is the response to a message. Without feedback, communication is less likely to be effective. When you order your pepperoni pizza and the server says in response, "That's a pepperoni pizza, right?" he has provided feedback to ensure that he decoded the message correctly.

Think of a Ping-Pong game. Like Ping-Pong balls, messages bounce back and forth. We talk; someone listens and responds; we respond to this response. This perspective can be summarized using a physical principle: For every action, there is a reaction.

Feedback can be intentional (applause at the conclusion of a symphony) or unintentional (a yawn as you listen to your uncle tell his story about bears again); verbal ("That's two burgers and fries, right?") or nonverbal (blushing after being asked for a date).

A second component recognized by the interaction perspective is **context**—the physical, historical, and psychological communication environment. All communication takes place in some context. As the cliché goes, "Everyone has to be somewhere." The literal or psychological "somewhere" of communication is the context. A conversation with your good friend on the beach would likely differ from one the two of you might have in a funeral home. Context encompasses not only the physical environment but also the number of people present, their past relationship with the communicators, the communication goal, and the culture in which the communicators are steeped. The psychological context includes the impact of what is going on in the minds of the communicators; the speaker's and listener's personalities and styles of interacting with others influence how messages are understood.

The communication-as-interaction model, as shown in Figure 1.2, is more realistic than the communication-as-action model, but it still has limitations. Although it emphasizes feedback and context, it does not quite capture the complexity of the communication process if the communication takes place *simultaneously*. The interaction model of communication still views communication as a linear, step-by-step process. But in many communication situations, both the source and the receiver send and receive messages at the same time.

feedback
The response to a message.

context
The physical, historical, and psychological communication environment.

Figure 1.2
A Model of Communication as Interaction
Interaction models of communication include feedback as a response to a message sent by a communication source and place the process in a context.

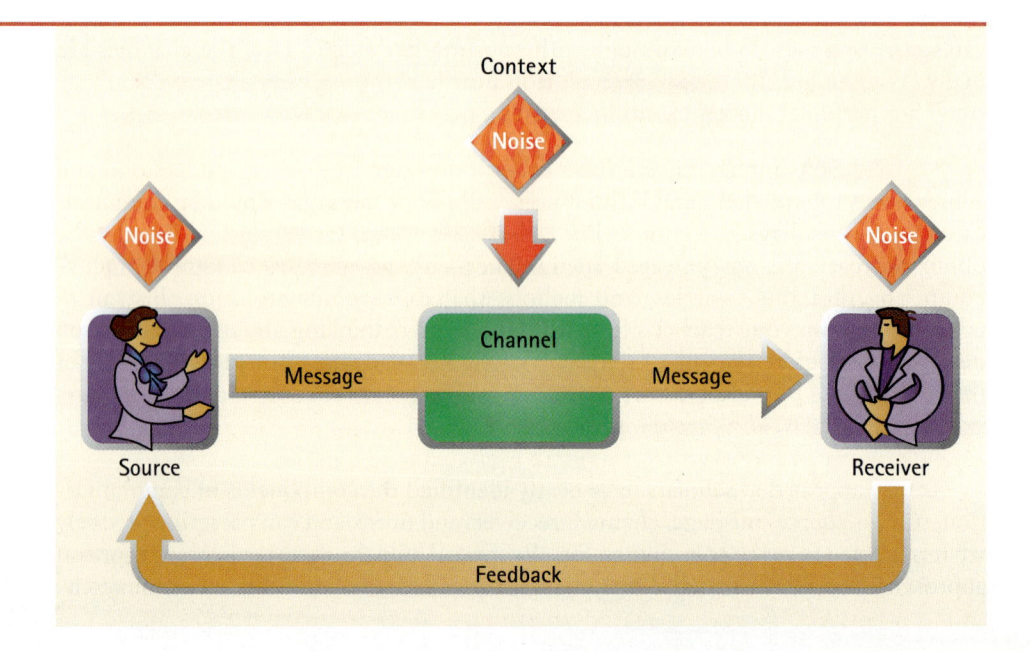

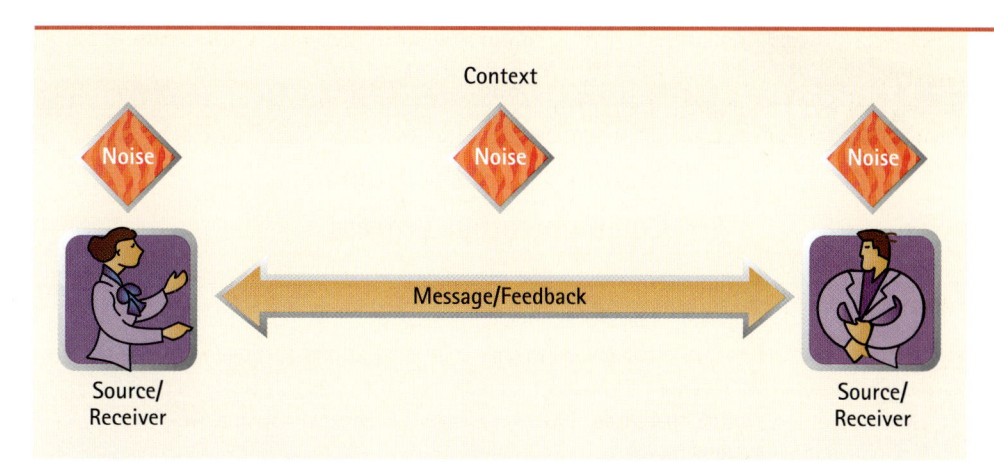

Figure 1.3
A Model of Communication as Transaction
The source and the receiver of a message experience communication simultaneously.

Communication as Transaction: Message Creation

The communication-as-transaction perspective, which evolved in the 1960s, acknowledges that when we communicate with another, we are constantly reacting to what our partner is saying and expressing. Most scholars today view this perspective as the most realistic model of communication. Although this model uses such concepts as action and interaction to describe communication, all of the interaction is simultaneous. As Figure 1.3 indicates, we send and receive messages concurrently. Even as we talk, we are also interpreting our partner's nonverbal and verbal responses. Transactive communication also occurs within a context, and noise can interfere with the quality and accuracy of our encoding and decoding of messages.

As we send a message, we simultaneously monitor the degree to which the other person understands the message. For example, if you ask your friend out for coffee but you're not sure she'd like to go with you, even as you're talking to her you carefully observe her reactions to determine if she's really interested in your invitation. If you'd really like her company and you sense she'd rather not go with you, you may try harder, using your best persuasive pitch to get your friend to join you. During each communication transaction you have with another person, you look for information about how your message is being received even before you finish talking.

One research team says that communication is "the coordinated management of meaning" through episodes during which the message of one person influences the message of another.[32] Technically, only the sender and receiver of those messages can determine where one episode ends and another begins. We make sense out of our world in ways that are unique to each of us.

Mediated Communication

Because of the power and pervasiveness of technology, we can easily and frequently communicate with people who are not physically present. Instead of relying on face-to-face contact for all of our communication today, we use various types of media (communication channels) to connect to others. The Internet has given the concept of being connected a new meaning; we are literally linked via the web. Whether we're using a phone, sending an e-mail, tapping out a text message, or seeking a relationship with someone on MySpace, we are establishing and maintaining relationships with people we may never meet in person. When we use media such as a cell phone or the Internet to carry our message, we are using **mediated communication**.

Even though connecting to others via the Internet seems to be a normal way to communicate for a significant and growing percentage of the world's population, there are times when relating to someone live and in person is best—especially for expressing feelings and emotions. There are other situations in which mediated communication, because of its ease and speed, is superior to face-to-face communication.

mediated communication
Any communication that is carried out using some channel other than those used in face-to-face communication.

Recap

Components of the Human Communication Process

Term	Definition
Source	Originator of an idea or emotion
Receiver	Person or group toward whom a source directs messages and who decodes the message
Message	Written, spoken, and unspoken elements of communication to which we assign meaning
Channel	Pathway through which messages pass between source and receiver
Noise	Any literal or psychological interference with the clear encoding or decoding of a message
Encoding	Translation of ideas, feelings, and thoughts into a code
Decoding	Interpretation of ideas, feelings, and thoughts that have been translated into a code
Context	Physical, historical, and psychological communication environment
Feedback	Verbal and nonverbal responses to a message

Can you really communicate *interpersonally* with someone on the Internet? Can relationships be developed with others without meeting them face to face? Yes, of course. You probably do so every day. There is evidence that some long-distance Internet relationships can be as satisfying as face-to-face relationships.[33] If you are attending a college or university away from family, friends, and loved ones, you may have found that sending text messages can help keep you in touch with others who are important to you. College freshmen and their parents report that e-mail connections reduce homesickness and the sadness parents often feel when their son or daughter leaves home. The past few years have seen an ever-increasing number of people meeting in Internet chat rooms or on Facebook or MySpace and eventually developing real-time relationships.

Of course, people have been communicating with others without being face to face for centuries; sending letters and other written messages to others is a long-standing human practice. The textbook you are currently reading provides a form of mediated "distance learning" in that the words were written some time ago and you are just now reading them. What's new today is that there are so many different ways of *immediately* connecting with someone, such as using a mobile phone, e-mail, text and instant messaging, and a host of other Internet-based ways of developing interpersonal relationships. Research has found that immediately after the terrorist attacks on September 11, 2001, not only the telephone but also the Internet was a prime means of spreading news of the attacks. People used e-mail not only to share the shocking news, but also to seek interpersonal support and reassurance from friends that their loved ones were safe. Other research suggests that we are increasingly using online communication channels to seek emotional support from others. We use the Internet to share information that is both dramatic and routine, as well as relationship-enriching.

How is mediated communication different from live, face-to-face conversation? There are four key differences:

- *Anonymity.* You may not always know precisely with whom you are communicating when you receive an e-mail message.
- *Personal appearance.* There is typically *less* emphasis on a person's physical appearance online. Yes, we may be curious about what our online partner looks like, and

> ### Recap
> #### An Evolving Model of Human Communication
>
> **Human Communication as Action**
> Human communication is linear, with meaning sent or transferred from source to receiver.
>
> **Human Communication as Interaction**
> Human communication occurs as the receiver of the message responds to the source through feedback. This interactive model views communication as a linear sequence of actions and reactions.
>
> **Human Communication as Transaction**
> Human communication is simultaneously interactive. Meaning is created based on mutual, concurrent sharing of ideas and feelings. This transactive model most accurately describes human communication.

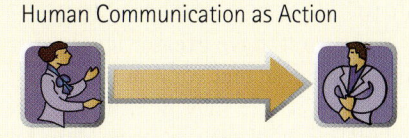

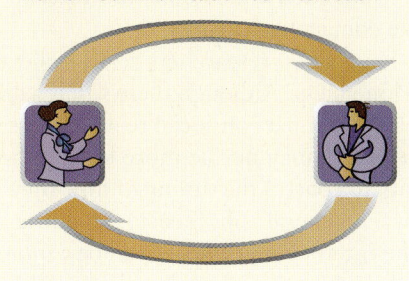

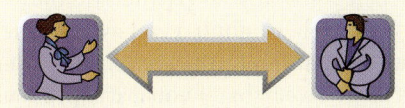

webcams let us see the person with whom we're communicating, but the majority of Internet communication occurs with people we don't see.
- *Distance.* Although we certainly can and do send e-mail and text messages to people who live and work in the same building, there is typically greater physical distance between people who are communicating online. Via the Internet, we can just as easily send a message to someone on the other side of the globe as we can to someone who is on the other side of town.
- *Time.* You have greater control over the timing and pacing of the messages you send and receive. You can decide, for example, when to retrieve e-mail messages and when to respond to them. Your interaction with others can be **asynchronous**, or out of sync; that is, there may be a time delay between when you send a message and when it is received. With **synchronous communication**, you communicate in real time; when you speak, someone immediately responds to your message.

asynchronous communication
Communication in which timing is out of sync; there is a time delay between when you send a message and when it is received.

synchronous communication
Communication in which messages occur in real time—when you speak or write, someone immediately responds to your message.

Do people who spend a lot of time online generally have more or less contact with other people face to face? A team of researchers led by Robert Kraut and Sara Kiesler made headlines when they published the results of their study, which concluded that the more people use the Internet, the less they interact with people in person.[34] They also found a relationship between people who said they were lonely and those who used the Internet. Yet two follow-up studies found that people who use the Internet are *more* likely to have a large number of friends; they are more involved with community activities and overall have greater levels of trust in other people.[35] The follow-up research seems to suggest that for some people—those who are already prone to being shy or introverted—there may be a link between Internet use and loneliness or feelings of social isolation. However, it may not be because of Internet use, but because they are less likely to make contact with others. For those who are generally outgoing and who like to interact with others, the Internet is another tool with which to reach out and make contact with others.

So what do researchers really believe about the relationship between Internet use and loneliness? Although there still is a difference of opinion about the role of the Internet and its impact on social relationships and loneliness, those people who spend much time online may not be more lonely; they may just feel more comfortable having the ability to control the timing of how they interact with others. There may also be a link between general apprehension about communicating with others face to face and use of the Internet. Cyberspace can be a more comfortable place to communicate with others if you are apprehensive about talking in face-to-face situations. If you're simply introverted or shy, you may reach out to others online because you prefer relationships in which you and your partner are only minimally interlinked or interdependent.

Researchers don't yet have all the answers about similarities and differences between communicating online and communicating face to face. They do have evidence, however, that if you are apprehensive about communicating in person, you will likely be more comfortable communicating via the Internet.

Communication Characteristics

Now that we have defined communication, noted its importance, and seen how our understanding of communication in general—and the pervasive influence of mediated communication in particular—evolved over the last half of the twentieth century, we turn our attention to describing how it works by examining the characteristics of communication. The following characteristics are evident when communication occurs: Communication is inescapable, irreversible, and complicated; it emphasizes content and relationships; and it is governed by rules.

Communication Is Inescapable

Opportunities to communicate are ubiquitous—they are everywhere. Even before we are born, we respond to movement and sound. With our first cry, we begin the process of announcing to others that we are here. And once we make contact with other humans, we communicate and continue to do so until death. Even though many of our messages are not verbalized, we nonetheless intentionally, and very often unintentionally, send them to others. As we noted earlier, some communication scholars question whether it is possible to communicate with someone unintentionally. What experts do agree on is this: Communication with others plays an ever-present role in our life. We spend most of our waking hours sending messages to or interpreting messages from others.[36] Even as you silently stand in line at a supermarket checkout line, your lack of eye contact with others waiting in line suggests you're not interested in striking up a conversation. Your unspoken messages may provide cues to which others respond. Even when you don't intend to express a particular idea or feeling, others may try to make sense out of what you are doing—or not doing. Remember: People judge you by your behavior, not your intent.

Communication Is Irreversible

"Disregard that last statement made by the witness," instructs the judge. Yet the clever lawyer knows that once her client has told the jury that her husband gave her a black eye during an argument, the client cannot really "take back" the message. In conversation we may try to modify the meaning of a spoken message by saying something like "Oh, I really didn't mean it." But in most cases, the damage has been done. Once created, communication has the physical property of matter; it can't be uncreated. As the helical model in Figure 1.4 suggests, once communication begins, it never loops back on itself. Instead, it continues to be shaped by the events, experiences, and thoughts of the communication partners. A Russian proverb nicely summarizes the point: "Once a word goes out of your mouth, you can never swallow it again."

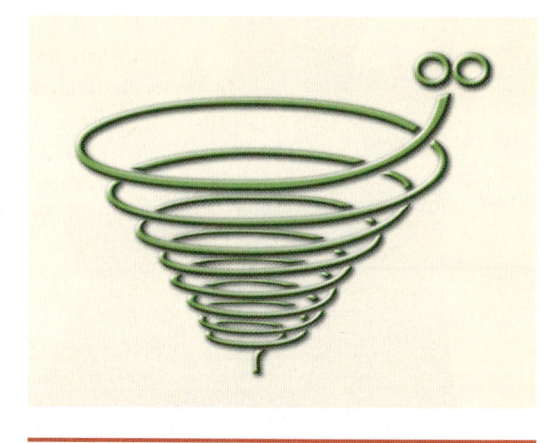

Figure 1.4
A Helical Model of Communication
Interpersonal communication is irreversible. This helical model shows that communication never loops back on itself. Once it begins, it expands infinitely as the communication partners contribute their thoughts and experiences to the exchange.

Source: Copyright © F. E. X. Dance in *Human Communication Theory* (Holt, Rinehart and Winston, 1967), 294. Reprinted with permission.

Communication Is Complicated

Pick up any morning newspaper and you will see that there is conflict brewing or erupting in some part of the world. Perhaps there is conflict and disagreement in your own home or in a relationship with someone you care about. Communicating with others is not simple. If it were, we would know how to reduce dramatically the number of misunderstandings and conflicts in our world. This book could also offer you a list of simple techniques and strategies for blissful management of your communication hassles. You won't find that list in this book or any other credible book. Human communication is complicated because of the number of variables and unknown factors involved when people interact. To illustrate the complexity of the process, communication scholar Dean Barnlund has suggested that whenever we communicate with another person, there are really at least six "people" involved: (1) who you think you are; (2) who you think the other person is; (3) who you think the other person thinks you are; (4) who the other person thinks he or she is; (5) who the other person thinks you are; and (6) who the other person thinks you think he or she is.[37] Whew! And when you add more people to the conversation, it becomes even more complicated.

Life is not only complicated, but also uncertain. There are many things we do not know. We seek information about such everyday things as the weather or about such questions as what others think about us. Several communication theorists suggest that we attempt to manage our uncertainty through communication.[38] In times of high uncertainty (when there are many things we do not know), we will communicate more actively and purposefully so as to manage our uncertainty. For example, we are likely to ask more questions, seek information, and listen intently when we are uncertain.

Adding to the complexity of communication and the problem of our own uncertainty is the fact that messages are not always interpreted as we intend them. Osmo Wiio, a Scandinavian communication scholar, points out the challenges of communicating with others when he suggests the following maxims:

1. If communication can fail, it will.
2. If a message can be understood in different ways, it will be understood in just the way that does the most harm.
3. There is always somebody who knows better than you what you meant by your message.
4. The more communication there is, the more difficult it is for communication to succeed.[39]

Although we are not as pessimistic as Professor Wiio, we do suggest that the task of understanding each other is challenging.

Communication Emphasizes Content and Relationships

What you say—your words—and how you say it—your tone of voice, amount of eye contact, facial expression, and posture—can reveal much about the true meaning of your message. If one of your roommates loudly and abruptly bellows, "Hey, dork! Clean this room!" and another roommate uses the same verbal message but more gently and playfully suggests, with a smile, "Hey, dork. Clean this room," both are communicating a message aimed at achieving the same outcome. But the two messages have different relationship cues. The first shouted message suggests that your roommate may be grumpy and frustrated that the room still harbors the remains of last night's pizza party, while roommate number two's more calmly expressed request suggests that he or she may be less frustrated and simply want the room tidied up a bit.

The **content** of communication messages is the new information, ideas, or suggested actions that the speaker wishes to express. The **relationship dimension** of a communication message is usually more implied; it offers cues about the emotions, attitudes, and amount of power and control the speaker directs toward the other.[40]

Another way of distinguishing between the content and relationship dimensions of communication is to consider that the content of a message refers to *what* is said. The relationship cues are provided in *how* the message is communicated. For example, when you read a transcript of what someone says, you can get a different meaning than you would if you actually heard the person's words.

The rules of both formal and informal play often call for a high five between teammates or friends.

Communication Is Governed by Rules

When you play Monopoly, you know that there are explicit rules about how to get out of jail, buy Boardwalk, or pass "Go" and get $200. The rules are written down. When you play a game with others, there may even be some unwritten rules, such as "When you play Monopoly with Grandpa, always let him buy Boardwalk. He gets grumpy as a bear before breakfast if he doesn't get to buy it." There are also rules that govern how we communicate with others. Most of the rules are imbedded in our culture or discussed verbally rather than written in a rulebook.

According to communication researcher Susan Shimanoff, a **rule** is a "followable prescription that indicates what behavior is obligated, preferred, or prohibited in certain contexts."[41] The rules that help define appropriate and inappropriate communication in any given situation may be explicit or implicit. For a class, explicit rules are probably spelled out in your syllabus. But your instructor has other rules that are more implicit. They are not written or verbalized because you learned them long ago: Only one person speaks at a time; you raise your hand to be called on; you do not pass notes.

Communication rules are developed by those involved in the interaction and by the culture in which the individuals are communicating. Most people learn communication rules from experience, by observing and interacting with others.

content
The new information, ideas, or suggested actions that a communicator wishes to express; *what* is said.

relationship dimension
The aspect of a communication message that offers cues about the emotions, attitudes, and amount of power and control the speaker directs toward others; *how* something is said.

rule
A followable prescription that indicates what behavior is required or preferred and what behavior is prohibited in a specific situation.

Communication Principles for a Lifetime

As you saw on page 2, underlying our description of human communication are five principles that provide the foundation for all effective communication, whether we are communicating with others one on one, in groups or teams, or by presenting a public speech to an audience. Throughout the book, we will emphasize how these principles are woven into the fabric of each communication context. We will expand on the discussion here with a brief introduction and then provide a more comprehensive discussion in the following five chapters to describe and illustrate the scope and power of these principles. Recall the five Communication Principles for a Lifetime that we presented at the beginning of this chapter:

Principle One:	Be aware of your communication with yourself and others.
Principle Two:	Effectively use and interpret verbal messages.
Principle Three:	Effectively use and interpret nonverbal messages.
Principle Four:	Listen and respond thoughtfully to others.
Principle Five:	Appropriately adapt messages to others.

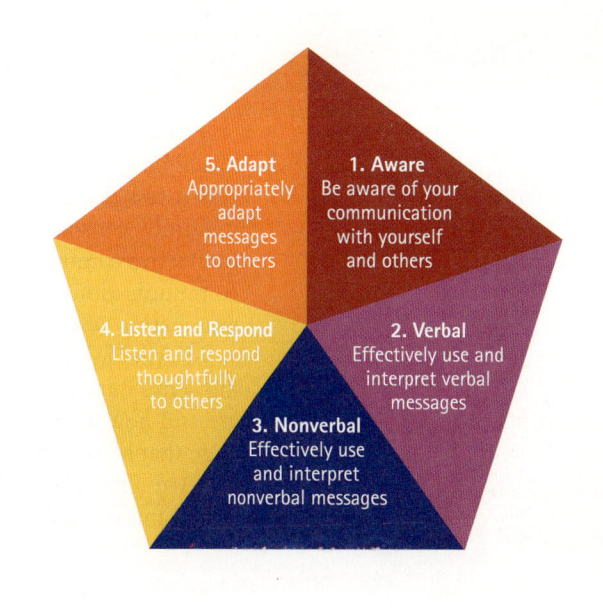

These five principles operate together rather than independently to form the basis of the fundamental processes that enhance communication effectiveness. The model in Figure 1.5 illustrates how the principles interrelate. Moving around the model clockwise, the first principle, being aware of your communication with yourself and others, is followed by the two principles that focus on communication messages, verbal messages (Principle Two) and nonverbal messages (Principle Three). The fourth principle, listening and responding, is followed by appropriately adapting messages to others (Principle Five). Together, these five principles can help explain why communication can be either effective or ineffective. A violation of any one principle can result in inappropriate or poor communication.

Throughout this book, we will remind you of how these principles can be used to organize the theory, concepts, and skills we offer as fundamental to human communication. Chapters 2 through 6 will each be devoted to a single principle. Chapters 7 through 15 will apply these principles to the most prevalent communication situations we experience each day—communicating with others interpersonally, in groups and teams, and when giving a talk or presentation.

To help you see relationships among the five communication principles for a lifetime and the various skills and content we will present in Chapters 7 through 15, we will place in the margin a small version of the model presented in Figure 1.5, like the one that appears in the margin here. We will also label which principle or principles we are discussing. Refer to the principles pentagon in Figure 1.5 as we introduce the principles.

Figure 1.5
Communication Principles for a Lifetime

1. Aware
2. Verbal
3. Nonverbal
4. Listen and Respond
5. Adapt

Principle One: Be Aware of Your Communication with Yourself and Others

The first foundation principle is to be aware of your communication with yourself and others. Effective communicators are conscious, or "present," when communicating. Ineffective communicators mindlessly or thoughtlessly say and do things that they may later regret. Being aware of your communication includes being conscious not only of the present moment, but also of who you are, your self-concept, your self-worth, and your perceptions of yourself and others. Being aware of your typical communication style is also part of this foundation principle. For example, some people realize that their communication style is to be emotional when interacting with others. Others may be shy.

As noted, self-awareness includes being conscious of your intrapersonal communication messages. By **intrapersonal communication,** we mean the communication

1. Aware

intrapersonal communication
Communication that occurs within yourself, including your thoughts and emotions.

that occurs within yourself, including your thoughts, your emotions, and your perceptions of yourself and others. Talking to yourself is an example of intrapersonal communication. Although our intrapersonal communication is often the focus of psychologists, our intrapersonal messages also form the basis of our communication with others.[42]

Competent communicators are aware of the choices they make when they communicate both intrapersonally and with others; incompetent communicators react to others' messages with thoughtless, quick, knee-jerk responses. Because they do not mindfully censor themselves, they may blurt out obscene, offensive, or profane words. Ineffective communicators operate in an unthinking "default" mode. Being aware of our communication is a foundation principle because all of the choices we make when communicating rest on our ability to make conscious choices when we respond to others.

Earlier in this chapter, we noted that human communication is the process of making sense out of the world and sharing that sense with others. Being aware of who we are and how we perceive, or "make sense" of, what we observe is a fundamental principle that helps explain both effective and ineffective communication. In the next chapter, we develop this principle and foreshadow how it relates to a variety of communication situations.

Principle Two: Effectively Use and Interpret Verbal Messages

The second principle we introduce here and elaborate on in Chapter 3 is to use and interpret verbal messages effectively. Verbal messages are created with language. A **language** consists of symbols and a system of rules (grammar) that make it possible for people to understand one another.

As we noted earlier, a symbol is a word, sound, gesture, or other visual signal that represents a thought, concept, object, or experience. When you read the words on this page, you are looking at symbols that trigger meaning. The word is not the thing it represents; it simply symbolizes the thing or idea.

Your reading skill permits you to make sense out of symbols. The word *tree*, for example, may trigger a thought of the tree you may be reading under now, a tree in your own yard or a nearby park, or a great sequoia you saw on your family vacation in Yosemite National Park. Effective communicators use appropriate symbols to create accurate meaning. Author Daniel Quinn once commented, "No story is devoid of meaning, if you know how to look for it. This is as true of nursery rhymes and daydreams as it is of epic poems."[43] Meaning is created when people have a common or shared understanding.

The effective communicator both encodes and decodes messages accurately; he or she selects appropriate symbols to form a message and interprets carefully the messages of others. The process of using and interpreting symbols is the essence of how we make sense out of the world and share that sense with others.

Words have power. The words we use to describe ourselves and our world have considerable influence on how we perceive what we experience. Any good advertising copywriter knows how to use words to create a need or desire for a product. Political consultants tell politicians how to craft sound bites that will create just the right audience response. And words can hurt us. Words have the ability to offend and create stress. For example, derogatory words about someone's gender or race can do considerable harm. Throughout this book, we will present strategies and suggestions for selecting the best word or symbol to enhance your listeners' understanding.

Principle Three: Effectively Use and Interpret Nonverbal Messages

Messages are also nonverbal. **Nonverbal communication** is communication by means other than written or spoken language that creates meaning for someone. Nonverbal messages can communicate powerful ideas or express emotions with greater impact than mere words alone. An optimistic hitchhiker's extended thumb and an irate driver's extended finger are nonverbal symbols with clear and intentional meaning. But not all

language
The system of symbols (words or vocabulary) structured by rules (grammar) that makes it possible for people to understand one another.

nonverbal communication
Communication by means other than written or spoken language that creates meaning for someone.

nonverbal symbols are clearly interpreted or even consciously expressed. You may not be aware of your frown when someone asks if he or she may sit next to you in a vacant seat in a restaurant. Or your son may excitedly be telling you about his field trip to the fire station while you stare into the pages of your newspaper. You have no intention of telling your son he is not important, but your lack of nonverbal responsiveness speaks volumes. Our nonverbal messages communicate how we feel toward others.

When there is a contradiction between what you say and what you do, your nonverbal message is more believable than your verbal message. When asked how your meal is, you may tell your server that the meal is "great," but your nonverbal message—facial expression and tone of voice—clearly communicates your unhappiness with the cuisine. As we noted when we discussed the concept of content and relationship messages, our nonverbal cues often tell people how to interpret what we are saying.

Effective communicators develop skill in interpreting nonverbal messages of others. They also monitor their own messages to avoid unintentionally sending contradictory verbal and nonverbal messages. It's sometimes hard to interpret nonverbal messages because they don't have a neat beginning and ending point—the flow of information is continuous. It may not be clear where one gesture stops and another begins. Cultural differences, and the fact that so many different nonverbal channels (such as eye contact, facial expression, gestures, posture) can be used at the same time, make it tricky to "read" someone's nonverbal message accurately. We amplify our discussion of the power of nonverbal messages in Chapter 4.

Principle Four: Listen and Respond Thoughtfully to Others

So far, our list of principles may appear to place much of the burden of achieving communication success on the person sending the message. But effective communication with others also places considerable responsibility on the listener. As we explained earlier in the chapter, because communication is a transactional process—both senders and receivers are mutually and usually simultaneously expressing and responding to symbols—listening to words with sensitivity and "listening between the lines" to nonverbal messages join our list of fundamental principles.

Listening can be hard because it looks easy. You spend more time listening than performing any other communication activity—probably more than any other thing you do except sleep.[44] Despite spending the greatest portion of our communication time listening, there is evidence that many if not most of us do not always listen effectively. What's tricky about listening? Both psychological, or internal, noise (our own thoughts, needs, and emotions) and external distractions (noise in the surroundings in which we listen) can create barriers to effective listening. The fact that it is perceived to be a passive rather than an active task makes listening and accurately interpreting information a challenge. Effective listening is *not* a passive task at all; the effective and sensitive listener works hard to stay on task and focus mindfully on a sender's message.

At the heart of this principle is developing sensitivity to others. We are not talking about the touchy-feely-emotional-what-I-hear-you-saying approach to interpersonal relationships. We are, however, suggesting that you develop an orientation or sensitivity to others when you listen and respond. When you are **other-oriented,** you consider the needs, motives, desires, and goals of your communication partners while

3. Nonverbal

4. Listen and Respond

other-oriented
Being focused on the needs and concerns of others while maintaining one's personal integrity.

still maintaining your own integrity. The choices you make in both forming the message and selecting when to share it should take into consideration your partner's thoughts and feelings.

Most of us are egocentric—self-focused. We are born with an innate desire to meet our own needs. As we grow and mature, we develop a consciousness of more than our own needs. Scholars of evolution might argue that it is good that we are self-focused; looking out for number one is what perpetuates the human race. Yet an *exclusive* focus on ourselves inhibits effective communication. Do you know anyone who is self-absorbed? Most of us find such a person tedious and uncomfortable to be around. People who are skilled communicators both listen and respond with sensitivity; they are other-oriented.

Principle Five: Appropriately Adapt Messages to Others

It is not enough to be sensitive and to accurately understand others; you must use the information you gather to modify the messages you construct. It is important to **adapt** your response appropriately to your listener. When you adapt a message, you make choices about how best to formulate it and respond to someone to achieve your communication goals. Adapting to a listener does not mean that you tell a listener only what he or she wants to hear. That would be unethical. Adapting involves appropriately editing and shaping your responses so that others accurately understand your messages and so that you achieve your goal without coercing or using false information or other unethical methods. To adapt a message is to make choices about all aspects of message content and delivery.

Regardless of whether you are giving a presentation, talking with a friend, or participating in a small-group meeting, as an effective communicator you consider who the listeners are when deciding what to say and how best to say it. One of the elements of a message that you adapt when communicating with others is the structure or organization of what you say. Informal interpersonal conversations typically do not follow a rigid, outlined structure. Our conversation freely bounces from one topic to another. Formal presentations delivered in North America, however, are usually expected to have a more explicit structure—an introduction, a body, and a conclusion. The major ideas of a formal presentation are expected to be clearly identified. North American audiences also seem to prefer a presentation that could be easily outlined. Other cultures, such as those in the Middle East, expect a greater use of stories, examples, and illustrations, rather than a clearly structured, outlined presentation. Knowing your audience's expectations can help you adapt your message so that it will be listened to and understood.

You also adapt the general style or formality of your message to the receiver. If you are speaking to your lifelong best friend, your style is less formal than if you are speaking to the president of your university. The language you use and jokes you tell when around your best friends will undoubtedly be different than your language and humor when you are attending a meeting with your boss or with faculty members from your school. Our point is that effective communicators not only listen and respond with sensitivity; they use the information they gather to shape the message and delivery of their responses to others. In Chapter 6, we will discuss this principle in greater detail by discussing the diverse nature of potential listeners and how to adapt to them. Adapting to differences in culture and gender, for example, may mean the difference between a message that is well received and one that creates hostility.

5. Adapt

adapt
To adjust both what is communicated and how a message is communicated; to make choices about how best to formulate a message and respond to others to achieve your communication goals.

Communicating with Others: Three Contexts

The five communication principles that we unveiled in this chapter operate whenever people communicate, regardless of the number of people present or the content of their messages. The three classic contexts to which communication researchers apply these principles are interpersonal communication, group communication, and presentational communication.

Each of the next five chapters is devoted to one of the five principles we've identified and relates these principles to the three most typical communication situations you will experience. As we've noted, a growing collection of research findings helps us understand how the Internet and other technological tools are affecting our communication. When appropriate, we'll offer some ideas and suggestions for interacting with others via mediated settings.

We now turn our attention to introducing these three contexts of communication: interpersonal, group, and presentational communication.

Interpersonal Communication

Interpersonal communication is a special form of human communication that occurs when we interact simultaneously with another person and attempt to mutually influence each other, usually for the purpose of managing relationships. At the heart of this definition is the role of communication in developing unique relationships with other people.[45]

For many years, communication scholars considered any two-person interaction interpersonal communication. Today interpersonal communication is defined not by the number of people who communicate but by the quality of communication that occurs when we express and interpret verbal and nonverbal messages. Interpersonal communication occurs not just when we interact with someone, but when we treat the other person as a one-of-a-kind human being.

Impersonal communication occurs when we treat people as objects, or when we respond to their roles rather than to who they are as unique people. Based on this definition, asking a server for a glass of water at a restaurant is impersonal rather than interpersonal communication. If you strike up a conversation with the server—say you discover it's her birthday, or you discover that you both know the same people—your conversation moves from impersonal to interpersonal. We're not suggesting that impersonal communication is unimportant or necessarily inferior or bad. Competent communicators are able to interact with others in a variety of situations.

Another attribute of interpersonal communication is that it is simultaneous. Both people are communicating at the same time and exerting mutual influence—both persons are reacting or involved in the process. Interpersonal communication is not a one-sided monologue; it's a dialogue in the sense that all communicators are influenced and meaning is created simultaneously.[46] Interpersonal communication reflects the characteristics of the transactional model of communication that we discussed earlier.

A final attribute, and among the most important, is that interpersonal communication is the fundamental means we use to manage our relationships. A relationship is an ongoing connection we make with others through interpersonal communication. To relate to someone is to give and take, listen and respond, act and react. When we talk about a good or positive relationship with someone, we often mean that we are "together" or "in sync." In an effective relationship, the individuals involved feel that their verbal and nonverbal messages are understood and that there is a relational harmony based on a common understanding between the communicators. We will apply the five principles of human communication to interpersonal communication in Chapters 7 and 8.

Group Communication

Each of us belongs to a gang of some type; it's just that some gangs are more socially acceptable than others. Comparisons between a rambunctious street gang and the local PTA may seem a stretch. But even though the street gang and the PTA have radically different objectives, both share similarities of function and form that make them a

We engage in interpersonal communication when we interact with another person.

interpersonal communication
Communication that occurs simultaneously between two people who attempt to mutually influence each other, usually for the purpose of managing relationships.

impersonal communication
Communication that treats people as objects, or that responds only to their roles, rather than to who they are as unique people.

Communication and Diversity

Communication Principles for a Lifetime: Principles for All Cultures?

We've suggested that our five Principles for a Lifetime constitute a framework for all human communication. Again, let's review the five principles:

Principle One:	Be aware of your communication with yourself and others.
Principle Two:	Effectively use and interpret verbal messages.
Principle Three:	Effectively use and interpret nonverbal messages.
Principle Four:	Listen and respond thoughtfully to others.
Principle Five:	Appropriately adapt messages to others.

The question is "How applicable are these five Principles for a Lifetime to communication in a variety of cultures?" Culture is the learned system of knowledge, behavior, attitudes, beliefs, values, and norms that is shared by a group of people. People who were born and raised in Asian countries, for example, have different cultural expectations than do people who were born and raised in North America. But do these five communication principles apply to *all* people everywhere, despite cultural differences and the wide variety of cultural traditions and backgrounds in the world? Is it true that all people should be aware of their communication, use and interpret verbal and nonverbal messages, listen and respond thoughtfully, and appropriately adapt their messages to others?

We're not suggesting that all cultures use and interpret verbal or nonverbal messages the same way (Principles Two and Three)—there are obvious differences from one culture to another in language and use of nonverbal cues. But we are suggesting that in all cultures, the use and interpretation of verbal and nonverbal messages is important in determining whether communication is effective. We are also not saying that people from all cultures adapt messages in the same way (Principle Five). There are clear cultural differences in the way people choose to adapt messages to others. But do people in all cultures adapt messages to others in some way, even though the interpretation of the adapted message varies from culture to culture? We suggest that these five fundamental principles may provide a common framework for talking about communication in a variety of cultures. Do you agree or disagree with this statement?

Engagement Questions

In your communication class, there are undoubtedly people from a variety of cultural backgrounds. Perhaps some of your classmates grew up in countries other than your own. Respond to the following questions, and then compare your answers with those of your fellow students.

1. How applicable are the five communication principles to your cultural experience?
2. Do any of the communication principles *not* apply in your culture?
3. Can you think of another fundamental communication principle that is not included in our list of five? If so, what is it?
4. Do you agree that these communication principles apply to all people?

---

group
A collection of people who have a common goal, feel a sense of belonging to the group, and influence each other.

small group communication
The transactive process of creating meaning among three to about fifteen people who share a common purpose, feel a sense of belonging to the group, and exert influence on one another.

dyad
Two interacting people.

team
A coordinated group of people intentionally organized to work together to achieve a common goal.

group: a collection of people who have common goals, who feel they belong to the group, and who influence each other.

Human beings are social, collaborative creatures. We do most of our work and play in groups. And today's globe-shrinking technology makes it possible for people to be linked with others in virtual groups even when they are in different physical locations. One focus of this book is the communication that occurs in groups—how we make sense out of our participation in groups and share that sense with others. We define **small group communication** as the verbal and nonverbal message transactions that occur among three to about fifteen people who share a common goal, who feel a sense of belonging to the group, and who exert influence on each other.[47]

A group must have at least three people; two interacting people are usually referred to as a **dyad**. What is the upper limit on the number of people for meaningful group discussion? Some scholars say fifteen, others say more.[48] The bigger the group, the less influence each person has on the group and the greater the chance that subgroups or splinter factions will emerge.

Our definition of group communication includes the notion that in order to be considered a group, people need a common goal—something that members all would agree is the reason for the group's existence. Group members also have a sense of belonging to the group. A collection of travelers waiting for the subway may have a common goal of catching the train, but they probably don't see themselves as belonging to a group with a single goal of going to the same place. Members of a small group need to have a sense of identity with the group; they should sense that it is their group.

What's the difference between a group and a team? Although some people use the two terms interchangeably, we see a distinction. A **team** is a coordinated group of individuals intentionally organized to work together to achieve a specific, common goal. To us, a team is more highly structured and organized than a group. Team members have clearly defined roles, duties, and responsibilities. Think of a sports team. Team members have assigned roles and well-thought-out assignments. Team members don't just show up and mill around and do what comes their way. They are focused. Teams also have clearly defined rules and explicit expectations for team operations. Their goals are well defined and measurable. And they coordinate their work efforts as they collaborate to achieve their well-articulated goals. In Chapters 9 and 10, we will discuss more thoroughly the five Communication Principles for a Lifetime as they apply to groups and teams.

Presentational Communication

For many people, speaking in public is a major source of anxiety. **Presentational communication** occurs when a speaker addresses a gathering of people to inform, persuade, or entertain. In this book, we will focus on applying the principles of communication when informing and persuading listeners. Effective presentational speakers are aware of their communication and how they interact with their audience. They also effectively use, interpret, and understand verbal and nonverbal messages; listen and respond to their audience; and adapt their message to their listeners.

Of the three contexts in which the principles we present in this book are applied, this context has the distinction of being the one that has been formally studied the longest. In 333 BC, Aristotle wrote his famous *Rhetoric*, the first fully developed treatment of the study of speech to convince an audience. He defined **rhetoric** as the process of discovering the available means of persuasion in a given situation. In essence, persuasion is the process of using symbols to persuade others. Today many communication departments have several courses that focus exclusively on how to persuade others, design and deliver both informative and persuasive messages, and evaluate the messages of others. Although we have certainly advanced in our understanding of informing and persuading others in the past two millennia, much of what Aristotle taught has withstood the tests of both time and scholarly research.

Our focus in Chapters 11 through 15 is on basic strategies for designing and delivering a speech to others. As with interpersonal and group communication, we will discuss presentational communication through the perspective of the five principles that anchor our study.

Are interpersonal, group, and presentational communication the only contexts in which communication takes place? The answer is no—communication takes place in a variety of situations. One of the most prominent forms of communication in our lives involves the media.

As we noted earlier, mediated communication is any communication that is expressed via some channel other than those that are used when we communicate in person. Some physical medium, such as a wire, a cable, a phone line, a cell phone, a TV set, a computer, or some other technology, carries the messages between sender and receiver. The channel of communication is not only physical but also electronic, in the form of the signal coming into your TV set, your phone, or your computer.

Mass communication occurs when a mediated message is sent to many people at the same time. A TV or radio broadcast is an example of mass communication. As we noted earlier in this chapter, our focus in this book is on unmediated communication. This is not meant to suggest that mass communication is not important, only that it is beyond the scope of this book. At some colleges and universities, mass communication is a focus of study in a separate department; at other colleges and universities, the study of mass communication is included in the same department that studies all human communication.

Many researchers study the communication that occurs in organizations such as businesses, government agencies, and nonprofits such as the Red Cross and other charities. **Organizational communication** is the study of human communication as it occurs within organizations. Although organizational communication includes

presentational communication
Communication that occurs when a speaker addresses a gathering of people in order to inform, persuade, or entertain them.

rhetoric
The process of using symbols to influence or persuade others.

mass communication
Communication accomplished through a mediated message that is sent to many people at the same time.

organizational communication
The study of human communication as it occurs within organizations.

applications of interpersonal, group, and presentational communication, there are unique ways in which communication functions in contemporary organizations.

Health communication, a growing area of communication study, examines the role and importance of communication that has an impact on our health. Health communication researchers study the interaction between health care workers (such as physicians, physician's assistants, and nurses) and patients. They also study how to best design campaigns to encourage healthy habits (messages about getting fit, losing weight, avoiding sexually transmitted diseases, or quitting smoking).

In the chapters ahead, we will analyze the five Communication Principles for a Lifetime as they apply to the three typical unmediated communication situations—interpersonal, group, and presentational communication. Our primary goal is to help you better understand your communication and improve your ability to communicate with others for the rest of your life.

health communication
The study of communication that has an impact on human health.

PRINCIPLES FOR A LIFETIME
Enhancing Your Skills

1. Aware

Principle One: Be aware of your communication with yourself and others.
- Be aware of your intrapersonal communication.
- Be conscious of how your own "self-talk" has an impact on your communication with others and your overall communication behavior.

2. Verbal

Principle Two: Effectively use and interpret verbal messages.
- Use clear and precise words to explain ideas and concepts to others.
- Make a concerted effort to accurately interpret the words of others.

3. Nonverbal

Principle Three: Effectively use and interpret nonverbal messages.
- Use nonverbal, unspoken cues to express feelings and emotions to others or to modify the explicit verbal message you are communicating to others.
- Make a conscious effort to accurately decode the nonverbal messages of others.

4. Listen and Respond

Principle Four: Listen and respond thoughtfully to others.
- Be other-oriented by taking special care to listen to both the verbal and the nonverbal messages of others.
- Be deliberate in how you provide feedback to those to whom you are listening.

5. Adapt

Principle Five: Appropriately adapt messages to others.
- Use your listening and nonverbal communication skills to help you appropriately adjust both your message and how you communicate it to others.
- Make ethical choices about how to best formulate a message and respond to others to achieve your communication goals.

Summary

Communication is essential for life. At its most basic level, communication is the process of acting on information. Human communication is the process of making sense out of the world and sharing that sense with others by creating meaning through verbal and nonverbal messages. It is important to learn about communication, because being a skilled communicator can help you obtain a good job and enhance the quality of your relationships, as well as improve your physical and emotional health. Early models viewed human communication as a simple message-transfer process. Later models evolved to view communication as interaction and then as simultaneous transaction. Key components of communication include source, receiver, message, channel, noise, context, and feedback.

Communication has five characteristics: It is inescapable; it is irreversible; it is complicated; it emphasizes content and relationships; and it is governed by rules.

Five principles are fundamental to good communication. First, be aware of your communication with yourself and others. Being mindful of your communication is important to help you improve your communication. Second, effectively use and interpret verbal messages. Words are powerful and influence our thoughts, our actions, and our relationships with others. Third, effectively use and interpret nonverbal messages. Unspoken cues provide important information about our emotions, feelings, and attitudes. Fourth, listen and respond thoughtfully to others. Being able to interpret accurately the messages of others enhances comprehension and relational empathy. Fifth, appropriately adapt messages to others. It is important to adapt messages to others to enhance both understanding and empathy.

These five principles are applicable to the most common communication contexts: interpersonal, group, and presentational communication. Interpersonal communication is a special form of communication that occurs when two people interact simultaneously and mutually influence each other, usually for the purpose of managing relationships. Small group communication is interaction among a small group of people who share a common purpose or goal, who feel a sense of belonging to the group, and who exert influence on the others in the group. Presentational communication occurs when a speaker addresses an audience for the purpose of informing, persuading, or entertaining.

Assessing Your Knowledge

For Discussion and Review

Principle One: Be aware of your communication with yourself and others.

1. What can you do to increase your awareness of internal and external noise that inhibits effective communication?

Principle Two: Effectively use and interpret verbal messages.

2. Explain how verbal messages are encoded and decoded.

Principle Three: Effectively use and interpret nonverbal messages.

3. When the verbal message and the nonverbal message presented by the same speaker contradict, which element of the message will be more believable?

Principle Four: Listen and respond thoughtfully to others.

4. Explain how improved listening skills can help make someone more other-oriented.

Principle Five: Appropriately adapt messages to others.

5. Explain the advantages of adapting messages to others and any potential disadvantages of being too adaptive to others.

Multiple Choice

Choose the *best* answer to each of the following questions.

1. Most contemporary communication scholars agree that the _____ model of communication is the most realistic model.

a. linear
   b. transactional
   c. interactional
   d. encoded

2. The pathway through which messages pass between source and receiver is the
   a. source.
   b. channel.
   c. receiver.
   d. context.

3. Susan arrives late for her date with Richard. He jumps from his chair and sarcastically says, "Glad you're here!" The relationship aspect of this message is communicated primarily by
   a. the words Richard said.
   b. Richard's sarcastic tone of voice.
   c. the time indicated on Richard's watch.
   d. both b and c

4. Telling the cashier at the gas station how much you owe and then paying her is an example of
   a. interpersonal communication.
   b. personal communication.
   c. team communication.
   d. impersonal communication.

5. Julie goes over in her mind what she wants to say during her upcoming job interview. This is an example of
   a. intrapersonal communication.
   b. interpersonal communication.
   c. impersonal communication.
   d. presentational communication.

6. A small group requires at least
   a. two members.
   b. three members.
   c. four members.
   d. five members.

7. The meaning of a message is
   a. created in the heart and mind of the sender.
   b. created in the heart and mind of the receiver.
   c. co-created by the sender and the receiver.
   d. determined solely by the symbols used.

8. Even though Phillip and Tim agreed to end their argument with each other by "starting over as if it had never taken place," each still felt angry toward the other. Phillip and Tim have failed to realize that
   a. communication is inescapable.
   b. communication is irreversible.
   c. communication involves content and relationship.
   d. communication is governed by rules.

9. When there is a contradiction between your verbal message and your nonverbal message,
   a. your verbal message is more believable than your nonverbal one.
   b. your nonverbal message is more believable than your verbal one.
   c. your verbal and nonverbal messages are equally believable.
   d. your verbal and nonverbal messages are equally unbelievable.

10. During times of high uncertainty, we attempt to manage our uncertainty by
    a. listening more and communicating less.
    b. communicating about the same as usual, but a little more slowly.
    c. communicating more actively and purposefully.
    d. paying more attention to verbal messages than nonverbal messages.

Answers to the questions in this practice test can be found at the end of the book.

Assessing Your Skill

Assessing Your Willingness to Communicate (WTC)

As you begin your study of communication, complete the following assessment measure to determine your willingness to communicate in several communication situations.

Directions: Below are twenty situations in which a person might choose to communicate or not to communicate. Presume you have *completely free choice*. Indicate in the space at the left what percent of the time you would choose to communicate in each situation (0 = *never*, 100 = *always*).

1. _____ Talk with a service station attendant.
2. _____ Talk with a physician.
3. _____ Present a talk to a group of strangers.
4. _____ Talk with an acquaintance while standing in line.
5. _____ Talk with a salesperson in a store.
6. _____ Talk in a large meeting of friends.
7. _____ Talk with a policeman/policewoman.
8. _____ Talk in a small group of strangers.
9. _____ Talk with a friend while standing in line.
10. _____ Talk with a waiter/waitress in a restaurant.
11. _____ Talk in a large meeting of acquaintances.
12. _____ Talk with a stranger while standing in line.
13. _____ Talk with a secretary.
14. _____ Present a talk to a group of friends.
15. _____ Talk in a small group of acquaintances.
16. _____ Talk with a garbage collector.
17. _____ Talk in a large meeting of strangers.
18. _____ Talk with a spouse (or girl/boyfriend).
19. _____ Talk in a small group of friends.
20. _____ Present a talk to a group of acquaintances.

Scoring Instructions:
The WTC score is designed to indicate how willing you are to communicate in a variety of contexts with different types of receivers. The higher your overall WTC score, the more willing you are to communicate in general. Similarly, the higher your subscore for a type of context or audience, the more willing you are to communicate in that type of context or with that type of audience.

The WTC assessment permits computation of one total score and seven subscores. The subscores relate to willingness to communicate in four common communication contexts, and with three types of audiences.

Subscore for Communication Context	*Scoring Formula*
Group discussions	Add scores for items 8, 15, 19; then divide by 3.
Meetings	Add scores for items 6, 11, 17; then divide by 3.
Interpersonal conversations	Add scores for items 4, 9, 12; then divide by 3.
Public speaking	Add scores for items 3, 14, 20; then divide by 3.

Subscore for Audience Type	
Stranger	Add scores for items 3, 8, 12, 17; then divide by 4.
Acquaintance	Add scores for items 4, 11, 15, 20; then divide by 4.
Friend	Add scores for items 6, 9, 14, 19; then divide by 4.

To compute your total WTC score, add the subscores for Stranger, Acquaintance, and Friend. Then divide by 3.

Norms for WTC scores

Group discussions	>89, high WTC; <57, low WTC
Meetings	>80, high WTC; <39, low WTC
Interpersonal conversations	>94, high WTC; <64, low WTC
Public speaking	>78, high WTC; <33, low WTC
Stranger	>63, high WTC; <18, low WTC
Acquaintance	>92, high WTC; <57, low WTC
Friend	>99, high WTC; <71, low WTC
Total WTC	>82, high overall WTC; <52, low overall WTC

Source: V. P. Richmond and J. C. McCroskey, *Communication: Apprehension, Avoidance, and Effectiveness* 5e (Boston: Allyn & Bacon, 1998).

Web Resources to Improve Your Knowledge and Skill

Most colleges and universities offer courses in communication and allow students to major or minor in communication, speech communication, or communication studies. The study of human communication may also be among the offerings of a department that focuses on mass communication, speech communication, and/or theatre. Students who select communication as a major or a minor pursue a wide variety of careers and professions, including business, law, government, education, and social services.

Several academic communication organizations offer a wealth of resources, information, and ideas about human communication. Chances are that the instructor for your communication course is a member of one or more of these organizations. The following web sites offer you a panoramic view of the communication discipline from an academic perspective.

- <www.natcom.org> is the web site of the National Communication Association.
- <http://facstaff.uww.edu/wca> is the web site of the World Communication Association.
- <www.icahdq.org> is the web site of the International Communication Association.
- <www.cios.org/encyclopedia/comlinks/websites.htm> is a comprehensive web site that lists dozens of sites on a variety of communication topics.

Marc Chagall, "The Painter," 1976. © 2008 Artists Rights Society (ARS), New York/ADAGP, Paris. © Scala/Art Resource/NY.

A person who buries his head in the sand offers an engaging target.

Mabel A. Keenan

Chapter 2

Self-Awareness and Communication

Chapter Outline

- Self-Awareness: How Well Do You Know Yourself?
- Self-Concept: Who Are You?
- Self-Esteem: What Is Your Value?
- Communication and the Enhancement of Self-Esteem
- The Perception Process
- When Perceptions Vary
- Communication and the Enhancement of Perceptual Accuracy
- Summary

Chapter Objectives

After studying this chapter, you should be able to

1. Discuss the importance of self-awareness in the process of improving one's communication skills.
2. Define attitudes, beliefs, and values as they relate to self-concept development.
3. Name and briefly describe the three types of selves, according to James's research.
4. Describe the four factors that affect the development of self-concept.
5. Describe Stewart's four characteristics of identity.
6. Explain the difference between self-concept, self-image, and self-esteem.
7. Describe how gender, social comparisons, self-expectations, and self-fulfilling prophecies affect one's self-esteem.
8. Provide examples of positive self-talk, visualization, and reframing that demonstrate the connection between these techniques and the enhancement of self-esteem.
9. Define perception and explain its three stages.
10. Explain why people differ in their perceptions of people and events.
11. Discuss three ways to enhance your perceptual accuracy.

Have you designed your own MySpace or Facebook page for purposes of social networking? If so, how did you make decisions as to what to include on your page? Did you provide photos of yourself with friends, family members, or even pets? How did you describe yourself—using physical characteristics, intellectual or personality aspects, or lifestyle elements like hobbies and interests? Do you think your page is an accurate representation of who you are as a person?

If you don't have a MySpace page or your own personal web site, perhaps you've experimented with an online dating service, such as <match.com> or <eharmony.com>, where you're asked a battery of questions about yourself. Your responses are then analyzed across multiple personality dimensions in an effort to match you with compatible potential partners who also use the service. If you've used such a service, did you learn anything about yourself in the process of answering all those questions?

Activities such as designing a MySpace page or responding to dating service questions rely on a central, important element: awareness. Stephen Covey, author of the best-selling book *The Seven Habits of Highly Effective People*, describes self-awareness as that which "allows us to stand apart and examine even the way we 'see' ourselves—our self-paradigm, the most fundamental paradigm of effectiveness. It affects not only our attitudes and behaviors, but also how we see other people."[1] Interpersonal communication scholar David Johnson suggests, "Self-awareness is the key to self-knowledge, self-understanding, and self-disclosure. Being open with another person begins with being aware of who you are and what you are like. To disclose your feelings and reactions, you must be aware of them."[2]

Figure 2.1 presents the model introduced in Chapter 1—our "Communication Principles for a Lifetime" model. You will no doubt become quite familiar with this model and its five principles as you read this book. As we said in Chapter 1, these integrative principles provide the foundation for effective communication in various contexts that you encounter throughout your life. In this chapter, we explore the first principle: *Be aware of your communication with yourself and others.* Developing self-awareness involves being conscious not only of the present moment, but also of who you are (your self-concept), your value in this life (your self-esteem), and your perception of yourself and others.

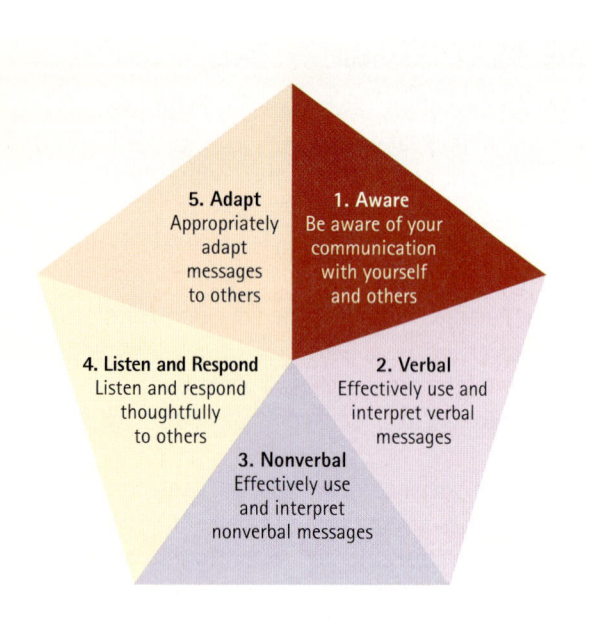

Figure 2.1
Communication Principles for a Lifetime

Self-Awareness: How Well Do You Know Yourself?

Many of us experience moments in our lives when we're acutely aware that we're learning something important—something that will change us in some profound way. (College years are typically full of these moments.) While a great deal of self-awareness comes gradually and simply, some is thrust upon us in dramatic fashion, and we take leaps in our maturity and understanding of ourselves. In this chapter, we deal with all forms of awareness—the simple and the profound, the casual and the dramatic—because any kind of awareness impacts how we communicate and respond to communication from others. Becoming more self-aware is a never-ending process in life. You don't reach a point where you've maxed out your self-awareness.

By one definition, *self-awareness* is "the capacity to observe and reflect upon one's own mental states."[3] A related view holds that self-awareness, sometimes referred to as **symbolic self-awareness,** is the unique human ability to develop a representation of oneself and communicate that representation to others through language.[4]

symbolic self-awareness
A unique human ability to develop and communicate a representation of oneself to others through language.

Sociologist Derek Layder outlines five properties of the self; it is our challenge to come to a greater understanding of each property within ourselves.[5] First, Layder suggests that the self is both social and psychological: "Something of the self always stands apart from the social world. At the same time the self can only exist within a social context." Second, he describes the emotional aspect of the self, our inner mental existence, which fuels our behavior. Next is the self as a focal point of action and control. Fourth, Layder describes the self as "flexible and pliable," in that people are complex and sometimes contradictory, evidencing various sides of their personalities that reflect a multifaceted self. Finally, Layder includes as an important component the spiritual or "higher" self, which some people ignore or resist and which is often overlooked in research.

The better we understand the complex, multilayered nature of the self, the more aware we will become of our own being; and this, we believe, is critical in becoming an effective communicator. A framework attributed to Abraham Maslow helps explain the process of becoming self-aware; it has also been used to explain the attainment of communication skill. The framework suggests that people operate at one of four levels:

1. *Unconscious incompetence.* We are unaware of our own incompetence. We don't know what we don't know.
2. *Conscious incompetence.* At this level, we become aware or conscious that we are not competent; we know what we don't know.
3. *Conscious competence.* We are aware that we know or can do something, but it has not yet become an integrated skill or habit.
4. *Unconscious competence.* At this level, skills become second nature. You know or can do something but don't have to concentrate to be able to act on that knowledge or draw on that skill.

Here's an example that will illustrate this framework. Let's say you have a coworker named Charlie who is really an okay guy, but he says the strangest things, oftentimes downright inappropriate things. It seems as though the guy was raised by wolves, because he simply does not know how to talk to people. But he's a hard worker, so everyone at work tolerates him. Charlie is at Maslow's level 1 when it comes to communication—he doesn't know that he communicates poorly. (This is the "ignorance is bliss" level, but it isn't "blissful" relationally.) He either hasn't thought much about his communication abilities or perhaps thinks he is good, or at least passable, at conversation.

The problem is that coworkers and customers are complaining to Charlie's supervisor. The supervisor calls Charlie into the office and reprimands him for his poor communication skills, requiring him to enroll in communication training at the corporate office to improve how he interacts with people. Now Charlie is at level 2 because he is conscious of his own incompetence as a communicator. Good for Charlie, because he embraces what he learns at communication training and actively works to improve how he relates to coworkers, bosses, and customers. His work is paying off—his supervisor and coworkers are noticing the changes he is making and are providing positive feedback. Charlie is now at level 3, in which he is conscious of his own competence as a communicator.

If Charlie continues to progress over time and receive feedback from people, at some point he may reach level 4, in which communication effectiveness is incorporated into his style and self-concept and is no longer something he has to make a conscious effort to achieve.

Almost any skill within the larger realm of communication can be described in terms of these four levels. And it is possible to be at one level with one skill and at another level with another skill. For example, a person may be skilled at meeting new people, but less skilled at managing conflict within a relationship. Someone may be very engaging in conversation with friends, but she or he would rather have a spinal tap than give a public presentation.

A couple of paragraphs ago, we described moments of heightened self-awareness and significant personal growth. Taking a communication course like the one you're enrolled in can spark such a moment. In this course, you will be challenged to think long and hard about your answers to the question "Who am I?" You'll be encouraged

1. Aware

to inventory what you believe about yourself and to think about the role such aspects as your gender, race or ethnicity, nationality, sexual orientation, and social class play in your view of self. You'll be challenged to consider how you communicate with others, how you are shaped and affected by those with whom you interact, and how you can use your powers of communication. But the key beginning point is awareness. Before attempting to communicate who you are to others, you must first be aware of yourself.

Self-Concept: Who Are You?

If someone were to say to you "Who are you?" how would you respond? You might start with basic demographic information like your age and where you're from; perhaps you would describe yourself in relation to groups and organizations to which you belong. Or you might talk about yourself according to various roles you assume, like "I'm a student at State" or "I'm so-and-so's daughter (or son)." Whatever answer you give will be incomplete, because you can't really convey the totality of who you are to others. But it's an interesting place to begin, considering just how you would answer the "Who am I" question.

Psychologist Karen Horney defines **self** as "that central inner force, common to all human beings and yet unique in each which is the deep source of growth."[6] Your "Who am I" responses are also part of your **self-concept**—your interior identity or subjective description of who you think you are, which remains relatively stable despite the changing world in which you live.[7] Some people use the term *self-image* synonymously with self-concept, but we want to avoid confusion over these terms. We subscribe to a narrower meaning for the term self-image, in that **self-image** is your view of yourself *in a particular situation*.[8] That view changes from situation to situation. For example, you may be extroverted in chemistry class but not at a party where you don't know too many people. You may become very nervous when talking to an authority figure but be quite comfortable communicating with people your own age. You have several self-images, because they change as the situation changes. These different self-images are part of the larger component we call self-concept. The self-concept is the way we *consistently* describe ourselves to others; it is deeply rooted and slow to change.

Self-Concept Components

Who you are is also reflected in the attitudes, beliefs, and values that you hold. An **attitude** is a learned predisposition to respond to a person, object, or idea in a favorable or unfavorable way. Attitudes reflect what you like and what you don't like. If you like sports, spaghetti, and history, you hold positive attitudes toward these things. You were not born with a fondness for sports; you learned to like them just as some people learn to enjoy the taste of exotic foods.

Beliefs are the way in which you structure your understanding of reality—what is true and what is false. Most of your beliefs are based on previous experience. You trust that the sun will rise in the morning and that you'll get burned if you put your hand on a hot stove.

Values are enduring concepts of good and bad, right and wrong. Your values can be difficult to identify because they are so central to who you are. But knowing what you value in your life is part of the principle of self-awareness that we focus on in this chapter. When you go to the supermarket, you may spend a few minutes deciding whether to buy chocolate or vanilla ice cream, but you probably do not spend much time deciding whether you will steal the ice cream or pay for it, because you value honesty over dishonesty. Other values may reflect your sense of loyalty, patriotism, justice and fairness, and love and caring for others. Our values are instilled in us by our earliest connections with others; for almost all of us, our parents are the first influences on our development of values. Of the three elements, attitudes are the most superficial and likely to change; values are more at the core of a person and least likely to change.

---

self
The sum of who you are as a person; your central inner force.

self-concept
Your interior identity or subjective description of who you think you are.

self-image
Your view of yourself in a particular situation or circumstance.

attitude
A learned predisposition to respond to a person, object, or idea in a favorable or unfavorable way.

belief
The way in which you structure your understanding of reality—what is true and what is false.

value
An enduring concept of good and bad, right and wrong.

Recap

Self-Concept Components

Component	Definition	Dimensions	Example
Attitude	Learned predisposition to respond favorably or unfavorably toward something	Likes–Dislikes	You like ice cream, video games, and free music downloads.
Belief	Way in which you structure reality	True–False	You believe your parents love you.
Value	Enduring concept of right and wrong	Good–Bad	You value honesty and truth.

One or Many Selves?

Shakespeare's famous line "To thine own self be true" suggests that you have a single self to which you can be true. But do you have just one self? Or is there a more "real you" buried somewhere within? "I'm just not myself this morning," sighs Sandy, as she drags herself out the door to head for her office. If she is not herself, then *who is she?*

Communication *and Diversity*

Self-Concept from East and West

In this section of the chapter, we define the term *self-concept* as an interior identity that remains relatively stable despite fluctuations in one's circumstances and the world. But are you aware that this definition reflects a Western perspective and that people who live in many countries in the Eastern hemisphere have quite a different way of looking at the self-concept?

International scholar Gabriel Bukobza offers an expanded view of the self-concept stemming from his cross-cultural research.[9] In general, we Westerners first use personal reflection and investigation to form the self-concept; then we pursue feedback from others in order to corroborate and validate our view of ourselves. We enjoy others' views of us that correspond with who we believe ourselves to be and tend to reject messages and withdraw from people who negate our self-concept. The knowledge we gather about ourselves constructs a coherent view of self from infancy through various situations, roles, and relationships in adulthood. Bukobza explains that when our experience is "congruent with the self-view it functions as a source of security and happiness, and contrarily, feelings of awkwardness and anxiety enter whenever the thread of consistency between experience and selfhood is interrupted."[10]

In contrast to the consistent and independent Western self-concept, many Eastern cultures view the self-concept as "malleable, contextual, inconsistent, relational, interdependent, and oriented to group hierarchy."[11] In Asian countries in particular, the self-concept is constructed around significant social groups, such as one's immediate family, extended family, or community, with each member feeling a strong commitment to group identity. Whereas actions and choices typically reflect individual preferences in Western cultures, in Eastern cultures a community's preferences are primary in a person's life. A central part of an Easterner's self-concept is harmonious interactions with others and fitting in or being an integral part of a collective.

In this global village in which we live, where access to members of other cultural groups is only a mouse click away, it's important to remember that even the most basic of elements—the self-concept—can vary interculturally. Those of us living in the United States likely hold independence and individuality as core positive qualities within our self-concepts, but we should refrain from sitting in judgment of someone from an Eastern culture whose core values within his or her self-concept include a strong tie to others and an emphasis on community over individual.

Engagement Questions

1. Do you have friends or acquaintances on campus who are from Eastern countries? If so, do you think the way they view themselves (self-concept) differs from how you view yourself and how your American friends view themselves?
2. What are some downfalls of developing an independent sense of self rather than a social or interdependent sense of self? What are some benefits?

The self-concept that we develop through communication with our family stays with us throughout our life.

Most scholars conclude that we have a core set of behaviors, attitudes, beliefs, and values that constitute our self—the sum total of who we are. But our *concept* of self can and does change, depending on circumstances and influences.

Perhaps the most enduring and widely accepted framework for understanding the self was developed by the philosopher William James. He identified three components of the self: the material self, the social self, and the spiritual self.[12]

The Material Self

Perhaps you've heard the statement "You are what you eat." The material self goes a step further by suggesting "You are what you have." The **material self** is a total of all of the tangible things you own: your body, your possessions, your home.

One element of the material self receives considerable attention in our culture: the body. Do you like the way you look? Most of us would like to change something about our appearance. Research has determined that in the United States, women experience more negative feelings about their bodies than men and experience significant self-esteem loss as a result.[13] Many women hold images of very thin women, such as supermodels and other media personalities, as ideals and develop dissatisfaction with their own bodies in comparison. Women's dissatisfaction with their bodies has markedly increased over recent decades. According to the Women's Sports Foundation in 2006, 56 percent of American women said that they were on a diet.[14] However, research also shows that men are not immune to body dissatisfaction, in that they compare their own bodies with ideal muscular male bodies displayed in the media and are concerned about what others want and expect them to look like.[15] When there is a discrepancy between our desired material self and our self-concept, we may respond to eliminate the discrepancy. We may try to lose weight, have a nose job, or get another tattoo.

We also attempt to keep up with the proverbial Joneses by wanting more expensive clothes, cars, and homes. By extension, what we own becomes who we are. The bigger, better, more "high-tech," and more luxurious our possessions, we may subconsciously conclude, the better *we* are.

The Social Self

Your **social self** is that part of you that interacts with others. William James believed that you have as many social selves as you have people who recognize you and that you change who you are depending on the friend, family member, colleague, or acquaintance with whom you are interacting. For example, when you talk to your best friend, you're willing to "let your hair down" and reveal more thoughts and feelings than you might in a conversation with your communication professor, your parents, or your boss. Each relationship that you have with another person is unique because you bring to it a unique social self. This means that you are multi-

material self
The element of the self reflected in all the tangible things you own.

social self
Your concept of self as developed through your personal, social interactions with others.

Recap

William James's Dimensions of Self

Dimension	Definition	Examples
Material Self	The component of self derived from physical elements that reflect who you are	The self you reveal through your body, clothes, car, home
Social Self	The variety of selves that appear in different situations and roles, reflected in interactions with others	Your informal self interacting with friends; your formal self interacting with your professors
Spiritual Self	The component of self based on introspection about values, morals, and beliefs	Belief or disbelief in a supreme being or force; regard for life in all its forms

faceted, not false with people, because you have different selves in relation to different people.

The Spiritual Self   Your **spiritual self** is a mixture of your beliefs and your sense of who you are in relationship to other forces in the universe. Note that this aspect of the self is termed "spiritual," not "religious." People who consider themselves religious most likely also consider themselves spiritual; however, many people view themselves as spiritual but not religious. The term *religious* implies adherence to a specific religion or faith, typically accompanied by a belief in a supreme being or creator. However, people who see themselves as spiritual often do not subscribe to any one religion, preferring to develop their views from an array of philosophies and belief systems. From William James's perspective, the spiritual self contains all of your internal thoughts and introspections about your values and moral standards. It is not dependent on what you own or with whom you talk; it is the essence of who you *think* you are and how you *feel* about yourself. It is your attempt to understand your inner essence, whether you view that essence as consciousness, spirit, or soul. Your spiritual self is the part of you that attempts to answer the question "Why am I here?"

How the Self-Concept Develops

Some psychologists and sociologists have advanced theories that suggest we learn who we are through four basic means: (1) our communication with other individuals, (2) our association with groups, (3) roles we assume, and (4) our self-labels.

Communication with Others   A valued colleague of ours often says, when he teaches communication courses, that every time you lose a relationship you lose an opportunity to see yourself. What he means is that we don't come to know and understand ourselves in a vacuum. We learn who we are by communicating with others, receiving their feedback, making sense out of it, and internalizing or rejecting all or part of it, such that we are altered by the experience. For example, let's say you like to think of yourself as a real comedian. Now think about it for a moment: How would you know you were funny if it were not for others' laughing at humorous things you say or do? Sure, you can crack yourself up, but the real test of whether you're funny or not is how others react to you.

In 1902, scholar Charles Horton Cooley first advanced the notion that we form our self-concepts by seeing ourselves in a figurative looking glass: We learn who we are by interacting with others, much as we look into a mirror and see our reflection.[16] Like Cooley, George Herbert Mead, author of *Mind, Self, and Society* and creator of symbolic

spiritual self
Your concept of self, based on beliefs and your sense of who you are in relationship to other forces in the universe; also includes your thoughts and introspections about your values and moral standards.

The verbal messages you send to others help to build your ascribed identity. In what ways can you make a concerted effort to use clear and precise words so that others understand the emotions and ideas you're trying to convey?

interactionism theory, also believed that our sense of who we are is a consequence of our relationships with others.[17] So when we form new relationships and sustain the old ones, we gain opportunities to know ourselves better.

Interpersonal communication scholar John Stewart and colleagues describe four characteristics of the self-concept or one's identity.[18] First, identities are multidimensional and changing. Human beings are complex. Some of a person's aspects are stable, such as his or her genetic profile or ethnicity, but most aspects of the self are constructed and therefore fluid, meaning that identity changes because of circumstances and, primarily, our interactions and relationships with others.

Second, identity involves responsiveness to others. We do not form our sense of self in a vacuum. Identities are negotiated, cocreated, reinforced, and challenged through communication with others.[19]

A third characteristic is that identities develop in both past and present relationships. Who you are today is greatly a function of your family background and relationships. Those early messages you received, nicknames you were given, and the ways family members related to you significantly influenced your view of self. While family relationships often remain important in our lives, these primary relationships may be replaced or de-emphasized, as present relationships with friends, romantic partners, classmates, and coworkers shape the self-concept and help to construct identity.

Finally, Stewart suggests that identities can be avowed and ascribed. An **avowed identity** is one you personally assign to yourself and portray, such as student, athlete, friend, and so forth. An **ascribed identity** involves characteristics others attribute or assign to you, and you may or may not agree with the assignment. For example, you think you have a great sense of humor, that your jokes and clownish behavior make you the life of every party. Your view of yourself as a person who can make other people laugh is part of your avowed self-concept. However, in a heart-to-heart conversation with a close friend, you learn that your friends think you're sort of humorous in a corny or folksy kind of way, but not "laugh out loud" hilarious. Their view of you is an ascribed identity—in this case, one that is in contrast with your avowed identity, the view you've personally assigned to yourself. When we face a contradiction like this between avowed and ascribed identities, one reaction is to simply dismiss the external information. But remember that we're after heightened self-awareness here—it's the focus of this chapter and Principle One of our Communication Principles for a Lifetime. We'll grow more and enhance our self-awareness by processing the ascribed identity: taking it in, contemplating why people see us the way they do, and considering whether any changes are necessary in the way we relate to others. Avowed and ascribed identities aren't static; they shift and are negotiated through our interactions with others.[20]

avowed identity
An identity you assign to yourself and portray.

ascribed identity
An identity assigned to you by others.

Association with Groups I'm a native New Yorker. I'm a soccer player. I'm a rabbi. I'm a real estate agent. I'm a member of the Young Democrats. Each of these self-descriptive statements answers the "Who am I" question by citing identification with a group or organization. Our awareness of who we are is often linked to those with whom we associate. Some groups we are born into; others we choose on our own. Either way, group associations are significant parts of our identities.

As you no doubt are aware, peer pressure is a powerful force in shaping attitudes and behavior, and adolescents are particularly susceptible to it. But adolescents are not alone in allowing the attitudes, beliefs, and values of others to shape their expectations and behaviors. Most adults, to varying degrees, ask themselves, "What will the neighbors think? What will my family think?" when they make choices.

Assumed Roles A large part of most people's answers to the "Who am I" question reflects roles they assume in their lives. Mother, aunt, brother, uncle, manager, salesperson, teacher, spouse, and student are labels that imply certain expectations for behavior, and they are important in shaping the self-concept.

Gender asserts a powerful influence on the self-concept from birth on. As soon as they know the sex of their child, many parents begin associating their child with a gender group by adhering to cultural roles. They give the child sex-stereotypical toys, such as catcher's mitts, train sets, or guns for boys, and dolls, tea sets, and "dress-up" kits for girls. These cultural expectations play a major role in shaping our self-concept and our behavior.[21] Research indicates that up until the age of three, children are not acutely aware of sex roles. Between the ages of three and five, however, behaviors reflecting masculine and feminine roles begin to emerge (as encouraged by parents), and they are usually solidified between the ages of five and seven.[22] By the time we reach adulthood, our self-concepts are quite distinguishable by gender, with men describing themselves more in terms of giftedness, power, and invulnerability and women viewing themselves in terms of likability and morality.[23]

Self-Labels Although our self-concept is deeply affected by others, we are not blank slates for them to write on. The labels we use to describe our own attitudes, beliefs, values, and actions also play a role in shaping our self-concept. Where do our labels come from? We interpret what we experience; we are self-reflexive. **Self-reflexiveness** is the human ability to think about what we're doing while we're doing it. We talk to ourselves about ourselves. We are both participants and observers in all that we do. This dual role encourages us to use labels to describe who we are.

When you were younger, perhaps you dreamed of becoming a rocker or an entrepreneur. People along the way may have told you that you were a great musician or had a head for business, but as you matured, you probably began observing yourself more

Recap

How the Self-Concept Develops

Communication with Others	The self-concept develops as we communicate with others, receive their feedback, make sense out of it, and internalize or reject all or part of it.
Association with Groups	We develop our self-concept partly because of and through our identification with groups or organizations.
Assumed Roles	The self-concept is affected by roles we assume, such as son or daughter, employee, parent, spouse, or student.
Self-Labels	The terms we use to describe our attitudes, beliefs, values, and actions play a role in shaping the self-concept.

self-reflexiveness
The human ability to think about what you are doing while you are doing it.

critically. You struck out with a couple of bands; your business ideas didn't pan out. So you self-reflexively decided that you were not, deep down, a rocker or a business owner, even though others may have labeled you as such. Sometimes, through self-observation, we experience a period of depression or disillusionment because who we thought we were does not reflect reality, and we confront the need to change. However, we may also discover strengths that encourage us to assume new labels.

Self-Esteem: What Is Your Value?

It may sound crass to consider our *value*, but we do this every day. Our assessment of our value as persons is termed **self-esteem.** Closely related to your self-concept, or your *description* of who you are, is your self-esteem, your *evaluation* of who you are. As Gloria Steinem described it in her book *Revolution from Within: A Book of Self-Esteem*, "It's a feeling of 'clicking in' when that self is recognized, valued, discovered, *esteemed*—as if we literally plug into an inner energy that is ours alone, yet connects us to everything else."[24]

While the self-concept pertains to one's enduring identity, self-esteem pertains more to one's current state of mind or view of self. But are the two aspects of the self related? Research continues to explore that very question, focusing on the notion of **self-concept clarity**, which Canadian psychologist Jennifer Campbell defines as the extent to which beliefs about oneself are clearly and confidently identified and stable over time.[25] This doesn't mean that you don't change as a person or that your view of yourself doesn't change; we know that people evolve as they mature and experience new things. But self-concept clarity relates to the stability associated with having a clear sense of who you are and being confident in your identity. One of the things Campbell and various colleagues have determined is that people who suffer from low self-esteem also tend to have a less clearly defined sense of self—in other words, they tend to have more questions about their identity.[26] So although the two concepts aren't synonymous, a lack of clarity in your self-concept is related to a lack of confidence and reduced self-esteem. If you suffer from low self-esteem, it might not stem from knowing yourself well but not liking yourself (as many people tend to believe); instead, it might stem from not knowing yourself very well in the first place. In those cases, perhaps some reflection and counseling toward a greater understanding of the basic self is in order.

Self-esteem can fluctuate because of relatively minor events, such as getting a high grade on a paper, or major upheavals, such as the breakup of an important relationship.[27] Self-esteem can rise or fall within the course of a day; sometimes just a look from someone (or someone's failure to notice you) can send you into a tailspin and make you feel devalued. Or a certain level of self-esteem can last for a while—you may have a series of months or even years that you look back on thinking "I felt pretty lousy about myself in those days. Glad that period is over." Researchers have identified four factors that provide clues about the nature of self-esteem: gender, social comparisons, self-expectations, and the self-fulfilling prophecy.

Gender

Sex and gender have an impact on self-esteem. Before exploring that impact, let's first clarify our use of the terms *sex* and *gender*, because many people use them interchangeably, and that can lead to confusion. One meaning for the term **sex** is the biological/physiological characteristics that make a person male or female. In another usage, *sex* can refer to sexual activity. The term used most often in this book is *gender*. In its most specific sense, gender refers to psychological and emotional characteristics of individuals that cause them to be masculine, feminine, or androgynous (having a combination of both feminine and masculine traits). Defined broadly, **gender** is a cultural construction that contains psychological characteristics but also includes your sex (being female or male), your attitudes about appropriate roles and behavior for the sexes

---

self-esteem
Your assessment of your worth or value as reflected in your perception of such things as your skills, abilities, talents, and appearance.

self-concept clarity
The extent to which beliefs about oneself are clearly and confidently identified and stable over time.

sex
The biological and physiological characteristics that make a person female or male.

gender
A cultural construction that includes one's biological sex, psychological characteristics (femininity, masculinity, androgyny), attitudes about the sexes, and sexual orientation.

in society, and your sexual orientation (to whom you are sexually attracted).[28] Because the term *gender* is more broad and all-inclusive, it's our preferred term in this book.

Research that has primarily focused on the development of self-esteem in childhood and adolescence documents ways that boys' self-esteem develops differently from girls'. In a patriarchal (or male-dominated) culture, such as that of the United States, women and girls suffer loss of self-esteem to a much greater degree than men and boys.[29] A survey of 3,000 schoolchildren, conducted by the American Association of University Women, showed that self-esteem decreases between elementary grades and high school, but this decrease is significantly more pronounced in girls.[30] Myra and David Sadker, authors of the book *Failing at Fairness: How America's Schools Cheat Girls*, explain how boys experience a "self-esteem slide," while girls' self-esteem loss is a "free fall."[31]

The difference in self-esteem levels seems to pertain to such factors as boys feeling better able to do things than girls. A related factor is the reinforcement boys receive from participating in athletics, which helps them cope with changes in their bodies better than girls. But this trend has begun to change, as we witness rising participation in and appreciation for women's athletics.[32]

Social Comparisons

One way we become more aware of ourselves and derive our sense of self-worth is by measuring ourselves against others, a process called **social comparison**.[33] I'm good at playing basketball (because I'm part of a winning team); I can't cook (because others cook better than I do); I'm good at meeting people (whereas most people seem to be uncomfortable interacting with new people); I'm not handy (but my dad can fix anything). Each of these statements implies a judgment about how well or badly you can perform certain tasks, with implied references to how well others perform the same tasks. A belief that you cannot fix a leaky faucet or cook like a chef may not in itself lower your self-esteem. But if there are *several* things you can't do or *many* important tasks that you cannot seem to master, these shortcomings may begin to color your overall sense of worth. If it seems as if you're a "jack of all trades, master of none" and everyone else is a "master," your self-esteem may suffer as a result.

One powerful social comparison that contributes to self-esteem loss in girls and women is fueled by images of physical attractiveness in the media. Mass media create and reinforce for consumers notions of what is physically attractive, and achieving that media-driven standard is next to impossible for most people.[34] One line of research has found that females of a wide range of ages—from preadolescents through college students—compare their own physical attractiveness to that of models in ads. When they perceive that they don't measure up, they often experience the "model trap." This trap is a continual cycle of viewing physically "perfect" models, hating them, then growing to like them, and loving them, followed by efforts to emulate them, failing in those efforts, resenting them again, and repeating the cycle.[35]

While this form of mediated social comparison has had a greater effect on females' than on males' self-esteem, advertisers have begun to target male consumers, too—so social comparisons to male models, and resulting self-esteem loss among males, are on the rise. In an analysis of *Men's Health* magazine, author Michelle Cottle explores increasing media attention being paid to male desires for physical beauty and

Research shows that the more a person feels committed to and positive about his or her ethnic group, the higher his or her levels of self-esteem tend to be. How do you feel about your own ethnic group? How are your messages and your interpretations of other people's messages affected by these feelings?

social comparison
Process of comparing oneself to others to measure one's worth in relationship to others who are similar.

Supportive relationships with friends can help young girls overcome feelings of low self-esteem.

effects on self-esteem. She explains, "With page after page of bulging biceps and Gillette jaws, robust hairlines and silken skin, *Men's Health* is peddling a standard of male beauty as unforgiving and unrealistic as the female version sold by those dewy-eyed pre-teen waifs draped across the covers of *Glamour* and *Elle*."[36]

It can be self-defeating to take social comparisons too far, to cause your self-esteem to suffer because you compare yourself unfairly or unrealistically to others. The wiser approach is to compare yourself to your friends and neighbors, people you know and who are similar to you in many ways, rather than to people who are obviously not like you. Expecting to be as wealthy as Microsoft Chair Bill Gates is unrealistic for most of us, so it's unwise to compare your income to his. You might, however, compare how much you make at your job with the incomes of others who have similar positions or abilities comparable to yours. A healthy sense of self-worth is derived in part from the conclusions we draw from realistic, fair comparisons.

Self-Expectations

Another factor that affects your self-esteem is an estimation of how well you accomplish your goals. **Self-expectations** are goals we set for ourselves, such as losing weight, developing a "buff" body, making better grades, being appointed or elected to an important office in an organization, graduating by a certain time, and acquiring wealth by a certain age. Self-esteem is affected when you evaluate how well you measure up to your own expectations. For instance, if you expect to receive all A's this semester and you don't achieve that, it's likely that your self-esteem will be affected negatively. You may have to readjust your goals and expectations, or just become more determined to achieve the straight-A goal next semester.

Some people place enormous expectations on themselves, probably because their parents had enormous expectations for them when they were growing up. We wish people who are stressed out all the time could give themselves a break, because they place such unrealistic, high demands on themselves. The popular achievement gurus will tell you that setting high goals is a good thing, that you will not accomplish much if you set easily attainable goals. But we are suspicious of that advice; we see too many people whose self-esteem is low because they place such pressure and unrealistic demands on themselves. When they can't live up to those demands, they feel guilty and begin to see themselves as failures. A downward trend involving expectation, failure, guilt, and low self-esteem takes a lot of work to reverse.

self-expectations
Goals you set for yourself; how you believe you ought to behave and what you ought to accomplish.

Communication and Technology

Searching for One's Self Online

Searching for one's self online isn't about googling oneself, just to see what comes up; it's about using mediated communication to better understand who you are. In Chapter 1, we explored the increasing impact of mediated communication (which includes online interaction) on the development of the communication skills necessary to form and maintain successful relationships. In that discussion, we reported that some researchers found that the more people use the Internet, the less they interact with other people in person; other studies showed that people believe that online relationships expand their circle of friends. Subsequent research has expanded this work, delving into the topic of self-concept development and online communication.

While our self-concept and self-esteem are still derived in large part through face-to-face interactions with people, now that so much more of our daily communication is mediated (particularly through computer usage), mediated communication can be an important source of information about ourselves. Canadian psychologist M. Kyle Matsuba has studied the connection between Internet use and psychological well-being, personal relationships, and self-concept (what he termed "ego identity").[37]

Over 200 students engaged in Matsuba's study, completing questionnaires about time spent online, forms of Internet use, motivation to engage in online communication, loneliness, quality of relationships, self-concept clarity, and identity. First, Matsuba found that subjects who reported high levels of loneliness were also the heaviest Internet users in the study; these students explained that they were motivated to use the Internet to connect with people, but in a controlled way not possible with face-to-face communication. Matsuba reported that extreme loneliness can lead to *pathological Internet usage (PIU)*, a term for people whose Internet use causes them to suffer academic, work-related, or interpersonal problems; depression; and withdrawal symptoms when they are offline. Subjects who reported having multiple online relationships were more likely to show symptoms of pathological Internet usage than those subjects who had no online relationships. Most pertinent for our discussion of the self, self-concept clarity and Internet usage were negatively correlated in the study. This finding means that the clearer college students are about their identities or views of self, the less they seek to establish relationships through the Internet as a means of helping them understand themselves better. As Matsuba explains, "People who lack self-clarity and who are searching for an adult identity may use the Internet to explore different facets of the self."[38]

What's your reaction to these research findings? Many people believe that online relationships are just as real and important as face-to-face relationships (the old-fashioned kind). People who are marginalized in their identities, who feel lonely and depressed, who feel challenged in forming face-to-face relationships, or who simply want to expand or diversify their circle of friends may be drawn to the relative safety, control, and anonymity of the Internet. They often use the Internet to experiment with their identity, exploring aspects of themselves through online communication. This process may actually be helpful if it leads to greater self-concept clarity, meaning a clearer sense of one's own identity.

Engagement Questions

1. How does the Internet allow us to explore and manipulate our self-concept in ways that face-to-face interaction does not?
2. What are some pros and cons to experimenting with identity online?
3. How did people accomplish self-concept clarity before the Internet was established?

Self-Fulfilling Prophecy

A concept related to the creation of self-expectations is the **self-fulfilling prophecy,** the idea that what you believe about yourself often comes true because you expect it to come true.[39] If you think you'll fail a math quiz because you have labeled yourself inept at math, then you must overcome not only your math deficiency but also your low expectations of yourself. If you hold the self-perception that you're pretty good at conversation, then you're likely to act on that assumption when you approach a conversation with someone. Your conversations, true to form, go well, thus reinforcing your belief in yourself as a good conversationalist.

Your level of self-esteem also affects the kinds of prophecies you make about yourself and colors your interpretation of events.[40] People with high self-esteem tend to anticipate or predict successes for themselves; they are then reinforced when they experience those successes. Conversely, persons with low self-esteem tend to interpret their successes as flukes; they attribute an achievement to luck rather than to their own efforts. Successes can enhance your self-esteem, but if you are in a downward spiral of low self-esteem, you may not recognize your own achievements to let them have a positive effect.

self-fulfilling prophecy The notion that predictions about one's future are likely to come true because one believes that they will come true.

Recap

Factors Affecting Self-Esteem

Gender	In male-dominated cultures, females suffer self-esteem loss to a much greater degree than men and boys, primarily as a result of males' feeling better able to do things than females.
Social Comparisons	Judgments about how well or poorly you can perform certain tasks compared to others can be self-defeating and can cause self-esteem to suffer.
Self-Expectations	Your estimation of how well you perform in comparison to your own goals or self-expectations has a profound impact on self-esteem.
Self-Fulfilling Prophecies	What you believe about yourself often comes true because you expect it to come true.

Communication and the Enhancement of Self-Esteem

We know the damage low self-esteem can do to a person—it can limit her or his ability to develop and maintain satisfying relationships, to experience career successes and advancement, and to create a generally happy and contented life. Teachers, psychologists, self-help gurus, clergy members, social workers, and even politicians suggest that many of our societal problems stem from our collective feelings of low self-esteem. Our feelings of low self-worth may contribute to our choosing the wrong partners; becoming addicted to drugs, alcohol, sex, or gambling; experiencing problems with eating and other vital activities; and opting, in too many cases, for death over life. So we owe it to society, as well as ourselves, to develop and work to maintain a healthy sense of self-esteem, as an integral part of the process of becoming more self-aware.

While no simple list of tricks can easily transform low self-esteem into feelings of being valued and appreciated, you can improve how you think about yourself. One thing is clear from research about self-esteem: Communication is essential in the process of building and maintaining self-esteem.[41]

Engage in Positive Self-Talk

Intrapersonal communication refers to how you take in information or stimuli in your environment and make sense out of it.[42] It also involves communication within yourself—**self-talk,** or what some scholars term "inner speech."[43] Your self-concept and level of self-esteem influence the way you talk to yourself about your abilities and skills. The reverse is also true, in that your inner dialogue has an impact on both your self-concept and your level of self-esteem. One of your authors recalls a snow-skiing experience. After several unsuccessful tries to manage an archaic ski-lift contraption (not your simple chair lift), she was determined to reach the top of the slope (just so she could fall down it). She remembers actively talking to herself throughout the climb to the top, willing herself not to fall off the lift, and feeling exhilarated upon achieving even this small piece of the process. The "you can do this" self-talk helped her keep focused on the task at hand and provided positive reinforcement of her self-concept.

Although becoming your own cheerleader may not enable you to climb metaphorical mountains quite so easily, there is evidence that self-talk, both positive and negative, is related to the building and maintaining of one's self-concept.[44] Realistic, positive self-talk can have a reassuring effect on your level of self-worth and therefore your interactions with others. Conversely, repeating negative messages about your lack of skill and ability can keep you from trying and achieving.

intrapersonal communication
How you take in stimuli in the environment or information and make sense out of it; also, thoughts and ideas that you say to yourself.

self-talk
Inner speech; communication with the self.

Positive self-talk is important in all forms of communication. When you communicate with someone, you probably also carry on an inner dialogue as you process what the other person is saying and doing and how you want to respond. In group meetings, self-talk enables group members to process the interaction. If the communication is excited or even heated, positive self-talk can motivate you to engage in the interaction, possibly offering disagreement with members' ideas. Another example of a situation that calls for positive self-talk is one that is challenging to most people—the presentational speaking context. Comedian Jerry Seinfeld commented a few years back that the number-one fear among Americans was of public speaking; people were more afraid of it than of death (which was number six). He joked that people would rather be in the coffin at a funeral than have to deliver the eulogy, or speech of tribute to the deceased.

Most speakers experience feelings that range from mild activation (feeling "jazzed" or "up" for the event) to debilitating, blinding fear. But don't worry—there are only a very few people at the upper end of the anxiety scale. When you make a presentation, you definitely need positive self-talk. You can create a negative self-fulfilling prophecy by telling yourself, "I can't do this; I won't be able to get through it. This speech is going to be lousy, and I'm going to fall flat on my face. My topic is lame; the audience will be bored and think I'm pathetic." Over years of teaching public speaking, we know that some students tell themselves just those kinds of negative messages.

But others have learned the power of getting psyched for presentations, just as an athlete would get psyched for a game or a performer for a show. These people harness the power of positive self-talk to get themselves pumped for a good outcome. When they hear negative messages creeping into their heads and creating self-doubt, they quash those messages before they have a chance to take hold. In any situation—from a mild challenge to the most pressure-filled circumstance you can envision—if you hear yourself start to say in your head, "I'm not sure I can do this" or "This isn't going to go well," stop right there and rephrase those statements. There's no need to completely turn the statement around ("This will be easy; a piece of cake") because you might not believe it. But simply tone down the negativity and say, "I can get through this; I'll be just fine. I CAN do this; I'll survive." While positive self-talk is not a substitute for preparation and effort, it can keep you on track by helping you focus and, ultimately, achieve your goal.

Visualize

Visualization—imagining oneself behaving in a certain way—takes the notion of self-talk one step further. Besides just telling yourself that you can achieve your goal, you can actually try to "see" yourself conversing effectively with others, performing well on a project, or exhibiting some other desirable behavior. Because the United States is such a visual culture, most of us have no trouble visualizing elaborate scenarios in our heads.

Research suggests that an apprehensive public speaker can manage her or his fears by visualizing positive results.[45] In fact, visualization reduces anxiety as well as negative self-talk or the number of debilitating thoughts that enter a speaker's consciousness.[46] If you are one of the many people who fears making presentations, try visualizing yourself walking to the front of the room, taking out your well-prepared notes, delivering a well-rehearsed and interesting presentation, and returning to your seat to the sound of applause from your audience. This visualization of positive results enhances confidence and speaking skill. The same technique can be used to boost your sense of self-worth about other tasks or skills. If you're nervous about a date, for example, visualize each step of the date (as realistically as you can). Think through what you might talk about on the date and how the night will progress. This mental rehearsal will help reduce your anxiety. In addition, visualizing yourself interacting or performing well can help you change long-standing feelings of inadequacy.

Reframe

The process of redefining events and experiences, of looking at something from a different point of view, is termed **reframing**. When a movie director gets different "takes"

visualization
The technique of imagining that you are performing a particular task in a certain way; a method of enhancing self-esteem.

reframing
The process of redefining events and experiences from a different point of view.

Communication and Ethics

Can You Have TOO Much Self-Esteem?

For decades, scholars, teachers, counselors, and others in helping roles in American culture have agreed that many people suffer from debilitatingly low levels of self-esteem. However, while many people still hold a less-than-positive view of themselves, growing evidence suggests that the efforts of self-help book authors, psychologists, and parents to build children's self-confidence may have paid off in a big way, perhaps too big of a way. Now some are wondering, "How much self-esteem is too much?"

While every day in our classes we still witness countless numbers of students whose self-esteem could use a shot of caffeine, we are also beginning to see the fruits of a "be all that you can be" generation. Some children have now grown into adults whose self-esteem is so healthy that, in some instances, it has led to narcissism or self-centeredness. Some people whose self-esteem took a pounding as they were growing up are now parents who reward (possibly over-reward) their children, making them feel like the center of the universe. This phenomenon is manifesting itself through a growing emphasis on physical attractiveness, with increasing numbers of cosmetic surgeries and procedures being performed each year on ever younger people; the expanding number of graduation ceremonies, where children are praised for such feats as "graduating from the fourth grade into the fifth grade" (which used to be just a transition, not an occasion); and rituals in which everyone in the league—even the losers—is rewarded with a trophy at the end of the season.

Some worry that if we coddle our young, they won't have healthy ways to deal with failure and they will grow up expecting the world to positively reinforce their every move. When inevitably it does not, they may be ill-equipped to respond. A rising level of self-esteem can certainly be positive, but is there or should there be a cap?

Jean Twenge, author of a book entitled *Generation Me: Why Today's Young Americans Are More Confident, Assertive, Entitled—and More Miserable than Ever Before*, has conducted extensive research on this topic. She contends:

> The society that molds you when you are young stays with you the rest of your life. Today's young people are experiencing that society right now, and they speak the language of the self as their native tongue. The individual has always come first, and feeling good about yourself has always been a primary virtue. Generation Me's expectations are highly optimistic: they expect to go to college, to make lots of money, and perhaps even to be famous. Yet this generation enters a world in which college admissions are increasingly competitive, good jobs are hard to find and harder to keep, and basic necessities like housing and health care have skyrocketed in price. This is a time of soaring expectations and crushing realities.[47]

"*Narcissism: A Cure?* by Luke Trent. Preface: "This book is dedicated to me! I totally acknowledge my invaluable contributions! Furthermore, I'd like to thank myself for . . .'"

Twenge is the lead investigator on research into college students and narcissism, a personality attribute that carries as its primary characteristic a positive but inflated view of self, especially regarding areas of one's own power, importance, and physical attractiveness. In their 2006 study of over 16,000 college students who completed the Narcissistic Personality Inventory, Twenge and colleagues found that student narcissism had sharply risen since 1982.[48] While some positive correlates of narcissism exist, such as enhanced self-esteem, extraversion, and levels of life satisfaction, the downside includes distorted judgment of one's abilities, risky decision making, potential addictive disorders and compulsions (e.g., alcohol abuse, compulsive shopping and gambling), and other negative consequences borne by people who are narcissists.[49]

Engagement Questions

1. How does one maintain a healthy level of self-esteem without becoming narcissistic?
2. Do your college peers seem to exhibit a high degree of narcissism, or is this something you've never thought about or noticed in others before?
3. How is the communication of narcissists different from that of non-narcissists?
4. If narcissism is on the rise and you view this development negatively, what communication strategies might you use to respond to narcissistic people?

---

or shots of the same scene, she or he is striving to get the best work possible. The director alters small details, like camera angles or actor movements, to get yet another look or vision for a scene. Just like that movie director, you can reframe your "take" on events or circumstances that cause you to lose self-esteem.

Here's an example: If you get a report from your supervisor that says you should improve one area of your performance, instead of engaging in self-talk that says you're terrible at your job, reframe the event within a larger context. Tell yourself that one negative comment does not mean you are a bad employee.

Of course, you shouldn't leave negative experiences unexamined, because you can learn and profit from your mistakes. But it is important to remember that our worth as human beings is not contingent on a single *anything*—a single grade, a single failed relationship, a single response from a prospective employer, or a single play in a football game. Looking at the big picture—at the effect this one event will have on your whole life, on society, on history—places negative experiences we all have in realistic contexts.

Develop Honest Relationships

The suggestion that you develop honest relationships may sound like the latest advice from Dr. Phil, but it is actually harder to accomplish than it sounds. Think about it: How many people are in your life who really give you the straight scoop about yourself? How many people are so solid in their relationship with you that they can tell you the things that are the hardest to hear, things that no one else would dare tell you? Most of us can count the number of those people on one hand. That doesn't mean we aren't honest with the many friends and acquaintances we have in our lives, but most of us really trust only a select few enough to deal with the tough stuff.

Having at least one other person who will give you honest feedback and help you objectively reflect on your virtues and vices can be extremely beneficial in fostering healthy, positive self-esteem. As we noted earlier, other people play a major role in shaping our self-concept and self-esteem. You don't want to find yourself at a point where you're oblivious to the feedback of others. That kind of attitude can make you narcissistic, unrealistic, and rigid, unable to adjust to life's changing circumstances. Most people who reject or overlook significant others' feedback end up isolated and with low self-esteem.

Surround Yourself with Positive People

Related to the development of honest relationships is a suggestion about the people you choose to associate with the most in your life. If you want to improve your self-esteem and to develop a more positive outlook, it's better to surround yourself with people who tend to have higher levels of self-esteem than with people who will bring you down. Granted, sometimes you don't have a choice; you get assigned a roommate in college, you end up with an instructor's choice of lab or study partner, and you rarely get to choose the people you work with. So we're not suggesting that you disassociate yourself from people who have low self-esteem, because that's unrealistic. Plus, we all suffer from bouts of low self-esteem at some time or another. People with low self-esteem need to be around uplifting people—those whose positive self-regard will rub off on them. What we mean is that it is hard enough to actively work on your self-esteem without constantly being around people with negative attitudes. Engaging in "pity parties" can lead to wallowing in poor self-esteem, which makes it doubly hard to alter that downward course. If you don't have a choice and must be around someone with low self-esteem, you can try to immunize yourself from his or her negativity—possibly by attempting to change a negative subject of conversation into a positive one.

As an example, we know an elderly woman, Hazel, who was in good enough health to be able to help the Meals on Wheels organization deliver food to shut-ins in her town. Hazel often talked about how sour many of the people on her route were, how their attitudes had "gone south" because of poor health, limited options, and fading hope. She felt that her main purpose wasn't to deliver a hot meal but to extend the gift of her positive outlook. She often told us about how many complaints she heard in the course of one day, but she was determined to stay optimistic and to offer hope to those she visited. One time Hazel described what she viewed as a personal triumph. The most sour person on her route—a woman with very low self-esteem and a cranky disposition, one who never did anything but gripe to Hazel when she visited—began to "thaw." One day when Hazel delivered her meal, the woman actually greeted her at the front door and seemed genuinely glad to see Hazel. She complained less often as she slowly began to enjoy the warm glow of Hazel's sunny disposition and empathic responses. Hazel felt that the woman's self-esteem had begun to improve, that her outlook on life had begun to change.

So this is what we mean by surrounding yourself with positive people whenever you feel a loss of self-esteem. Misery may love company, but misery gets old quickly and can degenerate into permanent low self-esteem, sometimes without your realizing it's happening.

Lose Your Baggage

Not making the team. Getting passed over for a key promotion at work. Seeing a long-term relationship end. Feeling like a failure. We've all had experiences that we would like to undo or get a second chance at, so that we could do it differently or so that we would *be* different. We all carry around experiential or psychological "baggage," but the key question is, How much space does that baggage take up within your self-concept? To phrase this another way, How negatively is your self-esteem affected by your baggage?

Individuals with low self-esteem tend to lock on to events and experiences that happened years ago and tenaciously refuse to let go of or move past them. Looking back at what we can't change only reinforces a sense of helplessness. Constantly replaying negative experiences only serves to make our sense of self-worth more difficult to repair. As Stephen Covey explains, with regard to his Highly Effective Habit #2, "Begin with the End in Mind," self-awareness leads us to an exploration of our values. The way we are living, our "script" as Covey terms it, may not be in harmony with our values, but we have the power to change. As Covey puts it, "I can live out of my imagination instead of my memory. I can tie myself to my limitless potential instead of my limiting past. I can become my own first creator."[50]

If you were overweight as a child, you may have a difficult time accepting that who you are today is not determined by pounds you carried years ago. A traumatic or defining experience in the past has a serious impact on your self-concept; it will probably always remain a part of you. But it doesn't have to affect your current level of self-esteem. Becoming aware of changes that have occurred in your life can assist you in developing a more realistic assessment of your value. It's important to take mental inventory of experiences in your past and then decide to let go of and move past those experiences that cause your present-day self-esteem to suffer.

The Perception Process

This chapter focuses on Principle One of our Communication Principles for a Lifetime: Be aware of your communication with yourself and others. Awareness involves developing greater understanding and skill by becoming more cognizant of yourself, others, and communication. In the first part of this chapter, we discussed self-concept (how we perceive ourselves) and self-esteem (how we value ourselves). We continue now by exploring how we perceive ourselves and our communication with others, as well as the many ways in which we perceive other people and their communication. But just what is perception?

On the most basic level, **perception** is the arousal of any of our senses. A sound travels through the air, vibrates in the eardrum, activates the nerves, and sends a signal to the brain. A similar sequence of events takes place when we see, smell, feel, or taste something. So perception begins with the process of attending to stimuli in the environment. The process of perception also includes structuring and making sense out of information provided by the senses. You come out of a building and see wet pavement

perception
The arousal of any of your senses.

Recap

Strategies for Enhancing Self-Esteem

Engage in Positive Self-Talk	If you want positive results, talk positively to yourself. If you are self-critical and negative, you may set yourself up for failure. Rephrase doubts and negative thoughts into positive, uplifting encouragement.
Visualize	In anticipation of a significant event, picture how you want the event to go, as a mental rehearsal. If you feel anxious or nervous, visualize success instead of failure.
Reframe	Try to look at experiences and events, especially those that can cause you to lose self-esteem, from a different point of view. Keep the larger picture in mind, rather than focusing on one isolated, negative incident.
Develop Honest Relationships	Cultivate friends in whom you can confide and who will give you honest feedback for improving your skills and abilities. Accept that feedback in the spirit of enhancing your self-esteem and making yourself a wiser, better person.
Surround Yourself with Positive People	Associating with persons with high self-esteem can help you enhance your own self-esteem and develop a more positive outlook.
Lose Your Baggage	Dump your psychological and experiential baggage: Work to move beyond the negatives of your past, so that you focus on the present and relieve your self-esteem of the burden of things you cannot change.

and puddles of water, hear thunder, smell a fresh odor in the air, and feel a few drops of water on your head. You integrate all those bits of information and conclude that it's raining and has been for a while.

Perceiving people, however, goes beyond the simple processing of sensory information. We try to decide what people are like, making judgments about their personalities, and we give meaning to their actions by drawing inferences from what we observe.[51] When you meet someone new, you notice certain basic attributes, like the person's sex, general aspects of physical appearance, the sound of her or his voice, whether or not he or she smiles, uses a friendly tone of voice, has an accent, and so forth. You also attend to specific details that the person communicates, verbally and nonverbally. Once you've chosen these stimuli to pay attention to, you then categorize the information into some sort of structure that works for you. Finally, you attempt to make sense out of your structured perceptions; you assign meaning to what you have perceived. Let's examine each of these three stages in the perception process.

Stage One: Attention and Selection

You are watching a group of parents at a playground with their children. The kids are playing, running around, laughing, and squealing, as children will do. You view the activity, hear the noise, feel the heat of the day on your skin, and perhaps smell hot dogs cooking on a grill. They smell so good you can almost taste them. After a moment, one of the parents who was sitting and chatting with other parents jumps up and runs over to comfort his or her child who has fallen down and is crying. You were watching the action but didn't see the particular incident and didn't register the child's cry amidst all the noise. But the child's parent did. How did this happen?

The ability of parents to discern their own child's voice from a chorus of voices is one of the mysteries of human nature, but it also exemplifies the first stage of perception. Our human senses simply cannot process all of the stimuli that are available at any given moment, so we select which sensations make it through to the level of awareness and ignore or filter out the rest. The activities of **attention** and **selection** constitute the first stage of the perception process. Have you ever listened to music in the dark

attention
The act of perceiving stimuli in your environment.

selection
The act of choosing specific stimuli in your environment to focus on.

Figure 2.2
What Do You See?

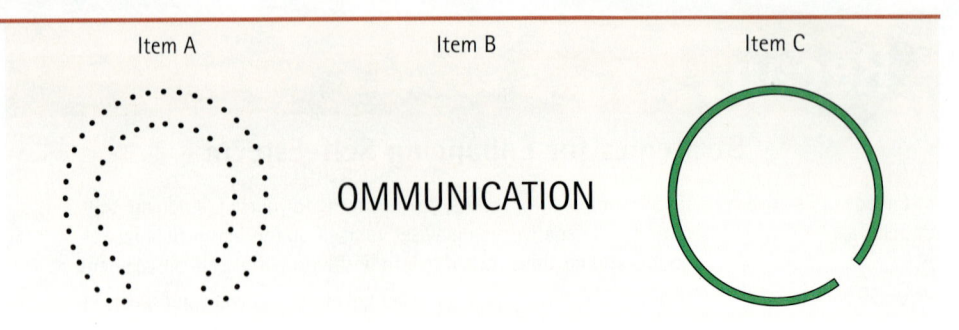

| Item A | Item B | Item C |

OMMUNICATION

so that you could eliminate visual sensations and focus only on what you were hearing? Have you ever watched TV with the sound turned off, just so you could enjoy the visual images without the "static" of sound? This is a particularly helpful strategy during televised sporting events, when the announcers continue talking over every bit of the action. (We believe this to be the original motivation for the development of the remote control's mute button.) What we're doing in these instances is selecting what we will and will not attend to.

Selectivity can also cause us to fail to perceive information that is important.[52] Jack and Jill are having an argument; Jack is so absorbed in making his points that he fails to see that Jill is crying. By selecting certain stimuli, we sometimes miss other clues that might be important, that might help us better understand what is happening and how to respond.

Stage Two: Organization

After we select stimuli to attend to and process, we start to convert the information into convenient, understandable, and efficient patterns that allow us to make sense of what we have observed. This activity, termed **organization,** makes it easier for us to process complex information because it allows us to impose the familiar onto the unfamiliar and because we can easily store and recall simple patterns.

Look at the three items in Figure 2.2. What does each of them mean to you? If you are like most people, you will perceive item A as a horseshoe, item B as the word *communication,* and item C as a circle. Strictly speaking, none of those perceptions is correct. For item A, you see a pattern of dots that you label a horseshoe because a horseshoe is a concept you know and to which you attach various meanings. The item really isn't a horseshoe; it could be an inverted U. It's actually a set of dots. But rather than processing a set of dots, it's much easier to organize the dots in a way that refers to something familiar. For similar reasons, we organize patterns of stars in the sky into various constellations with shapes, like the Big and Little Dippers.

In Figure 2.2, items B and C reveal our inclination to superimpose structure and consistency on what we observe. This tendency leads us to create a familiar word from the meaningless assemblage of letters in item B and to label the figure in item C a circle, even though a circle is a continuous line without any gaps. The process of filling in missing information is called **closure,** and it applies to our perceptions of people as well. When we have an incomplete picture of another human being, we impose a pattern or structure, classify the person on the basis of the information we do have, and fill in the gaps.

Perhaps you've sat in an airport or busy shopping mall watching people and tried to guess what they did for a living, what their personalities were like, or what their backgrounds were. Maybe you saw people you guessed were wealthy, hotheads, teachers, losers, athletes, loners, or surfer dudes. As you looked at people's clothing and saw how they walked or behaved, you made inferences about them. You superimposed some structure by using a general label and filling in the gaps in your information. This activity can get you into trouble, of course, but we'll save that discussion until the end of the chapter, when we focus on the problem of stereotyping.

organization
Converting information into convenient, understandable, and efficient patterns that allow us to make sense of what we have observed.

closure
The perceptual process of filling in missing information.

> ## Recap
> ### The Perception Process
>
> | Term | Explanation | Examples |
> |---|---|---|
> | Perception | The arousal of any of our senses | Tasting spicy food; hearing the sound of laughter; smelling smoke |
> | Attention and Selection | The first stage in the perception process, in which we perceive stimuli and choose which ones to focus our awareness on | Watching TV in your room while hearing giggling and laughter, and ignoring the TV show in order to eavesdrop on the giggler |
> | Organization | The second stage in the perception process, in which we structure stimuli into convenient and efficient patterns | Realizing that the laughter is coming from your younger sister, who's on the phone |
> | Interpretation | The final stage in the perception process, in which we assign meaning to what we have perceived | Deciding that your sister is talking on the phone to her boyfriend, because she only laughs like that when she talks to him |

Stage Three: Interpretation

Once we have organized stimuli, we are ready to assign meaning, a process termed **interpretation**. We attach meaning to all that we observe. In some cases, the meanings are fairly standardized, as they are for language, for example. But others are much more personalized. If you shake someone's hand and it feels like a wet, cold fish, what is your reaction and interpretation? If you notice someone you don't know staring at you from across a room, what thoughts go through your head? If a toddler is crying in a room full of people and a woman walks over and picks the child up, what do you assume about the woman? These examples all illustrate how we impose meaning on what we observe to complete the perceptual process.

Of course, our interpretations can be inaccurate or off-base; we may perceive a situation one way when in fact something entirely different is occurring. For example, the final scene in the movie *Swingers* is hilarious because it illustrates the faulty nature of human interpretation. The two leading male characters are sitting in a booth at a diner. One of them thinks that a woman several booths away is making eyes at him. She appears to be making flirtatious facial expressions and mouthing something which he interprets as a come-on. He's just about to make his move when he realizes that the woman is looking across her table at a baby in a portable carrier, positioned in the opposite side of the booth, and she's cooing and making faces at the child.

When Perceptions Vary

George and Martha have been married for, well, forever; they know each other very well, and each knows how the other thinks. So you'd think that their perceptions of things, events, and people would line up, right? Wrong. George and Martha are driving home from a party, chatting about what happened at the event. George believes that everyone had a good time, that the house was filled with interesting, pleasant, relatively good-looking people, and that he received positive responses from everyone he talked to. Martha saw the party differently. She tells George that the reason people looked good was that most of them either had had plastic surgery to "hold back Father

interpretation
Attaching meaning to what is attended to, selected, and organized.

Time," were botoxed beyond all recognition, or were younger, "replacement" partners for all the divorcees who attended the party. Some of the women brought younger men as their dates (a process known as "cougaring"), and many people at the party disliked each other so intensely that they stayed on opposite sides of the room all night. Martha's interpretation of events isn't based on prior or external knowledge, but on her perceptions from observing and interacting with people at the party. And about George's perception that everyone at the party liked him? Martha says, "Think again." She tells George that as soon as he left one group of men in a conversation and walked away, they signaled to one another with their "body language" that they thought George was a doofus. What's going on here? Who's right, George or Martha?

In actuality, no one's right or both people are right, because what this example illustrates are differing perceptions of the same reality. There's no "truth" to be found, only different "takes" on the same people and set of events. Both sets of perceptions are correct and valid, even though they differ, because varying perceptions are the norm in life. You know this to be true in your own life experience—even people you're very similar to and know quite well can differ from you dramatically in their perceptions of people and events.

One explanation for why perceptions vary—no matter whether we're similar to or different from another person—has to do with experience and background. Everyone's history and life experiences are different. So while you may hold opinions, attitudes, and values similar to those of another person, you aren't a carbon copy of that person. Your life experiences, how you were raised, and how you developed contribute a great deal to how you perceive things, events, and people in your life. These elements create a filter through which you observe and process the world around you.

For example, let's say that you grew up with a loving grandmother whose house you always looked forward to visiting, mainly because of the wonderful aromas of grandma's cooking. Now, as an adult, when you walk into any bakery, those wonderful smells trigger fond memories of your grandmother, so the smells are positive stimuli for you. But for someone who had a stern, abusive grandmother who also had great smells in her house, those smells might trigger a different response when she or he encounters them later in life. You may be drawn to bakeries not just for the sweets, but because the stimulus evokes memories of your grandmother; for someone else, the memories of grandmother associated with the smells might trigger negative feelings of fear, possibly even anger. That person would likely want to go nowhere near a bakery. Similar experiences can trigger different meanings in people, so we shouldn't be surprised when different reactions occur.

In addition, people are divergent in what they key in on when perceiving events and people. Research shows that the brains of men and women function differently in terms of how they process and interpret stimuli, leading to differences in how women and men respond verbally and nonverbally to others.[53] In general, men tend to perceive more of the general sense of a situation or have more global perceptions about people. In contrast, women tend to perceive more atomistically, finding meaning in detail. These tendencies are particularly pronounced when it comes to processing nonverbal information. The causes of these tendencies are complex and multifaceted: They include cognitive development, modeling (taking after the behaviors of, primarily, a same-sex parent), and socialization.[54] Women and girls are socialized toward connection and congruence with other people; thus, they tend to display, perceive, and interpret emotional cues more readily and accurately than men and boys. For example, women tend to detect nuances in people's facial expressions and eye behavior, attend to subtle changes in vocal cues, and remember people's appearance. The sex differences are consistent across U.S. and non-U.S. subjects and across age groups.[55]

Because of these differences, sometimes women can "miss the forest for the trees," while men may miss the fine points. You probably remember scenes in movies where a woman on a date covers the eyes of the man she's with and asks him for details about her appearance or the decor in the restaurant. When he can't do it, she's made her point about him "ignoring the little things." It's not that men intend to ignore small details, but that many men just tend to process stimuli more globally than women. But this difference is often bewildering, and it can become a sore spot for many heterosexual couples.

Communication and the Enhancement of Perceptual Accuracy

Our perceptions of others affect the way we communicate, just as others' perceptions of us affect the way they communicate with us. We continually modify the topics, language, and manner in which we communicate according to perceptions—ours and theirs.

Patrick sees Cliff at a party and thinks he is attractive; Cliff is nicely dressed and seems to be enjoying himself, laughing occasionally at a story someone is telling. Patrick thinks, "This might be someone I want to get to know," so he works his way over to join the conversation of Cliff and the group he's sitting with. Cliff notices Patrick coming over, because he has checked him out, too. However, not too long after joining the group, Patrick attempts to tell a humorous story, hoping to get a positive reaction from Cliff. Instead, he gets a cold stare from him, as though he didn't understand or appreciate his attempt at humor. Cliff walks away from the conversation thinking that Patrick is rude, while Patrick decides that Cliff is not as attractive as he first thought. In this example, the men both formed perceptions based on minimal information. They then experienced each other in the form of a brief conversation, and that bit of communication significantly altered their original perceptions. This process happens often in daily life.

The goal in the perception process is to form the most accurate perceptions you can, because then you have better, more reliable information on which to act. So what can you do to improve your ability to form accurate perceptions? We offer three suggestions: increase your awareness, avoid stereoytpes, and check your perceptions.

Increase Your Awareness

We've made this topic—awareness—our first of five Communication Principles for a Lifetime, and we've done so for a reason. As we discuss in the next two chapters, developing your skills in perceiving and then decoding others' verbal and nonverbal communication is critical as you strengthen existing relationships and establish new ones.

Exercise your senses, especially your sense of hearing. Work at really listening to people—fully listening, without interrupting them to put in your two cents' worth. Try to be more verbally and nonverbally aware, meaning monitor how you communicate with others and how people respond to you. If you don't like the responses you're getting from people, it may be time for a change in *your* behavior, not theirs. You also want to monitor the verbal and nonverbal cues others exhibit. Pay attention to contextual cues, such as where an interaction is taking place, the time of day, the perceived moods of those interacting, and any physical or psychological barriers that impede the communication exchange. Learn from your mistakes, rather than repeating them.

Avoid Stereotypes

"She's a snob." "He's a nerd." "They're a bunch of dumb jocks." All of these statements reflect **stereotypes**, or generalizations we apply to persons because we perceive them to have attributes common to a particular group.[56] Social psychologist Douglas Kenrick and his colleagues suggest, "Stereotyping is a cognitively inexpensive way of understanding others: By presuming that people are like other members of their groups, we avoid the effortful process of learning about them as individuals."[57]

What comes to mind when you hear the term *redneck?* (Maybe you think of the comedian Jeff Foxworthy, who has a repertoire of "you might be a redneck" jokes.) Do you associate with the term such qualities as being backward, ultra-conservative, or out of touch with what's happening in the world? If you perceive someone to have these qualities and you consider that person a redneck, then you have just invoked a stereotype.

First, let's examine the positive or functional aspects of stereotypes. They emerge from our human nature to simplify and categorize stimuli in our environment, which we described as components of the perception process. Further, they serve as a base-

stereotype
A generalization applied to persons perceived to have attributes common to a particular group.

line of information. If you know nothing else about a person other than she or he is a "northerner," for instance, then you can think about commonly held characteristics of other persons you've met from the northern part of the United States and go from there. But obviously, there's a serious downside.

Have you ever taken a class and, from day one, felt that the teacher pegged you a certain way? The teacher perceived you to be a slacker or uninterested in the course topic (on the negative side) or a straight-A student or future Ph.D. (on the positive side). The bottom line is that no one likes to be treated as a stereotype because it's limiting and impersonal. You can also feel pressure to try to live up to a stereotype, such as "all Asian students are exceptionally bright." Stereotypes are often degrading, as in age-old references to dumb blondes, bad women drivers, and dirty old men. Many of the worst stereotypes are related to gender, race/ethnicity, age, and physical appearance.

Scholars have been studying stereotypes for a couple of decades, examining how stereotypes emerge regarding race/ethnicity, gender, age, and sexual orientation, as well as among people who have feminine- and masculine-typed occupations, students who are high in academic achievement, and those who excel at so-called "intellectual sports" (like chess).[58] Research also explores the ways we try to inhibit stereotypical thoughts before they have a chance to affect our behavior.[59] For example, if you grew up hearing family members invoke stereotypes about different ethnic groups, you may decide as an adult that you will not follow suit—that assigning ethnic stereotypes is inappropriate. However, because it's part of your upbringing and ingrained in you, your first thoughts may be stereotypical when you encounter someone from an ethnic group other than your own. You have to assert mental control to suppress the stereotypical thoughts. But researchers have found that this suppression actually has the opposite effect than desired, in that stereotypical thoughts are highly likely to reappear subsequently with even stronger intensity, what the researchers term a *rebound effect*.[60] So it may be better to try not to let stereotypes form into expectations, rather than trying to rid ourselves of harmful stereotypical thinking after the fact. There's nothing inherently wrong with a stereotype, as a baseline of information. But the rigid way we enforce a stereotype, the expectations we form based on the stereotype, and our ensuing communication toward the stereotyped person are problematic.

Check Your Perceptions

You can check the accuracy of your perceptions and attributions indirectly and directly, so that you increase your ability to perceive things and people and respond to them effectively. **Indirect perception checking** involves an intensification of your own perceptual powers. You seek additional information to either confirm or refute your interpretations of someone's behavior. If you suspect that your romantic partner wants to end your relationship, for instance, you are likely to look for cues in his or her tone of voice, eye contact, and body movements to confirm your suspicion. You will probably also listen more intently and pay attention to the language your partner chooses to use. The information you gain is "checked" against your original perceptions.

Direct perception checking involves asking straight out whether your interpretations of a perception are correct. You can accomplish this in two ways: asking people directly for their interpretations of their own actions or asking other observers for their take on a situation (going to a third or outside party). Asking people directly is often more difficult than asking a third party for an interpretation. For one thing, we don't like to admit uncertainty or suspicions to others; we might not trust that they will respond honestly. And if our interpretations are wrong, we might suffer embarrassment or anger. But asking someone to confirm a perception shows that you are committed to understanding his or her behavior. If your friend's voice sounds weary and her posture is sagging, you may assume that she is depressed or upset. If you ask, "I get the feeling from your tone of voice and the way you're acting that you are kind of down and depressed; what's wrong?" your friend can then either provide another interpretation ("I'm just tired; I had a busy week") or expand on your interpretation ("Yeah, things haven't been going very well"). Your observation might also be a revelation: "Really? I didn't realize I was acting that way. I guess I am a little down."

---

indirect perception checking
Using your own perceptual abilities to seek additional information to confirm or refute your interpretations of someone's behavior.

direct perception checking
Asking someone else whether your interpretations of what you perceive are correct.

We have found over our years as professors that perception checking with our colleagues, as well as with family members and trusted friends, is an invaluable tool, particularly when emotions are involved. It can be very helpful to discuss situations with other people, to get their input as to what happened, why it happened, how they would feel about it if it happened to them, and what you might do about it. This is especially advisable in work settings, when the wisdom of someone else's perceptions can save you professional embarrassment or prevent you from losing your job. The "can I run something by you?" strategy gives you a broader perspective and a basis of comparison.[61]

PRINCIPLES FOR A LIFETIME
Enhancing Your Skills

1. Aware

Principle One: Be aware of your communication with yourself and others.
- Becoming aware of yourself, as you develop your self-concept, involves communicating with others, associating with groups with whom you identify, assuming social roles, and selecting self-labels that describe who you are.
- Inventory yourself for any negative self-fulfilling prophecies that can be detrimental to your self-esteem.
- Engage in positive intrapersonal communication, or self-talk, because a heightened awareness of how you talk to yourself can help you enhance self-esteem.
- Develop your perceptual abilities by becoming more aware of yourself and others.

Summary

This chapter is devoted to the first Communication Principle for a Lifetime: *Be aware of your communication with yourself and others.* Self-awareness is a process that continues throughout life, as we perceive and come to understand our own existence in the social world. The way we view ourselves is termed *self-concept* and includes our attitudes, beliefs, and values. William James viewed the self as containing three components: The material self includes our bodies and those tangible possessions that give us identity. The social self is the part that engages in interaction with others. The spiritual self is that part of the self-concept related to your beliefs and your sense of who you are in relationship to other forces in the universe.

Self-concept (who you think you are), self-esteem (your evaluation of who you are), and self-concept clarity (the extent to which your beliefs about yourself are clearly and confidently identified and stable over time) all affect how you interact with others, in both face-to-face and online contexts.

The self-concept develops through our interactions with other people and the groups with which we associate. The roles we assume are important in our view of self; they provide labels for who we are. Your gender has an effect on your self-esteem. When you compare yourself to others, especially others who are different from you, your self-esteem can be affected either positively or negatively. Your view of your own worth is also affected by those expectations or goals you set for yourself and how close you come to achieving them. You may set a goal for yourself that ends up creating a self-fulfilling prophecy. You may believe something about yourself and act in a way that reinforces that belief, and the cycle continues.

It is difficult to alter your self-esteem, but various techniques can prove helpful: engaging in positive self-talk, visualizing success instead of failure, avoiding inappropriate comparisons with others, reframing events and relationships from a different perspective, developing honest relationships with others, surrounding yourself with uplifting people, and letting go of the past by losing old baggage.

This chapter also pointed out that perception is the process of taking in stimuli through our senses, and it involves three components: attention and selection, organization, and interpretation. Our perceptions of others affect how we communicate, and how others perceive us affects how they communicate with us. Life experience shows us that people can vary dramatically in their perceptions of other people, things, and events. One reason for this phenomenon is diverse experiences and backgrounds. In addition, people differ in what they focus on when forming perceptions, with men and women often attending to and interpreting the same stimulus in different ways. If you want to increase your powers of perception so that you develop greater sensitivity and awareness, you first need to pay greater attention to things and people around you. Observe with more detail over time, so that you take in more data. Second, when you're in the organizing stage of perception, avoid imposing stereotypes on people or trying to fit them into rigid categories such that you expect certain behavior and exert pressure on individuals to behave as expected. Finally, conduct indirect and direct perception checks to determine the accuracy of your "take" on people and situations.

Assessing Your Knowledge

For Discussion and Review

Principle One: Be aware of your communication with yourself and others.

1. Why is it important to be aware of your self-concept and level of self-esteem when communicating with people?

Principle Two: Effectively use and interpret verbal messages.

2. What verbal messages have the most power to impact a person's self-esteem?

Principle Three: Effectively use and interpret nonverbal messages.

3. Explain how nonverbal cues such as eye contact, facial expressions, body movement, touch, the use of space, and vocal cues affect our perception of ourselves and others.

Principle Four: Listen and respond thoughtfully to others.

4. What role does effective listening play in the perception process?

Principle Five: Appropriately adapt messages to others.

5. How do stereotypes impede your ability to adapt your communication to people who are different from you?

Multiple Choice
Choose the *best* answer to each of the following questions.

1. The perception process consists of which of the following stages?
   a. attention and selection, organization, interpretation
   b. organization, visualization, interpretation
   c. attribution, organization, selection
   d. attention and selection, reframing, closure

2. "When I see our apartment is really messy, with your clothes thrown all over and dirty dishes stacked up in the sink, I don't know if you are so busy with school that you haven't had time to clean up or if you are hoping that I will clean up after you. What is the reason?" This statement is an example of
   a. indirect perception checking.
   b. intrapersonal communication.
   c. self-talk.
   d. direct perception checking.

3. "Why should I talk to the professor about my grade on the test? Professors never listen to students anyway." This statement is an example of
   a. a self-fulfilling prophecy.
   b. stereotyping.
   c. negative self-talk.
   d. social comparison.

4. Looking through your closet to find the "perfect" outfit for your job interview is an example of being influenced by your
   a. material self.
   b. social self.
   c. spiritual self.
   d. emotional self.

5. Learning to get over negative experiences that happened in your past is an example of
   a. self-talk.
   b. reframing.
   c. losing baggage.
   d. visualization.
6. Jorge rushes to clear the dishes from the dinner table because he knows *Sunday Night Football* is coming on in three minutes. Jorge's behavior is being influenced most by his
   a. attitude.
   b. belief.
   c. value.
   d. none of the above
7. The fact that our identities are assigned by ourselves and others and that they are negotiated through our communication with others reflects which characteristic of identity?
   a. Identities are multidimensional and changing.
   b. Identity involves responsiveness to others.
   c. Identities develop in past and present relationships.
   d. Identities can be avowed and ascribed.
8. Marie and Andrea are having lunch, and Marie says, "One of the things that I love about you is that you are such an optimist." With respect to Andrea's identity, being an "optimist" is a(n)_____ characteristic.
   a. avowed
   b. ascribed
   c. multidimensional
   d. responsive
9. According to this textbook, suppressing stereotypical thoughts
   a. is effective in helping to increase your perceptual accuracy.
   b. can overcome biases learned from family and friends during childhood.
   c. can make those thoughts stronger in the long run.
   d. is impossible because stereotypes are originally based on facts.
10. Kaitlyn suspected that her best friend, Alondra, wanted to break up with her boyfriend. Kaitlyn paid close attention to how Alondra complained about him, avoided his phone calls, and was late getting ready for dates with him, but did not say anything to Alondra about it. What method was Kaitlyn using to check her perception of Alondra?
    a. direct perception checking
    b. active perception checking
    c. indirect perception checking
    d. avoidant perception checking

Answers to the questions in this practice test can be found at the end of the book.

Assessing Your Skill

Generate statements that reveal common stereotypes about people in the following groups. Try to generate stereotypes that reflect positive as well as negative perceptions. We provide a couple of examples, just to get you started. Then focus on the damage that stereotypes can do to someone's self-esteem. Also, think about how your communication with someone from each group might be affected by stereotypes.

Group	Positive Stereotype	Negative Stereotype
elderly	Old people are wise.	Old people can't fend for themselves.
women	Women are naturally more loving and nurturing than men.	Women are terrible drivers.

Group	Positive Stereotype	Negative Stereotype
men		
blondes		
overweight people		
people of Irish descent		
athletes		
southerners		
politicians		
librarians		
professors		

Web Resources to Improve Your Knowledge and Skill

Self-esteem is such a pervasive and important topic that there is a national association devoted to its study. The National Association for Self-Esteem (NASE) is an organization whose purpose is, as described on its web site, "to fully integrate self-esteem into the fabric of American society so that every individual, no matter what their age or background, experiences personal worth and happiness." The web site for NASE offers links to books and CDs, as well as seminars, conferences, and educational programs on topics associated with self-esteem, such as parenting strategies that help foster positive self-esteem in children. Check out the web site at <www.self-esteem-nase.org>.

Galen Bodenhausen, a social psychologist at Northwestern University, and his international group of colleagues and students have developed a web site based on their years of research on stereotyping and social perception. The site describes major ongoing research efforts sponsored by their organization, the Social Cognition Laboratory. It also provides links to publications and classroom instruction on the topic, so you can view syllabi from courses devoted to the study of stereotyping and perception. Here's the URL: <www.psych.northwestern.edu/folks/bodenhausen/research.htm>.

Adolf Fenyes, "Brother and Sister." National Gallery, Budapest/ET Archive, London/© SuperStock.

Death and life are in the power of the tongue, and those who love it will eat its fruits.

Proverbs 18:21

Chapter 3

Understanding Verbal Messages

Chapter Outline

- Why Focus on Language?
- The Nature of Language
- The Power of Words
- Confronting Bias in Language
- Using Words to Establish Supportive Relationships
- Summary

Chapter Objectives

After studying this chapter, you should be able to

1. Describe the relationship between words (symbols) and meaning.
2. Explain the difference between denotative and connotative meanings people develop for words.
3. Explain the difference between concrete and abstract meanings of words.
4. Define culture-bound words and context-bound words.
5. Identify four primary ways in which words have power.
6. Describe the major ways in which biased language reveals attitudes about race, ethnicity, nationality, and religion.
7. Provide examples of language that reflects bias related to gender and sexual orientation.
8. Explain how biased language reveals attitudes about age, class, and ability.
9. Explain the difference between supportive and defensive ways to relate to others.

"in da beginnin God cre8d da heaven & da earth."
"God luvd da ppl of dis wrld so much dat he gave his only son."

No, this isn't a Bible lesson, but many of you will know how to decipher the above lines and will quickly recognize them as variations on Bible verses—specifically, Genesis 1:1 and John 3:16. A *New York Times* article reported on a religious charity in Australia, known as the Bible Society, that translated the *Contemporary English Version Bible* into the abbreviated language of text messaging.[1] The group offers free software and a search engine so that people can download Bible verses and text them to their friends. (If you're interested, check out <www.biblesociety.com.au>.) A spokesperson for the group believes that sending the entire Bible via texting would require over 30,000 messages.

Many students are familiar with and comfortable using this form of shorthand, which makes texting, instant messaging, and even e-mailing faster. These adaptations of the English language are becoming more popular in everyday communication.[2] However, parents and teachers alike have become concerned about the effects of such language shortcuts on students' writing ability and communication skills in general. Not only are words shortened, often by the omission of vowels, but numbers are substituted for letters, emoticons are prevalent, grammar rules are ignored, and standard punctuation and capitalization all but disappear. Some college professors of English composition courses have found it necessary to "un-teach Internet-speak," because students transfer online language shorthand to their written work.[3] A persistent use of slang may be fine when instant messaging with friends, but when it becomes such a habit that it slips into other written or oral communication—especially at inappropriate moments (like calling a potential boss at a job interview "dude")— then you've got a problem. When it comes to different uses of language, the key is to be able to develop "code-switching" abilities, meaning that you use more standard or formal language when appropriate (as in college papers, professional resumés, and job interviews) and relegate the shortcuts and "slanguage" to informal texting, online chats, e-mail, and conversations with friends who translate.[4]

Before diving into our discussion of language, let's review for a moment. Figure 3.1 depicts our five core principles of communication. In Chapter 2, where we discussed the first of our five Principles for a Lifetime, we explored ways to become more aware

Just as with other forms of communication, when texting someone, take the time to think before you reply. Often, people communicate electronically in ways they wouldn't dare do in person. When you text, do you make a conscious effort to consider the impact of your text messages? In what ways do you make an effort to accurately interpret the text messages sent to you by friends and acquaintances?

of yourself and your perceptions of things and people with whom you come into contact. An important step in this process of coming to know and understand yourself better is an honest, insightful examination of how you talk. How do you come across when meeting someone new? When talking with your best friends? What kind of communicator do your closest friends and family members think you are? How would they describe the way you talk?

Consider this: *What you say is who you are.* That may sound like a strong statement, but it's true that the words you use reveal who you are. Granted, you communicate with more than your words. Your background, culture, values, experiences, and the way you express yourself nonverbally reveal who you are as well. But as we explore the power of words, we challenge you to think about the incredible tool you have at your disposal: verbal communication. Take an inventory of your use of language as you read this chapter. Do you use language that accurately and effectively represents to other people who you are? Do some areas need improvement? Because of the tremendous potential of verbal communication—its power to reveal the self, to make and break relationships and careers, and to shape cultures—we've chosen to make this one of our five key Principles for a Lifetime.

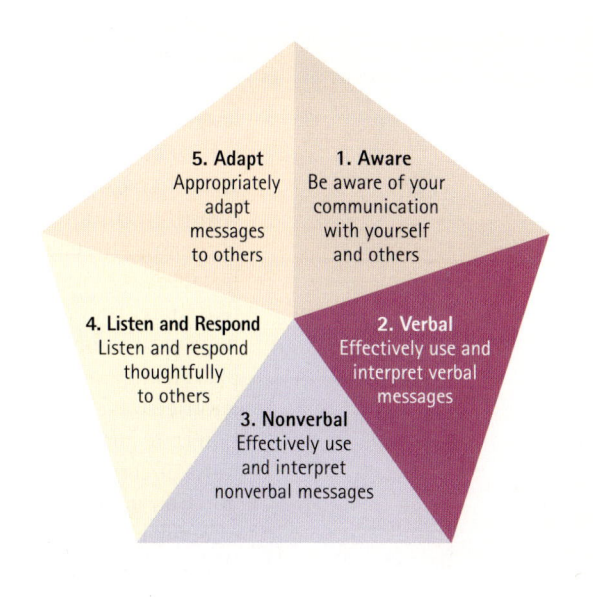

Figure 3.1
Communication Principles for a Lifetime

Why Focus on Language?

On occasion, we do stop to consider the effects of our language on others—usually when we're attempting to persuade or we've said something that has injured or angered someone else. We've all been in situations that made us wish we could get a conversational second chance or a "take 2." But it's important to keep in mind that every time we speak, every time we use language, we reveal our thoughts, our very selves to others—no matter how inane, superficial, or emotion-laden the conversation.

One of our main messages in this chapter is this: *Words are powerful.* They affect your emotions, thoughts, actions, and relationships. They affect how you are perceived by others. In fact, interviews with employers reveal their concern about college graduates' lack of language skills, attributed to growing up in a culture that is more visual than oral, stressing nonverbal cues over language.[5] The concern is that students' verbal skills, including both speaking and writing, are underdeveloped. This is clearly a negative trend, in light of other research that has determined that one's ability to use words to effectively participate in conversation with others is a key component in judgments about one's competence as a communicator. In this study, people who talked less in conversation were perceived by others as being less interpersonally skilled than people who comfortably and actively engaged in conversation.[6] If you better understand the nature and power of language, if you attend to your use of language and work to use words with forethought and skill, you can exert great influence and enhance your relationships.

Our second main theme in this chapter is this: *You choose language*. You don't use language involuntarily, in the way that your knee might jerk when rapped with a doctor's mallet as an involuntary reflex to a stimulus. You choose the language you use—even if you make that choice in the split second it takes your brain to select a symbol (word) to communicate your thought or impulse. At times we go into "default mode," choosing language we've chosen before. We're prone to patterns in our language because, as humans, we prefer regularity. We also choose particular words because we like them, they've worked well for us in the past, or we grew up with those words and have used them for many years. But pattern and history can breed too much comfort, preventing you from asking yourself, "Is this the best way to say this? Should I say this another way?" You have an incredible wealth of words from which to choose, and the power to make choices that allow you to communicate who you are to others in the most effective way possible.

Our goal in this chapter is to help you improve your ability to choose and use words effectively, as well as to interpret the verbal communication of others. To accomplish that goal we explore the nature of language, the power of words, and ways to expose subtle and not-so-subtle bias in language—bias that can inhibit your ability to present yourself to others in a manner you desire. Finally, we examine the role of verbal communication in establishing supportive relationships.

The Nature of Language

A **language** is a system of symbols (words or vocabulary) structured by grammar (rules and standards) and syntax (patterns in the arrangement of words) common to a community of people. Australian communication scholar Dale Spender explains that language is "our means of ordering, classifying, and manipulating the world. It is through language that we become members of a human community, that the world becomes comprehensive and meaningful, that we bring into existence the world in which we live."[7] That last phrase is particularly important, because it suggests that the very words we use help create our world.

One supposition about language relates to this notion of creating existence. Two language researchers, Edward Sapir and Benjamin Lee Whorf, developed what has come to be known as the Sapir–Whorf Hypothesis.[8] This hypothesis suggests that human language and thought are so interrelated that thought is actually rooted in and controlled by language. One implication of the supposition is that you cannot conceive of something for which you have no word. As a quick illustration of what we mean by this, think about colors. A woman describes her new dress to her friend using the term *puce*, but if the friend does not have the term *puce* in her frame of reference as a color term, she will be unable to conceive of the color her friend mentions. (For those of you with a possibly underdeveloped color-term repertoire, puce is a brilliant purplish-red color.)

To extend this notion further, one could argue that the quality of one's language reflects the quality of one's thought. More simply, your verbal communication reveals how you think and what you think about. This is only one supposition about how language and thought operate in human beings, but it is a provocative notion to consider that language has such a powerful influence on our everyday thinking processes.

People Use Words as Symbols

As we noted in Chapter 1, words are **symbols** that represent something else. Just as a flag is a symbol of a country, words are symbols that trigger thoughts, concepts, or feelings. For instance, what comes to mind when you see or hear the word *freedom*? Perhaps you think historically, remembering what you studied in grade school about

---

language
A system of symbols (words or vocabulary) structured by rules (grammar) and patterns (syntax) common to a community of people.

symbol
A word, sound, gesture, or visual image that represents a thought, concept, object, or experience.

Abraham Lincoln's freeing the slaves, or perhaps you picture American armed forces defending our national freedom. Or maybe you envision something a bit closer to home, like the feeling of freedom you get during a break between semesters at college.

People Attach Meanings to Words

Now imagine that you use the word *freedom* in a conversation, in an effort to convey to the other person the concept or image in your mind. You know what you're thinking when you say the word; the challenge is for the other person to understand your thoughts behind your choice of word. In communication terms, this is the process of creating **meaning.** The meaning of a word is a person's interpretation of that symbol—it is how the person makes sense of the symbol. Meanings don't reside in the words themselves but in the ways in which communicators use the words. You attach a meaning to the word *freedom*, the symbol you choose in conversation; your listener creates meaning for the word when he or she attempts to interpret what you've said. Words aren't the culprits in communication problems; the meanings people create for words lead to successful or problematic communication.

Sometimes a speaker's and a receiver's meanings do not correspond because the same words mean different things to different people; the term for this communication problem is **bypassing.** For example, have you ever found yourself at odds with someone because you had a different sense of what it meant to arrive "early" or "late" to an event? For some, getting there early means arriving at least half an hour before the event begins; for some, "early" means right on time. Being late can mean different things to different people as well. Some heated arguments can be boiled down to a simple difference in meaning.

People Create Denotative and Connotative Meanings for Words

As we have said, language is a vehicle through which we share with others our sense of the world and who we are. Through language, we convert our experience into symbols and then use the symbols to share that experience. But as you learned in Chapter 1, symbol sharing through language is not just a simple process of uttering a word and having its meaning clearly understood by another. People create meanings for language on two levels: the denotative and the connotative.[9]

The **denotative meaning** of a word conveys content. Denotation is the restrictive, or literal, meaning of a word. For example, one dictionary defines *apartment* as "a room or suite of rooms used as a residence."[10] This definition is a literal, or denotative, definition of the word *apartment;* it describes what the word means in U.S. culture.

By contrast, the **connotative meaning** of a word conveys feelings; people create personal and subjective meanings for words. To you, the word *apartment* might mean a comfortable place to relax at the end of the day or a setting in which to entertain friends. To others, though, the word *apartment* might engender feelings of guilt (if the apartment hasn't been cleaned in a while) or feelings of dread (if apartment rent is draining the wallet or relationships with roommates leave something to be desired). Clearly, the connotative level of language is more individual. While the denotative or objective meaning of the word *apartment* can be found in any dictionary, your subjective response to the word is probably not contained there.

People Convey Concrete and Abstract Meanings Through Words

Meanings for words can be placed along a continuum from concrete to abstract.[11] A word's meaning is **concrete** if we can experience what the word refers to (the referent) with one of our senses; if we can see it, touch it, smell it, taste it, or hear it, then it's concrete. If we cannot do these things with the referent, then the word's meaning is

---

meaning
A person's interpretation of a symbol.

bypassing
A communication problem that arises when the same words mean different things to different people.

denotative meaning
The restrictive, or literal, meaning of a word.

connotative meaning
The personal and subjective meaning of a word.

concrete meaning
Meaning that refers to something that can be perceived with one of the senses.

Communication and Technology

Computer Terms: Denotation and Connotation

What do you do when you "save" a "file" to a "file folder"? Do you insert a piece of paper into a manila container with a label at the top? Or do you save a document you've been drafting on your computer into the computer's memory, placing it in a location with other similar documents and giving it a name or label that will jog your own memory when you need the file again? Is what you're working on really a "document," or is a document only a piece of paper with words on it? Does your computer really have "memory," or is that a metaphor we use to represent the way we store computer work for safekeeping?

Think about how many metaphors emerge in simple, everyday computer use. What about the "mouse"? Do these important hardware devices look like scurrying mice? You can save documents, files, folders, and so forth to your "desktop," which isn't a literal desktop at all, but a means of organizing your computer information in the form of a screen display that appears when you turn on your computer. Think about why *desktop* is an interesting metaphor: When you want to grab something quickly, something you work with a lot or have worked with recently, you're likely to find it sitting on top of your desk somewhere, so it's not surprising that one of the most basic elements that computer users interface with is called a "desktop." But if you were working in a conference room with colleagues and someone asked you where to find a document that was needed for the meeting and you told him to go into your office and get it from your desktop, would your coworker look on your physical desktop or the one on your computer?

Most computer desktops display an icon that represents a storage area for discarded items. On some computers it's an open trash basket; on others, it's a trash can with a lid that is open or closed, depending on whether the user has "emptied the trash." If you're a Macintosh user, you "drag" items to the "trash," much as you might drag a heavy trash bag out to the curb for pickup. Many of us enjoy Microsoft Office, which isn't a physical office at all but software—means of organizing and accomplishing our computer work. The "office" metaphor helps us understand something new by relating it to something that's already familiar, something we can understand. If Microsoft had called the software Microsoft Frzshmez, we wouldn't relate so easily to this **neologism** (a new term introduced into a language); we would have trouble pronouncing and remembering it, so we would be less likely to buy it.

Just as the words we choose to use to communicate our meaning to other people in daily interactions have denotation and connotation, computer language is full of denotative and connotative meanings for terms that are largely metaphors, and using such language can get quite complicated. Metaphors are a bridge from the known and familiar to the new and different; they are commonly used in computing because so many novel concepts and mechanisms emerge that require terminology. Since metaphors are central to our language as well as our thought processes, they serve a useful communicative function. But they also pose a challenge, given that they lend variance to the denotative meanings of words. In the computer realm, connotations for widely used computer terms abound, but variation in denotation is a problem. A team of British information scientists explored this topic—specifically, the denotative meanings of the computer terms *save as* and *file*—to better understand how people use metaphors to interface with computers.[12] Condon, Perry, and O'Keefe explain, "There are problems for any interface that carries inappropriate connotations for the user, but confusion over the denotation of a standard computing term could carry much more serious consequences for the design of all computing systems."[13]

In Condon et al.'s study, the researchers pointed out the save as command to office employees who commonly used Microsoft Word for word processing and then asked each person "What is this for?" repeatedly until the employees had exhausted all the answers they could think of. Through this technique, the researchers received spontaneous expressions reflecting users' views of the computer system they used every day. They then analyzed responses and found significant variation in denotation among subjects who were employees versus managers. Despite the confusion surrounding the denotation of the save as command, Condon et al. believe that the term is too embedded in computer usage to be changed, but they hope that their results will be useful for people coping with human interface problems in the future. Wonder what term could best be applied to the process of hurling one's computer out a window after it freezes or crashes?

Engagement Questions

1. What other computer terms can you think of that are metaphorical? Have you ever considered the derivation of such terminology?
2. What are some computer terms that represent *neologisms*—new words introduced into a language? How long did it take you to learn to understand and use these new terms?
3. Will the denotation and connotation of computer terms continue to be a problem as technology continues to evolve?

---

neologism
A new term introduced into a language.

abstract meaning
Meaning that refers to something that cannot be perceived or experienced with one of the senses.

abstract. In general, the more concrete the language, the easier it is for others to understand. The more abstract a word, the more difficult it is to understand or agree on a meaning. For example, the word *patriotism* is abstract because we cannot hear or taste patriotism. But a word that suggests a demonstration of patriotism, such as *voting*, is more concrete, because we can physically perform the act of voting. It's wise to minimize the use of abstract words when you're trying to clarify a message. Concrete terms help make a message more clear.

Meanings Are Culture Bound

Culture is a learned system of knowledge, behavior, attitudes, beliefs, values, rules, and norms that is shared by a group of people and shaped from one generation to the next.[14] The meaning of a word, just like the meaning of any symbol, can change from culture to culture and across co-cultures (cultural groups with a larger culture). To a European, for example, a *Yankee* is someone from the United States; to a player on the Boston Red Sox, a *Yankee* is an opponent; and to an American from the South, a *Yankee* is someone from the North. Some years ago, General Motors sold a car called a *Nova*. In English, *nova* means "bright star," and in Latin, *nova* means "new"—both appropriate connotations for a car. In Spanish, however, the spoken word *nova* sounds like the words *no va*, which translates "It does not go." As you can imagine, this name was not a great sales tool for the Spanish-speaking market.

Meanings Are Context Bound

You were no doubt taught by an English or communication teacher about the pitfalls of taking someone's words out of context and how doing so can alter the meaning of a message. The context of verbal messages plays a central role in how accurately they are interpreted by receivers. The context includes all of our words, plus the nonverbal elements ever present in communication, like the environment or setting in which the communication occurs as well as the facial expressions, tone of voice, and other nonverbal cues that surround and accompany a verbal message and help us decode it.

In an election year, it's especially commonplace to hear a candidate say, "My comments were taken out of context," meaning either by the media or the opposition. When Republican presidential nominee Senator John McCain quipped in 2008 that U.S. armed forces might be in Iraq as long as a hundred years, he was roundly criticized. But McCain explained that those words were taken out of the context of an exchange he was having with a reporter at a press conference, and thus his meaning was distorted. Likewise, Democratic nominee for president Senator Barack Obama took heat for saying that, in tough times, people cling to their guns and religion. Focusing on that soundbite—the term for excerpting and highlighting a small piece of a greater text of what someone has said—took the comment out of the context of the answer Obama was giving to a question about the declining American economy.

Putting a soundbite under a microscope doesn't change the fact that the verbal message *was* said, but we all know that things look very different under a microscope than to the naked eye. Removing words from their context distorts the meaning. No matter their political persuasion, just about every day in the heated political context of a presidential election some candidates' words are likely to be taken out of context. Placing one's words back into context is next to impossible, once they've been extracted and scrutinized.

The Power of Words

No doubt you've heard the old schoolyard chant "Sticks and stones may break my bones, but words can never hurt me." We don't know who first came up with that statement, but we imagine it to be someone who never experienced the sting of name calling, the harmful effects of being labeled a "slow reader," or the legacy of an unfortunate family nickname. Words *do* hurt. They have the power to evoke a wide range of emotions in listeners. But words can also heal and inspire and transform the human spirit, which is another reason for making the effective use and interpretation of verbal

culture
A learned system of knowledge, behavior, attitudes, beliefs, values, rules, and norms that is shared by a group of people and shaped from one generation to the next.

Communication *and Diversity*

Code Switching as Linguistic Flexibility

On the first page of this chapter, we mentioned the term *code switching*, which refers to the practice of using one form of language and then switching to another form, usually seamlessly. But this linguistic practice warrants further exploration in a chapter undergirded by the principle of effectively using and interpreting verbal messages.

Two African American students were talking to each other in the elevator, recapping a class that had just let out. One said to the other, in regard to a classmate's behavior, "Can you believe she turn in she paper two weeks early?" to which the other replied, "She think she grades is above it all." A nerdy college professor (one of your book authors, but we won't identify which one), upon overhearing this exchange, asked the women to pardon the interruption, but would they mind answering a question: Did they use that form of language only with each other and their close friends, meaning did they use more standard English in class or when speaking directly to a professor? They explained that they would never say "She think she grades is above it all" to an authority figure or someone outside their peer group, because they realize that the language is perceived as nonstandard English. The incorrect (by standard English rules) usages of *she* instead of *her* as a possessive pronoun preceding *grades*, a plural verb (*think*) instead of a singular one (*thinks*), and the singular verb *is* after the plural noun *grades* are verbal markers that, if said to an authority figure like one's employer or professor, would make the students look uneducated, the two women explained. However, within the social context of their friendship, to use "proper" or "standard" English when talking among themselves would be just downright weird, as though they had something to prove or saw themselves as "uppity."

The brief exchange in the elevator illustrates code switching, which many of us perform in our own way at some point or another. While code switching is primarily an adaptive technique, as we explore in Chapter 6, many times such usage goes beyond adaptation to become an extension of ethnic or co-cultural identification.[15] Back in the 1990s, controversy arose over the teaching of and tolerance for *ebonics*, a term coined for what used to be called Black English, encompassing varied pronunciations of existing words, a relaxation of common grammatical rules, and the development of unique slang among some members of African American communities.[16] While some people, both inside and outside of the African American community, believed that ebonics went against standards of "correct" pronunciation and use of English and hurt the credibility of people who spoke and wrote it, others believed it to be an indicator of cultural pride and an expression of individuality. Proponents of ebonics believed that not only should African American "slanguage" be acceptable for students to use, but it should be taught in the schools.

Other forms of code switching have been explored by scholars as well. In South Texas, it's quite common to hear people who are bilingual switch in and out of Spanish and English, as one woman in a grocery store did when she asked a clerk, "Donde est la ice cream?" Researchers explain that bilingual code switching is quite common when two languages are frequently used in a particular environment and that the behavior is an indication of flexibility—the ability to choose the best word to convey meaning, regardless of one's primary or secondary language.[17] Code switching is sometimes used as a device to heighten an artistic effect in a song lyric and is common among signers and interpreters for people who are deaf, as interpreters often find it necessary to produce English words as well as American Sign Language signs in order to be more easily understood.[18]

Engagement Questions

1. Do you regularly or do you ever code-switch in interactions with people?
2. If so, what prompted you to code-switch, beyond the general goal of enhancing the likelihood that you would be understood by listeners?
3. Is your code switching a communication adaptation or a reflection of your identity?
4. How should people who don't know the "code" react to code switching? Are there drawbacks to this particular technique of verbal communication?

---

messages one of our five Principles for a Lifetime. Let's explore a few of the powerful attributes of words.

The Power to Create and Label Experience

How many diseases or medical conditions can you think of that are named after the person who discovered the condition? Some that come to mind include Alzheimer's, Parkinson's, and Tourette Syndrome. While you might not want your name associated with a disease, the point is that the name for a phenomenon labels the experience, thus making it more real.[19] It also etches it into history. As the English language continues to evolve, so does the need to name and describe new phenomena. For example, the term *sexual harassment* did not emerge until the 1970s; it was generated by feminists who wanted a term to correspond to a very real behavior many people experienced in

Recap

The Nature of Language

- People use words as *symbols:* Symbols represent something else.
- People create *meanings* for words: Meaning is a person's interpretation of a symbol.
- Words have both *denotative* and *connotative* meanings: The denotative meaning is a restrictive, or literal, meaning; the connotation is a personal and subjective meaning.
- People convey *concrete* and *abstract* meanings through words: A word's meaning is concrete if we can experience what the word refers to with one of our senses; if not, then the meaning is abstract.
- Meanings are *culture bound:* The meaning of a word can change from culture to culture.
- Meanings are *context bound:* The situation or context for communication aids people as they attach meanings to symbols.

the workplace.[20] Words give us tools to create and understand our world by naming and labeling what we experience.

Words also give us symbolic vehicles to communicate our creations and discoveries to others. For example, when you label something "good" or "bad," you use language to create your own vision of how you experience the world. If you tell a friend that the movie you saw last night was vulgar and obscene, you not only provide your friend with a film critique, but also communicate your sense of what is appropriate and inappropriate.

One theorist believes that you also create your moods and emotional states with the words you use to label your feelings.[21] If you get fired from a job, you might say that you feel angry and helpless or liberated and relieved. The first response might lead to depression and the second to happiness. One fascinating study conducted over a 35-year period found that people who described the world in pessimistic terms when they were younger were in poorer health during middle age than those who had been optimistic.[22] Your words and corresponding outlook have the power to affect your mental, emotional, and physical health.

The Power to Affect Thoughts and Actions

A line from a Shakespearean tragedy reads, "That which we call a rose by any other name would smell as sweet." Would it really? If the name for this fragrant flower were "aardvark," would it still be the flower of people in love? Can you imagine getting a delivery of a dozen long-stemmed red aardvarks?

A few decades ago, a weight-loss product called Ayds was introduced. Ayds were small, brown, chewy squares that helped reduce one's appetite (or so the manufacturers claimed). You can guess why this product disappeared in the 1980s; if it is still on the market, it has certainly been renamed. Given what we now know about the disease AIDS, who today would willingly ingest a product with a same-sounding name? Advertisers have long known that the way a product is labeled greatly affects the likelihood that consumers will buy it, because words affect the way we think about things and react to them.

Words not only have the power to affect how we think about and respond to something; they also affect policy and procedures. Consider the story about a young FBI agent who was put in charge

Studies show that people who describe their world in optimistic terms during their youth often enjoy good health in later life.

of the supply department. In an effort to save money, he reduced the size of memo paper. One of the smaller sheets ended up on Director J. Edgar Hoover's desk. Hoover didn't like the small size and wrote on the narrow margin of the paper, "Watch the borders." For the next six weeks, it was extremely difficult to enter the United States from Canada or Mexico.

The Power to Shape and Reflect Culture

If an impartial investigator from another culture were to study a transcript of all of your spoken utterances last week, what would she or he learn about you and the culture in which you live? If you frequently used words like *DVD* and *downloadings*, the investigator would know that these things are important to you. But he or she might not know what you mean if these things are not also part of his or her culture.

You've grown up within a culture; you've learned the language of that culture. And the way you use the language, the words and meanings you choose as well as the way you interpret others' communication, has the effect of shaping your culture. For example, during a 2008 debate in the Malaysian parliament, the deputy higher education minister (a native Malay speaker) addressed a member of parliament whose native language was Tamil. The minister attempted to say "Sit down" ("Ukarengeh" in Tamil) to the opposition member who was standing and arguing his point, but what he said instead was "Ukker," which translates into "Go [expletive] yourself." The deputy minister's words unleashed a flood of complaints because they were deemed unparliamentary and obviously offensive, even if unintentional in their use.[23]

Co-cultures (cultural groups within a larger culture) develop unique languages of their own as a way of forging connections and enhancing solidarity. For example, some gays and lesbians have reclaimed the once derogatory term *queer* and altered its meaning so that it's now a term of pride. Perhaps you've attended or seen news coverage of a gay pride parade or protest, in which participants can be heard chanting, "We're here; we're queer. Get used to it." Gang languages and symbols are also means of establishing an identity unique from other groups. This principle can even extend to two people in a romantic relationship who develop nicknames or other forms of language as secret codes. They don't dare use that language in the company of others; the privacy of the language and their shared experiences create a sort of co-culture—a co-culture of two.

The Power to Make and Break Relationships

Probably all of us have had the experience of saying something foolish, ridiculous, or embarrassing to another person. It seems that one of life's cruel ironies is the potential

Recap

The Power of Words to . . .

- *Create and Label Experience.* New experiences may lead to new words. For example, *texting* is a newly coined term for sendings text messages by call phone, pager, or PDA.
- *Affect Thoughts and Actions.* Words influence how we think. For instance, product names are critical to audience response and sales success. The critically acclaimed film *The Shawshank Redemption* was a box office failure, which some attributed to the film's obtuse title.
- *Shape and Reflect Culture.* Cultures change; language both creates and reflects the changing nature of culture.
- *Make and Break Relationships.* Verbal communication creates opportunities for us to know and be known by others. It's an important tool for establishing relationships and deepening them; it can also be a catalyst for a relationship to end.

for human beings to say things they later regret. But if you've ever said something so inappropriate that it cost you a relationship—either one that didn't get off the ground or one that ended because of what you said—then you know firsthand the power of words to make and break relationships. For example, people in love sometimes overstate things when they get emotional. That's understandable. But it's wise to try to avoid word barriers, such as **polarization**—the tendency to describe things in extremes or opposites without any middle ground. You might hear one romantic partner say to the other, "You either love me or you don't." These kinds of pronouncements can make people feel controlled, as though there were only two options and no compromise position. President George W. Bush was both praised and criticized for stating in his post–September 11, 2001, speech to Congress, "You're either with us or you're with the terrorists."

Confronting Bias in Language

We don't want to sound like the "language police"—that is, we don't want to dictate to you how you ought to talk. But we have found that oftentimes insensitive or stereotypical language usage arises out of ignorance or a lack of education. Even well-meaning, educated people can communicate bias through the language they choose to use. Words that reflect bias toward members of other cultures or groups can create barriers for listeners. In addition, such language ignores the fact that the world is constantly changing. In the following pages, we explore a few categories of language that illustrate the constant evolution of verbal communication and represent areas in which we can all heighten our sensitivity.

Biased Language: Race, Ethnicity, Nationality, and Religion

Think about whether you have ever said or overheard someone say the following:

"I got a great deal on a car; the sticker price was a lot higher, but I jewed the dealer way down."
"You can't have that back, you Indian giver!"
"She's a real Bible banger."
"He doesn't have a Chinaman's chance to make the team."
"That divorce settlement gypped me out of what's rightfully mine!"

That last statement tends to puzzle people more than the others. It includes the term *gypped*, which is derived from the word for the nomadic cultural group known throughout the world as gypsies. The stereotype relates to being suckered or cheated out of what one is due.

What would your impression be of a person who made one of these statements? The language used in each of these examples demonstrates an insensitivity to members of cultural groups. Such language reflects a word barrier known as **allness,** which occurs when words reflect unqualified, often untrue generalizations that deny individual differences or variations. In Chapter 6, we discuss the principle of adapting one's communication to maximize the effectiveness of our interactions with other people; there we make distinctions between what is meant by the terms *race* and *ethnicity*. We also stress the importance of avoiding classifying people by race or ethnicity because rigid classification systems lead to stereotyping, which often leads to prejudice and discrimination. But in this chapter where we examine our day-to-day language, it's important to think about how language reflects your attitudes and reveals how you think. If your attitudes regarding race, ethnicity, nationality, and religion have evolved, has your language kept pace? Or are you still using outdated terms out of habit or laziness or because this language business simply isn't on your personal radar?

You may remember that in 2007 shock jock Don Imus was fired from his radio program, which was simultaneously broadcast on the cable TV network MSNBC

polarization
The tendency to describe things in extremes, as though no middle ground existed.

allness
A word barrier created through the use of language that reflects unqualified, often untrue generalizations that deny individual differences or variations.

(whose owner also fired Imus), for using racially charged, derogatory language to describe the Rutgers women's basketball team, which the night before had clinched the national championship. While opinions varied about whether Imus's punishment fit his "crime," few disputed the egregious nature of the offense.[24]

Many of us try to stay current with our language, exhibiting sensitivity as we try to use appropriate terminology when referring to members of our own race and ethnicity, as well as members of other groups. But we're likely to hear—both off campus and on—racial language that is a throwback to an earlier time in our country's evolution; hearing or even hearing *about* that kind of language is always jolting.

Terms pertaining to certain racial and ethnic groups have certainly changed over time. Check out Table 3.1, which provides racial categories that appeared as options in the U.S. censuses of 1970, 1980, 1990, and 2000, and you'll see how much more specific our language has become in an attempt to better communicate racial and ethnic identity in this country. Sometimes it's a challenge to get your language to keep pace with the changing times. Just when you think you're using appropriate words, someone gets offended, which makes people of any cultural identity feel as if they're walking on eggshells. For example, some years back there was a movement to get white Americans to identify themselves as "European Americans" or the shortened version, "Euro Americans," terms that would be more uniform with common descriptors like Mexican American, African American, Asian American, and Native American. The terms were also designed to move the language away from an identification with skin color and to

A sensitive communicator keeps abreast of linguistic changes and adopts the most up-to-date designations preferred by members of various ethnic groups. In what ways can you improve your abilities to adapt, edit, and shape what you say and how you say it?

TABLE 3.1 U.S. Census Racial Categories

1970	1980	1990	2000
White	White	White	White
Negro or Black	Negro	Black	Black or African American
Indian (American)	Indian (American)	Indian (American)	American Indian or Alaska Native (specify tribe)
Japanese	Japanese	Japanese	Japanese
Chinese	Chinese	Chinese	Chinese
Filipino	Filipino	Filipino	Filipino
Hawaiian	Hawaiian	Hawaiian	Hawaiian
Korean	Korean	Korean	Korean
	Eskimo	Eskimo	
	Aleut	Aleut	
	Vietnamese	Vietnamese	Vietnamese
	Asian Indian	Asian Indian	Asian Indian
	Guamanian	Guamanian	Guamanian or Chamorro
	Samoan	Samoan	Samoan
		Other Asian Pacific Islander	Other Asian (print race)
			Other Pacific Islander (print race)
Other (print race)	Other (specify)	Other Race	Some Other Race (individuals who consider themselves multiracial can choose two or more races)

Source: Table based on information from M. Anderson and S. Feinberg, 2000, "Race and ethnicity and the controversy over the U.S. Census," *Current Sociology* 48(3): 87–110; National Research Council, *Measuring Racial Discrimination* (Washington, DC: National Academies Press, 2004); U.S. Census Bureau, 2001, "Population by race and Hispanic or Latino origin for all ages and for 18 years and over for the United States: 2000," <http://www.census.gov/PressRelease/www/2001/tables/st00_1.pdf>.

be less obtuse than "Caucasian," which was more something you'd see on an application form or survey than a self-identifier that people commonly used. But the Euro American designation never caught on; thus, it went by the wayside, as have other terms related to race and ethnicity. Another term that prevailed for a time as an alternative to black was "Afro American," but that term was soon replaced with "African American," which connects the identity more directly to Africa and avoids the connotation the former terminology had with a hairstyle.

A few years ago, a reader wrote to an African American columnist for the *Miami Herald*, asking about the appropriate term to use when referring to black people. Leonard Pitts addressed the question in his column by advocating for the evolution of vocabulary, no matter "how unwieldy, how imprecise, or how much of a PC pain in the backside." Pitts called for a saner world, in which such language obstacles would not be obstacles at all, because racial and ethnic differences would be minimized and thus would not command so much attention; the only term one would need to know to refer to another person would be the person's name.[25]

Complex explanations for language's deeply rooted association with identity can be found in any library or bookstore, but for our purposes the point is this: Be careful not to get lazy with language. It's important to inventory and revolutionize your language with regard to the racial, ethnic, national, and religious affiliations of people, because the language you choose to use is your primary tool for creating the reality of your existence, for revealing how you think, for being known by others, and for knowing them as well.[26]

The gender-neutral term *firefighter* describes both of these people, whereas the sexist term *fireman* excludes the person on the right.

Biased Language: Gender and Sexual Orientation

Language that reveals bias in favor of one sex and against another, termed **sexist** or **exclusive language,** is more prevalent than you'd think. Decades of effort, spurred by the women's liberation movement in the 1960s, have raised the consciousness of American culture regarding exclusive language. But many people still do not alter their language to reflect and include both sexes. In addition, insensitivity or intolerance toward persons who are gay, lesbian, or bisexual is often reflected in what is termed **heterosexist** or **homophobic language.** A person who uses heterosexist language speaks from an assumption that the world is heterosexual, as if romantic and sexual attraction to those of the same sex or to both sexes simply were not possible. Homophobic language more overtly denigrates persons of nonheterosexual orientations and usually arises out of a fear of being labeled gay or lesbian. We consider sexist and heterosexist forms of biased language below.

Language and the Sexes Even though women now constitute 50 percent of the U.S. population, to listen to the language of some people, you'd think it was still a man's world. Sexist language can reflect stereotypical attitudes or describe roles in exclusively male or female terms. Research indicates that exclusive language usage does the following: (1) maintains sex-biased perceptions, (2) shapes people's attitudes about careers that are appropriate for one sex but not the other, (3) causes some women to believe that certain jobs and roles aren't attainable, (4) contributes to the belief that men deserve more status in society than women do, and (5) mutes the voices of many women, because the words and norms formed by the dominant group don't allow for the articulation of women's experiences.[27] Even dictionaries fall into patterns of describing women and men with discriminatory language.[28] Included in the *Oxford English Dictionary* definition for *woman* are (1) an adult female being, (2) female servant, (3) a lady-love or mistress, and (4) a wife. Men are described in more positive and distinguished terms: (1) a human being, (2) the human creation regarded abstractly, (3) an adult male endowed with many qualities, and (4) a person of importance of position.

The most common form of sexism in language is the use of a masculine term as though it were **generic** (a term to describe all people). There are two primary ways in

---

sexist (exclusive) language
Language that reveals bias in favor of one sex and against another.

heterosexist language
Language that reveals an assumption that the world is heterosexual, as if homosexuality or bisexuality did not exist.

homophobic language
Language that overtly denigrates persons of nonheterosexual orientations, usually arising out of a fear of being labeled gay or lesbian.

generic language
General terms that stand for all persons or things within a given category.

which masculine-as-generic language typically appears in written and oral communication: in pronoun usage and man-linked terminology.

Consistent evidence from research on sexist language shows that people—particularly in U.S. culture—simply do not tend to think in neuter. We think in male or female, which is another example of the polarization aspect of language discussed earlier. We don't tend to think of living entities as *it*, and we rarely use that pronoun to refer to them. When most people read or hear the word *he*, they think of a masculine person, not a sexless person.[29] Using generic masculine language, in essence, turns all persons into male persons.

Sexist language can be so deeply embedded in some people's experience that it is used habitually, without much thought. For example, a student giving a speech on how to project a winning, confident style in a job interview said, "When you greet the boss for the first time, be sure to look him straight in the eye, give him a firm handshake, and let him know you're interested in the job." This language would be perfectly acceptable if the speaker were only describing a specific situation in which the job candidate was to meet a male boss. But his exclusive language choice only allowed for the possibility of a male boss, not a female boss, unless he meant the term *he* to stand for all persons—male and female bosses, in this case. What if the speaker had used only female pronouns, as in "look her straight in the eye, give her a firm handshake, and let her know you're interested in the job"? No doubt the exclusive female language would have drawn undue attention and perhaps distracted listeners. It's common for male terms to be used to refer to all persons, but less common for female language to serve as generic.

We don't know what you were taught in high school or in other college classes about generic language. Nevertheless, publishing standards today require the use of nonsexist language, which allows no masculine terms to stand for all persons.[30] You'll notice that we use inclusive language in this text—because it reflects our value system and because our publisher requires it.

The solution to the problem of sexist language is not to replace all *he*s with *she*s, which would be an equally sexist practice. The point is to use terms that include both sexes so that your language reflects the contemporary world. If you want to refer to one person—any person of either sex—the most clear, grammatical, nonsexist way to do that is to use either *she or he*, *he/she*, or *s/he*.[31] Other options include (1) omitting a pronoun altogether, either by rewording a message or by substituting an article (*a*, *an*, or *the*) for the pronoun; (2) using *you* or variations of the indefinite pronoun *one*; or (3) using the plural pronoun *they*.[32]

As with pronouns, research shows that masculine mental images arise when the term *man* is used, again rendering women invisible and reinforcing the male-as-standard problem.[33] Words such as Congress*man*, police*man*, and *man*kind ignore the fact that women are part of the workforce and the human race. Contrast these with *member of Congress* (or *senator* or *representative*), *police officer*, and *humankind*, which are gender neutral and allow for the inclusion of both men and women. Some progress has been made in this area, reflecting changed attitudes toward women in the professional arena. Compare some terms used in the past to describe workers to terms we now use (see Table 3.2).

A related issue concerns the generally accepted use of the phrase *you guys* as a generic reference. This language is not generic, since it includes the male term *guys*, but it is one of the most widely used, by both women and men, and unintentionally exclusive terms in everyday English. About using *you guys* to refer to a group of women, renowned author Alice Walker states, "I see in its use some women's obsequious need to be accepted, at any cost, even at the cost of erasing their own femaleness, and that of other women. Isn't it at least ironic that after so many years of struggle for women's liberation, women should end up calling themselves this?"[34]

Consciously remembering to use nonsexist, inclusive language brings several benefits.[35] First, inclusive language reflects inclusive attitudes. Your attitudes are reflected in your speech and your speech affects your attitudes. Monitoring your verbal communication for sexist remarks can help you monitor any sexist attitudes or assumptions

TABLE 3.2

Terms from the Past	Terms Used Today
stewardess	flight attendant
chairman	chair
fireman	firefighter
salesman	salesperson or clerk
mailman	mail carrier
female doctor or lady doctor	physician or doctor
girls at work or girl Friday	women at the office
Miss/Mrs.	Ms.
mankind	people, humans, or humankind

you may hold. Second, using gender-inclusive language helps you become more other oriented, which will have a positive impact on your relationships. Consciously ridding your language of sexist remarks reflects your sensitivity to others. Third, inclusive language makes your speech more contemporary and unambiguous. If you use *he*, for example, how is a listener to know if you are referring to a male person or any person in general? And finally, inclusive language strengthens your style and demonstrates sensitivity that can empower others. By eliminating sexist bias from your speech, you affirm the value of all individuals with whom you interact.

Language and Sexual Orientation We realize that sexual orientation is one of the more difficult topics to discuss, mainly because people tend to hold strong opinions about it. But no matter your views about sexuality, it is vital to use sensitive, appropriate communication with whomever you encounter.

Just as you have learned to avoid racially charged terms that degrade and draw attention to someone's ethnicity, it's important to learn to avoid language that denigrates a person's sexual orientation and draws undue attention to this element of cultural diversity. One of your authors was quite taken aback a few years ago when she received a paper from a first-year student in which the derogatory term *fag* frequently appeared. You've no doubt heard this term, probably bantered about in high school, but its use can be a signal of homophobia—the fear of being labeled or viewed as gay or lesbian. Heterosexist language is more subtle; it often emerges through omission, meaning what *is not* said, rather than commission, or what *is* said. For example, have you ever heard an instructor in one of your classes give a dating example using two persons of the same sex? Most examples about relationships that you read or hear about in courses such as interpersonal communication or introduction to psychology reflect heterosexual romantic relationships. As another example, how often do you hear or use the term *partner* instead of *husband* or *wife?* The first term, *partner*, is inclusive of all forms of couples, while the latter terms, at least in most states, refer only to heterosexual marriage. These forms of language usage can communicate a heterosexist bias and suggest that other sexual orientations are inappropriate or nonexistent.

Biased Language: Age, Class, and Ability

"Just turn the car, grandpa!" Ever heard a driver say this in irritation, or said it yourself? Ever call an elderly person a "geezer" or an "old-timer"? Just as some people contend that Americans are hung up on gender and racial diversity, many believe that Americans are hung up on age. We live in a culture that glorifies youth and tends to

Communication and Ethics

"That's So Gay!"

We've said in this chapter that the primary definition for the term *homophobia* is a fear of being labeled or viewed as homosexual. However, a secondary meaning for *homophobia* is a discriminatory attitude toward or hatred of people who are homosexual, and some forms of language certainly reflect this negativity.[36]

A few years ago, a language usage surfaced that can still be heard, albeit to a much lesser extent than when it first became popular: saying "That's so gay" in response to someone's choice of clothing, accessories, or furnishings (typically things not expected to be owned or used by members of one sex or the other) or in response to someone's communication or actions. The language was made popular by the then-hit TV show *Friends*, whose characters Chandler and Joey could often be heard criticizing something by saying "That's so gay." College students picked up this language, using the term *gay* to refer to anything disagreeable and often justifying its use by saying that it was just a funny thing to say, not meant to refer to homosexuals or to be discriminatory or inappropriate. Many communication professors, as well as gay rights activists and educators across the country, took a stand to curb the use of this form of language, contending that it was indeed homophobic and discriminatory.[37] You may not hear this language much any more; if so, we're glad that it's on its well-deserved way out of the lexicon, because here's the problem: Substitute any word for the term *gay* and see if it sounds derogatory. Would someone say "That's so Jew" or "That's so black" and dare to think that these phrases weren't racial/ethnic slurs?

Engagement Questions

1. Even if a person knows that he or she doesn't mean to discriminate against members of a particular group, does the person have a responsibility to potential listeners *not* to use biased language?
2. What is your responsibility if you hear someone using derogatory, biased language? Should you speak up and confront someone about his or her language?
3. What are some examples of language that is still in need of changing because of potential bias?

---

put its elders "out to pasture."[38] Age discrimination is a very real problem in the workforce—so much so that laws have been enacted to guard against someone's being denied professional opportunities because of age. Likewise, some older people may hold stereotypes of young people and may speak to them as though their youth exempted them from intelligence or responsible action. We recommend that you inventory your language for any terms that either show disrespect for elders or are patronizing or condescending to younger people.

Another factor influencing language that has received research attention of late is socioeconomic class.[39] Class distinctions typically are revealed in derogatory references to "blue-collar workers," "manual laborers," or "welfare recipients." Another class slur is the term "white trash." In the late 1990s, when Paula Jones filed a sexual harassment lawsuit against then-President Bill Clinton, she was called "white trash" and "trailer trash" as she was ridiculed in the press and in living rooms across the country. Avoid references that reveal a condescending or disrespectful attitude toward someone's education (or lack of it) and socioeconomic status.

Finally, an area of bias in language that most people became conscious of by the turn of the twenty-first century relates to ability. Some years ago, Helen Keller was described as "deaf, dumb, and blind." Nowadays, the appropriate term for her inability to communicate vocally would be *mute*. Be careful that your language doesn't make fun of or draw attention to someone's physical, mental, or learning disability, such as calling someone a "cripple," "retard," or "slow reader." Research has found that when people with disabilities were called demeaning names, they were perceived as less trustworthy, competent, persuasive, and sociable than when they were described in positive terms.[40] The researchers warn against using derogatory language that is offensive to persons with disabilities. Also, scholars who research communication and disability recommend that you use the reference "persons with disabilities" rather than "disabled persons." The former language usage makes the person primary and the disability secondary; the emphasis is on a person, who just happens to have some form of disability. The latter usage emphasizes the disability over the humanness of the person.[41]

> ## Recap
>
> ### Confronting Bias in Language
>
> Inventory your language for subtle and not-so-subtle indications of bias in several areas:
>
> - *Race, Ethnicity, and Nationality.* Avoid language that denigrates members of a racial or ethnic group; be careful not to overemphasize race or ethnicity or "mark" a person by using adjectives referring to national origin, as in "that Oriental student in my class."
> - *Religion.* Watch stereotypical language pertaining to religious affiliation, such as derogatory references to Jews, Muslims, or fundamentalist Christians, for example.
> - *Gender.* Include both sexes in your language, especially in your use of pronouns; avoid masculine generic pronouns and male-linked terms that exclude women.
> - *Sexual Orientation.* Be alert to the potential for heterosexism in your language—the assumption that everyone is heterosexual or that heterosexuality is the only possible orientation. Eliminate homophobic language that degrades and stereotypes gays, lesbians, bisexuals, and transgender individuals.
> - *Age.* Avoid calling too much attention to a person's age in your verbal communication. Be especially vigilant not to label or stereotype the elderly or to condescend to or glorify youth.
> - *Class.* Monitor references to socioeconomic differences, such as distinctions between blue-collar and white-collar workers.
> - *Ability.* Avoid verbal communication that draws attention to a person's physical, mental, or learning ability.

Using Words to Establish Supportive Relationships

As we said early on in this chapter, one reason that our Principle Two for a Lifetime is "Effectively use and interpret verbal messages" is because verbal communication has an impact on other people. Language is our primary tool for communicating who we are to others—for knowing them and being known by them. Relationships of all sorts bring life's greatest satisfactions, so the motivation for assessing and improving our verbal communication with others is obvious.

In our introductory communication classes, we often discuss **trigger words**—forms of language that arouse certain emotions in us. One student, Travis, was immediately able to identify a word his wife used during arguments that really sparked his frustration and anger more than anything else. When Travis would make a point that would frustrate his wife—one for which she had no comeback—she would look at him, toss her hand in the air, and say, "Whatever." Perhaps this word triggers you too, because it punctuates a conversation; it acts as a dismissal of the other person and her or his point. Do you know what words trigger your emotions? These words or phrases can incite positive as well as negative feelings, but they acutely illustrate the power of words in the context of relationships. Certain uses of language can make us feel accepted and appreciated or disrespected and hostile.[42]

For over four decades, communication scholar Jack Gibb's research has been used as a framework for both describing and prescribing verbal behaviors that contribute to feelings of either supportiveness or defensiveness.[43] Gibb spent several years listening to and observing groups of individuals in meetings and conversations, noting that some exchanges seemed to create a supportive climate whereas others created a defensive one. Words and actions, he concluded, are tools we use to let someone know whether we support them or not. Thus, Gibb defined **supportive communication** as communication that uses language to create a climate of trust, caring, and acceptance. The language used in **defensive communication,** in contrast, creates a climate of hostility

---

trigger word
A form of language that arouses strong emotions in listeners.

supportive communication
Language that creates a climate of trust, caring, and acceptance.

defensive communication
Language that creates a climate of hostility and mistrust.

and mistrust. When someone gets defensive, communication is seriously impeded. Think about times when your words made someone defensive and how hard you had to work (if you attempted it at all) to get the person to let the defenses down. In this section, we suggest ways to use verbal communication to create a supportive climate rather than an antagonistic one.

Describe Your Own Feelings Rather Than Evaluate Others

Most of us don't like to be judged or evaluated. Not only do we fear negative responses from others; we fear the potential that we will become defensive and say things we'll later regret. Criticizing and name calling obviously can create relational problems, but so can our attempts to diagnose others' problems or weaknesses. As Winston Churchill declared, "I am always ready to learn, although I do not always like being taught."

One way to avoid evaluating others is to attempt to use "I" statements instead of accusatory "you" statements. Statements such as "You always say you'll call, but you never do" or "You need to pick up the dirty clothes in your room" attack a person's sense of self-worth and usually result in a defensive reaction. Instead, use the word *I* to describe your own feelings and thoughts about a situation or event: "I find it hard to believe you when you say you'll call" or "I don't enjoy the extra work of picking up your dirty clothes." When you describe your own feelings instead of berating the receiver of the message, you take ownership of the problem. This approach leads to greater openness and trust because your listener is less likely to feel rejected or as if you are trying to control him or her.

Related to this point about description versus evaluation is the suggestion that you separate behaviors from persons in order to create a supportive climate. We probably all know people whose behaviors seem self-destructive, and we all do things from time to time that aren't in our own best interest. Maybe in reaction to getting dumped in a relationship that meant a great deal to you, you call that person's answering machine twenty times, just to hear the voice recording. Maybe you indulge in self-defeating behavior like drinking too much, overeating (or the opposite, starving yourself), or driving around late at night with the music blasting, feeling sorry for yourself. In these critical moments, do people respond to you or to your behavior? A supportive response focuses on the behavior, not the person. A supportive response sounds something like this: "Here's what I see you doing; I'm still your friend and I care about you, but this behavior isn't healthy. How can I help you?" Responses that engender defensiveness might sound something like "You're really out of control," "You've become someone I don't recognize," and "Stop acting like this or I won't be able to be around you or be your friend." The supportive response doesn't characterize the person as the embodiment of his or her destructive behavior; it focuses only on the behavior, because that's what's happening at the moment. In religious circles, the advice goes "Hate the sin, love the sinner."

Solve Problems Rather Than Control Others

When you were younger, your parents gave you rules to keep you safe. Even though you may have resented their control, you needed to know that the stovetop was hot, when not to cross the street, and how dangerous it was to stick your finger in a light socket. Now that you are an adult, when people treat you like a child, it often means they are trying to control your behavior, to take away your options.

Most of us don't like to be controlled. Someone who presumes to tell us what's good for us instead of helping us puzzle through issues and problems to arrive at our own solutions or higher understanding is likely to engender defensiveness. In truth, we have little or no control over others. Open-ended questions such as "What seems to be the problem?" or "How can we deal with this issue?" create a more supportive climate than critical comments such as "Here's where you are wrong" and "You know what your problem is?" or commands like "Don't do that!"

Be Genuine Rather Than Manipulative

To be genuine means honestly being yourself rather than attempting to be someone you are not. It also means taking a sincere interest in others, considering the uniqueness of each individual and situation, and avoiding generalizations or strategies that focus on your own needs and desires. A manipulative person has hidden agendas and her or his own concerns and interests most at heart. A genuine person has the other person's interests at heart and uses language to facilitate an open and honest discussion of issues and problems.

Empathize Rather Than Remain Detached from Others

Empathy, one of the hallmarks of supportive relationships, is the ability to understand and actually feel or approximate the feelings of others and then to predict the emotional responses they will have to different situations.[44] You work to put yourself in the other person's shoes, to experience as closely as you can what she or he is experiencing. The opposite of empathy is neutrality. To be neutral is to be indifferent or apathetic toward others. (Even when you express anger or irritation toward another, you are investing some energy in the relationship.) A statement that epitomizes this concept of neutrality is "I don't love you or hate you; I just *don't* you."

Remaining detached from someone when empathy is obviously called for can generate great defensiveness and damage a relationship. Here's an example: You're upset about an argument you just had with someone you're dating, so you seek the support and listening ear of a good friend. But that friend is in "party mode" or such a good mood that he or she chooses not to concentrate and listen to what's going on with you. Rather than engage in your situation, your friend remains detached and blows off your concerns. In situations like this, most of us become defensive and frustrated, and the quality of our friendship may suffer. Empathy takes work, but it is a building block of a supportive relationship.

Be Flexible Rather Than Rigid Toward Others

Some people are just *always* right, aren't they? (These people spend a lot of time alone, too.) Most people don't like someone who always seems certain that she or he is right. A "you're wrong, I'm right" attitude creates a defensive climate. This doesn't mean that you should have no opinions and go through life passively agreeing to everything. And it doesn't mean that there isn't a clear-cut right and wrong in a given situation. But instead of making rigid pronouncements, at times you may want to qualify your language by using phrases such as "I may be wrong, but it seems to me . . ." or "Here's something you might want to consider." Conditional language gives your opinions a softer edge that allows room for others to express a point of view; it opens the door for alternatives. Declarations tend to shut the door. Again, there are times when equivocation is not an appropriate or advisable way to communicate. But in those cases when you want to induce supportiveness and reduce the potential for defensiveness, conditional, flexible language works best.

Present Yourself as Equal Rather Than Superior

You can antagonize others by letting them know that you view yourself as better or brighter than they are. You may be gifted and extraordinarily intelligent, but it's not necessary to announce or publicize it. And although some people have the responsibility and authority to manage others, "pulling rank" does not usually produce a supportive climate. With phrases such as "Let's work on this together" or "We each have a valid perspective," you can avoid erecting walls of resentment and defensiveness. "We" language can be preferable to "you" language; it builds a sense of camaraderie and shared experience, and by using it you avoid setting yourself apart from listeners.

empathy
The ability to understand and feel what another person is feeling.

This memorial, constructed in remembrance of the bombing of the Murrah Federal Building in Oklahoma City, evokes strong emotions. Visitors to the site comfort each other and convey empathy as they mourn the deaths of innocent people.

Also, avoid using "high-falutin'" (or unnecessarily complicated) words just to impress others or to project some image. Sometimes referred to as "bafflegab," this kind of language can come in the form of words, phrases, or verbal shorthand that people use but no one understands. People with particular expertise may use abbreviated terms or acronyms (words derived from the first letters of several words in a phrase). The military is notorious for its use of language that doesn't easily translate outside of military circles. "Be sure to complete the Fit Reps on those Non-Coms ASAP before returning to the BOQ." Translation: "Be sure to complete the Fitness Reports on those Non-Commissioned Officers as soon as possible before returning to the Bachelor Officers' Quarters." If both speaker and listener are military personnel, then such a sentence may be a perfectly acceptable way to communicate. The problem comes when you use lingo no one understands, perhaps to create drama, exclude someone from the conversation, or posture. It's better to use informal language appropriate to the situation and your listeners than to attempt to talk over the heads of everyone in the room.

You can also create defensiveness by using language that is too simplistic for your listeners. Granted, when you communicate with someone from another culture or even from another U.S. co-cultural group, you may need to alter your message to get your meaning across. But this means that your verbal communication should be explicit, not condescending. For example, some people use oversimplified words when communicating with elderly persons. It's inappropriate to assume that aging diminishes one's capacity to understand. Try to use language to present yourself on equal ground with your listeners and establish a supportive, open climate for communication.

Avoid Gunny-Sacking

In one of his hit songs, Garth Brooks sings, "We buried the hatchet; we left the handle sticking out." Brooks makes mild reference here to a process known as gunny-sacking, which can be like an ax handle sticking out within easy reach; when grasped, it serves to remind you of a past conflict or wound. Gunny-sacking involves dredging up someone's past mistakes or problems and linking them to a current situation. The language comes from the imagery of reaching down into a bag (a gunny sack) to pull out something from the past. For example, suppose your best male friend has just been dumped by his "one true love," but you—being the good friend that you are—remind him that the last three women he dated were also his "one true love," at least at the time. Your friend wants empathy, but you respond by highlighting his tendency to turn

"Miss Right" into "Miss Right Now." Such an approach will likely make him feel criticized and engender defensive reactions in him. This kind of scenario rarely deepens a relationship.

However, in some situations, it may be wise to point out a pattern of destructive behavior that you observe in someone, especially if the person is someone you value highly and with whom you want to maintain a healthy, supportive relationship. Occasionally, people repeat behaviors that are not to their benefit, but they are unaware that a pattern is being established. A caring friend, romantic partner, or family member might use the supportive communication techniques highlighted in this chapter to describe past instances and reveal the pattern to the person. Once the negative patterns are revealed and explored, he or she may work to overcome them so that the destructive behavior isn't repeated.

Recap

Using Words to Create a Supportive Climate

- Describe your own feelings instead of evaluating the points of view or behavior of others.
- Keep the focus on problem solving, not control of others.
- Be genuine rather than manipulative in your approach.
- Show that you understand others' points of view instead of ignoring their feelings.
- Use conditional language and demonstrate flexibility rather than rigidity in your communication with others.
- Present yourself as an equal rather than as a superior. Make it clear that you don't have all the answers; avoid acting like a know-it-all. Don't attempt to talk over the heads of listeners or condescend to them, because either approach can breed defensiveness.
- Avoid gunny-sacking, or reminding someone of past mistakes or issues, unless you believe the person remains blind to his or her destructive patterns.

PRINCIPLES FOR A LIFETIME
Enhancing Your Skills

2. Verbal

Principle Two: Effectively use and interpret verbal messages.
- Realize that communication problems may not have to do with the words used, but with the meanings that people attach to the words.
- Recognize the difference between denotative and connotative language.
- Use concrete terms whenever appropriate, because abstract language is harder to understand than concrete language.
- Understand that meanings of words are affected by the culture within which the language is used.
- Pay attention to the words communicators choose to use and attempt to interpret those words in the spirit and context in which they were intended.
- Avoid biased language when speaking about race, ethnicity, nationality, religion, gender, sexual orientation, age, class, and ability.
- Use words to engender supportiveness, rather than defensiveness.

Summary

In this chapter, we explored the importance of effective verbal communication with others. The words we choose have great power to communicate who we are and to influence the relationships we establish. People use words as symbols for thoughts, and they create meanings for those symbols. We interpret their meanings in terms of the culture and context to which they belong. Communication is complex because people develop both denotative (literal) meanings and connotative (subjective) meanings for words and because meanings range from concrete to abstract.

The power of words stems from their ability to create images and to help us label and understand our experience. Words influence our thoughts and actions, as they both shape culture and are shaped by culture. Language also has the power to make and break relationships.

Biased language that is insensitive and exclusive of others creates noise that interferes with the meaning of a message; it also can create the impression that the user of such language is biased and can impede the development of satisfying relationships. The most common forms of biased language relate to race, ethnicity, nationality, religion, gender, sexual orientation, age, class, and ability.

The words you use can enhance or detract from the quality of relationships you establish with others. In contrast to defensive communication, supportive communication is descriptive rather than evaluative, problem oriented rather than control oriented, genuine rather than contrived or manipulative, empathic rather than neutral, flexible rather than rigid, equal rather than superior, and focused on current behaviors, not on past mistakes.

Assessing Your Knowledge

For Discussion and Review

Principle One: Be aware of your communication with yourself and others.

1. How can a heightened awareness of your use of language help make you a more effective communicator?

Principle Two: Effectively use and interpret verbal messages.

2. What forms of verbal messages reveal people's biases?

Principle Three: Effectively use and interpret nonverbal messages.

3. How do nonverbal cues work with verbal messages to improve the likelihood that a message will be understood by a receiver?

Principle Four: Listen and respond thoughtfully to others.

4. How can listening to someone else communicate enhance your own verbal communication abilities? Can you expand your vocabulary by listening to others?

Principle Five: Appropriately adapt messages to others.

5. Why is it important to adapt verbal messages to listeners?

Multiple Choice

Choose the *best* answer to each of the following questions.

1. The type of meaning for a word found in the dictionary is
   a. connotative.
   b. denotative.
   c. abstract.
   d. concrete.

2. Using general terms, such as *she* or *he*, to refer to all people is an example of
   a. defensive language.
   b. generic language.
   c. trivial language.
   d. supportive language.

3. Language that reveals an assumption that only a man and a woman can be involved in an intimate relationship is
   a. homophobic.
   b. heterosexist.
   c. homosexist.
   d. heterophobic.

4. Doug says to his employee, "Either we are going to build this front porch my way or we are not going to build it at all!" This is an example of
   a. defensive communication.
   b. supportive communication.
   c. empathic communication.
   d. problem-solving communication.

5. Sexist language
   a. is the same thing as generic language.
   b. perpetuates sex-biased perceptions.
   c. is the same thing as inclusive language.
   d. is not related to perceptions of men's and women's status.

6. To comfort his upset friend Hunter, Austin says, "I am so sorry that you lost your job this week. I can imagine that you are feeling very upset about it. Is there anything I can do to help you to feel better?" Austin's statement is an example of
   a. empathic communication.
   b. neutral communication.
   c. bypassing communication.
   d. concrete communication.

7. In referring to members of other ethnic groups, it's best to
   a. rely on traditional ethnic labels.
   b. use ethnic-neutral labels.
   c. use the current ethnic labels preferred by a group's members.
   d. use whichever term you are most comfortable with.

8. Trigger words
   a. convey a negative evaluation of another person.
   b. are used to control others.
   c. express sincere feelings.
   d. arouse both positive and negative emotions in us.

9. Meaning exists
   a. in the words themselves.
   b. in the way the communicators use the words.
   c. in the culture and context of the interaction.
   d. only in the mind of the receiver.

10. Bailey and Victoria are having an argument. Bailey says to Victoria. "I see you crossing your arms and rolling your eyes. When I try to talk to you, you turn your head away from me and sigh loudly. You do this all the time and then wonder why people don't like you. That's why Makayla doesn't like you anymore, and you know it. That's why you keep ending up alone." Bailey has violated which of Gibb's recommendations?
    a. Be descriptive rather than evaluative.
    b. Solve problems rather than control others.
    c. Empathize rather than remain detached from others.
    d. Avoid gunny-sacking.

Answers to the questions in this practice test can be found at the end of the book.

Assessing Your Skill

1. Below we review the differences between denotative and connotative meanings of words and provide examples.

Level	Definition	Examples
Denotative	Literal, restrictive definition of a word	*Teacher:* the person primarily responsible for providing your education
Connotative	Personal, subjective reaction to a word	*Teacher:* the warm, supportive person who fostered a climate in which you could learn OR the cold taskmaster who drilled lessons into you and made you feel inferior

For each of the following terms, provide a denotative, or dictionary-type, definition; then generate connotative meanings of your own.

work
parent
love
commitment
professionalism
loyalty

2. This activity illustrates how people reveal their biases through their use of language. Generate a list of stereotypical terms often associated with each of the words below. For example, for the word *Democrat*, you might think of positive and negative terms like "liberal," "tax and spend," "big government," "antiwar," and "populist."

conservatives
foreigners
homeless persons
the military
churchgoers
politicians

Web Resources to Improve Your Knowledge and Skill

If you decide that your vocabulary needs a bit of expansion, where do you turn? To the dictionary you got as a high school graduation present? To reruns of *South Park?* For a web site that will expand your capacity for English through its creative plays on words, visual puzzles, and innovative approaches to crosswords and word searches, try <www.puzzability.com>. For a site that offers anagrams and such services as A.Word.A.Day e-mails, try <http://wordsmith.org>.

If you encounter someone whose language is such "bafflegab" that a common dictionary won't help you decipher meanings, try the Extelligence Creative Word Dictionary at <www.extelligence.co.uk>. This web site offers seldom-used words and their definitions; you won't be stumped again by someone who is "ultracrepidarian" (acting or speaking outside one's experience, knowledge, or ability).

Here's an interesting web site to check out: <www.yforum.com>. This is the site for the National Forum on People's Differences, described as a no-holds-barred question-and-answer opportunity. Users can ask questions—either as postings or in a real-time chat format—that would be impolite or too embarrassing to ask in a face-to-face or even telephone format. Examples of questions that have been posted on the site include "What do retired people do all day?" "Is it disrespectful for a straight person to go to a gay bar?" "Why do Muslim women cover their hair?" "Is it considered offensive if a white person calls a black person 'black'?" It's interesting to observe the kinds of freedom the relative anonymity of the Internet provides.

Margie Livingston Campbell, "Barter." © M. L. Campbell/SuperStock, Inc.

We respond to gestures with an extreme alertness and, one might say, in accordance with an elaborate and secret code that is written nowhere, known by none, and understood by all.

Edward Sapir

Chapter 4

Understanding Nonverbal Messages

Chapter Outline

- Why Focus on Nonverbal Communication?
- The Nature of Nonverbal Communication
- Codes of Nonverbal Communication
- How to Interpret Nonverbal Cues More Accurately
- Summary

Chapter Objectives

After studying this chapter, you should be able to

1. Provide four reasons for studying nonverbal communication.
2. Describe the five ways in which nonverbal communication functions with verbal communication.
3. Discuss six elements that reveal the nature of nonverbal communication.
4. Be able to identify and explain the seven groupings of nonverbal communication codes.
5. Summarize major research findings regarding codes of nonverbal communication.
6. Explain Mehrabian's three-part framework for interpreting nonverbal cues.

"Don't use that tone of voice with me, mister; I don't need your sarcasm right now."
"Why are you looking at me like that? Did something happen?"
"I knew it was you coming down the hall; your footsteps are a dead giveaway."
"I'm sure I'll get over the argument, but right now I just need some space."

What do these statements have in common? They all have to do with a form of human communication that occurs without words—what we term *nonverbal communication*. As we explained in Chapter 1, **nonverbal communication** is communication other than written or spoken language that creates meaning for someone. The one exception to this definition is that to hearing persons, sign language appears to be nonverbal communication. However, to persons who are deaf, sign language is verbal communication, with certain movements, signs, and facial expressions conveying words, phrases, and emphasis.[1]

We know you're becoming familiar with our five-sided model of Communication Principles for a Lifetime, but let's do a quick recap (see Figure 4.1). In Chapter 2, we explored ways to become more aware of yourself and your perceptions of things and people with whom you come into contact. An important step in this process of coming to know and understand yourself better is an honest, insightful examination of how you talk. In Chapter 3, we challenged you to consider the power of words, to take inventory of your use of language, and to think about ways to improve your verbal communication so that you extend yourself to others and respond to them in an appropriate, effective manner. Now we get to what most people consider an even greater challenge—understanding and evaluating your nonverbal communication and improving your ability to interpret the nonverbal behavior of others. Nonverbal communication is of great importance; a person who can read others' nonverbal communication with sensitivity and skill makes a memorable impression on other people. Because of the power of nonverbal communication to complement verbal communication, to further reveal the self—particularly in those situations when talking is inappropriate, impossible, or inadequate—and to affect how you connect with others as you initiate and build relationships, we've chosen to make this the third of our five key Principles for a Lifetime.

We have two primary goals in this chapter. The first is to help you become more aware of your own nonverbal behavior—to help you understand how and why you behave as you do. Because much nonverbal communication behavior is subconscious, most people have limited awareness or understanding of it. Once you become more aware of this important form of communication, you will increase your ability to use nonverbal skills to interact more effectively with others. The second goal is to enhance your nonverbal receiving skills, or your ability to more accurately detect and interpret the nonverbal communication of others.

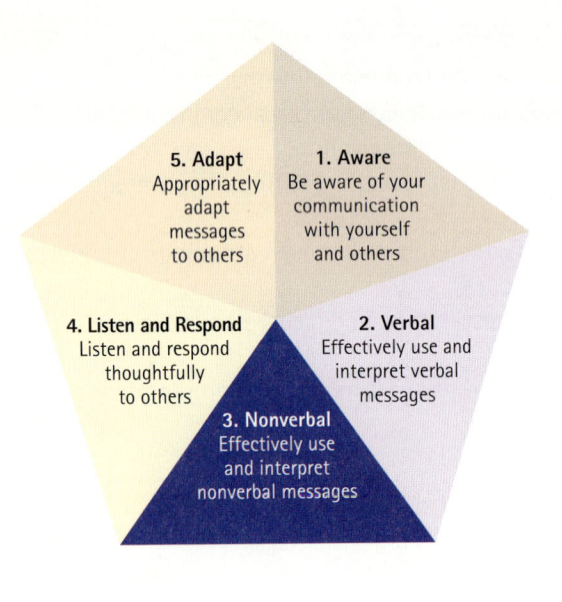

Figure 4.1
Communication Principles for a Lifetime

1. Aware — Be aware of your communication with yourself and others
2. Verbal — Effectively use and interpret verbal messages
3. Nonverbal — Effectively use and interpret nonverbal messages
4. Listen and Respond — Listen and respond thoughtfully to others
5. Adapt — Appropriately adapt messages to others

Why Focus on Nonverbal Communication?

nonverbal communication
Communication other than written or spoken language that creates meaning for someone.

Have you ever watched someone interact with someone else and thought, "That person just doesn't have a clue"? We've all seen or met people who appear not to pick up on the communication clues of others. For example, have you ever tried to end a conversation because you were late or needed to be somewhere else, and the person you were talking to just wouldn't let you out of the conversation? The person didn't seem to notice you looking at your watch, angling your body away, taking a few steps back, and making minimal vocal responses to what was being said. Now, we all have times when we can't "catch a clue," even if we consider ourselves to be fairly sensitive, perceptive people. Certain people, places, moods, or topics of conversation may impede our ability to give and receive nonverbal communication effectively. But we don't want to be clueless. We want to be able to exhibit effective nonverbal communication and to read and interpret the clues others give us more sensitively and accurately.

However, there's something very important to keep in mind as we proceed: No one can become a perfect interpreter of the nonverbal communication of others. It's unwise and inappropriate to assume that you can become an infallible judge of others' nonverbal cues, because human beings are unique, complicated, and ever-changing creatures. Although we encourage you to deepen your understanding of nonverbal communication, sharpen your powers of observation, and develop greater skill in interpreting the meanings behind others' nonverbal actions, we also suggest that you remain keenly aware of the idiosyncratic and complex nature of nonverbal communication. We hope that you catch more clues as a result of studying this topic, but avoid making the mistake of believing that your interpretations of nonverbal messages are always correct. To begin to explore this topic, let's look at four reasons for studying nonverbal communication.

Nonverbal Messages Communicate Feelings and Attitudes

What do you look like when you're happy and excited about something? When you're mad? When you're really worried about something? When you're surprised or disappointed? Recordings or pictures of yourself in different moods can be quite revealing, because your face, body, and voice communicate volumes about what's going on inside of you.

Nonverbal communication is a primary tool for conveying our feelings and attitudes and for detecting the emotional states of others. In the study of nonverbal communication, Albert Mehrabian is an expert. He concluded from his research that the most significant source of emotional information is the face, which can channel as much as 55 percent of our meaning. Vocal cues such as volume, pitch, and intensity convey another 38 percent of our emotional meaning. In all, we communicate approximately

How aware are you of the power of your nonverbal communication with others? Think back on confrontations you have had in the past. In your opinion, which communicates emotions most effectively: the volume, pitch, and intensity of the voice? Nonverbal gestures, facial expressions, and body positions? The meaning of the actual words spoken?

93 percent of the emotional meaning of our messages nonverbally; as little as 7 percent of the emotional meaning is communicated through explicit verbal channels.[2] Although these percentages do not apply to every communication situation, Mehrabian's research illustrates the potential power of nonverbal cues to communicate emotion and attitude.

Nonverbal Messages Are More Believable Than Verbal Ones

"Hey—are you mad or something?" asks Jonas.
(Big sigh.) "Oh, no. I'm not mad," responds Danita (in a subdued tone of voice and without making eye contact).
"You sure? Because you're acting funny, like you're ticked off." (One more try and then Jonas will likely give up.)
"I SAID I'M NOT MAD, OKAY? WILL YOU LEAVE IT ALONE PLEASE?"

Despite Danita's claim to the contrary, the real story is—she's mad. "Actions speak louder than words." This cliché became a cliché because nonverbal communication is more believable than verbal communication. Verbal communication is a conscious

Communication and Technology

Computer-Mediated Communication: Conveying Emotions

Without the usual nonverbal mechanisms that allow us to reveal our emotions to others in face-to-face communication, how do we let others at a distance know what we're feeling? Text messaging and e-mailing are so commonplace now that most people have learned the shorthand that allows us to send quick messages through our cell phone, personal data assistant (PDA), or computer. Acronyms and abbreviations such as "lol," "omg," and "bff" are speedy ways to get a message across. The sideways images made from punctuation marks, commonly referred to as emoticons, serve as nonverbal cues that help convey the meaning or emotion behind our messages. The most common emoticon is the happy face, or "smiley," which is typed by combining a colon, dash, and right parenthesis mark, as in :-). Here are some commonly used emoticons derived from various sources:[3]

:-(	Depressed or upset by a remark
:-I	Indifferent
:-|	Straight face
:-o	Surprise
;-)	Winking at a suggestive or flirtatious remark
:-/	Skeptical
:-P	Sticking your tongue out
:-D	Laughing
:-@	Screaming
8-)	Wearing sunglasses
::-)	Wearing regular glasses
(-:	Left-handed

Formatting options add nonverbal elements to our communication as well. For example, putting words in all caps, a technique known as shouting, typically reveals emphasis, frustration, or even anger. Another nonverbal element is the general look of the message itself; this applies more to e-mail and other computer-based exchanges than to text messages, since formatting options for texting are somewhat limited. While some reformatting occurs in the transmission of e-mail messages from computer to computer, most elements don't reformat. Research shows that styles of fonts (typefaces) convey different nonverbal cues that accompany our verbal messages.[4]

If someone sent you the following e-mail message, what would you guess the person was feeling, based on nonverbal cues conveyed through the choice of font and use of boldface?

I'VE HAD AN INTERESTING DAY, BUT WOULD LIKE TO HEAR ABOUT YOURS FIRST.

Might your sense of the message change if you received it in the font below?

I'VE HAD AN INTERESTING DAY, BUT WOULD LIKE TO HEAR ABOUT YOURS FIRST.

It's wise to consider the important, but often-overlooked nonverbal signals embedded in our communication when it is mediated by technology.

Engagement Questions

1. How well do emoticons, acronyms, and abbreviations help you convey emotion in text messaging and computer-mediated communication?
2. Have you ever thought about what emotion might be revealed in the font (typeface) you choose to use in e-mail messages or IM postings?

activity; it involves the translation of thoughts and impulses into symbols. Some nonverbal communication is conscious, but a great deal of it is generated subconsciously as we act and react to stimuli in our environment. It's easier to control your words than to control a quiver in your voice when you're angry, the heat and flush in your face when you talk to someone you're attracted to, or shaky knees when you're nervous.

When a person's verbal and nonverbal communication contradict, as in Danita's case, which should an astute observer believe? The nonverbal actions carry the truer message most of the time. When we can't catch a clue, it's most likely because we're wrapped up in ourselves or because we attend more to a person's verbal messages than to her or his nonverbal messages.

Nonverbal Messages Are Critical to Successful Relationships

One researcher suggests that as much as 65 percent of the way we convey meaning in our messages is through nonverbal channels.[5] Of course, the meaning others interpret from our behavior may not be the one we intended. But we begin making judgments about people just a fraction of a second after meeting them, based on nonverbal information. We may decide whether a date is going to be pleasant or dull during the first thirty seconds of meeting the person, before he or she has had time to utter more than "Hello."[6]

As another example, consider the handshake—a simple ritualistic greeting between two people, used in many cultures. Have you ever considered the power of a handshake to communicate? If you get a weak, half-handed, limp handshake from someone, what are you likely to conclude about that person? Research has focused on judgments Americans make about someone's personality based on this simple greeting ritual. William Chaplin and his colleagues determined characteristics of handshakes that contribute to what they term a handshake index.[7] These researchers examined such attributes as strength, vigor, completeness of grip, and duration. The high index or most positive handshake was strong (but not so strong as to cut off the blood supply), vigorous (meaning it conveyed an appropriate amount of energy), adequate in duration (not too brief or too long), and complete in its grip (meaning that the people gripped each other's hands fully, with palms touching). Next the researchers studied subjects' judgments of persons with a high handshake index versus those with a low handshake index. These researchers found that the higher a person's handshake index, the more extroverted, more open to experience, and less shy that person was believed to be. In addition to these traits, women with high handshake indexes were also perceived to be more agreeable than women with weak or poor handshakes. Subjects in the study also formed more favorable first impressions of those persons with high handshake indexes than those with low indexes. Thus, even a simple symbolic, culturally rooted gesture can have a definite and long-lasting impact on how others perceive you.

Nonverbal cues are important not only in the early stages of relationships, but also as we maintain, deepen, and sometimes terminate those relationships. In fact, the more intimate the relationship, the more we use and understand the nonverbal cues of our partners. Long-married couples spend less time verbalizing their feelings and emotions to each other than they did when they were first dating; each learns to interpret the other's subtle nonverbal cues. If a spouse is silent during dinner, the other spouse may deduce that the day was a tough one and decide to give the person a lot of space. In fact, all of us are more likely to use nonverbal cues to convey negative messages than to announce our explicit dislike of something or someone.[8] We also use nonverbal cues to signal changes in the level of satisfaction with a relationship. When we want to cool things off, we may start using a less vibrant tone of voice and cut back on eye contact and physical contact with our partner.

Nonverbal Messages Serve Multiple Functions

Nonverbal messages function in a variety of ways. First, nonverbal cues can *substitute for* verbal messages. Raising the forefinger and middle finger in the air can mean "peace," can signal "V" for victory, or can simply be someone's way of ordering two of something in a noisy, crowded environment where it's hard to be heard. When someone asks, "Where's the elevator?" we can point instead of voicing a response. In these instances, we substitute nonverbal cues for verbal messages.

Nonverbal cues delivered simultaneously with verbal messages *complement*, clarify, or extend the meaning of the verbal cues, conveying more information and allowing for a more accurate interpretation. When someone waves, makes eye contact, and says "hello," the gesture and eye contact serve as nonverbal complements to the verbal greeting. Complementary cues also help color our expressed emotions and attitudes. The length of a hug when you leave someone at the airport gives information about your feelings. A high-pitched chuckle may reveal your nervousness.

Sometimes, however, our nonverbal cues *contradict* rather than complement our verbal cues. Remember Danita, who said she wasn't mad even though she was acting and sounding mad? In an instance like this, the nonverbal cues contradict the verbal ones. The nonverbal message is almost always the one we should believe.

We also use nonverbal cues to *repeat* our words. You and your buddy separate after class, heading down the hallway in separate directions. You yell, "See you in the library to study around four," but your friend strains to hear you over the noise in the hall. When he looks at you—pointing to his ear, shaking his head, and looking confused—you simply raise your hand in the air, point in the direction of the library, and raise four fingers. Now he understands, because the nonverbal gestures and facial expressions repeat the verbal message.

Nonverbal cues also *regulate* our participation in conversation. In most informal meetings, it's not appropriate or necessary to signal your desire to speak by raising your hand. Yet somehow you're able to signal to others when you'd like to speak and when you'd rather not. You use eye contact, raised eyebrows, an open mouth, an audible intake of breath, a change in posture or seating position, or a single raised index finger to signal that you would like to make a point. If your colleagues don't see these signals, especially the eye contact, they may assume you're not interested in engaging in conversation.[9]

Finally, we use nonverbal behavior to *accent* or reinforce a verbal message. "We simply must do something about this problem," bellows the mayor, "or else we will all bear the blame." When the mayor says the word *must*, she pounds the podium and increases her volume for emphasis. When she says "all bear the blame," she uses a circling gesture with her arms to convey a shared responsibility among those in the room. These vocalizations and gestures serve to accent or add intensity to the verbal message.

The Nature of Nonverbal Communication

While the benefits of studying and improving one's facility with nonverbal communication are clear, deciphering unspoken messages is a tricky activity. Dictionaries help us interpret words, but no handy reference book exists to help decode nonverbal cues. Below are some of the challenges inherent in the interpretation of nonverbal communication.

When Donald Trump says, "You're fired" to a contestant on TV's *The Apprentice*, his words are accented by his signature hand gesture, often called "the cobra." How do you use nonverbal cues to accent or reinforce your verbal messages?

The Culture-Bound Nature of Nonverbal Communication

Some evidence suggests that humans from every culture smile when they are happy and frown when they are unhappy.[10] They also all tend to raise or flash their eyebrows when meeting or greeting others, and young children in many cultures wave to signal they want their parents, raise their arms to be picked up, and suck their thumbs for comfort. This evidence suggests that there is some underlying commonality in human emotion. Yet each culture tends to develop unique rules for displaying and interpreting the expression of emotion.[11]

It's important to realize that nonverbal behavior is culture bound. No common cross-cultural dictionary of nonverbal meaning exists. You will make critical errors in communicating nonverbally, as well as in attempting to interpret the nonverbal behavior of others, if you don't situate nonverbal actions within a cultural context. As intercultural communication scholars Richard Porter and Larry Samovar explain, one culture's friendly or polite action may be another culture's obscene gesture.[12] For example, during his second inaugural parade, President George W. Bush displayed the two-finger, "hook 'em horns" gesture to salute members of the University of Texas marching band as they passed by his stand. According to the Associated Press, a Norwegian newspaper expressed outrage over the gesture, since it is considered an insult or a sign of the devil in Norse culture. In sign language used by and for deaf persons, the gesture translates into "bull _____." In Mediterranean countries, the gesture implies that a man is the victim of an unfaithful wife. In Russia, it is considered a symbol for newly rich, arrogant, and poorly educated Russians; in many European countries, it serves to ward off the "evil eye"; and in some African nations, it's used to put a hex or curse on another person.[13] Concerns about potential international gaffes led Southern Methodist University to publish a pocket-size guide for its students studying abroad. Tips include sticking out your tongue as a way of saying hello in Tibet; making certain to take your hands out of your pockets when talking with someone in Belgium; and avoiding touching someone's head in Indonesia, where such an action would be considered a serious insult.[14]

> ## Recap
> ### Why Focus on Nonverbal Communication?
> - Nonverbal communication is our primary means of communicating feelings and attitudes toward others.
> - Nonverbal messages are usually more believable than verbal messages.
> - Nonverbal communication is critical in the initiation, development, and termination of relationships.
> - Nonverbal messages function to substitute for, complement, contradict, repeat, regulate, and accent verbal messages.

The Rule-Governed Nature of Nonverbal Communication

You operate according to many rules in your nonverbal communication. You may be unaware that you function according to these rules, but when your rules are violated, you definitely know it. For example, have you ever been in a conversation with someone who seemed as though he or she couldn't talk to you without touching you? Maybe it's just a series of simple touches on the forearm or shoulder, but it's not what you expect in casual conversation. For some reason, the other person's rule about appropriate touch is likely to be different from yours. Or perhaps you've been annoyed when people talk at the movie theater, as if they were sitting at home in their own living rooms instead of out in public. Maybe you have a rule that says people lower their voices and whisper at movie theaters, if they must talk at all; other people may not conform to that same rule.

One of the most prolific nonverbal communication researchers is Judee Burgoon, who developed a fascinating model for how nonverbal communication functions, termed the **expectancy violations model**.[15] The model suggests that we develop expectations for appropriate nonverbal behavior in ourselves and others, based on our cultural backgrounds, personal experiences, and knowledge of those with whom we interact. When those expectations (or rules) are violated, we experience heightened arousal (we become more interested or engaged in what's happening), and the nature of our interpersonal relationship with the other person becomes a critical factor as we attempt to interpret and respond to the situation. Because the expectancy violations model was first developed with regard to personal space, let's consider an example that deals with this form of nonverbal communication.

One *Seinfeld* episode depicted a person nicknamed the "close talker," because he got too close for most people's comfort when he talked to them. Most people within a given culture adhere to a widely agreed-on rule or expectation as to appropriate conversational distances. But there are those people who don't seem to catch the cultural clue—those who get too close to our face in casual conversation. Burgoon's model says that we register such a nonverbal violation and react in order to adjust to the circumstances. If the violating person is what Burgoon terms a "rewarding" communicator, meaning that the person has high credibility, status, and attractiveness (physically or in personality), we may view the behavior as less of a rule violation and simply adjust our expectations. We may even reciprocate the behavior. However, if the violator is not a rewarding communicator, we will use reactive nonverbal behaviors in an effort to compensate for or correct the situation. So if an attractive, credible, and high-status person stands too close to you while talking, you may adapt to the situation and not think negatively of the person. If the person has less attractiveness, credibility, and status, you may back away from the person or move to the side so as to increase the conversational distance, break eye contact, and so forth.

Our tendency in a rules violation situation is to attempt to adapt or correct the violation by nonverbal means before resorting to verbal communication. You're more

expectancy violations model
A model that suggests that we develop rules or expectations for appropriate nonverbal behavior and react when those expectations are violated.

likely to back away from a close talker than to say to her or him, "Please back up; you're violating my personal space." We all violate nonverbal rules from time to time; it is at those moments when we become acutely aware that rules or expectations of appropriateness have a powerful influence on nonverbal communication.

The Ambiguous Nature of Nonverbal Communication

Most words are given meaning by people within a culture who speak the same language. But the exact meaning of a nonverbal message is known only to the person displaying it; the person may not intend for the behavior to have any meaning at all. Some people have difficulty expressing their emotions nonverbally. They may have frozen facial expressions or monotone voices. They may be teasing you, but their deadpan expressions lead you to believe that their negative comments are heartfelt. Often it's a challenge to draw meaningful conclusions about other people's behavior, even if we know them quite well. One strategy that helps us interpret others' nonverbal cues is called **perception checking**, a strategy we mentioned in Chapter 2 in our discussion of self-awareness. Observe in detail the nonverbal cues, make your own interpretation, and then do one of two things (or both): (1) Ask the people you're observing how they feel or what's going on and/or (2) run your interpretation by another observer, to get a second opinion or more input before you draw a conclusion. Remember our earlier warning about not assuming that your interpretation is necessarily the right one; perception checking can enhance the likelihood that your interpretation will be accurate.

The Continuous Nature of Nonverbal Communication

Words are discrete entities; they have a beginning and an end. You can point to the first word in this sentence and underline the last one. Our nonverbal behaviors are not as easily dissected. Like the sweep of a second hand on a watch, nonverbal behaviors are continuous. Imagine you're standing in the hallway after class, talking to a classmate. You both give eye contact as you talk and make facial expressions that coordinate with what you're saying. You stand a certain distance apart, move and change your posture as the conversation flows, add a hand gesture or two to emphasize what you're saying, and change your pitch, volume, and rate of speaking to further make yourself understood. Your classmate's cell phone rings; the person apologizes, looks down into his or her bookbag to fish out the phone, and makes eye contact with you once again, along with a facial expression of apology. The person then signals to you with a hand gesture, while talking into the phone, that she or he has to go, and you understand that your conversation is over. You wave goodbye, break eye contact, and go your separate ways, and your nonverbal behaviors go with you. In this simple example, the nonverbal cues are flying faster than the verbal ones, but they're essential in getting the message across. The sheer volume and continuous flow of nonverbal cues—not to mention complications such as culture and emotion—make accurate interpretation a challenge.

The Nonlinguistic Nature of Nonverbal Communication

Even though some writers in the 1960s and 70s tried to make readers think otherwise, there is no "language of the body." Julius Fast, author of the 1970 book *Body Language*, believed that nonverbal communication was a language with pattern and grammar, just like verbal communication.[16] He suggested that if you were savvy and observant enough, you could quickly and easily interpret certain nonverbal behaviors to mean certain things—in any case, at any time. For example, Fast contended that if a woman sat cross-legged and pumped her foot up and down while talking to a man, that was a clear-cut sign of her romantic interest in him. If someone didn't make eye contact, she or he was automatically dishonest and untrustworthy. If people crossed their arms in front of them, that indicated hostility.

perception checking
The skill of asking other observers or the person being observed whether your interpretation of his or her nonverbal behavior is accurate.

The problem with this approach is that it didn't take into account the complexities of individual, contextual, and cultural differences. Pumping the foot might be an indication of nervousness, not attraction. Some people are shy; others come from a culture in which making direct eye contact is considered rude. It's important to remember that nonverbal communication doesn't conform to the patterns of a language.

The Multichanneled Nature of Nonverbal Communication

Have you ever tried to watch two or more TV programs at once? Some television sets let you see as many as eight programs simultaneously so that you can keep up with three ball games, two soap operas, the latest news, and your favorite sitcom. Like programs on a multichannel TV, nonverbal cues register on our senses from a variety of sources simultaneously. Just as you can really pay close attention to only one program at a time on your multichannel television, you actually attend to only one nonverbal cue at a time, although you can switch your attention very rapidly. Before you try to interpret the meaning of a single nonverbal behavior, look for clusters of corroborating nonverbal cues, in conjunction with verbal behavior, to get the most complete picture possible.

Codes of Nonverbal Communication

Because human nonverbal behavior is so diverse and vast, the need arises for classifications. Many individuals have long been fascinated with nonverbal communication, but those who have made perhaps the greatest contributions to our understanding are Paul Ekman and Wallace Friesen, sometimes referred to as the "great classifiers" of nonverbal behavior.[17] The primary categories or codes of nonverbal information researchers have studied include appearance; body movement, gestures, and posture; eye contact; facial expressions; touch; voice; and use of the physical environment, space, and territory. Although we concentrate on these codes as they are exhibited in mainstream Western culture, you should recognize that these behaviors are evidenced differently in other cultures. We introduce and explain each code, then provide a few research findings to illustrate how we can apply knowledge of nonverbal communication to further our understanding of human behavior.

Recap

The Nature of Nonverbal Communication

- *Nonverbal Communication Is Culture Bound.* Nonverbal behaviors vary widely across cultural and co-cultural groups. Interpret nonverbal cues within a cultural context.
- *Nonverbal Communication Is Rule Governed.* We develop rules or expectations for appropriate nonverbal behavior in ourselves and others.
- *Nonverbal Communication Is Ambiguous.* Nonverbal behavior is difficult to interpret accurately because the meanings for different actions vary from person to person.
- *Nonverbal Communication Is Continuous.* Unlike the stop-start nature of verbal communication, nonverbal messages flow from one situation to the next.
- *Nonverbal Communication Is Nonlinguistic.* Nonverbal communication does not have the regularities of vocabulary, grammar, and pattern that language has.
- *Nonverbal Communication Is Multichanneled.* Nonverbal cues register on our senses from a variety of sources simultaneously, but we can actually attend to only one nonverbal cue at a time.

Appearance

Many cultures around the world place a high value on appearance—body size and shape, skin color and texture, hairstyle, and clothing. We realize that we're writing from an American perspective, but it seems as though Americans place an undue emphasis on looks. For example, our views of and preferences for government leaders, especially presidents, are affected by their height.[18] College students perceive physically attractive teachers to be more approachable and give them higher evaluation scores.[19] We put such pressure on ourselves and others to be physically attractive that our self-esteem may decline when we realize we cannot match up with some perceived "ideal."[20] Americans elevate onto a pedestal people who are perceived to be highly physically attractive, whether or not they actually deserve this kind of accolade. We also attach all sorts of desirable qualities to highly attractive people. Research shows that we tend to think physically attractive people are more credible, happy, popular, socially skilled, prosperous, employable, persuasive, honest, poised, strong, kind, outgoing, and sexually warm.[21]

Clothing functions primarily to keep us warm and within society's bounds of decency. Another important function is to convey a sense of one's culture. Clothing such as baseball caps, baggy pants, and distinctive T-shirts, as well as other appearance aspects, termed **artifacts** (jewelry, tattoos, piercings, makeup, cologne, eyeglasses, and so on), are displays of culture. This is particularly detectable when you travel abroad or entertain foreign visitors in your home country. The brightly colored gowns and matching headpieces worn by some African women, the beautiful saris (draped dresses) many Indian women wear, and veils over the faces of Muslim women are but a few examples of clothing that reveals one's culture.

Although we don't believe that "clothes make the man," clothing and artifacts do affect how we feel about ourselves and how we are perceived by others.[22] Studies have attempted to identify a "power" look. Advertisers are constantly giving us prescriptions for ways to be attractive and stylish, but the fact is that there is no formula for dressing for success.[23] Styles and expectations about appearances change. We have only to look at the clothing norms of the 1950s, 60s, and 70s to note how they are different from those of today. Other interesting applications of what we know about appearance include the proliferation of "casual Fridays" in the corporate world, the connection between black uniforms and aggression in sports, and the growing trend in public schools to require school uniforms.[24]

Body Movement, Gestures, and Posture

Have you ever traveled in a country where you couldn't speak the language? Or have you ever tried to have a conversation locally with a person who didn't speak English or who was deaf and didn't read lips? What do you do in these situations? Chances are, you risk looking extremely foolish by using overexaggerated gestures or slowly and deliberately shouting words the listener cannot understand. These responses are nonverbal attempts to compensate for a lack of verbal understanding. Even when we do speak the same language as others, we often use gestures to help us make our point.

Kinesics is a general term for human movements, gestures, and posture. Technically, movements of the face and eyes are included in this category, but because one's face and eyes can produce such a wealth of information, we discuss them as separate codes. Researchers have long recognized that our kinesics provide valuable information to others. Have you ever seen someone and said "I just really like the way he carries himself"? We know that a person can't literally carry himself or herself, but what we are referring to in this description is the person's posture, stance, and walk. Posture is greatly affected by self-esteem and emotional state, such that when you're feeling upbeat and good about yourself, you're likely to carry yourself more upright and possibly exhibit a "spring in your step." Conversely, if you're having a bad day, your posture might be more slumped over or stooped, because some days it's just hard to hold your head and shoulders up.

artifact
Clothing or another element of appearance (e.g., jewelry, tattoos, piercings, makeup, cologne).

kinesics
Human movement, gesture, and posture.

When your clothing functions as an artifact rather than simply a way to cover your body, it conveys some sense of your culture.

Gestures are also a subset of kinesics and, as we've said earlier in this chapter, they are culture bound, context bound, and rule governed. Nancy Armstrong and Melissa Wagner are the authors of a book entitled *Field Guide to Gestures*, in which they describe and interpret a wide variety of gestures, particularly as used in U.S. culture.[25] They organize gestures into such categories as Arrival and Departure, Approval and Disapproval, Mating, and Offensive and Profane. Among the gestures in the Arrival and Departure category are the Bow, the Blown Kiss, the Fist-Chest Pound, and the Live Long and Prosper gesture (which needs no interpretation for *Star Trek* fans).

Various scholars and researchers have proposed models that we can use to analyze and code kinesics, just as we do spoken or written language.[26] In one of their most comprehensive contributions to nonverbal research, Ekman and Friesen classified movement and gestures according to their function. They identified five kinesic categories: emblems, illustrators, affect displays, regulators, and adaptors.[27]

Emblems Nonverbal cues that have specific, widely understood meanings in a given culture and may actually substitute for a word or phrase are called **emblems**. When you're busy typing a report that is due tomorrow and your roommate barges in to talk about weekend plans, you turn from your computer and hold up an open palm to indicate your desire for uninterrupted quiet. A librarian who wants people to stop talking in the stacks puts an index finger up to pursed lips. But remember that emblems emerge or are negotiated within cultures. A seemingly universal gesture can be used in a culturally specific way to mean something different from what you expect. Scholar Roger Axtell (1998), in his book *Gestures: Do's and Taboos of Body Language around the World*, explores kinesic behaviors across cultures.[28] One of Axtell's examples is the "come here" gesture, such as the signal a customer might make to a server in a restaurant. In the United States, a diner wanting service is likely to raise an arm slightly and curl the index finger in and out, as a signal for the server to come to the table. This simple "come here" gesture seems as though it would be universal, right? But in Indonesia and Australia, such a gesture is reserved for beckoning prostitutes! The "come here" gesture in many European and Latin American countries involves extending an arm with the hand out, palm down, and then making a scratching motion (curling the fingers back repeatedly), which people in the United States don't tend to do. This simple example teaches us that it's unwise to assume that nonverbal cues readily used by members of our own culture will be perceived as emblems by members of other cultures.

Illustrators We frequently accompany a verbal message with nonverbal **illustrators** that either contradict, accent, or complement the message.[29] Yawning while proclaiming that you're not tired is an example of a nonverbal illustrator that contradicts the ver-

---

emblem
A nonverbal cue that has a specific, generally understood meaning in a given culture and may substitute for a word or phrase.

illustrator
A nonverbal behavior that accompanies a verbal message and either complements, contradicts, or accents it.

bal message. Slamming a book closed while announcing "I don't want to read this any more" is a nonverbal accent to a verbal message. Frequent complementary illustrators are used when one person gives another directions to a location. You may even use them when you talk on the phone, although probably not as many as you use in face-to-face conversation.[30]

Affect Displays Nonverbal cues that communicate emotion are called **affect displays**. As early as 1872, when Charles Darwin systematically studied the expression of emotion in both humans and animals, scientists realized that nonverbal cues are the primary ways humans communicate emotion.[31] Facial expressions, posture, and gestures reveal our emotions.[32] Your face tends to express which *kind* of emotion you are feeling, while your body reveals the intensity or how *much* of the emotion you are feeling. If you're happy, for example, your face may telegraph your joy to others. The movement of your hands, the openness of your posture, and the speed with which you move tell others just how happy you are. Likewise, if you're depressed, your face reveals your sadness or dejection, unless you're very practiced at masking your emotions. Your slumped shoulders and lowered head indicate the intensity of your despair.

Regulators **Regulators** control the interaction or flow of communication between people. When we're eager to respond to a message, we're likely to make eye contact, raise our eyebrows, open our mouth, take in a breath, and lean forward slightly. When we do not want to be part of the conversation, we do the opposite: We tend to avert our eyes, close our mouth, cross our arms, and lean back in our seats or away from the verbal action.

Adaptors As teachers, we find it interesting to watch a group of students take an exam. Students who are nervous about the exam or who have general test anxiety exhibit their nervousness in many different ways. They shift frequently in their seats, tap their pencils or pens on the desktop (often unconsciously), or run their hands through their hair over and over again. Then there's the thigh shaker. Some students can make their legs quiver up and down at a high speed, and they don't usually realize they're doing it. All of these behaviors are examples of **adaptors**—nonverbal behaviors that help us to satisfy a personal need or adapt to the immediate situation.

What are some of the more interesting applications of the research on kinesics? Consider flirting. Even if you're married or in some other form of committed relationship, you probably find it interesting to think about how people flirt or show attraction and interest in one another. Research has explored verbal and nonverbal indications of attraction.[33] One study found 52 gestures and nonverbal behaviors that women use to signal their interest in men. Among the top nonverbal flirting cues were smiling, surveying a crowded room with the eyes, and moving closer to the object of one's affection.[34] However, other studies have found that men tend to view flirting as more sexual than women do, and men often misinterpret women's friendly behaviors as signs of sexual attraction and interest.[35] Studies have found that the likelihood for this kind of misinterpretation greatly increases as alcohol consumption increases.[36]

Another body of research along these lines has examined **quasi-courtship behavior**, those nonverbal actions we consciously and unconsciously exhibit when we are attracted to someone.[37] The first stage of quasi-courtship behavior is *courtship readiness*. When we are attracted to someone, we may alter our normal pattern of eye contact, suck in our stomach, tense our muscles, and stand up straight. The second stage includes *preening* behaviors, such as combing our hair, applying makeup, straightening our tie, pulling up our socks, and double-checking our appearance in the mirror. Research shows that women tend to preen more than men.[38] In stage three, we demonstrate *positional cues*, using our posture and body orientation to make sure we are seen and noticed by another person, as well as to position ourselves to prevent invasion by a third party. We intensify these cues in the fourth stage, termed *appeals to invitation*,

affect display
A nonverbal behavior that communicates emotions.

regulator
A nonverbal behavior that helps to control the interaction or level of communication between people.

adaptor
A nonverbal behavior that helps satisfy a personal need and allows a person to adapt or respond to the immediate situation.

quasi-courtship behavior
Nonverbal behaviors exhibited both consciously and unconsciously when we are attracted to someone.

Communication and Ethics

Lie Detectors

We have good information now as to how most people behave when they are being untruthful. Unless we have ice in our veins, most of us register some kind of higher activation in our bodies when we attempt to deceive, such as increased heart rate and elevated skin temperature. Lie detector machines track just such physiological changes as indications of deception.[39] Other instruments track patterns in the voice, such as vocal emphasis and rising intonation. Research has shown that most people's voices have a tendency to get higher in pitch when they try to deceive.[40] What lie detector professionals look for is a change in a person's normal behavior, any change from the baseline that is typically taken at the beginning of a lie detector session.

Engagement Questions

1. Do you think that modern lie detectors are sophisticated enough that the results of lie detector tests should be allowed as evidence in court trials?
2. Is is ethical to "wire up" a suspect in order to track bodily and vocal changes that might indicate deception?
3. Do you believe that someone can actually "beat" a lie detector?

---

using close proximity, exposed skin, open body positions, and direct eye contact to signal our availability and interest.

Eye Contact

Do you agree that the eyes are the "windows to the soul"? What can people tell about you by looking into your eyes? Are you comfortable making eye contact with most people or only with people you know well? Eye contact is extremely important in U.S. culture, as well as in many other cultures around the world. Americans, in particular, make all kinds of judgments about others—particularly about their trustworthiness and sincerity—on the basis of whether they make or avoid eye contact.[41] It's an interesting exercise to inventory your own eye behavior, thinking about when you're apt to look at someone and when you're apt to avert your gaze.

You are most likely to look at a conversational partner when you are physically distant from her or him, are discussing impersonal topics, have nothing else to look at,

Recap

Categories of Movements and Gestures

Category	Definition	Example
Emblems	Behaviors that have specific, generally understood meanings	Forefinger and middle finger raised to make the peace sign
Illustrators	Cues that accompany verbal messages and provide meaning	A speaker pounding on a podium to emphasize a point
Affect Displays	Expressions of emotion	Hugging to express love
Regulators	Cues that control and manage the flow of communication	Making eye contact when you wish to speak
Adaptors	Behaviors that help you adjust to your environment	Chewing your fingernails because you're nervous

are interested in your partner's reactions, are romantically interested in your partner, wish to dominate or influence your partner, come from a culture that emphasizes visual contact in interaction, are an extrovert, are listening rather than talking, or are female. You are less likely to look at your partner when you are physically close; are discussing intimate topics; have other objects, people, or backgrounds to look at; are not interested in your partner's reactions; are talking rather than listening; are not interested in or dislike your partner; come from a culture that does not value visual contact during interaction; are an introvert; are embarrassed, ashamed, sorrowful, sad, submissive, or trying to hide something; or are male.[42]

Research shows that eye contact plays a significant role in judgments of a public speaker's credibility.[43] In the first televised presidential debate, John F. Kennedy appeared comfortable and confident as he made eye contact with television cameras. It seemed as though he was making eye contact directly with the American public. In contrast, Richard Nixon darted his eyes nervously from side to side at times and generally made less eye contact with the camera and the viewing audience. This created a perception that Nixon was shifty, untrustworthy, and lacking credibility. American public speaking teachers emphasize eye contact as a key nonverbal element of speech delivery.

Studies on eye behavior continue to contribute to our understanding of deception and how people behave when they lie or mislead others.[44] Eye behaviors most often associated with deception include rapid blinking, diminished eye contact, and rapid eye movement.[45]

Facial Expressions

Actor/comedian Steve Carell has a very expressive face. Researchers suggest that the human face is capable of producing 250,000 different facial expressions.[46] Steve Carell can probably make all of them.

The face is the exhibit gallery for our emotional displays.[47] Suppose you buy an expensive new gadget and show it to your romantic partner or a friend. Or as an interviewer reads your resumé you sit in silence across the desk. In both of these situations, you scan the other person's face, eagerly awaiting some reaction. To interpret someone's facial expressions accurately, you need to focus on what the other person may be thinking or feeling. It helps if you know the person well, can see her or his whole face, have plenty of time to observe, and understand the situation that prompted the reaction.[48]

How accurately do we interpret emotions expressed on the face? Researchers who have attempted to measure subjects' skill in identifying the emotional expressions of others have found it a tricky business. According to Ekman and Friesen, the human face universally exhibits six primary emotions: happiness, sadness, surprise, fear, anger, and disgust or contempt. But these researchers note that, even though our faces provide a great deal of information about emotions, we quickly learn to control our facial expressions.[49] One fascinating study examined children's facial expressions when they received either wonderful, new toys or broken, disappointing toys.[50] When they received the disappointing toys, the children showed a flash of disappointment on their faces, but then very quickly they masked their disappointment and changed their facial expressions to reveal a more positive, socially appropriate reaction. Even very young children learn to control the way an emotion registers on their face. Another study found that abused children, sensitive to violence at home, are hypersensitive to anger in facial expressions. They are more likely to interpret sad or fearful facial expressions as angry.[51]

As adults, we come to realize that there are times when it is inappropriate and unwise to reveal our emotions fully, such as crying in front of superiors when we've been passed over for promotion or becoming visibly angry when a project doesn't come our way. But there are times when this learned masking of emotion—the development of a "poker face"—can endanger your relationships. Consider aloof, distant parents who can't separate themselves from their work to enjoy the company of their own children, or romantic partners who complain that they can't tell how their partners feel about them because emotional displays have been squelched. The best approach is a balance of control and spontaneity. You want to stay real and human, to be able to reveal to others what you feel, but there are times when doing so can be inappropriate or damaging.

Touch

Touch is the most powerful form of nonverbal communication; it is also the most misunderstood and carries the potential for the most problems if ill used. Consider some moments involving accidental touch. Standing elbow to elbow in an elevator or sitting next to someone in a crowded airplane, you may find yourself in physical contact with total strangers. As you stiffen your body and avert your eyes, a baffling sense of shame and discomfort floods over you. Why do we react this way to accidental touching? Normally, we touch to express affection and intimacy. When affection or intimacy is not our intended message, we instinctively react to modify the impression our touch has created.

Countless studies on touch, termed **haptics** in research, have shown that intimate human contact is vital to our personal development and well-being.[52] Infants and children need physical contact to confirm that they are valued and loved. Advocates of breast-feeding and infant massage suggest that these forms of intimate parent–child touch strengthen bonds.[53]

Think about your role models and the lessons you learned about touch while growing up. If you grew up in a two-parent family, did your parents display affection in front of you? If not, you may have grown up believing that affectionate touching should not be done in front of others. As an adult, you may be uncomfortable with public displays of affection. If you grew up with parents or family members who were affectionate with each other and their children, then, as an adult, your **touch ethic**—what you consider appropriate touching—is influenced by that experience.[54] We don't mean to insinuate that a touch ethic that accepts public affection is somehow more psychologically healthy than one that relegates touching to private moments. But what if you date or partner with someone whose experiences while growing up led to a very different touch ethic than yours? You may be headed for some conflict, but ideally some compromise as well.

haptics
The study of human touch.

touch ethic
A person's own guidelines or standards as to appropriate and inappropriate touch.

Communication and Diversity

Cultural Meanings of Silence

In his essay "Cultural Uses and Interpretations of Silence," communication scholar Charles Braithwaite explores the functions of silence "beyond one's own speech community" in an effort to discover cross-cultural generalizations.[55] He examined descriptions of the use of silence within many cultural groups and found two common themes:

- When people don't know each other very well or circumstances between them create a degree of uncertainty, silence may increase, but it is seen as expected and appropriate. This tendency emerged within cultural groups as diverse as some American Indian tribes, Japanese Americans in Hawaii, Americans in rural Appalachia, and native Japanese.
- Recognized status differences are associated with silence. When a difference in power level or status is detected, lower-status persons are expected to be silent and monitor when it is appropriate to engage in conversation. This tendency was particularly distinct within parent–child relationships, evidenced in such diverse peoples as the Anang of Southwestern Nigeria, the Wolof of Senegal, some urban African American women, the residents of the LaHave Islands (off the coast of Nova Scotia), some Indian tribes, and some American blue-collar workers.

Engagement Questions

1. How do members of your cultural group use silence to communicate? Is silence among those in your social circles perceived as awkward, or is it a sign of the level of comfort people feel with each other?

2. In your experience, what is the relationship between silence and status? Are people of lower social status more likely to use silence as a nonverbal cue than people of higher status?

When speaking publicly, the pitch, rate, and volume at which you speak tell your audience far more than your speech topic. How can you effectively use your voice to make your messages as clear and precise as possible?

The amount of touch we need, initiate, tolerate, and receive depends on many factors. As we've indicated, the amount and kind of touching you receive in your family is the biggest influence. Your cultural background has a significant effect as well. Certain cultures are high-contact—meaning that touching is quite commonplace—such as some European and Middle Eastern cultures in which men kiss each other on the cheek as a greeting. Other cultures are low-contact, like some Asian cultures in which demonstrations of affection are rare and considered inappropriate.[56]

Research on haptics has explored such topics as the role of touch in receiving sexual consent and how touch may be involved in behavior deemed sexually harassing.[57] Other research continues to focus on gender differences and touch. For years, studies showed that women touched members of both sexes more often and received more touches than men, leading to the conclusion that touch was more appropriate behavior for females than for males. Recent studies suggest that sex differences in the frequency of touch have diminished, but men and women still tend to differ in the meanings they assign to touch.[58]

The Voice

"We have nothing to fear but fear itself."
"Ask not what your country can do for you—ask what you can do for your country."
"I have a dream . . . I have a dream today."
"I am not a crook."
"Mr. Gorbachev, tear down this wall."

If you read these statements and recognize them as having been made by American leaders, you are likely to read them using the same pauses and changes in pitch, volume, and emphasis as did the famous speaker. John F. Kennedy greatly emphasized the word *not*, as in "Ask NOT what your country. . . ." Martin Luther King Jr. used rising pitch and increased volume as he uttered the word *dream* over and over again in his speech. These leaders learned to use the tremendous capacity and versatility of the voice to create memorable moments, even if those moments occurred in unpleasant circumstances.

Like your face, your voice is a major vehicle for communicating your thoughts and emotions. The pitch, rate, and volume at which you speak and your use of silence—elements termed **paralanguage** or **vocalics**—all provide important clues. Imagine that your spouse, romantic partner, or best friend modeled a new outfit and asked you what you think. If you really hated the person's new outfit, would you say enthusiastically,

paralanguage (vocalics)
Nonverbal aspects of voice (e.g., pitch, rate, volume, use of silence).

"That looks GREAT!"—which could be either an untruth designed to prevent hurt feelings or an expression of sarcasm? Or would you say, "That looks nice" in a half-hearted way? Or would you go into some long, careful explanation of why you thought the person should change clothes? Your ability to convey these different reactions is accomplished by the human voice.

The voice reveals our thoughts, emotions, and the nature of our relationships with others, but it also provides information about our self-confidence and knowledge and influences how we are perceived by others.[59] Most of us would conclude, as has research, that a speaker who mumbles, speaks very slowly and softly, continually mispronounces words, and uses "uh" and "um" is less credible and persuasive than one who speaks clearly, rapidly, fluently, and with appropriate volume.[60]

In addition to providing information about thoughts, emotions, self-confidence, and knowledge, vocal cues serve a regulatory function in conversation, signaling when we want to talk and when we don't.[61] When we're finished talking, we tend to lower the volume and pitch of our final words. When we want to talk, we may start by interjecting sounds such as "I . . . I . . . I . . ." or "Ah . . . um . . ." to interrupt the speaker and grab the verbal ball. We also may use more cues like "Sure," "I understand," "Uh-huh," or "Okay" to signal that we understand another's message and now we want to talk or end the conversation. These vocalizations, termed **back-channel cues**, are particularly useful in telephone conversations when no other nonverbal cues can help signal that we would like to get off the phone.

Sometimes it's not what we say or even how we say it that communicates our feelings. Pausing and being silent communicate volumes.[62] You may be at a loss for words or need time to think about what you want to contribute to a conversation, so pausing or being silent may be better than fumbling about for the right way to express yourself. When someone tells a lie, he or she may need a few moments to think up what to say. Nonverbal researchers have studied **response latency**, or how long it takes someone to formulate a response to a statement or question in conversation, to better understand vocal cues that may indicate deception.[63] You may be silent because you want to distance yourself from those around you or indicate that you don't want to engage in conversation. Silence can be a sign of respect, but it can also be an indication of anger (as when you give someone "the silent treatment") or discomfort (as in "an awkward silence"). At other times, you may feel so comfortable with someone that words aren't necessary; psychologist Sidney Baker calls these moments "positive silence."[64]

Physical Environment, Space, and Territory

Close your eyes and picture your bedroom as it is right now—whether it's a dorm room that you share with someone, the room you've lived in for many years in your parents' house, or a bedroom shared with a spouse or partner. Try to get a clear, detailed mental image of how that room looks right now. Then think about this: If one of your professors were to walk into your bedroom right now, what would she or he think about you? What impressions about you would he or she form, given the physical setup of that room? Does the room reveal your need for privacy? Are there hints as to who owns the space? Is the closet door in that room open or closed?

These questions all have to do with your interaction with the physical environment and the space around you. You may be unused to looking at the environment as a form of nonverbal communication, but the mini-world you create for yourself reveals a good deal about you. Also, your preferred amount of space, the level of ownership you attach to that space, and your behavior as you delineate and protect that space are fascinating nonverbal elements that researchers continue to study.[65]

back-channel cue
A vocal cue that signals when we want to talk and when we don't.

response latency
The amount of time it takes someone to formulate a response to a statement or question in conversation.

The Physical Environment
What's so great about a corner office with wall-to-wall windows? It's one of many indications in U.S. culture of high status. In a working world increasingly structured into cubicles, an employee's desk location serves as a symbol of importance.[66] As one scholar put it, "People cannot be understood outside of their environmental context."[67] In Chapter 3, we discussed several principles governing the use

of verbal language, one being that language is context bound—people derive the meaning of words in context. Likewise, nonverbal actions are only meaningfully interpreted when context is taken into account.[68] The environment is important to the study of nonverbal behavior in two ways: (1) The choices you make about the environment in which you live and operate reveal a good deal about who you are, and (2) your nonverbal behavior is altered by the various environments in which you communicate.

First, the physical environments in which we function can be seen as extensions of our personalities.[69] You may not be able to manipulate all elements of your environment, like the physical limitations of room size, but to whatever extent you are allowed, you will put your "signature" on your physical environs. Humans like to structure and adorn the settings in which they work, study, and reside to make them unique and personal. Rarely will you find an office, even a cubicle, that contains absolutely no personal artifacts.

Second, your behavior and perceptions are altered because of the physical environments in which you find yourself.[70] Your body may be more rigid, gestures more restrained, clothing more formal, and speech limited and whispered when you're in a church. (Obviously, this depends on the church.) In contrast, at a concert by a favorite musician, you move freely, wear comfortable clothing, and scream and applaud wildly.

The knowledge that humans react according to their interface with a physical environment has been put to some interesting uses. For example, in retail environments, colors that match shoppers' expectations have been found to enhance sales.[71] You probably wouldn't expect splashes of bright red, blue, and yellow or, conversely, dark, earthy tones in a Victoria's Secret lingerie shop; most of these stores use pastels or cool colors in their decor to help create a feminine atmosphere. You probably wouldn't expect pink walls and fixtures in a sporting goods store; if you did see such decor, it would likely defy your expectations, making you think that something was really odd about the place and discouraging you from spending your money there. The next time you're shopping, pay attention to the colors present in your favorite stores, since they are a form of nonverbal communication related to the environment.

Space Imagine that you are sitting alone at a long, rectangular table in your campus library. As you sit dutifully with your head in a textbook, you are startled when a complete stranger sits directly across from you at the table. Since there are several empty chairs at the other end of the table, you may feel uncomfortable that this unknown individual has invaded *your* area.

Every culture has well-established ways of regulating spatial relations. Normally we don't think much about the rules or norms we follow regarding space until those rules are violated. Violations can be alarming, possibly even threatening. How physically close we are willing to get to others relates to how well we know them, to considerations of power and status, and to our cultural background.

One of the pioneers in helping us understand personal space was Edward T. Hall. In his study of **proxemics**, the distances that people allow between themselves and objects or other people, Hall identified four spatial zones that we unconsciously define for ourselves, as shown in Figure 4.2.[72] Two people who are between 0 and 1½ feet apart are occupying an *intimate space*, in which the most personal communication occurs. This space is open only to those with whom we are well acquainted, unless we're forced to stand in an elevator or some other crowded space.

The second zone, ranging from 1½ to 4 feet from another person, is called *personal space*. Most of our conversations with family and friends occur in this zone. If someone we don't know well enters this space on purpose, we may feel uncomfortable. Zone three, *social space*, ranges from 4 to 12 feet from another person. Most formal group interactions, as well as many of our professional relationships, take place in this zone. *Public space*, the fourth zone, begins at 12 feet from another person. Interpersonal communication does not usually occur in this zone; many presentational speakers position themselves at least 12 feet away from their audiences.

The specific space that you and others choose depends on several variables, most specifically your cultural background.[73] But the more you like people, the closer you

proxemics
The study of how close or far away from people and objects we position ourselves.

Figure 4.2
Edward T. Hall's Four Zones of Space

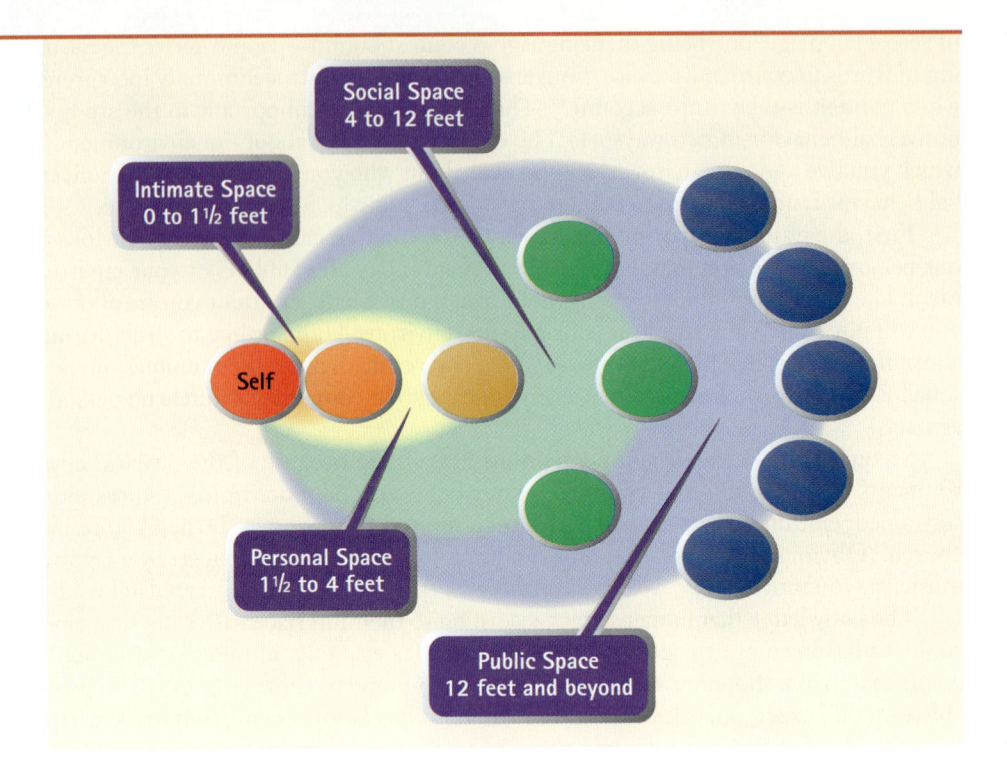

- Intimate Space: 0 to 1½ feet
- Personal Space: 1½ to 4 feet
- Social Space: 4 to 12 feet
- Public Space: 12 feet and beyond

will stand to them. Higher-status and larger persons are afforded more space than lower-status and smaller persons.[74] We also tend to stand closer to others in a large room than we do in a small room. In general, women tend to stand closer to others than men do.[75]

Territory The study of how people use space and objects to communicate occupancy or ownership of space is termed **territoriality**.[76] You assumed ownership of that table in the library and the right to determine who sat with you. You may have reacted negatively not only because your sense of personal space was invaded, but also because the intrusive stranger broke a cultural rule governing territoriality.

You announce your ownership of space with **territorial markers**—things and actions that signify an area has been claimed. When you arrive at class, for example, you may put your book bag on a chair while you get up and go out into the hall to make a call on your cell. That book bag signifies temporary ownership of your seat. If you returned to find that someone had moved your stuff and was sitting in your seat, you would probably become indignant. The most common form of territorial marker is a lock. We lock our doors and windows, cars, offices, briefcases, televisions (using V-chips), and computers so as to keep out intruders.

territoriality
The study of how humans use space and objects to communicate occupancy or ownership of space.

territorial marker
A thing or action that signifies an area has been claimed.

Recap
Edward T. Hall's Classification of Spatial Zones

Category	Definition	Distance Between Individuals
Zone One	Intimate Space	0–1½ feet
Zone Two	Personal Space	1½–4 feet
Zone Three	Social Space	4–12 feet
Zone Four	Public Space	12 feet and beyond

Recap

Codes of Nonverbal Communication

Appearance	Influences perceptions of credibility and attractiveness
Body Movement, Gestures, and Posture	Communicate information, status, warmth, credibility, interest in others, attitudes, and liking
Eye Contact	Conveys trustworthiness, sincerity, honesty, and interest
Facial Expressions	Reveal thoughts and express emotions and attitudes
Touch	Communicates intimacy, affection, and rejection
Voice	Communicates emotion and clarifies the meaning of messages through pitch, rate, and volume
Environment	Communicates information about the person who functions in that environment; provides context that alters behavior
Space	Provides information about status, power, and intimacy
Territory	Provides cues as to use, ownership, and occupancy of space

We also use markers to indicate where our space stops and someone else's starts. "Good fences make good neighbors," wrote the poet Robert Frost. When someone sits too close, we may try to erect a physical barrier, such as a stack of books or a napkin holder, or we might use our body as a shield by turning away. If we can't erect a physical barrier, we may erect a symbolic barrier to convey ownership, through the use of such things as partitions, objects, lighting, or elevation.[77] If an intruder doesn't get the hint that "this land is our land," we may ultimately resort to words to announce that the space is occupied.

While we traditionally think of space as a physical dimension, with increased accessibility and use of technology that links us with cyberspace we have recently begun to think of space differently.[78] What if someone hacked into your e-mail account and read your messages? You'd probably be very upset and view this as a territorial violation of your connections with other people in cyberspace. Most of us are highly territorial about our computer-mediated communication, as well as text messages on our cell phones or PDAs. If someone were to conduct a "phone dump" on our cell phone, allowing him or her to listen to our voice-mail messages, view the numbers we had called or texted, and see who had called or texted us, most of us would see such an action as a serious territorial violation.

How to Interpret Nonverbal Cues More Accurately

How do we make sense out of all the nonverbal cues we receive from others? Time and patience improve your receiving ability. If you earnestly want to accurately interpret and sensitively respond to someone's nonverbal communication, you must be willing to spend time and effort to develop this skill. You have already learned a good deal about nonverbal communication from reading this chapter, studying this topic in class, and living as many years as you have lived. But enhancing your interpretive skills requires, first, an awareness of the importance of nonverbal elements in the communication process. Many people make interpretive mistakes because they overemphasize the words people say. Verbal communication is important, but remember that the greater portion of someone's total message is conveyed nonverbally. A second requirement is the willingness and emotional maturity to make your own behavior secondary to that of someone else. In other words, if you're so wrapped up in yourself that you can only think about and deal with how *you're* feeling, what *you're* thinking, and what *you* want at a given moment, you can't possibly hope to take in others' nonverbal cues, interpret them accurately, and respond appropriately. As we discussed in Chapter 2, an awareness of oneself as a communicator expands with each interaction.

It's also important to remember to take into account the cultural backgrounds of those with whom you communicate. Be careful not to automatically attach your own cultural frame of reference when you decipher nonverbal cues. As we've stated, the context within which nonverbal cues are communicated plays an important role. It's wise to be aware of your surroundings and other situational factors when interpreting the meaning of nonverbal actions. Be prepared to fail. We all struggle to make sense of others' actions; no one has this skill down pat. Use your interpretive failures to learn lessons you can apply to the next encounter.

Beyond these suggestions, we recommend that you keep in mind a three-part framework developed by Albert Mehrabian to help you improve your nonverbal interpretive skills. Mehrabian found that we synthesize and interpret nonverbal cues along three primary dimensions: immediacy, arousal, and dominance.[79]

Immediacy

Why do we like some people and dislike others? Sometimes we can't put a finger on the precise reason. Mehrabian contends that **immediacy**—nonverbal behavior that communicates liking and engenders feelings of pleasure—is a probable explanation. The principle underlying immediacy is simple: We like and respond positively to people who tend to display immediacy cues and avoid or respond negatively to those who don't. Among the immediacy cues that show liking and interest are the following:[80]

- Proximity: close, forward lean
- Body orientation: face-to-face or side-by-side position
- Eye contact: eye contact and mutual eye contact
- Facial expression: smiling
- Gestures: head nods, movement
- Posture: open and relaxed, arms oriented toward others
- Touch: culture- and context-appropriate touch
- Voice: higher pitch, upward pitch

So how do you apply this information to help you improve your nonverbal receiving skills? Let's say that you go to a party and become attracted to someone there. You're introduced to the person and engage in a get-to-know-you kind of conversation. Your best bet is to attend to the person's nonverbal cues to determine if the person likes you. Although you can't know for sure that someone's nonverbal behavior translates into liking, immediacy cues can provide some information. Watch for a direct body orientation, as opposed to turning away from you and orienting toward the rest of the room. Watch for eye contact, smiling and other pleasant facial expressions, a rising intonation in the voice, and a forward lean toward you, rather than a backward lean, which can signal disinterest.

Arousal

When the term *arousal* is used in nonverbal research, it doesn't necessarily mean sexual arousal. According to nonverbal scholar Peter Andersen, the term relates to "the degree to which a person is stimulated or activated."[81] Arousal prepares the body for action, with such physiological indications as increased heart rate, blood pressure, and brain temperature. Arousal, in this sense, can occur when you drive fast or experience athletic exhilaration. Externally, the face, voice, and movement are primary indicators of arousal. If you detect **arousal** cues in someone, such as increased eye contact, closer conversational distances, increased touch, animated vocalics, more direct body orien-

---

immediacy
Nonverbal behaviors such as eye contact, forward lean, touch, and open body orientation that communicate feelings of liking, pleasure, and closeness.

arousal
Nonverbal behaviors such as vocal expression, facial expressions, and gestures that communicate feelings of interest and excitement.

tation (whether you are facing each other directly or not), and more smiling and active facial expressions, you can conclude with some degree of certainty that the other person is responsive to and interested in you or what you have to say. If the person acts passive or bored, as evidenced by few (or no) arousal cues, you can safely conclude that he or she is uninterested.

The next time you're at a party, become a people watcher for a moment. Check out which people look interested in the people they're talking to and which ones look bored or like they'd rather be somewhere else, anywhere else. You can tell how people feel about each other—not with absolute accuracy, but with a high degree of certainty—just by looking for things like body orientation, synchronized movement (meaning that when one shifts in position, the other shifts, as in a rhythmic response), smiling, laughter, and other arousal cues.[82]

Dominance

The third dimension of Mehrabian's framework communicates the balance of power in a relationship. **Dominance** cues communicate status, position, and importance. When interacting with a person of lower status, a higher-status person tends to have a relaxed body posture, less direct body orientation to the lower-status person, a downward head tilt, and less smiling, head nodding, and facial animation.[83] When you talk to professors, they may lean back in the chair, put their feet on the desk, and fold their hands behind their head during the conversation. But unless your professors are colleagues or friends, you will maintain a relatively formal posture during your interaction in their offices.

The use of space is another dominance cue. High-status individuals usually have more space around them; they have bigger offices and more "barriers" (human and nonhuman) protecting them. A receptionist in an office is usually easily accessible, but to reach the CEO of the company you probably have to navigate through several corridors and past several secretaries and administrative assistants who are "guarding" the door.

Other power cues are communicated by clothing, furniture, and locations. You may wear jeans and a T-shirt to class; the president of the university probably wears a business suit. You study at a table in the library; the college dean has a large private desk. Your dorm may be surrounded by other dorms; the president's residence may be a large house surrounded by a lush, landscaped garden in a prestigious neighborhood. You struggle to find a parking place within a half a globe of your classroom buildings;

Recap

Dimensions for Interpreting Nonverbal Behavior

Dimension	Definition	Examples
Immediacy	Cues that communicate liking, pleasure, and closeness	Eye contact, touch, forward lean, direct body orientation, physical closeness, smiling
Arousal	Cues that communicate active interest and excitement	Eye contact, varied vocal cues, increased touch, animated facial expressions, direct body orientation, movement, physical closeness
Dominance	Cues that communicate status and control	Larger and protected space, eye contact, initiated touch, relaxed posture, status symbols

dominance
Nonverbal behaviors such as relaxed posture, greater personal space, and protected personal space that communicate power, status, and control.

high-ranking campus administrators usually have reserved parking spots (sometimes with their names on them).

When you attempt to interpret someone's nonverbal communication, realize that there is a good deal of room for error. Humans are complex, and they don't always send clear signals. But the more you learn about nonverbal communication and the more you become aware of your own communication and the communication of others, the greater your chances of accurately perceiving and interpreting someone's nonverbal message.

PRINCIPLES FOR A LIFETIME
Enhancing Your Skills

3. Nonverbal

Principle Three: Effectively use and interpret nonverbal messages.
- Realize the importance of physical appearance and attractiveness in U.S. culture.
- Use culturally appropriate body movement, including posture and gestures, to convey messages.
- Work on making appropriate eye contact with others, given that eye contact is the key nonverbal behavior linked with credibility and trustworthiness.
- Become more aware of your facial expressions and the facial expressions of others, since this nonverbal channel is a primary one for conveying emotions.
- Use touch appropriately, given the cultural context within which you communicate.
- Become more aware of the potential you have for vocal expression and of how others use their vocal capacities to communicate emotions and ideas.
- Survey yourself to become aware of your own rules regarding space and territoriality, so that you may better understand and enact proxemic nonverbal behaviors in your interactions with others.
- Recognize that body movement, eye contact, facial expressions, touch, vocal behaviors, and use of space and territory can all communicate liking, interest, and dominance.

Summary

Successful communicators effectively use and interpret nonverbal messages. Nonverbal communication is central to our ability to function competently in relationships, because we convey our feelings and attitudes and detect the emotional states of others primarily through nonverbal channels. In most cases when verbal and nonverbal messages contradict, we should believe the nonverbal because it tends to carry the truer meaning of the message. (Again, leave open the option that you may be wrong.) Nonverbal cues are important not only in the early stages of relationships, but also as we maintain and deepen and sometimes terminate those relationships. Nonverbal messages function with verbal messages, in that they can substitute for, complement, contradict, repeat, regulate, and accent our words.

Accurately interpreting nonverbal cues is a challenge because of the nature of nonverbal communication. First, nonverbal communication is culture bound, meaning that we must account for the cultural context within which behavior occurs before making an interpretation of that behavior. Second, nonverbal communication is rule governed, in that we form rules or expectations as to appropriate behavior. Third, nonverbal communication is ambiguous; the exact meanings of nonverbal messages are truly known only to the person displaying them. Fourth, nonverbal communication is continuous; it flows in a steady stream without a definite starting and stopping point. Fifth, unlike verbal communication, nonverbal communication is not a language with a set pattern and rules of usage. Its nonlinguistic nature makes for more complicated interpretation. Finally, nonverbal communication is multichanneled, meaning that cues register on our senses from a variety of sources simultaneously.

Nonverbal cues have been categorized into separate codes. Personal appearance is a powerful communicator, especially in U.S. culture, where people make all sorts of judgments based on someone's looks. Kinesics, which include body movement, posture, and gestures, communicate both content and relational information when we use them as emblems, illustrators, affect displays, regulators, and adaptors. Eye contact is an important code for conveying liking and regulating interaction. Facial expressions and vocal cues provide a wealth of information about our thoughts, emotions, and attitudes. Touch is the most powerful nonverbal cue; it communicates the level of intimacy in a relationship, as well as liking and status. Finally, the way we react to and manipulate environments, as well as our use of space and territory, communicates a variety of messages related to power and status.

It is a challenge to assess our own nonverbal communication and to read and interpret others' nonverbal messages, but a general framework of three dimensions developed by Mehrabian can assist us in the process. Immediacy cues provide information about liking; arousal cues tip others off as to our interest and level of engagement with them; and position, power, and status are often communicated through dominance cues. Humans are complex, so the interpretation of nonverbal cues is never simple. However, the more we learn about this form of behavior and become aware of our own and others' nonverbal communication, the more sensitively and effectively we will interact with others.

Assessing Your Knowledge

For Discussion and Review

Principle One: Be aware of your communication with yourself and others.

1. Why is it important to be aware of nonverbal messages (your own and others') when communicating with people?

Principle Two: Effectively use and interpret verbal messages.

2. How do nonverbal messages function with verbal messages in effective communication?

Principle Three: Effectively use and interpret nonverbal messages.

3. Explain how nonverbal cues such as eye contact, facial expressions, body movement, touch, the use of space, and vocal cues reveal our thoughts, emotions, and attitudes.

Principle Four: Listen and respond thoughtfully to others.

4. If you improve your powers of sensitivity and accuracy in receiving and interpreting the nonverbal cues of other people, how will this enhanced skill impact your listening ability?

Principle Five: Appropriately adapt messages to others.

5. Explain why it is important to adapt your nonverbal behavior to the situation, the cultural context, and other people in a social setting.

Multiple Choice

Choose the *best* answer to each of the following questions.

1. Trinity is really angry with her girlfriend, so she refuses to sit near her while they are watching television. To communicate her anger, Trinity is relying on
   a. eye contact.
   b. haptics.
   c. vocalics.
   d. proxemics.

2. During a shopping trip, Logan bought T-shirts with his favorite sports team's emblem on the front, a new pair of jeans, and a pair of sunglasses. Logan was shopping for
   a. adaptors.
   b. territorial markers.
   c. emblems.
   d. artifacts.

3. According to Albert Mehrabian, the most significant nonverbal source of emotional information is
   a. vocal cues.
   b. the face.
   c. personal space.
   d. emblems.

4. Current research into the way men and women use touch during interactions reveals that
   a. men tend to touch others more than women do.
   b. women tend to touch others more than men do.
   c. men and women tend to interpret touching behavior in similar ways.
   d. men and women tend to interpret touching behavior in different ways.

5. A person of high dominance, when talking to a person lower in status, will
   a. have a more formal posture.
   b. face the other person directly.
   c. smile less.
   d. have more facial animation.

6. When your nonverbal message contradicts your verbal message, other people will tend to
   a. believe the nonverbal message.
   b. believe the verbal message.
   c. believe both the nonverbal and the verbal message.
   d. believe neither the nonverbal nor the verbal message.

7. The study of body motion and nonverbal behaviors related to body position is called
   a. kinesics.
   b. emblems.
   c. haptics.
   d. territoriality.

8. According to Edward T. Hall, your personal space zone where most of your conversations with others take place is anywhere from
   a. 0 to 1½ feet.
   b. 1½ to 4 feet.
   c. 4 to 12 feet.
   d. 12 feet on.

9. Immediacy, in nonverbal communication, refers to
   a. the physical distance between two people in conversation.
   b. the recency of the topic under discussion.
   c. how fast two people are talking to each other.
   d. feelings of liking between two people in conversation.

10. Stan is talking to Jenny about his trip to the mountains. Jenny wants Stan to keep talking, so she responds by smiling, nodding her head, and saying "uh-huh." The function of nonverbal communication, as it relates to verbal communication, best illustrated in this situation is
    a. accenting.
    b. contradicting.
    c. regulating.
    d. repeating.

Answers to the questions in this practice test can be found at the end of the book.

Assessing Your Skill

1. Suggest examples of body movements that reveal each of the six primary emotions listed below. Then generate possible alternative meanings for the movement. For example, we've said in this chapter that crossed arms might reveal either anger or that someone is closed off or not open to discussing something. We've provided an example below.

Emotion	Body Movements	Alternative Meanings
Embarrassment	Covering the face with one's hands	Could also indicate deception
Happiness		
Anger		
Surprise		
Fear		
Disgust		
Sadness		

2. We've explored the nonverbal codes of space and territory, and you should now have a better understanding of the range of people's reactions to perceived invasions of their space. Read each of the situations below, decide if a proxemic or a territorial violation has occurred, and then describe two tactics you would use in response to each situation. (Try to think of things you actually *would* do in each situation, not just what you *might* do. Be realistic.)
   a. You're at a bar or a club, sitting alone, waiting to order or for a friend to join you. A stranger sits down beside you and starts a conversation.
   b. You're a business executive. You enter your office after lunch and find your administrative assistant sitting at your desk.
   c. You're taking racquetball lessons and it's your turn on the court. A group of people gather to watch your lesson.
   d. You're interviewing for a part-time job. The interviewer moves from behind the desk toward you and touches you on the knee.

e. You want to wear your favorite sweater but can't find it. You discover it wadded up in the bottom of the laundry hamper, reeking of cigarette smoke, and you realize that your roommate or a family member wore it out to a bar without your permission.

Web Resources to Improve Your Knowledge and Skill

Are you a people watcher? Most of us who study communication become avid people watchers, because human beings are truly fascinating creatures, particularly in the realm of nonverbal communication. The human face is capable of producing an enormous number of expressions, most of which arise through a combination of movements of various areas of the face. The more aware you become of your own capacity for facial expression, the better able you will be to convey your emotions and thoughts to others. In addition, the more perceptive and sensitive a receiver and interpreter of others' facial expressions you become, the better a communicator you will become as you listen, respond, and adapt to other people.

To help you develop these skills, we direct your attention to a web site entirely devoted to the study of the human face: <www.face-and-emotion.com/dataface>. On this site, scholars who study the face for its communicative abilities explore its permanent and transient features; they also offer research citations and information about people who study this topic.

Edward Hopper, "Chop Suey." © SuperStock, Inc. With permission of Seattle Art Museum, Private Collection.

Listening, not imitation, may be the sincerest form of flattery.

Dr. Joyce Brothers

Chapter 5

Listening and Responding

Chapter Outline

- The Importance of Listening and Responding Skills
- How We Listen
- Listening Styles
- Listening Barriers
- Improving Your Listening Skills
- Responding Skills
- Responding with Empathy
- Summary

Chapter Objectives

After studying this chapter, you should be able to

1. Explain the principle of listening and responding thoughtfully to others.
2. Identify the elements of the listening process.
3. Describe four listening styles.
4. Identify and describe barriers that keep people from listening well.
5. Identify and use strategies that can improve your listening skills.
6. Identify and use appropriate responding skills.

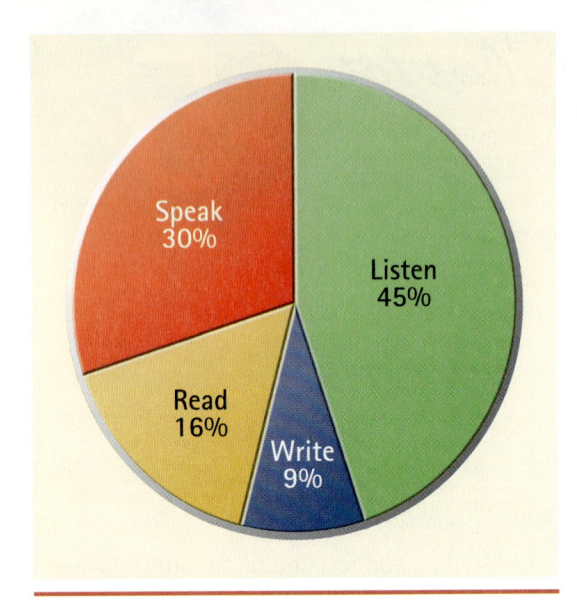

Figure 5.1
What You Do with Your Communication Time

It shows up on every list of what effective communicators do: They listen. You spend more time listening to others than doing almost anything else you do. Americans spend up to 90 percent of a typical day communicating with people, and they spend 45 percent of that communication time listening to others.[1] As shown in Figure 5.1, if you're typical, you spend the *least* amount of your communication time writing, yet you receive more training in writing than in any other communication skill. One of the hallmarks of an effective leader is being a good listener.[2] To be sensitive is to be aware of others and to be concerned about others. Increasing your skill in listening to others is one of the most productive ways to increase your communication sensitivity.

Most people have not had formal training in listening or responding. In this chapter, we focus on the principle of increasing your sensitivity to others by listening. Becoming sensitive to others includes more than just understanding and interpreting their words, thoughts, and ideas—sensitivity also involves understanding the emotions underlying the words and unspoken messages of others.

As shown in our familiar model of the Communication Principles for a Lifetime in Figure 5.2, effective communicators do more than absorb a message; they provide an appropriate response to the speaker. We'll address both listening and responding to others in this chapter.

The Importance of Listening and Responding Skills

Listening and responding skills are important for several reasons. Some researchers suggest that because listening is the first communication skill that we learn (we respond to sounds even while in our mother's womb), it's also the most important skill.[3] Listening plays a key role in helping us learn to speak.

Listening and responding thoughtfully to others is an important principle of communication, not only because you spend more time listening than in any other communication activity, but also because of its importance in establishing and maintaining relationships with others. In interpersonal communication situations, the essence of being a good conversationalist is being a good listener. Rather than focusing only on what to say, a person skilled in the art of conversation listens and picks up on interests and themes of others. Your skill as a listener has important implications for the relationships you establish with others. One research study found that a key difference between couples who remained married and those who divorced was the ability to listen to each other.[4] Partners in marriages that endure report that being a good listener is key to a satisfying marital relationship.

Being a good listener is also an essential skill when communicating with others in small groups. Whether you are the appointed or emerging leader of a group or a group or team member, your ability to listen and connect to others will affect your value to other group members.[5] Group members afflicted with bafflegab, those who verbally dominate group meetings, are not usually held in high esteem. Groups need

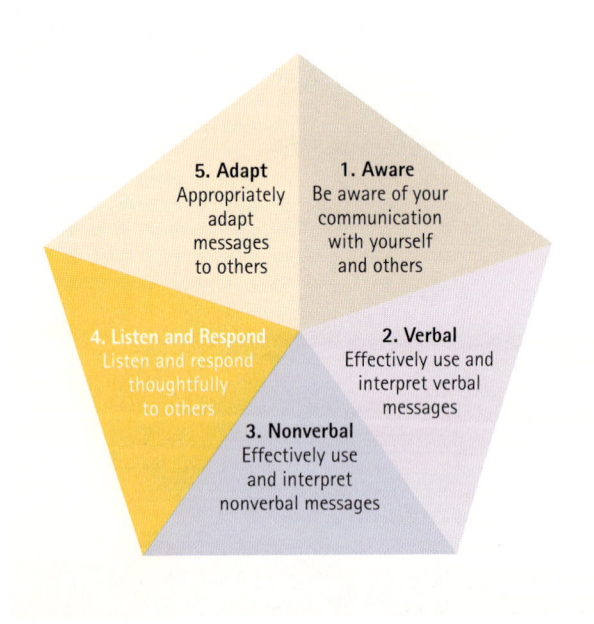

Figure 5.2
Communication Principles for a Lifetime

people who can listen and connect conversational threads that often become tangled or dropped in group dialogue.

It may be less clear how being an effective listener can enhance a presentational speaker's ability to connect with an audience. Effective speakers, however, are those who can relate to their listeners; good speakers know how to establish a relationship with the audience by listening to audience members one on one before a talk or lecture. Good speakers are also audience-centered. They consider the needs of their listeners first. They understand what will hold listeners' attention.

How We Listen

Do you know someone who is interpersonally inert? Interpersonally inert people are those who just don't "get it." You can drop hints that it's late and you'd rather they head home instead of playing another hand of cards, but they don't pick up on your verbal and nonverbal cues. They may *hear* you, but they certainly aren't listening; they are not making sense out of your symbols. **Hearing** is the physiological process of decoding sounds. You hear when the sound waves reach your eardrum and cause the middle ear bones (the hammer, anvil, and stirrup) to vibrate. Eventually, the sound vibrations are translated into electrical impulses that reach your brain. In order to listen to something, you must first select that sound from competing sounds.

Listening, defined succinctly, is the process we use to make sense out of what we hear; it is a complex process of receiving, constructing meaning from, and responding to verbal and nonverbal messages.[6] Listening involves five activities: (1) selecting, (2) attending, (3) understanding, (4) remembering, and—to confirm that listening has occurred—(5) responding.

Understanding these five elements in the listening process can help you diagnose where you sometimes get off track when listening. Having a framework to better describe the listening process can help you figure out how to get back on track and increase your listening skill.[7]

Selecting

To **select** a sound is to focus on one sound as you sort through the myriad of noises competing for your attention. Even now, as you are reading this book, there are probably countless sounds within earshot. Stop reading for a moment. What sounds surround you? Do you hear music? Is a TV on? Maybe there is the tick of a clock, a whir of a computer, or a whoosh of a furnace or an air conditioner. To listen—to be sensitive to another person—you must first select the sound or nonverbal behavior that symbolizes meaning. The interpersonally inert person does not pick up on the clues because he or she is oblivious to the information.

Attending

After selecting a sound, you attend to it. To **attend** is to maintain a *sustained* focus on a particular message. When you change channels on your TV, you first select the channel and then attend to the program you've selected. You may attend to the program or commercial for a moment and then move on or return to other thoughts or other sounds. Just as you tune in to TV programs that reflect your taste in information while you channel surf, you attend to messages of others that satisfy your needs or whims. Attending to a message is vital to being a good listener. There is clear evidence that a person who is skilled in maintaining sustained attention to a message (not interrupting and just listening) is perceived as a better listener than is someone with a "restless mind."[8]

hearing
The physiological process of decoding sounds.

listening
A complex process of receiving, constructing meaning from, and responding to verbal and nonverbal messages, which involves selecting, attending, understanding, remembering, and responding.

select
To focus on one sound as you sort through various sounds competing for your attention.

attend
To maintain a sustained focus on a particular message.

Communication and Technology

Listening When No One Is Home

Listening may be an even more important skill in the twenty-first century than in the past. Why? Communication researcher Sheila Bentley suggests that because of globalization and today's technology, listening skills are essential for professional and personal success.[9] The world is shrinking; no longer do vast distances keep us from communicating with people from around the globe. Cultural differences make listening an essential skill in relating to others who have a different cultural perspective from your own. In addition, today's technological tools make it possible for us to listen to others anytime and anywhere, including listening to vast numbers of recorded messages.[10]

There has been a huge increase in **asynchronous listening**, which is what you do when you listen to someone's recorded message on an answering machine, to voice mail, or to messages retrieved from your cell phone. You listen, yet no person is available to respond to your feedback. The inability to ask for clarification increases the potential for the message to be misunderstood.

In addition to making listening more important, increased globalization and advanced technology are also making it more challenging. How can you improve your skills in listening to and transmitting recorded messages?

When listening to a recorded message,

- *Focus.* Before playing the recorded message, stop what you are doing so that you can focus on the message; while driving, scurrying around the room, or coming in the door after a busy day may not be the best time to listen carefully to recorded messages.
- *Mentally summarize.* If you are listening to several recorded messages, mentally summarize the essence of the message you've just heard before playing the next one.
- *Increase redundancy.* If need be, replay the recorded message to ensure that you've absorbed the details.

When recording a message,

- *Slow down.* When you're leaving a recorded message for someone, speak slowly, clearly, and distinctly.
- *Keep it short.* Most people, when checking their messages, don't want to hear a lengthy story or detailed chronology of events. Make your message brief and to the point.
- *Leave follow-up information.* Do more than leave a phone number or e-mail address. Indicate when you're most likely to be available to receive a message in person, rather than encouraging a game of phone tag.

What holds our attention? Typically, conflict, new ideas, humor, or something that we can see or that is concrete holds our attention more easily than abstract ideas that don't relate to us. If you're having difficulty sustaining attention to a message, it may be because what you're listening to does not immediately seem to relate to you. So you may need to work a bit harder, either to concentrate on the message or to consider ways in which the message is relevant or important to you.

Understanding

It's been estimated that we hear over one billion words each year, but we understand a mere fraction of that number. To **understand** is to assign meaning to messages—to interpret a message by making sense out of what you hear. You can select and attend to sounds and nonverbal cues but not interpret what you see and hear. Hearing and seeing are physiological processes. Understanding occurs when you relate what you hear and see to your experiences or knowledge.[11] Perhaps you have heard the Montessori school philosophy: I hear, I forget; I see, I remember; I experience, I understand. It is when we can relate our experiences to what we hear and see that we achieve understanding.

Remembering

Remembering information is considered part of the listening process because it's the primary way we determine whether a message was understood. To **remember** is to recall information. Some scholars speculate that you store every detail you have ever heard or witnessed; your mind operates like a computer's hard drive, recording each life experience. But you cannot retrieve or remember all of the bits of information. Sometimes, even though you were present, you have no recollection of what occurred in a

---

asynchronous listening
Listening to recorded messages, such as those on an answering machine or voice mail, which do not allow an opportunity for you to get a response to your feedback.

understand
To assign meaning to messages.

remember
To recall information.

Once we select the sounds we want to listen to, we need to attend to—or focus on—those sounds for communication to take place. When you're communicating in a noisy, distracting setting, what skills can you use to take special care to focus on what others are saying?

particular situation. You can't consciously remember everything; your eye is not a camera; your ear is not a microphone; your mind is not a hard drive.

The first communication principle we presented in this book is to become self-aware. When we are not self-aware of our actions, thoughts, or what we are perceiving—when we are mindless—our ability to remember what occurs plummets. We increase our ability to remember what we hear by being not only physically present, but also mentally present.

You tend to remember what is important to you or something you try to remember or have practiced to remember (like the information in this book for your next communication test). You tend to remember dramatic information (such as where you were when you heard about the September 11, 2001, terrorist attacks) or vital information (such as your phone number or your mother's birthday).

Responding

As you learned in Chapter 1, communication is a transactive process—not a one-way, linear one. Communication involves responding to others as well as simply articulating messages. You **respond** to people to let them know you understand their message. Your lack of response may signal that you didn't understand the message. Your predominant response is often unspoken; direct eye contact and head nods let your partner know you're tuned in. An unmoving, glassy-eyed, frozen stupor may tell your communication partner that you are physically present, yet mentally a thousand miles away.[12] As you'll discover in the next section, most people have a certain style of listening and responding to others.

Listening Styles

Although we've described the typical elements in the listening process, not everyone has the same style or approach to listening. Your **listening style** is your preferred way of making sense out of the messages you hear and see. Some people, for example, prefer to listen to brief chunks of information. Others seem more interested in focusing on the feelings and emotions expressed.

respond
To confirm your understanding of a message.

listening style
A person's preferred way of making sense out of messages.

What's your listening style? Knowing your style can help you adapt and adjust your listening style when listening to others. Listening researchers Kitty Watson, Larry Barker, and James Weaver have found that people tend to listen using one or more of four listening styles: people-oriented, action-oriented, content-oriented, or time-oriented.[13]

People-Oriented Listening

People-oriented listeners tend to prefer listening to people's emotions and feelings. They are quite interested in hearing personal information from others. A people-oriented listener searches for common interests and seeks to empathize with the feelings of others—she or he connects emotionally with the sentiments and passions others express.[14] There is some evidence that people-oriented listeners are less apprehensive when communicating with others in small groups and interpersonal situations.[15]

Research shows that people-oriented listeners have a greater tendency to be sympathetic to the person they are listening to.[16] A sympathetic listener is more likely to voice concern for the other person's welfare when that person is sharing personal information or news about a stressful situation. A sympathetic listener says things like "Oh, I'm so sorry to hear about your loss" or "It's too bad that this has happened to you." Research also suggests that people who strongly prefer the people-oriented listening style are less anxious or apprehensive about listening, especially when listening to just one other person.[17] There is evidence that people-oriented listeners may be more empathic; they seem to have greater skill in understanding the thoughts and feelings of others.[18] One study found that jurors who are people-oriented listeners are less likely to find the plaintiff at fault in a civil court trial, perhaps because of their tendency to empathize with others.[19]

Action-Oriented Listening

Action-oriented listeners like information to be well organized, brief, and free of errors. While listening to a rambling story, the action-oriented listener may think, "Get to the point" or "Why should I be listening to this?" Action-oriented listeners want to do something with the information they hear; they want it to serve a purpose or function, and they become impatient with information that doesn't seem to have a "bottom line."

Action-oriented listeners tend to be a bit more skeptical and critical than are people-oriented listeners of the information they hear. Researchers call this skepticism **second guessing**—questioning the assumptions underlying a message.[20] It's called second guessing because the listeners don't always assume that what they hear is accurate or relevant; they make a second guess about the accuracy of the information they are listening to. Accuracy of information is especially important to action-oriented listeners, because if they are going to use the information in some way, the information should be valid.

Content-Oriented Listening

Content-oriented listeners are more comfortable listening to detailed, complex information than are those with other listening styles. A content-oriented listener is likely to perceive a message presented without details, facts, and evidence as less important and valuable than a message that includes rich content. Content-oriented listeners, like action-oriented listeners, are likely to second-guess the information they hear.[21] They are constantly checking messages for accuracy, because accurate, detailed information is highly valued. Content-oriented listeners are skilled at listening to arguments and debates, because they prefer to listen to messages with a significant amount of information in them.[22] They are less patient listening to stories, anecdotes, and illustrations that don't convey much information.

---

people-oriented listeners
Those who prefer to focus on the emotions and feelings communicated by others verbally and nonverbally.

action-oriented listeners
Those who prefer that the messages communicated by others contain information that is functional, well organized, brief, and accurate.

second guessing
Questioning the assumptions underlying a message.

content-oriented listeners
Those who prefer that messages communicated by others contain complex and detailed information.

Time-Oriented Listening

Time-oriented listeners like brief, short messages. They have much to do and don't want to waste time listening to lengthy talk. A time-oriented listener is likely to look at his or her watch and be conscious of how long it is taking to listen to a message. Whereas the content-oriented listener prefers to hear messages that are chock-full of details, the time-oriented listener would rather hear soundbites that quickly get to the point. Time-oriented listeners are typically busy people; they gauge their success by what they can accomplish, so they are more sensitive to the length of messages than are people with the other three listening styles.

How does knowing that most people have preferences for particular types of messages benefit you? There are at least three reasons to give some thought to your listening style and the listening styles of others. First, knowing your own listening style can help you adapt and adjust your listening style to fit the listening situation. If, for example, you are a people-oriented listener and you're listening to a message that has little information about people but lots of technical details, be aware that you will have to work harder to stay tuned in to the message.

Second, it's important to understand that you may have more than one style of listening. You may be wondering, "Do I have just one listening style, or do I have more than one style?" According to listening researchers Kitty Watson and Larry Barker, about 40 percent of all listeners have one primary listening style that they use, especially if they are under stress. Another 40 percent of listeners use more than one style—for example, they may prefer to listen to content (content-oriented listening style) and also want the information delivered in a short amount of time (time-oriented listening style). And about 20 percent of people do not have a specific listening style preference; these individuals may want to avoid listening altogether because they are shy and don't like to be around others in social situations, they may have receiver apprehension, or they may just have listener burnout—they are weary of listening to other people.[23] Evidence suggests that the situation, time, and place all have an impact on the listening style or styles people adopt.[24]

Finally, it can be useful to be aware of the listening style of others so that you can communicate messages that others are more likely to listen to. If you know your spouse is a content-oriented listener, then communicate a message that is rich in information; that's what your spouse prefers. Tell the content-oriented listener, "Here are three things I have to tell you." Then say those three things. The content preview tells your content-oriented listener that you are about to convey three pieces of information. Content-oriented listeners like to know that the message to be presented contains

Recap

Listening Styles

People-oriented listening style	Listeners prefer to attend to feelings and emotions and to search for common areas of interest when listening to others.
Action-oriented listening style	Listeners prefer to focus on information that is organized and accurate; they want a speaker to get to the point and emphasize what action should be taken with the information they hear.
Content-oriented listening style	Listeners prefer to hear complex, detailed information and expect facts and evidence to support key ideas.
Time-oriented listening style	Listeners prefer brief messages that are presented efficiently without digressions; they are busy listeners and don't want to spend a lot of time listening to long-winded stories and anecdotes.

time-oriented listeners
Those who prefer that messages communicated by others be brief.

Communication and Diversity

East and West Listening Styles

North American communication very often centers on the sender. Much emphasis is placed on how senders can formulate better messages, improve credibility, polish their delivery skills, and so forth. In contrast, the emphasis in East Asia has always been on listening and interpretation.

Communication researcher C. Y. Cheng has identified *infinite interpretation* as one of the main principles of Chinese communication.[25] The principle presumes that the emphasis is on the receiver and listening rather than on the sender and speaking. According to T. S. Lebra, "anticipatory communication" is common in Japan: Instead of the speaker's having to tell or ask explicitly for what he or she wants, others guess and accommodate his or her needs, sparing him or her the embarrassment that could arise if the verbally expressed request could not be met.[26] In such cases, the burden of communication falls not on the message sender but on the message receiver. A person who "hears one and understands ten" is regarded as an intelligent communicator. To catch on quickly and to adjust oneself to another's position before his or her position is clearly revealed is regarded as an important communication skill.

One thing that puzzles some foreign students from East Asia is why they are constantly being asked what they want when they are visiting in American homes. In their own countries, the host or hostess is supposed to know what is needed and to act accordingly. The difference, of course, is that in North America it is important to provide individual freedom of choice; in East Asia, it is important to practice anticipatory communication and to accommodate the speaker.

With the emphasis on indirect communication, the receiver's sensitivity and ability to capture the under-the-surface meaning and to understand implicit meaning become critical. In North America, an effort has been made to improve the effectiveness of message senders through such formal training as debate and public speaking, whereas in East Asia, the effort has been on improving the receiver's sensitivity. One achieves the greatest sensitivity when one empties the mind of preconceptions and makes it as clear as a mirror.[27]

Recently, there has been increased interest in listening in the United States. Both communication scholars and practitioners recognize that listening is necessary not only for the instrumental aspect of communication (comprehension) but also, and more importantly, for the affective aspect (granting the speaker the satisfaction of being listened to).[28]

useful information. Of course, it may be difficult to determine someone's listening style, especially if you don't know the person very well. But it is both easier and worth the time to consider the listening styles of people you *do* know well (your family members, your coworkers, your boss). Knowing your own and others' listening styles can help you adapt your communication to enhance the accuracy of your own listening and the appropriateness of the information you communicate to others.

Listening Barriers

Although we spend almost half of our communication time listening, some say we don't use that time well. One day after hearing something, most people remember only about half of what was said. It gets worse. Two days later, our listening comprehension drops by another 50 percent. The result: Two days after hearing a lecture or speech, most of us remember about 25 percent of what we hear.

Our listening deteriorates not only when we listen to speeches or lectures, but also when we interact interpersonally. Even in the most intimate relationships (or perhaps we should say *especially* in the most intimate relationships), we tune out what others are saying. One study reported that we sometimes pay more attention to strangers than to our close friends or spouses. Married couples tend to interrupt each other more often than nonmarried couples and are usually less polite to each other than are strangers involved in a simple decision-making task.[29]

What keeps us from listening well? The most critical elements are (1) self barriers—personal habits that work against listening well; (2) information-processing barriers—the way we mentally manage information; and (3) context barriers—the surroundings in which we listen.

Self Barriers

"We have met the enemy and he is us" is the oft-quoted line from the comic strip *Pogo*. Evidence suggests we are our own worst enemy when it comes to listening to others—whether it's listening to enjoy, learn, evaluate, or empathize. We mentally comment on the words we hear and the behavior we observe. Our internal thoughts are like a play-by-play sports commentator's description of the action in a sports contest. If our internal narration is focused on the message, then it may be useful. But we often attend to our own internal dialogues and diatribes instead of to others' messages; when we do that, our listening effectiveness plummets.

Self-Focus   That personal play-by-play commentary we may be carrying on in our minds is typically about us. "How long will I have to be here for this lecture?" "Wonder what's for dinner tonight?" "I've got to get that report finished." "She's still talking—will we be out of here in ten minutes?" "Do I have a school meeting tonight or is that tomorrow night?" Focusing on an internal message often keeps us from selecting and attending to the other person's message.

What can you do to regain your listening focus if you are focused on yourself rather than on the other person's message? Consider these suggestions:

- *Become aware of the problem.* Become consciously competent. Note when you find yourself drifting off, thinking about your agenda, rather than concentrating on the speaker.
- *Concentrate.* If your internal "announcer" is telling you that the message is boring, useless, or stupid, make sure you don't mindlessly tune the message out. Yes, some messages are boring, useless, and stupid. But the habit of quickly dismissing ideas and messages without making an effort to stay focused on them will keep you from being nominated for the Listening Hall of Fame.
- *Be active rather than passive.* The key to concentration is finding ways to be involved in the communication process. Taking notes when appropriate and providing nonverbal and even sometimes verbal feedback to the speaker can help keep your focus on the speaker rather than on you. If you don't understand something the speaker says, ask for clarification. Don't just sit there and "take it"; if you find your concentration waning, you'll more than likely "leave it."

Emotional Noise   Emotions are powerful. What we see and hear affects our emotions. **Emotional noise** occurs when our emotional arousal interferes with communication effectiveness. Certain words or phrases can arouse emotions very quickly; and, of course, the same word may arouse different emotions in different people. You respond emotionally because of your cultural background, religious convictions, or political philosophy. Words that reflect negatively on your nationality, ethnic origin, or religion can trigger strong emotional reactions. Cursing and obscene language may also reduce your listening efficiency. If you grew up in a home in which R-rated language was never used, then four-letter words may distract you.

Sometimes it's not just a word but a concept or idea that causes an emotional eruption. Third-trimester abortion and public school prayer, for example, are topics guaranteed to get radio talk show hosts' audiences involved in lively discussion. Whether you love him or hate him, TV talk show host Jerry Springer is a master at pushing emotional hot buttons for his talk show guests; and when emotions become heated, thoughtful listening is rare.

The emotional state of the speaker may also affect your ability to understand and evaluate what you hear. One researcher found that if you are listening to someone who is emotionally distraught, you will be more likely to focus on his or her emotions than on the content of the message.[30] Another researcher advises that when you are commu-

emotional noise
A form of communication noise caused by emotional arousal.

Some people find that yoga or quiet meditation helps dissolve the internal barriers that prevent effective listening. What strategies have you used to become more aware of your intrapersonal communication and any internal barriers to listening you may have experienced? What methods have you found helpful for making you conscious of the way your own "self-talk" affects your ability to listen to and communicate with others?

nicating with someone who is emotionally excited, you should remain calm and focused and try simply to communicate your interest in the other person.[31]

What are other strategies to keep your emotions from getting the best of you? Daniel Goleman offers several research-based strategies in his best-selling book *Emotional Intelligence*.[32] To be emotionally intelligent is to have the ability to understand, manage, and appropriately express emotions. For example, one simple yet powerful strategy to manage emotions when you find you may be ready to lose it is to take a deep breath. Yes, just breathe. Taking a deep, slow breath is a way of regaining control by calming down. It helps make you more conscious of your anger or frustration, much like the old technique of counting to ten.

Another strategy for managing emotions is to use the power of self-talk, a concept we discussed in Chapter 2. Tell yourself you won't get angry. Early detection of the emotions bubbling inside you can help you assess and then manage emotions before your nonrational, emotional impulses take control.

Sometimes, of course, expressing your frustration is appropriate. We do suggest that you become aware of the effect that emotions have on your listening ability; this is a constructive first step to avoid being ruled by unchecked emotions. The principle of self-awareness gives you *choice* and control. Your listening challenge is to avoid emotional sidetracks and keep your attention focused on the message. When emotionally charged words or actions kick your internal dialogue into high gear, make an effort to quiet it down and steer back to the subject at hand. Becoming consciously aware of our emotions and then talking to ourselves about our feelings is a way of not letting emotions get out of hand.

Criticism We usually associate the word *criticism* with negative judgments and attitudes. Although critiquing a message can provide positive as well as negative insights, most of us don't like to be criticized. Mother Teresa once said, "If you judge people, you have no time to love them."[33] Being inappropriately critical of the speaker may distract us from focusing on the message.

A person's appearance and speech characteristics can affect your ability to listen to him or her. Many a speaker's droning monotone, lack of eye contact, and distracting mannerisms have contributed to his or her ideas not being well received—even if the ideas are potentially life-changing for the listener. The goal of a sensitive communicator is to be conscious of when the delivery or other distracting features of the message or messenger are interfering with the ability simply to listen. In fact, now that you are studying principles of communication, you may find that this problem looms even larger, because you now pay more attention to nonverbal cues.

It would be unrealistic to suggest that you refrain from criticizing speakers and their messages. It is realistic, however, to monitor your internal critiques of speakers to make sure you are aware of your biases. Good listeners say to themselves, "While this speaker may be distracting, I am simply not going to let appearance or mannerisms keep my attention from the message." For example, Stephen Hawking is a prize-winning physicist at Cambridge University in England; because of a disability, he is able to speak only with the aid of computer-synthesized sounds. He is unquestionably brilliant. If you let his speaking delivery overpower you, you'd miss his marvelous message. Avoid using your mental energy to criticize a speaker unnecessarily; the longer your mental critique, the less you'll remember.

Information-Processing Barriers

In addition to self barriers that contribute to our loss of focus on messages, sometimes the way in which we use the information that comes to our eyes, minds, and hearts creates listening problems. The way in which we process the information we hear may keep us from being good listeners. Four information-processing listening barriers are (1) processing rate, (2) information overload, (3) receiver apprehension, and (4) shifting attention.

Mother Teresa understood the value of open listening without prejudging a person.

Processing Rate
One of the barriers to listening that has long been documented is the difference between our ability to process information and the rate at which information comes to us. The barrier boils down to this: You can think faster than people speak. Most people speak 125 words per minute, give or take a few words. You have the tremendous ability, however, to process four to ten times that amount of information. Some people can listen to 600 to 800 words a minute and still make sense out of what the speaker is saying; another estimate puts the processing rate up to 1,200 words per minute. Yet another estimate claims that we think not just in words but also in images and sounds: We can process 2,000 bits of information a minute for short periods of time. This difference between average speaking rate and your capacity to make sense out of words as they register in your cortical centers can cause trouble. You have extra time on your hands to tune in to your own thoughts, rather than focus on the speaker.[34]

You can use your information-processing rate to your advantage if you use the extra time to summarize mentally what a speaker is saying. By periodically sprinkling in mental summaries during a conversation, you can dramatically increase your listening ability and make the speech-rate/thought-rate difference work to your advantage.

Information Overload
Information abounds. Incoming messages and information on computers, fax machines, e-mail, cell phones, beepers, and other devices can interrupt conversations and distract us from listening to others. The amount of information coming at us on any given day also wears us out. The one word to describe many a poor listener is "weary." We spend 45 percent of our communication time listening, and the pace at which the information zips toward us exhausts us. The billion words that we hear each year contribute to our fatigue.

Again we recommend self-awareness. Be on the alert for drifting attention because of information overload. And when the encroaching information dulls your attentiveness, either take a break or consider conducting some *communication triage* (determining what's urgent and what's not urgent) so that you can focus on the information that is most important.

Receiver Apprehension   Just as some people are fearful of presenting a speech or speaking up during a meeting, research suggests that some people are fearful of receiving information. **Receiver apprehension** is fear of misunderstanding or misinterpreting the messages spoken by others or of not being able to adjust psychologically to messages expressed by others.[35] Some people may just be fearful of receiving new information because they worry about being able to understand it. Or apprehension may just be a characteristic of the way some people respond psychologically to information; they may not be able to make sense out of some of what they hear, which causes them to be anxious or fearful of listening to others.[36] If you are fearful of receiving information, you'll remember less information.

What are the implications for you of research on receiver apprehension? If you know that you are fearful of listening to new information, you'll have to work harder to understand the information presented. Using an audio recorder to record a lecture may help you feel more comfortable and less anxious about trying to remember every point. Becoming actively involved in the listening experience by taking notes or mentally repeating information to yourself may also help.

Shifting Attention   Can you multitask? Some people can easily do two things at once; some people can't. Emerging research evidence suggests that men are more likely to have difficulty attending to multiple messages: When they are focused on a message, they may have more difficulty than women in carrying on a conversation with another person.[37] Men have a tendency to lock on to a message, while women seem more adept at shifting between two or more simultaneous messages. When many men watch a TV program, they seem lost in thought—oblivious to other voices around them. Women, on the other hand, are more likely to be carrying on a conversation with one person and also focusing on a message they hear nearby. No, this difference doesn't mean that women are more likely to eavesdrop intentionally, but it does mean that some women have greater potential to listen to two things at once. What are the implications? It may be especially important for women to stop and focus on the messages of others, rather than on either internal or external competing messages. And men may need to be sensitive to others who may want to speak to them, rather than becoming fixated on their own internal message or on a single external message such as a program on TV.

Context Barriers

In addition to the barriers that relate to how you process information and those that occur when your emotions and thoughts crowd out a message, listening barriers can arise from the communication context or situation. Specifically, time, place, and outside noise can distract you from selecting, attending, understanding, remembering, and responding to messages.[38]

Barriers of Time and Place   The time of day can interfere with your listening acuity. Are you a morning person or an evening person? Morning people are cheerfully and chirpily at their mental peak before lunch. Evening people prefer to tackle major projects after dark; they are at their worst when they arise in the morning.

If you know you are sharper in the morning, whenever possible schedule your key listening times then. Evening listeners should try to shift heavy listening to the evening hours. Of course, that's not always practical. If you can't change the time of listening, you can increase your awareness of when you will need to listen with greater concentration.

Don't assume that because you are ready to talk, the other person is ready to listen. If your message is particularly sensitive or important, you may want to ask your listening partner, "Is this a good time to talk?" Even if he or she says yes, look for eye contact and a responsive facial expression to make sure the positive response is genuine.

External Noise   **Noise** is anything that interferes with your ability to listen to a message. Although you may think of noise as sounds you hear, noise can be processed

---

receiver apprehension
The fear of misunderstanding or misinterpreting the messages spoken by others or of not being able to adjust psychologically to messages expressed by others.

noise
Anything that interferes with your ability to listen to a message.

Recap

Managing Listening Barriers

Listening Barriers	What to Do
Self Barriers	
Self-Focus	• Shift attention back to the speaker.
	• Become actively involved in the message.
	• Take meaningful notes.
Emotional Noise	• Act calm to remain calm.
	• Use self-talk to stay focused on the message.
	• Take a deep breath if you start to lose control.
Criticism	• Focus on the message, not on the messenger.
Information-Processing Barriers	
Processing Rate	• Use the difference between speech rate and thought rate to mentally summarize the message.
Information Overload	• Realize when you or your partner is tired or distracted and not ready to listen.
	• Assess what is urgent and not urgent when listening.
Receiver Apprehension	• Record the message to be sure you capture it; review the audio later.
	• Take notes.
	• Make mental summaries of the information you hear.
Shifting Attention	• Make a conscious effort to remain focused on one message.
Context Barriers	
Barriers of Time and Place	• If possible, schedule difficult listening situations for when you're at your best.
External Noise	• Eliminate distracting noise.

by any one of your five senses. Not just sounds but also sights, the feeling of something touching you, even tastes and smells can affect your listening ability.

For most people, the best listening environment is one that offers as few distractions as possible. When you want to talk to someone, pick a quiet time and place, especially if you know you will be discussing a potentially difficult topic. Even in your own home, it may be a challenge to find a quiet time to talk. (Perhaps a good title for a text on listening would be *How to Turn Off the TV*.) Listening takes all the powers of concentration that you can muster. A good listener seeks a quiet time and place to maximize listening comprehension. Closing a door or window, turning off the television or radio, asking noisy or offensive talkers to converse more quietly or not at all, and simply moving to a less distracting location are steps that you may need to pursue to manage the noise barrier.

Improving Your Listening Skills

At the heart of listening is developing sensitivity to focus on the messages of others, rather than on your own thoughts. Improving your listening involves a set of skills that can increase your sensitivity toward others. At first glance, these skills may look deceptively simple—as simple as the advice given to most elementary students about crossing the street: (1) stop, (2) look, and (3) listen. Despite the appearance of simplicity, these three words summarize decades of research and insight about how to avoid being labeled "interpersonally inert." Those steps may seem like common sense, but they are not common practice. Let's consider each separately.

Stop: Turn Off Competing Messages

Many of the barriers to improved listening skill arise because we focus on ourselves and our own messages, rather than focusing on others. As we noted earlier, while you are "listening," you may also be "talking" to yourself—providing a commentary about the messages you hear. These internal, self-generated messages may distract you from giving your undivided attention to what others are saying. In order to select and attend to the messages of others, we need to become aware of our internal dialogue and stop our own running commentary about issues and ideas that are self-focused rather than other-focused.[39] Two listening researchers conducted a study to identify the specific behaviors that good listeners perform when listening.[40] What they discovered supports our admonition that the first thing you have to do to be a better listener is to stop focusing on your own mental messages and be other-oriented. Specifically, you should take the following actions during what the researchers called the *pre-interaction phase* of listening:

- Put your own thoughts aside.
- Be there mentally, not just physically.
- Make a conscious, mindful effort to listen.
- Take adequate time to listen; don't rush the speaker; be patient.
- Be open-minded.

Members of some religious groups take a vow to be silent and not talk to anyone else. They literally stop talking. Does this make them better listeners? One research team wanted to know the impact of various types of listening training, including being silent for twelve hours.[41] One group heard a lecture about how to be better listeners—probably like the lectures you hear in this course; the group then took a test to assess their overall listening skill. A second group promised not to talk to anyone for twelve hours—they literally gave others the "silent treatment." Then they, too, took a test to assess their listening ability. A third group both heard a listening lecture and were silent for twelve hours; then they also took the listening test. The results: There were no differences in listening test scores among the groups—all groups seemed to listen equally well, according to test results. But those who kept silent for twelve hours reported that they thought they were more attentive to others, more conscious of being good listeners. The researchers concluded that literally stopping to listen more and talk less can increase awareness of listening. Their research supports the maxim "You have been given two ears and one mouth so that you will listen more and talk less." We're not suggesting you not talk, but we are suggesting that you increase your awareness of how your own thoughts and talk can interfere with being a good listener. Stop—do your best to eliminate mental messages that keep you from listening well.

Try a process called social decentering. **Social decentering** involves stepping away from your own thoughts and attempting to experience the thoughts of another. In

social decentering
Stepping away from your own thoughts and attempting to experience the thoughts of another.

essence, you're asking yourself this question: "If I were the other person, what would I be thinking?" To decenter is to practice the first principle of communication—self-awareness—and to be aware that your own thoughts are keeping you from focusing on another's message, so that you can focus on the other person.[42] Of course, we are not suggesting that your own ideas and internal dialogue should be forever repressed; that would be both impossible and inappropriate. We are suggesting, however, that to connect to another, you must place the focus on the other person rather than on yourself.

The essence of the "stop" step is to become aware (our first Communication Principle for a Lifetime, which we discussed in Chapter 2) of whether you are listening or not listening to someone. You are either on task (focusing on another) or off task (oblivious to another and focusing on your own thoughts and emotions). The goal, of course, is to be on task—listening to others.

Look: Listen with Your Eyes

As you learned in Chapter 4, nonverbal messages are powerful, especially in communicating feelings, attitudes, and emotions.[43] A person's facial expression, presence or lack of eye contact, posture, and use of gestures speak volumes, even when no word is uttered. When words are spoken, the added meaning that comes from vocal cues provides yet another dimension to the emotion and nature of the relationship.

Sensitive listeners are aware of nonverbal as well as verbal messages; they listen with their eyes as well as their ears. A person's body movement and posture, for example, communicate the intensity of his or her feelings, while facial expression and vocal cues provide clues as to the specific emotion being expressed. A competent listener notices these cues, and an incompetent listener attempts to decode a message based only on what is said rather than "listening between the lines." When there is a contradiction between the verbal and nonverbal message, we will almost always believe the unspoken message; nonverbal cues are more difficult to fake.

By attending to your interpersonal partner's unspoken message, you are looking for the **meta-message**—the message about the message. *Meta-communication* is communication about communication. Accurately decoding unspoken or verbalized meta-messages helps you understand what people really mean. The nonverbal meta-message provides information about the emotional and relational impact of what a speaker is expressing with the verbal message.

Often a person will express a positive feeling nonverbally, such as by smiling, and also verbally, such as by saying "I'm happy to be here." But sometimes the nonverbal communication contradicts the verbal message. Your buddy may say, "Oh, that's just great" but use an exaggerated, sarcastic tone of voice that expresses just the opposite of the content of the verbal message. The sarcasm communicated by the tone of voice (a relationship cue) modifies the meaning of the verbal message (the actual content of the message). Your friend may not explicitly say that he is angry, upset, or irritated, but the nonverbal cues let you know that he is not happy.

How can you clarify the meaning of a nonverbal meta-message? Ask. For example, when you detect a smirk or a grimace from your listening partner, you can seek information about the communication: "Is what I'm saying bothering you?"

Besides looking at someone to discern his or her emotions and relational cues, it is important to establish eye contact, which signals that you are focusing your attention on your partner. Even though mutual eye contact typically lasts only one to seven seconds, when we carry on an interpersonal conversation, it is important to establish and reestablish eye contact to signal that you are on task and listening. We usually have more eye contact with someone when we are listening than when talking.[44]

In addition to eye contact, other nonverbal cues signal whether you are on task and responsive to the messages of others. If you look as if you are listening, you will be more likely to listen. Remaining focused, not fidgeting with your hands and feet, and even leaning forward slightly are other nonverbal cues that communicate to someone that you are listening. Appropriate head nods and verbal responses also signal that you are attending to your partner's message.[45]

> **meta-message**
> The message about the message.

Listen: Understand Both Details and Major Ideas

How do you improve your listening skill? Now that you've stopped your own internal dialogue and looked for nonverbal cues, it's time to listen. Here are six additional strategies for improving your listening skill.

Identify Your Listening Goal You listen to other people for a variety of reasons. Knowing your listening goal can increase your self-awareness of the listening process and increase your skill. If you're listening to Aunt Deonna talk about her recent trip to Northern Minnesota for the annual bear hunt, you need not worry about taking extensive notes and trying to remember all of the details of her expedition. But when your

Communication and Diversity

Who Are Better Listeners: Men or Women?

There is evidence that men and women can be equally good listeners, but research suggests that they sometimes (although not always) have different approaches to listening. The following chart summarizes research conclusions about feminine and masculine listening styles.[46]

	Feminine style	Masculine style
Differences in attending to information	• Tends to search for the relationships among separate pieces of information • Tends to identify individual facts and other isolated pieces of information	• Tends to look for a new structure or organizational pattern when listening • Tends to listen for the "big picture" and seek the major points being communicated
Differences in listening goals	• More likely to listen to new information to gain new understanding and new insights • Tends to use information to develop relationships with listening partners	• More likely to listen to new information to solve a problem • Tends to listen to reach a conclusion; shows less concern about relationship cues and more concern about using the information gained
Differences in attending to nonverbal cues	• Tends to emphasize meaning communicated through nonverbal cues • Typically uses more eye contact with the other person when listening	• Tends to emphasize the meaning of the words and information exchanged • Typically uses less eye contact with the other person when listening

So what does all this information mean? How is knowing differences in feminine and masculine listening styles useful to us? Although not all men and women fit into these categories of listening behavior, we think there are several good reasons to be mindful of gender-based differences in listening.[47] First, it's useful to be aware of different tendencies in listening so that we can be less critical and more accepting of others, should differences in communication arise. Conflicts may arise simply because you and your listening partner are focusing on different parts of the message expressed.

Second, by being aware of whether you fit the general profile of a masculine or feminine listener, you can determine whether you need to adapt your listening style. If, for example, you know that you have a tendency to be less interested in relational information and that you listen to get to the "bottom line" or solve a problem, being aware that your listening partner is not as focused on those objectives when listening can be helpful.

Third, the best listener may be one who is the most flexible and doesn't always default to his or her typical pattern or preferred listening approach, but rather combines listening approaches.[48] Make an effort to listen for both individual facts and the overall ideas. Listening for both relational and emotional meaning as well as for explicit content can also enhance listening skill. Be more aware of the way you tend to listen to others, and expand your listening repertoire to increase your ability to be other-oriented.

Finally, although we've noted differences in the way some men and women listen, we end our discussion by repeating our caution: Don't assume that all men or all women have typical masculine or feminine listening styles. Listening expert Stephanie Sargent suggests that studies of listening style differences between men and women may simply be measuring listening stereotypes.[49] Because it's often assumed that men and women listen differently, researchers may be documenting listening stereotypes or self-expectations. What may be occurring is a self-fulfilling prophecy—men and women assume they *are* listening the way they think they *should* listen.[50] But although there are some discernible patterns in masculine and feminine listening styles, the differences may not be as consistently pronounced as was once thought. Our conclusion: Differences in the way men and women listen may indeed exist, but these differences are only a few of a host of factors that explain why men and women sometimes have difficulty reaching a common understanding.

sociology professor tells a story to illustrate a sociological theory, you should be more attuned to the point he is making; the theory may be on a test. There are also times when you need to be on your guard to evaluate the message of a politician or salesperson. There are four primary listening goals: to enjoy, to learn, to evaluate, and to empathize.

- *Listening to enjoy.* Sometimes we listen just because it's fun. You might listen to music, watch TV, go to a movie, or visit with a friend. Because you know you won't be tested on Jay Leno's or Conan O'Brien's monologue, you can relax and just enjoy the humor; you don't have to worry about passing a test to remember each punch line.
- *Listening to learn.* Nothing snaps a class to attention more quickly than a professor's proclamation, "This next point will be covered on the test." Another key reason we listen is to learn. But you don't have to be a college student to listen to learn. Phone calls and conversations with family and friends contain information that we want to remember.
- *Listening to evaluate.* When you listen to evaluate, you try to determine whether the information you hear is valid, reliable, believable, or useful. One problem you may have when you listen to evaluate is that you may become so preoccupied with your criticism that you may not completely understand the message.
- *Listening to empathize.* The word *empathy*, which we introduced in Chapter 3 and will discuss in more detail later in this chapter, comes from a Greek word for "passion" and the German word *Einfühlung*, meaning "to feel with." To empathize with someone is to try to feel what he or she is feeling, rather than just think about or acknowledge the feelings. In effect, you act as a sounding board for the other person. Empathic listening serves an important therapeutic function. Just having an empathic listener may help someone out. No, we are not empowering you to be a therapist, but we are suggesting that simply listening and feeling with someone can help your communication partner sort things out.

If you were listening to someone give you directions to Centennial Hall, one of the oldest buildings on campus, you would listen differently than if your sister were telling you about her fears that her marriage was on the rocks. In the case of your sister, your job is to listen patiently and provide emotional support. In trying to get to Centennial Hall, you would be focusing on the specific details and making either mental or written notes.

One of the pleasures of developing good listening skills is the ability to listen for pure enjoyment. What nonverbal cues exhibited by the person pictured here let you know that she is listening for enjoyment? Based on what you can see from her nonverbal behavior, what sounds is she selecting? What sounds is she attending to?

Mentally Summarize the Details of the Message This suggestion may seem to contradict the suggestion to avoid focusing *only* on facts, but it is important to have a grasp of the details your partner presents. Yet to listen is to do more than focus on facts. Studies suggest that poor listeners are more likely to focus on *only* facts and data, rather than the overall point of the message.[51] To listen is to connect the details of the message with the major points. You can process words more quickly than a person speaks, so you can use the extra time to your advantage by periodically summarizing the names, dates, and facts embedded in the message. If the speaker is disorganized and rambling, use your tremendous mental ability to reorganize the speaker's information into categories or try to place events in chronological order. If you miss the details, you will likely miss the main point.

Link Message Details with the Major Idea of the Message Facts and data make the most sense when we can use them to support an idea or point. Mentally weave your summaries of the details into a focused major point or series of major ideas. So, as you summarize, link the facts you have organized in your mind with key ideas and principles. Use facts to enhance your critical thinking as you analyze, synthesize, evaluate, and finally summarize the key points or ideas your partner makes.

When a phone call comes at a time when you're busy with other things, it may be tempting to try to do two things at once. We have all tried to get away with a few "uh-huhs" and "mm-hmms" to indicate that we're listening to everything that's being said on the other end of the line. In this kind of situation, should you be honest and disclose that you're busy and would rather chat (and listen) when you can be more attentive? What sort of verbal strategies might you use?

Practice by Listening to Difficult or Challenging Material You learn any skill with practice. Listening experts suggest that our listening skills deteriorate if we listen only to easy and entertaining material. Make an effort to listen to news or documentary programs. As you listen to a lecture that seems chock full of content, make a conscious effort to stay focused, concentrate, and summarize facts and major ideas.

Work to Overcome Listening Barriers If you can avoid the listening barriers we presented earlier, you will be well on your way to improving your listening skill. Make it a deliberate goal not to be self-focused, let emotional noise distract you, or criticize a message before you've understood it. Watch out for information overload. And, when possible, take steps to minimize external noise and provide an environment more conducive to listening.

Don't Interrupt One of the best things you can do to be perceived as a good listener is to not interrupt a speaker when he or she is talking. When we interrupt someone, we are saying, "What I have to say is more important than what you have to say." This translates to the other person as "I'm more important than you are." Interrupting others when listening is more than just rude; it decreases your credibility and lowers your ability to understand the other person. Do you want to make sure you *don't* get hired based on the impression you make during a job interview? Interrupt your interviewer and you're less likely to get the job, according to one research study.[52] To listen without interrupting seems simple, but because thoughts are bouncing around in our head, we sometimes blurt them out.[53] Or we think we know what the other person is going to say, so we talk over her or him. Resist these temptations.

Recap

How to Listen Well

What to Do	How to Do It
Identify your listening goal.	Decide whether you are listening to enjoy, to learn, to evaluate, or to empathize. Your listening goal should determine the strategies you use to achieve it.
Mentally summarize the details of the message.	Every few minutes, take time to create your own mental recap of the key information presented. In just a few seconds, you can summarize much information.
Link message details with the major ideas of the message.	Consciously relate the bits of information you hear to the key points the speaker is developing, rather than focusing only on facts and details or only on major points.
Practice by listening to difficult or challenging material.	Periodically make an effort to listen to material that is complex and richer in detail and information than what you typically listen to; while listening to this more complex material, make a conscious effort to stop, look, and listen.
Work to overcome listening barriers.	Identify the key obstacles that keep you from listening at peak effectiveness (self barriers, information-processing barriers, or context barriers); make conscious efforts to overcome their underlying causes.
Don't interrupt.	Increase your awareness of whether you interrupt others. Wait until the other person has finished speaking before you speak.
Listen actively.	Be engaged in the listening process by maintaining good eye contact with the speaker and an alert posture (slight forward lean; sitting up rather than slouching).

Listen Actively Our suggestion that you listen actively is a distillation of the other recommendations we've offered. Active listeners are engaged listeners who listen with both their minds and their hearts. They are engaged physically and mentally in the listening process.[54] They are aware of what they are doing; they stop thinking about things that might take them off track.[55] They also have good eye contact with the speaker and communicate their interest with an intent facial expression and slight forward lean. By contrast, passive listeners are not involved listeners; they are detached and may fake attention with a frozen, nonexpressive facial expression. One listening research team noted that a passive listener receives information by being talked *to* rather than as an equal partner in the speaking-listening exchange.[56]

This same team described active listeners as people who

- Give full attention to others.
- Focus on what is being said.
- Expend considerable energy participating in the listening process.
- Have an alert posture.
- Maintain much direct eye contact.

It seems the best listeners are mentally alert, physically focused on the other person, and actively involved in seeking understanding. In short, they stop, they look, and they listen.

Responding Skills

To respond is to provide feedback to another about his or her behavior or communication. Your response can be verbal or nonverbal, intentional or unintentional.

Your thoughtful response serves several purposes. First, it tells a speaker how well you have understood his or her message. Second, your response lets a speaker know how the message affects you. It indicates whether you agree or disagree. Third, it provides feedback about statements or assumptions that you find vague, confusing, or wrong. It helps an individual keep the communication on target and purposeful. Finally, your response signals to the speaker that you are still "with" him or her—that you are still ready to receive messages. There is evidence that our ability to listen influences how we respond to others; when we are in the presence of someone whom we perceive to be a good listener, we're likely to respond with greater empathy and interest.[57] To respond appropriately and effectively, consider the following strategies.

Be Descriptive

"I see that from a different point of view" sounds better than "You're wrong, I'm right." Effective feedback describes rather than evaluates what you hear. Although one listening goal is to evaluate and make critical judgments about messages, evaluate once you're sure you understand the speaker. We're not suggesting that it's easy to listen from a nonevaluative perspective or that you should refrain from ever evaluating messages and providing praise or negative comments. Remember: Feedback that first acts like a mirror to help the speaker understand what he or she has said is more useful than a barrage of critical comments. Describing your own reactions to what your partner has said rather than pronouncing a quick judgment on his or her message is also more likely to keep communication flowing. If your partner thinks your prime purpose in listening is to take potshots at the message or the messenger, the communication climate will cool quickly. Listening researcher Eve-Anne Doohan not surprisingly found that when wives expressed negative emotions and critical evaluative comments to their listening husbands, the husbands were less satisfied with the overall quality of their relationships with their wives.[58] Being descriptive rather than evaluative encourages positive communication and has an impact on the overall quality of the relationship you have with another person.

Be Timely

Feedback is usually most effective at the earliest opportunity after the behavior or message is presented, especially if the purpose is to teach. Waiting to provide a response after much time has elapsed invites confusion.

Now let us contradict our advice. Sometimes, especially if a person is already sensitive and upset about something, delaying feedback can be wise. Use your critical-thinking skills to analyze when feedback will do the most good. Rather than automatically offering immediate correction, use the just-in-time (JIT) approach. Provide feedback just before the person might make another mistake, just in time for the feedback to have the most benefit.

Be Brief

Less information can be more. Cutting down on the amount of your feedback can highlight the importance of what you do share. Don't overwhelm your listener with details that obscure the key point of your feedback. Brief is usually best.

Be Useful

Perhaps you've heard this advice: "Never try to teach a pig to sing. It wastes your time, it doesn't sound pretty, and it annoys the pig." When you provide feedback to someone, be certain that it is useful and relevant. Ask yourself, "If I were this person, how would I respond to this information? Is it information I can act on?" Immersing your partner in information that is irrelevant or that may be damaging to the relationship may make you feel better but may not enhance the quality of your relationship or improve understanding.

Responding with Empathy

Empathy, as we noted earlier in the chapter, is the process of feeling what another person is feeling. To empathize is more than just to acknowledge that another person feels a particular emotion—being empathic involves making an effort to feel the emotion yourself.[59] Responding with empathy is especially important if you are listening to provide support and encouragement to someone. Being empathic is not a single skill but several related skills that help you predict how others will respond.[60] There is evidence that empathic listeners make better salespersons, teachers, counselors, and therapists and develop better relationships with others overall.[61]

Central to being empathic is being emotionally intelligent. As we noted earlier in this chapter, emotional intelligence is the ability to understand and express emotion, interpret emotions in yourself and others, and regulate or manage emotions.[62] Daniel Goleman suggests that people who are emotionally intelligent—sensitive to others, empathic, and other-oriented—have better relationships with others. Goleman summarizes the importance of emotions in developing empathy by quoting Antoine De Saint-Exupery: "It is with the heart that one sees rightly; what is essential is invisible to the eye."[63] Psychologist Carl Rogers suggests that empathic listening is more than a technique; it's a "Way of Being."[64] Effective empathic listeners make empathy a natural and normal way of interacting with others.

At the heart of empathic listening is the ability not only to know when to speak but also to know when to be silent. Henri Nouwen eloquently expressed both the challenge and the rewards of empathic listening:

> To listen is very hard, because it asks of us so much interior stability that we no longer need to prove ourselves by speeches, arguments, statements, or declarations. True listeners no longer have an inner need to make their presence known. They are free to receive, to welcome, to accept.... Listening is a form of spiritual hospitality by which you invite strangers to become friends, to get to know their inner selves more fully, and even to dare to be silent with you.[65]

Some people are simply better at being empathic than others. Just as you inherit physical qualities from your parents, there is also evidence that you inherit communication traits as well.[66] This does not mean that if you are not naturally empathic, you can never develop empathic skills; it does mean you may have to work a bit harder to enhance these skills. Can people be taught to be more empathic? Research suggests that the answer is a clear "yes." One goal of this book is to enhance your skill in appropriately adapting to others; empathy is at the heart of focusing on the needs and emotions of others.[67]

Four strategies that will help you respond empathically when you listen are understanding your partner's feelings, asking appropriate questions, paraphrasing message content, and paraphrasing emotions.

Understand Your Partner's Feelings

If your goal is to empathize, or "feel with," your partner, you might begin by imagining how you would feel under the same circumstances. If your roommate comes home from a hassle-filled day at work or school, try to imagine what you might be thinking or feeling if you had had a stressful day. If a friend calls to tell you his mother died, consider how you would feel if the situation were reversed. Even if you've not yet experienced the loss of your mother, you can identify with what it would be like to suffer such a loss. Of course, your reaction to life events is unlikely to be exactly like someone else's response. Empathy is not telepathically trying to become your communication partner.[68] But you do attempt to decenter—to consider what someone may be thinking—by first projecting how you might feel and then asking appropriate questions and offering paraphrases to confirm the accuracy of your assumptions. Considering how others might feel has been called the Platinum Rule—even more valuable than the Golden Rule ("Do unto others as you would have others do unto you"). The Platinum Rule invites you to treat others as *they* would like to be treated—not just as *you* would like to be treated.

Ask Appropriate Questions

As you listen for information and attempt to understand how another person is feeling, you may need to ask questions to help clarify your conclusions. Most of your questions will serve one of four purposes: (1) to obtain additional information ("How long have you been living in Buckner?"), (2) to check how the person feels ("Are you frustrated because you didn't get your project finished?"), (3) to ask for clarification ("What do you mean when you say you wanted to telecommute?"), or (4) to verify that you have reached an accurate conclusion about your partner's intent or feeling ("So are you saying you'd rather work at home than at the office?").

Another way to sort out details and get to the emotional heart of a dialogue is to ask questions to help you (and your partner) identify the sequence of events. "What happened first?" and "Then what did he do?" can help both you and your partner clarify a confusing event.

Your ability to ask appropriate questions will demonstrate your supportiveness of your partner and signal that you are interested in what he or she is sharing. Of course, if you are trying to understand another's feelings, you can just ask how he or she is feeling in a straightforward way—don't ask questions just for the sake of asking questions. Also, monitor how you ask your questions. Your own verbal and nonverbal responses will contribute to the emotional climate of your interaction.

Paraphrase Message Content

After you have listened and asked questions, check whether your interpretations are accurate by paraphrasing the content you have heard. **Paraphrasing** is restating in your own words what you think a person is saying. Paraphrasing is different from

paraphrasing
Checking the accuracy of your understanding by restating your partner's message in your own words.

repeating something exactly as it was spoken; that would be parroting, not paraphrasing. Your paraphrase can summarize the essential events, uncover a detail that was quickly glossed over, or highlight a key point. Typical lead-ins to a paraphrase include statements such as

"So here is what seems to have happened . . ."
"Here's what I understand you to mean . . ."
"So the point you seem to be making is . . ."
"You seem to be saying . . ."
"Are you saying . . . ?"

We are not suggesting that you paraphrase when clarification is not needed or appropriate; paraphrase only when you need to confirm your understanding of a murky message or to help the speaker sort out a jumbled or confusing situation. When a listener paraphrases the content and feelings of a speaker's message, the speaker is not only more likely to know that the message is understood but also more likely to trust and value the listener.

Paraphrase Emotions

The bottom line in empathic responding is to make certain that you understand your communication partner's emotional state.

"So you feel . . ."
"So now you feel . . ."
"Emotionally, you are feeling . . ."

These are typical lead-in phrases when paraphrasing feelings.

We have discussed empathic responses and the active listening process using a tidy, step-by-step textbook approach. Realize that, in practice, the process won't be so neat and tidy. You may have to back up and clarify content, ask more questions, and rethink how you would feel before you summarize how your partner feels. Or you may be able to summarize feelings without asking questions or summarizing the content of the message. A sensitive communicator tries not to let his or her technique show. Overusing paraphrasing skills can slow down a conversation and make the other person uncomfortable or irritated. But if used with wisdom, paraphrasing can help both you and your partner clarify message accuracy.

Reflecting on content or feeling through paraphrasing can be especially useful in the following situations:

Before you take an important action
Before you argue or criticize
When your partner has strong feelings
When your partner just wants to talk
When your partner is speaking "in code"—using unclear jargon or unclear abbreviations
When your partner wants to understand your feelings and thoughts
When you are talking to yourself (you can question and check your own emotional temperature)
When you encounter new ideas[69]

When you ask questions and paraphrase content and feelings, keep the following additional guidelines in mind:

Use your own words—don't just repeat exactly what the other person says.
Don't add to the information presented when paraphrasing.
Be brief.
Be specific.
Be accurate.

Don't use paraphrasing skills if you aren't able to be open and accepting; if you try to color your paraphrased comments to achieve your own agenda, you aren't being ethical.

Communication and Ethics

Expressing Honest Social Support to Others

A phony listener is someone who pretends to listen but isn't really attending to what the speaker is saying. Rather than just faking attention when listening to someone who has a problem or stressful "life issue," consider providing ethical and appropriate social support. You provide **social support** to someone when you sensitively and empathically listen to him or her and then offer messages of comfort or confirmation that let the person know that he or she is both understood and valued. Providing social support does not mean trying to solve the issue or problem your communication partner has; rather, it means communicating genuine concern instead of just going through the motions of listening. Effective social support is ethical in that you are doing what you can to provide assistance and comfort; you're not trying to fix the other person's problem.

What are the best ways to be a supportive, empathic listener when someone is experiencing sadness, disappointment, or trauma? One research study suggests that when we are experiencing stress we prefer what researchers called a mid-level amount of social support.[70] Most of us don't need over-the-top, dramatic expressions of support, nor do we like a mild or timid expression of support from others. We prefer a moderate level of positive, genuine, supportive communication. Research also suggests that females prefer a bit higher level of comforting social support than do males. The ability to listen empathically is important when you discern that people need positive, comforting social support.

What do researchers suggest are the best ways to provide supportive, empathic, comforting messages to others? Although there are no magic words or phrases that will always ease someone's stress and anxiety, here are some guidelines for developing social support messages that seem to be appreciated by others:[71]

- Clearly express that you want to provide support. ("I would really like to help you.")
- Appropriately communicate that you have positive feelings for the other person; explicitly tell the other person that you are her or his friend, that you care about her or him, or that you love her or him. ("You mean a lot to me." "I really care about you.")
- Express your concern about the situation that the other person is in right now. ("I'm worried about you right now because I know you're feeling _____ [stressed, overwhelmed, sad, etc.].")
- Indicate that you are available to help; you have time to support them person. ("I can be here for you when you need me.")
- Let the other person know how much you support him or her. ("I'm completely with you on this." "I'm here for you, and I'll always be here for you because I care about you.")
- Acknowledge that the other person is in a difficult situation. ("This must be very difficult for you.")
- Paraphrase what the other person has told you about the issue or problem that is causing stress. ("So you became upset when she told you she didn't want to see you again.")
- Consider asking open-ended questions to see if the other person wants to talk. ("How are you doing now?")
- Let the other person know that you are listening and supportive by providing conversational continuers like "Yes—then what happened?," "Oh, I see," or "Uh-huh."
- After expressing your compassion, empathy, and concern, just listen.

Some types of responses are *less* helpful in conveying social support. Here are a few things *not* to do, based on the conclusions of communication researchers:

- Don't tell the other person that you know exactly how he or she feels.
- Don't criticize or negatively evaluate the other person; she or he needs support and validation, not judgmental comments.
- Don't tell the other person to stop feeling what he or she is feeling.
- Don't immediately offer advice. First, just listen.
- Don't tell the other person that "it's going to get better from here" or that "the worst is over."
- Don't tell the other person that she or he really has nothing to worry about or that "it's no big deal."
- Don't tell the other person that the problem can be solved easily. ("Oh, you can always find another girlfriend.")
- Don't blame the other person for his or her problems. ("Well, if you didn't always drive so fast, you wouldn't have had the accident.")
- Don't tell the other person that her or his expression of feelings and emotion is wrong. ("Oh, you're just making yourself sick. Stop crying.")

Don't be discouraged if your initial attempts to use these skills seem awkward and uncomfortable. Learning to use any new set of skills well takes time. The instructions and samples you have seen here should serve as a guide, rather than as hard-and-fast prescriptions to follow every time. Being an empathic listener can be rewarding in both your personal and your professional life.[72] And here's some encouraging news about listening and responding skills: These skills can be improved. People who have received listening training show overall improvement in their ability to listen to others.[73] Reading this chapter, listening to your instructor give you tips on enhancing your skills, and participating in skill-building activities are well worth your time.

The poem on the following page, "Listen," by an unknown author, summarizes the essential ideas of how to listen and respond with empathy.

> **social support**
> Sensitive and empathic listening, followed by messages of comfort or confirmation, that lets a person know that he or she is understood and valued.

Listen

When I ask you to listen to me and you start giving advice, you have not done what I asked.

When I ask you to listen to me and you begin to tell me why I shouldn't feel that way, you are trampling on my feelings.

When I ask you to listen to me and you feel you have to do something to solve my problems, you have failed me, strange as that may seem.

Listen! All I asked was that you listen. Not talk or do—just hear me.

Advice is cheap: 50 cents will get you both Dear Abby and Billy Graham in the same newspaper.

And I can do for myself; I'm not helpless. Maybe discouraged and faltering, but not helpless.

When you do something for me that I can and need to do for myself, you contribute to my fear and weakness.

But when you accept as a simple fact that I do feel what I feel, no matter how irrational, then I quit trying to convince you and can get about the business of understanding what's behind this irrational feeling.

And when that's clear, the answers are obvious and I don't need advice.

Irrational feelings make sense when we understand what's behind them.

Perhaps that's why prayer works, sometimes, for some people, because God is mute, and doesn't give advice or try to fix things,

God just listens and lets you work it out for yourself.

So, please listen and just hear me, and, if you want to talk, wait a minute for your turn; and I'll listen to you.

—*Anonymous*

Recap

How to Respond with Empathy

Strategy	Action
Understand Your Partner's Feelings	Ask yourself how you would feel if you had experienced a similar situation or recall how you *did* feel under similar circumstances. Or recall how your *partner* felt under similar circumstances.
Ask Questions	Seek additional information to better understand your partner's message.
Reflect Content by Paraphrasing	Summarize for your partner the essence of the information, as you understand it.
Reflect Feelings by Paraphrasing	When appropriate, try to summarize what you think your partner may be feeling.

PRINCIPLES FOR A LIFETIME
Enhancing Your Skills

4. Listen and Respond

Principle Four: Listen and respond thoughtfully to others.
- Stop: Work to turn off competing mental messages that distract your listening focus.
- To overcome self barriers to listening effectively, consciously become aware of your drifting attention. Then, to get back in sync, use self-talk skills and emotion management skills (such as deep breathing) to remain calm and focused on the message, not the messenger.

- To overcome information-processing listening barriers, make mental summaries of the message you hear, recognize when you are tired and not at your listening best, take effective notes, and remain focused.
- To overcome context listening barriers, become aware of your best and worst times of the day for listening; consciously intensify your concentration if you know you're not at your listening best; and assertively take action, such as closing a door or a window, to reduce external noise when listening.
- Look: Listen with your eyes to discern nonverbal information that provides important information about emotions, attitudes, and relationship cues.
- Listen: Work to link facts and details with major ideas you hear.
- Respond: Use effective responding skills by providing feedback that is descriptive, timely, brief, and useful while remaining an active listener.
- Be empathic: Try to imagine how you would feel in a situation like the one your communication partner is in. To confirm your interpretation of his or her message, ask appropriate clarifying questions, then paraphrase both the content and the emotions expressed.
- Paraphrase by briefly summarizing the message in your own words while trying to accurately capture the essence of what your listening partner said; don't add to the information presented when paraphrasing.

Summary

An important principle of communication is to listen and respond thoughtfully to others. Listening is the process of receiving, constructing meaning from, and responding to verbal and nonverbal messages. It includes the processes of selecting, attending, understanding, remembering, and responding to others.

Each person develops a preferred listening style. The four listening styles are people-oriented, action-oriented, content-oriented, and time-oriented. Knowing your listening style can help you adapt your listening approach for maximum listening effectiveness.

Most people struggle with the skill of listening. Barriers to effective listening include focusing on our personal agenda, being distracted by emotional noise, criticizing the speaker, daydreaming, shifting attention, and being distracted by information overload and external noise.

To become a better listener, consider three simple steps: Stop, look, and listen. To stop means to be mindful of the message and avoid focusing on your own distracting inner "talk," which may keep you from focusing on the messages of others. To look is to listen with your eyes—to focus on nonverbal information that provides a wealth of cues about emotional meaning. To listen involves the skill of capturing the details of a message while also connecting those details to a major idea.

The other half of listening is responding to others accurately and appropriately. To respond thoughtfully means to stop and consider the needs of the other person. Check the accuracy of your listening skill by reflecting your understanding of what your partner has said. Responding skills are especially important if your listening goal is to empathize with and support others. Responding skills include understanding the feelings of others, asking appropriate questions, and paraphrasing the message's content and the speaker's feelings. Responding effectively does not mean being a parrot and repeating a message exactly as it was spoken. Paraphrasing means summarizing the gist of the message. The most effective responses to others are carefully timed, provide usable information, avoid cluttering details, and are descriptive rather than evaluative.

Assessing Your Knowledge

For Discussion and Review

Principle One: Be aware of your communication with yourself and others.

1. Explain the "stop" step of the process of improving your listening skill.

Principle Two: Effectively use and interpret verbal messages.

2. Identify and describe how to verbally respond to confirm your understanding of a message.

Principle Three: Effectively use and interpret nonverbal messages.

3. What should you be looking for when performing the "look" step of the process of improving your listening skill?

Principle Four: Listen and respond thoughtfully to others.

4. List several specific strategies presented in this chapter for performing the "listen" step of the process of improving your listening skill.

Principle Five: Appropriately adapt messages to others.

5. If your listening style is typically one of the four discussed in the chapter (people-oriented, action-oriented, content-oriented, or time-oriented), what strategies can you use to adapt your listening style to enhance your listening skill?

Multiple Choice

Choose the *best* answer to each of the following questions.

1. If you sit in class on Monday and listen to a lecture, how much of that lecture will you remember on Tuesday?
   a. about 25 percent
   b. about 50 percent
   c. about 75 percent
   d. almost all of it

2. Hearing refers to the _____ process of decoding sounds.
   a. psychological
   b. physiological
   c. affective
   d. behavioral

3. The stages of the listening process, in order, are:
   a. selecting and attending, understanding, interpreting.
   b. attending, selecting, understanding, rehearsing, responding.
   c. selecting, attending, understanding, remembering, responding.
   d. selecting, attending, interpreting, remembering, responding.

4. While you are giving your friend a detailed account of your weekend (the people you saw, the parties you went to, and what you did), your friend fidgets and keeps looking at the clock. Your friend likely has what type of listening style?
   a. people-oriented
   b. action-oriented
   c. content-oriented
   d. time-oriented

5. Peyton is telling Kamryn about his ideas for improving their service organization's recruiting efforts. Kamryn is responding skeptically and questioning the assumptions Peyton is making. This is likely due to
   a. an action-oriented listening style.
   b. criticism as a barrier to listening.
   c. difficulty with the remembering stage of the listening process.
   d. receiver apprehension.

6. The empathetic process of shifting attention away from your own thoughts to the thoughts of your communication partner is called
   a. a people-centered listening style.
   b. self-focus.
   c. active listening.
   d. social decentering.

7. Almost all speakers can
   a. speak faster than they can listen.
   b. listen faster than they can speak.
   c. speak and listen at about the same rate.
   d. speak fast, but only if they don't listen.

8. Christy is doing her best to pay attention in class, but the lecturer is unbelievably boring. So, instead of taking notes, Christy spends most of the class thinking about the test she has coming up next period. In this situation, Christy is giving in to
   a. emotional noise.
   b. information overload.
   c. self-criticism.
   d. self-focus.

9. Recent research seems to suggest that
   a. men can shift listening between messages better than women can.
   b. men are more likely than women to focus their listening on one message.
   c. men and women can shift listening between messages equally well.
   d. men and women both tend to focus their listening on one message.

10. While listening to Savannah talk about her new job, Connor notices that she has animated facial expres-

sions and open posture, is smiling a lot, is making direct eye contact, and is speaking with a raised pitch and tempo. When Savannah is done speaking, Connor says to her, "So you're feeling pretty good about this job. It's clear that you're really excited." Connor's statement reflects which guideline of responding effectively?
a. Be timely.
b. Be useful.
c. Paraphrase content.
d. Paraphrase emotion.

Assessing Your Skill

Take the following test to assess your level of receiver apprehension. Respond to each of the statements by indicating how much it describes you, using a 5-point scale: 5 = Strongly agree; 4 = Agree; 3 = Uncertain or sometimes; 2 = Disagree; 1 = Strongly disagree.

1. _____ When I am listening, I feel nervous about missing information.
2. _____ I worry about being able to keep up with the material presented in lecture classes.
3. _____ Sometimes I miss information in class because I am writing notes.
4. _____ I feel tense and anxious when listening to important information.
5. _____ I am concerned that I won't be able to remember information I've heard in lectures or discussions.
6. _____ Although I try to concentrate, my thoughts sometimes become confused when I'm listening.
7. _____ I worry that my listening skill isn't very good.
8. _____ I regularly can't remember things that I have just been told.
9. _____ I feel anxious and nervous when I am listening in class.
10. _____ I prefer reading class material rather than listening to it, so I don't have to be stressed about catching all the information the first time.

Scores range from 10 to 50. The higher your score, the more you're likely to experience some anxiety when you listen to others and the harder you'll have to work at developing strategies to improve your listening comprehension.

Source: L. Wheeless, "An Investigation of Receiver Apprehension and Social Context Dimensions of Communication Apprehension," *The Speech Teacher* 24 (1975): 261–268. Taylor & Francis Ltd. <http://www.tandf.co.uk/journals>

Web Resources to Improve Your Knowledge and Skill

Several web sites provide a wealth of information about how to improve your listening skills. There are also many Internet resources to bolster your responding and paraphrasing skills. The following web addresses give you tips, tools, and techniques to help you listen and respond better:

<http://conflict911.com/resources/Communication/Listening> is a site from Project911.com that provides resources and assistance in improving communication and listening skills.

<www.listen.org> is the web site of the International Listening Association. It offers a panoply of resources, quotations, and information about improving listening skills.

<http://web.cba.neu.edu/~ewertheim/interper/commun.htm#top> provides numerous practical tips and techniques to enhance listening and responding skills.

Christian Pierre, "Share the World." © SuperStock, Inc.

There are no ordinary people.

C. S. Lewis

Chapter 6

Adapting to Others: Diversity and Communication

Chapter Outline

- Understanding Diversity
- Ethically Adapting Your Communication to Others
- Culture and Communication
- Barriers to Bridging Differences and Adapting to Others
- Adapting to Others Who Are Different from You
- Summary

Chapter Objectives

After studying this chapter, you should be able to

1. Identify differences and similarities between male and female communication patterns.
2. Describe the importance of gender within the larger context of culture.
3. Describe how differences of gender, sexual orientation, ethnicty, and age influence communication.
4. Define *culture*.
5. Describe, compare, and contrast high-context and low-context cultures.
6. Describe five cultural values.
7. Illustrate five barriers that inhibit communication between individuals.
8. Describe six strategies that will help bridge differences between people and help them adapt to differences.

As C. S. Lewis observed, there are no ordinary people—which implies that each of us is unique. And the not-so-startling fact that people *are* different from one another provides the context for discussion of our final Communication Principle for a Lifetime: *Effective communicators appropriately adapt their messages to others.* We introduce this principle last because often people learn how to adapt only after they have learned the other communication principles. Figure 6.1 presents our now-familiar model, which includes this final principle of appropriately adapting messages to others. Being able to adapt to others suggests that you already have a sense of who you are and a consciousness of the presence of others—self-awareness and other-awareness, the components of the first principle we presented. We learn to use verbal and nonverbal messages as infants, though it may take several years to develop sophistication in using language and nonverbal symbols. Hearing and listening also develop early in our lives. Studies in developmental communication suggest that the ability to appropriately adapt our behavior to others evolves after we have become aware that there is a "me," after we have learned to use verbal and nonverbal symbols to communicate, and after we have developed an ability to hear and listen to others. To adapt to others requires a relatively sophisticated understanding of the communication process.

One of life's unprofound principles with profound implications for human communication is this: *We each have different backgrounds and experiences.*[1] As you learned in Chapter 2, we each see, hear, and experience the world differently. To some degree, we are each estranged from others.

In a world of ever-increasing tensions and conflict arising from differences in culture, religious beliefs, and political ideologies, being able to understand and appropriately adapt to others is of vital importance. When differences are heightened by attitudes of superiority and beliefs about being divinely ordained to dominate others, violence is the typical result.[2]

The goal of this chapter is to identify human differences that may inhibit communication with others and to suggest adaptive strategies that can improve the quality and effectiveness of our communication with others. Throughout the first five chapters, we have noted in our discussions (and in the Diversity and Communication boxed feature) that our differences affect our communication with others. In this chapter, we examine in more detail the influence of these differences on our lives and suggest some communication strategies for bridging these differences in our relationships with others.

As we focus on human differences and how to adapt to them, we will discuss the nature of differences in such areas as gender, sexual orientation, ethnicity, and age. We will also discuss how communication barriers that stem from cultural differences can help you better understand, appreciate, and adapt to people who are not just like you. Even though this chapter focuses on just a few of the ways we are different from one another, realize that there are countless differences that can divide people. Human differences in social class, religion, body type, and clothing choices have created tension in the past and probably will in the future. The challenge is not to let *any* human difference create a chasm so large that we can't find ways to ethically adapt our communication to create shared meaning. Our premise: In order to live comfortably in the twenty-first century, we must learn ways to appreciate and understand human differences, rather than ignore them, suffer because of them, or wish they would disappear. But simply understanding that there are differences is not enough to improve communication; it is important to learn how to use effective communication skills to adapt to those differences.

The principle of adapting to others is applicable to virtually all communication situations. The ideas and strategies for bridging differences in culture or gender that we suggest at the end of this chapter also apply to other differences that create conflict and tension.

Figure 6.1
Communication Principles for a Lifetime

- **5. Adapt** — Appropriately adapt messages to others
- **1. Aware** — Be aware of your communication with yourself and others
- **2. Verbal** — Effectively use and interpret verbal messages
- **3. Nonverbal** — Effectively use and interpret nonverbal messages
- **4. Listen and Respond** — Listen and respond thoughtfully to others

Understanding Diversity

Unless you have an identical twin, you look different from everyone else. Although you may have some things in common with a larger group of people (such as skin color, where you grew up, or language), you nonetheless are a unique individual, not only in your appearance but also in your personality and a host of other ways. There is no one exactly like you. Communication researchers have studied several major differences among humans that affect the way we interact with one another. To frame our discussion of diversity and communication, we'll note differences in gender, sexual orientation, ethnicity, and age and the implications these differences have on communication. Some of these differences are learned, some are based on biology—or, in the case of age differences, simply how long someone has lived—but they all have an effect on how we perceive and interact with others. Following our discussion of some of the classic ways we are diverse, we'll turn our attention to cultural differences and then note how human differences create communication barriers. We'll conclude the chapter by identifying strategies to enhance the quality of communication with others by appropriately adapting to our differences.

Gender

Perhaps the most obvious form of human diversity is gender—the division of human beings into female and male. As we pointed out in Chapter 2, a person's sex is determined by biology; gender is the culturally constructed and psychologically based perception of one's self as feminine, masculine, or **androgynous** (having both feminine and masculine traits). One's gender is learned and is socially reinforced by others, as well as by one's life experience and genetics. Some scholars prefer to study gender as a subset of culture (a co-culture), as a form of cultural diversity on the level of such other aspects as race, ethnicity, and religion. We view gender as one of many basic elements of culture; but because it so pervades our everyday existence, we choose to treat gender more fully in this chapter as we continue our focus on adapting to others.

At one time or another, you have probably thought, "Why doesn't she (or he) act like persons of *my* sex?" Have you ever heard yourself or someone else say, "You men are all alike" or "If women would just be more reasonable, like men are, life would be simpler"? You may also have heard (or said) "Vive la différence"—a French expression that celebrates the fact that men and women are different. Why celebrate? Because that difference makes us fascinating and mysterious, and it keeps the world from being awfully dull. Whatever your view of the relationship between the sexes, your day-to-day interaction with members of both sexes is a fact of life (unless you're a hermit). Women and men work, live, and play together, so it's important to explore the effects of gender on communication in order to improve our ability to relate to one another.

John Gray, author of the book *Men Are from Mars, Women Are from Venus*, would have us believe that the sexes are so different that we actually approach life from two distinct "planets," or spheres of perspective.[3] Although several of Gray's conclusions have been challenged by communication scholars because they are not supported by research, there are some research-documented differences in the ways men and women communicate.[4] Deborah Tannen, author of several books on the behavior of the sexes, views men and women as distinctly different cultural groups.[5] She suggests that female–male communication is cross-cultural communication, with all the challenges inherent in exchanging messages with persons of very different backgrounds and value systems. Perhaps these viewpoints are a bit extreme, and the sexes are actually more alike than different.

There are, however, some interesting differences based on research—not popular opinion or media hype—that are worthy of mention. We will discuss some of these below.

Research using multiple methods and originating in various disciplines consistently shows that differences in men's and women's communication have more to do with

androgynous
Exhibiting both masculine and feminine characteristics.

Have you ever been in a social situation like the one pictured here—in which friends, relatives, or loved ones seem to self-segregate according to gender? What does this common social phenomenon reveal about the nature of gender and communication? How can you appropriately adapt messages to others across gender lines?

why we communicate than *how*. Men tend to talk to accomplish something or complete a task. Women often use conversation to establish and maintain relationships.

Research also reveals that men tend to approach communication from a content orientation, meaning that they view the purpose of communication as primarily information exchange. You talk when you have something to say. This is consistent with the tendency for men to base their relationships, especially their male friendships, on sharing activities rather than talking. Women, research suggests, tend to use communication for the purpose of relating or connecting to others, of extending themselves to other persons to know them and be known by them. What you talk about is less important than the fact that you're talking, because talking implies relationship. There is a short way of summarizing this difference: *Men often communicate to report; women often communicate to establish rapport.*[6] So the point of difference isn't in the way the sexes actually communicate but in the motivations or reasons for communicating. The *how* may not be that different; the *why* may be very different.[7] Our instrumental and expressive orientations to the world translate into our communication behavior.

To bridge the gap, here's what we suggest you do:

- First, work to understand the differences we discuss.
- Second, make an insightful examination of your own behavior in light of the differences discussed and then determine how you conform to and differ from the description of members of your sex.
- Third, be a gender researcher yourself. Make a note of differences as well as similarities between you and members of the opposite sex. Be careful not to ascribe differences in communication only to gender, but to consider a host of other reasons such as age, personality, or culture.
- Finally, make a conscious effort to adapt your behavior appropriately. We don't mean that you have to always communicate as you think members of your sex would or should communicate, but be mindful of how you interact with others to enhance the quality of your relationships with them.

One reason adaptation is a premium skill is that by understanding both approaches to communication (content and relational) and by developing the ability to accomplish both, you broaden what you can do. Just because you're female doesn't mean that you have to take an expressive approach to every interaction; just because you're male doesn't mean that conversations are always about information exchange. In a conversation with a member of the opposite sex, try to assess the person's communication motivation. Analyze what the other person must view as the purpose for the conversation, and adjust your response accordingly. Sometimes it's wise simply to ask the person what he or she wants.

Sexual Orientation

The gay and lesbian community is an important subculture within the larger U.S. culture. Being gay has become a source of pride for some, but it is still a social stigma for others. There is evidence that gay and lesbian individuals continue to be judged negatively based solely on their sexual orientation.[8] Research further suggests that heterosexuals who have negative perceptions of gays and lesbians are more likely to have rigid views about gender roles and will assume that their peers also hold such rigid views and negative impressions of gays and lesbians.[9] In addition, those who hold negative attitudes toward gays and lesbians are less likely to communicate with them. It is because of the existence of these negative attitudes toward gays and lesbians, as well as anti-gay violence and harassment, that some gays and lesbians continue to live in the closet (conceal their sexual orientation).[10]

An effective and appropriate communicator is aware of and sensitive to issues and attitudes about sexual orientation in contemporary society. **Homophobia**, the fear of being labeled or perceived as gay or lesbian, continues to exist among many people. Just as you have been taught to avoid racially biased expressions that degrade someone's race or ethnicity, it is equally important to avoid using language that demeans a person's sexual orientation. Telling stories and jokes whose point or punch line relies on cruelly ridiculing a person because of his or her sexual orientation lowers perceptions of your credibility not only among gay and lesbian people, but also among people who dislike bias against gays and lesbians.

Without intending anything negative, sometimes we unintentionally offend someone through subtle use or misuse of language. For example, gays and lesbians typically prefer to be referred to as *gay* or *lesbian*, rather than as *homosexual*.[11] And the term *sexual orientation* is prefered over *sexual preference* in describing a person's sexual orientation. Our language should reflect and acknowledge the range of human relationships that exist. The key point is this: It is important to be aware of the range of human sexual expression and to be sensitively other-oriented as you interact with those whose sexual orientation is different from your own.

Recap

Gender-Based Approaches to Communication

Masculine Approach
- More instrumental—often characterized by assertiveness and getting things done
- Usually more emphasis on the content of messages
- More focus on the information being exchanged (the *what*) rather than on relational elements (the *how*) in the message
- More attention given to verbal than nonverbal messages

Feminine Approach
- More expressive—often characterized by an emphasis on connecting with others and fostering harmonious relationships
- Usually more emphasis on the relational elements of messages
- More focus on the quality of the relationship between communicators than on information exchanged
- More attention given to nonverbal elements—*how* something is said rather than *what* is said

homophobia
Fear of, aversion to, or discrimination against gays or lesbians.

Ethnicity

Ethnicity is a *social classification* based on a variety of factors, such as nationality, religion, and language as well as ancestral heritage (race), that are shared by a group of people with a common geographic origin. Simply stated, an ethnic group is a group of people who have identified themselves as such, based on a variety of factors that may or may not include ancestral heritage or biological characteristics such as skin color.

Ethnicity fosters common bonds that affect communication patterns. While ethnic groups bring vitality and variety to American society, members of these groups may experience persecution or rejection by members of other groups in our society.

A concept closely related to ethnicity is race, which is based on the genetically transmitted physical characteristics of a group of people who are also classified together because of a common history, nationality, or geographical location.[12] Skin color and other physical characteristics affect our responses and influence the way people of different races interact. A person's racial classification is typically based on such visible physiological attributes as phenotypes, which include skin color and other physical features including body type, hair color and texture, and facial attributes.

Although it may seem easy to classify individuals genetically as belonging to one race or another, it's not quite that simple. One geneticist has concluded that there is much more genetic variation *within* a given racial category than *between* one race and another.[13] There really aren't vast genetic differences between the people assigned to two racial categories. That's why many scholars suggest that we conceptualize race as a category that includes not only biological or genetic characteristics, but also such factors as cultural, economic, social, geographic, and historical elements.[14] The term *race*, therefore, is a fuzzy, somewhat controversial way of classifying people.

Making distinctions between race and ethnicity, Brenda Allen proposes that *ethnicity* be used to refer to "a common origin or culture based on shared activities and identity related to some mixture of race, religion, language and/or ancestry."[15] She suggests that ethnicity may include race, but that race is a separate category based on more genetic or biological factors; however, research has found that those genetic or biological distinctions are not clear-cut.[16] A key distinction between race and ethnicity is that ethnicity is a *socially constructed* category that emphasizes culture (learned behaviors, attitudes, beliefs, values, and norms shared by a group of people) and a host of factors other than racial or genetic background.[17] Not all Asians (race), for example, have the same socially constructed cultural background (ethnicity). Nationality and geographical location are especially important in defining an ethnic group. Those of Irish ancestry are usually referred to as an ethnic group rather than as a race. The same could be said of Britons, Norwegians, and Spaniards.

One of the most significant problems stemming from attempts to classify people by racial or ethnic type is the tendency to discriminate and unfairly, inaccurately, or inappropriately ascribe stereotypes to racial or ethnic groups. **Discrimination** is the unfair or inappropriate treatment of people based on their group membership. One of the goals of learning about diversity and becoming aware of both differences and similarities among groups is to eliminate discrimination and stereotypes that cause people to rigidly and inappropriately pre-judge others.

ethnicity
A social classification based on factors, such as nationality, religion, and language as well as ancestral heritage, that are shared by a group of people with a common geographic origin.

discrimination
The unfair or inappropriate treatment of people based on their group membership.

Age

Because different generations have experienced different cultural and historical events, they often view life differently. If your grandparents or great-grandparents experienced the Great Depression of the 1930s, they may have different attitudes about bank savings accounts than you or even your parents do. Today's explicit song lyrics may shock older Americans who grew up with such racy lyrics as "makin' whoopee." The generation gap is real and has implications for how we communicate with others.

There is considerable evidence that people hold stereotypical views of others based on others' perceived age.[18] You may see someone with graying or thinning hair and wrinkles and make assumptions about that person's preferences in music, food, or even politics. And older people who see someone with tattoos, piercings, and wildly colored hair may make stereotypical assumptions about a host of preferences of the younger person. (Even our example of old and young draws on stereotypes that run the risk of contributing to stereotypical images of appearance and a person's age.)

Regardless of the accuracy of the assumptions we make about others based on perceived age, a person's age has an influence on his or her communication with others, including how messages are processed. For example, one study found that older adults have greater difficulty in accurately interpreting the nonverbal messages of others than do younger people.[19] Older adults don't like to be patronized or talked down to (who does?).[20] And younger people seem to value social support, empathic listening, and being mentored more than older people do.[21]

Authors Neil Howe and William Strauss, two researchers who have investigated the role of age and generation in society, define a generation as "a society-wide peer group, born over a period roughly the same length as the passage from youth to adulthood, who collectively possess a common persona."[22] *Baby boomers* is the label for one such generation, of people born between 1943 and 1960, during the post-war years. Perhaps your parents or grandparents are "boomers." *Generation X* is the term used for people born between 1961 and 1981. If you were born between 1982 and 2002, you and other members of your generation have been labeled *millennials*. Researchers Howe and Strauss suggest that, as a group, "Millennials are unlike any other youth generation in living memory. They are more numerous, more affluent, better educated, and more ethnically diverse. More importantly, they are beginning to manifest a wide array of positive social habits that older Americans no longer associate with youth, including a focus on teamwork, achievement, modesty, and good conduct."[23] Table 6.1 summarizes the labels and common characteristics and values of several generational types.

TABLE 6.1 Summary of Generation Characteristics[24]

Generation Name	Birth Years	Typical Characteristics
Matures	1925–1942	• Work hard • Have a sense of duty • Are willing to sacrifice • Have a sense of what is right • Work quickly
Baby Boomers	1943–1960	• Value personal fulfillment and optimism • Crusade for causes • Buy now/pay later • Support equal rights for all • Work efficiently
Generation X	1961–1981	• Live with uncertainty • Consider balance important • Live for today • Save • Consider every job as a contract
Millennials	1982–2002	• Are close to their parents • Feel "special" • Are goal-oriented • Are team-oriented • Focus on achievement

Your generation of origin has important implications for communication, especially as you relate to others in both family and work situations. Each generation has developed its own set of values, anchored in social, economic, and cultural factors stemming from the times in which the generation has lived. Our values—core conceptualizations of what is fundamentally good or bad, right or wrong—color our way of thinking about and responding to what we experience. Generational and age differences may create barriers and increase the potential for conflict and misunderstanding. For example, one team of researchers, after investigating the role of generations in the workforce, suggests that Generation X workers are paradoxically both more individualistic (self-reliant) and more team-oriented than boomers.[25] In contrast, boomers are more likely to have a sense of loyalty to their employers, expect long-term employment, value a pension plan, and experience job burnout from overwork. Generation Xers, on the other hand, seek a more balanced approach between work and personal life, expect to have more than one job or career, value working conditions over other job factors, and have a greater need to feel appreciated.[26] Of course, these are broad generalizations and do not apply to all people in these categories.

Ethically Adapting Your Communication to Others

The key principle of adapting to others does not mean that you only do or say what others expect or that your primary goal in life is always to please others. You have a responsibility to ethically adapt your messages to others. To be ethical is to be truthful and honest while also observing the rights of others. Ethical communication is communication that is responsible, honest, and fair, that enhances human dignity, and that maintains listener options rather than coerces or forces someone to behave against his or her will. When we encourage you to adapt your messages to others, we are not recommending that you become a spineless jellyfish and say things only to make others happy. It would be unethical to abandon your own ethical principles and communicate only to please others.

Effective communicators are *appropriate* communicators—they are sensitive to others' needs while also communicating to enhance the probability that the message expressed will be the message interpreted. To be an appropriate communicator is to express your ideas in ways that fit the time, place, and situation.

Adapting your communication to others does not mean that you manipulate a conversation so that only *you* can accomplish your goals. Ideally both (or all) parties' goals are met. Several research studies document the importance and value of skillfully being able to adapt your communication behavior.[27] We do not advocate a form of adapted communication that is false or manipulative. Whether you are in an interpersonal interaction, a group, or a presentational speaking situation, adapting your message to others makes common sense. Even so, being sensitive to others and wisely adapting behaviors to others are often not so common.

Culture and Communication

Overheard from a student before class:

> I've had it with all this cultural diversity and gender stuff. It seems like every textbook in every class is obsessed with it. My music appreciation class is trying to force the music of other cultures down my throat. What's wrong with Bach, Beethoven, and Brahms? In English lit, all we're reading is stuff by people from different countries. And it seems my history prof talks only about obscure people I've never heard of before. I'm tired of all this politically correct nonsense. I mean, we're all Americans, aren't we? We're not going off to live

in Africa, China, or India. Why don't they just teach us what we need to know and cut all this diversity garbage?

Have you heard this kind of sentiment expressed before? Perhaps you've encountered this kind of "diversity backlash" among some of your classmates, or you may harbor this attitude yourself. It may seem unsettling to some that school curricula and textbooks are focusing on issues of culture and gender differences. But these changes are not motivated by an irrational desire to be politically correct. They are taking place because the United States is changing. The Communication and Diversity feature documents how diverse the United States is now and will continue to become in the future. There is evidence that the trend toward greater diversity will continue.[28] With this growing diversity comes a heightened awareness that learning about culture and gender differences can affect every aspect of our lives in positive ways. You may not plan to travel the world, but the world is traveling to you. Your employers, teachers, religious leaders, best friends, or romantic partners may have grown up with cultural traditions different from your own. School textbooks and courses are *reflecting* the change, not *initiating* it.

One statistician notes that if the world were a village of 1,000 people, the village would have 590 Asians, 122 Africans, 96 Europeans, 84 Latin Americans, 55 members of the former Soviet Union, and 53 North Americans.[29] Clearly, a global economy and the ease with which technology permits us to communicate with others around the world increase the likelihood that you will establish relationships with people who are different from you and who have cultural traditions different from your own. You need not travel abroad to encounter cultural differences; the world is here.

Communication and Diversity

Diversity Almanac

1. Two-thirds of the immigrants on this planet come to the United States.[30]
2. Hispanics accounted for almost half (1.4 million) of the U.S. population growth of 2.9 million on 2006.[31]
3. It is estimated that more than 40 million U.S. residents learned something other than English as their first language, including 18 million people for whom Spanish is their first language.[32]
4. Almost one-third of U.S. residents under the age of 35 are members of minority groups, compared with one-fifth of those age 35 or older. According to U.S. Census Bureau population projections, by the year 2025, nearly half of all young adults in this country will come from minority groups.[33]
5. If the current trend continues, by the year 2050 the proportion of the U.S. population composed of non-Hispanic whites will decrease to 53 percent, down from the current 72 percent. Asians will increase to 16 percent, up from 4.5 percent; Hispanics will more than double their numbers, to over 25 percent, up from just over 11.5 percent; and African Americans will increase their proportion slightly from the current 12 percent.[34]
6. "About one in three U.S. residents is a minority," said Census Bureau Director Louis Kincannon. "To put this into perspective, there are more minorities in this country today than there were people in the United States in 1910. In fact, the minority population in the U.S. is larger than the total population of all but eleven countries."[35]
7. Between 1995 and 2005, the combined population of African Americans, Native Americans, Asians, Pacific Islanders, and Hispanics grew thirteen times faster than the non-Hispanic white population.[36]
8. One out of every eight U.S. residents speaks a language other than English at home, and one-third of children in urban U.S. public schools speak a first language other than English.[37]
9. California has a minority population of 20.7 million—21 percent of the nation's total. Texas has a minority population of 12.2 million—12 percent of the nation's total.[38]
10. Non-Hispanic whites constitute a minority of the population in Texas, New Mexico, and California.[39]
11. Sixty percent of the residents of Miami, Florida, are foreign-born.[40]
12. There were 37.3 million people age 65 and older in 2006, accounting for 12 percent of the total population. In 2005, this group had numbered an estimated 36.8 million.[41]
13. Studies on gay and lesbian populations in the United States offer estimates that vary from 1 to 9 percent of the general male population, and from 1 to 5 percent of the general female population.[42]
14. There are more millennials (born between 1982 and 2002) than any other age group. The U.S. population in 2003 included 100 million millennials, 44 million Generation Xers (1961-1981), and 78 million baby boomers (1943-1960).[43]

Journalist Thomas Friedman argues that **globalization,** the integration of economics and technology that is contributing to a worldwide, interconnected business environment, is changing the way we work and relate to people around the world.[44] The world is now "flat" rather than round, suggests Friedman, because if you have a computer connected to the Internet or a cell phone, you can connect with anyone else in the world who also has those technologies. In saying that the world is flat, Friedman is using a metaphor to describe the interconnectedness of people throughout the world.

Globalization has increased the probability that you will communicate with someone today who has a cultural background different from your own. For example, when you call to get technical assistance with your computer or advice on fixing your TV, you are more likely to talk to someone in India than in Indiana. Although some suggest that because of globalization and the merging of cultural traditions the concept of a "national culture" is obsolete, nonetheless cultural differences do exist. To ignore the range of human cultural differences is to ignore a significant factor, which can mean the difference between effective communication and ineffective communication. Our point is not to debate the advantages or disadvantages of globalization, but only to suggest that one implication of a "flat" world is that you will increasingly communicate with people who have cultural backgrounds different from your own.

Defining Culture

Culture is a learned system of knowledge, behavior, attitudes, beliefs, values, and norms that is shared by a group of people and shaped from one generation to the next.[45] Communication and culture, says anthropologist Edward T. Hall, are inseparable—you can't talk about one without the other.[46] There is ample evidence that documents the influence of culture on how we work and live.[47] In the broadest sense, culture includes how people think, what they do, and how they use things to sustain their lives. Researcher Geert Hofstede says culture is the "mental software" that helps us understand our world.[48] Like the software and operating system in a computer, our culture provides the framework within which we interpret the data and information that enter our life.

Cultures are not static; they change as new information and new technologies modify them.[49] We no longer believe that bathing is unhealthy or that we should use leeches as the primary medical procedure to make us healthy. Through research, we have replaced both of these cultural assumptions with the values of personal hygiene and modern, sophisticated methods of medical care.

Some groups of individuals can best be described as a **co-culture**—a cultural group within a larger culture. Examples of co-cultures in the United States include the Amish and some communities in Appalachia. A person's gender places her or him in one of the co-cultures that researchers have used to analyze and investigate the influence of communication on our relationships with others. Gays and lesbians constitute another example of an important co-culture in our society.

globalization
The integration of economics and technology that is contributing to a worldwide, interconnected business environment.

culture
A learned system of knowledge, behavior, attitudes, beliefs, values, and norms that is shared by a group of people and shaped from one generation to the next.

co-culture
A culture that exists within a larger cultural context (e.g., gay and lesbian cultures, Amish culture).

Communication and Technology

Adapting to Cultural Differences When Communicating Electronically

It is increasingly likely that you communicate with people who are far away from where you work and live. It's not unusual to have e-mail conversations with people from around the globe. Nor are conference calls or video conferences among people thousands of miles apart rare or surprising. The world is indeed small when it comes to communicating with people from around the globe.

A team of communication researchers points out that when we communicate via e-mail or phone, it takes a bit longer to interpret information about relationships, because often there are fewer nonverbal cues available.[50] In the case of e-mail, we can't see or hear the person we're exchanging messages with. With a telephone call, we can hear a person, but we miss facial expressions and body posture information. Even during a video conference, we're not able to see all of a person's body posture or watch everyone participating 100 percent of the time. The potential for misunderstanding, already present because of cultural differences, a key focus of this chapter, is compounded by the lack of nonverbal information, which usually provides vital information about the nature of the relationship we have with others.

When nonverbal messages are diminished because we're not communicating with people face to face, it's important to seek other sources of information about the nature of the relationship with them. Specifically, what should you do?

- First, you may need to be more direct when responding or expressing how you feel; you may need to describe your emotional responses in writing.
- Second, you may need to ask more questions to clarify meanings.
- Third, it may be necessary to do more paraphrasing to confirm that you understand what others are saying.
- Finally, you simply may need to be more patient with others; relationships may take longer to develop because of the diminished nonverbal cues.

Intercultural communication occurs when individuals or groups from different cultures communicate. The transactional process of listening and responding to people from different cultural backgrounds can be challenging. As we stressed earlier, the greater the difference in culture between two people, the greater the potential for misunderstanding and mistrust. That's why it is important to understand the nature of culture and how cultural differences influence our communication with others. Such understanding helps us develop strategies to make connections and adapt to others with different "mental software."[51]

When you encounter a culture that has little in common with your own, you may experience **culture shock**, a sense of confusion, anxiety, stress, and loss.[52] If you are visiting or actually living in the new culture, your uncertainty and stress may take time to subside as you learn the values and message systems that characterize the culture. If you are trying to communicate with someone from a background quite different from yours—even on your home turf—it is important to consider the role of culture as you interact.

Our culture and life experiences determine our **worldview**—the general cultural perspective that shapes how we perceive and respond to what happens to us. A culture's worldview, according to intercultural communication scholar Carley Dodd, encompasses "how the culture perceives the role of various forces in explaining why events occur as they do in a social setting."[53] These beliefs shape our thoughts, language, and actions. Your worldview permeates all aspects of how you interact with society; it's like a lens through which you observe the world. If, as we noted in Chapter 1, communication is how we make sense out of the world and share that sense with others, our worldview is one of the primary filters that influence how we make sense out of the world. Two frameworks for describing how culture influences our worldview include cultural contexts and cultural values.

Cultural Contexts

The **cultural context** of any communication consists of the nonverbal cues that surround and give added meaning to the message. In this sense, *all* nonverbal cues are part

---

intercultural communication
Communication between people who have different cultural traditions.

culture shock
Feelings of confusion, loss, stress, and anxiety that a person may experience when encountering a culture different from his or her own.

worldview
A perspective shared by a culture or group of people about key beliefs and issues, such as death, God, and the meaning of life, which influences interaction with others; the lens through which people in a given culture perceive the world around them.

cultural context
Additional information about a message that is communicated through nonverbal and environmental cues rather than through language.

When we interact with people from cultures different from our own, we can discover new ways of thinking and fresh ideas. What kinds of verbal strategies can you use to clearly and precisely communicate your messages to people from cultures who don't share your language? How can you make a concerted effort to accurately interpret the words of others who are not from your own culture?

of a cultural context. Some cultures give more weight to the surrounding nonverbal context than to the explicit verbal message when interpreting the overall meaning of a message. Other cultures place less emphasis on the nonverbal context and greater emphasis on what someone says.

For example, when you interview for a job, you may be scanning the face of your interviewer and looking for nonverbal messages to provide cues about the impression you are making on the interviewer. These contextual cues (in this case, the nonverbal messages) give meaning to help you interpret the message of your interviewer. Edward T. Hall helped us understand the importance of cultural context when he categorized cultures as either high- or low-context.[54]

High-Context Cultures In **high-context cultures,** nonverbal cues are extremely important in interpreting messages. Communicators rely heavily on the context of subtle information such as facial expression, vocal cues, and even silence in interpreting messages—hence the term *high-context cultures,* to indicate the emphasis placed on the context. Asian, Arab, and Southern European peoples are more likely to draw on context for message interpretation.

Low-Context Cultures People in **low-context cultures** rely more explicitly on language and the meaning of words and use fewer contextual cues to send and interpret information. Individuals from low-context cultures, such as North Americans, Germans, and Scandinavians, may perceive people from high-context cultures as less attractive, knowledgeable, and trustworthy, because they violate unspoken low-context cultural rules of conduct and communication. Individuals from low-context cultures often are less skilled in interpreting unspoken contextual messages.[55] Figure 6.2 describes differences in communication style between high-context and low-context cultures.

Cultural Values

Ancient Egyptians worshiped cats. The Druids of England believed they could tap into spiritual powers in the shadow of the mysterious rock circle of Stonehenge at the summer solstice. Some would say contemporary Americans place a high value on accumulating material possessions and making pilgrimages to sports arenas on weekends. By paying attention to what a culture values, we can get important clues about how to respond to communication messages, establish relationships, and avoid making embarrassing errors when interacting with people from a given culture. Identifying what a given group of people values or appreciates can give us insight into the behavior of an

high-context culture
A culture in which people derive much information from nonverbal and environmental cues and less information from the words of a message.

low-context culture
A culture in which people derive much information from the words of a message and less information from nonverbal and environmental cues.

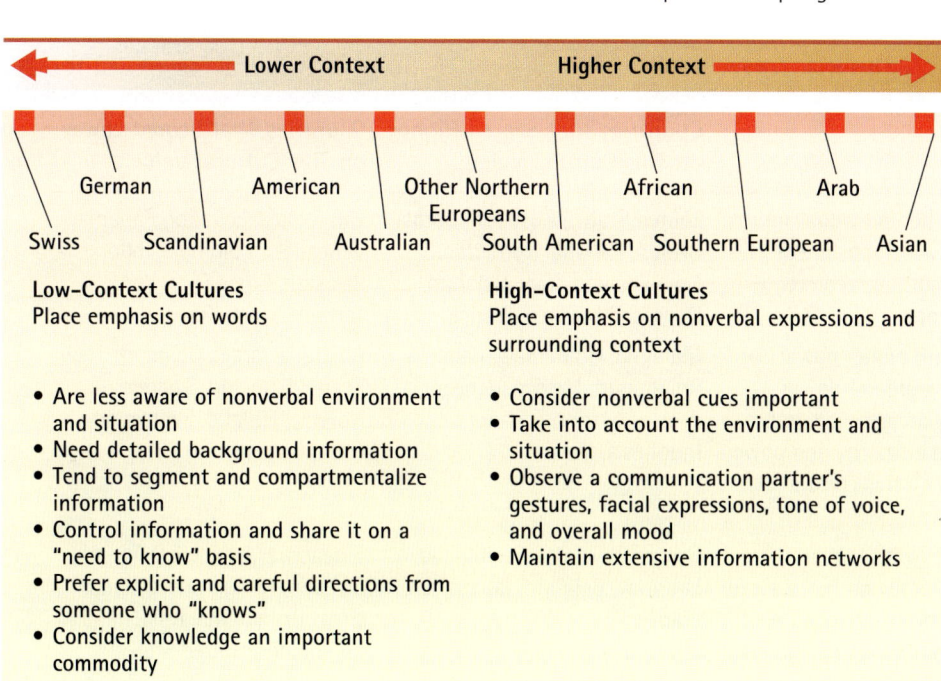

Figure 6.2
A Scale of High-Context and Low-Context Cultures

← Lower Context | Higher Context →

German, Swiss, Scandinavian, American, Australian, Other Northern Europeans, South American, African, Southern European, Arab, Asian

Low-Context Cultures
Place emphasis on words

- Are less aware of nonverbal environment and situation
- Need detailed background information
- Tend to segment and compartmentalize information
- Control information and share it on a "need to know" basis
- Prefer explicit and careful directions from someone who "knows"
- Consider knowledge an important commodity

High-Context Cultures
Place emphasis on nonverbal expressions and surrounding context

- Consider nonverbal cues important
- Take into account the environment and situation
- Observe a communication partner's gestures, facial expressions, tone of voice, and overall mood
- Maintain extensive information networks

individual raised within that culture. Although there are considerable differences among the world's **cultural values**—clearly, not all cultures value the same things—Geert Hofstede has identified five categories for measuring values that are important in almost every culture.[56] Even though his data were collected more than thirty years ago and only sampled employees (predominantly males) who worked at IBM—a large international company with branch offices in many countries—his research remains one of the most comprehensive studies to help us describe what people from a culture may value.

According to Hofstede's research, every culture establishes values relating to (1) individualism versus collectivism, (2) distribution of power (either centralized or shared), (3) avoidance of uncertainty versus tolerance for uncertainty, (4) masculine or feminine cultural perspectives, and (5) long-term and short-term orientation to time. An overview of Hofstede's research conclusions for several countries is included in Table 6.2. These generalizations are based on several surveys that he developed and administered to over 100,000 people. We'll consider each of these five categories of values in more detail.

As we discuss the five cultural values, keep in mind that we are applying generalizations to a cultural group; certainly not all of the people within the cultural group will hold the cultural values we will discuss. Think of these values as explaining cultural *group* differences viewed from an anthropological perspective, rather than *individual* differences viewed from a psychological perspective. There are vast differences *within* a culture as well as between cultural groups.

Individualistic and Collectivistic Cultural Values Which of the following two sayings better characterizes your culture: "All for one and one for all" or "I did it my way"? If you chose the first one, your culture is more likely to value group or team collaboration—it is what researchers call a **collectivistic culture**. Collectivistic cultures champion what people do together and reward group achievement. In contrast, the "I did it my way" phrase emphasizes the importance of the individual over the group.[57] A culture that celebrates individual achievement and in which individual recognition is important is an **individualistic culture**. The United States—with its Academy Awards; its reality TV shows in which contestants vie for the title of "American Idol" or try to be the lone "Survivor"; its countless sports contests; and its community awards to firefighters for dedicated service, to winners of spelling bees, to chefs for their barbecue recipes—perhaps epitomizes the individualistic culture.

cultural values
Whatever a given group of people values or appreciates.

collectivistic culture
A culture that places a high value on collaboration, teamwork, and group achievement.

individualistic culture
A culture that values individual achievement and personal accomplishments.

TABLE 6.2 Countries That Illustrate Five Categories of Cultural Values

Cultural Value	Countries That Scored Higher on This Cultural Value	Countries That Scored Lower on This Cultural Value
Individualism: Societies with higher individualism scores generally value individual accomplishment rather than the collective or collaborative achievement valued by societies with lower scores.	United States, Australia, Great Britain, Canada, Netherlands, New Zealand, Italy, Belgium, Denmark, Sweden, France	Guatemala, Ecuador, Panama, Venezuela, Colombia, Indonesia, Pakistan, Costa Rica, Peru, Taiwan, South Korea
Power Distribution: Societies with higher power distribution scores generally value greater power differences between people; they are generally more accepting of fewer people having authority and power than are those with lower scores on this cultural dimension.	Malaysia, Guatemala, Panama, Philippines, Mexico, Venezuela, Arab countries, Ecuador, Indonesia, India	Australia, Israel, Denmark, New Zealand, Ireland, Sweden, Norway, Finland, Switzerland, Great Britain
Uncertainty Avoidance: Societies with higher uncertainty avoidance scores generally prefer to avoid uncertainty; they like to know what will happen next. Societies with lower scores are more comfortable with uncertainty.	Greece, Portugal, Guatemala, Uruguay, Belgium, Japan, Peru, France	Singapore, Jamaica, Denmark, Sweden, Hong Kong, Ireland, Great Britain, Malaysia, India, Philippines, United States
Masculinity: Societies with higher masculinity scores value high achievement, men in more assertive roles, and more clearly differentiated sex roles than people with lower scores on this cultural dimension.	Japan, Australia, Venezuela, Italy, Switzerland, Mexico, Ireland, Jamaica, Great Britain	Sweden, Norway, Netherlands, Denmark, Costa Rica, Finland, Chile, Portugal, Thailand
Orientation to Time: Societies with higher scores have a longer-term orientation to time; they tend to value perseverance and thrift. Societies with lower scores have a shorter-term orientation to time; they value the past and present, respect for tradition, saving "face," and spending rather than saving money.	China, Hong Kong, Taiwan, Japan, Vietnam, South Korea, Brazil, India, Thailand, Hungary, Singapore, Denmark, Netherlands	Pakistan, Czech Republic, Nigeria, Spain, Philippines, Canada, Zimbabwe, Great Britain, United States, Portugal, New Zealand

Source: Adapted with permission from Geert Hofstede and Gert Jan Hofstede, *Cultures and Organization: Software of the Mind*, Revised and Expanded 2nd Edition (New York: McGraw-Hill, 2005). © Geert Hofstede BV.

Some researchers believe that the values of individualism and collectivism are the most important values of any culture—they determine the essential nature of every other facet of how people behave.[58] Other researchers, however, caution that cultures are complex and that it is dangerous to label an entire culture as "individualistic" or "collectivistic."[59] We agree—obviously, not everyone in a given culture fits a single label. But in trying to understand the role of culture and its impact on human communication, we believe that Hofstede's concept of cultural values, with special emphasis on individualism and collectivism, helps explain and predict how people may send and interpret communication.[60] Using Hofstede's five cultural values to describe a given culture or geographic region is a bit like flying over a country at 35,000 feet; at that height, you can't see the details and note nuances of difference, but you can gain a broad overview of the cultural landscape.

Traditionally, North Americans place a high value on individual achievements. People from Asian cultures are more likely to value collective or group achievement. Hofstede summed up the American value system this way:

> Chief among the virtues claimed . . . is self-realization. Each person is viewed as having a unique set of talents and potentials. The translation of these potentials into actuality is considered the highest purpose to which one can devote one's life.[61]

In a collectivistic culture, conversely, people strive to accomplish goals for the benefit of the group rather than the individual. Here's a description of the Kenyan culture's emphasis on group or team collaboration:

> ... nobody is an isolated individual. Rather, his [or her] uniqueness is a secondary fact. ... In this new system, group activities are dominant, responsibility is shared and accountability is collective. ... Because of the emphasis on collectivity, harmony and cooperation among the group tend to be emphasized more than individual function and responsibility.[62]

Decentralized and Centralized Approaches to Power and Cultural Values Some cultures are more comfortable with a broad distribution of power. People from such cultures prefer a decentralized approach to power. Leadership is not vested in just one person. Decisions in a culture that values decentralized power distribution are more likely to be made by consensus rather than by decree. Research suggests that people from Australia, Israel, Denmark, New Zealand, and Ireland typically prefer minimized power differences between others; they strive for more equal distribution of authority and control.[63]

Cultures that place a high value on centralized power are more comfortable with a more structured form of government, as well as managerial styles that feature clear lines of authority. Hierarchical bureaucracies are common, and the general assumption is that some people will have more power, control, and influence than others. Research by Hofstede suggests that people from Malaysia, Guatemala, Panama, and the Philippines are all high on the centralized power scale.[64]

Uncertainty and Certainty and Cultural Values "Why don't they tell me what's going on?" exclaims an exasperated student. "I don't know what my grades are. I don't know what my SAT score is. I'm in a complete fog." Many people like to know "what's going on." They like to avoid uncertainty and to have a general sense of what's going to happen. Too much uncertainty makes them uncomfortable.

Some people tolerate more ambiguity and uncertainty than others. Cultures in which people need certainty to feel secure are likely to develop and enforce more rigid rules for behavior and establish more elaborate codes of conduct. People from cultures with a greater tolerance for uncertainty have more relaxed, informal expectations for others. "It will sort itself out" and "Go with the flow" are phrases that characterize their attitudes.[65] As shown in Table 6.2, people from Greece, Portugal, and Guatemala generally do not like uncertainty, while people from Singapore, Jamaica, and Denmark are more comfortable not knowing what will happen next.

Again, we remind you that although there is evidence for the existence of the general cultural value of uncertainty avoidance, not all people in a given culture or country find this cultural value equally important. There is considerable variation within a culture as to how people respond to uncertainty.

Masculine and Feminine Cultural Values Some cultures emphasize traditional male values—such as getting things done and being assertive; other cultures place greater emphasis on traditional female values—building relationships and seeking peace and harmony with others. People from **masculine cultures** also tend to value more traditional roles for men and women. These values are not only about biological differences; they are general approaches to interacting with other people. People (both men and women) from masculine cultures value achievement, heroism, material wealth, and making things happen. Men and women from **feminine cultures** tend to value such things as caring for the less fortunate, being sensitive toward others, and enhancing the overall quality of life.[66] Later in this chapter, we will discuss how gender contributes to the development of a culture, but for now it is enough to realize that whole cultures can be typified by whether they identify with or emphasize masculine or feminine values.

We caution you to avoid making sweeping generalizations about every person in any cultural group. Just as there are differences between and among cultures, there are differences within a cultural group. For centuries, most countries have had masculine

masculine culture
A culture that values achievement, assertiveness, heroism, material wealth, and traditional male and female roles.

feminine culture
A culture that values being sensitive toward others and fostering harmonious personal relationships with others.

cultures. Men and their conquests are featured in history books and all aspects of society more than women are. But today's cultural anthropologists see some shift in these values. There is some movement toward the middle, with greater equality between masculine and feminine roles.

Long-Term and Short-Term Time Orientation and Cultural Values

A culture's orientation to time falls on a continuum between long-term and short-term.[67] People from a culture with a long-term orientation to time place an emphasis on the future and tend to value perseverance and thrift because these are virtues that pay off over a long period of time. A long-term time orientation also implies a greater willingness to subordinate oneself for a larger purpose, such as the good of society or the group. In contrast, a culture that tends to have a short-term time orientation values spending rather than saving (because of a focus on the immediate rather than the future), tradition (because of the value placed on the past), and preserving "face" of both self and others (making sure that an individual is respected and that his or her dignity is upheld) and has an expectation that results will soon follow the actions and effort expended on a task. Short-term cultures also place a high value on social and status obligations.

As shown in Table 6.2, cultures or societies with a long-term time orientation include many Asian cultures such as China, Hong Kong, Taiwan, and Japan. Short-term time orientation cultures include Pakistan, Czech Republic, Nigeria, Spain, and the Philippines. Both Canada and the United States are closer to the short-term time orientation than the long-term time orientation, which suggests an emphasis on valuing quick results from projects and greater pressure toward spending rather than saving, as well as a respect for traditions.[68]

Recap

Cultural Values

Individualistic vs. Collectivistic	• Individualistic cultures value individual accomplishments and achievement.
	• Collectivistic cultures value group and team collaboration.
Decentralized vs. Centralized Power	• Centralized power cultures value having power in the hands of a smaller number of people.
	• Decentralized power cultures favor more equality and a more even distribution of power in government and organizations.
Uncertainty vs. Certainty	• Cultures that value certainty do not like ambiguity and value feeling secure.
	• Cultures with a greater tolerance for uncertainty are comfortable with ambiguity and less information.
Masculine vs. Feminine	• Masculine cultures value achievement, assertiveness, heroism, material wealth, and more traditional sex roles.
	• Feminine cultures value relationships, caring for the less fortunate, overall quality of life, and less traditional distinctions between sex roles.
Long-Term vs. Short-Term Orientation to Time	• Cultures with a long-term orientation to time tend to be future-oriented and value perseverance and thrift.
	• Cultures with a short term orientation to time tend to value the past and present, respecting tradition, preserving "face," and fulfilling social obligations.

Barriers to Bridging Differences and Adapting to Others

Now that we've paid attention to how people are different from one another, let's identify barriers that increase the differences that exist between people. Differences, whether culture- or gender-based, often breed misunderstanding. And misunderstanding can lead to feelings of distrust, suspicion, and even hostility. Among the most common reasons for a woman to end up in an emergency room in the United States today is bodily harm inflicted by a male whom she knows.[69]

The front pages of newspapers continue to chronicle the prevalence of terrorism, war, and conflict around the globe, which are due, in part, to different cultural perspectives. Our hopes for harmony in our own country erode when we learn of hate crimes committed against members of co-cultural groups within the larger U.S. culture. Our hopes for peace and prosperity among all of the world's peoples are often dashed when we read of violent clashes between people of different religions, sexual orientations, and ethnicities.

Is it possible to develop effective relationships with people who are different from ourselves? The answer is "Of course." Although almost every relationship experiences some degree of conflict, most of the world's people do not witness annihilating destruction each day. Bridging culture and gender differences is possible.

The first step in bridging differences between people is to identify what hinders effective communication. Sometimes communication falters because of different meanings created by different languages or interpretations of nonverbal messages. And sometimes communication is not effective because of our inability to stop focusing exclusively on our own goals; we fail to consider the needs of our communication partners. To develop effective strategies to adapt to others who are different from ourselves, we'll examine some of the barriers that often separate us from one another.

Assuming Superiority

One of the most powerful barriers to adapting to others is the belief that one's own culture or gender is better than that of others. **Ethnocentrism** is the attitude that our own cultural approaches are superior to those of other cultures.[70] Extreme ethnocentrism is the opposite of being other-oriented. When fans from two rival high schools at a Friday-night football game scream, "We're number one!" they are hardly establishing quality communication. Competition is, of course, expected in sports; but when the mindset of unquestioned superiority is created through cultural or religious identification, the resulting mistrust and suspicion are breeding grounds for conflict. Ethnocentrism and cultural snobbery create a barrier that inhibits rather than enhances communication.

It would probably be impossible to avoid feeling most comfortable with our own culture and people who are like us. In fact, some degree of ethnocentrism can play a useful role in perpetuating our own cultural traditions; we form communities and groups based on common traditions, beliefs, and values. A problem occurs, however, if we become so extremely biased in favor of our own cultural traditions that we fail to recognize that people from other cultural traditions are just as comfortable with their approach to life as we are with ours. And when we mindlessly attack someone else's cultural traditions (which may be a prelude to physical aggression), we begin to erect communication barriers.

A person who assumes superiority may also assume greater power and control over others. Conflicts are often about power—who has it and who wants more of it. Differences in power, therefore, are breeding grounds for mistrust and conflict. The nineteenth-century British scholar Lord Acton said that absolute power corrupts absolutely; although this may not always be the case, an ethnocentric mindset that assumes superiority may add to the perception of assumed power over others. Although it's true that

ethnocentrism
The belief that one's own cultural traditions and assumptions are superior to those of others.

there are cultural differences in attitudes toward power (whether power is centralized or decentralized), world history documents that those who are consistently pushed and pulled and pummeled eventually revolt and seek greater equity of power.

Assuming Similarity

Just as it is inaccurate to assume that all members of the opposite sex or all people who belong to other social groups or classes are worlds apart from you, it is also wrong to assume that others will act and think just like you. Even if they appear to be like you, all people do not behave the same way.[71] Anthropologists Clyde Kluckhohn and Henry Murray suggested that every person is, in some respects, (1) like all other people, (2) like some other people, and (3) like no other people.[72] Our challenge when meeting others is to sort out how we are alike and how we are unique. Focusing on superficial factors such as appearance, clothing, and even a person's occupation can lead to false impressions. Instead, we must take time to explore the person's background and cultural values before we can determine what we really have in common.

On meeting a new acquaintance, we usually explore what we may have in common. "Do you know so and so?" "Oh, you're from Missouri. Do you know Mamie Smith from Buckner?" The search for similarities helps us develop a common framework for communication. But even when we find a few similarities, it's a mistake to make too many assumptions about our new friend's attitudes and perceptions. Because of our human tendency to develop categories and use words to label our experiences, we may lump people into a common category and assume similarity where no similarity exists. Our cultural worldview has a profound impact on how we describe ourselves and those in other cultures. Research has found that English-speaking people describe themselves and others by identifying individual personality traits ("Matt is friendly") rather than merely describing behavior ("Matt brings snacks to the meeting").[73] Each of us perceives the world through our own frame of reference. As one ancient Greek sage put it, "Every tale can be told in a different way." We not only see the world differently, but also express those differences in the way we talk, think, and interact with others. If we fail to be mindful that each of us is unique, we may take communication shortcuts, use unfamiliar words, and assume our communication will be more effective than it is.

Assuming Differences

Although it may seem contradictory to say so, given what we just noted about assuming similarities, another barrier that may keep you from bridging differences between yourself and someone else is to automatically assume that the other person will be different from you. It can be just as detrimental to communication to assume someone is essentially different from you as it is to assume someone is just like you. The fact is, human beings *do* share common experiences and characteristics despite their differences. So we suggest that while you don't want to assume everyone is just like you, it also hinders communication to assume you have nothing in common with others.

Cultural anthropologists have spent considerable effort to identify cultural differences among people. The gist of this entire chapter is that people are different—in culture, gender, and a host of other factors such as personality, age, sexual orientation, and innate talents. Yet if we don't seek to connect with those factors that make us all members of the human family, we may miss opportunities for bridging the real differences that exist.

The point of noting that humans have similarities as well as differences is not to diminish the role of culture as a key element that influences communication, but to recognize that despite cultural differences we are all members of the human family. The words *communication* and *common* resemble one another. We communicate effectively and appropriately when we can connect to others based on discovering what we hold in common. Identifying common cultural issues and similarities can also help you establish common ground with your audience.

How are we all alike? Cultural anthropologist Donald Brown has compiled a list of hundreds of "surface" universals of behavior.[74] According to Brown, people in all cultures

- have beliefs about death
- have a childhood fear of strangers
- have a division of labor by sex
- experience certain emotions and feelings, such as envy, pain, jealousy, shame, and pride
- use facial expressions to express emotions
- have rules for etiquette
- experience empathy
- value some degree of collaboration or cooperation
- experience conflict and seek to manage or mediate conflict

Of course, not all cultures have the same beliefs about death or the same way of dividing labor according to sex, but all cultures address these issues. Communication researcher David Kale believes that another universal value is the dignity and worth of other people. Thus, he suggests that all people can identify with the struggle to enhance their own dignity and worth, although different cultures express it in different ways.[75] Another common value that Kale notes is world peace. Intercultural communication scholars Larry Samovar and Richard Porter assert that there are other common elements that cultures share.[76] They note that people from all cultures seek physical pleasure as well as emotional and psychological pleasure and seek to avoid personal harm. It's true that each culture and each person decides what is pleasurable or painful; nonetheless, argue Samovar and Porter, all people operate within this pleasure-pain continuum.

Another advocate for common human values was the Oxford and Cambridge professor and widely read author C. S. Lewis. In his book *The Abolition of Man*, Lewis argued for the existence of universal, natural laws, which he called the Tao, that serve as benchmarks for all human values.[77] Lewis identified such common values as do not murder; be honest; hold parents, elders, and ancestors with special honor; be compassionate to those who are less fortunate; keep your promises; and honor the basic human rights of others.

What are the practical implications of trying to identify common human values or characteristics? If you find yourself disagreeing with another person about a particular issue, identifying a larger common value such as the value of peace and prosperity or the importance of family can help you find common ground so that the other person will at least listen to your ideas. It's useful, we believe, not just to categorize our differences but also to explore how human beings are similar to one another. Discovering how we are alike can provide a starting point for human understanding. Yes, we are all different; but we share things in common as well. Communication effectiveness is diminished when we assume we're all different from one another in every aspect, just as communication is hindered if we assume we're all alike. We're more complicated than that.

Members of high-context cultures are skilled in using nonverbal cues to communicate. Members of low-context cultures rely more on actual words to send and receive messages. What does your own cultural context reveal about your predisposition to effectively use and interpret nonverbal messages?

Communication and Ethics

Stereotyping Others

We've pointed out that being prejudiced toward others, as well as stereotyping people into predetermined, rigid categories (especially because of racial, ethnic, or cultural backgrounds), can hinder effective communication. Reaching conclusions about someone before you get to know him or her can result in a dishonest relationship. Most people are taught not to be prejudiced toward others. Yet might stereotypes sometimes serve a useful purpose, especially when a quick decision is needed and you have only partial information?

Imagine, for example, that you are driving your car late at night and have a flat tire in a neighborhood that's known to have a high crime rate. While wondering what to do, you see two people who have observed your plight and are moving toward you. Do you hop out of your car and seek their help? Or do you lock your doors and be thankful that you have your cell phone to call for assistance? Are there times when pre-judging a situation and reaching stereotypical conclusions about others may make common sense? Could a case be made that the ability to respond stereotypically may be useful in times of stress when quick thinking is needed? We never know all of the facts about a situation, and we sometimes (maybe even often) have to respond with only the partial information we have at hand. Some might argue that we sometimes need to make stereotypical, snap judgments. Malcolm Gladwell, author of *Blink: The Power of Thinking without Thinking*, describes how people often make quick, snap decisions and argues that sometimes these "thin-sliced," momentary decisions can be quite accurate.[78] Of course, sometimes snap judgments can be way off base. What do you think? Is it ever appropriate to hold stereotypical views of others and to make judgments about them without knowing all of the facts? When do stereotypical evaluations hinder communication? When is it preferable not to make stereotypical decisions?

Stereotyping and Prejudice

Closely related to ethnocentrism and feelings of cultural and gender superiority is the barrier of making a rigid judgment against a class or type of people.

> All Russians like vodka.
> All men like to watch wrestling.
> All Asians are good at math.
> All women like to go shopping.

These statements are stereotypes. They are all inaccurate. To **stereotype** someone is to place him or her in an inflexible, all-encompassing category. The term *stereotype* started out as a printing term to describe a process in which the typesetter uses the same type to print text again and again. When we stereotype, we "print" the same judgment over and over again, failing to consider the uniqueness of individuals, groups, or events. Such a "hardening of the categories" becomes a barrier to effective communication and inhibits our ability to adapt to others.

A related barrier, **prejudice,** is a judgment based on the assumption that we already know all of the information we need to know about a person. To pre-judge someone as inept, inferior, or incompetent based on that person's ethnicity, race, sexual orientation, gender, or some other factor is a corrosive practice that can raise significant barriers to effective communication. Some prejudices are widespread. Although there are more females than males in the world, one study found that even when a male and a female held the same type of job, the male's job was considered more prestigious than the female's.[79] Even though it is illegal in the United States to discriminate because of a person's gender, race, or age in offering employment or promotions, women and members of minority groups may still be discriminated against. In the workplace, stereotyping and prejudice are still formidable barriers to communicating effectively with others.

Mark Twain once said, "It is discouraging to try and penetrate a mind such as yours. You ought to get out and dance on it. That would take some of the rigidity out of it." Learning how to break rigid stereotypes and overcome prejudice is an important part of the process of learning how to adapt to others.

stereotype
To place a person or group of persons into an inflexible, all-encompassing category.

prejudice
A judgment of someone based on an assumption that you already know relevant facts or background information about the person.

Recap

Barriers to Bridging Differences and Adapting to Others

Assuming Superiority	Becoming ethnocentric—assuming that one's own culture and cultural traditions are superior to those of others
Assuming Similarity	Assuming that other people respond to situations as we respond; failing to acknowledge and consider differences in culture and background
Assuming Differences	Assuming that other people are always different from ourselves; failing to explore common values and experiences that can serve as bridges to better understanding
Stereotyping and Prejudice	Rigidly categorizing others and pre-judging others based on limited information

Adapting to Others Who Are Different from You

It is not enough simply to identify some of the common barriers that highlight our differences. Although becoming "consciously competent" about what may keep us from adapting and connecting with others is important, there are also some strategies that can help in our quest to adapt to others. Eleanor Roosevelt once said, "We have to face the fact that either we, all of us, are going to die together or we are going to live together, and if we are to live together we have to talk."[80] In essence, she was saying that we need effective communication skills to overcome our differences. It is not enough just to point to the barriers we have identified and say, "Don't do that." Identifying the causes of misunderstanding is a good first step, but most people need more concrete advice with specific strategies to help them overcome these barriers.[81]

To become competent at any task, you need three things: knowledge, motivation, and skill. To help you become competent in appropriately adapting to others, we suggest that you use two strategies to help you increase your knowledge about others: seek information about a culture and ask questions and listen to the responses. To maintain your motivation to adapt when communicating with others who are different from you, we encourage you to be patient and to strive to tolerate ambiguity and uncertainty; in addition, being mindfully aware of the differences between you and others can help you adapt. Finally, the key skills for communicating with people who are different from you include becoming other-oriented and then appropriately adapting your communication to others.

To have **intercultural communication competence** is to be able to adapt your behavior toward another person in ways that are appropriate to the other person's culture. Intercultural competence involves more than merely being aware of what is appropriate or sensitive to cultural difference. The interculturally competent person *behaves* appropriately toward others. But prior to behaving appropriately toward others, an individual needs to have knowledge about other cultures and the motivation to adapt or modify his or her behavior.

One team of intercultural communication researchers has developed a framework for describing the stages of interpersonal communication competence. The framework has six stages, progressing from least to most competent behavior.[82]

intercultural communication competence
The ability to adapt one's behavior toward another person in ways that are appropriate to the other person's culture.

Stage One: Denial	In this stage, a person believes there is only one real, authentic culture—his or her own culture. The interculturally incompetent person, characterized by extreme ethnocentrism, denies that there are other ways of doing things or other ways of behaving. The individual is oblivious to the fact that other people have a different cultural approach to the world.
Stage Two: Defense	In this stage, a person acknowledges the presence of other cultures, but still believes that his or her culture has the best way of doing things. The person believes that his or her own view of the world is best and other culturally based views are wrong. So, the person defends his or her own culture as the best culture.
Stage Three: Minimization	In this stage, a person recognizes that there are other cultural perspectives, but suggests that there are no real differences in the way people behave and interact. He or she simply doesn't see the nuances or the major differences reflected in culture. Thus, cultural differences are minimized.
Stage Four: Acceptance	In this stage, a person begins to realize that there are other culturally based ways of behaving. The person's ethnocentrism (perception of cultural superiority) is diminished, and he or she recognizes and accepts cultural differences.
Stage Five: Adaptation	In this stage, intercultural competence emerges in full blossom. A person consciously seeks to appropriately adapt his or her behavior in response to cultural differences.
Stage Six: Integration	At this highest stage of intercultural competence, a person moves freely in and out of his or her own cultural mindset while adapting to others. The person skillfully modifies his or her behavior to appropriately adapt to other cultures because the person's own cultural identity is minimized; the focus is on others.

The first three stages of this six-stage framework reflect an **ethnocentric cultural perspective**, in which a person assumes that her or his own culture is superior to all other cultures. The last three stages of cultural competence reflect a more enthnorelative cultural perspective. An **ethnorelative cultural perspective** requires an appreciation for and sensitivity to cultural differences; one's own cultural perspective is not viewed as always superior to other cultural perspectives.[83] The remaining portion of this chapter presents specific strategies to help you bridge differences between yourself and people who come from different cultures.[84]

Seek Information

Philosopher André Gide said, "Understanding is the beginning of approving." Prejudice often is the result of ignorance. Learning about another person's values, beliefs, and culture can help you understand his or her messages and their meaning. As you speak to a person from another culture, think of yourself as a detective, watching for implied, often unspoken messages that provide information about the values, norms, roles, and rules of that person's culture.

You can also prepare yourself by studying other cultures. If you are going to another country, start by reading a travel guide or another general overview of the culture. You may then want to learn more detailed information by studying the history, art, or geography of the culture. The Internet offers a wealth of information about the cultures and traditions of others. In addition to reading books and magazines and using cyber sources, talk to people from other cultures. If you are trying to communicate with someone closer to home who is from a different background, you can learn about the music, food, and other aspects of the culture. Given the inextricable link between

ethnocentric cultural perspective
The view that one's own culture is superior to all other cultures.

ethnorelative cultural perspective
An appreciation for and sensitivity to cultural differences.

Recap

A Model of the Stages of Intercultural Competence

Stage One: Denial	Stage Two: Defense	Stage Three: Minimization	Stage Four: Acceptance	Stage Five: Adaptation	Stage Six: Integration
A person denies that there are other cultural approaches to behavior beyond that of his or her own culture.	A person believes that his or her own culture is best.	A person minimizes cultural differences between himself or herself and others.	A person begins to realize that there are other culturally based ways of behaving.	A person consciously seeks to appropriately adapt his or her behavior in response to cultural differences.	A person is integrated into several cultures and minimizes his or her own cultural identity.

language and culture, the more skilled you become at speaking another language, the better you will understand the traditions and customs of the culture where it is spoken.[85]

Ask Questions and Listen

When you talk with people who are different from you, you may feel some discomfort and uncertainty. This is normal. We are more comfortable talking with people we know and who are like us. Communication, through the give-and-take process of listening, talking, and asking questions, helps to reduce the uncertainty present in any relationship. When you meet people for the first time, you are typically not certain about their likes and dislikes, including whether they like or dislike you. When you communicate with a person from another culture or co-culture, the uncertainty level escalates. As you begin to talk, you exchange information that helps you develop greater understanding. If you continue to ask questions, eventually you will feel less anxiety and uncertainty. You will be more able to predict how the person will behave. When you meet a person who is different from you, ask thoughtful questions, then pause to listen. This is a simple technique for gathering information and also for confirming the accuracy of your expectations and assumptions.

Just asking questions and sharing information about yourself is not sufficient to remove communication barriers and bridge differences in culture and background, but it is a good beginning. The skills of stopping (focusing on the message of the other person), looking (observing nonverbal cues), and listening (noting both details and major ideas) that we presented in the last chapter will serve you well in enhancing communication with people from cultural traditions different from your own.

Tolerate Ambiguity

Many people become uncomfortable with uncertainty and ambiguity—especially if they are from a low-context culture such as those in North America. As we discussed earlier in the chapter, people from low-context cultures prefer a more direct approach to getting information. North Americans, for example, often say things like "Tell it to me straight," "Don't beat around the bush," or "Just tell me what you want."

Communicating with someone from a culture that does not value such directness produces uncertainty. It may take time and several exchanges to clarify a message. If you are from a cultural tradition that values certainty, and you are uncomfortable with uncertainty, you may have to acknowledge the cultural difference. Be patient and work at tolerating more ambiguity. Don't be in a hurry to have all of the details nailed down. Remind yourself that the other person does not have the same attitudes about knowing the future or appreciating details.

Develop Mindfulness

To be **mindful** is to be aware of how you communicate with others. A mindful communicator puts into practice the first communication principle we presented in this book: *Be aware of your communication with yourself and others.* To be a mindful communicator, you should constantly remind yourself that other people are not like you. Also, you should be aware that other people do not use different communication strategies to offend or to be rude; they just have different culturally based strategies of interacting with others. Intercultural communication scholar William Gudykunst suggests that being mindful is one of the best ways to approach any new cultural encounter.[86] Mindfulness is a conscious state of mind, a realization of what is happening to you at a given moment. If you are not mindful, you are oblivious to the world around you. You are on mental cruise control.[87]

How can you cultivate the skill of being mindful? You can become more mindful through **self-talk,** something we discussed earlier in the book. Self-talk consists of messages you tell yourself to help you manage your discomfort, emotions, or negative thoughts about situations. For example, acknowledging cultural differences through self-talk, rather than emotionally and mindlessly becoming offended, can help you maintain your composure and communicate in a manner appropriate to the circumstances.

Become Other-Oriented

Scholars of evolution might argue that it is our tendency to look out for number one that ensures the continuation of the human race. But if we focus exclusively on ourselves, it is very unlikely that we will be effective communicators. As we noted earlier, assuming superiority is a major barrier to communicating with others. Most of us are **egocentric**—focused on ourselves.[88] Our first inclination is to focus on meeting our own needs before addressing the needs of others.[89]

In this chapter, we have emphasized the principle of adapting to others. If we fail to adapt our message to listeners, especially listeners who are different from us (and isn't everyone different from you?), it is less likely that we will achieve our communication goal. As we noted earlier, adapting messages to others doesn't mean that we tell others only what they want to hear. That would be unethical, manipulative, and ineffective. Nor does being considerate of others mean we abandon all concern for our own interests. **Other-oriented communication** is communication in which we take into account the needs, motives, desires, and goals of our communication partners while still maintaining our own integrity. In the choices we make in forming messages and selecting the time and place to deliver them, we should consider the thoughts and feelings of others.

Becoming other-oriented is not a single skill but a family of skills anchored in a willingness to try to understand others' thoughts and feelings. Research in emotional intelligence documents that focusing on the needs and interests of others is essential to adapting communication messages to others.[90]

Research also suggests that the level of empathy and social support we prefer is culturally determined. Research has found, for example, that people from Western European countries respond more positively to emotional support than do people from Eastern European nations and that people from Asian nations respond even less.[91] So when providing empathic social support it's important to consider not our own need for emotional support, but the preferences of others.

How do you become other-oriented? We suggest a two-stage process, using skills discussed previously. The first stage, which we previewed in Chapter 5, is called social

---

mindful
Aware of what you are doing and how you are communicating with others.

self-talk
Inner speech; communication with the self; the process of mentally verbalizing messages that help a person become more aware or mindful of how he or she is processing information and reacting to life situations.

egocentric
Focused on oneself and one's importance.

other-oriented communication
Communication in which we focus on the needs and concerns of others while maintaining our personal integrity; achieved through the processes of socially decentering and being empathic.

decentering—consciously *thinking* about another's thoughts and feelings. The second stage is developing empathy, a set of skills we also discussed in the last chapter. To empathize is to respond *emotionally* to another's feelings and actions. We'll discuss each of these two stages in more detail.

Social Decentering

Social decentering is a *cognitive process* through which we take into consideration another person's thoughts, values, background, and perspectives. It is seeing the world from the other person's point of view. To socially decenter is not to be a mind reader but to use past experiences and the ability to interpret the clues of others to understand what others may be thinking or how they may be perceiving issues or situations. According to Mark Redmond, a scholar who has extensively studied the process of social decentering, there are three ways to socially decenter.[92]

First, develop an understanding of the other person, based on how you have responded when something similar has happened to you in the past.[93] You know what it's like when you've been late for a meeting or an important appointment. When someone you know says he or she feels frazzled because he or she was late for a major meeting, you can think about what would be going through your mind if the same thing happened to you.

A second way to socially decenter is to base your understanding of what another person might be thinking on your knowledge of how that person has responded in the past. In communicating with someone who is different from you, the more direct experience you have interacting with that person, the better able you usually are to make predictions about how that person will react and respond. Suppose, for example, you have never seen one particular friend of yours be late for a meeting; you know how generally punctual your friend is. You therefore can guess that your friend would be quite frustrated by being late for a meeting.

A third way we socially decenter is to use our understanding of how most people, in general, respond to situations. If your roommate is from France, you probably have some general sense of the cultural differences between you and your French friend. You may harbor some general theories or assumptions about other French people. The trick, however, is to avoid rigid stereotypes or prejudices that confine or limit your perceptions. The more you can learn about others' cultural or gender perspectives, the more accurate you can become in socially decentering. It is important, however, not to develop inaccurate, inflexible stereotypes and labels for others or to base your perceptions of others only on generalizations.

Developing Empathy

Socially decentering involves attempting to understand what another person may be thinking. Developing **empathy,** a second strategy for becoming other-oriented, is feeling the *emotional* reaction that the other person may be experiencing. When we feel empathy, we feel what another person feels.

As we discussed in the last chapter, you develop the ability to empathize by being sensitive to your own feelings and assessing how you feel during certain situations and then projecting those feelings onto others.[94] To develop empathy, we suggested that you first *stop* focusing on only your own messages and thoughts and focus instead on the messages of others. We also recommended that you *look* for information about the emotional meaning of messages by focusing on nonverbal cues. Then *listen* by concentrating on what someone is telling you. In addition, *imagine* how you would feel if you were in your partner's position. Then *ask* appropriate questions, if you need to, to gain additional information. Finally, *paraphrase* your communication partner's message content and feelings and monitor his or her reactions to what you communicate.

Empathy is different from sympathy. When you offer **sympathy,** you tell others that you are sorry that they feel what they are feeling. When you sympathize, you acknowledge someone's feelings. When you empathize, however, you experience an emotional reaction that is similar to the other person's; as much as possible, you strive to feel what he or she feels.

The late author and theologian Henri J. M. Nouwen suggested that empathy lies at the heart of enhancing the quality of our relationships with others. As Nouwen

social decentering
A cognitive process through which we take into account another person's thoughts, values, background, and perspectives.

empathy
An emotional reaction that is similar to the reaction being experienced by another person.

sympathy
An acknowledgment that someone is feeling a certain emotion, often grief; compassion.

phrased it, in order to bridge our differences we need to "cross the road for one another":

> We become neighbors when we are willing to cross the road for one another. There is so much separation and segregation: between black people and white people, between gay people and straight people, between young people and old people, between sick people and healthy people, between prisoners and free people, between Jews and Gentiles, Muslims and Christians, Protestants and Catholics, Greek Catholics and Latin Catholics.
>
> There is a lot of road crossing to do. We are all very busy in our own circles. We have our own people to go to and our own affairs to take care of. But if we could cross the road once in a while and pay attention to what is happening on the other side, we might indeed become neighbors.[95]

Adapt to Others

Adapting to others gets to the bottom line of this chapter. After you have thought about how you may be different from others, considered culture and gender differences, and even identified potential barriers to communication, you reach this question: So now what do you *do*? What you do is appropriately adapt. To **adapt** is to adjust your behavior in response to the other person or persons you are communicating with. You don't just keep communicating in the same way you always did. You make an effort to change how you communicate, to enhance the quality of communication.

We adapt messages to others to enhance their understanding of the message, to help us achieve the goal or intended effect of our communication, to ensure that we are ethical in our communication with others, and to establish and develop satisfying relationships. Research documents the importance and value of being able to skillfully adapt your communication behavior.[96] To enhance understanding, you may need to slow your rate of speech or talk faster than you normally do. You may need to use more examples or to speak in a very structured, organized way. To ensure that you achieve your communication objectives, you may need to draw on statistics and other

Because the communication process may be difficult between members of different cultures, both parties need to work to understand each other. How have you adapted your communication skills when interacting with members of a different culture? In what ways can you improve your efforts to enhance understanding in such situations?

adapt
To adjust behavior in response to someone else.

Recap

How to Become Other-Oriented

Socially Decenter View the world from another person's point of view.
- Develop an understanding of someone, based on your own past experiences.
- Consider what someone may be thinking, based on your previous association with the person.
- Consider how most people respond to the situation at hand.

Develop Empathy Consider what another person may be feeling.
- Stop: Avoid focusing only on your own ideas or emotions.
- Look: Determine the emotional meaning of messages by observing nonverbal messages.
- Listen: Focus on what the other person says.
- Imagine: Consider how you would feel in a similar situation.
- Paraphrase: Summarize your understanding of the other person's thoughts and feelings.

forms of evidence to prove your point. Or your communication partner may not be impressed with statistics but might be quite moved by a story that poignantly illustrates your point. We also adapt messages to be ethical. Ethical communication gives your communication partner choices, rather than forcing or coercing him or her to do what you demand. Telling the truth, not withholding information, and identifying options are ways to adapt your message to be an ethical communicator. Finally, we adapt our communication to generate more positive feelings or regard for others, so as to enhance our relationships and improve our quality of life.

Can the skills and principles we have suggested here make a difference in your ability to communicate with others? The answer is a resounding "yes."[97] Communication researcher Lori Carrell found that students who had been exposed to lessons in empathy as part of their study of interpersonal and intercultural communication improved their ability to empathize with others.[98] There is evidence that if you master these principles and skills, you will be rewarded with greater ability to communicate with others who are different from you—which means everyone.[99]

It is not possible to prescribe how to adapt to others in all situations. We can suggest that you draw on the other four Communication Principles for a Lifetime that we have presented in this book. You will be more effective in adapting to others if you are aware of your own cultural traditions and gender-related behavior and how they are different from those of other people. Being able to use and interpret verbal and nonverbal symbols appropriately and effectively will also increase your ability to adapt and respond to others. The essential skills of listening and responding to others are key competencies in being able to adapt to others—to be other-oriented. To interpret spoken information accurately (as well as "listening" with your eyes to unspoken messages) is a linchpin of competence in adapting to others.

Adapting your messages to others does not mean you have to abandon your own ethical principles or personal positions. It would be unethical to change your opinions and point of view just to avoid conflict and keep the peace—like a politician who only tells his or her audience what they want to hear. It was President Harry Truman who said, "I wonder how far Moses would have gone if he'd taken a poll in Egypt?"[100] A spineless, wishy-washy approach to communication does not enhance the quality of your relationships with others. But you can be sensitive and mindful of how your comments may be received by others.

Recap

Adapting to Others

Develop Knowledge

Seek Information	Learn about a culture's worldview.
Ask Questions and Listen	Reduce uncertainty by asking for clarification and listening to the answer.

Develop Motivation

Tolerate Ambiguity	Take your time and expect some uncertainty.
Develop Mindfulness	Be consciously aware of cultural differences, rather than ignoring the differences.

Develop Skill

Become Other-Oriented	Put yourself in the other person's mental and emotional frame of mind; socially decenter and develop empathy.
Adapt to Others	Listen and respond appropriately.

Principles for a Lifetime
Enhancing Your Skills

5. Adapt

Principle Five: Appropriately adapt messages to others.

- It's important to learn to ethically adapt messages to others to enhance understanding, because we're all different for a variety of reasons (culture, age, background, experience, sexual preference, attitudes, beliefs, values).
- Appropriately adapt messages based on gender differences in communication by doing the following four things: (1) seek to understand differences between genders, (2) consider your own preferences, needs, and communication goals, (3) avoid assuming that differences between people are solely the result of gender, (4) consider both your needs and goals and those of the other person.
- Appropriately adapt your messages, paying particular attention to your verbal messages, to reflect differences in sexual orientation.
- Appropriately adapt your messages to respond to differences in age and ethnicity.
- Appropriately adapt messages to others based on whether an individual is from a high-context culture (in which an emphasis is placed on nonverbal messages and the surroundings) or a low-context culture (in which an emphasis is placed on words and explicitly communicated messages).
- Appropriately adapt messages to others based on the cultural value of individualism versus collectivism, preference for certainty versus tolerance of uncertainty, tendency to emphasize masculine versus feminine values, preference for centralized or decentralized power, and a long-term or short-term orientation to time.
- Avoid being ethnocentric—always assuming that your cultural traditions and approaches are superior to other cultural traditions.
- Don't assume everyone does things the same way you do or holds the same attitudes, beliefs, or values that you hold.
- Don't assume that because someone is from another culture or geographic area, you don't have anything in common with the person; seek to establish common ground.
- Avoid making rigid, inflexible stereotypes and pre-judgments of others based on limited information.
- Seek to bridge differences between yourself and others who speak a different language or have different interpretations for nonverbal expressions; learn the language of others.
- Bridge cultural differences by learning as much as you can about another culture.
- Listen and ask questions to enhance your understanding of others.
- Be patient and tolerate some ambiguity and uncertainty when you communicate with people who are different from you.
- Being mindful, or aware that differences will exist, can help you better tolerate differences.
- Develop your skills at being other-oriented: Focus on the needs and concerns of others while maintaining your personal integrity.
- Socially decenter: Think about how your communication partner would respond to information and situations; take into account people's thoughts, values, background, and perspectives.
- Empathize: Try to imagine how you would feel if you were in the other person's position.

Summary

Human differences result in the potential for misunderstanding and miscommunication. Differences in gender, sexual orientation, age, and ethnicity contribute to the challenge of communicating with others. The relevant communication principle is

Principle Five: *Effective communicators appropriately adapt their messages to others.* One concept that makes a difference when we communicate with others is taking into consideration cultural perspective or worldview. Culture is a system of knowledge that is shared by a group of people. Our worldview is the overarching set of expectations that helps us explain why events occur as they do and gives us a perspective for explaining what happens to us and others. Intercultural communication occurs when individuals or groups from different cultures communicate.

Culture and communication are clearly linked because of the powerful role culture plays in influencing our values. Cultural values reflect how individuals regard masculine perspectives (such as achieving results and being productive) and feminine perspectives (such as consideration for relationships), their tolerance of uncertainty or preference for certainty, their preference for centralized or decentralized power structures, the value they place on individual or collective accomplishment, and their long-term or short-term orientation to time.

Two gender-related cultural values are the masculine orientation, which involves assertiveness and action, and the feminine orientation, which emphasizes connection and the development of harmonious relationships and community. These orientations translate into communication behavior that differs depending on one's sex. Women tend to attend to the relational dimension of communication; that is, they focus on *how* something is said more than on *what*. Their purpose in communication typically is to establish and develop relationships and connections with others. In contrast, men tend to approach communication from a content perspective, meaning that they view communication as functioning primarily for information exchange. The principle of adaptation is quite useful in bridging gender differences in communication style. People can and should break out of sex-specific behavior to choose the best approach to communicating in a given situation.

Several barriers inhibit effective communication. When one culture or gender assumes superiority, communication problems often occur. Ethnocentrism is the belief that one's own cultural traditions and assumptions are superior to those of others. Sexism is the attitude that one sex is superior to the other. It is not productive when individuals or groups from different backgrounds or cultures assume that others behave with similar responses. But it is also important not to automatically assume that other people are different from you. We stereotype by placing a group or person into an inflexible, all-encompassing category. A related barrier is prejudice. When we prejudge someone before we know all the facts about him or her, we also create a potential communication problem. Stereotyping and prejudice can keep us from acknowledging others as unique individuals and therefore can hamper effective, open, honest communication. Differences in language codes and the way we interpret nonverbal messages interfere with effective communication.

Strategies for adapting to others include developing knowledge, motivation, and skill to bridge differences of culture and gender. To enhance understanding, actively seek information about others who are different from you, ask questions, and listen to the responses. Motivational strategies include being tolerant of ambiguity and uncertainty and being more conscious or mindful when interacting with others who are different from you. Finally, to develop skills in adapting to others, become other-oriented by socially decentering and emotionally empathizing with others. Then appropriately respond by adapting your messages to others; consider their thoughts and feelings.

Assessing Your Knowledge

For Discussion and Review

Principle One: Be aware of your communication with yourself and others.

1. How does the suggested skill of mindfulness enhance your ability to improve your intercultural communication competence?

Principle Two: Effectively use and interpret verbal messages.

2. How do words and labels contribute to making stereotypical judgments of others?

Principle Three: Effectively use and interpret nonverbal messages.

3. Explain the difference between high-context and low-context cultures in relation to the role and importance of nonverbal messages.

Principle Four: Listen and respond thoughtfully to others.

4. Discuss the value and importance of accurately listening and thoughtfully responding to others as a skill for enhancing intercultural competence.

Principle Five: Appropriately adapt messages to others.

5. How do the skills of socially decentering and empathy lead to the ability to appropriately adapt messages to others?

Multiple Choice

Choose the *best* answer to each of the following questions.

1. The cultural value of _____ means that people in the culture tend to value high achievement and differentiation in sex roles.
   a. uncertainty avoidance
   b. power distribution
   c. individualism
   d. masculinity

2. _____ cultures tend to value group achievement.
   a. Individualistic
   b. Decentralized
   c. Collectivistic
   d. Centralized

3. The likelihood that you will interact with individuals from different cultural backgrounds is greater now than in the past because of an increased interconnectedness referred to as
   a. culture shock.
   b. intercultural communication.
   c. globalization.
   d. decentralized values.

4. Kai is discussing an assignment with his professor, and the professor's office is rather cold. Instead of saying something to the professor, Kai crosses his arms, exaggerates his shivering, and hunches forward slightly. Kai then continues the conversation and waits for the professor to notice. Kai is likely from a/n _____ culture.
   a. high-context
   b. low-context
   c. ethnic
   d. diverse

5. According to your textbook, adapting your message to your audience means
   a. changing your message so that your audience will agree with it.
   b. going along with the ideas that are comfortable to the time, place, and situation.
   c. manipulating the way you express your ideas so that other interpret them correctly.
   d. doing what it takes to make sure that your goals are accomplished.

6. Cultures that tend to rely on explicit language to convey information are
   a. high power.
   b. low power.
   c. high context.
   d. low context.

7. To feel what another person is feeling is called
   a. superiority.
   b. egocentrism.
   c. intellectualism.
   d. empathy.

8. Because the Japanese culture is collectivistic,
   a. Japanese workers work better by themselves.
   b. Japanese workers value personal honors and awards.
   c. Japanese workers work better in teams.
   d. Japanese workers tend to be more loosely knit socially.

9. The tendency to believe that one's own culture is superior to other cultures is called
   a. ethnocentrism.
   b. egocentrism.
   c. stereotyping
   d. collectivism

10. On a recent Caribbean cruise, Cody commented to a friend, "I feel strange talking to the room stewards. They're all from interesting places and their English is excellent, but there's nothing we can talk about." Cody's dilemma can best be ascribed to
    a. different communication codes.
    b. assuming differences.
    c. prejudice.
    d. decentering.

Answers to the questions in this practice test can be found at the end of the book.

Assessing Your Skill

To assess your self-perceived level of ethnocentrism, complete the following Generalized Ethnocentrism (GENE) Scale.

Directions: Read the following statements concerning your feelings about your culture and other cultures. In the space provided, indicate the number that reflects the degree to which each statement applies to you by marking whether you (5) Strongly Agree, (4) Agree, (3) Are Undecided, (2) Disagree, or (1) Strongly Disagree with the statement.

There are no right or wrong answers. Some of the statements may seem very similar to another. Remember, everyone experiences some degree of ethnocentrism. Be honest. Work quickly and record your first response.

1. _____ Most other cultures are backward compared with my culture.

2. _____ My culture should be the role model for other cultures.
3. _____ People from other cultures act strangely when they come to my culture.
4. _____ Lifestyles in other cultures are just as valid as those in my culture.
5. _____ Other cultures should try to be more like my culture.
6. _____ I'm not interested in the values and customs of other cultures.
7. _____ People in my culture could learn a lot from people in other cultures.
8. _____ Most people from other cultures just don't know what's good for them.
9. _____ I respect the values and customs of other cultures.
10. _____ Other cultures are smart to look up to our culture.
11. _____ Most people would be happier if they lived like people in my culture.
12. _____ I have many friends from different cultures.
13. _____ People in my culture have just about the best lifestyles anywhere.
14. _____ Lifestyles in other cultures are not as valid as those in my culture.
15. _____ I am very interested in the values and customs of other cultures.
16. _____ I apply my values when judging people who are different.
17. _____ I see people who are similar to me as virtuous/good.
18. _____ I do not cooperate with people who are different.
19. _____ Most people in my culture just don't know what is good for them.
20. _____ I do not trust people who are different.
21. _____ I dislike interacting with the values and customs of other cultures.
22. _____ I have little respect for the values and customs of other cultures.

Scoring:
To determine your ethnocentrism score, complete the following four steps:

1. Add your responses to items 4, 7, and 9.
2. Add your responses to items 1, 2, 5, 8, 10, 11, 13, 14, 18, 20, 21, and 22.
3. Subtract the sum from Step 1 from 18 (i.e., 18 minus Step 1 sum).
4. Add results from Step 2 and Step 3. This is your generalized ethnocentrism score.

Higher scores indicate higher ethnocentrism. Scores higher than 55 points are considered to reflect high ethnocentrism.

Source: The GENE Scale, developed by James Neuliep and James C. McCroskey. See James W. Neuliep, *Intercultural Communication: A Contextual Approach* 2e (Boston: Houghton Mifflin, 2003), pp. 29–30.

Web Resources to Improve Your Knowledge and Skill

You need not travel to a foreign destination to experience another culture; opportunities to experience cultural differences may be as close as talking with your roommate, an instructor, or a good friend. To learn more about the role of culture in communication, check out one of the following web sites, which offer more information about intercultural communication.

<www.awesomelibrary.org> is the web address of Awesome Library. Once you're at this site, type the words "intercultural communication" in the Search box to access information and resources about intercultural communication skills and principles.

<www.takingitglobal.org/home.html> is the site for Taking It Global. It provides resources that focus on student travel, including cultural trips and ideas to facilitate better understanding between people from different cultures.

Unit Two

Interpersonal Communication

Diana Ong, "Sisy," © Diana Ong/SuperStock, Inc.

> The best of life is conversation, and the greatest success is confidence, or perfect understanding between sincere people.
>
> Ralph Waldo Emerson

Chapter 7

Understanding Interpersonal Communication

Chapter Outline

- What Is Interpersonal Communication?
- Initiating Relationships
- Maintaining Relationships
- Summary

Chapter Objectives

After studying this chapter, you should be able to

1. Define interpersonal communication and discuss its three unique attributes.
2. Define interpersonal attraction and discuss four factors to consider when acting on attraction.
3. Provide examples of verbal and nonverbal ways we reveal our attraction to others.
4. Explain uncertainty reduction and describe three strategies of information seeking to reduce uncertainty.
5. Describe some common verbal and nonverbal behavioral indicators of a self-absorbed communicator style.
6. Define self-disclosure and explain its role in relationship maintenance.
7. Discuss what is meant by reciprocity, appropriateness, and risk in self-disclosure.
8. Identify and explain two models of self-disclosure pertaining to relationship maintenance.
9. Discuss how emotional expression, as a form of self-disclosure, affects relationship maintenance.

"Hi. I'm _____. Nice to meet you." This simple statement can strike fear in the heart of even the most outgoing individual. Yet we know that meeting and getting to know people, as well as becoming known, are some of the most rewarding experiences in this life. If we cannot break out of our comfort zones to communicate with others, we won't survive. As we said in Chapter 1, communication is inescapable. We communicate—intentionally and unintentionally, verbally and nonverbally—to accomplish things great and small throughout our lifetimes. And the most common, everyday kind of communication we accomplish comes in the form of simple conversations with loved ones, friends, coworkers, acquaintances, and even strangers as we go about our daily routines.

Interpersonal communication is the form of communication we experience most often in our lives, and it involves all five of our Principles for a Lifetime (see Figure 7.1). *In the remaining chapters of the book, you will see a small version of the communication principles model in the margin to highlight our reference to one or more of the communication principles that we discuss.*

Effective interpersonal communication begins with an *awareness* of oneself. As you interact with people in your life, you make mental notes of what works well and not so well. You learn from these experiences and develop a personal style of communication. We continue this process by reassessing and reshaping our communication styles throughout our lives, with the goal of becoming better communicators. The second and third principles involve the *effective use of verbal and nonverbal messages.* We experiment with verbal and nonverbal communication as we interact with people, form relationships, develop those relationships, and, in some cases, let go of those relationships. A major element that enhances relationships is the ability to *listen and respond thoughtfully* to others, our Principle Four. Finally, few interpersonal relationships last without *adaptation*. We live in an extremely diverse world. It's imperative to learn to adapt our communication to others—to their cultural backgrounds and values, personalities, communication styles, needs, and goals—so that we form satisfying relationships that help us enjoy our lives to the fullest.

In this chapter, we examine interpersonal communication, distinguish it from other forms of human communication, and explore how interpersonal communication establishes and facilitates our relationships. As you work through this material, keep in mind those individuals who mean the most to you right now. Consider your communication with these valued people, assessing areas that are working well and areas that might need some attention. The more you personalize this information, the more you will gain from it.

1. Aware
2. Verbal
3. Nonverbal
4. Listen and Respond
5. Adapt

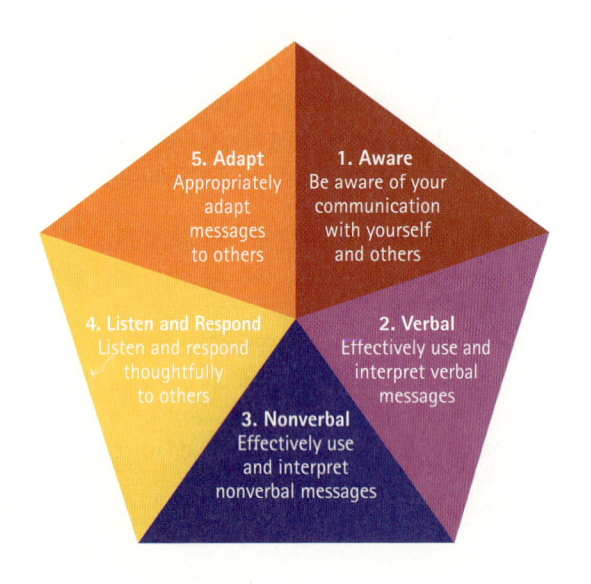

5. Adapt Appropriately adapt messages to others
1. Aware Be aware of your communication with yourself and others
2. Verbal Effectively use and interpret verbal messages
3. Nonverbal Effectively use and interpret nonverbal messages
4. Listen and Respond Listen and respond thoughtfully to others

Figure 7.1
Communication Principles for a Lifetime

What Is Interpersonal Communication?

In Chapter 1, we looked at three contexts in which communication most commonly occurs: interpersonal communication, group communication, and presentational communication contexts. In this chapter, we explore the interpersonal context in more depth. To review the definition provided in Chapter 1, **interpersonal communication** is a special form of human communication that occurs when two people interact simultaneously and attempt to mutually influence each other, usually for the purpose of managing relationships.

Traditionally, interpersonal communication research has focused primarily on the face-to-face (FtF) encounter, as researchers have attempted to better understand how people use conversation and nonverbal cues to initiate and maintain relationships. How-

interpersonal communication
Communication that occurs between two people who simultaneously attempt to mutually influence each other, usually for the purpose of managing relationships.

ever, given the immense popularity and increasing accessibility of the Internet, researchers are also studying interpersonal communication that occurs through this unique medium.[1] As our global society becomes more interconnected and we find we are able to "meet" all kinds of people worldwide through computer channels, it's important to examine how interpersonal communication functions online. So, as we proceed through the various topics related to interpersonal communication, we explore how online communication is similar to and different from FtF interpersonal communication. As you read, think about your own relationships, both FtF and online, and consider how interpersonal communication facilitates each one. To begin, we consider three unique attributes that help us better understand the nature of interpersonal communication.

Interpersonal Communication Involves Quality

Imagine you're having dinner at a restaurant with a friend. The communication you have with your friend is different from the communication you have with the person who waits on your table. (At least we certainly hope so; if not, your friendship may need some work!) Most likely, it is the quality of communication that differs.

Interpersonal communication occurs not just when we interact with someone, but when we treat the other as a unique human being. Conversely, **impersonal communication** occurs when we treat people as objects or respond to their roles rather than to who they are as unique people.[2]

In fact, aspiring doctors are now required by the National Board of Medical Examiners to pass a daylong test of "bedside manner," revealing their ability to establish rapport with patients, ask clear questions, and listen effectively to answers. Until medical students pass the bedside manner test, they are not allowed to practice medicine. So they must learn to treat patients as people, using interpersonal communication skills, rather than as objects who warrant only impersonal communication.[3]

We engage in a good deal of impersonal communication each day. We may pass people on the sidewalk and say hello, whether or not we know them. The first few days of a semester are always interesting because of the presence of so many people new to the campus, so we may find ourselves giving directions to various campus buildings. Giving directions or instructions is a common yet important form of impersonal communication. Many people's jobs involve a great deal of impersonal communication. In the online context, an e-mail message to a friend is an example of interpersonal communication. Posting a message on an electronic bulletin board would be impersonal communication, since it is likely you wouldn't know the receivers of your posting.

Interpersonal Communication Involves Mutual Influence

Interpersonal communication also involves attempts at mutual influence. This means that both partners are affected by the interaction. We don't mean to imply that interpersonal communication exclusively involves persuasion—changing someone's mind or swaying someone's opinion. We simply mean that people who interact affect each other. For example, during dinner, you ask your friend where he or she grew up, and you assume that your friend hears you. If so, you've both been affected by the question—there's something you want to know and information your friend can provide. But what if your friend doesn't hear you? In this case, interpersonal communication has not really occurred between you and your friend because there is no mutual interaction; only you have been affected by your attempt at communication.

Interpersonal Communication Helps Manage Relationships

Relationships are ongoing connections we make with others through interpersonal communication. For some people, the term *relationship* signals something serious and usually romantic. But we use the term *relationship* in a much broader sense in this text. You probably have a wide variety of relationships that include those with family

impersonal communication
Communication that treats people as objects or that responds only to their roles rather than to who they are as unique people.

relationship
An ongoing connection made with another person.

> ## Recap
> ### What Is Interpersonal Communication?
> - Interpersonal communication involves *quality*: The quality of communication within interpersonal relationships is superior to that of communication that occurs impersonally.
> - Interpersonal communication involves *mutual influence*: Both people in the relationship are affected by the interaction.
> - Interpersonal communication helps *manage relationships*: Communication facilitates the initiation, maintenance, and, in some cases, termination of interpersonal relationships.

members, coworkers, classmates, friends, and romantic interests. You may have some relationships that form and are maintained solely online. Many relationships involve a combination of FtF and online interaction.

We initiate and form relationships through communication. We seek to increase our interactions with people we would like to know better, and we interpersonally communicate to maintain those relationships. Occasionally, we use interpersonal communication to end relationships that we have decided are no longer viable or to transition them to a lower level of involvement.

Relationships form for different reasons. **Relationships of circumstance** form situationally—simply because our lives overlap with others' lives in some way or because a situation brings us into contact. Relationships with family members, teachers, classmates, and coworkers typically fall into this category. In contrast, relationships that we seek out and intentionally develop are termed **relationships of choice**. These relationships typically include those with friends, lovers, and spouses or relational partners. These categories of relationships are not mutually exclusive. Relationships of circumstance can change into relationships of choice: Your sister or brother can turn out to be your best friend. Conversely, you may be extremely close to a certain family member, but over time that relationship may become more distant and evolve into more of a relationship of circumstance than one of choice. Probably most of your relationships that involve online communication are relationships of choice. An online relationship of circumstance might be formed between members of a group, such as students enrolled in a class or employees of a company with several corporate locations, who interact online to discuss course topics or current projects.

We communicate differently in these two types of relationships because the stakes are different. Generally, relationships of choice are more important to us and central to our sense of well-being than relationships of circumstance. Also, we tend to be more intimate in relationships of choice, choosing to reveal more sensitive things about ourselves only with our closest friends or lovers. And with less intimate acquaintances or family members who have known us for some time, we might "get away with" some behaviors that would be intolerable or a source of conflict within a relationship of choice.

relationship of circumstance
A relationship that forms situationally, simply because one life overlaps with another in some way.

relationship of choice
A relationship that is sought out and intentionally developed.

Initiating Relationships

Some people make relationships look so easy; they just seem to meet people and make positive impressions effortlessly. For others, meeting and getting to know people is a huge challenge. We'll let you in on a little secret: Initiating relationships really isn't all that easy for anyone. Let's begin our discussion of relationship initiation by exploring the nature of attraction—what draws us into a conversation in the first place.

Attraction can emerge in a number of forms. How can you discover what traits in others are attractive to you?

Interpersonal Attraction: Why We Like Whom We Like

What does it mean to say that you are attracted to another person? Most of the time, we tend to think of physical or sexual attraction. But there are many forms of attraction besides physical and sexual, including intellectual, spiritual, and personality attraction. **Attraction**, in general, is a motivational state that causes someone to think, feel, and behave in a positive manner toward another person.[4] More specifically, **interpersonal attraction** is the degree to which you desire to form and possibly maintain an interpersonal relationship with another person. Remember that interpersonal relationships imply some form of ongoing connection, so we're not talking here about those instances when you can't breathe because an incredibly attractive stranger walks by. Whenever we feel a positive regard for another person or when we like someone, we can say that we feel attracted to that person, regardless of the sex of the person or our sexual orientation. However, the intensity of that attraction varies from relationship to relationship.

Interpersonal attraction occurs in both early stages and later stages of relational development. **Short-term initial attraction** is the degree to which you sense a potential for developing an interpersonal relationship. For instance, you might find one of your classmates interesting but never move to introduce yourself. Or you might interact with someone in a chat room and then decide that the person's comments attract you enough to begin private online exchanges. The information you gather in your first interaction with someone can generate a short-term initial attraction for a friendship or romantic relationship, which you may or may not pursue, depending on the circumstances.

Long-term maintenance attraction, on the other hand, is the type that sustains relationships like best friendships, marriages, or committed partnerings. It refers to a level of liking or positive feeling that motivates you to maintain or escalate a relationship. Short-term attraction gives way to long-term attraction as a relationship progresses. Rarely do you maintain a long-term intimate relationship solely on the basis of what you initially found attractive.[5] You usually need something more as you develop an interpersonal attraction and deepen a relationship. Several factors come into play when you decide to act on your attraction and establish a relationship.

Similarity What about the idea that "opposites attract"? Opposites certainly do attract, and differences between people can be interesting. They can also form the basis for a good friendship or coworker relationship—after all, we learn a great deal from people who are unlike us. But we like to add another phrase to the "opposites attract"

---

attraction
A motivational state that causes someone to think, feel, and behave in a positive manner toward another person.

interpersonal attraction
The degree to which one desires to form or maintain an interpersonal relationship with another person.

short-term initial attraction
The degree of potential for developing an interpersonal relationship with someone.

long-term maintenance attraction
The level of liking or positive feeling that motivates one to maintain or escalate a relationship.

cliché: "Opposites attract, but dramatic opposites seldom last." People who are opposites or significantly different in dispositions and preferences may intrigue each other and teach each other something in the short run, but similarity appears to be a more important factor in highly committed, long-term relationships than in short-term, noncommittal relationships.[6]

In general, you are attracted to people with whom you have **similarity**—those whose personality, values, upbringing, experiences, attitudes, and interests are similar to yours.[7] You may also be attracted more to persons who are similar to you in age, intelligence, and life goals. One of the most beneficial aspects of online communication is the unique structure of the Internet, which allows people with similar interests to find one another easily and form online relationships.[8] For example, new parents can find comfort in online chat rooms devoted to discussions of common experiences and predicaments in raising children. Interesting studies on dating partners and college roommates found that for both the partners and the roommates, similarity in the emotional dimensions of the relationship (such as comfort, ego support, conflict management, sincerity, and warmth) were more important than other dimensions of attraction and led to greater enjoyment of the relationship.[9]

In the initial stages of an online or FtF relationship, we try to emphasize positive information about ourselves to create a positive and attractive image. We reveal those aspects of ourselves that we believe we have in common with the other person, and the other person does the same.[10] Think about your initial interactions with strangers; typically, you spend the first few minutes trying to find topics of mutual interest. You discover that the person is from a place near your hometown, has the same taste in music or sports, has the same attitude about school, and on and on. But the depth of this information is limited. You're likely to save your revelations about important attitudes and issues for later, as your relationship progresses.

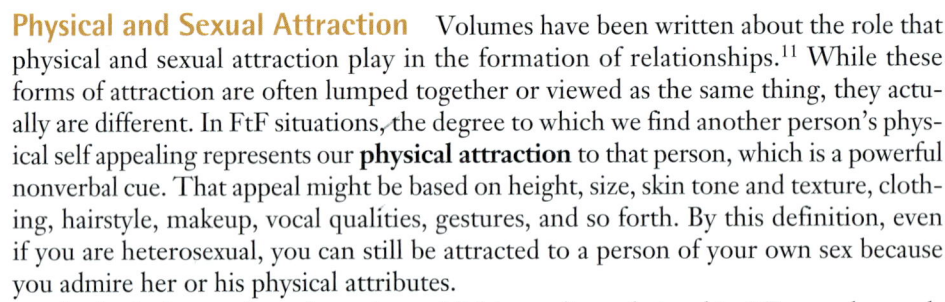

1. Aware

3. Nonverbal

Physical and Sexual Attraction
Volumes have been written about the role that physical and sexual attraction play in the formation of relationships.[11] While these forms of attraction are often lumped together or viewed as the same thing, they actually are different. In FtF situations, the degree to which we find another person's physical self appealing represents our **physical attraction** to that person, which is a powerful nonverbal cue. That appeal might be based on height, size, skin tone and texture, clothing, hairstyle, makeup, vocal qualities, gestures, and so forth. By this definition, even if you are heterosexual, you can still be attracted to a person of your own sex because you admire her or his physical attributes.

Is physical attraction a factor in establishing online relationships? Research reveals that many online communicators find the *lack* of emphasis on physical appearance and attractiveness in online relationships to be one of the most positive features of this approach to relationship development.[12] One set of researchers described the Internet as "a world where what you write, not how you look or sound, is who you are."[13]

Sexual attraction has been defined as "the desire to engage in sexual activity with someone," a desire that "typically is accompanied by feelings of sexual arousal in the presence of the person."[14] You may be physically attracted to someone but not sexually attracted, as we stated before. But can you be sexually attracted but not physically attracted? We're not sure about the answer to that one because it may be a uniquely individual judgment. You may find another person's online communication sexually arousing, even if you've never seen the person in the flesh. Suffice it to say that these two forms of attraction usually operate in tandem, even though they represent different kinds of appeal.

The adage "Beauty is in the eye of the beholder" is particularly true with regard to physical and sexual attraction. Each culture teaches and perpetuates its own definition of the physical ideal.[15] In the United States, for instance, advertisements and TV programs promote a slender ideal for both females and males. This ideal contributes to the American obsession with losing weight and getting fit.[16] However, in some cultures, and at various times throughout U.S. history, physical attractiveness was synonymous with bulkiness.

similarity
The degree to which one's characteristics, values, attitudes, interests, or personality traits are like those of another person.

physical attraction
The degree to which one finds another person's physical self appealing.

sexual attraction
The desire to have sexual contact with a certain person.

Communication and Diversity

Friendships: Thinking Outside the Race

How many friends do you have who are of a different racial or ethnic background than you? How many are a mixture of ethnic backgrounds? Whatever the numbers in your answers to these questions, they are probably quite a bit higher than those a college student like you would have given a few decades ago. We're not saying that previous generations of students were racists—political and social forces greater than the individual were at play, affecting the very potential for interracial friendships to occur. Times certainly have changed: Figures from the U.S. Census Bureau show that black-white marriages increased from 65,000 in 1970 to 422,000 by 2005; in 1970, only 2 percent of marriages in the United States were interracial, compared to 7 percent by 2005.[17]

Researchers offer helpful information about how interracial relationships develop and progress, as well as about special challenges the relational partners face.[18] Mark Orbe and Tina Harris are communication scholars and authors of the book *Interracial Communication*.[19] They write about the evolution of relationships—friendships as well as romantic relationships—between members of different races in the United States. Interracial friendships are on the rise, but they are complex because our society is still "racialized" (meaning it still draws distinctions among the races), although to a lesser degree than ever before in our country's history. Our socialization as children, adolescents, and adults occurs within the context of a culture that places attention on race and ethnicity, no matter what our family of origin's views and practices regarding race and ethnicity might be.

Orbe and Harris ask readers, "How have you been socialized to communicate (or not) with other racial/ethnic group members? Has your family or society socialized you to believe that such interactions are healthy and normal, or were you discouraged from having any type of interracial contact at all?" They go on to encourage, "Whatever your experience has been, it is our hope that you have become sensitized to how cultural group membership (e.g., dominant culture, U.S. nationality) influences our attitudes toward and beliefs about interracial contact."[20] While these scholars tout the benefits of within-race friendships, they also believe in the advantages and growth potential of having friends outside of one's own race or ethnic group.

Engagement Questions

1. What role does race/ethnicity play in how much you are drawn to strike up friendships with other people? Is it even a factor? If so, how much of a factor?
2. Do you tend to make friends more often with people whose racial/ethnic background is similar to yours, or do you seek friendships more often with members of other racial groups?
3. Do your closest friends tend to be of your same race, while less intimate friends and acquaintances reflect more racial/ethnic diversity?
4. What factors in your upbringing, as well as your current experiences, contribute to your tendencies regarding friendship?

Our perceptions about others' physical attractiveness reduce relationship possibilities. In general, while we may be attracted to a range of persons, we tend to seek out individuals who represent the same level of physical attractiveness we do.[21] In nonverbal communication research, this is termed the **matching hypothesis**.[22] Perhaps you perceive yourself to be average looking, not model-beautiful but not unattractive either. You may be physically or sexually attracted to extremely good-looking people; but if you are average-looking, you are more likely to seek someone who is also average-looking to date, and even marry or become partners with. Look around the next time you're in a public place, like an airport or a mall, and notice the couples—people who obviously look like they are together. Most couples will match each other in terms of physical attractiveness.

Proximity The principle of **proximity** in interpersonal relationships refers to the fact that we are more likely to be attracted to people who are nearer to us physically and geographically than to those who are farther away.[23] In your classes, you are more likely to form relationships with classmates sitting on either side of you than with someone seated at the opposite end of the room. Physical proximity increases communication opportunities, and opportunities to interact are likely to increase our attraction to those with whom we communicate. People involved in long-distance romantic relationships—those initiated through FtF encounters, but that continue even after the couple are geographically separated—understand the principle of proximity firsthand. They typically use multiple channels of communication to maintain their relationship, and the lack of proximity and accessibility to each other, over time, can become problematic.[24]

Relationship experts believe, "To meet people is not necessarily to love them, but to love them we must first meet them."[25] Of course, nowadays "meeting" someone

matching hypothesis
The theory that one tends to seek out individuals who represent the same level of physical attractiveness as oneself.

proximity
The likelihood of being attracted to people who are physically close rather than to those who are farther away.

need not refer to meeting someone physically. How many times have you heard someone say, "I met someone on the Internet"? They didn't actually meet in the physical sense, but that meeting is just as real (sometimes more real) and valuable to those involved as FtF meetings. Research suggests that proximity affects online relationships differently than it does FtF relationships.[26] The global presence and general accessibility of the Internet as a facilitator of interpersonal communication means that people can establish relationships even though they are geographically separated; without the Internet, they most likely would never meet. But the instantaneous and pervasive nature of online communication bridges the physical distance, creating a virtual closeness that FtF relationships may not achieve. Thus the impact of proximity—a long-standing predictor of relationship development and success—is minimized in an online relationship.

According to computer-mediated communication proponent Katrina Shonbeck, social networking sites like Facebook not only make it possible for people to develop friendships with people they will likely never meet, but also enable communication to occur before face-to-face meetings. Shonbeck describes what her younger sister did prior to heading off for college: Once she knew her university e-mail address, she used Facebook to make connections with other students who were getting ready to attend the same institution, thus creating a form of online proximity before a physical proximity was established. One advantage of this approach is the ability to interface with roommates or suite mates online prior to that first "move in" day at the dorms.[27]

Complementarity While we tend to like people with whom we have much in common, most of us wouldn't find it very exciting to spend the rest of our lives with someone who had identical attitudes, needs, and interests. We may tend to be attracted to someone similar to us in important things like human values, but for other things we may be more interested in someone with whom we share **complementarity** of abilities and needs.[28] For example, if you are highly disorganized by nature (and that's fine by you), you might be attracted to someone who is very organized because you appreciate that person's sense of structure.

Social psychologist Will Schutz identified three interpersonal needs that motivate us to form and maintain relationships with others: inclusion, control, and affection.[29] **Inclusion** is the need to include others in our activities or to be included in theirs. **Control** is the need to make decisions and take responsibility or the level of willingness to accept others' decision making. **Affection** is the need to be loved and accepted by others or the willingness to give love and acceptance to others. Most people are attracted to those whose interpersonal needs complement their own.

If you have a high need to control and make decisions and a general disrespect for or mistrust of others' decision making, you will be more compatible with someone whose need for control is minimal—a person who wants others to make decisions for her or him. Many committed couples reflect this pattern regarding finances. A person who is good at keeping track of bills and balancing the checkbook pairs with someone who is good at maintaining a budget, to create a strong personal finance team. If you have high affection needs, you're likely to be less attracted to someone who is distant or aloof and who doesn't show affection. If you resent it when someone you're dating spends time away from you with his or her friends, you're likely to be less attracted to that person over time because you may have different, noncomplementary inclusion needs. In essence, we can view pairs of individuals as teams in which each person's needs complement those of the other person in some way. In reality, there are no perfect matches, only degrees of compatibility.

Communicating Our Attraction

In general, the more we are attracted to someone, the more we attempt to communicate with him or her. So the amount of interaction we have with someone indicates the level of attraction in the relationship.

complementarity
The degree to which another person's different abilities, interests, and needs balance or round out one's own.

inclusion
The need to involve others in one's activities or to be involved in the activities of others.

control
The need to make decisions and take responsibility or the level of willingness to accept others' decision making.

affection
The need to be loved and accepted by others or the willingness to give love and acceptance to others.

Recap

Elements of Interpersonal Attraction

Short-Term Initial Attraction	This form of attraction involves a judgment that there is potential for an interpersonal relationship to develop with someone.
Long-Term Maintenance Attraction	This form of attraction is deeper and more long-lasting than short-term initial attraction and involves positive feelings that cause us to choose to maintain and escalate relationships.
Similarity	Attraction increases if our characteristics, values, attitudes, interests, and personality traits are similar to those of another person.
Physical Attraction	This form of attraction is based on another person's physical self.
Sexual Attraction	This form of attraction is based on the desire to have sexual contact with another person.
Proximity	We are more likely to be interpersonally attracted to people who are physically close to us.
Complementarity	We may be attracted to someone whose abilities, interests, and needs differ from but balance or round out our own.

When we are attracted to people, we use both indirect and direct strategies to communicate our liking, through nonverbal and verbal cues. Nonverbal cues are typically indirect and are often referred to as **immediacy**, which we discussed in Chapter 4 when we focused on Principle Four: *Effectively use and interpret nonverbal messages.*[30] Immediacy behaviors work to reduce the physical and psychological distance between people. For example, with people we are attracted to, we may sit closer, increase our eye contact and use of touch, lean forward, keep an open body orientation, use more vocal variety or animation, and smile more often than we normally do. Research also shows that individuals are more likely to preen as a means of attracting attention when in the presence of an attractive other.[31] For example, people may alter their posture to accentuate certain body parts, straighten or adjust their clothing, and fidget with their hair when interacting with someone they find attractive.

Most often, we communicate our attraction nonverbally. But how do we let our online partners know that we're attracted to them? If the nonverbal cues that primarily communicate attraction in face-to-face encounters aren't available in online interaction, how do we communicate our interest?

One study asked almost 6,000 people how they flirt in person as well as in online encounters.[32] The majority of people in the study reported that flirting was accomplished in basically the same way, whether the exchange was face to face or online. They described how they translate physical actions into online text. For example, body movements such as laughing in response to someone's humor are represented by an acronym, such as LOL (for "laugh out loud"), placed in the text of a message or in response to one. Eye behaviors associated with flirting, such as a wink, are communicated through the use of emoticons (symbols formed with combinations of keystrokes to represent an expression or substitute for an action). Survey respondents explained that other indications of attraction, such as closer proxemics and touch, had to be accomplished through descriptions in the text of messages, such as saying "I wish I could reach out and give you a hug right now."

On occasion, in both FtF and online contexts, we may communicate attraction verbally by using informal and personal language, addressing the person by her or his first name and often referring to "you and I" and "we." We ask questions to show interest, probe for details when our partner shares information, listen responsively, and refer

3. Nonverbal

2. Verbal
4. Listen and Respond

immediacy
Nonverbal cues, such as eye contact, forward lean, touch, and open body orientation, that communicate feelings of liking, pleasure, and closeness.

to information shared in past interactions, in an attempt to build a history with the person. All of these behaviors demonstrate that we value what the other person is saying.

Getting That First Conversation Going

In some ways, online interpersonal relationships have an advantage over FtF relationships, in that they develop out of conversation, meaning that an online conversation is probably what launched the relationship in the first place. In an FtF situation, the various steps of noticing someone interesting, realizing you're interested (either physically, sexually, or interpersonally), finding a way to meet the person (either by introducing yourself or through a third-party introduction), and starting up the first conversation can all be nerve-racking. But these steps don't happen the same way in online interactions. Initial online interactions are critical, in that they make or break future exchanges. With repeated virtual contact, online topics of discussion often become very personal, and intimacy often develops at a more rapid pace than it typically does in FtF relationships. If rapport develops, it may lead to telephone conversations or FtF meetings.[33]

In FtF settings, once you realize you're attracted to someone (and that realization usually happens very quickly), what do you do next? That's a question that we've all no doubt asked ourselves at times, when we feel that awkwardness about wanting to find a way to meet someone we find attractive and get to know her or him, either for simple friendship or for romantic possibilities. Research indicates that people who meet and have that all-important first conversation feel enduring effects of the encounter even months later, no matter what direction the relationship took (if it took any direction at all).[34] We have some practical suggestions for how to approach those first conversations, so that you feel confident and keep your self-esteem intact while communicating effectively to impress the other person positively.

Reducing Uncertainty Even though most of us like surprises from time to time, human beings are much more comfortable with certainty than with uncertainty. We prefer the known to the unknown, the predictable to the chaotic. Both FtF and online relationships involve uncertainty. One communication research team developed **uncertainty-reduction theory**, an explanation of how we use information as we endeavor to reduce our uncertainty, especially as it relates to communicating with people we don't know (or know well). Communication researchers Charles Berger, Richard Calabrese, and James Bradac contend that this driving motivation among humans to reduce our uncertainty prompts us to communicate.[35] We typically respond to uncertainty in three ways—using passive, active, and/or interactive strategies.

For an illustration of these strategies, let's consider an example. You're at a social gathering with some friends; a lot of people are there—some you know, some you don't. You spot an attractive person across the room and decide that you would like to know more about him or her. What's the first thing you would likely do in this situation? Charge right over to the person and introduce yourself? Maybe some of us would, but most of us respond less actively at first to an uncertain situation like this. The first thing most of us would do would be to scope out the situation—see who the "object of our affections" is talking with, watch to see if he or she seems to be with anyone at the party, and casually observe how the person communicates to get some sense of her or his personality. These are all **passive strategies**; we seek more information in order to reduce our uncertainty. Passive uncertainty reduction is related to the first of the Communication Principles for a Lifetime that we have discussed in this text—becoming more aware of yourself, your circumstances, and others.

After you've observed the person at the party, if you need more information before deciding what to do next, you might employ an **active strategy**. This approach involves

As online relationships grow more intimate, the partners' expectations for more emotional expression increase. How you do express your emotions online?

1. Aware

uncertainty-reduction theory
A driving human motivation to increase predictability by reducing the unknown in one's circumstances.

passive strategy
A noncommunicative strategy for reducing uncertainty by observing others and situations.

active strategy
A communicative strategy for reducing uncertainty by getting information from a third party.

perception checking, or getting information from a third party, such as asking your friends if they know the person, if he or she is dating anyone exclusively, what their opinions are about the situation or the person, and so forth. Finding out what your friends think of the person at the party increases your knowledge and helps you decide how to behave.

The final approach is termed an **interactive strategy**—going directly to the source who has the greatest potential to reduce your uncertainty. In our example, an interactive strategy would involve actually going over to the person and starting a conversation or joining one in progress. In some situations, uncertainty can be reduced enough through passive and active strategies; there may be no cause for an interactive strategy. At the party, you may learn enough about the person you saw across the room by watching and talking to others about her or him that you decide against initiating a conversation.

Uncertainty-reduction strategies aren't necessarily used in any particular order; you might bypass passive and active strategies and decide that the best way to cope with a situation is to get the information "straight from the horse's mouth." Interactive strategies are frequently used in online relationships, because starting up an online conversation or exchanging e-mails with someone tends to evoke less uncertainty than FtF first conversations. Online exchanges usually happen in private, with less potential for embarrassment than in FtF situations, when such factors as physical appearance and nervousness are in play.

But one element can inject uncertainty into the online situation: the potential for deception. Since you stare at a computer monitor rather than into someone's eyes when you "meet" online, you really don't know whom you're talking to. Research has shown people's tendencies to give false information or to omit pertinent facts in their online communication.[36] Subjects in studies reported lying about age, weight, details of physical appearance, marital status, and even their sex, meaning that some gender-bending experimentation certainly occurs. The uncertainty caused by the relative ease of online deception makes many a computer user gun-shy about getting involved with people through the Internet.

What Do You Say First? In some contexts, the first words you exchange with someone may be fairly scripted or expected. For example, in a job interview, introductions and ritualistic greetings typically take up the first few minutes. (See Appendix A for helpful information on communicating in interviews.) But what about situations in

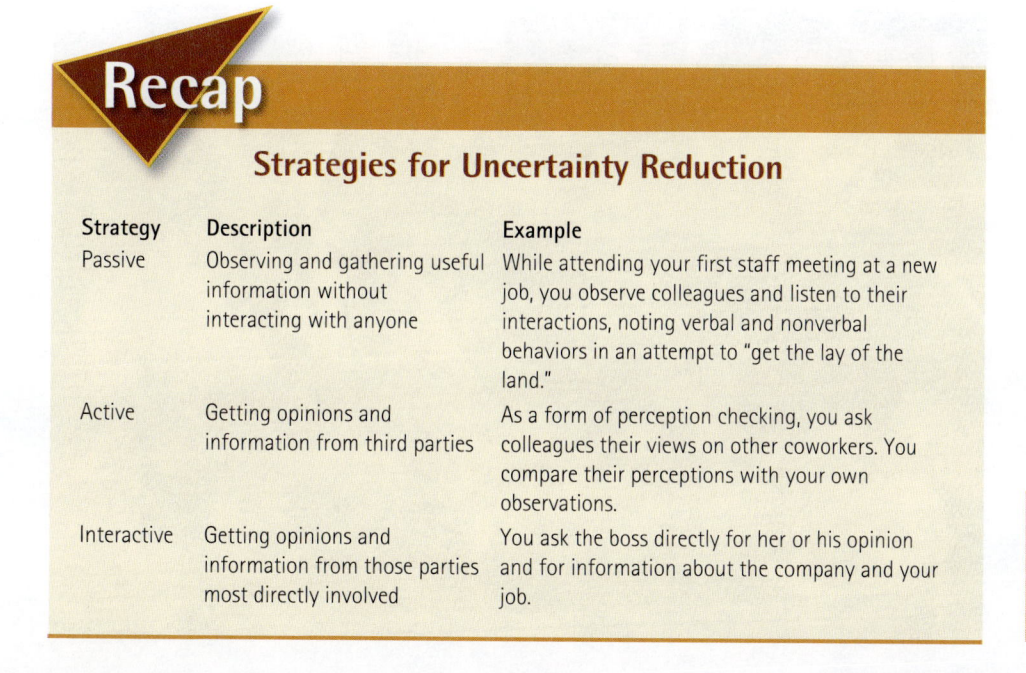

2. Verbal

Recap

Strategies for Uncertainty Reduction

Strategy	Description	Example
Passive	Observing and gathering useful information without interacting with anyone	While attending your first staff meeting at a new job, you observe colleagues and listen to their interactions, noting verbal and nonverbal behaviors in an attempt to "get the lay of the land."
Active	Getting opinions and information from third parties	As a form of perception checking, you ask colleagues their views on other coworkers. You compare their perceptions with your own observations.
Interactive	Getting opinions and information from those parties most directly involved	You ask the boss directly for her or his opinion and for information about the company and your job.

interactive strategy
A strategy of communicating directly with the source who has the greatest potential to reduce one's uncertainty.

"SORRY. YOUR INSTANT MESSAGE WASN'T CLEAR AND NOW YOU HAVE TO TALK TO ME."

which there are no prescribed, explicit rules or expectations for behavior? Our students tell us that the official "date" is a dying institution—that they just don't date much anymore. They still have romantic relationships and liaisons with people—they just accomplish those connections differently. More common than dating is the phenomenon no doubt known to you as "hanging out," in which two people meet somewhere or a group of people gather together, many of whom are "seeing each other" or have a special connection that goes beyond what they have with other people. For reasons as varied as the financial expense of dating, the difficulty of finding the time to make it happen, the uncomfortable formality often associated with dating, fear of the commitment that repeated dates can convey, and a preference for the image of being "unattached," dating is quickly being replaced by a lot of people just "hanging."

Any kind of social situation—a party, a date, or just hanging out with a mix of friends and new people—can create a level of anxiety in even the most confident among us, in part because of implicit rules and expectations that operate differently for different people. In a world where technological advances and social evolution continue to make the roles and rules different for women and men, it's sometimes hard to know what's expected and how to behave. It's especially tough when you're attracted to someone and want to have that all-important, impressive first conversation, because you know what's riding on it. In an age when it's equally acceptable for women to ask men out and to engage them in conversation for the purpose of making some kind of connection, members of both sexes need to work on their relationship initiation skills.[37] The ease of online dating and networking may offer some people a safe haven, socially speaking, but it may also make people less able to communicate effectively face to face.

This first-conversation business used to be easier, but perhaps not particularly satisfying. We won't stay on memory lane long, but first conversations used to be more true to script a few decades ago. Men were schooled at their fathers' knees on how to use opening or pickup lines to attract women; women were schooled by their mothers

Cute or flippant "pick-up" lines are not usually the best approach when meeting someone new. That's because effective communicators adapt their message to their listener—they don't use the same tired line in multiple communication encounters. What does using a standard pick-up line say about you when you're meeting new people? What strategies can you use in a first conversation to appropriately adapt your message to others?

as to how to respond (and how to ignore).[38] Lines like "Come here often?" "Haven't I seen you here before?" and (the all-time favorite) "What's your sign?" are now relegated to movie dialogue, as punch lines or flashback sequences. You probably don't have stock opening lines you rely on in social situations, because they are rarely effective. A "one size fits all" approach ignores the particulars of the situation and the unique qualities of each person you meet. As Principle Five (*appropriately adapt messages to others*) suggests, effective communicators adapt their communication to their listeners, so using the same approach in each new encounter is ill-advised. It's wise to do some thinking about how you come across—and how you *want* to come across—when meeting new people. You never know when you'll get to enjoy a fun night of speed dating or be on television meeting twenty-five new eligible dates, as in *The Bachelor* and *The Bachelorette*.[39]

Research has explored first-date plans and scripts (people's preferences and expectations as to how conversations should unfold), as well as strategies for first contact.[40] One of the best strategies, whether in an FtF or an online situation, is to find something you perceive you might have in common with the person. In person, we all give off a certain amount of "free" information that others can easily observe. If someone is wearing a T-shirt from a place you recognize or have visited or is carrying a book from a course you've taken or are taking, you can use that information as a starting point for conversation. If your online conversation springs from exchanges in a chat room, you have the commonality of the chat room to rely on to get the communication flowing.

The Art and Skill of Asking Great Questions When students ask us, as they frequently do, "What makes someone a good conversationalist?" a variety of things come to mind. All five of our Principles for a Lifetime could be reflected in our answer. But one important element is the ability to ask a great question of another person. This skill doesn't just magically appear—it takes time, maturity, and experience with a variety of people and relationships to develop fully.[41]

What do we mean by "asking great questions"? We don't mean tossing rapid-fire, superficial questions at someone, as though you were in the first five minutes of a job interview. You don't want someone to think that you're gathering data for the census. Asking a great question means, first, tailoring the question to the person as much as possible. Use what you've observed and learned from other sources to formulate your questions. Online, it's typical to ask basic information just to break the ice, but the use of too many "yes/no" questions or questions requiring one-word responses doesn't advance the conversation. Avoid questions that might be too personal or probing in the early stages of developing FtF and online relationships.

A second, very critical skill to develop is really listening to the person's answers to your questions. Then pose a follow-up question—one that is based on the person's response to your question. You can offer your opinion on something, but opinions work best when followed up with "Do you agree?" or "That's what I think, but what do you think?" Great conversationalists are great because they listen and then form responses that show they're listening—responses that are designed to draw other people out and let them shine.

Nowadays, a lot of people are going into coaching, and we don't mean the kind of coaching that involves a ball. Life coaching (also known as personal coaching) is becoming more popular as a profession or sideline and as an alternative to counseling or therapy. Individuals or teams of coaches are increasingly being hired by organizations to conduct training with employees on problem solving, team building, conflict management, communication skills, goal setting, self-actualization, and so forth. According to Laura Whitworth and her colleagues (a group of coaches who advocate a team, or "co-active," approach to coaching), a coach is "someone who cares that people create what they say they want, that they follow through when they choose. The coach is there to hold people accountable and keep them moving forward toward their dreams and goals."[42]

One of the primary communication skills people who wish to become life coaches are encouraged to learn relates to what we discussed in this section — in the coaching world, it's called "asking powerful questions." Whitworth describes the cornerstone of

5. Adapt

5. Adapt

4. Listen and Respond

coaching, the powerful question, as one that stems from sheer curiosity and that acts like a point on a compass. A powerful question sends a client in a general direction as opposed to a specific destination, allowing the client room for self-discovery. Powerful questions ask people to explain further what they meant or why they used particular language. Powerful questions "tend to stop people in their tracks, so there is often a sudden hush," according to Whitworth and colleagues.[43] These authors offer some examples of powerful questions, designed to evoke thinking and a response: "What does what you want look (or feel) like?" "What about that is important to you?" "What did you learn?" "What do you really want?" "Who do you need to be?" In order to pose an effective powerful question, you first have to listen intently while also processing your conversational partner's nonverbal cues. Then, to reinforce your question, the answer, and the other person, you have to listen and respond appropriately to the answer. Powerful questions are most easily generated and most effectively used within the context of an ongoing relationship, one that evolves over time, but powerful questions can also be useful in drawing someone out in a first conversation. While we don't mean to suggest that everyone turn into a mini life coach, we do believe that the average person can learn something about good old conversation from the coaching approach.

Avoiding Self-Absorption Too many people think the best way to be conversationally impressive is by talking glibly, smoothly, confidently, and virtually nonstop *about themselves.* In an online context, when one person's messages are consistently five times as long as the other's and the content rambles on and on about the person, it's a definite turnoff. Terms for this behavior include **conversational narcissism** and a **self-absorbed communicator style**.[44] For some people, this approach to communication is an outgrowth of a personality trait—a belief in oneself as the center of the universe.[45] Other times, it is a state, not a trait, meaning a temporary style of interacting rather than a more pervasive characteristic of a person. We can all be self-absorbed from time to time, but if the self-absorbed communication continues, if it moves from a temporary state into a more permanent trait or style of a person, then the likelihood that the person will be positively perceived seriously declines.

You probably know what self-absorption sounds like and looks like in another communicator. Some verbal indications include the number of times a person uses the pronoun *I* instead of *you* or *we*. Narcissistic communicators converse mostly about themselves and typically provide more detail in their narratives than necessary (because they enjoy the sound of their own voice or the clicking of the keys on their keyboard).[46] They talk more in statements than questions and constantly try to top someone's story or to draw the topic of conversation toward themselves, as in "Oh, you think *you're* tired—let me tell you about the kind of day *I* had." No one's day is as bad, no one's opinion as valuable or information as correct as the self-absorbed communicator's. The person may feign empathy in a conversation: "Oh, I know exactly how you feel." This usually leads to "The same thing happened to me," followed by a long story that takes attention away from the original communicator. Another indication of self-absorption is talking ad nauseam on topics about which one has some particular knowledge or expertise but that bore the socks off listeners. Many times, these types of communicators are driven by insecurity and uncertainty, rather than a belief that they truly are the center of the universe.

In FtF encounters, nonverbally self-absorbed communicators use vocal cues (such as increasing volume) and dominant body postures to hold their turns at talk and stave off interruptions from others. They may even physically block another person from attempting to leave the conversation and are generally insensitive to others' nonverbal cues. Online, self-absorbed chatters attempt to dominate the contributions of other chatters, make their postings more frequent and lengthier, and control the topic of conversation. People with self-absorbed personalities soon find themselves with few FtF or online friends, because few of us can tolerate such an out-of-balance relationship.

4. Listen and Respond

1. Aware

3. Nonverbal

conversational narcissism
A communication style emerging from the view that one is the center of the universe.

self-absorbed communicator style
A dominating communication style in which one focuses attention on oneself.

So, in sum, the best conversationalists aren't great talkers—they're great listeners and responders (as we've articulated in Principle Four). In other words, it's not what *you* say, but how you respond to what *others* say that makes you a good conversationalist.

The Art and Skill of Giving and Receiving Compliments Sometimes it seems as though people don't comment about one another unless it's to criticize. That's unfortunate, because positive reinforcement and support from others is central to our self-esteem. So let's discuss the lost art of the compliment. Are you a person who compliments others? If so, what do you tend to compliment people for—their appearance, hard work, scholarly achievement, athletic prowess? If you are a person who tends not to compliment others, why is that the case?

British linguistic scholar Janet Holmes calls compliments "social lubricants."[47] She explains that the most common purpose of a compliment is to make someone feel good by offering praise and encouragement, but an important byproduct is a sense of increased goodwill and solidarity between the complimenter and the receiver. Research shows that compliments between romantic partners can enhance self-esteem and are viewed as a form of intimate talk, and that the sharing of positive feelings is linked to how satisfied partners are with the relationship.[48] In heterosexual relationships, women tend to be more aware of the presence and absence of compliments than men, although men and women are equal in believing that compliments are important in a relationship. However, research shows that men tend to compliment women more for their appearance than for their competence, while women tend to compliment men for their abilities rather than their appearance.[49]

Giving compliments is a tricky business, because some attempts at flattery can be taken in ways other than you intend. For example, many female professionals tire of receiving workplace compliments on their appearance while their male coworkers are more often complimented on their work-related achievements. Some compliments are too personal and can make people feel uncomfortable. A pattern of personal compliments may be grounds for a claim of sexual harassment. But these are extreme examples. We encourage you to think about complimenting as a communication skill and a strategy particularly useful in first conversations, whether online or face to face. You don't want to come across as a phony or a predator, but a well-thought-out compliment can open the door to further conversation.

It's also important to know how to receive a compliment graciously—not by agreeing with the complimenter (and sounding cocky) or by disagreeing or attempting to talk the person out of his or her compliment, as in "This old outfit? I've had it for years—I just threw it on today." The best response is a simple "thank you" that acknowledges that something nice was said about you.[50]

Maintaining Relationships

Many forms of interpersonal communication are necessary to maintain successful, satisfying relationships. In this section, we explore a few of the most central forms, which represent some of the most heavily researched topics in the communication discipline.

Self-Disclosure: Revealing Yourself to Others

Imagine you're on a first date. (Even if people "hang out" now more than "date," use your imagination. For those of you who have been married for quite a while, this will take some work, but try it anyway.) Things are going fairly well. You find that you like the other person, and you become more comfortable as the evening progresses. But while you're engaged in conversation, your date manages to turn the topic of discussion to sex. The person starts describing sexual details about his or her last date or romantic partner—information that is just too intimate and private for a first date or,

4. Listen and Respond

2. Verbal

4. Listen and Respond

As relationships develop, the expectation is for deeper and more frequent self-disclosure to emerge. In what ways can you carefully attend to another person's self-disclosure?

4. Listen and Respond

self-disclosure
Voluntarily providing information to others that they would not learn if one did not tell them.

reciprocity
Sharing information about oneself with another person, with the expectation that the other person will share information that is similar in risk or depth.

appropriateness
An aspect of self-disclosure related to the propriety of revealing certain information to another person.

by some people's standards, for *any* date. Have you ever been in a situation where your date told you "TMI" (too much information)? How did you feel about the person after that experience? Did the inappropriate disclosure stop a relationship from getting off the ground?

Self-disclosure, originally studied by psychologist Sidney Jourard, occurs when we voluntarily provide information to others that they would not learn unless we told them.[51] People can learn our approximate age, height, and weight by just observing us. But they can't learn our exact age, height, or weight unless we disclose it. Communication scholar David Johnson provides eight reasons why people self-disclose:

1. We begin and deepen a relationship by sharing reactions, feelings, personal information, and confidences.
2. Self-disclosure improves the quality of relationships.
3. Self-disclosure allows us to validate our perceptions of reality.
4. Self-disclosure increases self-awareness and clarifies our understanding of ourselves.
5. The expression of feelings and reactions is a freeing experience.
6. We may disclose information about ourselves or not as a means of social control.
7. Self-disclosing is an important part of managing stress and adversity.
8. Self-disclosure fulfills a human need to be known intimately and accepted.[52]

Reciprocity in Self-Disclosure One thing we expect when we self-disclose is **reciprocity**, meaning that when we share information about ourselves with other people, we expect them to share information that is similar in risk or depth about themselves. If you introduce yourself to someone and give your name, you expect that person to respond by telling you his or her name. If you reveal to someone online where you're from, you expect similar information to be revealed in the person's response. This cultural rule allows us to use disclosure as a way of gaining information and reducing uncertainty.

If the other person doesn't reciprocate, however, you might feel embarrassed or resentful. Sharing information about yourself gives others a certain amount of power over you. If the other person reciprocates by disclosing similar information, it helps maintain an equal balance of power. But if one person shares information and the other doesn't, the resulting imbalance may cause discomfort. Over time, unreciprocated self-disclosure may cause someone to end a relationship.

Relationship experts John Harvey and Ann Weber describe relationship maintenance as "minding the close relationship," which they define as "thought and behavior patterns that interact to create stability and feelings of closeness in a relationship."[53] In a "well-minded" relationship, partners facilitate self-disclosure by questioning each other about feelings and behaviors, utilizing effective listener responses (such as head nods, eye contact, and vocalizations like "uh-huh" when face to face or emoticons online), accurately repeating or paraphrasing their partner's disclosure, and remembering their partner's opinions and preferences.[54]

Appropriateness in Self-Disclosure **Appropriateness** is another key variable related to self-disclosure. Certain kinds of information are inappropriate to disclose at an early stage of relational development but appropriate at a later stage. However, people vary a good deal on this dimension. It's sometimes hard to gauge what is appropriate to talk about and what is not while you're in the process of getting to know someone. Sometimes unwanted disclosures emerge because one person misjudges the nature of the relationship, assuming or wanting a greater level of intimacy than his or her partner assumes or wants.

Be sensitive to your partner when you choose what and when to disclose. Consider how the other person will react to the information. Although you may not think of

Communication and Technology

"High-Tech" Self-Disclosure

MySpace, Facebook, Friendster, blogging. You probably know what these things are, but have you ever viewed them as "high-tech" delivery systems for self-disclosure? In this book, we've already talked about the creation of online identities as extensions of the self, but as we examine interpersonal communication, it's worthwhile to think about relatively new methods of self-disclosing that college students are drawn to in droves.

When you create a profile for a MySpace page, for example, you may not include your most personal information (we hope not), but many people do describe their personalities, likes/dislikes, hobbies/interests, and so forth, along with opinions and attitudes. Once you are "friended" on Facebook (meaning someone gives you access to his or her page), you enter a social network where you can read people's postings and get to know them better. Revelations of this kind are a form of online self-disclosure.

You may not think of a blog (short for "web log") as a format for self-disclosure, as many blogs don't contain private information about the blogger, but they do reveal the author's thoughts, opinions, and feelings about a range of subjects. You wouldn't know the person's views unless she or he told them to you, so blogging meets the basic criteria for self-disclosure, even if the identity of the blogger is masked.[55]

While the principle of reciprocity operates a bit differently in the online arena, it does apply to several forms of computer-mediated communication (CMC), including responding to people you choose to "friend" on social networking sites. College student and author Katrina Shonbeck explains, "If you do not perceive that the other person is reciprocating—replying in an appropriate length of time, staying on topic, responding to your away message, 'poking' you on Facebook, sending you e-cards, e-vites, and so on—chances are you will discontinue or greatly reduce the amount of time devoted to that person using CMC."[56]

We don't have to warn you about the need to retain your privacy; the dangers of putting too much personal information on social networking pages or revealing yourself too fully online are well known. Terrible stories of "online gone wrong" are in the news frequently, and university officials and professors always encourage students to exercise caution when creating and disseminating their profiles or sharing personal information. But let's consider the upside of computer-mediated self-disclosure for a moment. As Shonbeck explains, "Facebooking people" allows you to "learn about each other before talking to them in person, which changes the subsequent interaction that both have with one another."[57]

Earlier in this chapter, you read about uncertainty reduction—how people use communication to reduce their uncertainty so that they function more comfortably with other people. Reading someone's profile, postings, or blog reduces uncertainty about that person, so if you do meet the person eventually, you'll feel you have a "leg up" in the typical get-to-know-you process. Another positive aspect is the decrease in feelings of isolation that many people experience when they develop online networks. For some, self-disclosure in person is difficult; they know that it's a building block for relationships, but they are too shy or reticent to share information about themselves. For these folks, online self-disclosure serves as a relatively safe way to develop their disclosure abilities, to perhaps practice self-disclosure so that they can more readily accomplish it in face-to-face situations.

Of course, there are downsides to online disclosure, such as the sharing of inappropriate information or having information used in ways not foreseen by the originator. Some boundary issues emerge, as in those instances when people (like professors, potential employers, or unscrupulous characters) gain access to your network, profile, or blog when you didn't mean for them to.[58] On occasion, poorly chosen words or inappropriate photographs posted online, oftentimes innocently, have cost someone a relationship, job, or chance at advancement.[59] But researchers will continue to study new CMC formats for self-disclosure because people will continue to want new and improved ways of connecting in cyberspace.

---

some information as intimate, the other person may. Conversely, when your partner reveals information, try to determine whether it is highly personal to her or him. You could upset the other person if you fail to treat the information appropriately.

Assessing the Risks of Self-Disclosure Self-disclosure can be extremely rewarding because of its potential to deepen a relationship and enhance trust, but it is not without its risks.[60] For example, even in a society that seems to be becoming more accepting of homosexuality, bisexuality, and transgenderism, "coming out of the closet" as a form of self-disclosure is still a very risky prospect. Relationships with family members and friends can be hurt at the revelation, and the potential for rejection of and hostility toward the discloser is very real.[61] When we disclose, we make ourselves vulnerable and forfeit control of information. We might hurt or insult the other person by saying things she or he finds offensive, signal an unintended level of intimacy, or damage the relationship with ill-timed and inappropriate disclosures. Typically, in

5. Adapt

relationships we seek a balance between the potential risks and rewards of disclosing personal information.

What is high self-disclosing for one person may be low self-disclosing for another. In judging what, when, and how much to disclose, it's important to realize that different people have different standards or expectations. For example, some individuals are quite comfortable talking about their personal problems with relative strangers, whereas others engage in such discussions only in the most intimate relationships, if at all.

Relationships typically include frequent periods of self-disclosure early in the development process.[62] However, while the *level* of intimacy (or risk) of the information increases over time, the *amount* of disclosure tends to decrease as the relationship becomes more intimate. As a relationship proceeds, we share a good deal of low-risk information fairly rapidly, move on to share higher-risk information, and then, finally, share our most intimate disclosures. The more intimate the relationship becomes, the more intimate the information that is disclosed. Holding back from sharing intimate information may signal a reluctance to develop a relationship.

Self-Disclosure, Intimacy, and Gender   Interpersonal communication research is extensive on the topic of self-disclosure and the development of intimacy in a relationship. But just what is intimacy? Experts use such terms as *bonding*, *closeness*, and *emotional connection* when referring to the sharing of personal, private information and experiences over time.[63] We especially like the definition developed by couples therapist Jeffrey Fine: "To be intimate is to be totally transparent, emotionally naked in front of another who is equally transparent. You want to see into the other's heart. What people should mean when they say *intimacy* is in-to-me-see."[64]

Conventional wisdom, borne out by early studies, contends that relationships cannot fully develop into intimacy unless both partners share (ideally, with equal frequency and depth) information about themselves.[65] Without self-disclosure, we form only superficial relationships. However, research on gender and self-disclosure calls the conventional wisdom and prior findings into question.[66]

Consider for a moment men's friendships with other men. Think about golfing buddies, a group of guys who gather over lunch a few times a week to shoot some hoops, or men who enjoy one another's company over a few beers. Do these relationships tend to be based on an intimate sharing of personal information? Or are they based on shared experiences, on doing things together or having interests in common? Now think about how women's friendships form, in general. Do they form more through shared activities or through communication? It's not a stereotype: Women's friendships with other women *are* more often developed through interpersonal communication, particularly self-disclosure, than through common experiences.[67]

So, if men's friendships tend to form on the basis of shared activities, are they any less meaningful than relationships that develop through communication? Research has

> ## Recap
> ### Self–Disclosure
>
> . . . is providing someone with information about yourself that she or he couldn't learn about you unless you revealed it.
>
> . . . should be reciprocal, meaning that the person you reveal something to should respond with information about himself or herself that is similar in depth. The frequency with which partners self-disclose should be reciprocal as well.
>
> . . . should be appropriate, meaning that it can be a mistake to reveal information that is too personal too soon in the development of a relationship.
>
> . . . involves some risk, because knowledge is power. By revealing information to another person, you give that person a degree of power over you.
>
> . . . is highly rewarding, in that it is a building block of relational intimacy.

attempted to discover what constitutes intimacy for men, how men's friendships form, and what makes them meaningful.[68] Most men describe their friendships with other men as forming quite differently than their friendships with women, but being just as satisfying and important.[69] Men's friendships more often develop by doing, while relationships among female friends involve more talking. Men who experience the terror of battle together form powerful bonds, developed from shared experience rather than shared personal information down in the trenches. To suggest that only superficial relationships can be accomplished by doing, while deep ones must be accomplished by communicating, is to measure relational intimacy with a feminine yardstick.[70]

Two Models of Self-Disclosure

Research has explored the way in which self-disclosure works to move a relationship toward intimacy. Here, we examine two of the more prominent models that illustrate the process by which this happens.

The Social Penetration Model
A pair of researchers, Irwin Altman and Dalmas Taylor, developed the **social penetration model**, which illustrates how much and what kind of information we reveal in various stages of a relationship.[71] According to their theory, interpersonal communication in relationships moves gradually from the superficial to the more intimate. Two aspects of this communication increase: the breadth of the information (the variety of topics discussed) and the depth (the personal significance of what is discussed).

Their model is a configuration of rings, or concentric circles (see Figure 7.2). The outermost circle represents breadth, or all the potential information about yourself that you could disclose to someone—information about athletic activities, spirituality, family, school, recreational preferences, political attitudes and values, and fears. Then there are a series of inner circles, which represent the depth of information you could reveal about yourself. The innermost circle represents your most personal information.

As an online or FtF relational partner interacts with you, that interaction can be seen as a wedge that is at first narrow (few topics are discussed) and shallow (topics are fairly superficial). People who have just started dating might talk about commonalities (like being students at the same college), hobbies, interests, and favorite activities. As the relationship progresses, the wedge becomes broader (as more topics are discussed) and deeper (as more personal topics are discussed). After several dates or conversations about hobbies and interests, topics might turn more to values, like the importance of family and friendships or attitudes about politics or social issues. Self-disclosure causes your layers to be penetrated, as you penetrate the layers of the other person.

Each of your relationships exhibits a certain degree of social penetration, determined by the extent to which the other person has entered your concentric circles.

social penetration model
A model of self-disclosure that asserts that both the breadth and the depth of information shared with another person increase as the relationship develops.

Figure 7.2
Altman and Taylor's Model of Social Penetration

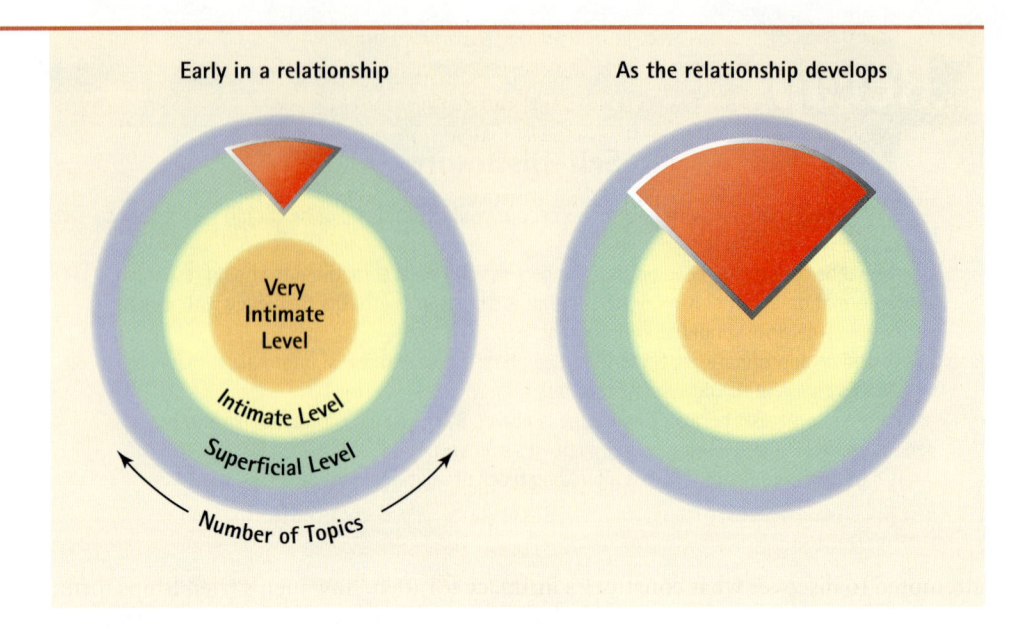

Early in a relationship | As the relationship develops

Very Intimate Level
Intimate Level
Superficial Level
Number of Topics

Some relationships, such as those with professors, distant family members, and acquaintances, may reflect a narrow, shallow wedge. The relationship does not involve a great deal of personal disclosure. A few relationships represent almost complete social penetration, the kind you achieve in an intimate, well-developed relationship, in which a large amount of in-depth self-disclosure has occurred. But many contend that no one can ever completely know another person; complete social penetration is unattainable. This model is a helpful way to assess your relationships in terms of whom you allow or encourage to get close to you and why. It may also help you diagram the level of intimacy you have in online and FtF relationships with others, as you attempt to penetrate their layers.

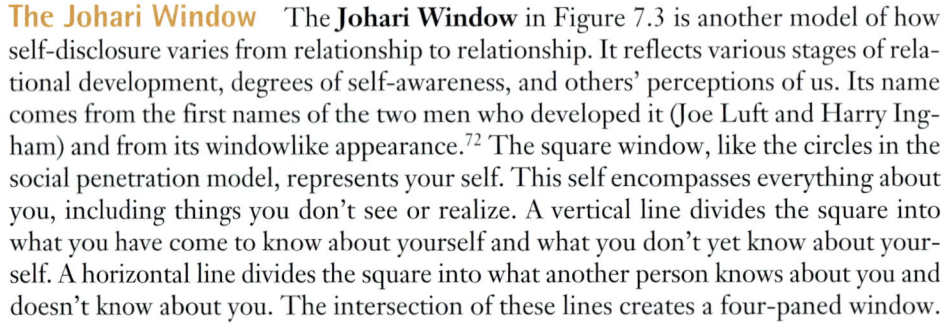

The Johari Window The **Johari Window** in Figure 7.3 is another model of how self-disclosure varies from relationship to relationship. It reflects various stages of relational development, degrees of self-awareness, and others' perceptions of us. Its name comes from the first names of the two men who developed it (Joe Luft and Harry Ingham) and from its windowlike appearance.[72] The square window, like the circles in the social penetration model, represents your self. This self encompasses everything about you, including things you don't see or realize. A vertical line divides the square into what you have come to know about yourself and what you don't yet know about yourself. A horizontal line divides the square into what another person knows about you and doesn't know about you. The intersection of these lines creates a four-paned window.

The *Open* quadrant represents that part of yourself that you know and have revealed to the other person. As a relationship becomes more intimate, the Open quadrant grows larger. The *Hidden* quadrant is information you know about yourself but have not shared with the other person. This quadrant is fairly large initially, but as you self-disclose, it shrinks and the Open quadrant grows. The information in the *Unknown* quadrant is that part of yourself that you have yet to discover or realize. As you learn and self-disclose more or as others learn more about you, this quadrant becomes smaller. Individuals who are not very introspective and do not have a very well-developed sense of self have larger Unknown areas than do those who have made a concerted effort to come to know themselves.

Your closest friends can probably tell when you're attracted to someone. Perhaps they detect a rising pitch in your voice or overhear you talking really fast. Maybe they notice that your skin is a bit flushed and that you don't know what to do with your arms and feet. These nonverbal cues are represented by the *Blind* quadrant. This quadrant includes real aspects of ourselves that we fail to recognize. The Blind quadrant is usually small when someone doesn't know us very well; it grows larger as that person

1. Aware

Johari Window
A model that explains how self-disclosure varies from relationship to relationship; the model reflects various stages of relational development, degrees of self-awareness, and others' perceptions.

observes more information that is in our Unknown quadrant. However, as the relationship becomes more intimate, the other person is more likely to reveal his or her perceptions of us, so the Unknown and the Blind quadrants shrink as the information becomes known and accessible to us. As you can see, then, intimate relationships play an important role in the growth of self-knowledge.

Expressing Emotions

Expressing emotions is another powerful way we reveal ourselves to others and deepen our relationships. Such expression comes more easily to some people than others, but it's a skill that can be improved in both your online and your FtF relationships.[73] However, there are cultural barriers to achieving this skill, in that many cultures designate particular emotions as appropriate for only some people to display in certain situations.[74] If you placed emotional expression on a continuum according to cultural groups, with one end being an open approach to emotional display and the other end being the suppression of emotional display, U.S. culture would fall somewhere in the middle. Some cultural groups (such as Latin cultures) are comfortable with and accepting of emotional display, while other groups (such as Asian cultures) value emotional inhibition more than people in the United States do.[75] People from countries where the norm is emotional inhibition often think that Americans "wear their hearts on their sleeves," while people from some other cultures view Americans as being "pent up" emotionally.

Families teach children very specific rules about the appropriateness of emotional display. One fascinating nonverbal communication study found that, at very young ages, children learn to mask disappointment in order to be socially appropriate.[76] We also perpetuate gender distinctions regarding emotions.[77] Many American men are taught to contain their emotions for fear that emotional expression may make them appear weak. Acquiring a "poker face" is a goal. Men are allowed to show anger and jealousy (short of physical violence), but it is frowned on for men to reveal sadness, fear, or great joy—unless they reveal it in a sporting context. (Some believe that this is one reason so many men are drawn to sports; the sporting context allows them emotional release that would most likely be considered inappropriate or "unmanly" in other contexts.) In fact, the male tendency to suppress emotion is so pronounced, it led Sidney Jourard (who first studied self-disclosure) to entitle one of his book chapters "The Lethal Aspects of the Male Role."[78] Jourard found that men who had difficulty express-

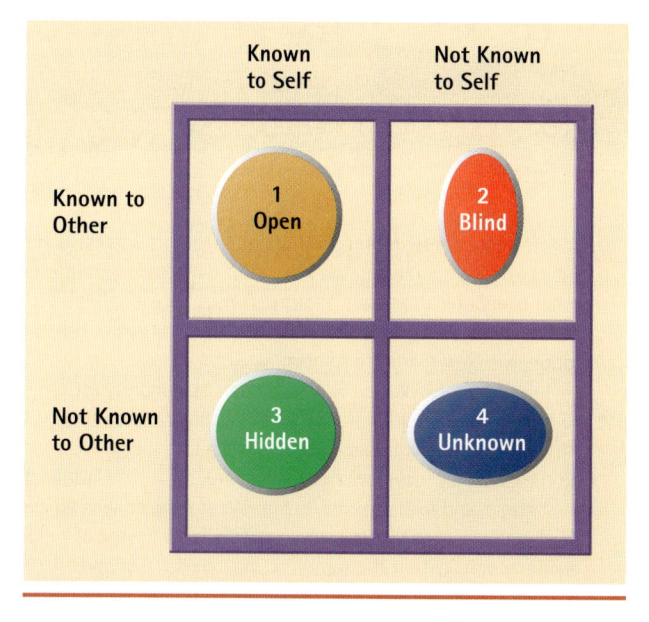

Figure 7.3
Johari Window

3. Nonverbal

Research suggests that men's relationships with other men often develop out of shared activities or common experiences—like sporting events—whereas women's relationships tend to rely more on verbal communication. Is this true in your experience? Why do you think this is the case?

Communication and Ethics

PostSecret

One of our students, Angela Huddleston, got us interested in the subject of secrets recently, as a result of a discussion in interpersonal communication class about self-disclosure and relationship development. We want to share what we learned from that conversation, with our thanks to Angela.

In 2004, Frank Warren wanted to do a community art project, so he began leaving blank postcards in public places and giving them to strangers, with one simple request—that they write a secret on the card that they have not told anyone, make sure not to sign their name, and mail the card to him. What resulted was an overwhelming response that has now grown into somewhat of a global phenomenon. Within the first year, Warren received over 10,000 postcards carrying secrets. He has published multiple books, including *PostSecret, My Secret, A Lifetime of Secrets*, and *The Secret Lives of Men and Women*, all filled with pages and pages of anonymous people's secrets submitted on personally decorated, highly artistic postcards. The secrets range from fairly low-level, humorous confessions like "I waste office supplies because I hate my boss" to private passions and eccentricities to humiliating accounts of abuse and suffering. If you'd like to see a sampling of the kinds of funny, heartwarming, sad, and intimate secrets people across the globe have shared with Warren, visit <www.postsecret.blogspot.com>.

Since people submit postcards to Warren anonymously and willingly, there's no ethical breach in sharing the secrets with readers, but this "movement" started us thinking about secrets as a unique form of self-disclosure and the ethics involved in keeping secrets. Is it safe to assume that everyone has at least one secret that he or she has never told anyone? What is it about the very nature of secrets that makes many of us want to *tell* them? We all know that it's unethical to tell other people's secrets that were told to us in confidence, but we also know how hard it is for people to keep a secret. In many ways, that's the beauty of Warren's work—the release that PostSecret provides someone, in that she or he can tell a secret to the world without the risk involved in telling a friend or family member. As Warren writes in his introduction to *PostSecret*, "Secrets have stories; they can also offer truths. After seeing thousands of secrets, I understand that sometimes when we believe we are keeping a secret, that secret is actually keeping us."[79]

Engagement Questions

1. If you were to submit a secret on a postcard to Frank Warren, what would it be?
2. If you don't have a secret that you've never told a single solitary soul, why is that? Are you likely to tell close friends and family members what happens to you or what you think or feel, rather than keeping secrets?
3. What's your ethical view of secrets and the telling of others' secrets?

---

2. Verbal

ing their feelings had high levels of stress-related disease. Research suggests that if and when men do disclose their feelings to someone, most seek women as listeners because they report feeling safer expressing emotions to women than to other men.[80]

Women in American culture, in most settings, are allowed the emotional display of crying that can be prompted by sadness, fear, or joy. (Exceptions include some professional settings, where "keeping one's cards close to the vest" is valued and displaying emotion is deemed inappropriate.) But many women receive negative reactions when they display anger. The view persists that an angry woman is "out of control" or "hormonal," while an angry man is behaving more in line with societal expectations for members of his sex. While these trends and expectations have changed somewhat with recent generations, there is still a significant tendency for men (and many women as well) to believe that emotional expression of any kind is more appropriate in women than men.[81]

As relationships become more intimate, we have a greater expectation that our partner will disclose emotions openly. The amount of risk associated with such emotional disclosure varies from person to person. Most of us are comfortable sharing the emotions of happiness and joy but are more reserved or hesitant about sharing fear or disappointment. While emotional expression can sometimes be difficult to handle, we generally want to know how our partners in intimate relationships are feeling, even if those feelings are negative.[82]

In this chapter, we've explored several aspects of interpersonal communication, yet we've only scratched the surface of the complexities of relationships—those entities that give us life's greatest joys, as well as challenges. In the next chapter, we examine key aspects of communication that are critical to ongoing relationships, with regard to our five Communication Principles for a Lifetime. Perhaps the information provided here and in Chapter 8 will whet your appetite enough that you'll enroll in an interpersonal or relational communication class next semester.

PRINCIPLES FOR A LIFETIME
Enhancing Your Skills

1. Aware

Principle One: Be aware of your communication with yourself and others.
- Attraction emerges in several different forms; it's important to discover what traits in other persons are attractive to you.
- Early in an online or FtF relationship, be aware of aspects of your personality that you want to emphasize to another person in order to create a positive and attractive image.
- One strategy to reduce uncertainty in interpersonal contexts is to be aware of your surroundings and situation as you passively observe others' interactions.
- The Johari Window and social penetration model can help you become more aware of your relationships and your interpersonal communication.

2. Verbal

Principle Two: Effectively use and interpret verbal messages.
- In initial interactions, honest, direct approaches are preferable to "canned" opening lines.
- When initiating online or FtF relationships, use questions that will engage and draw out another person.
- You may verbally reveal your liking for another person by using informal, personal, and inclusive language.
- You may verbally reveal your liking for another person by asking questions, probing for further information, and directly expressing your feelings.
- An active strategy to reduce uncertainty in interpersonal contexts is to ask third parties for their perceptions and knowledge.
- An interactive information-seeking strategy involves direct communication with the source who has the greatest potential for reducing your uncertainty.
- Asking great questions in a conversation draws a person out and helps a communicator avoid creating a perception of being self-absorbed.
- Practice giving sincere compliments generously and receiving others' compliments graciously.
- One of the key variables in relationship development is self-disclosure.
- As relationships grow more intimate, the expectation of deeper, more personal self-disclosure increases.
- Women's relationships tend to rely more on verbal communication, and especially on self-disclosure, while men's relationships with other men more often develop out of shared activities or common experiences.
- As online and FtF relationships grow more intimate, the expectation of emotional expression increases.

3. Nonverbal

Principle Three: Effectively use and interpret nonverbal messages.
- Physical attraction is the degree to which you find another person's physical self appealing, while sexual attraction is the desire to have sexual contact with a certain person.
- In an FtF relationship, you may nonverbally reveal your liking for another person through the display of immediacy cues.
- In an online relationship, acronyms and emoticons help convey interest.
- Certain nonverbal behaviors, such as increasing the volume of your voice to keep someone from interrupting you or posting multiple lengthy messages in a chat rooom, can signal a self-absorbed style of interpersonal communication.
- As children, we learn early on to mask some emotions (disappointment, for example) so as to behave "appropriately."

4. Listen and Respond

Principle Four: Listen and respond thoughtfully to others.
- Early in online and FtF relationships, it's important to concentrate on and listen to your partner's responses to your questions, so that you can offer an appropriate follow-up response.

- You may verbally reveal your attraction and liking for other people by listening, asking questions to elicit more detail, and then responding appropriately and sensitively to the added information.
- The best conversationalists aren't great talkers; they're great listeners and responders.
- The formulation of great questions and powerful questions in conversation requires listening carefully and responding appropriately to someone's communication.
- It's important to attend carefully to someone's self-disclosure, because it comes with an expectation of reciprocity, meaning that the receiver is expected to self-disclose in response to the sender's self-disclosure.

Principle Five: Appropriately adapt messages to others.

- Adapt to others' communication, especially in first conversations, by attending to what is said and following up with great questions.
- A self-absorbed style of communication involves very little adaptation to others.
- Adapt your self-disclosure to the other person and the context, so that your revelations are appropriate.

5. Adapt

Summary

In this chapter, we explored the important topic of interpersonal communication—the form of communication that we use most frequently in our lives. Effective interpersonal communication is intricately related to one's ability to enact the five Communication Principles for a Lifetime. We first defined interpersonal communication as a special form of human communication that occurs when we interact with another person and attempt to mutually influence each other, usually for the purpose of managing online or FtF relationships. We then differentiated interpersonal communication from impersonal communication and relationships of circumstance from relationships of choice.

We all know that relationships are important, but just how do they begin? In this chapter, we explored the concept of attraction in its various forms, distinguishing interpersonal attraction as the form that causes us to forge ongoing connections with others. Four primary factors play a role in interpersonal attraction: how similar we perceive ourselves to be to our relational partners, how physically and/or sexually attracted we are to them, our proximity to them, and whether our personality traits, values, and needs are complementary to theirs. We explored ways that we verbally and nonverbally communicate our attraction to others, as we attempt to form friendships, relationship with coworkers, romances, and committed partnerings.

Once you acknowledge that you are attracted to another person and desire a relationship with her or him, how do you use communication to get that relationship off the ground? Whether our relationships form online or in person, most of us face a degree of uncertainty when meeting new people. We attempt to reduce that uncertainty by seeking information in passive, active, and/or interactive ways. We then must call on our best communication skills to get to know the other person. Rather than communicate about ourselves in a self-absorbed or narcissistic fashion, it is better to ask questions of the other person that will draw him or her out and get a conversation going. Learning to give and receive compliments graciously and sincerely is something we can all benefit from, because the compliment is a unique form of interpersonal communication that can have a profoundly positive effect on a relationship.

One of the most important forms of interpersonal communication that facilitates our online and FtF relationships is self-disclosure, defined as revealing something about ourselves to another person that she or he would not otherwise know if we did not reveal it. The rate and depth of self-disclosure vary as a relationship progresses, but we expect self-disclosure to be reciprocal. This means that if we share something about ourselves, we expect our partners to respond in kind, in both frequency and depth of information. Self-disclosure is also expected to be appropriate to the level of intimacy of the relationship. And self-disclosing involves a degree of risk.

One way to develop intimacy in a relationship is to disclose personal information, but self-disclosure is not the only road to intimacy. Gender affects how one develops relationships, in that men may develop close friendships with other men more through shared activities while women are more likely to deepen relationships by disclosing information. We discussed two models of self-disclosure: the social penetration model, which focuses on how one's personal layers are revealed to others, and the Johari Window, which illustrates our level of self-awareness and relational partners' perceptions of us. Another form of disclosure is the expression of emotions to friends and relational partners. The degree to which we feel safe discussing or displaying our emotions with others is a measure of intimacy in a relationship.

Assessing Your Knowledge

For Discussion and Review

Principle One: Be aware of your communication with yourself and others.

1. What aspects of yourself must you become more aware of in order to become a more effective communicator in interpersonal relationships?

Principle Two: Effectively use and interpret verbal messages.

2. What forms of verbal messages are most critical in successful interpersonal relationships?

Principle Three: Effectively use and interpret nonverbal messages.

3. What nonverbal cues are central to such interpersonal skills as listening, responding, asking great questions, self-disclosing, and expressing emotions?

Principle Four: Listen and respond thoughtfully to others.

4. Explore the role of listening and responding in the development of successful interpersonal relationships.

Principle Five: Appropriately adapt messages to others.

5. If someone doesn't adapt her or his communication to others, what's likely to happen to her or his interpersonal relationships?

Multiple Choice

Choose the *best* answer to each of the following questions.

1. When asking questions of someone you have just met, you should
   a. limit yourself to yes/no questions.
   b. focus on questions that are personal in nature.
   c. ask questions quickly, moving from one to the next.
   d. tailor the questions to what you have observed about the other person.

2. Susan does not feel comfortable communicating with others, but her boyfriend loves socializing. Susan appreciates this about him because he takes "center stage" when they are with people and she can stay in the background. This exemplifies which principle of interpersonal attraction?
   a. proximity
   b. matching hypothesis
   c. similarity
   d. complementarity

3. According to Altman and Taylor's social penetration model, intimate relationships are characterized by self-disclosures that are
   a. broad but not deep.
   b. deep but not broad.
   c. broad and deep.
   d. neither broad nor deep.

4. Derek spots an attractive woman at a party and asks his friend whether he knows her. This illustrates what type of uncertainty reduction strategy?
   a. active
   b. passive
   c. interactive
   d. third party

5. One of Jim's first assignments at his new job is to complete a project with his coworker Sally. Sally and Jim work well together during the project, but once it is complete they rarely see each other. The relationship between Jim and Sally is best described as a
   a. relationship of choice.
   b. relationship of attraction.
   c. relationship of circumstance.
   d. relationship of emotion.

6. Luke will talk with anyone about both his background and his current activities and interests. This information is in Luke's
   a. blind area.
   b. unknown area.
   c. hidden area.
   d. open area.

7. Morgan has a crush on Brody. When he is around, she moves to sit closer to him, increases her eye contact, smiles more, and fidgets with her hair. In order to communicate her attraction to Brody, Morgan is using
    a. nonverbal immediacy.
    b. complementarity.
    c. passive strategies.
    d. active strategies.

8. Physical and sexual attraction
    a. are the same thing.
    b. are different kinds of appeal.
    c. are not influenced by culture.
    d. remain fairly constant over time.

9. The direct expression of emotion occurs
    a. only in the early stages of a relationship.
    b. primarily in the middle stages of a relationship.
    c. typically at the later stages of a relationship.
    d. typically throughout the entire relationship.

10. Brayden has decided to rush a social fraternity. As part of deciding which fraternity he would like to pledge, he attends a number of meetings and parties and watches the way the active members interact. He also listens in on their conversations with one another in the cafeteria. Brayden's uncertainty reduction strategies can best be described as
    a. passive.
    b. active.
    c. reactive.
    d. interactive.

Answers to the questions in this practice test can be found at the end of the book.

Assessing Your Skill

1. Because we think that learning to ask great questions is so important, we want to provide you with an opportunity to practice this art and skill. For each of the situations and snippets of conversations below, generate effective follow-up questions that would deepen and extend the conversation. We've provided a complete example to get you started.

    Sample Situation and Conversation: The situation is a first conversation between two classmates who have never met; they are seated in the classroom before class begins.

    Bob: Hi. My name's Bob. What's yours?
    Sue: Hi. I'm Sue.
    Bob: I've never taken a philosophy course before, have you? What do you think this course will be like?
    Sue: Well, I've never taken a philosophy course either, but I expect there will be lots of reading. And I've heard that the professor's tests are pretty tough.
    Bob: Oh, great; is it too late to drop?! When you say the tests are tough, tough in what way? Do you mean they cover lots of material, the prof's a hard grader, or what?

    a. *Situation:* At a fraternity/sorority mixer, a woman and a man are introduced to each other for the first time by other members of their organizations.
    b. *Situation:* After a staff meeting, two new coworkers who will be working on the same important project introduce themselves to each other.

2. As a class, develop a list of categories of information for self-disclosure. For example, categories could include academic achievement, religion, family background, cultural heritage, romantic experiences, and sexuality. Then have each class member write down (privately) something pertaining to each category that the person *would* and *would not* feel comfortable disclosing to another person. For example, under the category of family background, an item that might be disclosed could be that one's parents were divorced; an item that might not be disclosed could be that one suffered emotional or physical abuse in one's family. This activity will help you clarify your own "rules" about self-disclosing personal information.

Web Resources to Improve Your Knowledge and Skill

How do people who are looking for romantic relationships meet other people? While singles bars and personal ads in newspapers are still around, people are turning increasingly to the web to meet others. If you're interested in virtual dating, here are a few sites to try. (But be careful: Some services charge fees just to access the site and get started.)

<www.eHarmony.com>   <www.Matchmaker.com>
<www.Match.com>   <www.eCrush.com>

Here's some sound advice about Internet dating services.[83]

1. Browse the dating services to find the one that best suits you. Sites often focus on people with particular interests and profiles.
2. Do a free trial, if the site offers one, to see if you like the process before becoming a paying member.
3. Once you choose to invest time and money in a particular site, be as honest as possible in completing your profile. Don't describe yourself as you'd like to *think* you are; answer as you *really* are.
4. Provide a recent, realistic, yet flattering picture of yourself, even if you feel insecure doing so. You will receive more replies than if you choose not to include a picture (which can set off alarm bells for some people).
5. Don't be discouraged by the responses you receive; it's typical to receive some rude or inappropriate messages from people whose motives are questionable.
6. If you do make a connection with someone and begin to exchange e-mail messages, pay attention to what is communicated, as well as what is *not* communicated.
7. If you decide to meet face to face with someone you've been e-mailing, be careful. Meet in a public place and have your own transportation so that you can make a safe departure if need be. Make sure a friend or family member knows what you're doing, where you're going, and when you're meeting the person.
8. Once you meet, if you don't feel a romantic connection, don't be shy about telling the person you're really not interested. Be assertive and firm, but not rude, in expressing your desire not to pursue things further. No one likes to be strung along.

Does self-disclosure, as a tool for enhancing intimacy in relationships, operate the same way in cyberspace as it does face to face? Apparently; according to research on Internet usage, people are telling other people all kinds of things about themselves over the web. Revealing personal information about oneself isn't as threatening to many people when it is accomplished through machines to someone in another location, rather than in face-to-face encounters. What's your view of self-disclosure and relationship development in cyberspace? Have you shared personal information with an online partner, or has someone shared personal information with you? If you haven't, but you're daring enough to try, here are a couple of sites to check out:

<www.love.com> This site, created by America Online, contains close to 200,000 personal ads. Chat rooms at this site serve as meeting places and arenas for exploring relationships. If you are a member of AOL, you also have access to their site Love@AOL.[84]

<luvcoach@aol.com> Robert Bruce Starr is known as the "Luvcoach" at America Online. He opens his chat room, called "Relationship Coaching," a few times a week and gives relationship advice to computer users. Users also chat with each other about a wide variety of relational issues.[85]

Bergander, Rudolf, "Young People." © 2008 Artists Rights Society (ARS), New York. Bildarchiv Preussischer Kulturbesitz /Art Resource, NY

> Relationship is a pervading and changing mystery ... brutal or lovely, the mystery waits for people wherever they go, whatever extreme they run to.
>
> Eudora Welty

Chapter 8

Enhancing Relationships

Chapter Outline

- The Importance of Friendship
- The Importance of Family
- The Importance of Colleagues
- Stages of Relationship Development
- Tensions in Relationships: The Dialectical Perspective
- Managing Interpersonal Conflict
- Summary

Chapter Objectives

After studying this chapter, you should be able to

1. Explain how the five Communication Principles for a Lifetime apply to interpersonal communication among friends, family members, and coworkers.
2. Identify the interpersonal communication skills that are most critical for effectiveness in the workplace.
3. Identify and describe the five stages of relational escalation.
4. Identify and describe the six stages of relational de-escalation.
5. Discuss relational dialectics and the three primary tensions in relationships.
6. Define interpersonal conflict and identify eight types of conflict.
7. Discuss power dynamics in complementary, symmetrical, and parallel interpersonal relationships.
8. Explain the difference between assertive and aggressive communication.
9. Explain the key characteristics of nonconfrontational, confrontational, and cooperative styles of conflict management.
10. Discuss the major ways to manage emotions, information, goals, and problems in conflict situations.

What makes you happy in this life? Think a bit before answering that question. What really gives you enjoyment? Staring at a computer screen? Working on a project for your job? Reading a great book? Playing a video game? Being by yourself, writing in your journal? Taking a long walk? Let us venture a guess: While any one of these things might bring some level of pleasure into your life, none of them could be considered *the* thing in life that gives you the most enjoyment. Probably most of us would answer that question with some response that involves other people or, perhaps, only one other person. Our family members, friends, and coworkers are very important to us.

To some degree, we all come from dysfunctional families—there is no such thing as a perfect, or "functional," family. As Tolstoy said, "Happy families are all alike; every unhappy family is unhappy in its own way." But no matter how imperfect our families are, no matter how crazy our siblings used to make us (or still make us), or how far apart we feel we may have grown from family members, almost all of us would agree that family relationships are extremely important. Likewise, when people talk about their jobs and what they like best about where they work, most often they talk about the people they work with. So, disregarding the few true hermits out there, most of us are "people who need people." It may sound corny, but we all know that our relationships with other people are what bring us joy.

In Chapter 7, we examined some fundamental aspects of interpersonal communication that help us initiate online and face-to-face relationships. In this chapter, we move forward to discuss interpersonal communication as it occurs in ongoing relationships. Where appropriate, we discuss online relationships, but our primary focus in this chapter is the good old-fashioned face-to-face relationship.

First, let's reconsider our five Communication Principles for a Lifetime as they pertain to certain relationships. Most of our examples in this chapter and the previous one tend to focus on romantic relationships, but friendships, family relationships, and relationships with colleagues are all critical in our lives.

1. Aware
2. Verbal
3. Nonverbal
4. Listen and Respond
5. Adapt

The Importance of Friendship

One of the best definitions of a friend, attributed to Aristotle, is "a soul that resides in two bodies." A friend is someone we like and who likes us. We trust our friends and share good and bad times with them. We enjoy being with them, so we try to make time for that purpose. We expect a certain level of self-sacrifice from our friends. For example, you know you've got a good friend when that person gives up something (like a hot date) just to help you through a tough time.

Researchers have examined some differences among friendships at four stages in life: childhood, adolescence, adulthood, and old age.[1] When we start to talk (around the age of two), we begin to play and interact with others and perceive playmates as those who can help meet our needs. Our first friendships are typically superficial, self-centered, and fleeting, because they are based on momentary sharing of activities.[2] As we grow, we develop more of a give-and-take in friendships. During adolescence, we move away from relationships with parents and toward greater intimacy with our peers. At this point in our development, peer relationships are the most important social influence on our behavior.

Adult friendships are among our most valued relationships, even though they may be few in number. Research has found that, on average, adults have ten to twenty casual friends, four to six close friends, and only one to two best friends.[3] Rather than progressing through a series of stages in which intimacy deepens, which is typical of romantic relationships, friendships often alternate between periods of development and deterioration.[4]

As Americans continue to spend more hours at work each year, we often find that our closest friends are also our coworkers.[5] We share common interests, concerns, and schedules with coworkers, so it's natural for colleagues to fulfill each other's social needs as well. No doubt some of you reading this text are working a job, taking classes that demand significant blocks of time, and juggling all of this with a home and family life. Given all this activity, you may find that friendships get less of your attention. Unless we make maintaining friendships a priority, we may find ourselves becoming too busy to "work them in" and, sadly, losing them over time.

One type of friendship that has received attention recently from researchers and the popular press is the "friends with benefits" relationship (FWBR), also referred to as the "booty call." Sexual liaisons between people who are "just friends" have been popularized through such television shows as *Sex and the City*, *Grey's Anatomy*, and a *Seinfeld* episode entitled "The Deal." Communication scholars Mikayla Hughes, Kelly Morrison, and Kelli Jean Asada define the friends with benefits relationship as one that emerges from a pre-existing friendship but that evolves to include sexual activity. The sexual contact doesn't change the friendship into a romantic relationship or imply a commitment; in fact, the people involved in an FWBR don't want anything more from their partners than what they have. These researchers explain that "these types of relationships are distinct in that they combine ... the benefits of friendship with the benefits of a sexual relationship, yet avoid the responsibilities and commitment that romantic sexual relationships typically entail."[6]

The FWBR differs from a "hookup" (a casual one-night sexual encounter), which has also been observed among college student populations, in that it is more long-lasting and stable because it builds on a pre-existing friendship.[7] Hughes and her colleagues discovered that FWBRs are relatively common on college campuses today, that participants in such relationships perceive them as important, and that the relationships function effectively, provided both participants adhere to the following rules:

1. FWBR participants must maintain their original friendship, meaning that sexual activity doesn't change the friendship and the participants continue to do things together that they typically did as friends.
2. Emotions don't become involved, or the FWBR will be at risk.
3. The FWBR is maintained in secret, even if, for some people, this means that their romantic/sexual partners don't know about the FWBR.
4. The relationship may be renegotiated, with either participant opting out at any time.[8]

Friendships are extremely important in old age.[9] During retirement, when many individuals have more time for socializing, friendships become increasingly critical. Older adults tend to rely on enduring friendships and to maintain a small, highly valued network of friends.

Many people find that the friendships they maintain over the years are the most valuable. How can being aware of your own interests, likes, and dislikes as you expand your circle of friends now help you build on those friendships so that they have the potential to last many years?

Communication Principles for a Lifetime: Enhancing Friendships

Noted author and motivational speaker Dale Carnegie suggested, "You can make more friends in two months by becoming interested in other people than you can in two years by trying to get other people interested in you."[10] Attraction is what draws you to potential friends, just as various forms of attraction draw you to potential dates or romantic partners. Like many other things, friendship development begins with an awareness of yourself—Principle One. Knowing your own interests, likes, and dislikes is a first step if you are trying to expand your circle of friends. If, for example, you consider yourself a spiritual person, then you're more likely to make new friends with those kinds of people at a church gathering or in a yoga and meditation class than in some other setting.

We need communication to initiate and maintain friendships. Principles Two and Three, which involve the effective use of verbal and nonverbal communication, are essential in friendship. Our verbal communication tends to become more frequent and to deepen as friendships develop. We also use immediacy cues to establish friendships—behaviors that reveal our liking of other people, such as leaning forward, moving closer, making eye contact, smiling, and nodding.

Listening and responding are important communication skills in friendship. Most of us don't stay friends with people who don't seem to listen to us or who listen but respond inappropriately. With friends, it's important to be aware of what they *say* as well as what they *do*, as we attempt to read what's going on with them and determine the best response. Probably no other communication skill develops a friendship more than the ability to listen and respond appropriately.

Finally, we learn to adapt to our friends or they probably don't stay our friends for very long (Principle Five). This means that we extend different parts of ourselves and communicate differently with various friends. You may enjoy your dancing buddies because you can let a creative, wilder side of yourself show with them, while you communicate more seriously as you study with a group of classmates who have become your friends.

1. Aware
2. Verbal
3. Nonverbal
4. Listen and Respond
5. Adapt

The Importance of Family

Of all the relationships we experience in our lifetimes, none are more complicated than family relationships. Family members have the power to shape our self-concepts and affect self-esteem more than other people. Granted, at some point we can choose to stop or lessen the effect family members can have on our lives. But for most of us, those early messages we received as children still remain in our psyches and affect who we are today.

To say that family life has changed is an understatement. Family units are dramatically different than they were when the predominant profile was a two-parent, father-as-bread-winner, mother-as-homemaker arrangement.[11] In the 1980s, the New York Supreme Court provided a very broad definition of a family, stating, "The best description of a family is a continuing relationship of love and care, and an assumption of responsibility for some other person."[12] The most common profile of the American family in the twenty-first century is the step-family, or blended family.[13]

Communication Principles for a Lifetime: Enhancing Family Relationships

Growing up in families, we begin to discover who we are and how we should communicate with others. Virginia Satir has conducted extensive research on family communication.[14] She suggests that, in healthy families, "the members' sense of self-worth is high; communication is direct, clear, specific, and honest; rules are flexible, humane, and subject to change; and the family's links to society are open and hopeful." In such families, Satir notes, people listen actively; they look *at* one another, not *through* one another or at the floor; they treat children as people; they touch one another affectionately regardless of age; and they openly discuss disappointments, fears, hurts, angers, and criticism, as well as joys and achievements. The degree to which parents and children can reveal what they are thinking and feeling is a measure of family cohesiveness. Another aspect Satir highlights corresponds to our Principle Four, that of listening and responding. Healthy family relationships are built on foundations of trust, which involves listening to one another and responding helpfully. Many conflicts arise because family members don't listen well to one another and respond based on that faulty listening.

Finally, family relationships involve a good deal of adaptation, particularly when, as adults, we visit our parents. Sometimes our parents and extended family members talk a certain way mainly because they've always talked that way. But if, for example, you're the family member who's moved away, attended college, and adapted your communication to meet the changing times, connect with friends, and demonstrate professionalism at work, it can be quite awkward to be immersed once again in the family setting and realize how much you've changed. Adaptation can be challenging in such a situation, but it's necessary if your goal is effective communication.

4. Listen and Respond

5. Adapt

The Importance of Colleagues

For many of us, our work is our livelihood, our most time-consuming activity. In fact, many Americans are working longer hours—10 percent more time on the job in the twenty-first century than thirty years ago. And according to the web site of the AFL-CIO, Americans are already working almost a full week's worth of hours more per year than they were at the beginning of the twenty-first century.[15] Many things make a job worthwhile and rewarding, but most working people say that relationships with people they work with make the most difference between job satisfaction and dissatisfaction.

What are the most important skills people need to be successful on the job? Year after year, the number-one skill employers look for in new hires is the ability to communicate effectively with others.[16] You land your job through a face-to-face interview (in most cases). You keep your job based on your ability to do the work and get along with coworkers and bosses, which usually involves a large amount of interpersonal interaction.

Communication Principles for a Lifetime: Enhancing Workplace Relationships

Getting accustomed to a new job takes a while. There are the rudimentary things to discover and adjust to, such as finding out where to park or which subway to take, learning what makes the organization function, and observing general office protocol. Then there are the more important things, like learning how to do your job well, ascertaining the chain of command, and discovering which colleagues have the potential to develop into friends.

When most of us enter a new situation, such as a new job, we experience uncertainty. We discussed in Chapter 7 how the motivation to reduce uncertainty causes us to seek information. On the job, our uncertainty will most likely be reduced by those who hired us, those who are assigned to train or orient us to the new situation, and coworkers who are at our same level within the organization. We are most likely to use passive strategies first, meaning that we observe our surroundings and how people interact on the job, as a way of becoming more aware so that we will know how to behave appropriately (Principle One). Perception checking with colleagues also increases awareness. For example, after attending your first staff meeting, you might

1. Aware

Listening and responding appropriately are key skills potential employers value. What can you do to listen and respond thoughtfully and successfully to others in the workplace?

2. Verbal
3. Nonverbal

4. Listen and Respond

5. Adapt

want to ask a few colleagues whether the gathering was typical of the kind of staff meetings the organization holds.

As we begin to interact with people of varying status in the organization, we draw on our most effective verbal and nonverbal communication skills so that we make positive impressions on others (Principles Two and Three). The higher you go in an organization, the more your job involves communicating with others, both online and in person.

One skill that makes for an effective worker is the ability to listen and respond effectively to colleagues (Principle Four). It's important to listen patiently, fully, and nonjudgmentally at work and to exercise caution before responding, so that you respond appropriately.

Finally, our Principle Five about adaptation is critical to successful coworker relationships. You cannot hope to be successful on the job if you communicate the same way to your boss as you do to your peers on the job, your subordinates, and others in your life—including long-term friends, intimates, and family members. This may seem obvious, but we find that people sometimes experience isolation on the job because they cannot get along with coworkers. Or they've trusted coworkers too much and revealed personal information, only to have that information used against them later. Some people don't realize that they can't talk at work about everything they talk about at home. They don't adapt to the situation, and it often costs them their jobs.

Stages of Relationship Development

In this chapter, we explore aspects of communication that are critical to the successful functioning of ongoing relationships, but it is helpful to first understand that relationships tend to develop in discernible stages.[17] While the research on relational stages is most often applied to dating or romantic relationships, the information can also apply to other types of relationships.

Understanding relationship stages is important for several reasons. First, interpersonal communication is affected by the stage of the relationship. For instance, individuals in an advanced stage discuss topics and display nonverbal behaviors that rarely appear in the early stages of a relationship. Second, interpersonal communication facilitates movement between the various stages. Relationships change and are continually

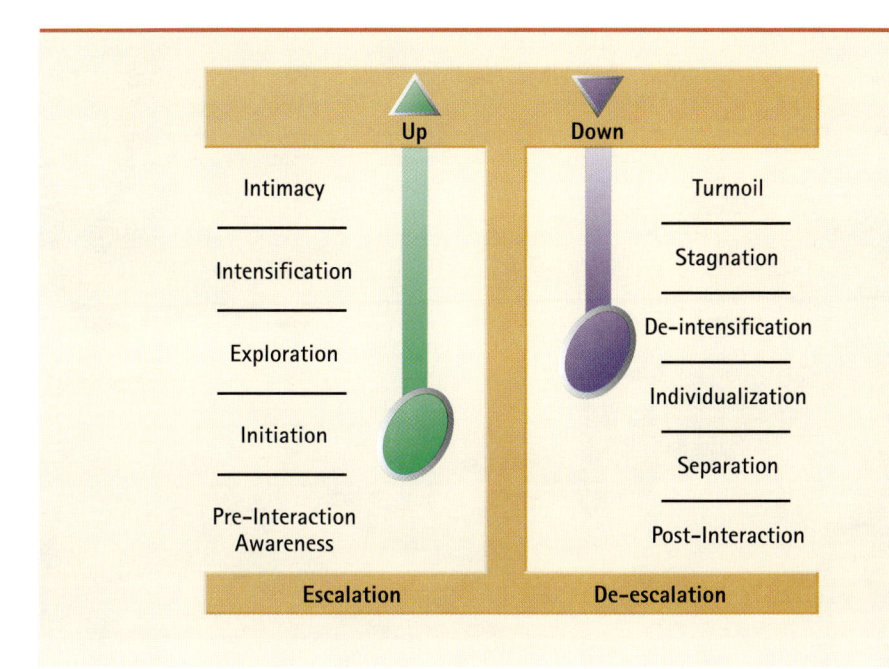

Figure 8.1
Relationship Stages

Source: From Steven A. Beebe, Susan J. Beebe, and Mark V. Redmond, *Interpersonal Communication: Relating to Others*, 5th edition. Published by Allyn & Bacon, Boston, MA. Copyright © 2008 by Pearson Education. Reprinted by permission of the publisher.

renegotiated by those involved. Interpersonal communication moves a relationship forward as we progress from being acquaintances to friends, to lovers, and, possibly, to marital or committed partners. Ideally, communication should move a relationship back from partners to friends as well, although regressing a relationship is difficult to accomplish.

It's helpful to think of relational stages as floors in a high rise (see Figure 8.1). The bottom floor represents a first meeting; the penthouse is intimacy. Relational development is an elevator that stops at every floor. As you ascend, you might get off the elevator and wander around for a while before going to the next floor. Each time you get on, you don't know how many floors up the elevator will take you or how long you'll stay at any given floor. In fact, sometimes you never get back on the elevator, electing instead to stay at a particular stage of relational development. This may represent stability or stagnation. Stability is not the same as stagnation; it may simply mean that a relationship has reached a comfortable point for both partners. But if one partner feels the relationship has stabilized and the other partner feels the relationship has stagnated, dissatisfaction and conflict are often the result.

If you fall head over heels in love, you might want to escalate quickly from floor to floor toward intimacy, possibly even skipping some floors. In contrast, the process of de-escalating a relationship does not always occur, but if it does, it may be a slow or quick descent through various floors. The best approach to relationship development is to share this elevator with your partner or friend, so that the two of you make decisions about how high you will ride, how long to stay at each floor, and whether to take the elevator back down. Often partners do not share decisions about movement within the relationship. Sometimes one of the partners rides the elevator alone.

Relational Escalation

As depicted in Figure 8.1, the first level of relational development is termed the **pre-interaction awareness stage**. In this stage, you might observe a person or even talk with others about that person without having any direct interaction. You might not move beyond the pre-interaction awareness stage if your impressions of the person aren't favorable or the circumstances aren't right.

If you are attracted to the other person and the circumstances are right, you might proceed to the **initiation stage**. First conversations typically involve each person

1. Aware

pre-interaction awareness stage
The stage of becoming aware of one's attraction to another person and observing that person but not actually interacting.

initiation stage
The first contact with a person with whom one desires a relationship; usually characterized by asking and answering questions.

At the intensification stage, a couple's relationship becomes the central focus of their lives.

2. Verbal
3. Nonverbal
4. Listen and Respond

exploration stage
The stage that involves more in-depth interactions.

intensification stage
The stage in which partners begin to depend on each other for self-confirmation; characterized by more shared activities, more time spent together, more intimate physical distance and contact, and personalized language.

intimacy stage
The stage in which partners provide primary confirmation of each other's self-concept; characterized by highly personalized and synchronized verbal and nonverbal communication.

responding to the other's questions as they both try to determine what they have in common. Nonverbal behavior also indicates interest.

If you decide to go to the **exploration stage**, you'll begin to share more in-depth information. You'll probably have minimal physical contact, and you may limit the amount of time you spend together because you're building a relationship. But some relationships move through stages very quickly. For example, we probably all know people whose relationships were extremely physical, and perhaps sexual, from the very start. Are those relationships doomed because they didn't follow set or prescribed paths for development? No; some relationships may just proceed through stages faster than others. However, relationships that are extremely physical or sexual may burn out quickly because they lack the emotional foundation necessary to survive.

If you proceed to the **intensification stage**, you will start to depend on each other for self-confirmation, meaning that your partner's opinion of or feelings about you weigh more heavily than those of others. Partners tend to spend more time together, increase the variety of activities they share, adopt more intimate physical distance and contact, and personalize their language. The frequency and level of shared personal information increase, and the couple may decide to label their connection.

The top level of relationship escalation is the **intimacy stage**. Partners who are in this stage provide primary confirmation of each other's self-concept, and communication is highly personalized and synchronized. Partners talk about anything and everything, and a commitment to maintaining the relationship might even be formalized and socially recognized, such as with a decision to marry. The partners share an understanding of each other's language and nonverbal cues and have a great deal of physical contact. They use fewer words to communicate effectively because they understand each other without words. Reaching this stage takes time—time to build trust, share personal information, observe each other in various situations, and create an emotional bond and commitment.

Relational De-Escalation

Sometimes relationships begin to unravel; this can happen for a variety of reasons. Some unravel to the point of termination. But as you may already know, ending a relationship is not as simple as going down the same way you came up; it is not a mere reversal of the escalation process.[18]

Recap

Relational Escalation

Stage	Explanation
Pre-Interaction Awareness	You become aware of your attraction to someone and begin to observe that person.
Initiation	You initiate contact with the person with whom you want a relationship.
Exploration	Interactions deepen as questions and answers elicit more information from partners.
Intensification	Partners begin to depend on each other for confirmation of their self-concepts. They spend more time together, engage in more intimate touch, and personalize their language.
Intimacy	Partners provide primary confirmation of each other's self-concept. Verbally, language is highly personalized; nonverbal behaviors are synchronized.

Communication scholar Mark Knapp provides a model for how relationships come apart.[19] When an intimate relationship is not going well, it usually enters a stage of either turmoil or stagnation. The **turmoil stage** involves an increase in conflict, as one or both partners find more faults in the other. The definition of the relationship loses its clarity, and mutual acceptance declines. The communication climate is tense; interactions are difficult and forced. The **stagnation stage** occurs when the relationship loses its vitality and the partners become complacent, taking each other for granted. Communication and physical contact between the partners decrease; they spend less time together but don't necessarily engage in conflict. Partners in a stagnating relationship tend to go through the motions of an intimate relationship without the commitment or the joy. But a stagnating relationship can be salvaged; individuals can repair, redefine, or revitalize the relationship and return to intimacy.

If the turmoil or stagnation continues, however, a couple will likely experience the **de-intensification stage**. This involves significantly decreased interaction; increased physical, emotional, and psychological distance; and decreased dependence on the other for self-confirmation. The partners might discuss the definition of their relationship, question its future, and assess each other's level of dissatisfaction. The relationship can be repaired and the individuals can move once again toward intensification and intimacy, but it's more difficult to accomplish at this point.

After de-intensification, the **individualization stage** occurs. Partners tend to define their lives more as individuals and less as a couple or unit. Interactions are limited; both partners tend to turn to others for confirmation of their self-concepts; physical intimacy is at an all-time low, if not nonexistent; and nonverbal distance is easily detected.

In the **separation stage**, individuals make an intentional decision to minimize or eliminate further interpersonal interaction. If they share custody of children, attend mutual family gatherings, or work at the same place, the nature of their interaction changes. They divide property, resources, and friends. Interactions in this stage are often tense and difficult, especially if the relationship has been intimate.

Although interaction may cease, the effect of a relationship is not over. Relationships—even failed ones—are powerful experiences in our lives. The final level in relational de-escalation is termed the **post-interaction stage**. This level represents the lasting effects the relationship has on the self, and therefore on other interactions and relationships. Relationship scholar Steve Duck explains that in this final stage of terminating relationships, we engage in "grave-dressing"—we create a public statement for

---

turmoil stage
The stage characterized by increased conflict, less mutual acceptance, a tense communication climate, and an unclear relationship definition.

stagnation stage
The stage in which a relationship loses its vitality, partners begin to take each other for granted, and communication and physical contact decline.

de-intensification stage
The stage involving significantly decreased interaction, increased distance, and decreased dependence on one's partner for self-confirmation.

individualization stage
The stage in which partners define their lives more as individuals and less as a couple.

separation stage
The stage in which individuals make an intentional decision to minimize or eliminate further interpersonal interaction.

post-interaction stage
The bottom, or final, stage in relational de-escalation, which represents the lasting effects of a relationship on the self.

Communication and Ethics

How Easy Should a Breakup Be?

In one memorable episode of the hit cable TV show *Sex and the City*, the Carrie Bradshaw character woke up to find a Post-it note next to her bed, with a scribbling from Berger (her boyfriend at the time) saying that he was sorry but he was breaking up with her. She was outraged at his cowardice in ending a relationship via something so impersonal as a yellow sticky note.

An interpersonal communication class was discussing the subject of breakups one day, and it seemed everyone had experiences to offer. Some had gone through long, drawn-out episodes of arguing, breaking up, getting back together, and then breaking up again. But then one student revealed that, in his last romantic relationship, he'd been "dumped" over the Internet, through an apologetic but hurtful e-mail message. That comment led another student to say that she'd learned she'd been dumped via a MySpace page. Still another student trumped both of these stories by saying that she'd been dumped by her boyfriend via text message—he'd had the nerve to text her while she was in class and break up with her, even knowing that he'd soon see her on campus. Hers had not been a short-term relationship, either—not that the length of the relationship should determine the means of breaking up, but the text-message breakup might have been at least a bit more understandable if the couple hadn't been together for long.

Are these high-tech equivalents of the "Dear John" letter ethical? We know that some people don't use interpersonal communication at all when they want to break up; the relationship just sort of fades away because one or both partners don't call or come around anymore. Perhaps computer-mediated communication is preferable to no communication at all, but just what are the ethics involved in such situations?

Engagement Questions

1. What do you believe is a person's ethical obligation when she or he wishes to terminate a relationship?
2. Communicating through technology allows for a certain level of impersonality, but is sending a text message or posting a breakup notice on a MySpace page an appropriate way to end a relationship? Might the impersonality be helpful, in that the "dumpee" can save face and not have to confront the "dumper" in person?
3. If you wanted to break up with someone, would your method of breaking up depend on how long you'd been with the person? How intimate the relationship was? How often you'd have to see or be around that person in the future?

---

people who ask why we broke up or why we're no longer friends with someone. It also means that we come to grips with losing the relationship.[20] Sometimes our sense of self gets battered during the final stages of a relationship; we have to work hard to regain a healthy sense of self.

Research over several decades has shed light on how people prefer to end relationships, as well as how they prefer someone to end a relationship with them.[21] In most relationships, the breakup is unilateral (done by one party) rather than bilateral (agreed to by both parties). Studies show that most people use and prefer indirect breakup strategies, such as avoidance, requests for "distance" or "space" in the relationship, a general fading away rather than an abrupt or definite breakup, and the staging of a conflict that leads to blaming and relationship termination. Direct breakup strategies, typically accomplished face to face, are probably the most interpersonally communicative but not the most preferred by most people in relationships. Being told we're being dumped just isn't something many of us prefer to experience. If you're really sheepish about breaking up with someone and you have some money to burn, a payment of $50 to the web site BreakUpService.com will buy you the services of someone who will call or write a letter and break up your relationship for you. An employee of the service will even pick up any possessions you've left in the care of your ex and make sure they get returned to you. The service's employees report a significant increase in business just after major holidays.

What typifies each of the different relational stages of escalation and de-escalation is the communication—verbal and nonverbal—that is present or absent. Interpersonal communication facilitates movement through the stages of escalation; lack of communication moves people through the stages of de-escalation.

Communication and Technology

Cheating in Cyberspace

Research reveals that the primary use for the home computer is keeping in touch with family members and friends.[22] Another, less mainstream, use is to establish "liaisons" outside one's primary relationship.[23] Typically, these liaisons don't begin as sexual relationships. They may begin through common interests, such as those you share with someone who posts frequently in a chat room; after a while, you decide to begin exchanging comments with only that person in a private chat room. Since these exchanges are anonymous (chatters most often use pseudonyms), a private exchange between two chatters seems harmless, but this form of cyber-relationship can escalate and take on another level of intimacy and meaning.

You've probably heard of cybersex—sexual activity that occurs online, but without any physical contact between participants—but you may not have thought about the damage cybersex can do to a monogamous, committed relationship. Most people have negative reactions to marital infidelity, whether they have experienced it themselves or know someone who has; even those who haven't experienced it say that they would respond negatively to a partner's infidelity if it were to happen.[24] But few people in committed, monogamous relationships think much about cyber-infidelity—until it happens to them. No physical contact has taken place; the sexual activity is accomplished through verbal exchanges within virtual reality—so how real is virtual reality?

Putting a positive spin on this situation, some research suggests that people who form sexual liaisons online are able to explore their sexuality with little concern that friends, coworkers, and spouses will discover their activities.[25] People may feel sexually hindered in their face-to-face relationships, so in a sense, the Internet becomes the arena in which their "true" sexual selves find expression. They may come to understand themselves better sexually because they feel under less pressure, and the benefits of such discovery can carry over into their face-to-face relationships. Some are drawn to the Internet for sexual gratification if their in-person relationships are in turmoil or decline and their opportunities for sexual expression and gratification are limited. In addition, since online sexual exchanges don't occur in person, the eroticism is based on other factors, such as emotional intimacy and verbal expressiveness, rather than on physical attractiveness. Concerns about STDs or unwanted pregnancies disappear. A final benefit cited in research relates to the fact that if a virtual sexual liaison goes awry, participants don't suffer such consequences as in-person retribution or confrontation, since online exchanges, for the most part, remain anonymous, with true identities withheld.

One study asked participants about their online sexual activity, including what initially motivated them to engage in cybersex, why they continued to engage in it, the role it played in their lives, and the effects it had on them.[26] Interestingly enough, 41 percent of subjects revealed that they did not believe that online sexual activity constituted cheating on a partner under any circumstances. Fourteen percent believed it to be cheating if a person engaged in cybersex repeatedly with the same person. Smaller percentages of participants believed that online sex was cheating only if interactive video cameras were used or if the online sex led to phone sex. Thirty-three percent of subjects believed that online sex was cheating and that it was just as much an act of infidelity as in-person sex with someone other than one's partner.

Engagement Questions

1. What's your view of cybersex? Is it a breach of faith or just simple, harmless "sexploration"?
2. Should someone who is in a monogamous, committed, face-to-face relationship be seeking sexual liaisons over the Internet?
3. The downsides of cybersex (online infidelity) are obvious, but do you agree that there are upsides to such activity?
4. Should cyber-infidelity affect a committed relationship as much as in-person infidelity, or is it somehow different?

Tensions in Relationships: The Dialectical Perspective

Relationships are living, breathing, dynamic entities, and no two relationships are the same. Relationships are constantly changing, in both small and large ways. One way to approach relationships, known as **relational dialectics** or the dialectical perspective, was developed by communication scholars Leslie Baxter and Barbara Montgomery (and extended by other researchers).[27] Dialectics help us understand the up-and-down, ebb-and-flow, messy, oftentimes illogical nature of interpersonal relationships. In this section of the chapter, we discuss a set of tensions that people in relationships commonly face—but by *tensions*, we don't mean to imply something that is necessarily negative. A

relational dialectics
A perspective that views interpersonal relationships as constantly changing rather than stable and that revolves around how relational partners manage tensions.

Recap

Relational De-Escalation

Stage	Explanation
Turmoil	Partners take each other for granted and have more conflict. They exhibit less mutual acceptance, their communication climate is tense, and their relationship definition is unclear.
Stagnation	The relationship loses its vitality, partners begin to take each other for granted, and communication and physical contact decline.
De-Intensification	Partners significantly decrease their interaction and their dependence on each other for self-confirmation; they increase their physical distance.
Individualization	Partners define their lives more as individuals and less as a couple.
Separation	Partners make an intentional decision to minimize or eliminate further interpersonal interaction.
Post-Interaction	This is the bottom or final level in relational de-escalation; it represents the lasting effects of a relationship on the individuals.

dialectical perspective suggests that relationship issues are better understood in terms of push–pull dynamics or points on a continuum, rather than opposite poles or fixed entities. While tensions can occur in all sorts of relationships—among family members, between coworkers, within friendships—they are arguably most revealing of the romantic relationship.

Romantic relationship tensions arise from the decision making a couple faces in developing and defining their relationship, not necessarily because of the individuals in the relationship. With each tension, it's not a matter of "either/or" ("either we're committed or we're not"), but a matter of degree or "both/and" ("we're both committed and independent"). If partners can recognize the presence and shifting nature of the tensions, they can talk about them and either resolve them or decide that they just aren't suited for each other. While multiple tensions have been identified in research, for our purposes we will focus on three primary issues that most relational partners face: integration–separation, stability–change, and expression–privacy.

Integration–Separation: Autonomy versus Connection

The first dialectic Baxter and Montgomery identified is integration–separation, more easily understood as the tension of autonomy versus connection. While people want to be connected to others and feel that they are part of a couple or group, they also want to be self-sufficient and independent. The amount of autonomy partners desire within a relationship varies widely within the people themselves and also over the course of the relationship; thus, autonomy is one of the most difficult issues to confront. In the early stages of romance, the tendency is to spend as much time together as possible. This creates a sense that your life together operates almost in a vacuum, sheltered from the outside world. After a while, the rest of life usually intrudes (reality sets in) and begins to whittle time away from the people in the relationship, and the tension of autonomy versus connection can arise.

Since finding a balance between personal freedom and shared activities is one of the single toughest issues in a relationship, talking it out isn't easy. It's particularly problematic in the initial stages of romantic relationships, when a pattern of spending great amounts of time together has been set and conflict is the last thing either partner wants. When a time-consuming activity occurs or when the "first night out without you" arises, a relational partner is likely to feel a degree of betrayal or have problems dealing with the contrast from doing everything together. In anticipation of this tension, partners can benefit from an honest, open, nondefensive conversation about the amount of time they expect to spend together versus time apart. Talking about this tension won't necessarily ensure a perfect balance or prevent the problem from arising, but it will allow partners to know each other better and will open the door to further discussion.

Stability–Change: Predictability versus Novelty

While people are drawn to stability and consistency in a relationship, they are also drawn to excitement and unpredictability, so becoming comfortable with the ebb and flow of these aspects within a relationship can be a challenge. At times, stability may feel comforting and secure; at other times, it may feel stagnant and stifling. Change can be scary, but also energizing.

The tension of stability versus change can manifest itself in a couple of ways. Typically, at the start of a relationship, a relational partner is happy with the status quo; but over time, as the novelty wears off, one partner may try to change the other. At the onset of a relationship, we have a tendency to emphasize our partner's positive points and gloss over personality traits or behaviors that we don't like. But as a relationship progresses and the "sheen" fades, we may have difficulty accepting our partner as he or she is or may believe that we know what's best for him or her. So we start exerting a bit of control or persuasion, in an effort to change our partner into the person we think he or she should be or to get him or her to do what we think should be done.

A second way this tension emerges is described by communication theorists Lynne Turner and Richard West in terms of a couple's approach to planning.[28] When relational partners make plans to be together, the plans reinforce the relationship and begin to establish a routine. But if partners feel compelled to "go according to plan," they may come to feel stifled by the level of predictability in the relationship. If partners stay flexible, knowing that plans can change, the tension is better managed. Again, being aware that this tension is likely to emerge at some point—or several points—within a relationship is key, because it's hard to anticipate and even harder to fix something that you don't recognize as a problem.

Expression–Privacy: Openness versus Closedness

Each of us is different in how open we wish to be—or feel comfortable being—and our need for privacy. If the two people in a relationship are dramatically different on this count, they will have to be proactive and work hard to manage this tension, or else it can be a deal breaker. Many couples feel a push–pull regarding how much they reveal to each other, with some partners wanting complete openness and others wanting to retain a degree of privacy lest they be criticized, judged, or abandoned for revealing their innermost thoughts and feelings. For some, revealing a good deal of information signifies trust and a combining of the individuals into one entity: the couple. For others, a good relationship means that each partner retains some of his or her individual identity, keeping some thoughts and behaviors private even from the person he or she feels closest to. Again, the goal is to attain some sort of balance on this front.

Often in the early stages of a relationship, the topic of past relationships/lovers comes up; this situation provides a perfect illustration of this particular tension. One partner may want to reveal all and know all, while the other may not wish to bring the past into the present, preferring to start anew without dragging relational baggage into the new situation. Both positions—and all points in between—are legitimate, but they are indicative of a relational tension that typically has to be addressed for a relationship to flourish.

2. Verbal

1. Aware

Managing Interpersonal Conflict

A World of Conflict

We live in a world full of conflict. You can hardly watch the news on TV, listen to a radio talk show, or read a newspaper online without being confronted with another story of conflict. Whether it's the Middle East, a political coup in a country in Africa, or a disturbance generated by extremist groups right here at home, conflict on a global scale seems inevitable. While conflicts have always existed throughout the world, the events of September 11, 2001, launched the United States into a series of intense conflicts across the globe. How can we understand conflict on such a scale? What can we learn about conflict that might help mediate its destructive effects across the world? Developing an understanding of conflict and effective communication skills to manage it begins one on one, in our day-to-day relationships. Conflict is rooted in interpersonal communication.

Do you know the three most important words a person can say to someone? The answer isn't "I love you"; the answer is "I was wrong." These words are actually better to hear than "I'm sorry," because saying you're sorry could mean that you're sorry you're having a disagreement or you're sorry you got caught doing something that caused the conflict, or it could be just something to say in an attempt to end the conflict. It's quite hard for most of us to admit that we were at fault, but it's very meaningful in a conflict situation when someone admits that she or he was wrong.

Interpersonal conflict is a struggle that occurs when two people cannot agree on a way to meet their needs. If needs or goals are incompatible, if there are too few resources to satisfy them, or if individuals opt to compete rather than to cooperate to satisfy them, then conflict occurs. Suppose you are trying to find a place to park in an overcrowded lot on campus. Just as you find an empty spot, another student zips into "your" space. Your blood boils and you get out of your car fighting mad. The intensity of a conflict usually relates to the intensity of the unmet needs. The bedrock of all conflict is differences—different goals, experiences, expectations, and so forth.[29] Your goal collides head-on with someone else's, and you feel as if you have lost control of the situation.

Communication scholar Peter Kellett researches conflict by studying people's stories or accounts of arguments or conflicts with other people. One coworker might say to another, "You'll never guess what my wife said to me last night; she actually had the nerve to tell me . . . ," and the story proceeds to unfold from one person's perspective. Kellett explains that we rarely know the full story of a conflict, but he suggests that "smart interpretive guesswork can often lead to some keen insights into the various layers and dimensions of a given conflict. In understanding these layers and their interrelationships lies the wisdom to know why the conflict takes the form that it does and possibly insight into how to manage it more effectively based on that wisdom."[30] Kellett processes conflict by first hearing someone's story, then asking what he calls "smart questions" about the narrative, and then making recommendations for changing people's conflict behavior. Before we explore how to better manage and resolve conflict, let's first examine the nature of conflict and how it functions in interpersonal relationships.

Types of Conflict

While we all probably know people who enjoy conflict for conflict's sake, most of us want to better understand conflict so that we're more fully equipped to manage it, rather than letting it manage us. Realizing that several forms of conflict exist is a first step.

Conflict can be constructive or destructive. To construct something is to build or make something new. Characterized by cooperation in dealing with differences,

---

interpersonal conflict
A struggle that occurs when two people cannot agree on a way to meet their needs.

constructive conflict can help identify which elements of a relationship need to change or be improved, so that new patterns are established. Here's an example:

> Jake: You know, I'm getting tired of always going to your mother's on Sundays. It's like we're in a rut or something. Just one weekend, I'd like to have a Sunday with no schedule or agenda.
>
> Julie: Jake, I thought you liked going over there, because my mom's such a good cook and you and dad are working on that project together. Plus, it's one of the few times I get to spend time with my folks.
>
> Jake: Well, I do like going over there, but not every weekend.
>
> Julie: I didn't realize you were starting to resent it or feel like you were in a rut. Let's talk more about this, and figure something out.

Note that Julie recognizes the need for further dialogue about Jake's complaint. She transforms the issue of disagreement into a topic for discussion and relational adjustment. If Jake hadn't expressed his dissatisfaction, the issue might have taken on larger proportions. He might have expressed his feelings of being in a rut in a cruder, more hurtful way later on. Many times these expressions contain more venom than we intend or actually feel. A well-managed disagreement that includes expressing one's own needs or revising goals can lead people to examine and then revitalize their relationship. Constructive conflict enables both people to view a disagreement from different perspectives, even if the information shared seems negative at first.

A rapidly spiraling **destructive conflict** can do as much damage as a tornado churning through a trailer park. A conflict may start over a seemingly small issue but can increase in intensity as other issues and differences are brought into the discussion. Such destructive escalation blocks off options for managing differences and makes a win–win solution more elusive. The primary characteristic of destructive conflict is a lack of flexibility in responding to others.[31] Combatants view their differences from a win–lose perspective, rather than looking for solutions that allow each individual to gain. This form of conflict dismantles relationships without restoring them. If both individuals are dissatisfied with the outcome of the conflict, then it has been more destructive than constructive.

In their book on interpersonal conflict, William Wilmot and Joyce Hocker discuss six hallmarks of constructive conflict.[32]

1. *People change.* In relationships, people are involved with each other. In conflict, people must work hard to stay involved with each other, because an interaction that escalates into conflict can pull people apart. Flexibility and a willingness to change are key.
2. *People interact with an intent to learn instead of an intent to protect themselves.* You can learn a great deal about yourself, your partner, and your relationship if you approach conflict as a learning experience—one that will take your relationship forward instead of allowing it to stagnate or regress. Protecting yourself against conflict doesn't help a relationship grow.
3. *People don't stay stuck in conflict when the conflict is constructive.* Destructive conflict can make you feel stuck in one place in a relationship. Constructive conflict is a dynamic process that emerges, plays out, and recedes.
4. *Constructive conflict enhances self-esteem in the participants.* You probably don't associate conflict with enhanced self-esteem, because most of us think of conflict as negative and destructive. However, constructive conflict brings energy and productivity to a relationship and provides each partner with a more honest, complete picture of himself or herself.
5. *Constructive conflicts are characterized by a relationship focus instead of a purely individualistic focus.* If parties in a conflict focus on the relationship instead of themselves, then the conflict will more likely be constructive than destructive. Participants should emphasize the "we" over the "I," so that conflict is seen as an experience that builds the relationship.

5. Adapt

4. Listen and Respond

constructive conflict
Conflict characterized by cooperation in dealing with differences; helps build new insights and patterns in a relationship.

destructive conflict
Conflict characterized by a lack of cooperation in dealing with differences; dismantles relationships without restoring them.

6. *Constructive conflict is primarily cooperative.* Conflict built on competition, power struggles, and self-interest will destroy a relationship. Conversely, a cooperative, win–win approach to conflict will open the door for greater growth.

Communication scholars Gerald Miller and Mark Steinberg categorize conflict as having three forms.[33] First, **pseudoconflict** reflects a basic lack of understanding; one person misunderstands the meaning in a message. Second, **simple conflict** stems from differences in ideas, definitions, perceptions, or goals. Third, when conflict gets personal, such that people attack each other's self-esteem, it's **ego conflict**. One form of conflict can morph into another. For example, two people could start out with a simple misunderstanding about the time they were supposed to meet (pseudoconflict). But if it escalates, with one person accusing the other person of something deeper than a mere misunderstanding (for example, telling the other that he or she is "always like this" or that misunderstanding the timing was "done on purpose, just to make me mad"), then an ego conflict is likely to erupt out of the more basic pseudoconflict.

Have you ever been involved in an argument when you suddenly realized that the true point of the conflict was not what you were arguing about at all, but something deeper? Sometimes this kind of awareness never comes—we think that what we're arguing about really is the point or actual issue. But perhaps later, sometimes *much* later, we realize or have it pointed out to us that the momentary issue wasn't the actual issue, that the conflict was an outgrowth of a much more important concern. Kellett writes about this phenomenon of **symbolic displacement**, defined as "(1) when people engage in one conflict through, or in place of, another symbolically related one or (2) when a participant's behavior is an expression of displaced or unconscious meaning of which either or both may be unaware."[34] Kellett explains that when a conflict is displaced (ignored, unspoken, buried, tabled), the volatile energy that builds up as a result can create "hot buttons" for people—language or topics that are highly likely to trigger conflict. A reaction to a "hot button issue" can be a clue to a displaced conflict. Let's say that one partner in a relationship nags the other about cleaning junk out of a spare room; the nagging escalates into a full-blown, "knock down, drag out" argument about the lack of action on the project. The conflict issue or topic at hand is the project, but the actual displaced issue might be a feeling of being judged as a lazy procrastinator, of being criticized for never following through on one's goals, of being "all talk and no action." The deeper issue might be a fear of failure, which has little to do with the junky spare room.

Two other types of conflict are worthy of note. First, people in ongoing relationships often have **serial arguments**, defined as "argumentative episodes focused on a given issue that occur at least twice."[35] How many times have you heard someone complain, "We have this same argument over and over"? Serial arguments typically involve repetitious, highly negative verbal communication (such as name calling) and negative nonverbal cues (yelling, aggressive movements). They usually spiral and are rarely productive; they engender mutual hostility in the partners and create a pattern that is very hard to break. Over time, unchecked serial arguments have an adverse effect on relationships and can erode self-esteem. Another form of conflict that occurs within interpersonal relationships is what communication scholar Courtney Waite Miller terms the **irresolvable conflict**.[36] In such a conflict, one or both of the parties deem the conflict impossible to resolve. A person who holds the view that an argument is irresolvable may not necessarily state that view out in the open, choosing simply to believe that compromise is impossible. She or he may adopt a "go along to get along" approach if relationships with people in an ongoing conflict are worth managing through appeasement or tolerance rather than confrontation. Gays and lesbians often report irresolvable conflicts with family members who don't understand or approve of what they see as a lifestyle, not an orientation. In a situation like this, the gay person who wishes to retain a relationship with her or his parents may simply view the conflict as something that's never going to change, or a "dead issue." The conflict still exists, but the issue isn't dealt with or talked about because doing so is perceived to be futile.

---

1. Aware

pseudoconflict
Conflict stemming from a lack of understanding.

simple conflict
Conflict over differences in ideas, definitions, perceptions, or goals.

ego conflict
Conflict based on personal issues in which people attack each other's self-esteem.

symbolic displacement
A phenomenon that occurs when people engage in one conflict through or in place of another symbolically related one or when a participant's behavior is an expression of displaced or unconscious meaning.

serial arguments
Argumentative episodes focused on the same issue that occur at least twice.

irresolvable conflict
A conflict in which one or both parties deem the conflict impossible to resolve.

Communication and Diversity

Conflict and Culture

Interpersonal conflict is difficult to manage, but cross-cultural conflict can be even more overwhelming. Some people are trained in negotiation and mediation techniques, so that they can facilitate peaceful relations between nations and peoples. But what if you're not planning on becoming an international negotiator? What if you simply want to know a few things to keep from being tossed in jail in a foreign country?

Intercultural communication scholar Stella Ting-Toomey has written extensively on this subject and produced some insightful information that can help you anticipate and avoid intercultural conflict.[37] People from individualistic cultures, such as the United States, emphasize the importance of the individual over the group. Those in collectivistic cultures, such as Japanese people, emphasize group rather than individual achievement. These differing values contribute to intercultural conflict.

So what should members of individualistic cultures know when interacting with members of collectivistic cultures? Note below seven assumptions about conflict that individualistic cultures hold; compare this list with seven assumptions about conflict that collectivistic cultures hold, assessing the differences.

Not only do members of different cultural groups have different views of conflict; they have different ways of dealing with or managing conflict. It's wise to do some research on the country you will be visiting or moving to, so that you understand how basic cultural values differ from those of your home country.

Individualistic Cultures	Collectivistic Cultures
1. The purpose of conflict is to air out major differences and problems.	1. Conflict is damaging to self-respect and relational harmony; it should be avoided as much as possible.
2. Conflict can be either functional or dysfunctional.	2. For the most part, conflict is dysfunctional.
3. Repressed, unconfronted problems can lead to dysfunctional conflict.	3. Conflict signals emotional immaturity and a lack of self-discipline.
4. Functional conflict provides an opportunity for solving problems.	4. Conflict provides a testing ground for skillful negotiation and "face-saving."
5. Substantive and relational issues in conflict should be handled separately.	5. Substantive and relational issues are always intertwined.
6. Conflict should be handled directly and openly.	6. Conflict should be handled discreetly and subtly.
7. Effective conflict management should be a problem-solving activity with a win–win outcome.	7. Effective conflict management should be a face-saving negotiation game with a win–win outcome.

How Conflict Functions in Relationships

Conflict is a normal, inevitable element within relationships. One of the most important topics to learn about in order to enhance relationships of all sorts is conflict—how conflict functions; how each person in a relationship approaches, processes, and responds to conflict; and how we can better manage conflict when it inevitably arises. The more meaningful the relationship, the greater the potential for conflict, because we aren't as likely to voice disagreement with people who don't matter very much to us.

It's surprising (and disconcerting) when people in relationships say, "We just get along so well; we belong together because we've never even had a fight." While we don't advocate staging or picking a fight with a partner as an experiment, we do believe that it's worrisome to commit to a person when you don't know how she or he handles conflict. If your partner or close friend is a "screamer" and you prefer to walk away from a conflict in silent protest, your relationship is headed for very rough waters. People's responses to conflict must be known quantities if a relationship is to be successful.

Conflict Involves Power One of the most significant elements within interpersonal relationships is power. We might not realize it, but distributing power between partners requires a lot of subtle negotiation. Without this negotiation, conflict can become rampant. Power has been defined in a variety of ways, but for our purposes, **interpersonal power** means the ability to influence another in the direction we

> **interpersonal power**
> The ability to influence another in the direction one desires; getting another person to do what one wants.

"LISA KNOWS WHAT I'M GOING TO SAY BEFORE I DECIDE I'D BETTER NOT SAY IT."

desire—to get another person to do what we want.[38] It also involves the ability to resist others' influences on us.[39] Perhaps it is easier to think of it in terms of who has more *control* in a relationship, rather than to use the term *power*.

All interactions, including conflicts, involve some level of power or control. If you ask a friend to go to a movie with you, you attempt to influence him or her. If the answer is no, your friend is mustering resistance and demonstrating power over you. If you don't like the negative response, you might attempt to assert control once more, perhaps by offering to buy your friend's ticket or to drive.

Romantic relationships can be typified by power dynamics.[40] In what is termed a **complementary relationship**, one partner willingly and continuously cedes power to the other. For example, suppose two friends open a small business together. One partner is the artistic or creative force behind the business; the other plans most of the details surrounding the business, like the physical space, merchandising, employee hiring, and so forth. That partner also handles money matters and tends to make most of the decisions about the future of the enterprise. Some business partners appreciate an arrangement like this because it plays to each person's strengths. If, however, the balance of power or control shifts over time to the money partner, the artistic partner may start to feel as though she or he has little influence over the most critical decision making for the business and may come to resent this setup.

Symmetrical relationships are characterized by similar degrees of control on the part of each person. In the entrepreneur example, both partners may compete in an effort to dominate the other and assert control, or both may relinquish control to the other to avoid making decisions or committing to something she or he may later have to take responsibility for. In the first instance, partners may argue over every business decision, from what color paint to put on the walls to the overarching company philosophy. These kinds of power struggles can be quite common among independent, strong-willed people. In the second instance, partners are reluctant to express preferences, instead engaging in endless exchanges of "I don't know—whatever you want." In addition to being time-consuming and fatiguing, this kind of constant negotiation can be paralyzing and ineffective when quick decisions are needed.

In a **parallel relationship**, power continually shifts from one partner to the other, depending on the nature of the interaction or situation. One partner may take control because he or she is more experienced or equipped to handle a particular circumstance. This doesn't mean that one partner is constantly in an out-of-power position; rather, partners alternate being in control according to their strengths and weaknesses. For instance, if one partner is in charge of keeping the finances straight, she or he will have more power in budgetary decisions. If the other partner is better at working with people, he or she probably will exert more power over decisions about hiring. This form of give and take works extremely well in relationships, but partners need to agree on (and integrate into their self-concepts) who is really better suited to take control in certain situations.

Conflict May Involve Assertive or Aggressive Communication

Sometimes our emotions cause us to communicate aggressively when assertive communication would be preferable. You may tend to think of assertive and aggressive communication as being the same thing, but they are actually different. The best way to distinguish between the two is this: **Assertive communication** takes the other person's feelings and rights into account; **aggressive communication** does not. Let's say that you experience a mix-up with a close friend over plans for the weekend. You get your signals

---

complementary relationship
A relationship in which one partner willingly and continuously cedes power to the other.

symmetrical relationship
A relationship characterized by similar control behaviors in partners; partners compete to dominate each other or both relinquish control to the other to avoid making decisions.

parallel relationship
A relationship in which power continually shifts from one partner to the other.

assertive communication
Communication that takes a listener's feelings and rights into account.

aggressive communication
Self-serving communication that does not take a listener's feelings and rights into account.

Recap

Relationship Types Based on Power Dynamics

Relationship Type	Symbols	Explanation
Complementary	↑ ↓	One up, one down; one partner is almost always in power, and the other is almost always out of power.
Symmetrical	↑ ↑ ↓ ↓	Both up or both down; partners either compete for power and control or relinquish power.
Parallel	→ ←	Give and take; power alternates between partners, depending on who is better equipped or more adept in certain situations.

crossed and don't end up going out together. When you next see your friend, you have the choice of responding to your frustration over the situation in a passive, assertive, or aggressive manner. You could be passive and say nothing about the mix-up. While this may sound like an unrealistic response, some people choose not to communicate even when they have been wronged, a phenomenon known as self-silencing.[41] They're afraid or unwilling to engage in any form of confrontation, no matter how benign or superficial, with strangers and intimates alike. A passive approach tends merely to internalize frustration, which may build into a destructive rage that later erupts.

Another option is to blow up at your friend. This is an aggressive, self-oriented approach because it doesn't take into account the rights of the recipient of such communication. Unfortunately, this is the tactic of choice for some people, especially if they have a great deal of anxiety and feel justified taking out their frustrations on others. An aggressive approach rarely achieves one's objectives.

Verbal aggression, also termed verbal abuse, has received much research attention in recent years. Communication scholars Dominic Infante and Andrew Rancer and various colleagues suggest that verbal aggression is a form of communication violence because it attacks the heart of a person's being, her or his self-concept.[42] Conflicts that are prompted by or degenerate into verbal aggression can be characterized by insults ("You wouldn't say that if you had half a brain"), ridicule ("You're just too selfish to understand"), merciless teasing with an angry edge to it, character assassination ("You're low class"), and profanity.[43] Typically, the verbally aggressive person claims that the other person is the source or cause of the problem. Rather than focusing on the problem, the verbal aggressor gets personal.

We can more easily fend off verbal aggression from those who don't matter much to us, but we can be deeply wounded, and the relationship can be permanently damaged, by verbal aggression from someone important to us, whom we care about.[44] Unfortunately, verbally aggressive tactics are used widely in conflicts, according to research. One study surveyed dating partners and found that more than 70 percent reported using or experiencing some form of verbal aggression in their relational conflicts.[45] When the verbally aggressive tactics were used only occasionally—as lapses into "bad" behavior—partners were able to weather the aggression without much damage to the relationship. However, when the verbal aggression was more frequent, it signaled a relationship in trouble. Another study of verbal aggression among 5,000 American college-age couples found that women and men are equally capable of producing verbally aggressive communication when in conflict.[46] Research has also determined a connection between verbal aggression and physical aggression or abuse.[47]

Clearly, an assertive approach to conflict is best—for ourselves and for the people we interact with. It's important to assert yourself and express your perception of a problem to the person who can best correct or clear it up rather than blowing off steam to

2. Verbal

The best communicators have learned to solve conflict through the use of assertive communication rather than aggressive communication. What steps can you take to adapt your communication accordingly from aggressive to assertive?

1. Aware

nonconfrontational style
A conflict management style that involves backing off, avoiding conflict, or giving in to the other person.

an innocent bystander or third party. Communicating assertively means that you explain your concerns or cause for disagreement in a direct and firm manner, staying in control of your emotions but not allowing yourself to be bullied or discounted as you take the receiver's rights into account.

An assertive response to the mix-up with your friend might be something like this: "Hey, Jane, we were supposed to get together last weekend, but you never called. What happened?" In this statement, you express your perception of the situation, but ask the other person for her perception, rather than aggressively saying something in an angry tone that would make the other person defensive, such as "Why did you leave me hanging when we made definite plans?" If the person offers a lame excuse for not getting together, an assertive follow-up comment might be "Well, I just want you to know that I don't like what happened; it's no big deal, but I just hope it doesn't happen again." If you communicate in this manner, you're far more likely to reach a positive resolution to any conflicts than if you behave passively or aggressively, violating the receiver's right to be treated humanely.[48]

Styles of Managing Conflict

Scholars in the communication discipline like to talk about conflict in terms of *management*, meaning that interpersonal communication can help people work through and handle conflict so that something positive results. What's your approach to managing interpersonal conflict: fight or flight? Do you tackle conflict head on or seek ways to remove yourself from it? Most of us don't have a single way of dealing with disagreements, but we do have a tendency to manage conflict by following patterns we learned early in life and have used before.[49] The pattern we choose depends on several factors, including our personality, the individuals with whom we are in conflict, and the time and place of the confrontation.

Researchers have attempted to identify styles of conflict management. One widely accepted approach organizes conflict styles into three types: (1) nonconfrontational; (2) confrontational or controlling; and (3) cooperative (also known as a *solution orientation*).[50]

Nonconfrontational Style One approach to managing conflict is to back off, either avoiding the conflict or giving in to the other person. Placating, distracting, computing, withdrawing, and giving in are responses that typify a **nonconfrontational style**.

A *placating* response is an attempt to please; placaters are uncomfortable with negative emotions and may adopt this approach because they fear rejection if they rock the boat. Typically, they seek approval and try to avoid threats to their sense of self-worth. Placaters never seem to get angry, are so controlled that they seem unresponsive to the intensity of the situation, quickly agree with others to avoid conflict, and try to avoid confrontation at all costs.

Another nonconfrontational style is called *distracting*. Distracters attempt to change the subject or make a joke to avoid conflict or stress, rather than face issues directly. They hope that eventually the problem will just go away if it can be put off long enough.

A third nonconfrontational style is called *computing*. Human computers remove themselves from conflict by remaining aloof and cool. They avoid emotional involvement and refuse to be provoked or ruffled, even under intense pressure. This detachment allows them to avoid expressing genuine feelings about issues and ideas. Instead, they respond to emotional issues with impersonal words and phrases, such as "One would tend to become angry when one's car is dented, wouldn't one?" The computing style is characterized by low empathy and minimal involvement with the issues at hand.

Withdrawing from conflict, either physically or psychologically, is another non-confrontational approach. "I don't want to talk about it," "It's not my problem," and the one-word "Whatever" are typical responses from someone who uses this style.

Finally, some people consistently *give in* when faced with conflict. They are so uncomfortable that they surrender before the conflict escalates. Skip hates romantic movies. Yet when his girlfriend wants to rent *The Notebook*, Skip agrees, just to avoid a conflict. A nonconfrontational or avoidant style often leads to a perpetuating conflict cycle that has a chilling or silencing effect on a relationship.[51] In addition, research shows that when conflict arises during problem-solving discussions, people who exhibit a nonconfrontational style of responding to the conflict are perceived as incompetent.[52]

Confrontational Style   Each of us has some need to control others, but some people always want to dominate and make sure that their objectives are achieved. In managing conflict, people with a **confrontational style** have a win–lose philosophy. They want to win at the expense of the other person, to claim victory over their opponents, and to control others. They focus on themselves and usually ignore the needs of others. Confronters often resort to blaming or seeking a scapegoat, rather than assuming responsibility for a conflict. "I didn't do it," "Don't look at me," and "It's not my fault" are typical responses. If this strategy doesn't work, confronters may try hostile name calling, personal attacks, or threats.

Cooperative Style   Those who have a **cooperative style** of conflict management view conflict as a set of problems to be solved, rather than a competition in which one person wins and another loses. They work to foster a win–win climate by using the following techniques:[53]

- *Separate the people from the problem.* Leave personal grievances out of the discussion. Describe problems without making judgmental statements about personalities.
- *Focus on shared interests.* Emphasize common interests, values, and goals by asking such questions as "What do we both want?" "What do we both value?" "Where do we already agree?"
- *Generate many options to solve the problem.* Use brainstorming and other techniques to generate alternative solutions.
- *Base decisions on objective criteria.* Try to establish standards for an acceptable solution to a problem. These standards may involve costs, timing, and other factors.

Conflict Management Skills

As we saw in the previous section, nonconfrontational and confrontational styles of conflict management do not solve problems effectively, nor do they foster healthy

Recap

Conflict Management Styles

Nonconfrontational	A person avoids conflict by placating (agreeing), distracting, computing (becoming emotionally detached), withdrawing from conflict, or giving in to another person.
Confrontational	A person wants to manipulate others by blaming and making threats; this approach sets up a win–lose framework.
Cooperative	A person seeks mutually agreeable resolutions to manage differences, and works within a win–win framework. A cooperative approach • Separates people from problems; • Focuses on shared interests; • Generates many options to solve problems; • Bases decisions on objective criteria.

confrontational style
A win–lose approach to conflict management in which one person wants control and to win at the expense of the other.

cooperative style
A conflict management style in which conflict is viewed as a set of problems to be solved, rather than a competition in which one person wins and another loses.

"Well, if it doesn't matter who's right and who's wrong, why don't I be right and you be wrong?"

long-term relationships. The skills we review here are those we touched on in our discussion of the cooperative style.[54]

Managing conflict, especially emotionally charged conflict, isn't easy. Even with a fully developed set of skills, you shouldn't expect to melt tensions and resolve disagreements instantaneously. The following skills can, however, help you generate options that promote understanding and provide a framework for cooperation.

Manage Emotions For weeks, you have been working on a group project for an important class; your group has a firm deadline that the professor imposed. You submitted your portion of the project to your fellow group members two weeks ago. Today you check in with the group for a progress report and discover that very little has been done. The project is not much further along than when you completed your portion two weeks ago. Your grade is on the line; you feel angry and frustrated. How should you respond? You may be tempted to march into the next group meeting and scream at your classmates. You might consider going to the professor and complaining. Our best advice is this: Try to avoid taking action when you're in such an emotional state. You may regret what you say and you will probably escalate the conflict, making the situation worse.

Often the first sign that we're in a conflict situation is a combined feeling of anger, frustration, and fear that sweeps over us. Emotions aroused in us during conflict situations are understandable and to be expected. As psychotherapist Jeffrey Rubin explains, "Your feelings are your reality," meaning that the feelings conflict generates are real and should not be ignored.[55] In actuality, anger is not the predominant emotion generated by conflict. Many of us are unprepared for the aching, lonely, sad, and forlorn feelings that can emerge in conflict.[56] As tall an order as it is, it's important to try to understand the other person's feelings and to take the emotion of the situation seriously.[57]

Expressing our feelings in an emotional outburst may make us feel better for the moment, but it also may exacerbate the situation and close the door to negotiation. Until we can tone down (not eliminate) and channel our emotions, we'll find it difficult to use appropriate communication skills to resolve conflict. Here are some specific strategies that you can draw on when an intense emotional response to conflict clouds your judgment and decision-making skills.[58]

- *Select a mutually acceptable time and place to discuss a conflict.* If you're upset or tired, you're at risk for an emotion-charged confrontation. If you ambush someone with an angry attack, you can't expect her or him to be in a productive frame of mind. Give yourself time to cool off before you try to resolve a conflict. In the case of the group project, you could call a meeting for later in the week. By that time, you could gain control of your feelings and think things through.
- *Plan your message.* If you approach someone to discuss a disagreement, take care to organize your message, perhaps even on paper. Identify your goal and determine what outcome you would like; don't barge in unprepared and dump your emotions on the other person.
- *Monitor nonverbal messages.* Your nonverbal communication plays a key role in establishing an emotional climate. Monitor nonverbal messages—your own and those of others—to help defuse an emotionally charged situation. Speak calmly, use direct eye contact, and maintain a calm facial expression and body position to signal that you wish to collaborate rather than control. Try to place yourself on the same level as other people involved in the conflict. Standing while others sit, for example, can serve as a power cue and an impediment to resolving conflict.
- *Avoid personal attacks, name calling, profanity, and emotional overstatement.* Threats and derogatory language can turn a small conflict into an all-out war. When people feel attacked, they usually respond by becoming defensive in an effort to protect themselves. It's also important to avoid exaggerating your emotions. If you say you're irritated or annoyed rather than furious, you can still communicate your feelings, but you will take the sting out of your description.
- *Use self-talk.* Back to the problem of the group project: At the next meeting, what if a member lashes out at you, suggesting that you're a big part of the problem? Instead of lashing back at that person, the best course would be to pause, take a slow deep breath, and say to yourself, "I could get really mad, but that won't make things better. I'll respond calmly and coolly, so we keep the problem in proportion." You may think that talking to yourself is an eccentricity, but nothing could be further from the truth. Thoughts are directly linked to feelings; the messages we tell ourselves play a major role in how we feel and respond to others.[59]

Manage Information Because uncertainty, misinformation, and misunderstanding are often byproducts of conflict and disagreement, skills that promote mutual understanding are important components of cooperative conflict management. The following skills can help you enhance the quality of communication during conflict.

- *Clearly describe the conflict-producing events.* Instead of blurting out complaints in random order, try to deliver a brief, well-organized presentation. Public speaking teachers recommend that, for certain speech topics, you describe events in chronological order. The same technique works well when describing a conflict. In our example of the group project situation, you could offer your perspective on what created the conflict, sequencing the events and describing them dispassionately so that your fellow group members end up sharing your understanding of the problem.
- *"Own" your statements by using descriptive "I" language.* In Chapter 3, we described the use of "I" language instead of "you" language in order to create a supportive climate. The same advice applies to dealing with conflict. "I feel upset when it seems as if little is getting done and we're running the risk of not making our deadline." This is an example of an "I" statement that you could say to your group members. The statement describes your feelings as your own and keeps the issue manageable. Saying "You guys aren't pulling your weight and you're gonna blow our deadline" has an accusatory sting that will likely make members defensive, escalating the conflict. Also notice that, in the second statement, you don't take

any responsibility for the problem but suggest that it belongs to several other people. This "ganging-up" approach almost always heightens people's defensiveness.

- *Use effective listening skills.* Managing information is a two-way process. Whether you're describing a conflict situation to someone or that individual is bringing a conflict to your attention, good listening skills are invaluable. Give your full attention to the speaker and make a conscious point of tuning out your internal messages. Harvard psychologist Howard Gardner suggests that people "listen charismatically," which involves paying careful attention to what is not said (nonverbal cues) and rephrasing what conflict partners say in a tentative, nonthreatening manner.[60]
- *Check your understanding of what others say and do.* Checking perceptions is vital when emotions run high. If you're genuinely unsure about facts, issues, or major ideas addressed during a conflict, ask questions to help you sort through them instead of barreling ahead with solutions. Then summarize your understanding of the information; don't parrot the speaker's words or paraphrase every statement, but check key points to ensure that you comprehend the message. Your response and that of your conflict partner will confirm that you understand each other.

Manage Goals As we have seen, conflict is goal-driven. Both individuals involved in an interpersonal conflict want something. And, for some reason—competitiveness, scarce resources, or lack of understanding—the goals appear to be in conflict. To manage conflict, it is important to seek an accurate understanding of these goals and to identify where they overlap. Here are a couple of techniques to help you accomplish just that.

- *Identify your goal and your partner's goal.* After you describe, listen, and respond, your next task should be to identify what you would like to have happen. What is your goal? Most goal statements can be phrased in terms of wants or desires. Continuing with the group project example, you express to your fellow group members your goal of turning the project in on time. Next, it's useful to identify the goals of other people involved in the conflict. Use effective describing, listening, and responding skills to determine what each conflict partner wants. Obviously, if goals are kept hidden, it will be difficult to resolve the conflict.
- *Identify where your goals and your partner's goals overlap.* Authorities on conflict negotiation stress the importance of focusing on shared interests when seeking to manage differences.[61] Armed with an understanding of what you want and what your partner wants, you can then determine whether the goals overlap. Suppose that after you explain your goal about the project deadline, another group member states that her or his goal is to make the project the best it possibly can be. These goals may be compatible, so you've identified a commonality that can help unify the group, rather than keep it splintered. But what if that goal of making the project the best means that your group will have to ask the professor for an extension on the deadline? Now you may have competing goals. But at least you've identified a central part of the problem. Framing the problem as "how can we achieve our mutual goal" rather than arguing over differences of opinion moves the discussion to a more productive level.

Manage the Problem If you can view conflicts as problems to be solved rather than battles to be won or lost, you will better manage the issues that confront you in your relationships with others. Of course, not all conflicts can be easily managed and resolved. But using a rational, logical approach to conflict management is more effective than emotionally flinging accusations and opinions at someone. Structuring a disagreement as a problem to solve helps manage emotions that often erupt; a problem-solving orientation to conflict also helps keep the conversation focused on issues rather than personalities.

The problem-solving process is relatively simple: Define the problem, analyze the problem, generate possible solutions, evaluate the pros and cons of the solutions under consideration, and then select the solution that is agreeable to all concerned. The best solution is one that meets the goals of the persons involved in the conflict. As you apply the problem-solving approach to managing conflict, consider the following suggestions:

- *Resist developing solutions to manage the conflict until you and the other person fully understand the precise nature of the problem as well as each other's goals.* When there is a problem to be solved, we typically want to head directly for solutions. Resist that temptation. Before blurting out solutions, realize that you're more likely to reach agreement on the solution to a problem if you each understand the specific issues that trigger the problem.
- *The more possible solutions you identify and consider, the greater the likelihood that the conflict will be managed successfully.* If you're just batting around one or two solutions, you're limiting your options in managing the conflict. Rather than making the conflict a tug of war with only two ends of the rope pulling against each other, consider multiple creative strategies for achieving what you both want.
- *Systematically discuss the pros and the cons of the possible solutions together.* After you have a list of possible solutions, honestly identify advantages and disadvantages of each solution. How do you know which is the best solution? If you discussed the goals that each of you seek to achieve, you're well on your way to developing a vision of the future that can help you sort out the advantages and disadvantages of the potential solutions you're considering. Determine which solution or combination of solutions best achieves the goals you and your feuding partner are trying to accomplish.

We emphasize again that there are no sure-fire techniques that will manage or resolve the interpersonal conflicts that will inevitably occur even in the best of relationships. In reality, you don't simply manage your emotions and then march easily on to coolly communicate your ideas, followed by neatly sorting out goals and then rationally solving the problem that created the conflict. Conflict management is messier than this step-by-step process suggests. Our suggestions for managing emotions, information, goals, and the problem will not eliminate conflict from your life. Turning conflicts into problems to solve and seeking mutually agreeable solutions may, however, provide the structure necessary to help you manage conflict constructively.

PRINCIPLES FOR A LIFETIME
Enhancing Your Skills

1. Aware

Principle One: Be aware of your communication with yourself and others.
- Know your own interests, likes, and dislikes as you expand your circle of friends.
- Awareness and an understanding of self begin in your family as you grow up.
- Perception checking with colleagues increases your awareness of yourself and your workplace.
- The first stage of relational escalation, the pre-interaction awareness stage, begins with an awareness of the self and the other person to whom you are attracted.
- Even after relationships terminate, they still have an effect on our self-concept; be aware of the effect of relationships (even failed ones) on your view of yourself.
- It's important to know your conflict management style, especially if your style is different from that of other people involved in a conflict.

- Self-talk is appropriate in conflict, because it can help you manage your emotions and think clearly.
- Check your perceptions of a conflict with trusted others.
- Be aware of your own goals, as well as the goals of others, in conflict situations.

Principle Two: Effectively use and interpret verbal messages.
- Language patterns we learn as children in our families stay with us into adulthood.
- People in advanced stages of relationships tend to use verbal communication to discuss topics that typically are not discussed in early stages.
- Relational partners should use effective verbal communication to work through relational dialectics, or tensions in a relationship.
- Assertive communication takes a receiver's rights into account; aggressive communication does not.
- Managing the verbal expression of your emotions in conflict situations is an important skill.
- Plan your message carefully in a conflict situation.
- Avoid personal attacks, name calling, profanity, and emotional overstatements in conflict situations.
- Use "I" language instead of "you" language in a conflict, so as to lessen defensiveness.

Principle Three: Effectively use and interpret nonverbal messages.
- Nonverbal immediacy behaviors, such as eye contact and forward body lean, are important in the maintenance of friendships, family relationships, and workplace relationships.
- People in advanced stages of relationships tend to display nonverbal behaviors that typically are not in evidence in early stages.
- Nonverbal skills are important in your first conversations with people, as you attempt to establish and escalate relationships.
- Nonverbal immediacy cues diminish when a relationship is in de-escalation.
- Monitor and adapt your nonverbal behaviors in conflict situations.
- Monitor the nonverbal behaviors of other people involved in your disagreement.

Principle Four: Listen and respond thoughtfully to others.
- Listening is important in friendships, family relationships, and workplace relationships.
- Listening and responding appropriately are key skills that potential employers value.
- Destructive conflict is characterized by a lack of listening.
- Conflict often escalates because the parties don't listen to one another; continue to listen, even if you feel yourself becoming emotional in the conflict.

Principle Five: Appropriately adapt messages to others.
- It's important to learn to adapt our communication in friendships, family relationships, and workplace relationships.
- Adaptation is critical for couples who face relational tensions.
- In conflict situations, partners often have to adapt to each other and admit that they were wrong. Destructive conflict often involves a reluctance to adapt to the other person and see the problem from her or his point of view.
- Be flexible and adapt to other cultures' approaches to conflict; don't assume that your home culture's approach to conflict management is applicable in conflicts with members of other cultural groups.
- After checking your perceptions of a conflict with trusted others, adapt your communication accordingly.
- One way to adapt in a conflict is to look for overlaps between your goals and the goals of your conflict partner.

Summary

In this chapter, we focused on interpersonal communication that enhances relationships and discussed three types of relationships that have tremendous impact on our lives: friendships, family relationships, and workplace relationships. We reviewed the five Communication Principles for a Lifetime in light of each of these three forms of important relationships.

Most relationships develop in stages, characterized by the type and presence (or absence) of interpersonal communication. Once relationships are initiated, they begin to escalate if the partners want the relationship to develop and become more intimate. Relationships also de-escalate as they move away from intimacy.

The relational dialectics perspective is useful for understanding the up-and-down, sometimes illogical nature of interpersonal relationships. Three sets of tensions are common in relationships: integration–separation; stability–change; expression–privacy.

Conflict is a significant element within interpersonal relationships. The chapter described eight different types of conflict in relationships and explored six building blocks of constructive conflict. Power and control create patterns that can lead to harmony or strife in relationships. We contrasted assertive communication (which takes receivers' rights into account) with aggressive communication (which ignores the rights of receivers). We examined three conflict management styles—nonconfrontational, confrontational, and cooperative—and discussed the forms of communication that characterize these styles. In a final section on conflict management skills, we suggested that you view conflicts as manageable events rather than as personal battles. We also offered suggestions for effective ways to manage emotions, information, goals, and problems, so that the resolution of conflict can make your relationships stronger.

Assessing Your Knowledge

For Discussion and Review

Principle One: Be aware of your communication with yourself and others.

1. How can you manage your emotions in a conflict situation so that you remain aware of how you're communicating, as well as how others are communicating?

Principle Two: Effectively use and interpret verbal messages.

2. What forms of verbal messages constitute an assertive approach to conflict management? An aggressive approach?

Principle Three: Effectively use and interpret nonverbal messages.

3. What nonverbal cues are central to relational escalation? Relational de-escalation?

Principle Four: Listen and respond thoughtfully to others.

4. Explore the role of listening and responding in the resolution of conflict.

Principle Five: Appropriately adapt messages to others.

5. How should an effective communicator adapt her or his messages in a cooperative style of conflict management?

Multiple Choice

Choose the *best* answer to each of the following questions.

1. A conflict management style that seeks a win–win resolution is called
   a. cooperative.
   b. confrontational.
   c. nonconfrontational.
   d. passive.

2. When power in a romantic relationship continually shifts from one person to the other, the relationship is said to be
   a. complementary.
   b. symmetrical.
   c. parallel.
   d. elliptical.

3. Lola says to her romantic partner, "I don't think we should see each other as much. I need to spend more time with my friends, and I am getting behind in school. Maybe we can see each other just on the

weekends." From her talk, it appears the relationship is entering which stage of relationship de-escalation?
   a. de-intensification stage
   b. intensification stage
   c. separation stage
   d. post-interaction stage

4. _____ communication takes into consideration the listener's feelings and rights.
   a. Passive
   b. Assertive
   c. Aggressive
   d. Complementary

5. In an intimate relationship that is not going well, the partners typically
   a. end the relationship at the current stage.
   b. progress back through the stages they have already experienced.
   c. enter a turmoil or stagnation stage.
   d. merely reverse the escalation process.

6. Those in individualistic cultures believe that conflict
   a. should be handled directly and openly.
   b. can only be dysfunctional.
   c. should deal with substantive and relational issues together.
   d. should result in a winner and a loser.

7. According to William Wilmot and Joyce Hocker, constructive conflict
   a. involves protecting yourself against situations where conflict might arise.
   b. demands a more rigid approach to relationships.
   c. focuses on finding a winner of the conflict.
   d. emphasizes learning instead of self-protection.

8. When one person in a romantic relationship continually allows the other to have most of the power, the relationship is said to be
   a. complementary.
   b. symmetrical.
   c. parallel.
   d. elliptical.

9. Dominic Infante's research has determined that people who are highly verbally aggressive
   a. recognize their aggressiveness and want to find ways of diminishing it.
   b. recognize their aggressiveness and do not want to change it.
   c. view their aggressiveness as an asset and wish they were even more aggressive.
   d. commit communication violence by attacking another person's self-concept.

10. The main difference between assertive and aggressive communication is
    a. nonverbal, mainly based on tone and volume of speech.
    b. that assertive communication focuses on the other person's feelings and not your own.
    c. that assertive communication focuses on your own feelings and not the other person's feelings.
    d. that assertive communication focuses on both your own feelings and the other person's feelings.

Answers to the questions in this practice test can be found at the end of the book.

Assessing Your Skill

Sometimes it's hard to discern the difference between assertive and aggressive communication. To gain some practice, consider the following situations. For each one, first generate aggressive and inappropriate communication. Then rethink the situation and generate an assertive form of communication that would be more effective. We've provided an example to get you started.

Sample Situation: You are expecting a raise at work but find out that another coworker, who has less time on the job than you, received a raise and you did not.

Aggressive Communication: You interrupt a staff meeting that your boss is holding, storm about the room, and demand an explanation of why you did not receive the expected raise.

Assertive Communication: You make an appointment with your boss for a meeting outside the office. At the meeting, you calmly ask the boss to assess your value to the company, leading up to the question of why you did not receive the expected raise.

Situation: Two people have been in a monogamous dating relationship for several months when one partner finds out that the other person has cheated.

Situation: A student receives a disappointing grade on a paper. After reading the papers of a few fellow classmates and finding that lesser quality papers received higher grades, the student decides to confront the teacher about the grade.

Web Resources to Improve Your Knowledge and Skill

Perhaps you've heard, in the news or in connection with some incident that happened at work or school, of someone's "going to mediation." A new cottage industry, centers for mediation services are springing up with increasing frequency across the country. When people in conflict cannot resolve that conflict, they may turn to mediation before taking a more formal (and expensive) step, such as going to court.

Many universities now offer mediation services for students, faculty, and staff members. The Ombuds Office at Stanford University defines mediation as a "voluntary meeting of disputing parties to attempt to reach their own solution with the help of a neutral person." The University of Virginia's mediation service was founded in 1996 to give students and community members an alternative for conflict resolution. This student-operated service is available only for students enrolled in the university. The web site for Texas State University's Mediation Program quotes people who have used its mediation services for roommate grievances, problems within student organizations, and graduate student issues. This program engages trained faculty and staff from the university as mediators.

To read more about sample university mediation programs and services, visit these web addresses:

<www.vpfss.txstate.edu/personnel/mediation.htm>
<www.student.virginia.edu/~mediate>
<www.umich.edu/~sdrp>
<www.campus-adr.org>
<www.stanford.edu/dept/ocr/ombuds>

Unit Three
Communicating in Groups and Teams

Patricia Ossa, "Citizens," © SuperStock, Inc.

The best way to have a good idea is to have a lot of ideas.

Linus Pauling

Chapter 9

Understanding Group and Team Performance

Chapter Outline

- Groups and Teams Defined
- Understanding Types of Groups and Teams
- Understanding Group and Team Dynamics
- Understanding Phases of Group and Team Development
- Summary

Chapter Objectives

After studying this chapter, you should be able to

1. Define and note similarities and differences between a group and a team.
2. Identify and describe types of small groups.
3. Identify and appropriately perform task and social roles in groups and teams.
4. Avoid performing individual roles in a group.
5. Describe group rules and norms.
6. Define and differentiate between status and power.
7. List strategies to enhance group cohesiveness.
8. Recognize group and team interaction patterns.
9. Identify the four stages of group development.

Do you like working with others in groups? Although you may be one of those people who relish working on team projects and going to meetings, many people don't like collaborating with others. Here are some typical sentiments people sometimes have about working in groups:

> To be effective, a committee should be made up of three persons. But to get anything done, one member should be sick and another absent.
> A committee is a group of people who individually can do nothing and who collectively decide nothing can be done.
> A group task force is a collection of the unfit chosen from the unwilling by the incompetent to do the unnecessary.

Whether you are one of those people who like group work or one who finds it frustrating and a waste of time, the evidence suggests that groups are here to stay. Human beings collaborate. We are raised in groups, educated in groups, and entertained in groups; we worship in groups and work in groups. Today's technology makes it easier for us to collaborate in teams, even when we're not meeting face to face. There is evidence that most of you reading this book will spend about one-third of your time on the job working in groups or teams and attending meetings or preparing for meetings.[1] And if you aspire to upper-management leadership positions, you'll spend up to two-thirds of your time in meetings.[2] Your work will be based on that kindergarten skill called "getting along with others."

To help you with the inevitable group and team projects that will come your way, this chapter offers descriptions of how groups and teams work. In the next chapter, we'll offer specific strategies for improving group and team performance. As we examine concepts and strategies of group skills and theories, we'll remind you how the core of group communication research can be discussed in terms of the five principles we've used to frame our presentation of human communication:

1. *Be aware of your communication with yourself and others.* Your awareness of your own behavior and the behavior of other group members is often the first step in understanding why you and other group members behave as you do and adjusting your behavior for improved group performance.
2. *Effectively use and interpret verbal messages.* The verbal messages you and other group members use are pivotal in shaping the roles you assume and how the group accomplishes its work.
3. *Effectively use and interpret nonverbal messages.* The social climate of a group is influenced by the way group members behave nonverbally; eye contact, tone of voice, facial expression, and the use of space and time influence what it feels like to be in a group.
4. *Listen and respond thoughtfully to others.* The quintessential skill of listening and responding to others is vital for an effectively functioning group; how group members interact (or don't interact) is directly shaped by group members' skill in listening and responding to what others say and do. One survey found that effective listening was the skill most valued by those who work in groups and teams.[3]
5. *Appropriately adapt messages to others.* The ability to modify messages and adjust to the behavior of others is especially important when communicating with three or more people in a small group.

1. Aware
2. Verbal
3. Nonverbal
4. Listen and Respond
5. Adapt

Groups and Teams Defined

What makes a group a group? Is a collection of people waiting for an elevator a group? How about students assigned to a class project—do they meet the technical definition of a group? And what about the term *team*? Teams are often viewed as a management innovation that can improve both productivity and morale. Is there a difference between a group and a team? By exploring these questions, you can better understand what groups and teams do and develop strategies for improving group and team performance.

Many important workplace decisions are made within small groups of coworkers. As a member of this kind of group, how could you verbally help clarify the group's goals? What nonverbal cues would you look for to help you interpret group norms?

Communicating in Small Groups

A **small group** consists of three to fifteen people who share a common purpose, who feel a sense of belonging to the group, and who exert influence on one another.[4] Let's look at this definition more closely.

A Group Consists of a Small Number of People
How many people does it take to be a group? We suggest at least three people. Two people do not usually exhibit the characteristics of group behavior that we will present later in this chapter, such as the formation of group member roles and norms. If a group becomes too large, it typically operates as a collection of subgroups rather than as a single body. When more than fifteen people meet together, it is difficult for all members to participate; usually, when the group gets so big that it is impractical to give everyone a chance to talk, a few people monopolize the discussion. Large groups need formal rules, such as parliamentary procedure, to provide structure that will help the group stay focused on the task at hand.

A Group Has a Common Purpose
In order to be a group, people need to be united by a common goal or purpose. They must all seek the same thing. A collection of people waiting for an elevator may all want to go somewhere, but they probably haven't organized their efforts so that they all are going the same place. If you are assigned to a class project by an instructor, your classmates do have a common goal—to complete the project and earn a good grade. This class-project group would meet our definition of a group.

Group Members Feel a Sense of Belonging
In order to be a group, the members must realize that they are part of the group. Again, people waiting for the elevator doors to open probably do not feel an obligation to others around them. Group members develop a sense of identity with their group. They know who is in their group and who is not in the group.

Group Members Exert Influence on Others in the Group
When you are in a group, your presence and participation influence other people in the group. Group members are interdependent; what one group member says or does affects other group members. Your comments and even your silence help shape what the group does next. Your nonverbal messages have a powerful effect on personal relationships. Each mem-

small group
Three to fifteen people who share a common purpose, feel a sense of belonging to the group, and exert influence on one another.

ber of a group potentially has some influence on others. Even silence, facial expressions, and eye contact (or lack of it) affect what the group does.

Small group communication is the transactive process of creating meaning among three to fifteen people who share a common purpose, who feel a sense of belonging to the group, and who exert influence on each other. Communicating in small groups is sometimes a challenge because of the potential for misunderstanding. But don't assume that working in a group will inevitably be a frustrating experience. People accomplish much when working together. It was anthropologist Margaret Mead who said, "Never doubt that a small group of concerned citizens can change the world. Indeed, it's the only thing that ever has." In this chapter and the next chapter, we'll provide concepts and strategies to enhance the quality of your collaborations with others.

Communicating in Teams

Most of us have participated on a sports team at some time. The goal of a sports team is usually to win the game or competition. A work team has some of the same characteristics as a sports team.[5] Instead of winning the game, the goal may be to get the contract, build the best mousetrap, or achieve some other objective. A **team** is a coordinated group of people organized to work together to achieve a specific, common goal.[6]

Often the terms *team* and *group* are used interchangeably. Is there a difference? Yes. Given the increased importance teams have in the workforce today, it's important to know precisely how groups and teams are different from each other. Although both groups and teams are made up of a small number of people who work to achieve a goal, teams are often structured deliberately to achieve the goal. Also, teams spend a great deal of time coordinating their efforts to accomplish the goal.[7] Every team is a group, but not every group is highly organized or coordinated enough to meet the definition of a team. Let's consider several specific characteristics of teams.

Teams Develop Clearly Defined Responsibilities for Team Members
On a sports team, most team members have specifically assigned duties, such as shortstop, pitcher, quarterback, or fullback. On a work team, team members' duties and roles are usually explicitly spelled out. Team members may perform more than one function or role, but they nonetheless have well-defined duties.[8]

Teams Have Clearly Defined Rules for Team Operation
Team members develop explicit rules for how the work should be done. A rule is a followable prescription for acceptable behavior.[9] Just as there are written rules in the game of Monopoly, there are usually explicit rules for how a team will function. For example, a team may establish a rule that a member who will be absent from a meeting must tell another team member beforehand. Team members know what the rules are and know how those rules affect the team.

Teams Develop Clear Goals
A third way to characterize a team is to look at the importance and specificity of the team goal.[10] A team goal is usually stated in such a way that the goal can be measured: to win the game, to sell more cornflakes than the competition, or to get to the North Pole before anyone else, for example.

Teams Develop a Way of Coordinating Their Efforts
Team members spend time discussing how to accomplish the goals of the team. Their work is coordinated to avoid duplication of effort. A sports team spends considerable time practicing how to work together. Watching a sports team at work is like watching a choreographed dance. Team members have developed a system of working together rather than at cross-purposes. Just as a football team develops a list of the plays to get the ball down the field, a work team develops collaborative strategies to achieve its goal.

Although we have differentiated between groups and teams, don't get the idea that they are completely exclusive entities. Both groups and teams are made up of a small

---

small group communication
The transactive process of creating meaning among three to fifteen people who share a common purpose, feel a sense of belonging to the group, and exert influence on each other.

team
A coordinated group of people organized to work together to achieve a specific common goal.

number of people striving to achieve a goal. Since every team is a small group, whenever we refer to a team we are also suggesting that it's a group as well. Think of groups and teams as existing on a continuum; some deliberations will make the people seem more like a group, whereas other behavior—a more coordinated and structured process, with clear rules and explicit goals—will make the people appear to be a team.

Characteristics of Effective Team Members You may still wonder, "But what do effective team members do?" Several communication researchers have sought to answer that question by asking seasoned team members what they consider to be the characteristics of an excellent team. Here's what they found.[11]

- *Experience.* Effective team members have "been there, done that." They have practical experience in collaborating with others. More experienced team members were better able to see the big picture; less experienced members tended to lack the technical background needed to be successful at their collaborative work.
- *Problem-solving ability.* Team members who were effective were perceived as decisive. It wasn't just that they made quick decisions; they carefully analyzed information and issues while staying focused on the problem. Their ability to examine a problematic situation and select effective strategies for managing it set skilled team members apart from less skilled collaborators.
- *Openness.* Have you ever worked on a team and found one or more members not willing to express ideas and opinions honestly, yet tactfully? Communication researchers Frank LaFasto and Carl Larson found that openness was an essential characteristic for team success. Effective team members were willing to discuss delicate and sensitive issues and topics in an appropriate way that didn't make people defensive. Team members who were more secretive and participated less were perceived as less important to team success.
- *Supportiveness.* Supportive team members listened to others. They didn't just stand by and watch someone else work; they found out what needed to be done, then pitched in and did it. Nonsupportive team members tended to focus on their individual agendas, rather than being aware of the needs of the team as a whole.
- *Action orientation.* "Just do it!" That advertising slogan sold lots of tennis shoes for a sports equipment company. It's also a good motto for effective team members. Ineffective team members hung back and watched others do the work.
- *Positive personal style.* You may have heard the story about a boy who awoke on the morning of his birthday to find only a large pile of manure where he'd hoped to find birthday presents. But undaunted, he smiled and said, "With this much horse manure, there's got to be a pony here somewhere!" Effective team members were optimistic. Even in bad times, they found something to be positive about. Their encouraging, patient, enthusiastic, and friendly attitude contributed to their being well liked by other team members. Here's how to be perceived as an ineffective team member: Argue with others frequently, be intolerant and impatient, and cultivate skills that will help you win the "pain-in-the-neck" award.
- *Positive overall team perceptions.* Effective teams and effective team members believed they were effective; they were optimistic that they had the skills and resources to accomplish their task. Teams that were less effective thought they were less effective. Was the team effective because of a self-fulfilling prophecy (just expecting to be effective caused the team to act effectively)? Or did team members think they were effective because they really were top notch? We're not quite sure what the precise cause-and-effect relationship is between self-perceptions of being effective and actually being effective. But it does appear that teams that have a positive, can-do attitude perform better than those teams whose members have doubts, worries, and uncertainties about whether they will get the job done. The bottom line: Optimism enhances effectiveness.

4. Listen and Respond

You may wonder whether the attributes of team effectiveness that we've described can be enhanced through study and training. We have good news. Evidence suggests

Recap

Comparing Groups and Teams

	Groups	Teams
Roles and Responsibilities	Individual responsibilities of group members may not always be explicitly defined.	Expectations, roles, and responsibilities of team members are clearly developed and discussed.
Rules	Rules are often not written down or formally developed; rules evolve, depending on the group's needs.	Rules and operating procedures are clearly identified to help the team work efficiently and effectively.
Goals	Group goals may be discussed in general terms.	Clearly spelled out goals are the focus of what the team does.
Methods	Group members may or may not decide to divide the work among group members.	Team members develop clear methods of collaborating and coordinating their efforts to achieve the team's goals.

that by learning more about teams and participating in training development courses, you can improve your team skills.[12]

When Not to Collaborate in Groups and Teams

Although we've joined the chorus singing the praises of working in groups and teams, there are times when one head may be better than two or more. What are those situations in which it may be best to not collaborate? Here are four situations in which it is better to work individually rather than collectively:[13]

- *When the group or team has limited time.* If a very quick decision must be made, delegating an individual to make the decision may be better than convening a group. Sometimes you may not have time to gather a group together to discuss options; action may be needed immediately. In times of extreme crisis or emergency, it may be best to have a leader ready to provide some initial direction.
- *When an expert already has the answer.* You don't need a group to hash through the process of finding an answer if an individual already has the answer. If you want to know what tomorrow's weather will be, ask a meteorologist. Don't collaboratively puzzle through questions that can be readily answered by someone else.
- *When the information is available from other research sources.* Using the power of the Internet, you can find vast amounts of information. If you want a bit of data, a specific date, or more information about something, doing individual research may be better than commissioning a group, team, or task force to get the answers. Some groups find it useful for individual members to gather information and then meet with the rest of the group to analyze and discuss the information. But if you just need information and need it fast, head to the library or click your mouse.
- *When the group or team is entrenched in unmanageable conflict.* We don't suggest that you avoid group and team conversations just because they may arouse conflict and disagreement. In fact, it's normal for groups to experience conflict. An absence of conflict can be a sign of an ineffective group. But if the conflict is so entrenched that group members can't listen and thoughtfully respond, it may be advisable to take a break from group deliberations. Convening a dysfunctional group or team that can't or won't work together may not be the best way to reach a decision. What may be needed is a more structured conversation, such as mediation or nego-

tiation with a trained facilitator, to help sort things out. Don't give up on a group or team just because there is conflict. But if the conflict is so pervasive that no progress is likely, seek other ways of moving forward rather than having the group engage in more contentious talk.

Understanding Types of Groups and Teams

Groups and teams are formed for a variety of reasons. The type of group is determined by its purpose. The following group descriptions focus on the different goals or purposes of groups.

Primary Groups

A **primary group** exists to fulfill basic human needs. One of the best examples of a primary group is your family. While some families may have a family business or have other goals, in most family discussions one person does not whip out an agenda while the rest of the group follows a process to achieve a specific outcome. As in other primary groups, family communication is informal. People talk just because they are together.

Study Groups

As a college student, you probably don't need this type of group defined for you. A **study group** meets to learn new ideas. Learning theory suggests you are more likely to learn when you actively participate in the learning process. Students sometimes form study groups because they know that by participating in the give and take of a discussion, they'll be more likely to remember what is discussed. Teachers, too, often assign students to groups as a means of accomplishing what is called *collaborative learning*. Assigning students to small groups and inviting participation is a time-proven strategy to help students learn. Such groups are also training grounds for the groups and teams students will participate in during their careers.

primary group
A group, such as a family, that exists to fulfill basic human needs.

study group
A group that exists to help group members learn new information and ideas.

Communication and Ethics

Ethically Achieving a Team Goal

Teams have a strong sense of purpose and a well-structured, clear, coordinated plan to achieve the goals of the team. Without a clear goal, teams falter. But sometimes you may be part of a team whose goal or means of achieving the goal you don't support. Suppose, for example, you are a valued and skilled member of a soccer team that has a "win at all costs" mentality. The team wants to win so badly that team members bend some of the rules to enhance their chance of winning: They knowingly allow someone to play who, because of poor grades, is not eligible. Team members let the person play because the person's skill will increase the team's chances of winning. You're the only person who seems concerned about the rule violation. What would you do? Would you continue to participate on the team and not let the other members of the team down, even though permitting an illegal player to participate violates your own ethical standards? Do the ends justify the means? Is winning more important than following the rules?

Here's another example: What if it's not a sports team but a work group? Assume you're a salesperson and part of a sales team. To get a raise in salary, everyone on the team has to meet the sales goal assigned to the team. One team member consistently lies to customers about the company's product to get a sale; that team member's sales success helps make the whole team look good in terms of sales, but look bad in terms of ethics. What would you do? Would you keep quiet and enjoy the benefits of being part of a "successful" sales team? Or would you bring the unethical behavior of the team member to the attention of your supervisor, even though it would place other team members in jeopardy for knowingly "going along to get along"? Are team goals more important than individual ethical standards?

Therapy Groups

therapy group
A group that provides treatment for problems that group members may have.

Therapy is treatment designed to solve a personal concern or problem or to resolve an issue. A **therapy group** exists to provide treatment for the personal problems that group members may have. Weight Watchers, Alcoholics Anonymous, and Gamblers Anonymous are examples of therapy groups. People gain insight by being in a group with others who have similar needs. Also, the feedback people receive from the therapy group leader and other group members is an important part of the treatment. We learn about ourselves from the perceptions of others.

Problem-Solving Groups

problem-solving group
A group that meets to seek a solution to a problem and achieve a goal.

A **problem-solving group** exists to resolve an issue or overcome an unsatisfactory situation or obstacle and achieve a goal. Problem-solving groups are the most common type of groups in businesses and other organizations. In business, the problem a group focuses on often is "How can we overcome an obstacle to make more money?" A problem-solving group or team in a hospital or health clinic will focus on ways to make people healthy. Most problems boil down to something you want more of or less of. The problem-solving group goal is often to figure out how to get more or less of something (time, money, help from others) in order to achieve the goal of the group or organization.

Focus Groups

focus group
A group that is asked to discuss a particular topic or issue so that others can better understand how the group members respond to the topic or issue presented to them.

A **focus group** is a small group of people who are asked to discuss a particular topic or issue so that others can better understand how these group members respond to the

virtual group or team
A group or team whose members are not together in the same physical location but who are typically connected via an electronic channel such as the Internet, a telephone, or a video conference.

Communication *and Technology*

Does Virtual Group Communication Improve Decision Making?

The chances are increasing that you will work in a **virtual group or team**—a group or team that doesn't meet face to face but is instead connected via some electronic channel, such as a telephone, the Internet, or a video conference. A growing body of research notes advantages and disadvantages of working in virtual groups and teams. Here are some key research conclusions about virtual group and team communication:[14]

Benefits of Working in Virtual Teams

- Electronically mediated communication seems to work best for more structured, linear tasks.
- In computer-mediated meetings, ideas can be captured and recorded with speed and accuracy.
- Because it's possible to submit ideas and information anonymously, team members may feel more comfortable sharing creative and innovative ideas with the team.

Cautions about Working in Virtual Teams

- The application of computer and e-technology does not inherently result in better solutions and decisions. Problems are solved and decisions are made by people.
- The increased speed of information transfer allows less time for reflection. Thus, technology may sometimes help us make mistakes faster.
- Some group members do a *less* thorough job of evaluating the pros and cons of alternatives when using computer-mediated technology than when interacting in face-to-face settings.

Although there are some clear advantages of using virtual teams, such as saving travel time and the expense of meeting face to face, the use of technology does not mean teams will always make better decisions. Technology may allow greater access to accurate information, help structure the process, and keep a group focused on facts, but decisions will continue to be made by people skilled in the art and science of decision making and problem solving.[15]

So what is the answer to our question—does virtual group communication improve decision making? The answer is both "yes" and "no." Yes, it can, because the technology can help track ideas, connect people over long distances who might not be able to participate in the decision-making process otherwise, and structure the conversation. Evidence suggests that although we may start out having less trust in virtual team members, over time we develop as much trust in our virtual colleagues as we would if we were meeting face to face.[16] So it just may take a bit more time for trust to develop when we communicate via computer or other mediated methods. But no, the use of technology does not replace the intellectual energy exerted by human beings. People, not machines, need to make sense out of information, turn information into communication, and then develop creative options.

topic or issue presented. One person usually acts as the moderator or facilitator and asks open-ended questions and then gives group members a chance to share their views on the issue at hand. Many advertising agencies will present a new advertising campaign to a focus group and then listen to the responses of the group members to assess the impact or effectiveness of the campaign. Before launching a new kind of potato chip, a snack company may use reactions from a focus group to guide them in marketing the new product. Politicians often use focus groups to determine the effectiveness of a political strategy or new policy. In some ways, a focus-group discussion is like a group interview. The purpose is to listen to group members' ideas about and responses to whatever is being discussed.

Social Groups

Some groups exist just for the joy of socializing with others. Such a group is a **social group**. Travel groups, dinner clubs, or music groups are often formed because group members enjoy the fellowship of interacting and meeting with others. They also like the activity that the group supports. In most cases, people could still do the activity (eat, travel, play music) without a group—but a group makes the experience more enjoyable.

A final note about group types: Although we've identified several different types of groups and teams, don't get the idea that a group or team fits into only one category. The types of groups we've identified can overlap. You could, for example, be in a study group for a class but, during your conversation, discuss a problem and recommend solutions. These categories of groups give you a general idea of the goals that many different types of groups develop during the course of their existence. But they are not mutually exclusive.

Understanding Group and Team Dynamics

Groups and teams are dynamic; their structure changes. Those dynamic or changing factors that fuel groups to achieve goals include how group members interact with and relate to one another. The study of group dynamics includes a discussion of the roles, norms, status, power, and cohesiveness of groups. We'll examine each concept and note how it is related to the five Principles of Communication.

Roles

Your **role** is the consistent way you communicate with others in a group. It is based on your expectations of yourself and the expectations others place on you. Do you often become a leader of a group, or are you more comfortable just blending in and taking directions from others? Or are you the one who makes sure the group gets the work done instead of just having a good time? And then there are those group members who seem especially gifted at smoothing conflict and disagreement. Or perhaps there is no typical pattern to what you do in a group; your role depends on the group and who else is in it. There are three classic categories of group roles:

- **Task roles** are behaviors that help the group achieve its goal and accomplish its work; gathering and sharing research conclusions with the group, taking minutes of meetings, and writing ideas on a chalkboard are examples of task-role behaviors.
- **Social roles** focus on behavior that manages relationships and affects the group climate; these roles help resolve conflict and enhance the flow of communication.

social group
A group that exists to provide opportunities for group members to enjoy an activity in the company of others.

role
The consistent way a person communicates with others in a group.

task role
A role that helps a group achieve its goal and accomplish its work.

social role
A role that helps a group manage relationships and affects the group climate.

A therapy group can be more effective than individual therapy sessions for treating many personal problems.

Smoothing hurt feelings and helping the group celebrate its accomplishments are examples of social-role behavior.

- **Individual roles** focus attention on the individual rather than the group. These are roles that do *not* help the group; they emphasize individual accomplishments and issues rather than those of the entire group. Dominating group discussions to talk about personal issues or concerns, telling frequent jokes that get the group off track, and constantly complaining or whining about how one's individual needs aren't being met are examples of individual roles.

The role of leader, a person who influences others in the group, is a special kind of role, which more than one person can assume. Some leaders focus on assisting with the team's task and therefore assume more task roles to get the job accomplished. Other leaders assume more social roles to help manage the quality of relationships in the group. Usually, a person who assumes an individual, self-focused role doesn't emerge as a natural leader. Being overly dominant or aggressive or blocking the team's progress may focus attention on an individual, but such self-focused behavior doesn't wear well over time, and people who focus on themselves rather than the team aren't perceived as effective leaders.

More than sixty years ago, Kenneth Benne and Paul Sheats came up with a list of group roles that remains a classic way of dividing up the roles that group and team members typically assume.[17] Table 9.1 (pages 242 and 243) presents a summary of these roles. As you review the roles and their descriptions, note whether you usually assume roles in the task, social, or individual category. Or perhaps you'll see yourself in a variety of roles in all three categories.

As you look at the list of roles in Table 9.1, you may think, "Yes, that's what I usually do. That's the role I usually take." You can probably see roles that fit other group members. Most group members don't assume only one or two roles during group meetings. Most of us assume several roles when we interact in a group. A role is worked out jointly between us and the group, and the roles we assume change depending on which group we're in. There is also evidence that your personality and the personality characteristics of other team members have a major influence on team role development.[18] Effective group members adapt their behavior to what is happening or needed in the group. In some groups, your expertise may give you the confidence to give information and share your opinions freely. In other groups, you may assume a role to maintain social harmony and peace.

5. Adapt

individual role
A role that focuses attention on the individual rather than on the group.

What are the best or worst roles to assume? We don't recommend that you assume any individual role; by definition, these roles focus attention on an individual rather than the group. The group needs a balance of task and social roles, not attention drawn to an individual.

What is the proper balance between task and social concerns? Some experts recommend a 60:40 balance between task and social roles.[19] What is clear is that groups seem to operate most effectively when it's not all work and no play. Conversely, an out-of-balance group that focuses just on having a good time is not going to achieve its task goals. In general, more comments need to be about getting the work done than about having fun or managing the social climate, but don't neglect making sure that there are good working relationships among group members.

The action steps for you: Monitor what roles are being assumed and not assumed in your group. Be aware of your communication. Then help meet a need. Adapt your behavior to the needs of the group. If your group seems unduly focused on the task and members are insensitive to the harmony of the group relationships, the group will not be as effective as it might be.

1. Aware
5. Adapt

Rules

As we noted both in Chapter 1 and earlier in this chapter, rules are followable prescriptions that indicate what behavior is expected or preferred.[20] Rules also clearly specify what behavior is inappropriate. Leaders or members of groups and teams often develop rules that specify how people should behave. Think of rules as serving the same function as the U.S. Constitution or the laws of your state or community.

Teams, in particular, often develop team ground rules that help a team function more smoothly. **Team ground rules** are just another way of talking about the behaviors that are expected of group members. They are important to help manage uncertainty when working with others. Imagine playing on a sports team if there were no written rules; it would be chaos. Highly structured teams need rules to ensure that they are both efficient and effective. While most informal groups do not develop explicit, written rules, more formal teams may take time to develop such rules as the following: Everyone should attend all meetings; meetings will start on time; each team member should follow through on individual assignments. Making the rules explicit makes it easier to foster appropriate behavior and prevent inappropriate behavior.

2. Verbal

Norms

While not all groups develop explicit rules, most groups and teams develop norms. **Norms** are general standards that determine what is appropriate and inappropriate behavior in a group. Is it normal for group members to raise their hands before speaking in your group? Is it okay to move around while the group is in session or to go get a cup of coffee while someone is talking? Norms reflect what's normal behavior in the group; they influence how group members are supposed to behave—such as the type of language that is acceptable, the casualness of the clothes they wear, or whether first names are used.

How do you know what the norms of any group are? Watch the group. Listen and observe any repeated verbal or nonverbal behavior patterns. Note, for example, consistencies in the way people talk or dress. Consider the following questions:

- What are group members' attitudes toward time (do meetings start and stop on time)?
- How do group members dress?
- Is it acceptable to use informal slang terms or to use obscenity?
- What kind of humor is acceptable?
- How does the group treat the leader?

Noting when someone breaks a norm can also help you spot a norm. If a member waltzes into a meeting twenty minutes late and several folks grimace and point to their

team ground rules
The behaviors that are expected of team members, often spelled out in explicit rules of acceptable behavior developed by team members working together.

norms
Standards that determine what is appropriate and inappropriate behavior in a group.

TABLE 9.1 A Classification of Group Roles

Task Roles	Description	Example
Initiator/contributor	Offers new ideas or approaches to the group; suggests ways of getting the job done.	"How about developing an agenda to help us organize our work?"
Information seeker	Asks for additional clarification, facts, or other information that helps the group with the issues at hand.	"Can anyone tell me how many times the university has threatened to close the fraternities and sororities on campus because of the problem of underage drinking?"
Opinion seeker	Asks group members to share opinions or express a personal point of view.	"So, what do you all think of the new dress code the school board is proposing?"
Information giver	Provides facts, examples, statistics, or other evidence that relates to the task confronting the group.	"Within the past year, the vice president for student affairs has given a special award to three fraternities and one sorority for developing a program to combat underage drinking."
Opinion giver	Offers opinions or beliefs about what the group is discussing.	"I think the new school dress code proposed for first graders is unworkable."
Elaborator	Provides comments or examples to extend or add to the comments of others.	"Tom, that's a good point. I had the same thing happen to me when my children were attending a private school in New York last year."
Coordinator	Clarifies and notes relationships among the ideas and suggestions that have been offered by others.	"Tyrone, your ideas sound a lot like Juanita's suggestion. Juanita, why don't you elaborate on your idea so that Tyrone can decide whether he agrees or disagrees with you?"
Orienter	Summarizes what has occurred and seeks to keep the group focused on the task at hand.	"I think we're getting a bit off track here. Let's go back to the issue on the agenda."
Evaluator/critic	Assesses the evidence and conclusions that the group is considering.	"How recent are those statistics? I think there are newer figures for us to consider."
Procedural technician	Helps the group accomplish its goal by handling tasks such as distributing reports, writing ideas on a chalk board, or performing other tasks.	"I'll write your ideas on the board as you suggest them. After the meeting, I'll copy them and summarize them in an e-mail message to each of you."
Recorder	Makes a written record of the group's progress by writing down specific comments, facts, or the minutes of the meeting.	"I'll take the minutes of today's meeting."

Social Roles	Description	Example
Encourager	Offers praise and support and confirms the value of other people and the ideas they contribute.	"You're doing a wonderful job."
Harmonizer	Manages conflict and mediates disputes among group members.	"Tynesha, you and Mandy seem to be agreeing more than you are disagreeing. Both of you want the same goal. Let's brainstorm some strategies that can help you both get what you want."
Compromiser	Resolves conflicts by trying to find an acceptable solution; seeks new alternatives.	"Jane, you want us to meet at 7:00 PM, and Sue, you'd like us to start at 8:00. What if we started at 7:30? Would that work?"

TABLE 9.1 (continued)

Social Roles	Description	Example
Gatekeeper	Encourages people who talk too much to contribute less and invites those who are less talkative to participate.	"Tim, we've not heard what you think. What do you suggest we do?"
Follower	Goes along with the suggestions and ideas of other group members.	"I can support that option. You have summarized the issues about the same way I see them."
Emotion expresser	Verbalizes how the group may be feeling about a specific issue or suggestion.	"We seem to be frustrated that we are not making more progress."
Group observer	Summarizes the group's progress or lack of progress.	"We are making great progress on all of the issues except how much salary we should offer."
Tension reliever	Monitors stress within the group and offers suggestions for breaks, using humor or other appropriate strategies.	"Hey, what we need is a good laugh. Here's a joke I saw on the Internet today."

Individual Roles	Description	Example
Aggressor	Deflates or disconfirms the status of other group members or tries to take credit for the work of others.	"Lee, your idea is the pits. We all know that what I suggested two meetings ago is the only way to go."
Blocker	Is negative, stubborn, and disagreeable without an apparent reason.	"I just don't like it. I don't have to tell you why. I just don't like it."
Recognition seeker	Seeks the spotlight by dwelling on his or her personal accomplishments; seeks the praise of others.	"Don't you remember this was my idea? And say, did you see my picture in the paper? I won the grand prize at the science fair."
Self-confessor	Uses the group as a forum to disclose unnecessary personal feelings and personal problems unrelated to the group's task.	"Let me tell you how my parents are so unfair. They won't let me live off campus next year. My parents just don't understand me."
Joker	Wants to crack jokes, tell stories, and just have fun instead of focusing on the task or what the group needs.	"Hey, let's forget this project and go to the mall. Then I'll tell you the gossip about Professor Smith. What a kook!"
Dominator	Tries to take control of the group, talks too much, and uses flattery or aggression to push his or her ideas off on the group.	"Now, here's what we're going to do: Marcie, you will take notes today; Phil, you go get us some pizza; and Russ, I want you to just sit there in case I need you to run an errand."
Special-interest pleader	Seeks to get the group to support a pet project or personal agenda.	"My service club would like it if we would support the new downtown renovation project. I'll stand a good chance at club president if I can get you on board."
Help seeker	Seeks to evoke a sympathetic response from others; often expresses insecurity stemming from feelings of low self-worth.	"I don't know if I can participate in this project. I'm not very good with people. I just feel like I don't relate well to others or have many friends."

watches, that's a sure sign that a norm has been violated. The severity of the punishment corresponds to the significance of the norm.[21] Mild punishment is usually unspoken—such as silent glances or frowning stares. More serious punishment might include a negative comment about the behavior in front of other group members or even expulsion from the group. You don't have to worry about whether your group will have norms or not; norms happen. You should, however, monitor the group norms to ensure that your behavior doesn't distract from the work of the group and to note the possible development of any unproductive group norms (such as spending too much time socializing) that the group should talk about.

How do norms differ from rules? Rules are more explicit. Group and team rules are written down or at least verbalized. Here's an example of a rule: If you have more than three absences in this course, you lose ten points. Here's another: Any member of this team who does not pay his or her dues on time will pay an extra $5 in dues. Norms, on the other hand, are more general standards or expectations that are not as clearly spelled out. It may be a norm in your group that no one uses four-letter words; there's probably no written policy that prohibits expletives, and group members may never have said, "No one should ever use a curse word during our discussions." But even without such specific admonitions, group members don't use offensive or obscene words. Norms develop based on norms that you and other team members have experienced in other groups, as well as on behavior that occurs naturally as group members interact. If after a couple of meetings no one is telling off-color jokes or stories, then a norm has begun to gel.

Status

As she walks into the room, all eyes are fixed on her. Group members watch every move. As the chairperson, she has much influence. Without her support, no new issues will come before the board. She has high status. **Status** refers to an individual's importance and prestige. Your status in a group influences whom you talk to, who talks to you, and even what you talk about. Your perceived importance affects both your verbal and your nonverbal messages. A person with high status typically

- Talks more than low-status members.
- Directs comments to other high-status group members.
- Has more influence on the decisions the group makes.
- Is listened to by group members.
- Addresses more comments to the entire group.[22]

Because high-status people enjoy more privileges, most people want to be in the "in group"—the group with status and influence. Being aware of status differences can help you predict who talks to whom. If you can discern status differences, you'll also be better able to predict the type of messages communicated. Although some people underestimate their perceived level of status and influence in a group, research suggests that you are probably quite perceptive at knowing your own status level when communicating with others.[23]

But just because a person has status does not mean that his or her ideas are good. Some groups get into trouble because they automatically defer to the person with more status, without reviewing the validity of the ideas presented. Status influences group communication, but don't let status differences influence your perceptions of and critical thinking about the merit of the ideas presented. Conversely, don't dismiss ideas out-of-hand because the person who suggested them doesn't have status or prestige. Focus on the quality of the message, not on the messenger.

Power

Status refers to perceived importance, whereas power refers to whether the status influences behavior. **Power** is the ability to influence others' behavior. Although status and power often go hand in hand, a group member can have status and still not be able to

2. Verbal
3. Nonverbal

status
An individual's importance and prestige.

power
The ability to influence other people's behavior.

influence how others behave. People have power if they can affect what others do. Their power stems from the resources available to them to influence others. Who does and doesn't have power in a group influences how people relate to one another.

A power struggle often creates ripples of conflict and contention through a group. Power struggles also often focus attention on individual group members rather than on the group as a whole. People with less power tend to participate less in group discussion unless they're trying to gain power. A group that is not power balanced may have problems; the "power people" may dominate the discussion. In any group or team, when one or more members dominate the discussion, the group loses the contributions and insights of others. Research supports the conclusion that groups with equal power distribution usually have better quality outcomes.[24]

According to a classic discussion of how individuals become powerful, there are five power bases: legitimate, referent, expert, reward, and coercive power. These power bases explain why certain people have power and why others don't.[25]

Based on what you can see in this photo, how many sources of power would you think the leader of this group exerts?

Legitimate Power
You have **legitimate power** if someone elected or appointed you to a position of power. Your power source comes from holding a position of responsibility. The president of your university or college has the legitimate power to establish and implement school policy. U.S. senators, police officers, and parent/teacher association (PTA) presidents are other examples of people who have legitimate power. A group or team member who has been elected chair or president of the group is given legitimate power to influence how the group operates.

Referent Power
You have **referent power** if people like you. Put simply, people we like have more power over us than people we do not like. If you are working on a committee with your best friend, your friend exerts power over you in the sense that you will tend to give more credence to what your friend recommends. Just the opposite occurs if you are working with someone you don't like; you will be more likely to ignore the advice that comes from someone you don't admire.

Expert Power
Knowledge is power. People who have **expert power** are perceived as informed or knowledgeable. They have more influence in a group or team than do people who are perceived as uninformed. Suppose you are working with a group to develop strategies to clean up the river that runs through your town. Your colleague who is majoring in aquatic biology will probably have more power than other, less knowledgeable group members.

Reward Power
People who can grant favors, money, or other rewards have more power than people who can't provide such rewards; those who can bestow rewards have **reward power**. People who have greater power to reward are typically sent more positive, supportive messages than people who don't have the ability to reward others. Someone also has reward power if he or she can take away a punishment or other unpleasant experience. But reward power is effective only if the person being rewarded finds the reward satisfying or useful. What is rewarding to one person may not be rewarding to another person.

Coercive Power
You have coercive power if you can punish others. **Coercive power** is the flip side of reward power. The ability to influence comes from the ability

legitimate power
Power that stems from being elected or appointed to a position of authority.

referent power
Power that stems from being liked.

expert power
Power derived from having expertise and information.

reward power
Power that comes from the ability to provide rewards or favors.

coercive power
Power that stems from being able to punish others.

to make others uncomfortable. If someone can cut your salary, lower your grade, demote you, or force you to do unpleasant jobs, then that person has coercive power. The power results from the perception that the person with the power will actually use the power. If a person has the authority to punish but group members don't perceive that the person will use this power, then there really is no coercive power.

Even though we have categorized power into five different types, don't get the idea that group members may exert just one type of power. In reality, group or team members often have more than one type of power. For example, because a group member may be the elected leader (legitimate power), he or she may also be able to offer more rewards (reward power) or punishments (coercive power).

Cohesiveness

If you have ever read about the Three Musketeers or seen a movie about them, you know that their motto was "One for all, and all for one." They were a cohesive group—they liked to be around one another. **Cohesiveness** is the degree of attraction that members of a group feel toward one another and the group. In a highly cohesive group, the members feel a high degree of loyalty to one another; the goal of the group is also the goal of the individual. Cohesive group members listen to one another. Members of a cohesive group are more likely to use words and phrases that have a unique meaning to group members; they are also more likely to tell "inside jokes"—jokes that mean something only to them.[26]

Groups become cohesive because of a variety of forces that attract people to the group and to one another. Similarity of goals, feelings of genuine liking, and similarity of backgrounds and culture are variables that influence group cohesiveness.

What makes groups and teams cohesive? Table 9.2 summarizes some strategies that enhance group cohesiveness and other strategies that make a group less cohesive. The common element in cohesive groups is the manner in which group members communicate with one another. Cohesiveness is more likely to occur if group members have the opportunity to talk with one another freely about a goal all members have in common and if this interaction increases group members' affection and liking for each other. Teams that have greater control over how they conduct their work are also likely to be more cohesive.[27]

4. Listen and Respond

cohesiveness
The degree of attraction group members feel toward one another and toward their group.

Recap

Types of Power

Legitimate Power	Power that results from being elected, appointed, or ordained to lead or make decisions for a group or a team.
Referent Power	Power that results from being popular and well liked.
Expert Power	Power that results from having information or being knowledgeable about issues or ideas.
Reward Power	Power that results from having the resources to bestow gifts, money, recognition, or other rewards that group members value.
Coercive Power	Power that results from having the ability to punish others.

Chapter 9 Understanding Group and Team Performance 247

TABLE 9.2 Suggestions for Enhancing Group Cohesiveness[28]

Cohesive Groups	Uncohesive Groups
Talk about the group in terms of "we" rather than "I"; stress teamwork and collaboration.	Emphasize the individual contributions of group members; stress individual accomplishment.
Reinforce good attendance at group meetings.	Make little effort to encourage group members to attend every meeting.
Establish and maintain group traditions.	Make little effort to develop group traditions.
Set clear short-term and long-term goals.	Avoid setting goals or establishing deadlines.
Encourage everyone in the group to participate in the group task.	Allow only the most talkative or high-status members to participate in the group task.
Celebrate when the group accomplishes either a short-term or a long-term goal.	Discourage group celebration; make sure group meetings are all work and little or no fun.

Can a group be too cohesive? Yes. If group members are focused only on developing a positive, cohesive relationship to the exclusion of getting their work done, group productivity can suffer. If the group becomes obsessed primarily with having fun and enjoying one another's company, they will produce *less* work. Although usually cohesiveness is a good thing, a group can have too much of a good thing. Strive for group cohesiveness, but balance it with concern for accomplishing the group's task.

Communication Interaction Patterns

Do you have a Facebook or MySpace page? If you do, or if you're connected to someone else's page, you have a sense of how we form connections with other people. Sometimes you're invited to join someone else's social network. Or you may discover that you have a lot in common with some people and just naturally connect to their pages. Just as you may interact with some people's Facebook pages more than others, when not communicating in cyberspace you communicate with some people more than others. When you participate in a group or team, you'll find that you talk more with some people than with others. Group communication scholars have studied and classified the various distinct patterns that emerge when people talk to one another in groups. A **communication interaction pattern** is a consistent pattern of who talks to whom. Some groups have an equal distribution of interaction among group members, while others develop distinct patterns of interaction.[29]

In most groups, we often speak to specific people in the group rather than to the group as a whole. And we tend to speak to people who have power and status, more often directing communication to those in leadership positions than to those who have less influence in the group. In addition, we talk to people we like more than people we don't like. However, there will also be more communication directed toward someone in the group who holds an opinion different from that of the rest of the group. This person is called a **group deviate**. Other group members may spend considerable time trying to change his or her opinion.

A group in which everyone talks to everyone else is called an all-channel network. All channels are open and used, as you can see in the first model in Figure 9.1. There is considerable interaction, and no cliques or small subgroups emerge. A **clique** is a smaller group of people within a group who form a common bond among themselves. Perhaps in your social, service, or religious groups you have special friends whom you seek out and who seek you out when you attend meetings. During meetings, you probably sit together, share private jokes and stories, and talk about other members. Although there is nothing wrong with having special friends and colleagues, cliques can become detrimental to a group or team if they foster rivalries within the group or

2. Verbal

communication interaction pattern
A consistent pattern of who talks to whom.

group deviate
A group member who holds an opinion, attitude, or belief that is different from that of other group members.

clique
A smaller, cohesive group within a group.

1. Aware

if they inhibit the flow of communication with others. Groups should avoid dividing into subgroups or cliques that can develop divisive power plays that foster conflict. You don't want cliques or groups to ratchet up the emotional tension as the group seeks to deliberate rationally. How do you avoid being in a clique? Become aware that you are in a subgroup that could be detrimental to the larger group.

The chain network in Figure 9.1 illustrates a form of group communication in which people convey a message to one person at a time rather than communicating with all group members at once. In organizations, it is typical to find a hierarchical chain communication pattern. Here's an example: The president of the company sends a message to the vice president, who talks to the director. The director then talks to the manager, who eventually gives the message to the other employees. As you might suspect, passing a message through many different ears and minds often results in misunderstanding by the time the message reaches the last person in the chain.

The wheel network pattern occurs when one group member receives most of the messages. This pivotal communicator is also the prime source of information to other group members. Perhaps one member of your family always seems to know what's going on. The wheel pattern emerges when there is a strong leader or when the group members do individual tasks and need someone to keep them informed of what others are doing, without interacting with those others.

What's the best interaction pattern? It depends. The most effective leaders and group members adapt their interaction pattern to fit the task and the time constraints

Figure 9.1
Small Group Communication Networks

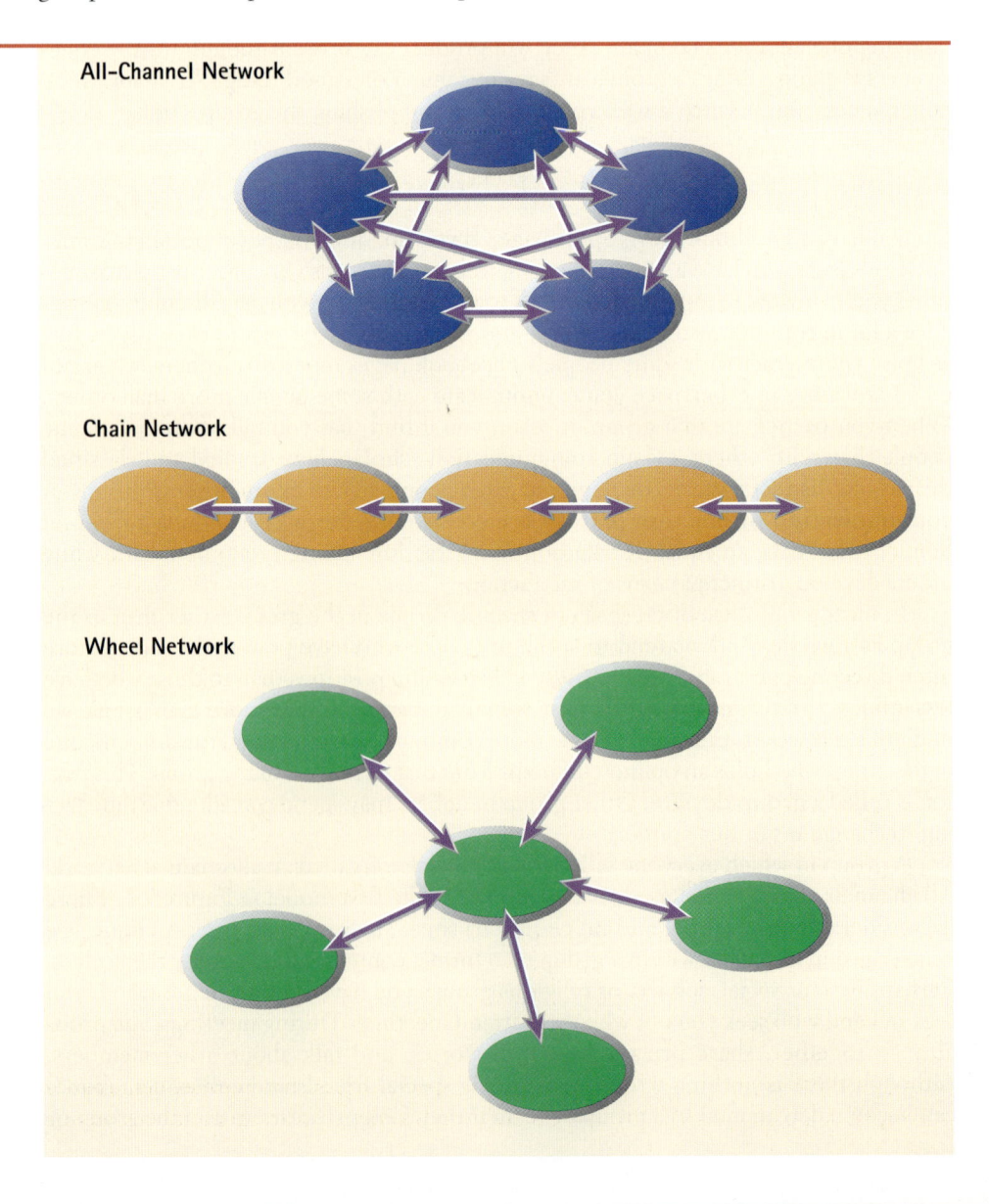

All-Channel Network

Chain Network

Wheel Network

of the project at hand. Sometimes, the efficiency and structured nature of the chain or wheel pattern may be called for. For example, during the huddle before a football play, the quarterback usually does most of the talking while others listen (wheel network). But most teams function best if there is an all-channel pattern of communication, especially when the group is trying to generate new, creative ideas. Breaking into smaller groups can be a useful divide-and-conquer strategy and enhances efficiency for some tasks. If the group is not too large, the all-channel pattern serves most groups well. As you participate in or lead group meetings, be aware of the general pattern of communication. Are all members participating? Do some people whisper their ideas only to a few and not share with the rest of the group? Is a group deviate monopolizing the conversation? By being observant of interaction patterns, you can help the group enhance cohesiveness and develop appropriate roles to get the work done.

Understanding Phases of Group and Team Development

Sometimes, small group communication can be a disorganized, messy process—especially if the all-channel network is the predominant communication pattern. Although the free flow of ideas is a good thing, it may seem as though there is no order or structure to the way group members interact. But what may look like chaotic talk may, in fact, be just a normal aspect of how groups behave.

Researchers have found that some groups go through certain phases or sequences of talk when they meet to solve a problem or make a decision.[30] Some researchers have found three phases; most have found four. One of the most descriptive four-phase models was developed by communication researcher Aubrey Fisher.[31] His four phases of group talk are (1) orientation, (2) conflict, (3) emergence, and (4) reinforcement. To understand the sequence of these four phases can be like having a group map. By listening to what people are saying, you can identify where the group is. We will describe these phases so that you can identify them when they occur in your group.

Orientation

As you might suspect, when people first get together in a group, they enter the **orientation phase**, in which they adjust to at least two things: who's in the group (group process) and what they will be doing (group task).

When you join a group for the first time, you have high uncertainty about how the group will be organized, who's in charge, and exactly how things will work. Research on the orientation phase suggests that your earliest communication is directed at orienting yourself to others, as well as to the group's task. What happens during this first phase is often referred to as **primary tension**. This is the tension that results from the uncertainty and discomfort people experience when they meet for the first time.[32] Just as you may have some anxiety when you give a speech, some uncertainty and anxiety occur in a group when group members are trying to figure out who is supposed to do what, who's in charge, and why they are there. Some group members who don't like uncertainty at all and are eager to start sorting things out will suggest an agenda: "Hello, my name is Steve. Let's each introduce ourselves." Other group members are quite content to sit quietly in the background and let others take the lead. As people begin to become acquainted and start talking about the group's purpose, typical groups experience the second phase—conflict.

Conflict

As we've pointed out, people are different—and nowhere is that more evident than in a group discussion after the group gets down to business. As group members become

orientation phase
The first phase of group interaction, in which members become adjusted to one another and to the group's task.

primary tension
Tension arising from the uncertainty and discomfort that occur when a group first meets.

During the conflict phase of group development, tensions may emerge if there is a struggle for leadership.

conflict phase
The second phase of group interaction, in which group members experience some degree of disagreement about social and task issues.

secondary tension
The conflict that occurs, after the members of a group have become acquainted with one another, over group norms, roles, leadership, and differences among member opinions.

emergence phase
The third phase of group interaction, in which conflict or disagreement is managed, decisions are made, and group problems begin to be solved or managed.

reinforcement phase
The fourth phase of group interaction, in which group members express positive feelings toward each other and toward the group.

more comfortable and oriented toward the task and one another, they start asserting opinions about what the group should be doing and who should be doing it. They have tested the water in the first phase and are now ready to jump in. This second phase, which is characterized by increased disagreement, is known as the **conflict phase**, and the conflict that arises in the phase is sometimes called **secondary tension**. This tension or conflict occurs when there is a struggle for leadership or when group members disagree with each other.

Conflict is not always bad—it occurs when people are honest about sharing their opinions. If there is no conflict, it usually means people aren't honest about how they really feel. As journalist Walter Lippman once said, "When we all think alike, then no one is thinking." The conflict phase is necessary for solving problems and maintaining group relationships. When ideas aren't challenged and tested, groups are more likely to make unwise decisions. We are not suggesting that you celebrate when you have conflict, only that you take some comfort in knowing that conflict is an expected part of group deliberations. The amount and intensity of the conflict vary, depending on how important the issues are to the group. The more important the issues are to group members, the greater the intensity of the conflict is likely to be.

Research suggests that when intense conflict arises in your group, especially conflict that results in heightened emotions and tension because of cultural differences, it may be best to "cool it."[33] Taking time to back off, rather than continuing to hash out issues verbally, may be helpful in managing the tension. Regardless of the issue or trigger for the conflict, when emotions are aroused, rational discussion is hard to achieve. Especially if the group you're in includes people from a variety of cultural backgrounds, letting the group "breathe" rather than continuing to hammer out meaning with more talk may be best. We're not suggesting that all conflict should be managed by avoiding it; we are suggesting that when emotions become aroused it's difficult to make headway on the issues with words that may fan the flames of the conflict.

When conflict in virtual groups and teams stems from differences in cultural values or perceptions, it's important that team members feel connected to the team and empowered to participate rather than marginalized or discounted. Research suggests that having virtual team members vote on decisions or the value and importance of contributions is a useful way of keeping them engaged with the team.[34]

Emergence

You know you are in the **emergence phase** when the group begins to solidify a common point of view. Decisions emerge; conflict is reduced. Though conflict is still evident in this third phase, what sets the emergence phase apart from the conflict phase is the way in which group members manage conflict. Norms, roles, and leadership patterns that have been established in the group now help the group get work accomplished. In the emergence phase, the group settles on norms and moves closer to agreement. The group begins to get a clearer glimpse of how issues will be resolved and what the group outcome will be.

Not all of what emerges may be productive. The group could decide that the conflict is so intense that the best decision is to disband the group. Or an individual could decide to leave the group.

Reinforcement

Group members become more unified in the **reinforcement phase**. During the orientation, conflict, and emergence phases, group members struggle through getting acquainted, developing cohesiveness, competing for status and prominence, and puzzling over action the group could take. The group eventually emerges from those struggles and develops a new sense of direction. This accomplishment results in a more positive feeling about the group. The group more clearly develops a sense of "we." In fact, one of the ways you can identify the reinforcement phase is when group members use more collective pronouns *(we, us, our)* than personal pronouns *(I, me, my)* to talk about the group.

The Process Nature of Group Phases

Even though we have identified four distinct phases that groups can experience, don't get the idea that all groups progress neatly through these phases in exactly the same way. They don't.[35] Some researchers have found that only about one-third of all groups experience these distinct stages.[36] Other studies have difficulty identifying four phases and find just one or two. Even if you have trouble identifying these phases in your group, you will probably see some elements of the four phases during your group meetings. Some groups get stuck in one of the phases. For example, have you ever participated in a group that could never quite figure out what it was supposed to do? It was stuck in the orientation phase.

Some groups remain in the conflict phase for long periods of time, perhaps bouncing between orientation and conflict. The group either seems torn by personal conflict between group members or just can't reach agreement or make a decision.

Eventually something will emerge from the group (phase three), even if it is not a wise decision or quality solution. The group may decide, for example, to disband and never meet again because it is so dysfunctional. Although not the original objective of the group, something emerged—the group members quit.

Reinforcement is likely to occur because we like to make sense out of what happens to us. Even if the group disbands, we are likely to celebrate its demise or reinforce the decision to disband. Because of our culture's emphasis on efficiency and productivity, many groups quickly gloss over the reinforcement aspects of group celebration. Wise group leaders and participants make sure that accomplishments are celebrated and both group and individual efforts are recognized. The cohesiveness and positive feelings that result from such celebrations will be helpful as the group prepares for its next task.

Recap

A Map of Group Phases

Phase	Characteristics
Phase One: Orientation	• What are we doing here? • What is our goal? • Who are these people? • What is my role?
Phase Two: Conflict	• Who put him/her in charge? • I see the goal differently. • I have different ideas. • I have different strategies.
Phase Three: Emergence	• Something happens. • Decisions are made. • Issues are managed. • The group moves forward.
Phase Four: Reinforcement	• The group is aware it is making progress. • Members seek to justify their actions. • Members reward others. • The team celebrates its success or rationalizes its failure.

Communication and Diversity

The Impact of Individualism and Collectivism on Groups and Teams

As you recall from Chapter 6, individualistic cultures tend to focus on individual achievement. Most North Americans value individual accomplishment over group or team achievement. In general, people from the dominant cultural groups in the United States, Great Britain, and Australia savor and celebrate individual accomplishment. Collectivistic cultures emphasize group or team accomplishment rather than individual achievement. Research suggests that the collectivist mindset is prevalent in Asian countries, Latin America, and some parts of Eastern Europe.[37]

These two perspectives have important implications for group and team collaboration. People who hold individualistic cultural values may find it more difficult to work collaboratively than people from collectivistic cultures. The following summary compares individualistic assumptions with collectivistic assumptions about working in groups and teams.[38] These differences can sometimes explain why groups and teams have difficulty accomplishing their tasks. If you're from a culture that places a high value on individual achievement, you may find it challenging to work collaboratively with others.

Individualistic Assumptions	Collectivistic Assumptions
The best decisions are made by individuals.	The most effective decisions are made by teams.
Planning should be done by leaders.	Planning is best done by the entire group.
Individuals should be rewarded.	Groups or teams should be rewarded.
Individuals should work primarily for themselves.	Individuals should work primarily for the team.
Healthy competition among group and team members is more important than teamwork.	Teamwork is more important than competition.
Meetings are for sharing information with others.	Meetings are for making group or team decisions.
To get something accomplished, you should work with individual people.	To get something accomplished, you should work with the entire group or team.
The prime objective of meetings is to advance your own ideas.	The prime objective of meetings is to reach consensus or agreement.
Group or team meetings are often a waste of time.	Group or team meetings are the best way to achieve a quality goal.

How Real Groups and Teams Interact in Organizations

Textbooks have a tendency to describe things in tidy ways, which may make it appear as if the world were neatly organized into clear categories. Although we've noted in this chapter that there are distinctly different types of groups, roles, communication networks, and goals, groups and teams—as they operate in real-world businesses and other organizations—don't always fit textbook categories.

It is likely that in today's multitasking workforce you will be participating in many different types of teams and groups *at the same time*. Most people do not belong to just one team and focus all of their energy and talent on one primary task. The **bona fide perspective** of groups suggests that the context and boundaries for the groups in which we participate move and change. The term *bona fide* simply means authentic, true, or genuine. Thus, a bona fide perspective is concerned with how groups actually operate within organizations.

According to communication scholar Linda Putnam, who has done extensive research and writing about bona fide groups, we need to be more sensitive to how groups really operate in natural settings.[39] Most groups and teams do not work in isolation from other groups and from the organization in which they exist. Groups and teams are connected to and genuinely influenced by what else is happening in the organization. If, for example, an organization is losing money and on a tight budget, then the lack of money will affect how a group operates within the organization. Therefore, Putnam suggests that two elements need to be addressed when considering bona fide groups: (1) how the group is connected to other groups and the organization and (2) how the group operates in relationship to its external context.

bona fide perspective
A perspective that focuses on how groups actually operate within organizations.

How can we apply a bona fide perspective to help us with the groups and teams to which we belong? Consider these observations:

- If you're a leader or manager in an organization, a bona fide perspective suggests that you need to be aware that the people who work under your supervision have multiple roles and multiple jobs. Just as your instructor needs to remember that you're likely taking more than one class, so should a manager realize that her or his employees are working on multiple projects at the same time.
- Remember that the teams you're working with today may not be the same teams you'll be working with tomorrow. Team membership changes. The changing composition of the group may require that the group go through numerous periods of reorientation, as new group members come and other group members go.
- When some members participate in a team via e-mail or phone rather than face to face, special effort must be made to integrate these long-distance group members into the fabric of the team.
- Remember that when you work on a group or team task, you're bound by the constraints of the larger organization in which you work. You're not just working in isolation—you're connected to the whole, although all you may experience is the interaction in the group or team in which you're working.

Naturally occurring groups are complex, with changeable boundaries and changeable group members. The bona fide, or authentic, approach to groups and teams reminds us to be realistic when we apply principles and practices of group theory to groups and teams.

PRINCIPLES FOR A LIFETIME
Enhancing Your Skills

Principle One: Be aware of your communication with yourself and others.
- Be knowledgeable of the definitions of and differences between groups and teams.
- Be aware of your role and the roles of others in groups and teams.
- Be aware of how you and your group develop and maintain group norms.
- Be mindful of how your power and the power of others influence group interaction.
- Be aware of the forces that affect group and team cohesiveness.
- Be aware of and sensitive to the stages of orientation, conflict, emergence, and reinforcement that influence group interaction.
- Be aware that your group does not operate in isolation.

Principle Two: Effectively use and interpret verbal messages.
- Be verbally supportive of other team members so as to foster a collective sense of team spirit.
- Verbally help clarify team goals; clear, elevating goals are the hallmark of an effective team.
- Express realistic optimism when working with others in groups and teams; groups and teams with a positive outlook are more effective than those with a pessimistic perspective.
- Verbally help to clarify individual member roles and your own roles.
- Help the group or team set clear ground rules and clarify norms that may be ambiguous.
- Set short-term as well as long-term goals to help enhance cohesiveness.
- Talk about your group or team in terms of "we" rather than "I."

3. Nonverbal

Principle Three: Effectively use and interpret nonverbal messages.
- Watch for nonverbal cues to help you understand group and team norms.
- Observe group and team members' use of space, touch, and eye contact to pick up clues about status and power.
- Be supportive of other group members nonverbally as well as verbally; reinforce statements with positive facial expressions, eye contact, and head nods to indicate agreement when appropriate.
- Use supportive nonverbal messages to help groups and teams manage both the primary tension (early tension that occurs when a group first meets) and the secondary tension (conflict that emerges about leadership, norms, rules, or roles) that typically is present in groups.

4. Listen and Respond

Principle Four: Listen and respond thoughtfully to others.
- Being a good listener is one of the most important ways to help a group; listening skills help you identify your roles and the roles of others.
- Listen to others to help identify group and team norms and rules.
- Listen attentively to other group members to help foster a climate of cohesiveness.

5. Adapt

Principle Five: Appropriately adapt messages to others.
- Be sensitive to the needs of your group so that you can adapt your messages to help the group achieve its goal.
- Adapt to the group by paying attention to roles, norms, rules, and status differences.
- Adapt to help the group become oriented to the task, manage conflict, facilitate emergent decisions, and reinforce group behavior.
- Adapt appropriately to cultural differences within the group.

Summary

Groups and teams are an ever-present aspect of our lives. Small group communication is the transactive process of creating meaning among a small number of people (three to fifteen people) who share a common purpose, who feel a sense of belonging to the group, and who exert influence on one another. Groups and teams are similar in that they are collections of a small number of people who meet to achieve a goal. A team can be differentiated from a group in that it is more highly organized and the members' collaborative efforts are more coordinated to achieve the team goal. Groups exist for a variety of reasons. Some primary groups, such as families, exist to meet basic human needs; other types of groups include study groups, therapy groups, focus groups, problem-solving groups, and social groups.

Groups and teams are dynamic. This means that a variety of factors influence the ever-changing nature of what occurs when you interact with others in groups and teams. The role you assume in a group, the consistent way you communicate with others, influences your behavior and the behavior of others. There are three primary types of roles in small groups and teams: task roles—those that help the group do its work; social roles—those that help the group members relate to one another; and individual roles—those that inappropriately divert the group's focus to individual concerns rather than group concerns. Other factors that affect the dynamic nature of groups and teams include norms (standards of what is normal or expected), rules (explicit statements about appropriate and inappropriate behavior), status (a person's importance or prestige), power (the ability to influence others), cohesiveness (the degree of loyalty and attraction the group members feel toward one another), and interaction patterns (the consistent communication networks that emerge based on who talks to whom).

Group communication may sometimes seem chaotic, but researchers have noted that many (though not all) groups experience predictable phases. During the orientation phase, group members get acquainted with both the task and one another. The second phase, conflict, occurs when group members recognize that they have differing ideas and opinions about both the group's task and its procedures for accomplishing the task. The third phase, emergence, is evident when the group begins to make decisions and starts completing the task. The reinforcement phase occurs when the group has accomplished its task and takes some time to recognize and confirm the group's actions; the reinforcement phase may be brief, especially in groups that don't take time to celebrate their success or attend to the social dynamics of the group.

Groups operate in real-world organizations and don't always fit textbook categories. Group members and leaders need to be sensitive to differences in cultural expectations that may affect groups and teams and adapt accordingly. In the next chapter we identify practical strategies to help you make decisions and solve problems as a group member, lead a group, or organize a meeting. Throughout our discussion, we will continue to interweave the five foundation principles that are fundamental to communicating with others, including in groups and teams.

Assessing Your Knowledge

For Discussion and Review

Principle One: Be aware of your communication with yourself and others.

1. How does being aware of the role or roles you typically play in a group help you enhance your communication in groups and teams?

Principle Two: Effectively use and interpret verbal messages.

2. Why do clearly defined rules and goals enhance teamwork?

Principle Three: Effectively use and interpret nonverbal messages.

3. How does accurately interpreting nonverbal messages help you identify group and team norms, as well as status differences in a group?

Principle Four: Listen and respond thoughtfully to others.

4. What is it about the process of interacting with others in a group or team that makes listening and responding skills among the most valued competencies when working collaboratively with others?

Principle Five: Appropriately adapt messages to others.

5. What are some suggestions for adapting your behavior during each of the four phases of group and team development (orientation, conflict, emergence, reinforcement) that often (but not always) occur during group and team discussions?

Multiple Choice

Choose the *best* answer to each of the following questions.

1. The group roles that are of the least benefit to the group's objective are
   a. task roles.
   b. social roles.
   c. individual roles.
   d. focus roles.

2. Which of the following is not one of the common characteristics in the definition of small group communication?
   a. Members exert influence on each other.
   b. Members number more than fifteen.
   c. Members feel a sense of belonging.
   d. Members have a common purpose.

3. In comparison to groups, teams generally have
   a. more clearly defined rules of operation, but less clearly defined responsibilities for members.
   b. less clearly defined rules of operation, but more clearly defined responsibilities for members.
   c. more clearly defined rules of operation and responsibilities for members.
   d. less clearly defined rules of operation and responsibilities for members.

4. As group cohesiveness increases, group productivity tends to
   a. increase.
   b. decrease.
   c. increase, unless the group becomes too cohesive.
   d. remain unchanged; cohesive groups are not productive.

5. Michelle says to the rest of her group, "I think we need to finish discussing the problem with parking

on campus before we get into possible solutions." Michelle's role in the group is best described as
   a. a task role.
   b. a social role.
   c. an individual role.
   d. a negative role.

6. The stage of group problem solving in which conflict is diminished and the group solidifies a point of view is called
   a. orientation.
   b. conflict.
   c. emergence.
   d. reinforcement.

7. When group members get into disagreements, David helps them work through the conflict. His role in the group is best described as
   a. encourager.
   b. coordinator.
   c. procedural technician.
   d. harmonizer.

8. In order for a group to be most effective, some experts recommend a balance of
   a. 90% task roles, 10% social roles.
   b. 60% task roles, 40% social roles.
   c. 40% task roles, 60% social roles.
   d. 10% task roles, 90% social roles.

9. When advertisers test-market a new product, they often rely on input from a
   a. primary group.
   b. therapy group.
   c. problem-solving group.
   d. focus group.

10. A group member who is able to influence the behavior of other members in the group has
    a. high power, but not necessarily high status.
    b. high status, but not necessarily high power.
    c. high power and status.
    d. neither power nor status.

Answers to the questions in this practice test can be found at the end of the book.

Assessing Your Skill

1. **Agree–Disagree Statements:** Read each of the following statements once. Take four or five minutes to do this. Then, in small groups, try to reach consensus about each statement (everyone either agreeing or disagreeing with the statement). Try especially to find reasons for differences of opinions. If your group cannot reach consensus, you may change the wording in any statement enough to promote unanimity. Mark A on the line preceding a statement if you agree, D if you disagree.[40]

   1. _____ Despite its flaws, a meeting is the best way to get work done in an organization.
   2. _____ There are often occasions when an individual who is a part of a working team should do what he or she thinks is right, regardless of what the group has decided to do.
   3. _____ Sometimes it is necessary to move people in the direction you yourself think is right, even if they object.
   4. _____ It is sometimes necessary to ignore the feelings of others in order to reach a group decision.
   5. _____ When the leader is doing his or her best, one should not openly criticize or find fault with his or her conduct.
   6. _____ In most team conflicts, someone must win and someone must lose. That's the way conflict is.
   7. _____ Much time is wasted in talk when everybody in the group has to be considered before making a decision.
   8. _____ Almost any job that can be done by a committee can be done better by having one individual responsible for the job.
   9. _____ Body language and nonverbal messages are more important than verbal messages when communicating with others in team meetings.
   10. _____ If people spend enough time together, they will find something to disagree about and will eventually become upset with one another.
   11. _____ Most hidden agendas are probably best kept hidden to ensure a positive social climate and manage conflict.
   12. _____ If you disagree with someone in a group, it is usually better to keep quiet than to get the group off-track with your personal difference of opinion.
   13. _____ When a team can't reach a decision, members should abide by the decision of the group leader if the leader is qualified and competent.
   14. _____ Some people produce more conflict and tension than others. These people should be restricted from decision-making meetings.

2. **Assessing Your Group's Cohesiveness:** Invite each member of a group you participate in to use the classic Seashore Index of Group Cohesiveness to measure group cohesiveness. After each person has completed the scale, summarize the results and compare impressions about the degree of cohesiveness present in your group.

Seashore Index of Group Cohesiveness

Check one response for each question.

1. Do you feel that you are really a part of your work group?

   _____ Really a part of my work group

   _____ Included in most ways

_____ Included in some ways, but not in others
_____ Don't feel I really belong
_____ Don't work with any one group of people
_____ Not ascertained

2. If you had a chance to do the same kind of work for the same pay in another work group, how would you feel about moving?

_____ Would want very much to move
_____ Would rather move than stay where I am
_____ Would make no difference to me
_____ Would want very much to stay where I am
_____ Not ascertained

3. How does your work group compare with other similar groups on each of the following points?

	Better than most	About the same as most	Not as good as most	Not ascertained
a. The way the members get along together	_____	_____	_____	_____
b. The way the members stick together	_____	_____	_____	_____
c. The way the members help each other on the job	_____	_____	_____	_____

Source: S. Seashore, *Group Cohesiveness in the Industrial Work Group* (Ann Arbor: University of Michigan Institute for Social Research, 1954).

3. Assessing Group Communication Skills: Communication researchers Katherine Hawkins and Bryant Fillion surveyed personnel managers to find out what the managers considered the most important skills necessary for successful groups and teams. The items in the following scale are among the skills the personnel managers deemed important. Rate each member of a group you are in on the following skills, using a scale from 1 to 5 (1 = not at all effective; 2 = generally not effective; 3 = uncertain; 4 = effective; 5 = very effective).

Scoring: Total the score for each group member. A perfect score is 65; the lowest possible score is 13. Your instructor may invite you to share your ratings of other group members anonymously. Or, if you don't share your ratings, simply note how you evaluate your skill in comparison to your

Skill	Group Member A	B	C	D	E
1. Listens effectively	_____	_____	_____	_____	_____
2. Understands roles and responsibilities	_____	_____	_____	_____	_____
3. Actively contributes to the group	_____	_____	_____	_____	_____
4. Asks clear questions	_____	_____	_____	_____	_____
5. Establishes and maintains rapport with others	_____	_____	_____	_____	_____
6. Is sensitive to people with different cultural backgrounds	_____	_____	_____	_____	_____
7. Uses clear, concise, accurate, and professional language	_____	_____	_____	_____	_____
8. Communicates well with people who have different professional backgrounds	_____	_____	_____	_____	_____
9. Gives clear and accurate instructions	_____	_____	_____	_____	_____
10. Presents a positive professional image nonverbally (through appropriate grooming and attire)	_____	_____	_____	_____	_____
11. Helps resolve conflicts	_____	_____	_____	_____	_____
12. Accurately summarizes information for the group	_____	_____	_____	_____	_____
13. Gives brief, clear, well-organized, and informative presentations to the group when appropriate	_____	_____	_____	_____	_____
Total	_____	_____	_____	_____	_____

Web Resources to Improve Your Knowledge and Skill

For a collection of resources and strategies to help you work with others in small groups and teams, check out the Allyn & Bacon web site: <www.abacon.com/commstudies/groups/group.html>. This site provides tips to help you investigate key small group communication concepts. You can also participate in an interactive activity or take a quick quiz to test your knowledge of groups and teams.

Ben Shahn, "Four Piece Orchestra," 1944. © Copyright VAGA, NY. Fundacion Coleccion Thyssen-Bornemisza, Madrid, Spain. © Estate of Ben Shahn/Licensed by VAGA, New York, NY. © Scala/Art Resource. NY.

Never doubt that a small group of concerned citizens can change the world; it's the only thing that ever has.

Margaret Mead

Chapter 10

Enhancing Group and Team Performance

Chapter Outline

- What Effective Group Members Do
- Structuring Group and Team Problem Solving
- Enhancing Group and Team Leadership
- Enhancing Group and Team Meetings
- Summary

Chapter Objectives

After studying this chapter, you should be able to

1. Identify six functions that effective group members perform.
2. List and describe the five steps of group problem solving (reflective thinking).
3. Compare and contrast the trait, functional, styles, situational, and transformational approaches to understanding leadership.
4. Develop and use an agenda to ensure that meetings have appropriate structure.
5. Use strategies to maintain appropriate discussion and dialogue to ensure that meetings include appropriate interaction.

What's so great about groups? Why does every organization, from the U.S. Congress to the local Parent Teacher Association, use groups, teams, and committees to get something done? The simple fact is that groups work. Collaborating with others produces clear benefits that just don't happen when you give a task to an individual. Research clearly supports the following conclusions:

- Groups and teams come up with more creative solutions to problems than a person does working alone.
- Working with others in groups improves group members' comprehension of the ideas presented.
- Group and team members are more satisfied with the group's conclusions and recommendations if they participated in the discussion.
- Groups have access to more information when they tap into the experience of group members.[1]

All of these advantages sound wonderful. But these benefits of collaboration don't just occur automatically when people work in groups and teams. Sometimes there are significant disadvantages to working collaboratively.

- Overly talkative or insensitive, overbearing people may speak too much; the advantage of working collaboratively is lost when one or more people dominate the conversation.
- Group members sometimes feel pressure to conform to what other group members are doing and saying; it can be difficult to stick up for your own ideas when everyone else sees issues differently.
- Some group members just sit back and wait for others to do the work; it may be easy for some people to loaf and not do their share of the work. If not enough people carry part of the load, then the advantages of working together as a group don't materialize.
- Working in groups and teams takes more time than working individually; it takes time to talk and listen.[2]

This chapter is designed to help you achieve the advantages of working in groups and minimize the disadvantages of working collaboratively. We can't claim that if you follow all of the strategies we suggest, your life will be free of unpleasant and unproductive group experiences. We do believe that group members who both understand how groups work (see Chapter 9) and know principles and strategies for enhancing the quality of group work are much more likely to avoid the pitfalls and reap the benefits of working in groups. Working in groups will usually involve more time than working by yourself, but the benefit of improved decision quality can far outweigh the disadvantage of investing more time.

What Effective Group Members Do

1. Aware
2. Verbal
3. Nonverbal
4. Listen and Respond
5. Adapt

"I hate groups," mutters an exasperated group member who has just finished a two-hour meeting in which nothing was accomplished. "Not me," chirps another group member. "Meetings and team projects are fun. I like the energy and productivity that occur when we work together." What is it the second person knows that the first one doesn't? As we noted at the start of the last chapter, working in groups can be frustrating, but it doesn't have to be if you and other group members learn some fundamental ways to perform effectively as group members.

Underpinning all of the suggestions we offer in this chapter are the same five Communication Principles for a Lifetime that we introduced in Chapter 1 and have been discussing throughout the book. Effective group members are aware of what they are doing. They effectively use verbal and nonverbal messages, listen and respond, and then appropriately adapt their messages to others.

Some tasks, like a barn-raising, cannot be completed without the cooperation of all the group members involved in the task. How can you adapt your leadership and group membership styles to achieve the goals of a group when total cooperation on a given task is required?

Identify and Implement Key Functions to Achieve Results

Effective group and team members help to ensure that key functions or communication behaviors that enhance the overall quality of the group are put into practice. Researchers have found that when these critical functions are not performed, the group is less effective. This **functional approach** to group communication describes the kinds of behaviors or functions that lead to better quality solutions and decisions in group deliberations.[3]

Researchers have spent several years trying to identify the key functions of high-performing groups and teams so that you can make sure you enact them in your group. The primary means by which researchers have identified these functions is by comparing the way group members in high-performing groups talk with the way group members in low-performing groups talk.

The essence of these functions involves group members being vigilant thinkers.[4] **Vigilant thinkers** pay attention to the *process* of how problems are solved. A vigilant thinker assesses, evaluates, and tests ideas; he or she effectively uses verbal messages and listens to what others are saying. Communication researcher Randy Hirokawa and his colleagues identified four essential questions that vigilant-thinking group members should consider:

1. What goal does the group want to achieve?
2. Does something in the present situation need to be changed in order to achieve the goal?
3. What options does the group have that will help achieve the goal?
4. What are the positive and negative implications of the options?[5]

Even though these questions are usually discussed in the order listed, some productive, vigilant-thinking groups don't always follow this sequence.[6] What is clear, however, is that if one or more of these critical questions is not discussed, the group is less effective in solving problems and making wise decisions. These questions lead to the achievement of the following six critical functions that effective groups need to consider.

Identify a Clear, Elevating Goal

What are we trying to do? Note that the first question that a vigilant-thinking group asks relates to the group's goal. Articulating a clear and elevating goal is one of the early functions that group members should make sure to accomplish in their group. According to one research team, the goal should be not only clear, but also *elevating*, or exciting to the group.[7] The group needs to know that it is pursuing a goal that is significant; the group goal needs to be something more exciting and important than anything an individual could achieve on his or her own. A professional baseball team during spring training camp may hang up signs in the locker room that say "World Series

2. Verbal

functional approach
An approach to group problem solving that assumes that to achieve a group goal, group members should perform certain communication functions.

vigilant thinker
A group member who pays attention to the process of how problems are solved, is sensitive to the need to make changes, identifies the goal of the group, identifies options the group has, and evaluates the positive and negative implications of the options.

Champs!" A professional football team may see itself as a Super Bowl contender at the beginning of summer training camp. Groups, too, need to identify a clear, exciting, yet realistic goal that drives all aspects of what the group does. Without a goal and a results-driven structure to achieve the goal, group performance sputters.[8]

Develop a Results-Driven Structure

A group with a **results-driven structure** is organized around the action steps that it needs to take to achieve its goal.[9] At any given moment during group discussion, the group is either on task or off task in working to achieve the group goal. Perhaps you've been part of a group or team that was quite busy but didn't seem to accomplish much; that kind of activity reflects a non–results-driven structure. A group that structures itself for results makes sure that the work is clearly linked to the desired outcome.

A group or team may have a clear goal, such as winning the Super Bowl, getting an A on a group assignment, or selling more widgets than other groups in the company—but just having a clear, elevating goal doesn't mean that the group will achieve what it wants to achieve. The old saying "If wishes were horses, then beggars would ride" comes to mind. Just wishing something to happen won't make it happen. Results-driven action has to follow goal setting. The action that must be taken should be focused on the group goal; the group should be driven by results. If you want to win the Super Bowl, you have to invest time in becoming physically fit and working on executing successful football plays. If you want to get an A on the assignment, you need to be doing those things that the instructor wants you do to, rather than socializing and just having fun. To be results-driven means that you "keep your eye on the prize" and then develop a group or team structure to achieve the prize.

Gather and Use Information Effectively

Computer programmers are familiar with the acronym GIGO—"Garbage in, garbage out." If you develop a computer program using bad information or a bad program command (garbage), you're likely to come out with low-quality output (more garbage). Information is the fuel that makes a group function well. High-performing groups and teams don't just rely on the unsupported opinions of group members; group members conduct research and find relevant information to accomplish the goal. Effectively functioning groups ask, "Does something need to be changed?" They gather information and analyze the situation to answer that question.

If a group or team's purpose is to solve a problem, it gathers information to help analyze the problem. To analyze an issue, an effective group should do at least three things:

1. Gather the information the group members need.
2. Share the information with group and team members.
3. Draw accurate conclusions from the information.

Group members who don't gather and use information effectively are more likely to make bad decisions. Having too little evidence—or no evidence at all—is one of the reasons groups sometimes fail to analyze their current situation correctly.[10] Even if group members do have plenty of evidence, it may be bad evidence or they may not have tested the evidence to see whether it is true, accurate, or relevant.

Develop Options

Another hallmark of an effectively functioning group is that group members generate many ideas and potential solutions *after* gathering information and analyzing a situation. Effective groups don't just settle on one or two ideas and then move on. They list multiple creative approaches.

Sometimes groups get stuck and ideas just don't flow. Rather than continuing to hammer away at the problem, the group may want to take a break from the difficult

---

results-driven structure
A structure that causes a group to focus its efforts on the actions it needs to take to achieve its goals.

issues or knotty problems. Perhaps you've had a great idea come to you when you were taking a walk or driving. Taking a break gives your mind a chance to thrash through some of the issues and generate a breakthrough solution. The principle of self-awareness operates here: As a group member, you have a responsibility to become aware of the group's ability to generate high-quality ideas. Be sensitive to the group's need to take a fresh look at the problem or issue.

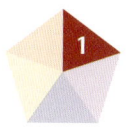

1. Aware

Evaluate Ideas

High-performing groups know a good idea when they see it. They are able to evaluate evidence, opinions, assumptions, and solutions to separate good ideas from bad ones. Low-performing groups are less discriminating. A group that is too eager to make a decision just so it can get a job done and that does not critically evaluate ideas usually comes up with lower-quality decisions.

An effectively functioning group examines the advantages and disadvantages of an idea, issue, or opinion.[11] When the group is zeroing in on a particular course of action, the effective group has at least one member who suggests, "Let's consider the positive and negative consequences of this decision." Research suggests that it's especially important to talk about the negative consequences of a specific proposal.[12] Some groups use a chalkboard or flip chart and make a written list of the pros and the cons. Groups that do this are likely to come up with a better decision than groups that don't systematically evaluate the good and bad aspects of a potential solution or decision.

Develop Sensitivity Toward Others

Most of the functions we've described so far focus on getting work done effectively and efficiently; but group success is about more than just focusing on the task. In effectively functioning groups, members also listen and are sensitive to one another's needs. Group members are aware of how the comments they make might be perceived by other members. Effectively functioning group members make comments that confirm the value of others' contributions and nonverbally show that they are genuinely interested in what others are saying. Fostering a climate of fairness and supportiveness is essential to developing a well-functioning team.[13]

Effective group members balance concern for the task with concern for the feelings of others. Being solely task-oriented is not beneficial to the functioning of a group.

2. Verbal
3. Nonverbal
4. Listen and Respond

For meetings to be effective, group members must use sound verbal and nonverbal communication skills. When you are in a group meeting, what types of verbal and nonverbal messages do you use to contribute to a positive group setting?

> ## Recap
> ### What Effective Group and Team Members Do
>
> | Group Function | Description of Function |
> |---|---|
> | Identify and Implement Key Functions to Achieve Results | Getting a handle on key functions helps the group
• Identify the goal
• Identify what needs to be changed
• Identify options
• Identify positive and negative implications of the options |
> | Identify a Clear, Elevating Goal | A clear, elevating, or important goal anchors the purpose of group discussion. |
> | Develop a Results-Driven Structure | Structure helps the group stay on task and do those things that will help it achieve its goal. |
> | Gather and Use Information Effectively | Conducting research and using accurate information are important elements in the deliberation of any group or team. |
> | Develop Options | Effective groups expand the number of alternatives or options before choosing a course of action. |
> | Evaluate Ideas | Effective groups or teams examine the pros and cons of an option before implementing the strategy. |
> | Develop Sensitivity Toward Others | Group members do more than focus on the task; they express sensitivity to the needs and concerns of group members by using appropriate verbal and nonverbal messages, listening, responding, and adapting messages to others. |

Group members also listen to what each group member has to say—even members who hold a minority opinion. One of the benefits of working in a group is that you can hear a variety of ideas. If opinions of others are quickly squelched because they are not what most other group members think or believe, the group loses the power of many different points of view.

Structuring Group and Team Problem Solving

"Just tell me what to do. What I want to know is, what techniques will help me solve the problem? Make it simple." We usually want simple techniques or steps that will help us achieve our goal. The truth is, however, that there are no magic techniques that will enable a group or team always to come up with the right solution to a problem.

The functional approach to group problem solving that we just discussed is based on the assumption that high-performing groups and teams perform certain functions or communication behaviors that ineffective groups and teams don't enact. We now turn our attention to a more structured, prescriptive approach to solving problems. You will note some obvious similarities between the two approaches. But the more prescriptive approach to group problem solving we present now offers a sequence of steps and techniques to help your group stay on task and remain productive while still being sensitive to group members. Just as a prescription from your doctor is based on the assumption that a specific dose of medicine will help remedy an ailment, a prescriptive approach to problem solving is based on the assumption that there are specific things you can do to enhance the communication health of the group.

Communication researcher Arthur Van Gundy suggests that problems can be classified on a continuum from *structured* to *unstructured*.[14] A structured problem is one to which there is a single best correct solution. A math problem is structured in the sense that there is one right answer. When group members are highly uncertain about how to solve a problem, have little information about how to proceed, and are confused, they are facing an unstructured problem. Problems such as how to "save" Social Security, how to solve the parking problem on campus, and how to increase teachers' salaries without raising taxes are examples of unstructured problems; there is more than one way to tackle each one. The more uncertainty there is (or the less structured the problem), the greater the need for a structured approach to help the group manage their uncertainty. Leaders who give the group structure by setting goals, keeping track of the time, and suggesting procedures enhance the group's perceived effectiveness.

More than seventy methods or sequences of prescriptive steps and techniques have been identified for structuring problem solving in groups and teams.[15] Several researchers have sought to identify the sequence that works best. Their conclusion? *No single prescriptive method or series of steps works best in every situation. But having some structured sequence of steps or questions works better than having no structure.*[16]

Structure is the way a group or team discussion is organized to follow a prescribed agenda. Because of the number of people working together to solve a problem, groups need structure to avoid hopping from topic to topic. According to one researcher, groups that engage in free-ranging discussion without an agenda change topics about once a minute.[17]

Can a group have too much structure? Yes. If you've been to a meeting or group discussion that seemed more like a seminar than an interactive discussion, then there was too much structure. If a meeting is so controlled that one or two people do most of the talking, you're not at a meeting—you're at a speech. The goal is to balance the amount of structure with group interaction.

Interaction includes give-and-take discussion and the responsiveness of group members to the comments of others. In an interactive group, there are fewer long utterances, more people contribute, and more people take turns talking. In a highly structured meeting, there is more control over who talks, about what, and for how long; overly structured meetings include less interaction. As suggested in Figure 10.1, the key is to find the right balance between structure and interaction. When there is too much interaction, the group experiences the chaos of unbridled talk which may not be focused; group and team members may need help in focusing on one idea at a time, rather than bouncing from topic to topic. When there is too much structure, however, the group loses the freedom to listen and respond with sensitivity to what others are saying.

structure
The way a group or team discussion is organized, focusing on the group's agenda and the task that needs to be achieved.

interaction
The give-and-take discussion and responsiveness to other group members.

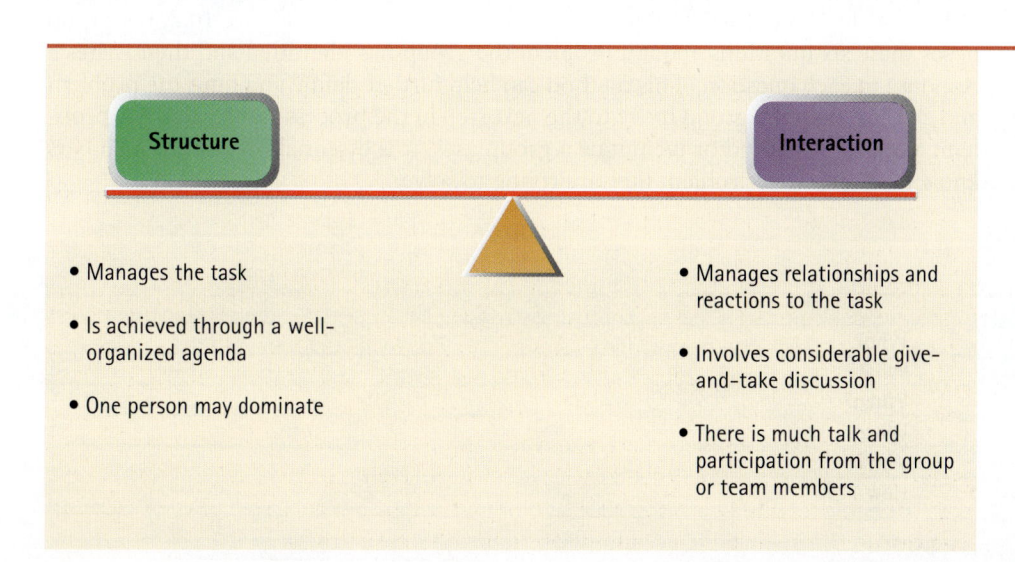

Figure 10.1
Groups Need a Balance of Structure and Interaction

Structure
- Manages the task
- Is achieved through a well-organized agenda
- One person may dominate

Interaction
- Manages relationships and reactions to the task
- Involves considerable give-and-take discussion
- There is much talk and participation from the group or team members

In the pages that follow, we present a set of steps that can help you develop a sequence of things group members should be talking about. These five steps are inspired by educator and philosopher John Dewey, who in 1910 wrote a book called *How We Think*.[18] His book described how individuals go about the problem-solving process; in essence, he described the scientific method that scientists still use to solve problems: defining and analyzing a problem, identifying solutions, picking a solution, and putting the solution into practice. He called this process **reflective thinking.** We present these steps here, not as a one-size-fits-all prescription that you should always follow, but as a way of structuring the problem-solving process to manage uncertainty and also to ensure that the key functions we talked about earlier are accomplished during your discussion. In addition to describing each step of the reflective thinking process, we present several techniques to help you structure discussion.

2. Verbal

Step 1: Identify and Define the Problem

"What's your problem?" Groups work best when they have identified a clear, elevating goal that unites their problem-solving effort. To reach a clear statement of the problem, consider asking the following questions:

- What is the specific problem that concerns us?
- What do we want more of or less of?
- What terms, concepts, or ideas do we need to define in order to understand the problem?
- Who is harmed by the problem?
- When do the harmful effects of the problem occur?

Most group experts recommend that an effective way to give your problem-solving task appropriate structure is to phrase your problem in the form of a policy question. A policy question is phrased so that the group will recommend some action (policy) to eliminate, reduce, or manage the problem. Policy questions begin with the words "What should be done about . . ." or "What could be done to improve . . . ."

Here are some examples:

- What should be done to lower the cost of tuition at our university?
- What could be done to decrease property taxes in our state?
- What should be done to make health care more affordable for all U.S. citizens?

One specific technique for structuring the discussion so as to identify a problem is to use the Journalists' Six Questions method.[19] Most news reporters are taught to include the answers to six questions when writing a news report: Who? What? When? Where? Why? and How? Using a simple chart like the one in Figure 10.2, the group poses these six questions about a problem the group has identified and then writes a response to each question. This method can help further define and limit the problem and can also help the group move to the next step in the process—analyzing the problem. Whatever method or technique a group uses, it is essential that group members know precisely what problem they are trying to solve.

reflective thinking
A problem-solving process based on the scientific method.

Figure 10.2
Journalists' Six Questions

Who?	
What?	
When?	
Where?	
Why?	
How?	

Step 2: Analyze the Problem

To analyze something is to break it down into smaller pieces; to analyze a problem is to consider the causes, effects, symptoms, history, and other information that will inform the group about how to best solve the problem. Many groups want to "cut to the chase" quickly and start spinning out solutions, without taking the time to analyze the problem thoroughly. Resist this temptation. Analyzing a problem well is an important prerequisite to finding an effective solution. When analyzing a problem, group members will need to spend time in the library or on the Internet to gather information and determine how experts view the problem. Essential questions that can help you analyze problems include the following:

- How long has the problem been in existence?
- How widespread is the problem?
- What are the causes of the problem?
- What are the effects of the problem?
- What are the symptoms of the problem?
- Who is harmed by the problem?
- What methods already exist for managing the problem?
- What are the limitations of existing methods?
- What obstacles keep the group from achieving the goal?

In addition to considering these questions, group members should develop criteria for an acceptable solution. **Criteria** are standards for an acceptable solution to a problem. Identifying clear criteria can help you spot a good solution when you see one. Sample criteria for solutions include the following:

- The solution should be inexpensive; the cost should not exceed a specified percentage of the budget.
- The solution should be implemented by a certain date.
- The solution should be agreed on by all group members.
- The solution should be agreed on by all persons affected by the recommendations.

Don't rely on your memory when you verbalize criteria. Write down on a chalkboard or flip chart the list of criteria your group has identified and include the list in the minutes or notes that summarize the meeting.

After you have gathered information and developed criteria, your group may need to develop a systematic way of analyzing the information you've gathered. One technique that can help structure the analysis of your problem and also help your team identify criteria is the **force field analysis technique**.[20] This technique works best when your group has identified a clear goal and needs to assess what is happening now that would increase the probability that the goal will be achieved.

Here's how to conduct a force field analysis. After identifying a goal, the group lists all of the driving forces currently at work that would help achieve the goal. Then the group does just the opposite: It identifies the restraining forces that are keeping the group from achieving the goal. When complete, the analysis can help the group see what needs to be increased (the forces that currently favor achieving the goal) and what needs to be decreased (the forces working against the goal). Figure 10.3 shows an example of a force field analysis conducted by a group that wanted to increase the number of students who volunteer for community projects; the goal is written on the top. On the left side of the diagram is a list of all of the factors that the group identified as increasing the chances of achieving the goal—getting more students to volunteer. On the right side is a list of the restraining forces, or forces that keep the group from achieving the goal. The task of the group in developing solutions is now clear: Increase the driving forces and decrease the restraining forces.

One final observation: Be careful not to spend so much time overanalyzing data that you forget the purpose of the group—to solve the problem. Beware of "the killer inch" problem. This occurs when group members agree on the major points but are distracted by minor details; they've traveled a long way to reach their goal, but get distracted in the last inch of the journey. Avoid analysis paralysis.

2. Verbal

2. Verbal

criteria
Standards for an acceptable solution.

force field analysis technique
A method of analyzing a problem or issue by identifying forces that increase the likelihood that the desired goal will occur (driving forces) and forces that decrease the probability that the goal will occur (restraining forces).

Figure 10.3
Force Field Analysis
Source: Adapted from Julius E. Eitington, *The Winning Trainer* (Houston: Gulf Publishing, 1989). Used with permission. All rights reserved.

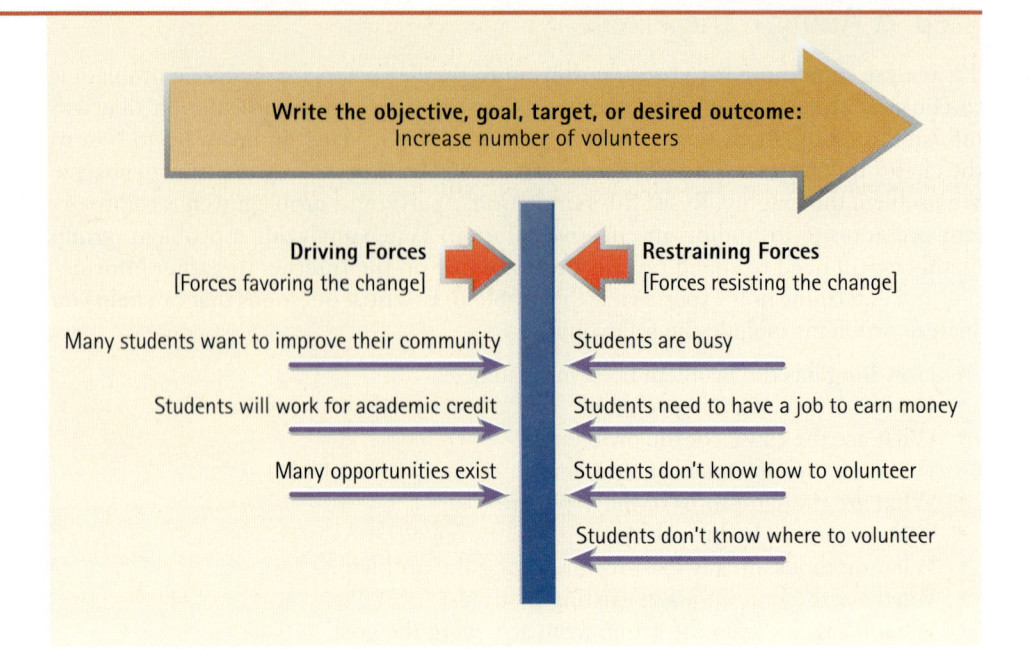

Write the objective, goal, target, or desired outcome:
Increase number of volunteers

Driving Forces
[Forces favoring the change]

Restraining Forces
[Forces resisting the change]

Many students want to improve their community — Students are busy

Students will work for academic credit — Students need to have a job to earn money

Many opportunities exist — Students don't know how to volunteer

— Students don't know where to volunteer

2. Verbal
3. Nonverbal

Step 3: Generate Creative Solutions

Now that you've identified a specific problem, analyzed its causes and history, and established clear criteria for solutions, you're ready to generate creative options to solve the problem. **Creativity** is the generation, application, combination, and extension of new ideas. Researchers have found that your entire group is more likely to be creative if individual group members are creative; it's important not to rely on others to be creative, but to develop your own creative skill. It's simply not true that only a few gifted and talented people are creative; creative ideas can come from anyone. Author Malcolm Gladwell believes that our powers of intuition and creativity harbor the greatest potential for generating the breakthrough ideas that can change the world.[21] Your group is more likely to be creative if you do the following things:[22]

- Make sure everyone knows the precise nature of the problem.
- Review and summarize the analysis of the problem.
- Promote a climate of freedom; let people experiment and play with ideas.
- Don't judge and evaluate the ideas of others prematurely.
- Listen to minority points of view; you never know who may have the next great insight.
- Provide enough time for creativity to occur; don't rush the creative process.

Brainstorming is the classic technique for identifying possible solutions to a problem. This technique was developed by an advertising executive over forty years ago to encourage a group to be creative.[23] You've probably used brainstorming before. Many groups, however, don't use the technique effectively.

The key to making brainstorming work—to generating many creative ideas—is to *separate the generation of ideas from the evaluation of ideas.* This means group members are supposed to feel free to offer ideas without fear of criticism, snickering, or being made to feel foolish. Reality, however, may be quite different. When group members start suggesting ideas, there may be either verbal or, more likely, nonverbal evaluation of ideas. People may laugh at the more offbeat suggestions; or, when someone announces a suggestion, others may frown, sneer, or voice an editorial comment. Another subtle form of evaluation occurs when some group ideas are praised and some are not. Group members whose ideas are not praised may feel that their ideas are considered stupid. Clearly, when ideas are evaluated as soon as they're offered, brainstorming doesn't work well; members may be reluctant to share ideas. This is especially true of group members who are shy or uncomfortable talking in a group; these people, however, may have great ideas that are worth sharing.

One solution to this problem is to have a period of **silent brainstorming** before members share their ideas verbally. Another name for silent brainstorming is the **nominal group technique**.[24] For a few moments, people work individually—for that period of time, they are a group in name only (hence the name *nominal*). After group members have brainstormed individually, they share their ideas with the group.

The same rules apply, whether you are brainstorming out loud or silently:

- Set aside judgments and criticism when people offer ideas.
- Think of as many ideas as possible; volume is important.
- Piggyback off someone else's idea.
- Try to identify one or more zany or wild ideas—this triggers creativity and may lead to a less zany but workable idea.
- Record the ideas on a flip chart or chalkboard when people share them. It's usually best to go around the group one at a time to have group members share what they have written down.
- Evaluate the ideas *after* all of the group members have finished sharing.

You may ask group members to do some individual brainstorming before they come to the group meeting. For example, you could say, "Each group member should bring five or ten suggestions for solving our problem." Or you could just invite group members to brainstorm ideas silently for a few minutes and then move into small groups to share and piggyback off ideas. If everyone has e-mail access, ask group members to do some private brainstorming and e-mail their responses to either the group leader or other group members. Another creative way to generate ideas is to have group members first write each idea or suggestion on a sticky note.[25] Once the ideas are on the sticky notes, group members can stick them to the wall and then arrange them in groups. Seeing other group members' ideas may trigger additional creative ideas from

When seeking a consensus decision from group members, what strategies can you employ to effectively express your sensitivity to others' ideas and opinions? What can you do to be sure your own contributions are considered?

2. Verbal

Recap

Brainstorming Steps

1. Select a problem that needs to be solved.
2. Discuss the history, causes, and background of the problem. Make sure the group knows precisely what options are needed.
3. Tell the group to develop a creative mindset:
   - Put aside judgments and evaluations.
   - Stress quantity of ideas.
   - Avoid criticizing ideas, including your own.
   - Try to come up with one or more wild ideas—stretch your imagination; it's easier to modify wild ideas.
   - Piggyback off someone else's ideas.
4. Start brainstorming. Give the group a time limit.
5. To reduce the possibility that people will evaluate ideas, consider using a period of silent brainstorming before having people verbalize their ideas.
6. Write all of the ideas on a chalkboard or flip chart.
7. Keep reminding the group not to evaluate the ideas of others when they are first expressed.
8. Evaluate the ideas after all ideas have been presented.

creativity
The generation, application, combination, and extension of new ideas.

brainstorming
A technique for generating many possible solutions to a problem by withholding evaluation while group members suggest ideas; ideas are evaluated after suggestions have been offered.

silent brainstorming (nominal group technique)
A method of generating creative ideas; group members brainstorm individually and write down their ideas before meeting together to share them.

the group. The goal is to separate generating or listing ideas from critiquing the ideas. When those two parts of brainstorming get mixed together, fewer ideas flow because of group members' fear of being criticized.

Step 4: Select the Best Solution

The next step is to evaluate the ideas your group has identified and pick the best solution. The group members now take the long list of ideas generated and determine which ones best meet the criteria they identified when they analyzed the problem. They also determine which solutions best achieve the clear, elevating goal they identified. This means it's really important that group members have both a clear goal and specific criteria—without them, they will have difficulty recognizing a good solution when they see it.

It is usually easier for groups to expand alternatives (brainstorm) than to narrow alternatives. The methods used by groups to whittle a long list down to a manageable number for more serious debate include these five approaches:

1. *Decision by expert.* Let someone who has high credibility narrow the list.
2. *Rank.* Tell group members to rank their top five choices from 1 to 5.
3. *Rate.* Ask group members to evaluate each solution on a scale from 1 to 5; the solutions rated best get the most serious discussion.
4. *Majority vote.* Group members vote for the ideas they like.
5. *Consensus.* Group members seek a solution that all group or team members can accept.

Consensus occurs when there is enough agreement that group members will all support a decision. Consensus doesn't mean everyone agrees enthusiastically and completely with what the group has decided—but at least group members won't stand in the way of what the group has decided. Reaching a consensus decision has the advantage that all group members can verbalize support for the decision. But reaching consensus takes time.

Three primary strategies can help groups reach consensus:

1. *Be goal-oriented.* Keep the outcomes in mind as you talk.[26] Because groups often bounce from topic to topic, it's important to keep the group oriented toward the goal. When you see the group starting to stray from its task, remind group members what the goals are. It also helps to write ideas and facts on a flip chart or chalkboard; this helps keep the group focused.
2. *Listen.* Work to clarify misunderstandings. When you do agree with something that is said, say so. Maintain eye contact with the speaker, and give him or her your full attention.
3. *Promote honest dialogue and discussion.* True consensus is more likely to occur if many ideas are shared and group members don't just give in to avoid conflict.

Table 10.1 compares what effective group members do to achieve consensus with ineffective strategies for reaching agreement.

Be cautious if all group members agree too quickly. You may be experiencing groupthink instead of consensus. **Groupthink** occurs when group members seemingly agree but primarily just want to avoid conflict. On the surface, it seems as though group members have reached consensus—but it's an illusion of agreement. Another way of describing groupthink is to call it faulty consensus; too little disagreement often reduces the quality of group decisions. If a group does not seriously examine the pros and cons

consensus
Agreement among all members of a group or team to support an idea, proposal, or solution.

groupthink
A faulty sense of agreement that occurs when members of a group fail to challenge an idea; a false consensus reached when conflict is minimized and group members do not express concerns or reservations about an idea or proposal.

TABLE 10.1 Suggestions for Reaching Group and Team Consensus[27]

Effective Group Members	Ineffective Group Members
Keep the Group Oriented Toward Its Goal	
Remind the group what the goal is.	Go off on tangents and do not stay focused on the agenda.
Write facts and key ideas on a flip chart or chalkboard.	Fail to summarize or rely on oral summaries to keep group members focused on the goal.
Talk about the discussion process; ask questions that keep the group focused on the agenda.	Do little to help clarify group discussion.
Listen to the Ideas of Others	
Clarify misunderstandings.	Do not clarify misunderstandings or check to see whether others understand their message.
Emphasize areas of agreement.	Ignore areas of agreement.
Maintain eye contact when listening to someone and remain focused on the speaker without interrupting.	Do not have eye contact with the speaker, and do not focus attention on the speaker; interrupt the speaker.
Promote Honest Dialogue and Discussion	
Seek out differences of opinion.	Do not seek other opinions from group members.
Do not change their minds quickly to avoid conflict.	Quickly agree with other group members to avoid conflict.
Try to involve everyone in the discussion.	Permit one person or just a few people to talk too much and dominate the conversation.

of an idea, it's likely that the quality of the decision it makes will suffer because the group has not used its full power to analyze and evaluate ideas.

Failure to test ideas and the resulting groupthink can have serious consequences in the form of wrong, dangerous, or stupid decisions. The following list identifies a few well-known disasters or problems in which groupthink was a key factor.

- In 1986, American viewers watched in horror as the *Challenger* space shuttle exploded on live TV. The tragedy resulted from both faulty engineering and groupthink: Some people knew the shuttle wouldn't fly in cold temperatures, but because of pressure to stay on schedule decided not to stop the launch.[28]
- In 1999, several students were killed in a traditional pre-football game bonfire at Texas A&M University in College Station, Texas. Some thought the bonfire construction unsafe before the accident occurred, but because of tradition the bonfire continued to be built, and tragedy was the result.[29]
- The commission that investigated the terrorist attacks of September 11, 2001, concluded that groupthink was one of the factors contributing to the nation's not being prepared for the attacks.[30] The 9/11 commission believed there was pre-existing evidence of a terrorist threat, yet not enough action was taken to address the problem fully.
- In 2003, the *Columbia* space shuttle disintegrated on re-entry into the earth's atmosphere because of damage sustained during takeoff. Some thought there might be a problem but didn't speak up, so no corrective action was attempted.

The headlines are not the only places to look for examples of groupthink. If you think about it, you'll find plenty of examples in groups and teams you've worked with.

What causes groupthink? Sometimes it occurs because group members are not particularly interested in the topic or are tired and want to get on with other work. If a group has a highly revered leader, someone with high status whom all group members respect, the group is likely to agree with the leader, rather than test and challenge

Communication and Ethics

Managing Conflict in Groups and Teams

Some people think of conflict as bad and detrimental to a group. Yet, in our discussion of groupthink—a false sense of agreement arrived at when people fail to challenge ideas and conclusions—we note that it's important for group members to challenge ideas. Being too uncritical and failing to raise reservations about group conclusions can breed a climate of groupthink. The question is, however, how do you know when to challenge ideas?

Moya knows that she doesn't like to disagree with other members of her project team. When working with this group, she consistently tries to find something positive or pleasant to say about others' comments. When she does disagree with an idea or suggestion of another group member, she usually doesn't voice her opinion. Is it ethical to remain silent because you want to maintain peace when you actually disagree with an idea suggested? When is it best to keep quiet rather than express disagreement that could escalate to more intense conflict? What are your personal criteria for expressing disagreement with others in a group or team? Specifically, when do you speak up, and when do you avoid creating a fuss?

---

the leader's ideas. Groupthink also occurs when group members feel they can do no wrong. Rather than take time to test and evaluate ideas, the group that feels invincible may quickly decide that their decision is a good one. Groupthink can also occur when (1) the group feels apathetic about its task, (2) group members don't expect to be successful, (3) one group member has very high credibility—group members tend to believe what he or she says, (4) one group member is very persuasive, and (5) group members don't usually challenge ideas—it's expected that group members will agree with one another.[31] Be on the lookout for these symptoms in your groups and teams.

Of course, as the saying goes, "Hindsight is 20/20." After the fact, it can be easy to spot an example of groupthink. The hard part is to be aware of groupthink when it occurs in your group. Knowing the causes and symptoms of groupthink can help you spot it if it occurs in your group and then put an end to it.

To overcome groupthink, consider the following strategies.[32]

- Don't agree with someone just because he or she has high status; examine the ideas of others carefully, regardless of their position.
- Consider asking someone from outside the group to evaluate the group's decisions and decision-making process.
- Assign someone to be a devil's advocate—to look for disadvantages to a proposed idea.
- Ask group members to break into smaller teams or pairs to consider both the pros and the cons of a proposed solution.

An easy way to structure the discussion suggested in the last item above is to use a T-chart like the one in Figure 10.4. Write the possible solution at the top of the chart

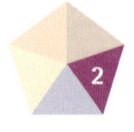

2. Verbal

Figure 10.4
T-Chart

Pros	Cons

Recap

Top Six Reasons Groups and Teams Sometimes Make Stupid Decisions

No Common Goal	Group does not begin with the end in mind—no collective vision.
Analysis Paralysis	Team members overanalyze unimportant details; talk is valued more than action.
Jumping to Solutions	People propose solutions before the facts are known.
Topic Hopping	There is a lack of agenda and structure; discussion is not focused on the goal.
Killer Inch	People agree on major points but argue over minor details.
Groupthink	Group and team members agree too quickly; ideas are not questioned or challenged.

(on a flip chart, chalkboard, or transparency using an overhead projector), and then list both the pros and the cons. This technique will help you look at the positive and negative consequences of an action before you leap into a specific recommendation.

Step 5: Take Action

Once you have identified your solution(s), your group needs to consider the question "Will it work?" You may want to do a pilot test (practice test) or ask a small group of people what they think of your idea before you "go public" with it. Bouncing your proposed solution off an expert and checking to see if the solution has been successful when others have adopted it can help you test the solution's effectiveness.

If your group has to not only identify a solution but also put it into action, your group will need structure to make sure that details don't get overlooked in getting the job done. Perhaps you know the people in the following story:

> This is a story about four people: Everybody, Somebody, Anybody, and Nobody. There was an important job to be done, and Everybody was asked to do it. Everybody was sure Somebody would do it. Anybody could have done it, but Nobody did it. Somebody got angry about that because it was Everybody's job. Everybody thought Anybody could do it, but Nobody realized that Everybody wouldn't do it. It ended up that Everybody blamed Somebody when actually Nobody asked Anybody.

Make a written list of who should do what. Follow up at the next group meeting to see whether the assignments have been completed. Effective groups and teams develop an action plan and periodically review it to make sure Anybody asked Somebody.

Enhancing Group and Team Leadership

Leadership is the ability to influence others through communication. Some view a leader as someone who delegates and directs the group. Others see a leader as someone who is primarily responsible for ensuring that whatever task is assigned or designed by the group is completed. Actually, most groups have many leaders—not just one person who influences others. In fact, each group or team member undoubtedly influences what the group does or does not achieve. Regardless of who serves as leader, research suggests that the quality of group and team leadership has a significant impact on how satisfied team members are.[33] Members of an effectively led team feel greater satisfaction,

leadership
The ability to influence the behavior of others through communication.

Recap

Reflective-Thinking Steps and Techniques

Steps	Techniques
1. Identify and define the problem.	• Phrase the problem as a policy question. • Use the Journalists' Six Questions (Who? What? When? Where? Why? How?) to help define the issues.
2. Analyze the problem.	• Use force field analysis to identify driving and restraining forces. • Develop clear criteria that clarify the issues and can help in evaluating solutions.
3. Generate creative solutions.	• Use brainstorming. • Use silent brainstorming (nominal group technique) or electronic brainstorming.
4. Select the best solution.	• Narrow alternatives using ranking, rating, majority vote, or expert decision. • Reach consensus by being goal-oriented, listening, and promoting honest dialogue.
5. Take action.	• Develop a clear action plan. • Make a written list of who should do what.

are more productive, and are less likely to be absent.[34] The quality of team leadership influences virtually every aspect of what it feels like to be a team member. The prevailing approaches to analyzing the behavior of effective leaders are the trait, functional, styles, situational, and transformational approaches to leadership.

Trait Approach

Are leaders born or made? The **trait approach to leadership** suggests that there are certain attributes or traits that make leaders. According to this approach, if you are born with these traits or if you cultivate leadership skills, then you will be a leader. Researchers have identified intelligence, confidence, social skills, general administrative skill, physical energy, and enthusiasm as some of the traits effective leaders possess.[35] Researchers have also found that effective leaders develop persuasive arguments and are comfortable expressing their ideas to others.[36] Although many leaders do seem to have traits or special skills that can enhance their ability to influence others, just having these traits does not mean you will be an effective leader. Many of these attributes that researchers have found may be important, but they are not sufficient to make a leader effective. Another research study found support for two of the Communication Principles for a Lifetime that we've presented in this book: Effective leaders are self-aware and adapt to the people they lead and the context in which they lead.[37] But these traits alone will not ensure effective leadership behavior. Leadership is more complicated than that.

Functional Approach

Rather than identifying personality characteristics or other traits, the **functional approach to leadership** categorizes the essential leadership behaviors or functions that need to be performed to enhance the workings of a group. According to the functional approach, there are two broad leadership functions: (1) task functions and (2) process functions. These two functions should look familiar. They are similar to the types of group roles that we discussed in the last chapter.

---

trait approach to leadership
A view of leadership that identifies specific qualities or characteristics of effective leaders.

functional approach to leadership
A view of leadership that identifies the key task and process roles that need to be performed in a group.

Task functions include behaviors that help the group or team get the work done. Whether the leader is appointed or elected, one of the responsibilities of leaders is to ensure that the group completes the task it is tackling. The functional approach to leadership suggests that several people can share the leadership functions. These are some of the jobs that often need to be done:

- Helping to set the group's agenda
- Recording what the group does
- Determining when meetings begin and end
- Preparing and distributing handouts
- Initiating or proposing new ideas
- Seeking and giving information
- Suggesting options
- Elaborating on the ideas of others
- Evaluating ideas

In most groups, these key functions are assumed by many if not most group members. A group member who rarely helps with any of these tasks often earns the uncoveted title of "slacker."

Process functions are the second major type of function leaders assume in groups. Process leaders help maintain a harmonious group climate by fostering amiable relationships in the group and encourage team members to share information with one another. They seek to maintain a friendly environment that promotes honest, frank discussion. Process leaders have "people skills." They listen sensitively to others and are observant of nonverbal cues. They focus on managing relationships by adapting to the needs of individual members. Another key process leadership task is to seek support from people and resources outside the team. An effective team leader keeps the team informed about how external influences affect the team's work goals.[38] Although a single person can perform all these functions, just as with task leadership, more than likely several people will help maintain the group's process. Specific process roles include the following:

- Energizing the team by encouraging team members to keep at it
- Mediating conflict
- Compromising or helping others to compromise
- Gatekeeping: monitoring discussion to ensure that some members don't talk too much and others too little

In most groups or teams, these process roles are not formally assigned. Although some of the task functions may be explicitly assigned to others ("Daria, would you make copies of this report?"), process roles are assumed when needed; they emerge based on the needs of the group and the personality, skills, sensitivity, and past experiences of the group members who are present. It is unlikely that you will start a meeting by saying, "Okay, Janice, you're in charge of settling the arguments between Ken and Daryl. And Carl, you try to encourage Muriel and Russell to talk more." Effective leaders are on the lookout for opportunities to enhance the overall climate of the group; they try to catch people doing something right and then offer sincere praise and recognition.

Styles Approach

The **styles approach to leadership** suggests that leaders operate in one of three primary styles: (1) authoritarian, (2) democratic, or (3) laissez-faire. The methods used to influence group members usually fall into one of these broad categories, outlined in Table 10.2.[39]

Authoritarian leaders influence by giving orders and controlling others. Dictators and military officers assume this leadership style. But you don't have to be in the military or living in a dictatorship to experience an authoritarian leadership style. Perhaps you've felt like mumbling, "Who put *her* in charge?" during a group meeting. Or

3. Nonverbal
4. Listen and Respond

task function
A leadership behavior that helps a group accomplish its job.

process function
A leadership behavior that helps maintain a positive group climate.

styles approach to leadership
A view of leadership that identifies three methods of interacting when leading others: authoritarian, democratic, and laissez-faire.

authoritarian leader
One who leads by directing, controlling, telling, and ordering others.

TABLE 10.2 Leadership Styles

Authoritarian	Democratic	Laissez-Faire
The leader makes all policy decisions.	The leader discusses all policy decisions with group members. The group makes decisions by consensus.	The leader gives minimal direction to discussions of policy decisions. Group members must initiate discussions about policy and procedures.
The leader determines what will happen one step at a time; future steps are unclear or uncertain.	The group discusses what steps need to be taken. Group members work together to develop both short-term and long-term action steps.	The leader may supply information about what steps need to be taken, if asked. The leader does not volunteer information.
The leader tells people what to do.	The leader serves as a facilitator to develop a collaborative approach to accomplishing the group's work.	The leader does not participate in making work assignments.

maybe you have observed that some action needed to be taken and asked someone in the group to do what you thought was needed. As we discussed, groups need a certain amount of structure. The authoritarian leader assumes he or she knows the type and amount of structure the group needs and proceeds to tell others what to do. Authoritarian leaders may be self-aware and may use appropriate verbal and nonverbal messages, but they are not always known for listening and responding to others; they also may not be worried about adapting their messages to those whom they lead. They often speak and expect others to follow. Of the three primary leadership styles, the authoritarian leader is least effective over a long period of time.[40] Yet when a group or team experiences increased stress, a decisive leader is perceived as more charismatic.[41] Group members don't like an authoritarian leader all of the time, but they may tolerate or even appreciate a bold, charismatic leader when there's a need for someone to make an important decision quickly.

The **democratic leader,** as you might guess from the name, consults with the group before issuing edicts. The democratic leader listens and adapts messages to others. This type of leader seeks to join in the process of influencing without bulldozing or shoving the group into action it may resent. Sometimes formal votes are taken in larger groups or assemblies; but in smaller groups, the leader or leaders gauge the reaction of the group through dialogue and nonverbal cues. The democratic leader leads by developing a consensus, rather than telling people what to do or think.

The **laissez-faire leader** takes a hands-off, laid-back approach to influencing. This type of leader shies away from actively influencing the group. He or she influences only when pushed to lead. Like the authoritarian leader, this type of leader often does not adapt to the needs of the group. A laissez-faire approach is easiest to spot when an elected or appointed leader simply won't lead. Some laissez-faire leaders fear making a mistake. Others just want to be liked and don't want to ruffle anyone's feathers. But as the slogan goes, "Not to decide is to decide." The laissez-faire leader is influencing the group by his or her silence or inactivity. The team may have a problem to unravel, but the laissez-faire leader is reluctant to act.

Which leadership style works best? It depends. During times of crisis, a group needs a decisive leader who can help manage uncertainty and provide appropriate structure.[42] During a military battle, the commander doesn't ask for a democratic vote; someone needs to lead the group to take decisive action. If the group's task is to solve a problem or make a decision collaboratively, then the democratic leadership style is what the group needs. An authoritarian or dictatorial leader may squelch the free flow of ideas needed to analyze issues and identify a solution. If a group's goal is primarily social or creative, a laissez-faire leader may be best. Rather than needing structure and agendas to come up with a creative idea, such a group may function best with no direct influence from a leader.

democratic leader
One who leads by developing a consensus among group members; a leader who asks for input and then uses the input when leading and making decisions.

laissez-faire leader
One who fails to lead or who leads or exerts influence only when asked or directed by the group.

The effective leader adapts his or her style to fit the needs of the group and the task at hand. The principle of adapting to others gives rise to the situational approach to leadership. Remember, leadership in groups and teams is usually shared by several people. Even when someone has been appointed or elected to be "the leader," leadership roles are often assumed by several group members.

Situational Approach

The **situational approach to leadership** views leadership as an interactive process in which such factors as culture, time limitations, group member personalities, and the work the group needs to do determine a particular style of leadership. Sometimes a group needs a strong, authoritarian leader to make decisions quickly so that the group can achieve its goal. Although a democratic leadership style is preferred by most groups, leaders sometimes need to be more assertive, especially in times of crisis or high uncertainty.

Groups with highly structured goals and a high level of stress may operate best with a more authoritarian leadership style. For example, a military troop experiences high stress during combat, and the task is quite clearly structured—survive. In this situation, the group needs decisive authoritarian leadership. But a book club that is trying to select its next reading selection has less structured goals (there are many possible options) and a less stressful situation (no one is shooting at them!). This less structured and less stressful task calls for a more participative democratic style of leadership. So, according to the situational approach, the answer to the question "What's the best leadership style?" is "It depends."[43]

One simple rule for determining your leadership style is this: When the leader emerges naturally from the group or leads a one-time-only group, then the group will permit him or her to be more directive. If the group will be together for some time and the quality of group relations is important to the functioning of the group, a more participative, democratic leadership style is in order.[44]

Regardless of which style of leadership you find yourself adopting, given the increased use of virtual teams it's likely that you'll have the opportunity to lead groups that don't meet face to face. What are the best practices for leading a virtual team, which may be dispersed around your building, city, state, or country or even around the globe? A team of communication scholars has summarized the research and made the recommendations in Table 10.3 for leading a virtual team.[45]

Transformational Leadership

One of the newest leadership approaches to emerge is called the **transformational approach to leadership**.[46] The transformational leader influences the group or organization by *transforming* the group—giving it a new vision, energizing or realigning the group culture, or giving the group a new structure. The leader leads by helping the group see all the possibilities within the group. The transformational leader also develops a relationship with those whom he or she leads.[47] Author Peter Senge suggests three fundamental skills of transformational leadership: (1) Build a shared vision, (2) challenge existing ways of thinking, and (3) be a systems thinker—help a group or team see that everything is connected to everything else.[48] Emerging research suggests that transformational leaders can enhance team cohesiveness and improve perceptions of team performance.[49] They achieve these benefits by linking with other groups and teams either inside or outside the organization; they help the group span boundaries and stay connected with issues and forces that influence the group.[50] Another skill of transformational leaders is the ability to help a team or organization grow and develop by encouraging new ideas. Transformational leaders help teams adopt new ideas and information. Teams that emphasize learning do a better job of both accomplishing the task and fostering positive, supportive interpersonal relationships.[51]

Articulating a collective vision is an important part of what a transformational leader does. An authoritarian leader would just tell the group, "Here's your vision; now

---

situational approach to leadership
A view of leadership as an interactive process in which a leader gauges how to lead based on such factors as the quality of the relationships among group members, the power of the leader, the nature of the task, and the maturity of the group.

transformational approach to leadership
A view of leadership that defines a leader as one who leads by shaping the vision of the group and by developing trust through quality interpersonal relationships with group members.

TABLE 10.3 Recommendations for Leading a Virtual Team

What Virtual Team Leaders Should Do	Best Practices for Leading a Virtual Team
Maintain trust	• Be aware of team norms. • Revise and adjust team norms when needed. • Make sure no geographic area suffers more than others (for example, one team should not always be the one that has to be up in the middle of the night to participate in virtual meetings).
Appreciate diversity	• Let people use e-mail and other asynchronous means to express ideas so that someone with a different cultural perspective has a chance to think about a message before responding. • Rotate team members so that everyone has a chance to work with others from a variety of cultural and ethnic backgrounds. • Develop a directory of team-member expertise so that members know the strengths of other members.
Manage meeting structure	• At the beginning of an electronic meeting, allow time for relationship building; encourage meeting participants to engage in "off-task" talk, communicating about personal information. • During the meeting, ensure that every person is heard from and that all are engaged and participating in the meeting. • Shortly after the meeting, have the meeting minutes distributed to each participant.
Use technology to monitor team progress	• Have team members provide progress reports via e-mail. • Have team members talk to one another during synchronous, real-time meetings so that they can ask each other questions about progress reports.
Enhance the external visibility of the team	• Provide periodic reports to the team sponsor or supervisor. • Use a web page to summarize the ongoing progress of the team.
Reward team members	• Hold virtual reward ceremonies; with all team members logged on or "present," provide rewards and recognition to both individuals and the entire team. • Recognize good work at the beginning and end of team meetings. • Make sure each team member's "real-location" supervisor is aware of the excellent work the team member is doing.

1. Aware
4. Listen and Respond

get to work." The democratic leader would ask, "What vision do you want?" The laissez-faire leader would do nothing about a vision unless asked to do something. The situational leader would say, "Let me see what type of group I'm leading and listen to group members, and then I'll share a vision." The transformational leader paints a picture of the future for the group by getting to know individual members in the group. Drawing on the approaches of both the democratic leader and the situational leader, the transformational leader leads by establishing quality interpersonal relationships with others. Transformational leaders provide inspiration, motivation, and intellectual stimulation for the group by being aware of individual needs. A wise leader will also consider the cultural backgrounds of those whom she or he leads. Research supports the important role of culture in influencing the style of leadership that seems to be best suited to a team.[52] A group with a collective cultural framework seems to appreciate more participative styles of leadership.

Transformational leadership is less a set of prescribed skills or techniques than a general philosophy that says people can be trusted and can be motivated to achieve important goals if they have someone they can trust to help them see the possibilities. Transformational leaders like to think of themselves as coaches or mentors rather than leaders who dictate or even just facilitate interaction; they are sometimes viewed as the "guide on the side" rather than the "sage on the stage."

Can transformational leadership skills—or any leadership skills—be taught, the way you can teach someone to drive a car? Some suggest that experience is the best

> ## Recap
>
> ### Leadership Approaches
>
> | Approach to Leadership | Guiding Principle |
> |---|---|
> | Trait | Leaders possess certain traits or characteristics that contribute to leadership effectiveness. |
> | Functional | Leaders influence others through two primary functions:
• Task functions, which help accomplish the work
• Process functions, which help establish a positive climate |
> | Styles | Leadership is enacted in three primary styles:
• Authoritarian leaders direct and control others.
• Democratic leaders solicit input from others and seek to lead by involving others in the decisions.
• Laissez-faire leaders intentionally influence others only when asked or directed by others to lead. |
> | Situational | Leadership is an interactive process in which a leader adapts his or her approach based on such factors as
• The quality of group member relationships
• The nature of the task
• Time limitations |
> | Transformational | A leader influences others by
• Developing a shared vision
• Using listening and relationship-building skills to create a climate of trust |

teacher.[53] You can learn how to communicate, listen, relate, and solve problems, but having an opportunity to practice these skills in real-life settings may be the best way to develop your leadership skills. Whether you learn leadership skills and principles from a book or from the "school of life," the role of a good leader is that of a servant, helping others accomplish a goal. This ancient description of a wise leader offers considerable insight into what makes a leader great:

> The wicked leader the people despise.
> The good leader the people revere.
> Of the great leader the people say,
> "We did it ourselves."
>
> —Lao Tsu

Enhancing Group and Team Meetings

Humor columnist Dave Barry said, "If you had to identify, in one word, the reason why the human race has not achieved, and never will achieve, its full potential, that word would be *meetings*."[54] Meetings are an inescapable fact of life for most people and will undoubtedly be inescapable for you as well.

Why does meeting participation inspire such a negative reaction—not only from Dave Barry, but from many people? Often, it's because meeting leaders and participants have not mastered the principles we've stressed as fundamental to communication success in any context. Meetings are more productive if participants are aware of their behaviors and the behavior of others. Using and interpreting verbal and nonverbal messages effectively is also vital for meeting effectiveness, as is listening and

1. Aware
2. Verbal
3. Nonverbal
4. Listen and Respond
5. Adapt

Communication and Diversity

Differences in the Use of Time in Groups and Teams

Mark was frustrated. He was sure the meeting was supposed to start at 11:00 AM. But it was now 11:15 AM, and no one else was there. About five minutes later Gilbert arrived; Samantha showed up a few minutes after that. Then Joe arrived at about 11:30. "Where were you guys?" Mark asked, exasperated.

"Oh, we thought you knew. When we say 11:00 AM in our organization, that means we'll actually start twenty or thirty minutes after that," said Joe. While Mark now had at least some insight, he was still frustrated and puzzled. Mark and his colleagues had different assumptions about time.

Have you ever worked with people who just never quite seemed to be punctual, didn't pay attention to deadlines, and took their own sweet time getting things done? Yet other people never miss a deadline and are always punctual. One cultural characteristic that makes a difference in how we communicate in groups and teams is the way we use time.

Some people are **monochronic;** they like to do only one thing at a time, pay attention to deadlines and schedules, and make plans to use time efficiently. Others are **polychronic;** they do many things at a time, don't worry about deadlines and schedules, believe relationships are more important than work, change plans frequently, and are less concerned about deadlines than are monochronic individuals.[55]

People from North America and Northern Europe tend to be more monochronic; deadlines and timelines are valued. Research suggests that for North Americans, monitoring the clock and being aware of how much time there is to accomplish the work can enhance productivity.[56]

Latin Americans, Southern Europeans, and Middle Easterners are often more polychronic; deadlines and strict adherence to schedules are less important. Western cultures have a tendency to approach a discussion of problems in groups or teams in a linear, step-by-step manner. Structuring, scheduling, and agendas are important. In Eastern cultures, such as China and Japan, problem-solving approaches often follow a less structured, more narrative approach.[57] One team of scholars found that North Americans tend to believe that only one thing can or should be done at a time.[58] People from Latin American cultures, in contrast, are more comfortable working on multiple tasks simultaneously.

If you find you're in a group whose members have different cultural approaches to time, what should you do? Consider these suggestions:

- Don't pounce on other team members and accuse them of being laggards (or slave drivers). Let them know some of your assumptions about how the work should be done.
- Take some time to talk about those differences. Conversation and compromise can accomplish a lot when you find yourself facing cultural differences.

---

monochronic
Preferring to do one thing at a time, pay attention to deadlines and schedules, and use time efficiently.

polychronic
Preferring to do many things at once, place less emphasis on deadlines and schedules, and consider relationships to be more important than work and meeting deadlines.

responding to messages with sensitivity. Because of the complexity and uncertainty that arise when people collaborate, being able to adapt message content and message structure is essential. We conclude this chapter by providing some tips for managing one of the most likely collaborative contexts you'll encounter—meetings.

The participants at this meeting likely have all three of the most common goals of meetings: giving information, discussing information, and taking action.

What specific problems occur most frequently in meetings? Based on a survey of meeting participants, the most common meeting "sin" is getting off the subject.[59] The second biggest problem is not having clear goals or a meeting agenda. Meeting goers also reported that often meetings were too long, people weren't prepared, nothing really happened, meetings started late, and there were no follow-up action plans.

Meetings need two essential things in order to be effective: *structure* and *interaction*. Sound familiar? As we noted earlier in the chapter, groups also need a balance of these two things.

Many of the meeting problems we've described stem from a lack of clear structure—no written agenda, no one helping to keep the group on track. Too many unstructured interactions lead to unfocused discussion. Consequently, nothing gets done. Being prepared to adapt to the need for structure and interaction is a fundamental principle of meeting management. The essential tool for giving a meeting structure is the agenda. To manage interaction, meeting leaders need to be good facilitators of talk. We'll look more closely at how to provide the two essentials of structure and interaction.

Manage Meeting Structure

As we just noted, the essential weapon to combat disorganized, rambling meetings is a clear, well-developed agenda. An **agenda** is a list of the key issues, ideas, and information that will be discussed, in the order of discussion. How do you develop a well-crafted agenda? Consider these three steps.

Step One: Determine Your Meeting Goals
Every meeting seeks to accomplish something. (If you don't have something to accomplish, don't hold a meeting!) Most meetings have one or more of the following three goals: (1) giving information, (2) discussing information, and (3) taking action.

- *Giving information.* An information-giving meeting is like a briefing or a series of short speeches. If the only task is to share information, you may not really need a meeting at all—a written memo or an e-mail message will suffice. But if you want to share information with others face to face to emphasize its importance, then giving information is an appropriate primary meeting goal.
- *Discussing information.* An information-discussion meeting is one in which there is considerable give and take. The key to this type of meeting is not to let it become a series of long-winded speeches. Also, if you're not careful, discussions digress off the topic. The meeting leader or meeting participants should be aware of the goals of the discussion so that the comments remain relevant.
- *Taking action.* A meeting may involve making a decision, solving a problem, or implementing a decision or solution. If the purpose of the meeting is to take action, it's helpful if group members know before they arrive for the meeting that they will be asked to take some action.

Step Two: Identify What Needs to Be Discussed to Achieve the Goal
After you have determined your goal(s), you need to determine how to structure the meeting to achieve the goal. What topics need to be covered to achieve the goal? What information do you need? What issues do you need to focus on? Brainstorm answers to these questions, but don't worry about the precise order of the items yet; focus on organizing the agenda after you know what you need to discuss.

Step Three: Organize the Agenda
Once you have identified your meeting goals (giving information, discussing information, taking action) and assessed what you need to talk about, take time to arrange the items in the most effective way to achieve your goals. There are several strategies for organizing effective meetings.[60]

- Organize the agenda around your meeting goals. If you're meeting to solve a problem, you could use the five problem-solving steps as an agenda-setting guide: (1)

agenda
A written plan for achieving the goals during a group meeting, which typically includes items for discussion, action, and information.

identify and define the problem, (2) analyze the problem, (3) generate creative options, (4) select the best option, and (5) take action. A single meeting may focus on only one or two of those steps; don't feel you have to cram all five problem-solving steps into every meeting.

- Use subheads of "Information Items," "Discussion Items," and "Action Items" as you construct your agenda to signal to group members the goal of the discussion, as shown in the sample meeting agenda.
- Consider putting your most important agenda item first, because usually what is introduced first takes the most time.
- There may be times when you will want to put your most challenging issue for discussion in the middle of the meeting; this gives the group a chance to get oriented at the beginning and ease out of the discussion at the end.[61]
- Consider making your first agenda item something that will immediately involve all meeting participants in active discussion. If you start with routine reports (a common practice), you establish a norm of passivity, and boredom is the usual result.
- If you are going to discuss a conflict-producing topic, you may want to put that agenda item after an issue on which you think the group will reach agreement; groups may be more likely to reach agreement on a contentious issue if they have already reached agreement on another point.
- Start the meeting by asking meeting participants if they have any other agenda items to consider. That way you aren't as likely to be surprised by people who want to add something after you've planned the meeting agenda.
- After you've prepared your agenda, estimate how long you think the group will take to discuss each agenda item. Most groups take more time than you would expect to talk about issues and ideas.

A sample agenda is shown below. Note that the meeting has clear goals. Also note how many of the agenda items are phrased as questions. Questions give an agenda focus and help to manage discussion.

Sample Meeting Agenda

Meeting Goals:

1. Discuss new product proposal: evaluate the pros and cons
2. Decide whether to implement the personnel policy and mentor program
3. Receive updates from committees

    I. Discussion Items
        A. How should we revise today's agenda?
        B. Identify new problems: What new issues or problems have you identified?
        C. React to new product team proposal (distributed by e-mail): What are the pros and cons of the proposal?

    II. Action Items
        A. Should we approve the new personnel policy (distributed by e-mail)?
        B. Issue: Should we implement the new mentor program? If so, what should the program policies be?

    III. Information Items
        A. New employee orientation report
        B. Planning committee report
        C. Finance committee report
        D. Announcements

Recap

Making Meeting Agendas Useful

Potential Meeting Agenda Problem	Suggested Meeting Agenda Strategy
Meeting participants tend to spend more time on the first or second agenda item.	Make sure the early agenda items are something the group needs to spend time on.
Meeting participants want to talk, even if the meeting leader wants them to just listen.	Take advantage of the desire to participate by inviting input and discussion early in the meeting rather than trying to squelch discussion or interrupt group members.
Meeting participants aren't prepared. They haven't done their "homework."	Take a few minutes for silent reading. Let members get up to speed by reviewing information or quickly looking at key pieces of data.
Meeting participants won't stick to the agenda.	Continue to remind the group of the agenda and the overall goal of the meeting. Make sure to distribute a written agenda ahead of the meeting.
There is an agenda item that may produce conflict and disagreement.	Help the group develop a sense of success by putting one or more noncontroversial items on the agenda ahead of the item that may produce conflict. Build on the group's ability to reach agreement.

When your job is to lead the meeting, you have several specific tasks to perform, including the following:

1. Call the group together; find out when is the best time to meet (finding time is often a major problem for busy people).
2. Develop an agenda, using the steps already described.
3. Determine whether there is a **quorum**—the minimum number of persons who must be present at a meeting to conduct business.
4. Call the meeting to order.
5. Use a flip chart, chalkboard, or dry-erase board to summarize meeting progress; written notes of the meeting become the "group mind" and help keep the group structured.
6. Decide when to take a vote.
7. Prepare a final report or delegate to a group member the preparation of a report or minutes.

Manage Meeting Interaction

Interaction, as you recall, is the back-and-forth dialogue and discussion in which participants engage during meetings. Without interaction, meetings would be like a monologue, a speech, or a seminar, rather than a lively discussion. But too much unfocused interaction can result in a disorganized, chaotic discussion. To keep a meeting on track, meeting leaders and participants need facilitation skills. The most important facilitation skills include being a gatekeeper, using metadiscussion, monitoring discussion time, and structuring discussion techniques to keep discussion focused.

- *Use gatekeeping skills.* A gatekeeper helps to encourage less-talkative members to participate and tries to limit long-winded contributions by other group members. Gatekeepers need to be good listeners so that they can help manage the flow of conversation. Gatekeepers make such comments as "Ashley, we haven't heard your

quorum
The minimum number of persons who must be present at a meeting to conduct business.

4. Listen and Respond

2. Verbal

metadiscussion
Discussion about the discussion process; comments that help the group remain focused on the goals of the group or that point out how the group is doing its work.

"I" message
A message in which you state your perspective or point of view.

"you" message
A message that is likely to create defensiveness in others because it emphasizes how another person has created a problem, rather than describing the problem from one's own perspective ("I" message).

ideas yet. Won't you share your thoughts with us?" or "Mike, thanks for sharing, but I'd like to hear what others have to say." Polite, tactful invitations to talk or limit talk usually work. You may need to speak privately with a chronic oververbalizer to let him or her know that you'd appreciate a more balanced discussion.

- *Use metadiscussion.* **Metadiscussion** literally means "discussion about discussion."[62] It's a comment about the discussion process rather than about the topic under consideration. Metadiscussional statements include "I'm not following this conversation. What is our goal?" or "Can someone summarize what we've accomplished so far?" or "Peggy, I'm not sure I understand how your observation relates to our meeting goal." These comments contain information and advice about the communication *process*, rather than about the issues that are being discussed.

  Metadiscussional phrases are helpful ways to keep the team or group focused on the task. Obviously, metadiscussional statements should not be phrased to personally attack others. Don't just blurt out "You're off task" or "Oh, let's not talk about that anymore." Instead, use tactful ways of letting other group members know you'd like to return to the issues at hand. Use "I" messages rather than "you" messages to bring the group back on track. An **"I" message** begins with the word *I*, such as "I am not sure where we are in our discussion" or "I am lost here." A **"you" message** is a way of phrasing a message that makes others feel defensive—for example, "You're not following the agenda" or "Your point doesn't make any sense." Another way to express these same ideas, but with less of a negative edge, is to use "I" messages such as "I'm not sure where we are on the agenda" or "I'm not sure I understand how your point relates to the issue we are discussing." The ability to carry on metadiscussion is an exceptionally powerful skill, because you can offer metadiscussional statements even if you are not the appointed leader.

- *Monitor time.* Being sensitive to the time the group is spending on an issue is yet another skill necessary to manage meeting interaction. Think of your agenda as a map, helping you plan where you want to go. Think of the clock as your gas gauge, telling you the amount of fuel you have to get where you want to go. In a meeting, keeping one eye on the clock and one eye on the agenda is analogous to focusing on the map and the gas gauge on a car trip. If you are running low on fuel (time), you will need to either get more gas (budget more time) or recognize that you will not get where you want to go. Begin each meeting by asking how long members can meet. If you face two or three crucial agenda items and one-third of your group has to leave in an hour, you may need to reshuffle your agenda to make sure you can achieve your goals.

- *Use structure to manage interaction.* Another way to manage interaction is to use some of the prescriptive structures that we talked about earlier. For example, using silent brainstorming is a way to gain maximum participation from everyone. Yet another strategy is to ask people to come to the meeting with written responses to questions that you posed in the agenda, which group members received in advance of the meeting. This signals that you want people to prepare for the meeting rather than doing their "homework" at the meeting. An essential task of the meeting facilitator is to orchestrate meaningful interaction during the meeting so that all group or team members have the opportunity to share. Another structured method of inviting involvement is to have group members first write individually and then share their ideas with the group. Having members write before speaking is like providing them with a script, which can be effective in garnering contributions from *all* group members—not just the people who talk the most or who aren't shy about speaking up.

One of the best ways to ensure appropriate interaction as a meeting participant when you are not assigned the specific role of leader is to consider the following suggestions from Roger Mosvick and Robert Nelson in their book *We've Got to Start Meeting Like This!*.[63]

- Organize what you say. Don't ramble.
- Speak to the point. Make sure your contributions are relevant to the goal.
- Make one point at a time.
- Speak clearly and forcefully. Weak, timid suggestions mumbled to the group will probably not be listened to.
- Support your ideas with evidence. Don't just assert opinion without data or expert opinion backing you up.
- Listen. Listen. Listen. Connect your comments to those of others.

What are the best strategies to make yourself a valuable meeting leader or participant? The five Communication Principles for a Lifetime that we've emphasized throughout the book will serve you well. In general, be aware of your own behavior and the behavior of others. Monitor your verbal and nonverbal messages to make sure you are making comments relevant to the task at hand, but also be sensitive to the needs of the people in your group. You develop that sensitivity by listening to others and thoughtfully responding. Ineffective meeting participants make little effort to link their comments to what others are saying. They also don't adapt to the messages of others. Effective communicators adapt what they say and do to help achieve the goals of the group.

2. Verbal

4. Listen and Respond

1. Aware
2. Verbal
3. Nonverbal
4. Listen and Respond
5. Adapt

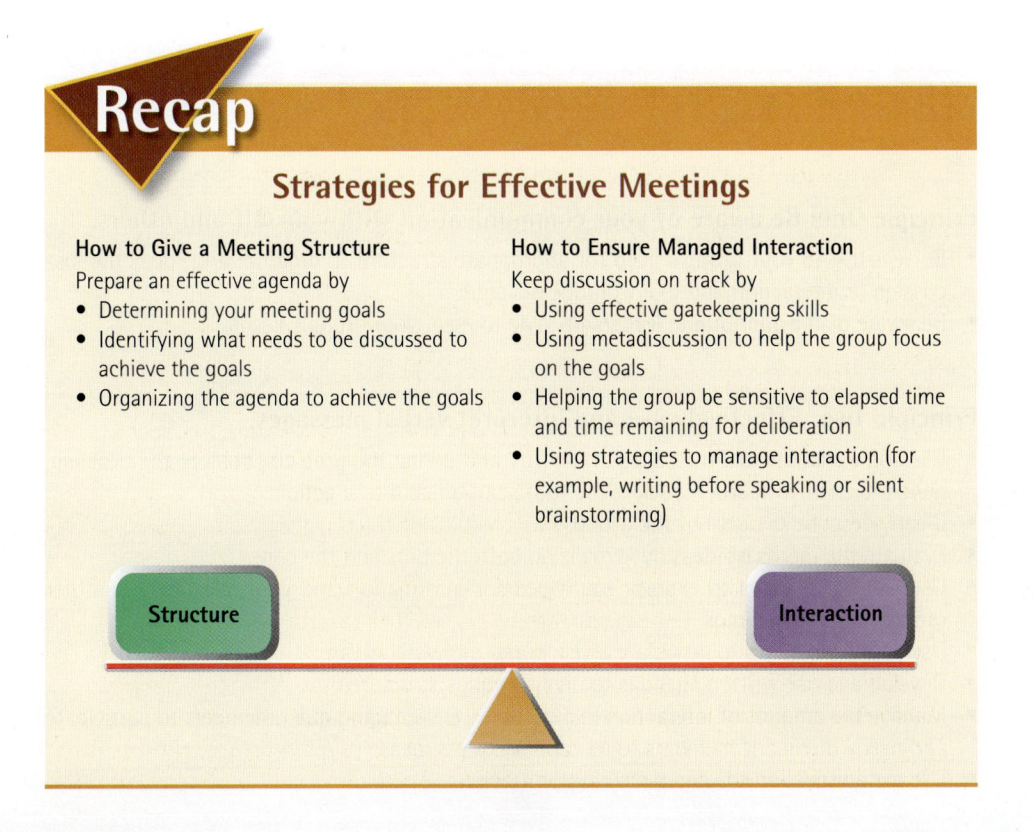

Recap

Strategies for Effective Meetings

How to Give a Meeting Structure
Prepare an effective agenda by
- Determining your meeting goals
- Identifying what needs to be discussed to achieve the goals
- Organizing the agenda to achieve the goals

How to Ensure Managed Interaction
Keep discussion on track by
- Using effective gatekeeping skills
- Using metadiscussion to help the group focus on the goals
- Helping the group be sensitive to elapsed time and time remaining for deliberation
- Using strategies to manage interaction (for example, writing before speaking or silent brainstorming)

Structure — Interaction

Communication and Technology

Participating in Virtual Meetings

A virtual meeting occurs when you use the Internet or some other electronic means of connecting with others, rather than meeting face to face. Increased globalization of the economy, rising travel costs, and technological advances in electronic collaboration make it likely that you will hold meetings in cyberspace. What are ways to maximize your e-collaboration? Here are several research-supported tips to help you make the most of mediated meetings.[64]

- *Get down to business early; don't procrastinate.* Because it sometimes takes longer for team members to get to know one another when meeting virtually, it's a good idea to dive right into your work agenda. The conversation that you have about the issues and topics facing the team will help you develop relationships with other team members.
- *Communicate frequently.* Don't hesitate to send virtual meeting members short notes and messages. Resist the temptation to hold on to information until you have a longer message. Frequent communication helps virtual meeting participants get to know one another.
- *Work on several parts of your agenda at once.* Researchers suggest that it's easier to multitask when participating in mediated meetings than when communicating face to face. So it's OK for the team leader to have some team members identify the problem, others research the history of the problem, and still others gather background information about the issue you're discussing. Divide and conquer.
- *Let other members know that you have read their messages.* When other team members send you e-mail messages, reply with a short note saying "Thanks" or "Got it" or "I understand." Acknowledging other members' messages helps develop relational rapport and provides necessary feedback that members are involved and engaged in the communication process.
- *Be explicit about what you are doing and thinking.* Since team members may not be able to see what you are doing and won't know your thoughts, provide brief updates about what you are doing (or not doing), as well as thoughts and ideas you have about your project. Team members shouldn't have to guess what you're thinking; tell them.
- *Set and keep deadlines.* Deliver what you promise. Having both short-term and long-term deadlines provides needed structure for the work that you are doing. Celebrate when you've accomplished your short-term goals. And keep tabs on your progress toward longer-term outcomes.

PRINCIPLES FOR A LIFETIME
Enhancing Your Skills

1. Aware

Principle One: Be aware of your communication with yourself and others.
- Be sensitive to your group's need for appropriate structure to organize and focus the discussion or interaction and to encourage dialogue.
- Be aware of the appropriate leadership style to meet your group's needs.

2. Verbal

Principle Two: Effectively use and interpret verbal messages.
- Use appropriate verbal messages to identify and define the problem, analyze the problem, generate creative solutions, select the best solution, and take action.
- Clearly describe the goal of the group.
- Evaluate the merits of ideas by verbalizing both the pros and the cons.
- Use verbal messages to express your need for information and your sensitivity to other group members' feelings.
- Use verbal messages to articulate a vision and motivate a team.
- Develop and use written agendas to give meetings structure.
- Manage the amount of interaction in a group by encouraging quiet members to participate and overly dominant members to let others express ideas.
- Use metadiscussion to keep a meeting on track.

Principle Three: Effectively use and interpret nonverbal messages.

- Use appropriate nonverbal messages to establish and maintain a positive group climate.
- Do your best to avoid nonverbally expressing your evaluation of others' ideas when brainstorming.
- Communicate your sensitivity to other group members through your nonverbal behavior.
- Use eye contact and other nonverbal cues to regulate the flow of interaction in group and team meetings.

Principle Four: Listen and respond thoughtfully to others.

- Listen to other group members to determine whether your group is accomplishing the appropriate group functions.
- Listen and respond to others to express your sensitivity to others' ideas and opinions.
- Listen and respond to others to provide appropriate leadership.
- Listen and respond to provide appropriate contributions to group meetings and problem-solving discussions.

Principle Five: Appropriately adapt messages to others.

- Adapt your comments to ensure that your group spends an appropriate amount of time on the six functions of effective groups.
- Adapt your leadership and group membership styles to achieve the goals of the group.
- Adapt your messages to help the group identify, define, and analyze the problem; create solutions; select the best solution; and take action.
- Adapt your messages to give group meetings appropriate structure and to foster interaction.

Summary

Specific strategies can help groups and teams operate at peak performance levels. Research has identified several essential functions that, when carried out in a group, enhance group performance. Effective group members identify the goal, develop a results-driven structure, gather and use information effectively, develop options, evaluate ideas, and are sensitive to group social and relationship concerns.

Groups perform best if they have appropriate structure to make an often-bumpy process smoother. Although group communication researchers have identified different steps, methods, and procedures, there is no single series of steps that will ensure high performance. In his book *How We Think*, John Dewey described five problem-solving steps: (1) Identify and define the problem, (2) analyze the problem, (3) generate creative solutions, (4) select the best solution, and (5) take action.

High-performing groups have competent group leaders. Researchers have devised several approaches to analyzing leadership. The trait approach to leadership seeks to identify certain characteristics or traits that all leaders possess. Ensuring good leadership is more complicated than finding leaders with just the right traits, however. The functional approach to leadership suggests that leaders need to be concerned with both task functions and group process functions. The functional leadership approach identifies specific roles that leaders should perform. A third approach to understanding leadership, the styles approach, identifies leaders as authoritarian, democratic, or laissez-faire. No one style seems to work all of the time. The situational leadership approach suggests that the best leadership style depends on a variety of factors, including the readiness of the group, the urgency of the problem, and the type of issue the group is discussing. Finally, transformational leadership is an approach that encourages leaders to help shape the vision and goals of the group by being in touch with followers. Groups can be transformed if the leaders help articulate a vision for the future that takes the group in new directions yet builds on the vision and goals of the group.

Assessing Your Knowledge

For Discussion and Review

Principle One: Be aware of your communication with yourself and others.

1. How does being aware of the amount of structure or interaction needed during group deliberation enhance group communication?

Principle Two: Effectively use and interpret verbal messages.

2. What techniques and strategies can be used to structure verbal messages during group and team collaborations?

Principle Three: Effectively use and interpret nonverbal messages.

3. What strategies or techniques can be used to discourage group members from nonverbally evaluating ideas and creative suggestions made during brainstorming sessions?

Principle Four: Listen and respond thoughtfully to others.

4. What symptoms should you listen for to detect whether groupthink is occurring in your group?

Principle Five: Appropriately adapt messages to others.

5. What is the situational approach to group and team leadership, and how can leaders appropriately adapt their messages to enhance group and team performance?

Multiple Choice

Choose the *best* answer to each of the following questions.

1. The key to making brainstorming work is to
   a. focus more on evaluating ideas and less on generating more ideas.
   b. have group or team members offer only their best ideas.
   c. focus both on evaluating ideas and on generating more ideas.
   d. focus solely on generating ideas and avoid evaluating ideas.

2. The first step in planning an effective meeting is
   a. organizing the agenda.
   b. distributing the agenda before the meeting.
   c. identifying the discussion topics.
   d. identifying the meeting goal.

3. Mary Lynn says to her group, "How long has parking been a problem on campus? Does it really affect a lot of students?" Given Mary Lynn's question, her group is most likely in what phase of the problem-solving process?
   a. identifying the problem
   b. analyzing the problem
   c. generating creative solutions
   d. selecting the best solution

4. For a group or team goal to be "elevating," it should be
   a. beyond the capabilities of the group.
   b. easily accomplished
   c. something that could not be achieved without team effort.
   d. surprising to the group members.

5. Bill is a task-oriented leader. He develops the group's agenda and does not tolerate deviations from the agenda. He assigns tasks to members and encourages them to make the decisions he prefers. Bill's style of leadership is
   a. democratic.
   b. authoritarian.
   c. laissez-faire.
   d. trait.

6. When evaluating ideas, it is best for group members to
   a. talk about the positives and negatives of any proposal.
   b. focus solely on the best suggestions.
   c. zero in on a course of action as quickly as possible.
   d. focus solely on the worst suggestions.

7. A group discussion that ends up with everybody talking at the same time is characterized by
   a. too much structure and interaction.
   b. too much structure and too little interaction.
   c. too little structure and too much interaction.
   d. too little structure and interaction.

8. Group members will tend to get defensive if you rely on
   a. "I" messages.
   b. "you" messages.
   c. metadiscussional messages.
   d. structural messages.

9. A leader who helps group members mediate conflict with one another is focusing on
   a. trait leadership.
   b. task functions.
   c. laissez-faire leadership.
   d. process functions.

10. Oftentimes, it is important for groups to talk about how they discuss issues within the group. What is this type of group discussion called?
    a. "I" message
    b. "you" message
    c. metadiscussion
    d. structure

Answers to the questions in this practice test can be found at the end of the book.

Assessing Your Skill

Assessing Group and Team Problem-Solving Competencies[65]

Use the evaluation form on pages 290–291 to assess the presence or absence of small group communication competencies in a group or team discussion. Competencies are specific behaviors that group and team members perform. This assessment form includes nine competencies organized into four general categories. Here's how to use the form:

1. Observe a group or team that is attempting to solve a problem. Write the names of the group members at the top of the form. (If the group includes more than five group members, photocopy the form so that each group member can be evaluated.)

2. When using the form, first decide whether each group member has performed each competency. Circle NO if the group member was not observed performing the competency. Circle YES if you did observe the group member performing the competency (e.g., defining the problem, analyzing the problem, identifying criteria, and so on).

3. For each competency for which you circled YES, determine how effectively the competency was performed. Use a scale from 0 to 3:

   0 = The group member performed this competency but did so inappropriately or inadequately. For example, the person observed tried to define the problem but did so poorly.
   1 = Overall, the person's performance of this competency was adequate.
   2 = The person performed this competency twice.
   3 = The person performed this competency three or more times.

4. Total the score for each group member in each of the four categories.

   The first category, *Problem-Oriented Competencies*, consists of items 1 and 2. These are behaviors that help the group or team define and analyze the problem. If a group member performed the competencies, his or her total number of points will range from 0 to 6. The more points he or she scores, the better the individual performed this competency.

   Solution-Oriented Competencies include items 3, 4, and 5; the total number of points for this category can range from 0 to 9. These competencies focus on how well the group or team member helped develop and evaluate a solution to the problem.

   Discussion Management Competencies, competencies that helped the group or team remain focused or helped the group manage interaction, are items 6 and 7. The total points for this category can range from 0 to 6.

   Relational Competencies are behaviors that focus on dealing with conflict and developing a positive, supportive group climate. Items 8 and 9 reflect this competency; points for this category can range from 0 to 6.

5. You can also assess the group's or team's overall ability to perform these competencies. The column marked "Group Assessment" can be used to record your overall impressions of how effectively the group or team behaved. Circle NO if no one in the group performed a particular competency. Circle YES if at least one person in the group or team performed this competency. Then evaluate how well the entire group performed this competency, using the scale already described.

Sometimes it is difficult to make so many judgments about group competencies by just viewing a group discussion once. Many people find that it's easier to videotape the group discussion so that they can observe it more than once.

Web Resources to Improve Your Knowledge and Skill

When you lead a meeting, you need all the help you can get. An informative web site called The Virtual Meeting Assistant provides a list of skills and strategies that adds to the discussion in this chapter about facilitating a meeting. Here's the web address: <www.ku.edu/~coms/virtual_assistant/vma/vms.htm>.

Another site that offers information to help you conduct a meeting via the Internet is <www.learnthenet.com/english/html/30conf.htm>. Here you'll find an introduction to software and other resources that will enhance your ability to conduct a virtual meeting.

COMPETENT GROUP COMMUNICATOR

Problem-Solving Group Communication Competencies	Group Member A	Group Member B
Problem-Oriented Competencies		
1. **Defined the problem** the group attempted to solve.	NO YES 0 1 2 3	NO YES 0 1 2 3
2. **Analyzed the problem** the group attempted to solve. Used relevant information, data, or evidence; discussed the causes, obstacles, history, symptoms, or significance of the problem.	NO YES 0 1 2 3	NO YES 0 1 2 3
Solution-Oriented Competencies		
3. **Identified criteria** for an appropriate solution to the problem.	NO YES 0 1 2 3	NO YES 0 1 2 3
4. **Generated solutions** or alternatives to the problem.	NO YES 0 1 2 3	NO YES 0 1 2 3
5. **Evaluated solution(s):** Identified positive or negative consequences of the proposed solutions.	NO YES 0 1 2 3	NO YES 0 1 2 3
Discussion Management Competencies		
6. **Maintained task focus:** Helped the group stay on or return to the task, issue, or topic the group was discussing.	NO YES 0 1 2 3	NO YES 0 1 2 3
7. **Managed group interaction:** Appropriately initiated and terminated discussion, contributed to the discussion, or invited others to contribute to the discussion. Didn't dominate or withdraw.	NO YES 0 1 2 3	NO YES 0 1 2 3
Relational Competencies		
8. **Managed conflict:** Appropriately and constructively helped the group stay focused on issues rather than personalities when conflict occurred.	NO YES 0 1 2 3	NO YES 0 1 2 3
9. **Maintained climate:** Offered positive verbal comments or nonverbal expressions that helped maintain a positive group climate.	NO YES 0 1 2 3	NO YES 0 1 2 3

Scoring   NO = Not observed   YES 0 = Overall inappropriate or inadequate performance of competency   1 = Overall adequate performance of competency

Problem-Oriented Competencies (0–6)
Solution-Oriented Competencies (0–9)
Discussion Management Competencies (0–6)
Relational Competencies (0–6)

Group Member C	Group Member D	Group Member E	Group Assessment
NO YES 0 1 2 3	NO YES 0 1 2 3	NO YES 0 1 2 3	NO YES 0 1 2 3
NO YES 0 1 2 3	NO YES 0 1 2 3	NO YES 0 1 2 3	NO YES 0 1 2 3
NO YES 0 1 2 3	NO YES 0 1 2 3	NO YES 0 1 2 3	NO YES 0 1 2 3
NO YES 0 1 2 3	NO YES 0 1 2 3	NO YES 0 1 2 3	NO YES 0 1 2 3
NO YES 0 1 2 3	NO YES 0 1 2 3	NO YES 0 1 2 3	NO YES 0 1 2 3
NO YES 0 1 2 3	NO YES 0 1 2 3	NO YES 0 1 2 3	NO YES 0 1 2 3
NO YES 0 1 2 3	NO YES 0 1 2 3	NO YES 0 1 2 3	NO YES 0 1 2 3
NO YES 0 1 2 3	NO YES 0 1 2 3	NO YES 0 1 2 3	NO YES 0 1 2 3
NO YES 0 1 2 3	NO YES 0 1 2 3	NO YES 0 1 2 3	NO YES 0 1 2 3

2 = Person performed this competency twice

3 = Person performed this competency three or more times

Unit Four
Presentational Speaking

Jacob Lawrence. "The Library," 1960. Tempera on fiberboard, 24" × 29 7/8". Artwork © 2008 The Jacob and Gwendolyn Lawrence Foundation, Seattle/Artists Rights Society (ARS), New York. Photo credit: Photograph courtesy of Gwendolyn Knight Lawrence/Art Resource, NY.

Freedom of speech is of no use to a man who has nothing to say.

Franklin D. Roosevelt

Chapter 11

Developing Your Presentation

Chapter Outline

- An Overview of the Presentational Speaking Process
- Understanding Speaker Anxiety
- Managing Speaker Anxiety
- Selecting and Narrowing Your Topic
- Identifying Your Purpose
- Developing Your Central Idea
- Generating Main Ideas
- Gathering Supporting Material
- Summary

Chapter Objectives

After studying this chapter, you should be able to

1. Explain the practical value of presentational speaking skills.
2. List the nine components of the audience-centered public speaking model.
3. Define speaker anxiety, explain what causes it, and offer at least three suggestions for managing it.
4. Suggest three questions and three strategies that can help a speaker discover a topic.
5. List the three general purposes for presentations.
6. Explain how to write an audience-centered specific-purpose statement.
7. List and explain four criteria for a central idea.
8. Explain how to generate main ideas from a central idea.
9. Describe three sources and five types of supporting material for a presentation and offer guidelines for using each type effectively.
10. List six types of library resources.

A good friend of ours who has lived in Hong Kong for several years recently remarked that she found traveling back to the United States exhausting. Her reason? Not so much the long plane trip or the thirteen-hour time difference, but, as she explained, "When I begin to hear airport public announcements in English instead of Cantonese, I suddenly feel compelled to pay attention to every word. All that listening wears me out!"

Few of us can take for granted that others will listen to us merely because we are speaking their native language. However, when we study the presentational speaking process and learn its component skills and principles, we certainly increase the likelihood that others will listen to us out of genuine, compelling interest.

Far from being a rare talent possessed only by an inspired few, public speaking, or presentational speaking, is a teachable, learnable process—a process of developing, supporting, organizing, and orally presenting ideas. It is a process that has much in common with expository writing. Yet preparing an oral presentation and writing a paper are not exactly the same. For one thing, the language you use when you speak is less formal and more conversational than the language you use when you write. You are likely to use shorter words, more first- and second-person pronouns (*I* and *you*), and shorter sentences when you speak than when you write.

Second, while a writer can rely on parenthetical citations and Works Cited pages to document his or her sources, a speaker must document sources orally, within the text of the speech itself. And third, perhaps the most important way in which presentational speaking and writing differ is that speaking is more redundant than writing. What might seem unnecessary repetition in a paper is essential in a presentation. A person listening to a presentation does not have the luxury of rereading something he or she missed or did not understand the first time. Nor can the listener rely on paragraphing to indicate when a speaker is moving on to another point or idea. Instead, the listener must depend on the speaker to repeat important ideas and to provide oral organizational cues, such as transitions, previews, and summaries. Certainly you can apply to presentational speaking some of the skills and strategies you have learned as a writer. But you will also learn new and sometimes slightly different ones. As with the writing process, the more you practice, the easier and more "natural" the presentational speaking process will become.

> **public speaking (presentational speaking)**
> A teachable, learnable process of developing, supporting, organizing, and orally presenting ideas.

Still not convinced that you want or need to learn presentational speaking? Perhaps you will feel more motivated if you consider that the skills you will develop as you study presentational speaking will be of practical use in the future. They will give you an edge in other college courses that require oral presentations. They may help you convince some current or future boss that you deserve a raise. And they may even land you a job. Ethernet inventor Bob Metcalf recently told a group of MIT students (who expected, no doubt, to hear technology-related advice) that "Communication is key" to their success.[1] Young entrepreneurs in technical fields need presentation skills, Metcalf pointed out, to "secure funding, win customers, recruit talented employees, and talk with the media."

The communication skills that Metcalf was talking about are grounded in the five Communication Principles for a Lifetime and can be learned and practiced in the various stages of the presentational speaking process. Let's begin our discussion of presentational speaking with an overview of that process. Then—because even if you are fully convinced of the value of learning to speak in public, you may still feel nervous about delivering a presentation—we will explore why you feel that way and offer suggestions for managing your anxiety and developing confidence. In the final pages of this chapter, we will focus more closely on the first five stages of the public speaking process: selecting and narrowing your topic; identifying your purpose; developing a central idea; generating main ideas; and gathering supporting material for your presentation.

An Overview of the Presentational Speaking Process

Chances are that you didn't complete a driver-education course before you got behind the wheel of a car for the first time. Similarly, you don't have to read an entire book on public speaking before you give your first presentation. An overview of the presentational speaking process can help you with your early assignments, even if you have to speak before you have a chance to read Chapters 12 through 15.

Figure 11.1 illustrates the presentational speaking process. Viewing the model as a clock, you find "Select and narrow topic" at 12 o'clock. From this stage, the process proceeds clockwise in the direction of the arrows, to "Deliver presentation." Each stage is one of the tasks of the public speaker:

1. Select and narrow topic.
2. Identify purpose.
3. Develop central idea.
4. Generate main ideas.
5. Gather supporting material.
6. Organize presentation.
7. Rehearse presentation.
8. Deliver presentation.

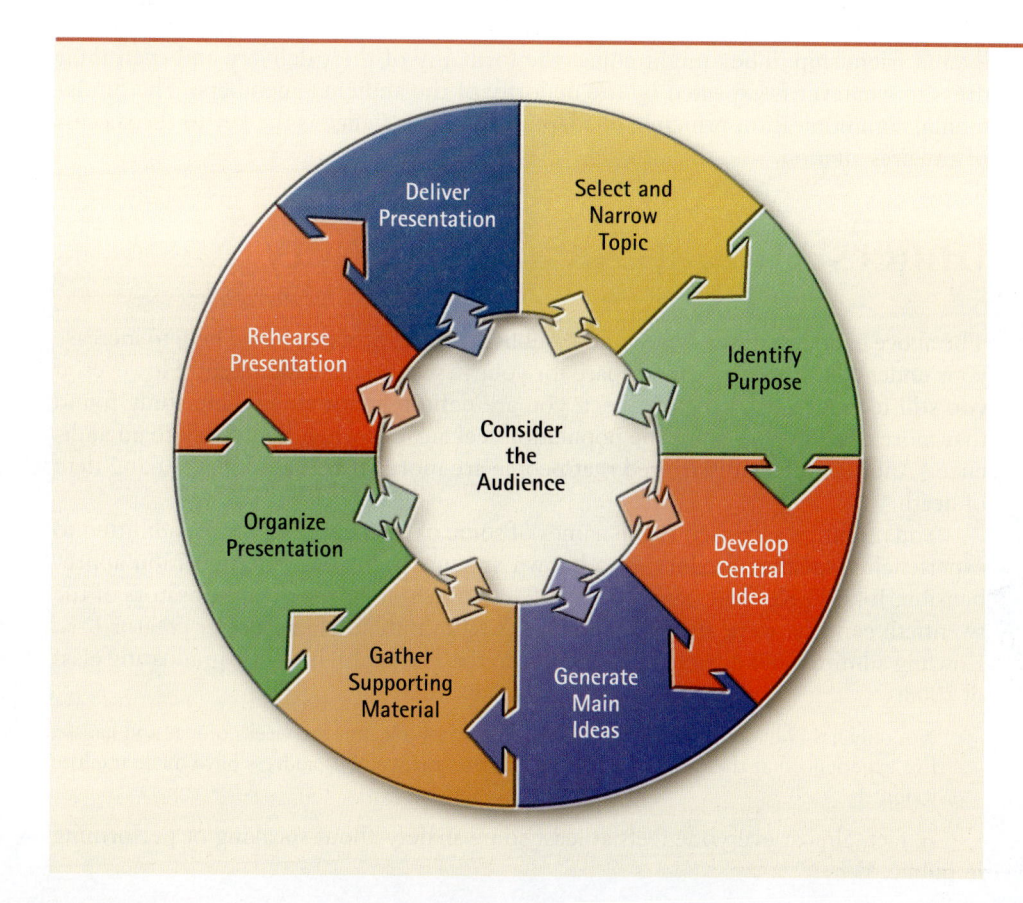

Figure 11.1
An Audience-Centered Model of the Presentational Speaking Process

DEVELOPING YOUR PRESENTATION
Step by Step

Considering Your Audience

A well-known Chinese proverb says that a journey of a thousand miles begins with a single step. Developing and delivering a presentation may seem like a daunting journey. But we believe that if you take it one step at a time and keep your focus on your audience, you'll be rewarded with a well-crafted and well-delivered message.

To help you see how the audience-centered presentation process unfolds step by step, we will explore each step of that process by showing how one student prepared and delivered a presentation. Maggie Yancey, a student at The University of Texas, competes in intercollegiate individual speaking events. Her persuasive presentation "Cyberterrorism" is outlined in Chapter 12.[2] In the pages ahead, we will walk you through the process Maggie used to develop her award-winning presentation.

Maggie thought about her audience even before selecting her topic. Realizing that her listeners would include both students and faculty, she decided to look for a topic that was relevant to both groups. And she knew that she could discuss complex issues, using a fairly advanced vocabulary. The Developing Your Presentation Step by Step feature will provide a window through which you can watch Maggie at work on each step of the presentational speaking process.

---

5. Adapt

Note that a ninth component, "Consider the audience," appears at the center of the model. Double-headed arrows connect this center with every other stage, illustrating that at any point you may revise your ideas or strategies as you learn more about your audience. Your audience influences every decision you make.

Audience-centered presentational speakers are inherently sensitive to the diversity of their audiences. While guarding against generalizations that might be offensive, they acknowledge that cultural, ethnic, and other traditions affect the way people process messages. They apply the fundamental principle of appropriately adapting their messages to others. How? They might choose to use pictures to help them communicate. They might select topics and use illustrations with universal themes such as family and friendship. They might adjust the formality of their delivery and even their dress to whatever is expected by the majority of the audience members. The fundamental communication principle of adapting to the audience is the key to the success of any presentation.

Understanding Speaker Anxiety

The above overview of the stages of the public speaking process should help to increase your understanding of how to prepare for your first speaking assignment. However, if you still feel nervous at the prospect, you are definitely not alone. One study found that more than 80 percent of the population feel anxious when they speak to an audience.[3] Another survey discovered that people are more afraid of public speaking than of death![4]

You might be surprised at the names of some of the people who have admitted to experiencing **speaker anxiety**, also known as stage fright or communication apprehension. John F. Kennedy and Winston Churchill, among the greatest orators of the twentieth century, were anxious about speaking in public. Harry Potter creator J. K. Rowling admitted her anxiety in an address to the Harvard University graduating class of 2008:

> Not only has Harvard given me an extraordinary honour, but the weeks of fear and nausea I've experienced at the thought of giving this commencement address have made me lose weight.[5]

In fact, almost everyone feels at least some anxiety about speaking or performing in public. Why?

---

audience-centered presentational speaker
Someone who considers and adapts to the audience at every stage of the presentational speaking process.

speaker anxiety
Also known as stage fright; anxiety about speaking in public that is manifested in physiological symptoms such as rapid heartbeat, butterflies in the stomach, shaking knees and hands, quivering voice, and increased perspiration.

Harry Potter creator J. K. Rowling has admitted experiencing speaker anxiety; we all need to take positive steps to control anxiety before a performance.

To answer this question and to manage your own anxiety, you need both accurate information and practical advice. Even if the prospect of giving a presentation makes you feel a sense of heightened excitement rather than fear, you can use these suggestions to make your excitement help you, rather than distract you.

It is important to understand that speaker anxiety results from your brain signaling your body to help with a challenging task. The body responds by increasing its breathing rate and blood flow and by pumping more adrenaline, which in turn results in the all-too-familiar symptoms of a rapid heartbeat, butterflies in the stomach, shaking knees and hands, quivering voice, and increased perspiration.

Although these physical symptoms may annoy and worry you, remember that they indicate that your body is trying to help you with the task at hand. The same increased oxygen, blood flow, and adrenaline that cause the uncomfortable symptoms can actually be helpful. You may find that you speak with heightened enthusiasm. Your brain thinks faster and more clearly than you would have believed possible. Your state of increased physical readiness can help you speak better.

Keep in mind, too, that most speakers feel more nervous than they look. Although the antiperspirant advertising slogan "Never let 'em see you sweat" suggests that our increased perspiration, along with our shaking hands and knocking knees, is likely to be visible to our audience, rarely is this true. Communication researchers call this mistaken belief the **illusion of transparency** and have found that simply informing speakers that their nervousness is not as apparent as they think can improve the quality of their speeches.[6]

Speaker anxiety is a normal physiological reaction. It can actually help us in our speaking tasks. Its physical symptoms are seldom apparent to anyone else; rarely does it become so severe that it is actually debilitating. Still, it can be uncomfortable. Some practical tips can help you manage that discomfort and further build your confidence in your speaking ability.

Managing Speaker Anxiety

illusion of transparency
The mistaken belief that the physical manifestations of a speaker's nervousness are apparent to an audience.

Perhaps you've read books or magazine articles that address the topic of speaker anxiety with such advice as "Look over the audience's heads, rather than at them" and "Imagine that your audience members are naked." Interesting though they may be, these techniques are not particularly helpful in reducing speaker anxiety. (After all, wouldn't you be pretty anxious if you had to talk to a group of naked people?) In addition, these strategies create new problems. Gazing at the back wall robs you of eye contact with your audience, an important source of information about how they are responding to your speech. And your audience can tell if you are looking over their heads instead of at them. Rather than pay attention to your speech, they may begin to glance surreptitiously over their shoulders to find out what in the world you're staring at.

If these techniques won't help, what will? Fortunately, several proven strategies exist for managing anxiety.

Know How to Develop a Presentation

Communication researchers have found that public speaking instruction decreases students' perception of their own speaker anxiety.[7] If you have read the first part of this chapter, then you have already taken this first step toward managing anxiety—learning about the public speaking process. Just knowing what you need to do to develop an effective presentation can boost your confidence in being able to do it.

Be Prepared

Being well prepared will decrease anxiety. Communication researchers have found that one way for speakers to manage anxiety is to follow the recommended steps for preparing a speech, which include developing a logical and clear outline.[8] Being prepared also involves selecting an appropriate topic and researching that topic thoroughly. Perhaps most important, it includes rehearsing your presentation. Research suggests that people who experience high speaker anxiety typically spend less time rehearsing than do those who report lower speaker anxiety.[9]

When you rehearse your presentation, imagine that you are giving it to the audience you will actually address. Stand up. If you cannot rehearse in the room where you will deliver the presentation, at least imagine that room. Practice rising from your seat, walking to the front of the room, and beginning your presentation. Speak aloud, rather than rehearsing silently. Thorough preparation that includes realistic rehearsal will increase your confidence when the time comes to deliver your presentation.

Focus on Your Audience

5. Adapt

The fundamental communication guideline of being audience-centered is key to reducing speaker anxiety. As you are preparing your presentation, consider the needs, goals, and interests of your audience members. As you rehearse your presentation, visualize your audience and imagine how they may respond; practice adapting your presentation to the responses you imagine. The more you know about your audience and how they are likely to respond to your message, the more comfortable you will feel about delivering that message. And as you finally deliver your presentation, focus on connecting to your listeners. Look especially for positive, reinforcing feedback from audience members.[10] The more you concentrate on your audience, the less you attend to your own nervousness.

Focus on Your Message

Focusing on your message can also be a constructive anxiety-reducing strategy. Like focusing on your audience, it keeps you from thinking too much about how nervous you are. In the few minutes before you begin your presentation, think about what you are going to say. Mentally review your main ideas. Silently practice your opening lines and your conclusion. Once you are speaking, maintain your focus on your message and your audience, rather than on your fears. Communication researchers have found that most public speakers become progressively more comfortable as they speak, a phenomenon they term **habituation**.[11]

Give Yourself a Mental Pep Talk

Even if you focus primarily on your audience and your message, you are bound to have some lingering thoughts about your performance. Rather than allowing yourself to dwell on how worried or afraid you are, make a conscious effort to think positively. Remind yourself that you have chosen a topic you know something about. Give yourself a mental pep talk before getting up to speak: "I know I can give this presentation. I have prepared and practiced, and I'm going to do a great job." Researchers have suggested that such "pre-speaking exercises" may be the most effective antidotes for anxiety both before and during the speech.[12]

Use Deep-Breathing Techniques

Two of the physical symptoms of nervousness are shallow breathing and rapid heart rate. To counter these symptoms, take a few slow, deep breaths before you get up to speak. As you slowly inhale and exhale, try to relax your entire body. These simple strategies will increase your oxygen intake and slow your heart rate, making you feel calmer and more in control.

Take Advantage of Opportunities to Speak

As you gain public speaking experience, you will feel more in control of your nervousness. Past successes build confidence. Your communication course will provide opportunities for frequent practice, which will increase your skill and confidence.

Seek Professional Help

For a few people, the above strategies may not be enough help. These people may still experience a level of speaker anxiety that they consider debilitating. If you feel that you may be such a person, ask your communication instructor where you might turn for additional help. Some college or university departments of communication maintain communication labs that teach students various additional strategies to help manage counter-productive anxiety.

One such strategy is **systematic desensitization**, which helps you learn to manage anxiety through a combination of general relaxation techniques and visualization of successful and calm preparation and delivery of a presentation.[13]

Another proven strategy is **performance visualization:** viewing a videotape of a successful, effective speaker; becoming familiar enough with the videotaped presentation that you can imagine it; and eventually visualizing yourself as the speaker. This process may offer one of the best long-term strategies for managing speaker anxiety. Studies suggest that student speakers who practice performance visualization view

2. Verbal

1. Aware

habituation
The process of becoming more comfortable as you speak.

systematic desensitization
An anxiety management strategy that includes general relaxation techniques and visualization of success.

performance visualization
An anxiety management strategy that involves viewing a videotape of a successful presentation and imagining oneself delivering that presentation.

> ## Recap
> ### Managing Speaker Anxiety
>
> - Know how to develop a presentation.
> - Be prepared.
> - Focus on your audience.
> - Focus on your message.
> - Give yourself a mental pep talk.
> - Use deep-breathing techniques.
> - Take advantage of opportunities to speak.
> - Seek professional help.

themselves as more positive, vivid, and in-control speakers both immediately after performance visualization and up to several months later.[14]

Additional services may be available through university counseling or other student support services. If you think that you might benefit from professional help, find out what is available and use it.

Selecting and Narrowing Your Topic

Sometimes a speaker is invited or assigned to speak on a certain topic and doesn't have to think about selecting one. At other times, however, a speaker is given some guidelines—such as time limits and perhaps the general purpose for the presentation—but otherwise allowed freedom to choose a topic. When this happens to you—as it almost certainly will in your communication class—you may find your task made easier by exploring three questions: Who is the audience? What is the occasion? What are my interests and experiences?

Who Is the Audience?

5. Adapt

As we have noted several times throughout this book, the principle of appropriately adapting messages to others is central to the communication process. In presentational speaking, that adaptation begins with topic selection. Who are the members of your audience? What interests and needs do they have in common? Why did they ask you to speak?

One professional speaker calls the answers to such questions "actionable intelligence"—information that you can use as you select your topic.[15] Your college classmates are likely to be interested in such topics as college loans and the job market. Older adults might be more interested in hearing a speaker address such topics as the cost of prescription drugs and investment tax credits. Thinking about your audience can often yield an appropriate topic.

What Is the Occasion?

You might also consider the occasion for which you are being asked to speak. A Veteran's Day address calls for such topics as patriotism and service to one's country. A university centennial address will focus on the successes in the institution's past and a vision for its future.

1. Aware

What Are My Interests and Experiences?

Self-awareness, another communication principle you already know, can also help you discover a topic. Exploring your own interests, attitudes, and experiences may suggest

When selecting a topic, think about the needs of the audience who will be listening to your presentation. How can you effectively anticipate and consider their knowledge, interests, and expectations?

topics about which you know a great deal and feel passionately and result in a presentation that you can deliver with energy and genuine enthusiasm. One speaker's thinking about her own interests and experiences quickly produced the following list of possible topics:

San Diego, California: city of cultural diversity
Hybrid cars
The reconstructed Globe Theatre
Working at Six Flags
What a sociologist does

Even after considering audience, occasion, and personal interests and experiences, you may still find yourself facing a speaking assignment for which you just cannot come up with a satisfactory topic. When that happens, you might try silent brainstorming, scanning web directories and web pages, or listening and reading for topic ideas.

Conducting Silent Brainstorming

Silent brainstorming, discussed in Chapter 10 as a technique used by small groups to generate creative ideas, is a useful strategy for generating possible topics for presentations. A silent brainstorming session of about three minutes yielded the following list of eleven potential topics:

Gargoyles
Gothic architecture
Notre Dame
French food
Disney's *The Hunchback of Notre Dame*
Collecting Disney movie celluloids
Grammy Award winning movie themes
Academy Award winning movies of the 1940s
The Motion Picture Academy's Lifetime Achievement Award
John Wayne
The California Gold Rush

Having generated a list of topics, you can now go back and eliminate topics that don't have much promise or that you know you would never use. For example, you may not have any real interest in or reason for discussing the California Gold Rush. However, perhaps your film course has given you good background for discussing Academy Award winning movies of the 1940s or some other decade. Keep the topics you like in your class notebook. You can reconsider them for future assignments.

Scanning Web Directories and Web Pages

You know how addicting it can be to surf the web—to follow various categories and links out of interest and curiosity. What may seem an idle pastime can actually be a good way to discover potential speech topics. For example, a recent random search on Yahoo! Everything at <everything.yahoo.com>, starting with the general menu heading Learn, yielded the following categories and possible topics, arranged from broad to narrow:

> Green
> Living green
> Environmental news
> Bacteria may unlock mysteries of human body

An additional advantage of this strategy is that you now have both a broad topic and one or more potential sources for your presentation.

Listening and Reading for Topic Ideas

It is not unusual to see on television or read in a newspaper something that triggers an idea for a presentation. For example, the following list of quite varied topics was suggested by the headlines in a recent daily newspaper:

> Housing foreclosures
> Record prices at fine art auctions
> Monitoring locations of cell phone users
> Political fundraising
> Repairing the International Space Station

The nightly news is not the only media source of potential topics. You might also get topic ideas from television talk shows or from general interest or news magazines. Or you might get an idea from a book. Perhaps you have just read *Newsweek* columnist Fareed Zakaria's book *The Post-American World*. You might decide to give a speech on the meteoric rise of the economies of China and India.

You might also find a topic in material you have studied for a class. Perhaps you recently had an interesting discussion of minimum mandatory sentencing in your crim-

4. Listen and Respond

DEVELOPING YOUR PRESENTATION
Step by Step

Selecting and Narrowing Your Topic

While scanning the latest issue of *Newsweek* one Sunday afternoon, Maggie happens on an article that catches her interest. She settles down to read the article, which discusses the threat posed to national security by cyberterrorism. Maggie is surprised. She had no idea that the government's technology infrastructure was so vulnerable. As she finishes the article, another thought goes through her mind: Maybe cyberterrorism would make a good topic for her upcoming persuasive presentation.

> ## Recap
> ### Select and Narrow Your Topic
> - Consider the audience, the occasion, and your interests and experiences.
> - Practice silent brainstorming.
> - Scan web directories and web pages.
> - Listen and read for topic ideas.
> - Narrow your topic by generating increasingly specific categories and subcategories.

inology class. It might make a good topic for a presentation. And your instructor would probably be happy to suggest additional resources.

Even a topic that comes up in casual conversation with friends may make a good speech topic. Perhaps everyone in your dorm seems to be sniffling and coughing all at once. "It's sick-building syndrome," gasps one. Sick-building syndrome might be an interesting topic for a presentation.

The point is to keep your eyes and ears open. You never know when you might see or hear a potential topic. If you do, write it down. Nothing is so frustrating as knowing you had a good idea for a topic but not being able to remember what it was!

If you discover potential topics through brainstorming, surfing the web, or listening or reading, you should still consider the communication principles of adapting to your audience and being aware of your own interests and experiences before you make your final topic selection. And you will also need to consider the time limits of the speaking assignment. Many good topics need to be narrowed before they are appropriate for a given assignment. Be realistic. Although many beginning speakers worry about how they will ever fill three minutes, in reality, more speakers run over their time limits than under.

One strategy for narrowing topics is to construct the kinds of categories and subcategories created by web directories. Write your general topic at the top of a list, making each succeeding word or phrase more specific and narrow. For example, in order to narrow the topic "animals," write it down and then write an increasingly specific list of topics under it:

Animals
Pets
Reptiles
Bearded dragons
Caring for a bearded dragon

If you have ten minutes for your presentation, you might decide that the last topic is too narrow. If so, just go back one step. In ten minutes, you may be able to discuss the characteristics and habits of bearded dragons, as well as how to care for them.

1. Aware
5. Adapt

Identifying Your Purpose

Now that you have a topic in mind, you need to clarify your purpose for your presentation. If you are unclear about exactly what you hope to accomplish, you probably won't accomplish anything, except to ramble about your topic in some sort of vague way. A clear purpose, on the other hand, can help you select main ideas, an organizational strategy, and supporting material, and can even influence the way in which you deliver the presentation. You should determine both your general purpose and your specific purpose for every presentation that you give.

General Purpose

Your **general purpose** is the broad reason for giving your presentation: to inform, to persuade, or to entertain. When you inform, you teach. You define, describe, or explain a thing, person, place, concept, or process. You may use some humor in your presentation; you may encourage your audience to seek out further information about your topic. But your primary purpose for speaking is to give information.

If you are using information to try to change or reinforce your audience's ideas or convictions or to urge your audience to do something, your general purpose is persuasive. The insurance representative who tries to get you to buy life insurance, the candidate for state representative who asks for your vote, and the coordinator of Habitat for Humanity who urges your fraternity to get involved in building homes all have persuasive general purposes. They may offer information about life expectancy, the voting record of an incumbent opponent, or the number of people in your community who cannot afford decent housing, but they use this information to convince you or to get you to do something. Their primary purpose is persuasive.

The speaker whose purpose is to entertain tries to get the members of his or her audience to smile, laugh, and generally enjoy themselves. For the audience members, learning something or being persuaded about something is secondary to having a good time. Most after-dinner speakers speak to entertain. So do most stand-up comedians and storytellers.

In your speech class, the general purpose for each assignment will probably be set by your instructor. Because the general purpose influences the way you develop and organize your presentation, as well as the way you deliver it, it is important that you be aware of your general purpose throughout the process of developing and delivering your presentation.

1. Aware

Specific Purpose

Knowing whether you want to inform, persuade, or entertain clarifies your general purpose for speaking. You also need to determine your specific purpose. A **specific purpose** is a concise statement of what your listeners should be able to do by the time

DEVELOPING YOUR PRESENTATION
Step by Step

Identifying Your Purpose

Maggie's assignment is to prepare and deliver a persuasive presentation, so she knows that her general purpose is to persuade. She will have to try to change or reinforce her audience's attitudes and beliefs about cyberterrorism and perhaps also get her listeners to take some sort of action.

Maggie also knows that her specific purpose should begin with the phrase "At the end of my presentation, the audience will . . . ." So she jots down,

> At the end of my presentation, the audience will know about cyberterrorism.

As Maggie thinks further about her draft specific purpose, she sees some problems with it. How can she determine what her audience "knows" at the end of her presentation? And just what is it the audience should know about cyberterrorism? She edits her purpose statement to read,

> At the end of my presentation, the audience will be able to explain what cyberterrorism is and offer examples of its occurrence.

This version is more specific, but perhaps more appropriate for an informative speech than a persuasive one. What does she want her audience to *do* about the problem? Maybe a better statement would be

> At the end of my presentation, the audience will take steps to strengthen the cybersecurity of government servers and communications systems.

Maggie is pleased with this third version. It is a concise statement of what she wants her audience to do at the end of her speech. She is ready to move to the next step of the process.

Recap

Identify Your Purpose

General Purpose

- To inform — To define, describe, or explain a thing, person, place, concept, or process
- To persuade — To change or reinforce audience members' ideas or convictions, or to urge them to do something
- To entertain — To amuse an audience

Specific Purpose

- Specifies what you want audience members to be able to do by the end of your presentation
- Guides you in developing your presentation
- Uses the words "At the end of my presentation, the audience will . . . ."

Examples of General Purposes	**Examples of Specific Purposes**
To inform	At the end of my presentation, the audience will be able to list two benefits for adults of learning to play a musical instrument.
To persuade	At the end of my presentation, the audience will enroll in a music appreciation course.
To entertain	At the end of my presentation, the audience will be laughing at my misadventures as an adult cello student.

---

you finish your presentation. In other words, a specific purpose is an audience-centered behavioral goal for your presentation. It is not intended to become part of your speech, but to guide your own preparation of the speech.

You can begin a specific-purpose statement for any presentation with the words

> At the end of my presentation, the audience will . . .

And then specify a behavior. For example, if you are giving an informative presentation on eating disorders, you might state,

> At the end of my presentation, the audience will be able to explain the causes and most successful treatments for anorexia and bulimia.

If your topic is Zen meditation and your general purpose is to persuade, you might say,

> At the end of my presentation, the audience will try Zen meditation.

Wording your specific purpose as in the examples above will help you keep your audience foremost in your mind during the entire presentation preparation process.

Every subsequent decision you make while preparing and delivering your presentation should be guided by your specific purpose. As soon as you have formulated it, write it on a note card and keep it with you while you are working on your presentation. Think of it as a compass pointing true north—toward your audience. Refer to it often.

Developing Your Central Idea

While your specific purpose indicates what you want your audience to know or do by the end of your presentation, your **central idea** makes a definitive point *about* your topic. It focuses on the content of the speech.

general purpose
The broad reason for giving a presentation: to inform, to persuade, or to entertain an audience.

specific purpose
A concise statement of what listeners should be able to do by the time the speaker finishes the presentation.

central idea
A definitive point *about* a topic.

Professional speech coach Judith Humphrey explains the importance of a central idea:

> Ask yourself before writing a speech . . . "What's my point?" Be able to state that message in a single clear sentence. Everything else you say will support that single argument.[16]

Sometimes, as in the following example, wording the central idea can be as simple as copying the part of the specific purpose statement that specifies what the audience should be able to do.

TOPIC: Foreign-language education
SPECIFIC PURPOSE: At the end of my presentation, the audience will be able to explain two reasons foreign-language education should begin in the elementary grades.
CENTRAL IDEA: Foreign-language education should begin in the elementary grades.

Even though they may seem similar, the specific purpose and central idea are used quite differently. While the specific purpose guides you as you prepare your presentation, the central idea will guide the audience as they listen to the presentation. Although the specific purpose is never actually stated in the presentation itself, the central idea is usually stated at or near the end of the speaker's introduction. The most successful central ideas are audience-centered, reflect a single topic, are complete declarative sentences, and use direct, specific language.

An Audience-Centered Idea

5. Adapt

If your specific purpose is audience-centered, your central idea probably will be, too. It should reflect a topic in which the audience has a reason to be interested and should provide some knowledge they do not already have or make some claim about the topic that they may not have previously considered. The second of the following central ideas is more appropriate to an audience of college students than the first.

INAPPROPRIATE: Taking Advanced Placement classes in high school can help fulfill your general education requirements. *(Inappropriate because taking Advanced Placement classes is something college students either did or did not do in the past. They cannot make any decisions about them at this point.)*

APPROPRIATE: Taking web-based classes can help fulfill your general studies requirements. *(Appropriate because students are probably looking for various options for completing required courses. They can choose to take courses on the web.)*

A Single Topic

A central idea should reflect a single topic. Trying to cover more than one topic, even if the multiple topics are related, only muddles your presentation and confuses the audience.

MULTIPLE TOPICS: Clubbing and running in marathons are two activities that appeal to many college students.
SINGLE TOPIC: Clubbing appeals to many college students.

Effective speakers state their central idea during their introductory remarks to help their audience focus on the main points covered in the body of the speech.

DEVELOPING YOUR PRESENTATION
Step by Step

Developing Your Central Idea

Maggie knows from reading Chapter 11 of *Communication: Principles for a Lifetime* that her central idea should be a complete declarative sentence that states a single audience-centered idea. She knows, too, that sometimes you can develop your central idea by copying the part of your specific purpose statement that specifies what the audience should do. So she writes,

> We should take steps to strengthen the cybersecurity of government servers and communications systems.

A Complete Declarative Sentence

Your central idea should be more than just the word or phrase that is your topic—it should make a claim about your topic. Questions may help you come up with a central idea, but questions themselves are not good central ideas, because they don't make any kind of claim. A central idea should be a complete **declarative sentence**—not a topic and not a question.

TOPIC: Study abroad
QUESTION: Should students consider opportunities to study abroad?
CENTRAL IDEA: Study abroad provides significant advantages for students in most fields of study.

Direct, Specific Language

A good central idea uses direct, specific language, rather than qualifiers and vague generalities.

VAGUE: Crop circles are not what they seem to be.
SPECIFIC: Although they have been variously attributed to alien forces and unknown fungi, crop circles are really just a clever hoax.

Recap
The Central Idea Should . . .

Be audience-centered.
Reflect a single topic.
Be a complete declarative sentence.
Use direct, specific language.

Generating Main Ideas

If the central idea of a presentation is like the thesis statement of a paper, the **main ideas** of a presentation correspond to the paragraph topics of a paper. They support or subdivide the central idea and provide more detailed points of focus for developing the presentation.

declarative sentence
A complete sentence that makes a statement, as opposed to asking a question.

main ideas
Subdivisions of the central idea of a presentation, which provide detailed points of focus for developing the presentation.

Getting from the central idea to related but more specific main ideas can seem a challenging task, but actually you can use the central idea to generate main ideas. Here's how.

Write the central idea at the top of a sheet of paper or a word-processing document. Then ask yourself three questions:

1. Does the central idea have *logical divisions?*
2. Can I think of several *reasons* the central idea is true?
3. Can I support the central idea with a series of *steps* or a *chronological sequence?*

You should be able to answer yes to one of these questions and to write down the corresponding divisions, reasons, or steps. Let's apply this strategy to several examples.

Does the Central Idea Have *Logical Divisions?*

Suppose that your central idea is "Most accomplished guitarists play three types of guitars." The phrase *three types* is a flag that indicates that this central idea does indeed have logical divisions—those being, in this case, the three types of guitars. You list the three that come to mind:

1. Acoustic
2. Classical
3. Electric

You don't need to use Roman numerals or to worry particularly about the order in which you have listed the types of guitars. Right now, you are simply trying to generate main ideas. They aren't set in concrete, either. You may revise them—and your central idea—several times before you actually deliver the presentation. For example, you may decide that you need to include steel guitars in your list. So you revise your central idea to read "four types of guitars" and add "steel" to your list. If your central idea has logical divisions, you may organize those logical divisions topically, spatially, or according to cause–effect or problem-and-solution, organizational strategies that will be discussed in Chapter 12.

Can You Think of Several *Reasons* the Central Idea Is True?

If your central idea is "Everyone should study a martial art," you may not be able to find readily apparent logical divisions. Simply discussing judo, karate, and taekwondo would not necessarily support the argument that everyone should study one of them. However, the second question is more productive: You can think of a number of *reasons* everyone should study a martial art. You quickly generate this list:

1. Martial arts teach responsibility.
2. Martial arts teach self-control.
3. Martial arts teach a means of self-defense.

Unlike the list of types of guitars, this list is written in brief complete sentences. The purpose of your first list of main ideas is just to get the ideas in written form, whether words, phrases, or sentences. You can and will revise them later. If your main ideas are reasons your central idea is true, you will probably organize them according to effect–cause.

Can You Support the Central Idea with a Series of *Steps* or a *Chronological Sequence?*

"The events of September 11, 2001, were the climax of a decade of deadly terrorist attacks against the United States." It seemed like a pretty good central idea when you came up with it. But now what do you do? It doesn't have any logical divisions. You couldn't really develop reasons that it is true. However, you could probably support this central idea with a chronological sequence or a history of the problem. You jot down the following list:

1. 1993—Bomb explodes in the underground parking garage of the World Trade Center, killing six people.
2. 1995—Car bomb in Riyadh, Saudi Arabia, kills seven people, five of them American military and civilian National Guard advisors.
3. 1996—Bomb aboard a fuel truck explodes outside a U.S. Air Force installation in Dhahran, Saudi Arabia, killing nineteen U.S. military personnel.
4. 1998—Bombs destroy the U.S. embassies in Nairobi, Kenya, and Dar es Salaam, Tanzania. Three hundred one people are killed, including thirteen Americans.
5. 2000—Bomb damages the *USS Cole* in the port of Aden, Yemen, killing seventeen American sailors.
6. 2001—Hijacked airliners crash into the World Trade Center in New York, the Pentagon in Washington, D.C., and a field in Pennsylvania, killing more than 3,000.[17]

These six fatal terrorist attacks, arranged in chronological order, could become the main ideas of your speech.

How many main ideas should you have? Your topic and time limit will help you decide. A short presentation (three to five minutes) might have only two main ideas. A longer one (eight to ten minutes) might have four or five. If you find that you have more potential main ideas than you can use, decide which main ideas are likely to be most interesting, relevant, and perhaps persuasive to your audience. Or combine two or more closely related ideas.

DEVELOPING YOUR PRESENTATION
Step by Step

Generating Your Main Ideas

With her central idea in hand, Maggie knows that she next needs to generate main ideas for her presentation. She asks three questions:

- Does the central idea have logical divisions?
- Can I think of several reasons the central idea is true?
- Can I support my central idea with a series of steps or a chronological sequence?

Maggie's central idea does not seem to have logical divisions, but she can certainly provide reasons it is true. She jots down her central idea and writes *because* at the end of it:

We must take steps to strengthen the cybersecurity of government servers and communications systems because

And then she adds,

1. Cyberterrorism is a growing threat.
2. The targets of cyberterrorism are unpredictable.
3. Government servers and communications systems are insufficiently protected.

Maggie thinks at first that these might make three good main ideas for her speech. Then she realizes that ideas 2 and 3 are actually subpoints of idea 1. Both are reasons the first idea is true; they explain *why* cyberterrorism is a growing threat. Additionally, glancing back at her purpose statement reminds her that she wants her listeners to take steps to strengthen cybersecurity. So she revises her original list of main ideas to read,

1. Cyberterrorism is a growing threat.
2. The threat is growing because the targets of cyberterrorism are unpredictable and because government servers and communications systems are insufficiently protected.
3. To urge the government to restructure cybersecurity, individuals should contact their local newspapers and representatives to voice their concerns.

Now Maggie has main ideas that both support her central idea and fulfill her specific purpose.

Gathering Supporting Material

By the time you have decided on your main ideas, you have a skeleton presentation. Your next task is to flesh out that skeleton with **supporting material**, both verbal and visual. Verbal supporting material includes illustrations, explanations, descriptions, definitions, analogies, statistics, and opinions—material that will clarify, amplify, and provide evidence to support your main ideas and your thesis. Visual supporting material includes objects, charts, graphs, posters, maps, models, and computer-generated graphics. You can also support your speech with audio aids such as music or sounds from your iPod or a CD. The speaker who seeks out strong verbal and visual supporting material is adhering to the fundamental communication principles of effectively using verbal and nonverbal messages.

Sources of Supporting Material

Like a chef who needs to know where to buy high-quality fresh fruits and vegetables for gourmet recipes, you need to know where to turn for supporting material that will effectively develop your presentation and achieve your specific purpose. We will discuss three potential sources of supporting material: yourself, the Internet, and the library.

Yourself If you were self-aware as you selected your topic, you may be your own source. You may have chosen a topic about your hobby—collecting CDs, raising cockatiels, or cooking. Or, you may have chosen a topic with which you have had some personal experience, such as undergoing plastic surgery or negotiating a favorable apartment lease.

The point is that you don't necessarily need to consult the Internet or run to the library for every piece of supporting material on every topic on which you speak. It is true that most well-researched presentations will include some objective material gathered from the Internet or from library resources. But you may also be able to provide an effective illustration, explanation, definition, or other type of support from your own knowledge and experience. As an audience-centered speaker, you should realize, too, that personal knowledge or experience has the added advantage of heightening your credibility in the minds of your listeners. They will respect your authority if they realize that you have firsthand knowledge of the topic on which you are speaking.

The Internet Only a few short years ago, the Internet was more of a research curiosity than a serious source of supporting material. Now it is the first place many of us turn when faced with a research task. You have probably accessed material on the web—the Internet's information-delivery system—with *Google* or *Yahoo!*, both of which offer both directory and search engine capabilities. A **directory** allows you to click on subject categories, which are, in turn, broken down into ever-more-specific subcategories; a **search engine** uses subject or keyword searches.

Before the Internet became available, students often struggled to find enough information for speeches and papers. One of the ways in which the Internet has changed research is that today's students are more likely to find themselves overwhelmed by too much material.

One tool that can help you narrow a search is a specialized **vertical search engine** such as *Google Scholar*, which indexes academic sources, or *Indeed*, which indexes job web sites. One technical writer explains the difference between general-purpose and vertical search engines this way:

> Regular search . . . is a "horizontal" search in that you are searching across a wide spectrum of material. Information from sports sites, news sites, medical sites, shopping sites—the entire horizontal spectrum of topics is represented.
>
> With vertical search, you slice down vertically through one topic area. You search only against the news sites or against the medical information, for example. This type of focus can make for more relevant results.[18]

---

1. Aware

supporting material
Verbal or visual material that clarifies, amplifies, and provides evidence to support the main ideas of a presentation. Verbal support includes illustrations, explanations, descriptions, definitions, analogies, statistics, and opinions; visual support includes objects, charts, graphs, posters, maps, models, and computer-generated graphics.

directory
An Internet site that offers the user ever-more-specific categories through which to search the World Wide Web.

search engine
An Internet site that works much like a traditional card catalog or index, allowing the user to perform a subject or keyword search of the World Wide Web.

vertical search engine
A web site that indexes information on the World Wide Web in a specialized area.

Communication and Technology

A New Kind of Search Engine

Over the past few years, vertical search engines—designed to select only certain types of information from the Internet—have been increasing in both number and popularity.

One such engine is Ziggs, which can help you find people with certain specific characteristics. For example, one user explains, "It might help you find a lawyer in Washington specializing in international trade, or an alumnus of Brandeis University who lives in Delaware."[19]

Newer vertical search engines include Surgeryfindit, where surgeons can access such resources as medical journals, medical schools, and surgical device suppliers, and BizAg, which searches U.S. and Canadian business-for-sale listings on multiple sites.[20]

Another way to narrow your search is to do a **Boolean search**. A Boolean search lets you enclose phrases in quotation marks or parentheses so that the search yields only those sites on which all the words in the phrase appear together, rather than sites that contain the words at random. You can also insert the word *or* between two parenthetical phrases, directing your search to include documents in which either phrase appears. Or you can insert the word *and* between parenthetical phrases to indicate that you wish to see results that contain both phrases. Boolean searches also let you exclude words or phrases from your search or restrict the dates of documents to a specified time frame. These relatively simple strategies can help you narrow thousands or even millions of hits to a more workable number.

A third strategy for sorting through information you discover on the World Wide Web has to do with the principle of appropriately interpreting verbal and nonverbal messages. Specifically, you need to evaluate the sites you discover, according to a consistent standard. The following six criteria can serve as such a standard:[21]

1. *Accountability.* Find out what organization or individual is responsible for the web site. A good place to start is to examine the domain, indicated by the last three letters of the site's URL. The following domains are used by the types of organizations indicated:[22]

.com or **.net**	commercial sites
.org	nonprofit groups
.edu	educational institutions
.gov	government agencies
.mil	military groups

   You can also try entering the name of the organization, enclosed in quotation marks, in a search engine. If you cannot identify or verify the author or sponsor of a web site, be extremely wary of the information on the site. If no one is willing to be accountable for the information, you cannot be accountable to your audience for using it.

   The criterion of accountability explains why Wikipedia, the free online encyclopedia generated as the first hit by many online searches, is generally not considered a reliable academic source. Anyone, regardless of expertise, can add a Wikipedia entry or edit the content of any existing entry; no single entity is accountable for its content. Search elsewhere.

2. *Accuracy.* Sources of facts should be documented on a web site just as they are in a print source. An additional advantage of the web is that it can provide a **hyperlink** to the original source. Hyperlinks are usually colored, underlined words or images in the text. Clicking with your mouse on a hyperlink will take you directly to the linked site.

---

2. Verbal
3. Nonverbal

Boolean search
A web search that ties words together so that a search engine can hunt for the resulting phrase.

hyperlink
A highlighted word or graphic on a web page that takes a user who clicks on it directly to the site to which it refers.

Web sites should also be relatively free of errors in grammatical usage and mechanics. If a site contains such errors, it might also contain errors in content.
3. *Objectivity.* As noted above, you need to know who has posted the site. Consider the philosophy and possible biases of the organization or individual responsible for the site. Are those beliefs, interests, and biases likely to slant the information? The more objective the author, the more credible the facts and information.
4. *Date.* At the bottom of many sites is information about when the site was posted and when it was last updated. If you do not find a date there, you may be able to find it under Properties or Page Info in your menu, depending on the computer you are using. In most cases, when you are concerned with factual data, the more recent, the better.
5. *Usability.* If you have spent much time exploring the Internet, you have probably at one time or another called up a site that contained such complex graphics that it took a long time to load or even caused your computer to crash. Frames, graphics, and multimedia resources can enhance a site, or they can simply complicate it. Consider the practical efficiency of the sites you explore.
6. *Sensitivity to diversity.* A diversity-sensitive web site will be free of bias against either gender; against any ethnic, racial, or sexual-preference subgroup; and against people with disabilities.[23]

Federal agencies are required by law to make their web sites accessible to people with disabilities. For example, federal web sites must be accessible in a mode that allows people with low vision to view them without relying on audio input.[24] Other requirements include making sure hyperlinks can be detected by color-blind users and providing audio and video clips with written captions for people with hearing disabilities.[25]

The Library Despite the explosion of World Wide Web resources in recent years, the library remains a rich source of supporting material. Most libraries, from the largest research university library to the smallest village public library, house the following kinds of resources:

Books
Periodicals
Full-text databases
Newspapers
Reference resources
Government documents
Special services

Books The word *library* is almost synonymous with the word *book*. In spite of the predictions of some that electronic resources will someday make books obsolete, for now books remain central to the holdings of most libraries.

A library's books are housed in the **stacks**, often several floors of shelves of books. Books are organized in the stacks according to **call number**, a reference number

stacks
The collection of books in a library.

call number
The numerical code by which a book in a library is identified.

> ### Recap
> **Using the Internet as a Source of Supporting Material**
> 1. Use a directory or search engine to find relevant sites.
> 2. Look beyond Wikipedia, which is not a reliable source.
> 3. Evaluate web sites according to six criteria: accountability, accuracy, objectivity, date, usability, and sensitivity to diversity.

Figure 11.2
Entry from an Electronic Card Catalog

Author:	Strike, Kenneth A.
Title	Ethics and college student life : a case study approach / Kenneth A. Strike, Pamela A. Moss.
Publication Info.	Upper Saddle River, N.J. : Pearson/Prentice Hall, c2008.
Edition	3rd ed.
URL to This Record:	http://catalog.library.txstate.edu:80/record=b1702331a

Table of contents only

Location	Call No.	Status
General Collection, Floor 6	LA229 .S665 2008	AVAILABLE

Description	viii, 280 p. ; 24 cm.
Bibliography	Includes bibliographical references and index.
Subject	College students -- United States -- Conduct of life.
	Ethics -- United States.
	Moral education -- United States.
Local Subject	0868AL
Additional Author	Moss, Pamela A.
ISBN	9780132343312 (pbk.)
	0132343312 (pbk.)

assigned to each book, which encodes the subject or topic, as well as the author. Most libraries use the **Library of Congress classification system** of call numbers.

A library's central catalog of all its books is called the **card catalog**. Today, most card catalogs are electronic ones. Banks of computer monitors in a central location in the library provide directions for looking up the books you need. Many college, university, and public library card catalogs these days are also accessible from remote locations, meaning that you can search them online and build preliminary bibliographies of books and call numbers before ever going to the library building itself. Figure 11.2 illustrates a sample entry from a computerized card catalog.

Books will be important sources as you prepare your presentations. They can provide in-depth coverage of topics, which is not possible in shorter publications. However, because most books are written two or three years before they are published, they are inherently outdated. If your presentation addresses a current topic or if you want to use current examples, you will probably not find the information you need in books. You will turn instead to periodicals and newspapers.

Periodicals The term **periodicals** refers both to magazines, such as *Time, Consumer Reports,* and *Sports Illustrated,* and to professional journals, such as *College English* and the *Quarterly Journal of Economics.* Both types of periodicals can be useful for presentations.

Periodical indexes are the equivalent of card catalogs in helping you locate information you need. A number of such indexes cover many topics and most of the thousands of periodicals published. Many periodical indexes are available on CD-ROM, and many can be accessed either from the library or from remote locations. In most periodical indexes, entries are indexed alphabetically according to both subject and author. Most people use them by searching for subjects or keywords, much as they would conduct a World Wide Web search. Some periodical indexes are **full-text databases**, meaning that you can access not only bibliographical information but also the texts of the articles themselves.

Following are some frequently used periodical indexes and full-text databases:

- *The Reader's Guide to Periodical Literature* is the oldest periodical index and the one that many researchers first learn to use. It indexes popular magazines and a few

Library of Congress classification system
The most commonly used system of call numbers.

card catalog
A file of information about the books in a library, whether an index-card file or a computerized system.

periodical
A popular magazine or professional journal.

periodical index
A listing of bibliographical data for articles published in a group of magazines or journals during a given time period.

full-text database
An indexing system that provides not only bibliographic data but also full texts of entries.

trade and professional journals; articles are alphabetized according to both subject and author. Libraries can subscribe to the *Reader's Guide* either in hard copy or as an electronic database.
- *Academic Search Complete* is the largest multidisciplinary full-text database, providing full texts of more than 5,500 periodicals from virtually every academic field. Coverage is updated daily and currently goes as far back as 1865.
- *ABI/Inform Global* provides full texts from more than 1,800 periodicals in such fields as business, health care, human resources, insurance, real estate, and telecommunications. Articles date from 1971 to the present.
- *Education Research Complete* offers full texts from more than 750 journals relating to the field of education. This database also includes full text for more than a hundred books and monographs, as well as full text for numerous education-related conference papers. Dates of coverage vary.

Your university library's web page probably has a link to online databases. Use this link or contact your library directly to find out what full-text databases are available to you, as well as how to access them from remote sites.

Newspapers   You can find information that is only hours old by reading the latest edition of a daily newspaper. Newspapers also offer the most detailed coverage available of current events.

Newspapers today exist in three formats. The first is the traditional newsprint format. However, libraries usually keep only the most recent newspapers (probably less than a week old) in their racks because they take up so much storage space. Back issues are kept on microfilm, the second format. And in recent years, many newspapers, from major national newspapers to local and college newspapers, have also become available online.

Of course, before you can consult a newspaper, you have to figure out where to look. To find relevant information on your subject, you need to consult a **newspaper index** or database. *Newspaper Source* provides full texts of selected articles from some thirty U.S. and international newspapers and more than two hundred regional U.S. newspapers. It also provides full-text television and radio news transcripts from CBS News, CNN, CNN International, FOX News, NPR, and other news providers.

Reference Resources   A library's **reference resources** include encyclopedias, dictionaries, directories, atlases, almanacs, yearbooks, books of quotations, and biographical dictionaries. As a speaker, you may at one time or another use most of these types of materials. Like periodicals, newspapers, and microfilm, reference resources usually are available only for in-house research and cannot be checked out.

Government Documents   Government agencies at all levels publish information on almost every conceivable subject, as well as keeping records of most official proceedings. Once a dauntingly complex collection of pamphlets, special reports, and texts of

---

newspaper index
A listing of bibliographical data for articles published in a newspaper (or group of newspapers) during a given time period.

reference resources
Material housed in the reference section of a library, such as encyclopedias, dictionaries, directories, atlases, almanacs, yearbooks, books of quotations, and biographical dictionaries.

Communication *and Ethics*

A Question of Speechwriting

An online "speech mill" advertises that for $8.95 per page, "highly qualified writers" will prepare a custom presentation for you. The ad goes on to claim that because the presentation is customized to your requirements and written "from scratch," it is not plagiarized.

Would it be ethical to use this or a similar site to prepare a presentation for a class assignment? Are you comfortable with the claim that such a presentation is not plagiarized?

speeches and debates, **government documents** today are much more readily accessible through the World Wide Web.

The most important index of government documents has long been the *Monthly Catalog of U.S. Government Publications*, available online in recent years. At present, several government agencies continue to work toward developing a comprehensive and authoritative *National Bibliography of U.S. Government Publications*.[26]

Special Services Interlibrary loan and reciprocal borrowing privileges are among the special services that can help you find resources not otherwise available through your own library or online.

Say you are reading an article and discover a reference to a book you would like to see. Your library does not own the book. You might be able to use **interlibrary loan** to locate the book at another library and have it sent to your library within a few days. Or, if your library has **reciprocal borrowing privileges** with another library, you may be able to go to that library yourself and locate the book.

Types of Supporting Material

If you have explored your own knowledge and insights and those of people you know, discovered material on the Internet, and examined a variety of library resources, you probably have a wealth of potential supporting material. Now you will need to decide what to use in your presentation. Keeping in mind your audience's knowledge, interests, and expectations will help you to determine where an illustration might stir their emotions, where an explanation might help them to understand a point, and where statistics might convince them of the significance of a problem. Let's discuss these and other types of supporting material and consider suggestions for using them effectively.

Illustrations **Illustrations** offer an example of or tell a story about an idea, issue, or problem a speaker is discussing. They can be as short as a word or phrase or as long as a well-developed paragraph. Sometimes speakers will offer a series of brief illustrations, as President George W. Bush did in his final State of the Union address in January 2008:

> In the past seven years, we've also seen images that have sobered us. We've watched throngs of mourners in Lebanon and Pakistan carrying the caskets of beloved leaders taken by the assassin's hand. We've seen wedding guests in blood-soaked finery staggering from a hotel in Jordan, Afghans and Iraqis blown up in mosques and markets, and trains in London and Madrid ripped apart by bombs. On a clear September day, we saw thousands of our fellow citizens taken from us in an instant.[27]

Other speakers offer longer and more detailed illustrations. Speaking to the Association for Education in Journalism and Mass Communication, veteran journalist Bill Moyers offered this extended illustration of a fellow journalist who died for his craft:

> Chauncey Bailey believes journalism matters. The editor of the *Oakland Post* was murdered a week ago on the streets of his city. The 19-year-old suspect told police he ambushed and killed Bailey for writing negative stories about a local bakery that may have been responsible for more questionable activities than baking bread. Fifteen hundred people turned out this week for his funeral, believing that journalism matters.[28]

Bush's and Moyers's illustrations are true examples. However, sometimes a speaker will use instead a **hypothetical illustration**—one that has not actually occurred. If you decide to use a hypothetical illustration, it is important to make clear to your audience that the scene you describe never really happened. Note how Matthew uses the word *imagine* to make clear to his audience that his illustration is hypothetical:

> Imagine an evening outing: You and your two children decide to have a fun night out. You look up to your rearview mirror to see a car slam into the back of your car—WHAM—killing your children. You survive the crash and so does the individual who rear-ended you.[29]

2. Verbal

government documents
Material published by the government, including records of official proceedings, pamphlets, texts of speeches, and statistical data.

interlibrary loan
A borrowing/lending arrangement between one library and another that allows patrons to have materials from another library sent to their own.

reciprocal borrowing privileges
A borrowing/lending arrangement among libraries that allows patrons of any one library to use the resources of the others on site.

illustration
A story or anecdote that provides an example of an idea, issue, or problem the speaker is discussing.

hypothetical illustration
An example or story that has not actually occurred.

DEVELOPING YOUR PRESENTATION
Step by Step

Gathering Supporting Material

With a draft of her specific purpose, central idea, and main ideas in hand, Maggie begins to research cyberterrorism. Fortunately, she kept the *Newsweek* article that gave her the idea for the topic, so she has one source already. Because this first source is a news publication, Maggie decides to check out newspapers next.

She goes online to her university library's web site, where she accesses the database *Newspaper Source* and discovers another article entitled "Asymmetric Cyber Threat," in the November 13, 2007, issue of the *Washington Times. Newspaper Source* provides the full text of that article. While Maggie is online, she uses Google to search for additional information on her topic and discovers the web site of the United States Institute of Peace. The site identifies the Institute as "an independent, nonpartisan, national institution established and funded by Congress." Maggie decides it is another credible source.

Maggie records in MLA format on note cards the essential bibliographical information for these and other sources she discovers. Then she begins to read carefully and take notes. As she does so, she puts quotation marks around any material she copies verbatim and makes sure she has copied it accurately.

2. Verbal

Whether you choose to use brief or extended illustrations, true or hypothetical ones, remember this principle: Everybody likes to hear a story. An illustration almost always ensures audience interest. In addition, communication researchers have found that listeners are less likely to generate counterarguments to a persuasive message supported by examples and personal narratives.[30]

The following suggestions should help you use illustrations effectively in your presentations:

- Be sure that your illustrations are directly relevant to the idea or point they are supposed to support.
- Choose illustrations that are typical, not exceptions.
- Make your illustrations vivid and specific.
- Use illustrations with which your listeners can identify.
- Remember that the most effective illustrations are often personal ones.

Descriptions and Explanations   Probably the most commonly used forms of supporting material are descriptions and explanations. A **description** provides detailed images that allow an audience to see, hear, smell, touch, or taste whatever you are describing. Descriptions can make people and scenes come alive for an audience. In her Nobel Prize acceptance speech, writer Doris Lessing described Africa as she remembered it:

> . . . the banks of the Zambesi, where it rolls between pale grassy banks, it being the dry season, dark-green and glossy, with all the birds of Africa around its banks. . . . elephants, giraffes, lions and the rest . . . the sky at night, still unpolluted, black and wonderful, full of restless stars.[31]

An **explanation** of how something works or why a situation exists can help an audience understand conditions, events, or processes. Justice Ruth Bader Ginsburg explained during a lecture how to interpret the U.S. Supreme Court's delivery of dissenting opinions:

> Typically, when Court decisions are announced from the bench, only the majority opinion is summarized. Separate opinions, concurring or dissenting, are noted, but not described. A dissent presented orally therefore garners immediate attention. It signals that, in the dissenters' view, the Court's opinion is not just wrong, but importantly and grievously misguided.[32]

---

description
A word picture.

explanation
A statement that makes clear how something is done or why it exists in its present or past form.

This speaker effectively uses an electronic presentation aid to complement his use of descriptions and explanations.

Although descriptions and explanations are part of most presentations, they lack the inherent interest factor that illustrations have. The following suggestions may help you to keep audiences from yawning through your descriptions and explanations:

- Avoid too many descriptions and explanations.
- Keep your descriptions and explanations brief.
- Describe and explain in specific and concrete language.

Definitions   Speakers should offer **definitions** of all technical or little-known terms in their presentations. However, they do not need to define terms with which most or all audience members are likely to be familiar. If you determine that you should define a word or phrase for your audience, consider whether you can best define it by **classification**, the format of a standard dictionary definition, or by an **operational definition**, explaining how the word or phrase works or what it does. Discussing his role in an investigation of unlawful interrogation practices, New York attorney Scott Horton used this operational definition of *torture*:

> . . . the following techniques were the focus of our concern: waterboarding, long-time standing, hypothermia, sleep deprivation in excess of two days, the use of psychotropic drugs and the sensory deprivation/sensory overload techniques first developed for the CIA at McGill University.[33]

To use definitions effectively, consider the following suggestions:

- Use definitions only when necessary.
- Be certain that your definitions are understandable.
- Be sure that any definition you provide accurately reflects your use of the word or phrase throughout the presentation.

Analogies   An **analogy** demonstrates how unfamiliar ideas, things, and situations are similar to something the audience already understands. Speakers can use two types of analogies in their presentations. The first is a **literal analogy**, or comparison of two similar things. Kristen uses a literal analogy to offer a solution to America's complex income tax system:

> According to many experts, following in Europe's fiscal footsteps could bring the American tax system up to speed. With a flat income tax, the U.S. could keep fairness while gaining simplicity and efficiency in its taxing burden.[34]

2. Verbal

definition
A statement of what something means.

classification
A type of definition that first places a term in the general class to which it belongs and then differentiates it from all other members of that class.

operational definition
A definition that shows how a term works or what it does.

analogy
A comparison between two ideas, things, or situations that demonstrates how something unfamiliar is similar to something the audience already understands.

literal analogy
A comparison between two similar things.

2. Verbal

The second type of analogy is a **figurative analogy**, a comparison of two seemingly dissimilar things that in fact share a significant common feature. In his much-acclaimed "Last Lecture," Carnegie Mellon professor Randy Pausch created a memorable figurative analogy between one's outlook on life and the outlooks of two beloved characters from *Winnie the Pooh*:

> . . . you just have to decide if you're a Tigger or an Eeyore. I think I'm clear where I stand on the great Tigger/Eeyore debate. Never lose the childlike wonder. It's just too important.[35]

Two suggestions can help you use analogies more effectively in your presentations:

1. Be certain that the two things you compare in a literal analogy are very similar.
2. Make the similarity between the two things compared in a figurative analogy apparent to the audience.

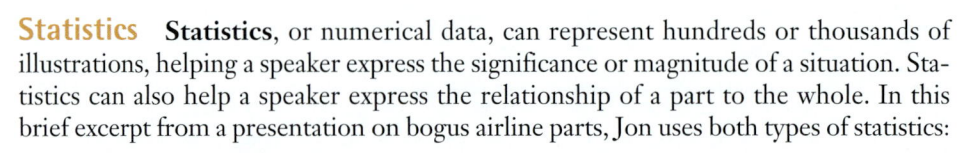

2. Verbal

Statistics Statistics, or numerical data, can represent hundreds or thousands of illustrations, helping a speaker express the significance or magnitude of a situation. Statistics can also help a speaker express the relationship of a part to the whole. In this brief excerpt from a presentation on bogus airline parts, Jon uses both types of statistics:

> . . . 26 million parts are installed on airplanes every year in the U.S., and the FAA estimates that at least 2% of these parts are counterfeits.[36]

Skilled speakers learn how to use statistics to their greatest advantage. For example, they try to make huge numbers more dramatic for their audiences. AFL-CIO pres-

Communication *and Diversity*

Adapting to Diverse Audiences

One of the principles we've stressed throughout this book is the importance of adapting your message to others. Many, if not most, of the presentations you give will be to audiences that represent a mix of cultures and backgrounds rather than a single cultural tradition. Although you may not have immediate plans to deliver a presentation in Singapore, Moscow, Tokyo, or Warsaw, it will not be unusual for you to face audience members who come from one of these cities when you speak on campus or in your hometown.

People from the predominant culture in North America usually prefer a structured presentation that follows an outlined pattern; they also prefer an introduction that previews the ideas you'll present and a conclusion that crisply summarizes the essential points you've made. But a Russian or Eastern European audience would expect a less tightly structured presentation. When you're in doubt about listener preferences, we recommend being structured and organized. But realize that not all audience members may expect information to be presented as *you* prefer. One study found that members of some cultures prefer a more formal oratorical style of delivery than the conversational, extemporaneous style that is usually taught in American presentational speaking classes.[37] For example, Japanese speakers addressing a predominantly Japanese audience begin a presentation by making respectful references to their audience.

You may still be wondering, "So, what should I do when I speak to people who have a cultural background different from my own?" Here are some ideas that may help you.[38] First, consider using a variety of different types of supporting materials. A mix of stories, examples, statistics, and other supporting illustrations can appeal to a wide range of audience backgrounds. Also consider the power of images over words. Use visual aids to illustrate your talk. Pictures and images can communicate universal messages—especially emotional ones. Telling a good story to illustrate your ideas is another effective strategy to appeal to a wide range of audience preferences. Most audiences value a good story with a point or moral that is relevant to the point you want to make. Our overarching suggestion: Be aware of who will be in your audience. If you're unsure of your listeners' speaking-style preferences, ask for tips and strategies from audience members or people you trust, before you design or deliver your presentation.

ident John J. Sweeney dramatized the danger of unsafe bridges in the United States by making a statistic personal:

> Since I was coming to work from Washington to New Rochelle this morning, I asked my staff to check out my route.
> We found that traveling the I-95 corridor between Washington, D.C. and New York City, I would cross or come within two-tenths of a mile of 30 bridges that are rated either functionally obsolete or structurally deficient.[39]

Another speaker made statistics about alcohol-related deaths more dramatic by **compacting** them—limiting them so that they were more meaningful to his listeners:

> . . . in 2005 the number of alcohol-related traffic deaths increased 41%, and in 2006, of the 39,000 fatal car crashes, nearly half of them were alcohol-related. To put that in a better perspective, this is someone being killed every 31 minutes because of an alcohol-related crash.[40]

In addition to dramatizing and compacting statistics, you can use statistics more effectively if you utilize the following three suggestions:

1. Round off large numbers.
2. Use visual aids to present your statistics.
3. Cite the sources of your statistics.

Opinions The opinions of others can add authority, drama, and style to a presentation. A speaker can use three types of opinions: expert testimony, lay testimony, and literary quotations.

Expert testimony is the type of opinion most frequently employed by speakers. If you lack authority on your topic, cite someone who can offer such expertise. In preparing her speech on the college credit card crisis, Jeni realized that her audience might not believe that the misuse of credit cards by college students is a widespread problem. So Jeni quoted an expert:

> Ruth Suswein, executive director of the Bankcard Holders of America, told the . . . *Pittsburgh Post Gazette*, "I defy you to go on any college campus and find any student who doesn't know some other student who has messed up using credit cards."[41]

After the devastating earthquake that killed tens of thousands in central China in May 2008, television audiences around the world were moved by the reports of people who had witnessed firsthand the disaster and its aftermath. For a speaker, as well as a news organization, such **lay testimony** can provide the most memorable moments of a presentation, stirring an audience's emotions.

Finally, speakers may wish to include **literary quotations** in their presentations. In a speech on how technology is changing television broadcasting, NBC Universal chief executive Jeff Zucker quoted Henry David Thoreau's concern about the inventions of his day:

> They are but improved means to an unimproved end . . . . We are in great haste to construct a magnetic telegraph from Maine to Texas; but Maine and Texas, it may be, have nothing important to communicate.[42]

Whether you use expert testimony, lay testimony, or literary quotations, consider the following suggestions for using opinions effectively in your presentations:

- Be certain that any authority you cite is actually an expert on the subject you are discussing.
- Identify your sources.
- Cite unbiased authorities.
- Cite opinions that are representative of prevailing opinion. If you cite a dissenting viewpoint, identify it as such.
- Quote or paraphrase your sources accurately, and note the context in which the remarks were originally made.
- Use literary quotations sparingly.

2. Verbal

figurative analogy
A comparison between two seemingly dissimilar things that share some common feature on which the comparison depends.

statistics
Numerical data that summarize examples.

compacting
Breaking down a statistic so that it is more meaningful to your audience.

expert testimony
The opinion of someone who is an acknowledged expert in the field under discussion.

lay testimony
The opinion of someone who experienced an event or situation firsthand.

literary quotation
A citation from a work of fiction or nonfiction, a poem, or another speech.

Acknowledgment of Supporting Material

Once you have supporting material in hand, you must decide whether it must be credited to a source. Some information is so widely known that you may not need to acknowledge a source. For example, you need not credit a source if you say that former FBI official Mark Felt has been identified as the long-anonymous Watergate informant "Deep Throat." This fact is general knowledge and is widely available in a variety of sources. However, if you decide to use any of the following, then you must give credit:

- Direct quotations, even if they are only brief phrases
- Opinions, assertions, or ideas of others, even if you paraphrase them rather than quote them verbatim
- Statistics
- Any nonoriginal visual materials, including graphs, tables, and pictures

To cite your source, you can integrate an **oral citation** into your presentation. For example, you might say,

> *The New York Times* of March 4, 2008, explains that a superbug staph infection is spreading in locations that millions of Americans visit daily, like college campuses and gyms, where incidental skin-to-skin contact is inevitable.[43]

Recap

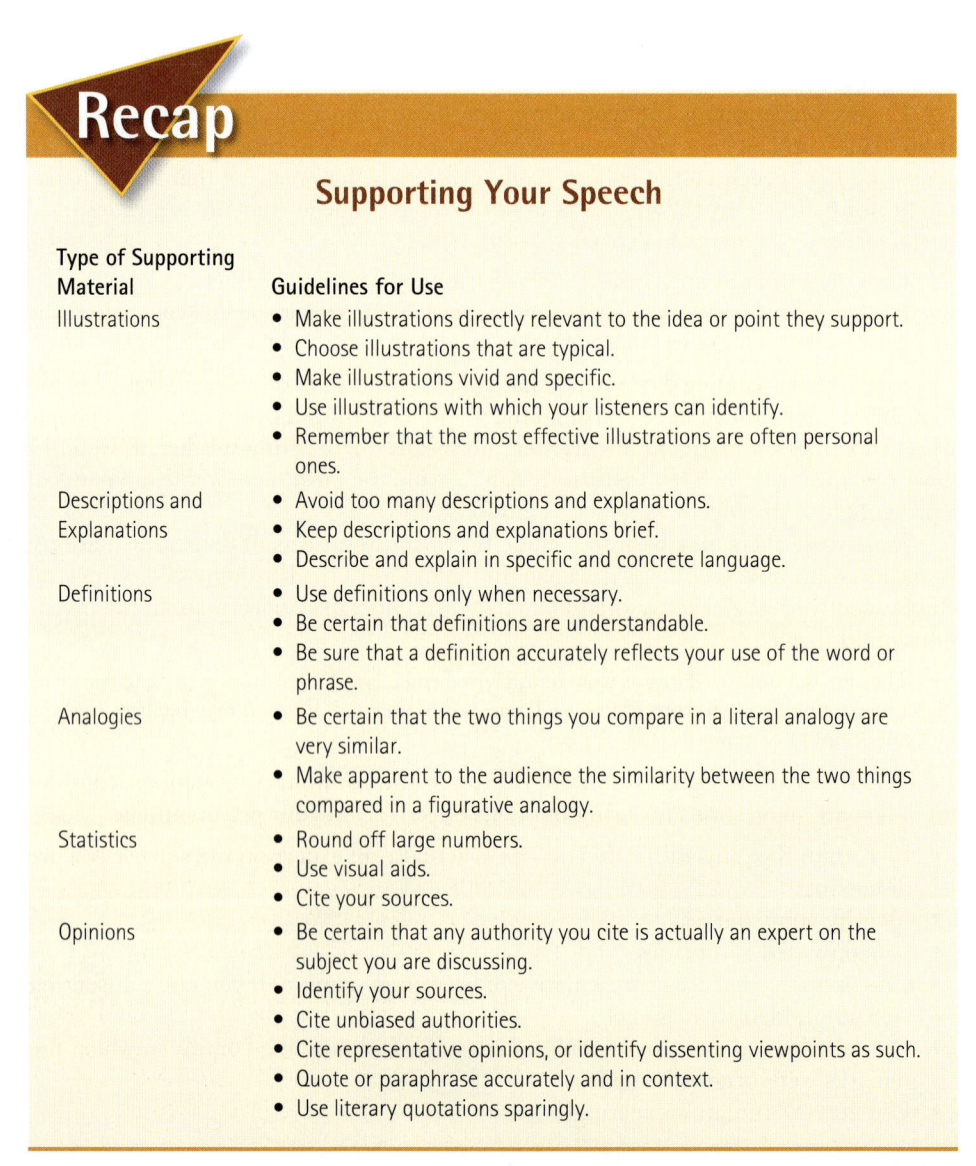

Supporting Your Speech

Type of Supporting Material	Guidelines for Use
Illustrations	• Make illustrations directly relevant to the idea or point they support. • Choose illustrations that are typical. • Make illustrations vivid and specific. • Use illustrations with which your listeners can identify. • Remember that the most effective illustrations are often personal ones.
Descriptions and Explanations	• Avoid too many descriptions and explanations. • Keep descriptions and explanations brief. • Describe and explain in specific and concrete language.
Definitions	• Use definitions only when necessary. • Be certain that definitions are understandable. • Be sure that a definition accurately reflects your use of the word or phrase.
Analogies	• Be certain that the two things you compare in a literal analogy are very similar. • Make apparent to the audience the similarity between the two things compared in a figurative analogy.
Statistics	• Round off large numbers. • Use visual aids. • Cite your sources.
Opinions	• Be certain that any authority you cite is actually an expert on the subject you are discussing. • Identify your sources. • Cite unbiased authorities. • Cite representative opinions, or identify dissenting viewpoints as such. • Quote or paraphrase accurately and in context. • Use literary quotations sparingly.

oral citation
The oral presentation of such information about a source as the author, title, and publication date.

As you select your illustrations, descriptions, explanations, definitions, analogies, statistics, and opinions, be guided not only by the suggestions provided in this chapter for each type of supporting material but also by the five Communication Principles for a Lifetime. The best supporting material reflects self-awareness, taking advantage of your own knowledge and experience. Effective verbal supporting material is appropriately worded, concrete, and vivid enough that your audience can visualize what you are talking about. Effective visual supporting material enhances, rather than detracts from, your verbal message. Sensitivity to your audience will help you choose the verbal and visual supporting material that is most appropriately adapted to them. If a presentation is boring, it is probably because the speaker has not used the fundamental principles of communication as criteria for selecting supporting material.

1. Aware
2. Verbal
3. Nonverbal
4. Listen and Respond
5. Adapt

PRINCIPLES FOR A LIFETIME
Enhancing Your Skills

1. Aware

Principle One: Be aware of your communication with yourself and others.
- Give yourself a pep talk before getting up to speak.
- Consider your own interests and experiences when searching for a topic.
- Remember that the most effective illustrations are often personal ones.

2. Verbal

Principle Two: Effectively use and interpret verbal messages.
- Focus on your message to help manage speaker anxiety.
- Search for topics on the web, in the media, and in books.
- Word your specific purpose in terms of your audience to help you keep your focus on them.
- Make sure your central idea reflects a single topic, is a complete declarative sentence, and uses specific language.
- Consider the accountability, accuracy, objectivity, date, usability, and sensitivity to diversity of verbal material you find on web sites.
- Look beyond Wikipedia, which is not a reliable source.
- Be sure that your illustrations are directly relevant to the idea or point they are supposed to support.
- Make your illustrations vivid and specific.
- Avoid too many descriptions and explanations.
- Keep descriptions and explanations brief.
- Describe and explain in specific and concrete language.
- Make your definitions readily understandable, and be certain they accurately reflect how you use the word or phrase in the speech.
- Round off statistics to make them more readily understandable.
- Cite unbiased authorities.
- Cite opinions that are representative of prevailing opinion.
- Quote or paraphrase accurately and in context.
- Use literary quotations sparingly.
- Integrate oral citations of your sources into your presentation.

3. Nonverbal

Principle Three: Effectively use and interpret nonverbal messages.
- Remember that the physical symptoms of speaker anxiety are rarely visible to an audience.
- Consider the accountability, accuracy, objectivity, date, usability, and sensitivity to diversity of pictures and graphics you find on web sites.
- Use visual aids to present statistics.

4. Listen and Respond

Principle Four: Listen and respond thoughtfully to others.

- Seek out information about your audience and how they are likely to respond to your message to increase your comfort with speaking in public.
- Listen for topic ideas in the course of casual conversation with friends.

5. Adapt

Principle Five: Appropriately adapt messages to others.

- Revise your ideas or strategies at any point in the presentation-preparation process, as you seek out and learn more about your audience.
- Be audience-centered to reduce speaker anxiety.
- Be sensitive to and adapt to the diversity of your audience.
- Consider your audience's interests and expectations as you select the topic for your presentation.
- Keep in mind your audience's knowledge, interests, and expectations as you select supporting material for your presentation.
- Use illustrations with which your audience can identify. Consider making your audience members part of the scenario in a hypothetical illustration.
- Make the similarity between the two things compared in a figurative analogy apparent to your audience.

Summary

Public speaking is a teachable, learnable process of developing, supporting, organizing, and presenting ideas. Presentational speaking skills can help you in other college courses and in the workplace.

The stages of the public speaking process center around consideration of the audience, who influence every decision a speaker makes. A speaker's tasks include selecting and narrowing a topic, identifying a general and specific purpose for speaking, developing the central idea of the presentation, generating main ideas, gathering supporting material, organizing the presentation, and, finally, rehearsing and delivering the presentation.

Nearly everyone feels some anxiety about speaking in public. Speaker anxiety triggers physiological responses that may be worrisome but are actually your body's attempt to help you. Focusing on your audience and message and giving yourself mental pep talks can help you manage speaker anxiety, as can knowing how to develop a presentation, being well prepared, and seeking out opportunities to speak. Professional help is available for those few who continue to suffer debilitating speaker anxiety.

As you begin to prepare your presentation, you will first have to select and narrow your topic, keeping in mind the audience, the occasion, and your own interests and experiences. You may find helpful such strategies as silent brainstorming, scanning web directories and web pages, and listening and reading for topic ideas. Once you have a topic, you need to identify both your general and your specific purpose. General purposes include to inform, to persuade, and to entertain. Specific purposes are determined by the general purpose, the topic, and the audience. You will also need to decide on the central idea for the presentation. You can use that central idea to help you generate your main ideas, which are usually logical divisions of the central idea, reasons the central idea is true, or a series of steps or a chronological sequence that develops the central idea.

Next, you will need to discover support for your main ideas. As a presentational speaker, you have at least three potential sources of supporting material: yourself, the Internet, and the library. Personal knowledge and experience increase the likelihood that the audience will find you a credible speaker. To supplement your own knowledge and experience, you might turn to the vast resources available on the Internet. And most likely, you will still use library resources—books, periodicals, newspapers, reference resources, government documents, and various special services—as sources of supporting material.

The types of supporting material you can use in a presentation include illustrations, descriptions and explanations, definitions, analogies, statistics, and opinions. Simple guidelines can help you use each of these types of supporting material effectively and cite your sources correctly.

Assessing Your Knowledge

For Discussion and Review

Principle One: Be aware of your communication with yourself and others.

1. Explain what causes the symptoms of speaker anxiety.

Principle Two: Effectively use and interpret verbal messages.

2. With what phrase should an audience-centered specific purpose begin?

Principle Three: Effectively use and interpret nonverbal messages.

3. Explain how to evaluate pictures and graphics you find on the Internet.

Principle Four: Listen and respond thoughtfully to others.

4. Give an example of a topic for a presentation that might come from a conversation with friends.

Principle Five: Appropriately adapt messages to others.

5. Discuss how the interests and expectations of your listeners might affect your choice of topic for a presentation.

Multiple Choice

Choose the *best* answer to each of the following questions.

1. Which of the following identifies what your audience should know or be able to do at the conclusion of your presentation?
   a. general purpose
   b. specific purpose
   c. central idea
   d. supporting material

2. In your presentation, you should cite a source for all of the following except
   a. historical events if they are well known.
   b. others' opinions that you have paraphrased.
   c. statistics.
   d. direct quotations if they are very brief.

3. Destiny gave an informative presentation in class with the following central idea: "Good study habits and time management skills are key to a successful college experience." Her instructor deducted points from her grade because Destiny's central idea
   a. is not a complete declarative statement.
   b. is not audience-centered.
   c. uses vague and abstract language.
   d. should be a single topic.

4. Research in the area of speaker anxiety has found that approximately _____ of speakers experience anxiety.
   a. 20%
   b. 40%
   c. 60%
   d. 80%

5. Informing, persuading, and entertaining are the three types of
   a. general purposes.
   b. specific purposes.
   c. central ideas.
   d. supporting material.

6. Whenever Linda gets nervous about giving a presentation, she takes a look at a video of Martin Luther King's "I Have a Dream" presentation so that she can imagine herself being that effective. Linda is practicing
   a. systematic desensitization.
   b. focusing on her audience.
   c. performance visualization.
   d. deep-breathing techniques.

7. Dallin is planning to use information about population growth in the United States in his speech. From which top-level domain should he gather his information if he uses the Internet?
   a. .com
   b. .org
   c. .gov
   d. .mil

8. During a speech on alternative energy, Luis says, "The American Petroleum Institute's web site explains that the need for alternative energy sources

is exaggerated because the current known oil supplies are expected to last for almost a hundred more years." Which standard for evaluating web sites did Luis most likely overlook?
   a. accountability
   b. objectivity
   c. accuracy
   d. date

9. The comparison of two seemingly dissimilar things in order to reveal a common feature is known as a(n)
   a. definition.
   b. literal analogy.
   c. figurative analogy.
   d. illustration.

10. During a speech on global warming, Rosalinda says, "Imagine spending spring break on the Gulf Coast, but instead of going to South Padre Island, you drive to Austin, Texas." What type of support is Rosalinda using?
    a. description
    b. hypothetical illustration
    c. literal analogy
    d. opinion

Answers to the questions in this practice test can be found at the end of the book.

Assessing Your Skill

Personal Report of Communication Apprehension (PRCA-24)

The best known and most frequently used measure for assessing communication apprehension is James C. McCroskey's Personal Report of Communication Apprehension, which assesses anxiety in the context of a number of communication activities, including presentational speaking (the "Public" category).

Directions: This instrument is composed of twenty-four statements concerning your feelings about communication with other people. Please indicate in the space provided the degree to which each statement applies to you by marking whether you (1) Strongly Agree, (2) Agree, (3) Are Undecided, (4) Disagree, or (5) Strongly Disagree with each statement. There are no right or wrong answers. Many of the statements are similar to other statements. Do not be concerned about this. Work quickly, just record your first impression.

1. _____ I dislike participating in group discussions.
2. _____ Generally, I am comfortable while participating in a group discussion.
3. _____ I am tense and nervous while participating in group discussions.
4. _____ I like to get involved in group discussions.
5. _____ Engaging in a group discussion with new people makes me tense and nervous.
6. _____ I am calm and relaxed while participating in group discussions.
7. _____ Generally, I am nervous when I have to participate in a meeting.
8. _____ Usually I am calm and relaxed while participating in meetings.
9. _____ I am very calm and relaxed when I am called upon to express an opinion at a meeting.
10. _____ I am afraid to express myself at meetings.
11. _____ Communicating at meetings usually makes me uncomfortable.
12. _____ I am very relaxed when answering questions at a meeting.
13. _____ While participating in a conversation with a new acquaintance, I feel very nervous.
14. _____ I have no fear of speaking up in conversations.
15. _____ Ordinarily I am very tense and nervous in conversations.
16. _____ Ordinarily I am very calm and relaxed in conversations.
17. _____ While conversing with a new acquaintance, I feel very relaxed.
18. _____ I'm afraid to speak up in conversations.
19. _____ I have no fear of giving a speech.
20. _____ Certain parts of my body feel very tense and rigid while giving a speech.
21. _____ I feel relaxed while giving a speech.
22. _____ My thoughts become confused and jumbled when I am giving a speech.
23. _____ I face the prospect of giving a speech with confidence.
24. _____ While giving a speech I get so nervous, I forget facts I really know.

SCORING:
Group = 18 − (1) + (2) − (3) + (4) − (5) + (6)
Meeting = 18 − (7) + (8) + (9) − (10) − (11) + (12)
Dyadic = 18 − (13) + (14) − (15) + (16) + (17) − (18)
Public = 18 + (19) − (20) + (21) − (22) + (23) − (24)
Overall CA = Group + Meeting + Dyadic + Public

Source: J. McCroskey, *An Introduction to Rhetorical Communication* 9e (Boston: Allyn and Bacon, 2006).

Web Resources to Improve Your Knowledge and Skill

The Internet can be a useful source when you are searching for an interesting speech topic. Remember: The best topic is one that relates to your audience, the occasion, and your own interests and background.

Consider using a web directory such as Yahoo! to help you find a topic that meets the three criteria we've noted. Here's the address: <www.yahoo.com>.

Another interesting source of speech ideas is current headlines. Here's a source that has links to many media outlets, including most major news networks: <www.totalnews.com>.

Pollock, Jackson, "Male and Female." © 2008 Artists Rights Society (ARS), New York. The Philadelphia Museum of Art/Art Resource, NY

Don't agonize. Organize.

Florynce R. Kennedy

Chapter 12

Organizing and Outlining Your Presentation

Chapter Outline

- Organizing Your Main Ideas
- Organizing Your Supporting Material
- Organizing Your Presentation for the Ears of Others
- Introducing and Concluding Your Presentation
- Outlining Your Presentation
- Summary

Chapter Objectives

After studying this chapter, you should be able to

1. List and explain five strategies for organizing main ideas in a presentation.
2. Define the principles of recency, primacy, and complexity and explain how each can be applied to organizing main ideas.
3. List and explain six strategies for organizing supporting material in a presentation.
4. Explain three ways to organize a presentation for the ears of others.
5. List and explain the six functions of a presentation introduction.
6. Suggest at least five strategies for getting an audience's attention in a presentation introduction.
7. List and explain the four functions of a presentation conclusion.
8. Define a preparation outline and explain how a speaker would use one.
9. Outline a presentation according to standard outline format.
10. Explain how to create speaking notes from a preparation outline.

Developing a presentation is like building a house. Just as a building contractor frames out a house early in the building process, a speaker frames out a presentation by completing the first four stages of the speech preparation process—selecting and narrowing a topic, identifying a general and a specific purpose, determining a central idea, and generating main ideas. Framing completed, the contractor assembles all the materials needed for the house: windows, doors, cabinets, hardware, and flooring; the speaker finds and adds supporting material to the presentation "frame," the fifth stage of the process. Once the house is framed out and the building materials are ready, the contractor must organize the work of the electricians, plumbers, carpenters, and carpet layers. Similarly, the speaker must organize ideas and supporting material.

In this chapter, we will discuss strategies for organizing and outlining your presentation, and we will explore ways to introduce and conclude your presentation effectively. Grounded in the five Communication Principles for a Lifetime with which you are now familiar, these suggestions and strategies will result in an essentially complete "house"—a presentation that is ready to be rehearsed and delivered.

Organizing Your Main Ideas

You have already completed the first five stages of audience-centered presentation preparation:

- Select and narrow a topic.
- Determine your purpose.
- Develop your central idea.
- Generate main ideas.
- Gather supporting material.

Now it is time to put your presentation together, organizing the ideas and information you have generated and discovered.

Logical organization is one way you can communicate your verbal message effectively. A logically organized presentation has three major divisions—an introduction, a body, and a conclusion. The introduction catches the audience's attention and previews the body. The body presents the main content of the presentation. The conclusion summarizes the main ideas and provides memorable closure to the presentation.

Professional speaker Larry Tracy suggests a strategy he calls "3-1-2" for drafting the organization of a presentation.[1] It works like this:

1. Take a stack of 3 × 5 cards. Label one card "3" and write on it your "bottom line" message. This is the core of your conclusion.
2. Label another card "1" and write on it where the presentation will go—your preview.
3. Next, place the supporting points that flow from "1" to "3" on a series of cards marked "2a," "2b," "2c," etc. These will become the main ideas of the body of your presentation.

The advantage of the "3-1-2" strategy, says Tracy, is that it clarifies from the start of the drafting process where the presentation is going, ensuring more logical structure. He adds, "Just remember: You draft 3-1-2, but . . . you deliver 1-2-3."

Regardless of whether you use Tracy's drafting process, one recommended by your public speaking instructor, or one of your own devising, you will need to consider early on how best to organize your main ideas. Then you will organize your supporting material for maximum impact, and devise signposts to lead your audience through your presentation. Finally, you will need to develop an effective introduction and conclusion. Once you have made the necessary decisions about these component parts, you will be ready to outline the entire presentation.

2. Verbal

Organizing Ideas Topically

If your main ideas are logical divisions of your central idea, you will probably arrange them according to **topical organization**, the strategy used most frequently. Topical organization may be simply an arbitrary arrangement of main ideas that are fairly equal in importance. For example, if you are giving an informative presentation on the various instrument families in the modern symphony orchestra, your main ideas will probably be strings, woodwinds, brass, and percussion. The order in which you discuss these instrument groups may not really matter.

At other times, topical organization is less arbitrary. The principle of **recency** suggests that audiences remember best what they hear last. If you want to emphasize the string section of an orchestra, you will purposefully place that instrument family last in your informative presentation.

Another principle that can help guide your topical organization is the principle of **primacy**. Primacy suggests that you discuss your most convincing or least controversial idea first. To adapt to an audience who may be skeptical of some of your ideas, discuss first those points on which you all agree. If you are speaking to an anti–gun-control audience about ways to protect children from violence in schools, don't begin by advocating gun control. Instead, begin by affirming family values and education in the home, perhaps move on to the importance of small classes and adequate counseling in schools, and only then discuss gun control as a possible preventive measure.

One other type of topical organization is organization according to **complexity**, moving from simple ideas and processes to more complex ones. Many skills you have learned in life have been taught by order of complexity. In first grade, you learned to read easy words first, then moved on to more difficult ones. In third grade, you learned single-digit multiplication tables before moving on to more complex double- and triple-digit multiplication problems. In junior high school, you learned to use the library's catalog before you began a research project. And in high school, you learned to drive by practicing simple maneuvers in the parking lot before going out on the highway. Similarly, if you are giving a presentation on how to trace your family's genealogy, you might discuss readily available, user-friendly Internet sources before explaining how to access old courthouse records or parish registries of births, deaths, and baptisms.

Organizing Ideas Chronologically

If you determine that you can best develop your central idea through a series of steps, you will probably organize those steps—your main ideas—chronologically. **Chronological organization** is based on time or sequential order, according to when each step or event occurred or should occur. If you are explaining a process, you will want to organize the steps of that process from first to last. If you are providing a historical overview of an event, movement, or policy, you might begin with the end result and trace its history backward in time.

Examples of topics that might lend themselves to chronological organization include the process for stripping and refinishing a piece of furniture, the three deadliest U.S. tornadoes on record, and the history of higher education for women.

Organizing Ideas Spatially

"Go down the hill two blocks and turn left by the florist. Then go three blocks to the next stoplight and turn right. The place you're looking for is about a block farther, on your right." When you offer someone directions, you organize your ideas spatially. **Spatial organization** means arranging items according to their location, position, or direction. It is another strategy by which you might organize main ideas that are logical divisions of your central idea.

Presentations that rely on description are especially good candidates for spatial organization. For example, a discussion of the route taken by Sir Edmund Hillary and Tenzing Norgay when climbing Mt. Everest in 1953 or the molecular structure of

---

topical organization
Organization determined by the speaker's discretion or by recency, primacy, or complexity.

recency
Arrangement of ideas from least important to most important or from weakest to strongest.

primacy
Arrangement of ideas from most important to least important or from strongest to weakest.

complexity
Arranging ideas from simple to more complex.

chronological organization
Organization by time or sequence.

spatial organization
Organization according to location, position, or direction.

DNA would lend itself to spatial organization. Or, rather than organizing your presentation on the three deadliest U.S. tornadoes chronologically (by year), you might choose to organize it spatially, according to where each tornado occurred.

Organizing Ideas to Show Cause and Effect

Cause-and-effect organization actually refers to two related patterns: identifying a situation and then discussing the resulting effects (cause–effect) and presenting a situation and then exploring its causes (effect–cause). If your main ideas are logical divisions of your central idea, you might organize them according to cause–effect. If your main ideas are reasons your central idea is true, you will probably organize them according to effect–cause.

A speaker discussing the consequences of teenage pregnancy might use a cause–effect pattern, first establishing that teenage pregnancy is a significant social issue and then discussing various consequences or effects. On the other hand, a speaker who wanted to explore the reasons for the high rate of teen pregnancy would probably use an effect–cause pattern, first discussing teenage pregnancy as an effect and then exploring its various causes. As the recency principle would suggest, a cause–effect pattern emphasizes effects; an effect–cause pattern emphasizes causes.

Organizing Ideas by Problem and Solution

If, instead of exploring causes or consequences of a problem or issue, you want either to explore how best to solve the problem or to advocate a particular solution, you will probably choose **problem-and-solution organization**. It is another strategy appropriate for organizing logical divisions of a central idea. For example, if you were speaking on how listeners can protect themselves from mountain lion attacks in the American West, you might first establish that a significant problem exists, then talk about solutions to that problem. Or if you were talking about ending discrimination against overweight people, you could first establish that such discrimination exists and is harmful, then talk about the solutions. Although you can use problem-and-solution organization for either informative or persuasive presentations, you are more likely to use it when your general purpose is to persuade—to urge your audience to support or adopt one or more of the solutions you discuss.

Note that the topics in both of the above examples also lend themselves to organization by cause and effect. You could, for example, discuss mountain lion attacks as an effect and explore why the frequency of such attacks has increased in recent years (causes). Or you could talk about discrimination against the overweight as a cause and discuss the harmful effects of such discrimination. How do you decide which organizational pattern to use? Return to your specific purpose. If it is for your audience to be able to explain how to end discrimination against overweight people, select the problem-and-solution organizational strategy. If it is for your audience to be able to explain the harmful effects of discrimination against those who are overweight, use the cause-and-effect strategy of organization. Let both your general and your specific purpose continue to guide your presentation as you organize your main ideas.

cause-and-effect organization
Organization by discussing a situation and its causes or a situation and its effects.

problem-and-solution organization
Organization by discussing first a problem and then various solutions.

Organizing Your Supporting Material

Once you have organized your main ideas, you are ready to organize the supporting material for each idea. Suppose you find that you have two brief illustrations, a statistic, and an opinion in support of your first main idea. How should you organize these materials to communicate your verbal message most effectively?

Recap

Organizing Your Main Ideas

Strategy	Description	Applicable to main ideas that are . . .
Chronological	Organization by time or sequence	Steps or a chronological sequence
Topical	Arbitrary arrangement of topics or organization according to recency, primacy, or complexity	Logical divisions
Spatial	Organization according to location or position	Logical divisions
Cause-and-effect	Organization by discussing a situation and its causes (effect-cause) or a situation and its effects (cause-effect)	Reasons (effect-cause) Logical divisions (cause-effect)
Problem-and-solution	Organization by discussing a problem and then various solutions	Logical divisions

The same organizational patterns you considered as you organized your main ideas can also help you organize your supporting material. For example, you might arrange a group of brief illustrations *chronologically*. At other times, you might find it more useful to organize supporting material according to the principle of recency, primacy, or complexity. You would employ the principle of *recency* if you saved your most convincing statistic for last. You would use *primacy* if you decided to present first the opinion with which you were certain your audience would agree. And you might arrange two explanations according to the principle of *complexity*, presenting the simplest one first and working up to the more complex one. Two additional principles that may help you organize supporting material are specificity and arrangement from "soft" to "hard" evidence.

Sometimes your supporting material includes both specific illustrations and more general explanations or statistics. The principle of **specificity** suggests that you group your specific information and either offer it first, followed by your general explanation or statistics, or give your general explanation or statistics first and then follow with your specific illustrations. In a presentation on raising awareness about poverty, Kerlin provides statistics before moving to a specific illustration:

> . . . in New Orleans, 38% of children live in poverty, which is more than double the national child poverty rate of 17%. In the state of Louisiana, 13% of children live not in poverty—but extreme poverty.
>
> Let me tell you about the 6-year-old hero in the aftermath of Katrina. Deamonte Love was born and raised in a poor family. According to the *Los Angeles Times* of September 5, 2005, that 6-year-old boy walked down the road, holding a 5-month-old infant. He had no clues whatsoever where his parents were, while surrounded by five toddlers, and one was wearing only diapers.[2]

Another principle that can help you organize your supporting material is moving from "soft" evidence to "hard" evidence. Hypothetical illustrations, descriptions, explanations, definitions, analogies, and opinions are usually considered **soft evidence**. **Hard evidence** includes factual examples and statistics. In his speech on de facto segregation in U.S. schools, Christopher moves from soft evidence to a hard statistic and then compacts that statistic for even more impact:

> . . . 1955 was a pivotal year for America's education system. The Supreme Court decided in *Brown v. the Topeka Board of Education* that schools must integrate. . . . [B]ut due to the

specificity
Organization from specific information to a more general statement or from a general statement to specific information.

soft evidence
Hypothetical illustrations, descriptions, explanations, definitions, analogies, and opinions.

hard evidence
Factual examples and statistics.

Communication and Diversity

Acknowledging Cultural Differences in Organizing Messages

What's the shortest distance between two points? Why, going in a straight line, of course. In organizing a message, it may seem that the most logical strategy is to develop a structure that moves from one idea to the next in a logical, "straight" way. But not every culture organizes ideas using that logic. In fact, each culture teaches its members unique patterns of thought and organization that are considered appropriate for various occasions and audiences. In general, U.S. speakers tend to be more linear and direct than do Semitic, Asian, Romance, or Russian speakers.[3] Semitic speakers support their main points by pursuing tangents that might seem "off topic" to many U.S. listeners. Asians may allude to a main point only through a circuitous route of illustrations and parables. And speakers from Romance and Russian cultures tend to begin with a basic principle and then move to facts and illustrations that only gradually are related to a main point. The models in Figure 12.1 illustrate these culturally diverse patterns of organization.[4] Of course, these are very broad generalizations. As an effective speaker who seeks to adapt to your audience, you should investigate and perhaps acknowledge or even consider adopting the customary organizational strategy of your particular audience. In addition, when you are listening to a presentation, recognizing the existence of cultural differences can help you appreciate and understand the organization of a speaker from a culture other than your own.

Figure 12.1 Organizational Patterns by Culture

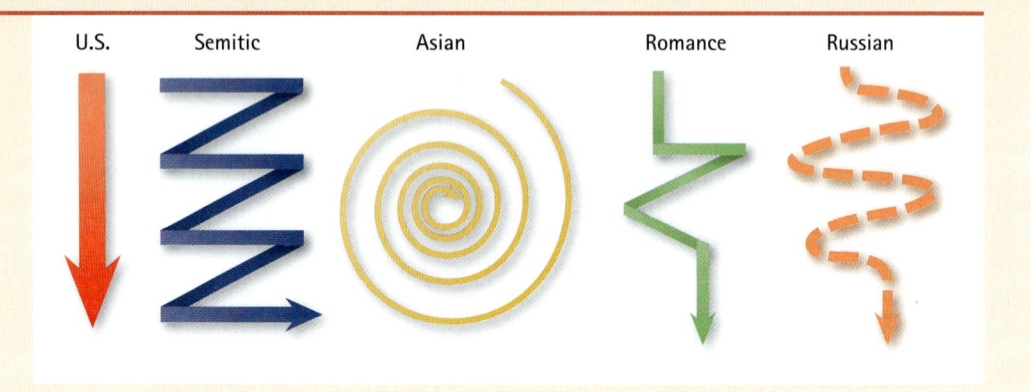

language used in the ruling, schools did not have to act immediately or in a timely manner to desegregate. In fact, according to *Salon.com*, "In education today 70% of American schools are comprised 60% or more of only one race." This means that in a school of 1,000 students, 600 students are, say, black, while the remaining 400 students are made up of white, Hispanic, Asian, Native American, and other ethnicities.[5]

Recap

Organizing Your Supporting Material

Strategy	Description
Chronology	Organization by time or sequence
Recency	Most important material last
Primacy	Most convincing or least controversial material first
Complexity	From simple to more complex material
Specificity	From specific information to general overview or from general overview to specific information
"Soft" to "hard" evidence	From hypothetical illustrations and opinions to facts and statistics

Organizing Your Presentation for the Ears of Others

You now have a fairly complete, logically organized plan for your presentation. But if you tried to deliver it at this point, your audience would probably become confused. What are your main ideas? How is one main idea related to the next? What supporting material develops which main idea? To adapt your logically organized message to your audience, you need to provide **signposts**, or organizational cues for their ears. You do this by adding previews, transitions, and summaries that allow you to move smoothly from one idea to the next throughout the presentation.

5. Adapt

Previews

A **preview** "tells them what you're going to tell them"—it is a statement of what is to come. Previews help your audience members anticipate and remember the main ideas of your presentation. They also help you move smoothly from the introduction to the body of your presentation and from one main idea to the next. The **initial preview** is usually presented in conjunction with, and sometimes as part of, the central idea. Note how Abby states her central idea and then previews her three main ideas near the end of the introduction to her presentation on the ongoing war on cancer:

> The leaders in cancer research in this country are more interested in controlling cancer rather than curing it. . . . So today, in order to treat the cancer problem, we must first understand the problems, unearth the causes, and implement the solutions to change the course of cancer in America.[6]

In addition to offering an initial preview, a speaker may also offer **internal previews** at various points throughout a presentation. These previews introduce and outline ideas that will be developed as the presentation progresses. Meleena provides an internal preview just before the final main idea of her presentation on sexual harassment in schools:

> Now . . . we can look at some things that we can all do, as parents, teachers, and students, to stop sexual harassment in our schools. There are two ways to prevent these causes from recurring. The first is education and the second is immediate action.[7]

When Meleena delivers this preview, her listeners know that she is going to talk about two possible solutions to the problem she has been discussing. Their anticipation increases the likelihood that they will hear and later remember these solutions.

Verbal and Nonverbal Transitions

A **transition** signals to an audience that a speaker is moving from one idea to the next. Effectively using verbal messages includes using **verbal transitions**, words or

---

signpost
A verbal or nonverbal organizational signal.

preview
A statement of what is to come.

initial preview
First statement of the main ideas of a presentation, usually presented with or near the central idea.

internal preview
A preview within the speech that introduces ideas still to come.

transition
A word, phrase, or nonverbal cue that indicates movement from one idea to the next or the relationship between ideas.

verbal transition
A word or phrase that indicates the relationship between two ideas.

Communication and Ethics

The Ethics of Primacy and Recency

Jessica knows that, according to the principle of recency, she should discuss last what she wants her audience to remember best. However, in her presentation on the risk of counterfeit prescription drugs, Jessica thinks that it may be more ethical to reveal immediately to her audience how costly the problem is in terms of both dollars and human lives. Is it ethical for Jessica to save that important statistic for last?

phrases that show relationships between ideas in your presentation. They include simple enumeration (*first, second, third*); synonyms or pronouns that refer to earlier key words or ideas (the word *they* at the beginning of this sentence refers to the phrase "verbal transitions" in the previous sentence); and words and phrases that show relationships between ideas (*in addition, not only . . . but also, in other words, in summary, therefore, however*). As you begin to rehearse your presentation, you might need to experiment with various verbal transitions to achieve a flow that seems natural and logical to you. If none of the verbal alternatives seems quite right, consider a nonverbal transition.

Nonverbal transitions are sometimes used alone and sometimes in combination with verbal transitions. An effective **nonverbal transition** might take the form of a facial expression, a pause, a change in vocal pitch or speaking rate, or movement. Most good speakers will use a combination of verbal and nonverbal transitions to help them move from one idea to the next throughout their presentations.

nonverbal transition
A facial expression, vocal cue, or physical movement that indicates a speaker is moving from one idea to the next.

summary
A recap of what has been said.

internal summary
A recap within the presentation of what has been said so far.

Summaries

Like previews, a **summary**—a recap of what has been said—provides an additional opportunity for the audience to grasp a speaker's most important ideas. Most speakers use two types of summaries: internal summaries and a final summary.

Internal summaries, like internal previews, occur within and throughout a presentation. You might want to use an internal summary after you have discussed two or three main ideas, to ensure that the audience keeps them firmly in mind as you move into another main idea. You can combine an internal summary with an internal preview. In his "Last Lecture," Carnegie Mellon professor Randy Pausch combined an internal preview and summary in this way:

Professor Randy Pausch effectively used signposts in his now-famous "Last Lecture," delivered shortly before his death. How can you use verbal transitions to show the relationship between ideas in your presentations?

All right, so now the third part of the talk. Lessons learned. We've talked about my dreams. We've talked about helping other people enable their dreams. Somewhere along the way there's got to be some aspect of what lets you get to achieve your dreams.[8]

You may also want to provide your audience with a final opportunity to hear and remember your main ideas, in the form of a **final summary** in your conclusion. While your initial preview gave your audience their first exposure to your main ideas, your final summary will give them their last exposure to those ideas. Near the end of Stephanie's presentation on cruise ship violence, she provides this final summary of her three main ideas:

> Today we outlined violence on cruise ships and the need for recourse; we then discussed the nature of these criminal environments and lack of laws; and finally, we explored solutions for handling or avoiding these crimes even if the authorities are not supportive.[9]

Adding previews, transitions, and summaries to your well-organized presentation applies the fundamental principles of using both verbal and nonverbal messages effectively and of adapting your message to others, increasing the likelihood that your audience will grasp your main ideas and the logic of your organizational strategy.

2. Verbal
3. Nonverbal
5. Adapt

Introducing and Concluding Your Presentation

At this point, you have pretty well developed the ideas and content of the body of your presentation, and you have strategies for organizing that material. But you have not yet given much thought to how you are going to begin and end the presentation. That's okay. Even though you will deliver it first, you usually plan your introduction last. You need to know first what you're introducing—especially your central idea and main ideas. Once you do, it is time to plan how you are going to introduce and conclude your presentation. While they make up a relatively small percentage of the total presentation, your introduction and conclusion provide your audience with first and final impressions of you and your presentation. They are important considerations in adapting your message to others.

5. Adapt

final summary
A recap of all the main points of a presentation, usually occurring just before or during the conclusion.

introduction
Opening lines of a presentation, which must catch the audience's attention, introduce the topic, give the audience a reason to listen, establish the speaker's credibility, state the central idea, and preview the main ideas.

Introductions

Your **introduction** should convince your audience to listen to you. More specifically, it must perform five functions: get the audience's attention, introduce the topic, give the audience a reason to listen, establish your credibility, state your central idea, and preview your main ideas. Let's briefly consider each of these six functions.

Get the Audience's Attention
If an introduction does not capture the audience's attention, the rest of the presentation may be wasted on them. You have to use verbal messages effectively to wake up your listeners and make them want to hear more.

There are several good ways to gain an audience's attention. One commonly used and quite effective way is to open with an illustration. Buey Ruet opens his speech on the bloodshed in Sudan with this moving personal illustration:

> On October 15, 1994, a woman by the name of Workinsh Admasu opened a letter, which required her 8- and 13-year-old boys to immediately report to military training camp. Three weeks after basic training, the boys, along with another 300,000 8- to 14-year-olds, strapped on AK47s that were half of their body weight and headed off to fight in Sudan's civil war. . . . That 8-year-old boy was me. . . . My 13-year-old brother and I were forced to experience things that no other child should ever have to experience.[10]

Other strategies are to ask a rhetorical question, relate a startling fact or statistic, quote an expert or a literary text, tell a humorous story, or refer to historical or recent events. Former U.S. Poet Laureate Billy Collins used humor to assure the 2008 graduates of Rollins College that his commencement address would be brief:

> Like people who attend poetry readings, you need to be assured that this will be a finite experience.[11]

Democratic presidential candidate Barack Obama combined references to place and historical event in the opening words of his March 2008 address in Philadelphia:

> "We the people, in order to form a more perfect union."
> Two hundred and twenty-one years ago, in a hall that still stands across the street, a group of men gathered and, with these simple words, launched America's improbable experiment in democracy.[12]

Still other speakers might get their audience's attention by referring to a personal experience, referring to the occasion, or referring to something said by a preceding speaker. While not all of these strategies will work for all presentations, at least one of them should be an option for any presentation you make. And with a little practice, you may find yourself being able to choose from several good possibilities for a single presentation.

Introduce the Topic Within the first few seconds of listening to you, your audience should have a pretty good idea of what your topic is. The best way to achieve this objective is to include a statement of your central idea in your introduction.

2. Verbal

As an audience member, what efforts can you make to take into consideration the cultural differences in the organization of speeches by speakers from cultures other than your own?

Give the Audience a Reason to Listen
Not only do you have to get your audience's attention and introduce your topic—you have to motivate your listeners to continue to listen. Show the audience how your topic affects them and those they care about. Catherine uses rhetorical questions to drive home to her audience the relevance and importance of her speech on a healthy diet:

> What if I told you that, by decreasing one food item in your and your loved ones' diet, you could significantly lessen the chance for metabolic syndrome (or obesity); heart disease; coronary artery disease; osteoporosis due to calcium depletion; high blood pressure; colon, kidney, breast, prostate, and liver cancer? Would you change the menu at your and your loved ones' next meal?[13]

By the end of your introduction, your audience should be thinking, "This concerns *me*!"

Establish Your Credibility
A credible speaker is one whom the audience judges to be believable, competent, and trustworthy. Be aware of the skills, talents, and experiences you have had that are related to your topic. You can increase your credibility by telling your audience about your expertise. For example, in your introduction to a persuasive presentation on studying abroad, you might say:

> I know firsthand how studying abroad can broaden your worldview, increase your understanding of another culture, and enrich your academic studies. Last fall, I studied at the Sorbonne in Paris.

State Your Central Idea
Your central idea usually appears at or near the end of your introduction, as in the following example from Aaron's speech on post-traumatic stress disorder:

> Hundreds of combat veterans . . . are being dismissed from the Armed Services without the medical benefits needed to treat combat stress.[14]

Preview Your Main Ideas
Previewing your main ideas allows your listeners to anticipate and begin to listen for those main ideas. You can provide your initial preview immediately after your central idea. Here is the initial preview of main ideas that follows Aaron's central idea, quoted above:

> So in today's speech we will uncover the problems associated with the denial of benefits to discharged veterans suffering from Post-Traumatic Stress Disorder. Next we will investigate the causes of these problems before finally understanding what can be done to solve this flaw in the policies of the VA.[15]

Conclusions

While your introduction creates a critically important first impression, your **conclusion** leaves an equally important final impression. Long after you finish speaking, your audience will hear the echo of effective final words. An effective conclusion serves four functions: to summarize the presentation, to reemphasize the main idea in a memorable way, to motivate the audience to respond, and to provide closure. Let's consider each of these functions.

Summarize the Presentation
The conclusion offers a speaker a last chance to repeat his or her main ideas. Most speakers summarize their main ideas between the body of the presentation and its conclusion or in the first part of the conclusion.

Reemphasize the Central Idea in a Memorable Way
The conclusions of many famous speeches contain many of the lines we remember best:

> . . . that government of the people, by the people, for the people, shall not perish from the earth. (*Abraham Lincoln*)[16]

conclusion
Closing lines of a presentation, which leave a final impression.

Effective speakers save their most important idea—the one they want the audience to walk away with—for last. If you are concerned that your audience may be skeptical of your message at first, how can you organize your presentation so that it adapts to their potential skepticism and builds to a last point that leaves them motivated to respond?

2. Verbal

2. Verbal
3. Nonverbal

closure
The sense that a presentation is finished.

Old soldiers never die; they just fade away. *(General Douglas MacArthur)*[17]

Free at last! Free at last! Thank God almighty, we are free at last! *(Martin Luther King Jr.)*[18]

Use your final verbal message effectively. Word your thoughts so that your audience cannot help but remember them.

Motivate the Audience to Respond
Think back to your specific purpose. What do you want your audience to be able to do by the end of your presentation? If your purpose is to inform, you may want your audience to think about your topic or to seek more information about it. If your purpose is to persuade, you may want your audience to take some sort of action—to write a letter, make a phone call, or volunteer for a cause. Your conclusion is where you can motivate your audience to respond. Travis closes his presentation on sleep deprivation with this admonition:

> Before we are all, literally, dead on our feet, let's take the easiest solution step of all. Tonight, turn off your alarm, turn down your covers, and turn in for a good night's sleep.[19]

Provide Closure
You may have experienced listening to a presentation and not being certain when it was over. That speaker did not achieve the last purpose of an effective conclusion: providing **closure**, or a sense that the presentation is finished.

One good way to provide closure is to refer to your introduction by finishing a story, answering a rhetorical question, or reminding your audience of your introduction. Steven had opened his presentation on reducing DUI occurrences with an extended illustration about a Wyoming highway patrol officer forced to kill a woman in self-defense after the inebriated woman brutally attacked him. He provides memorable closure to his presentation by finishing the story:

> Whenever I heard about someone being killed during an alcohol-related traffic incident, I used to shrug it off, thinking, "How does this affect me?" . . . When the Wyoming highway patrolman took the life of Alyssa Harriet, I learned how drinking and driving affects me, because that highway patrolman is my brother.[20]

You can also achieve closure by using verbal and nonverbal signposts. For example, you might use such transitions as *finally* and *in conclusion*, as you move into your conclusion. You might pause before you begin the conclusion, slow your speaking rate as you deliver your final sentence, or signal by falling vocal inflection that you are making your final statement. Experiment with these strategies until you are certain that your presentation "sounds finished."

> ### Recap
> **The Purposes of Introductions and Conclusions**
>
> Your introduction should... Get your audience's attention.
> Introduce your topic.
> Give your audience a reason to listen.
> Establish your credibility.
> State your central idea.
> Preview your main ideas.
>
> Your conclusion should... Summarize your presentation.
> Reemphasize your central idea in a memorable way.
> Motivate your audience to respond.
> Provide closure.

Outlining Your Presentation

With your introduction and conclusion planned, you are almost ready to begin rehearsing your presentation. By this point, you should have your preparation outline nearly complete. A **preparation outline** is a fairly detailed outline of central idea, main ideas, and supporting material and may also include the specific purpose, introduction, and conclusion. A second outline, which you will prepare shortly, makes up the speaking notes from which you will eventually deliver your presentation.

Preparation Outline

Although few presentations are written in manuscript form, most speakers develop a fairly detailed preparation outline that helps them to ensure that their main ideas are clearly related to their central idea and are logically and adequately supported. A speaker who creates a preparation outline is applying the first fundamental principle of communication: becoming increasingly aware of his or her communication. In addition to helping the speaker judge the unity and coherence of the presentation, the preparation outline also serves as an early rehearsal outline and is usually the outline handed in as part of a class requirement.

Instructors who require students to turn in a preparation outline will probably have their own specific requirements. For example, some instructors ask you to include your introduction and conclusion as part of your outline, while others ask you to outline only the body of the presentation. Some ask that you incorporate signposts into the outline or write your specific purpose at the top of the outline. Be certain that you listen to and follow your instructor's specific requirements regarding which elements to include.

Almost certainly, your instructor will require that you use **standard outline format**. Standard outline format lets you become more aware of the exact relationships among various main ideas, subpoints, and supporting material in your presentation. Even if you haven't had much experience with formal outlines, the following guidelines can help you produce a correct outline.

Use Standard Numbering
Outlines are numbered by using Roman and Arabic numerals and uppercase and lowercase letters followed by periods, as follows:

   I. First main idea
      A. First subdivision of I
      B. Second subdivision of I
         1. First subdivision of B
         2. Second subdivision of B

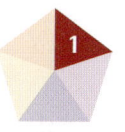

1. Aware

preparation outline
A detailed outline of a presentation that includes the central idea, main ideas, and supporting material, and may also include specific purpose, introduction, and conclusion.

standard outline format
Conventional use of numbered and lettered headings and subheadings to indicate the relationships among parts of a presentation.

Communication and Technology

Using Outlining Software

Word-processing programs such as Microsoft Word have features that allow you to set the style of, and various levels within, an outline. The feature will then apply the appropriate number, letter, and indentation to each heading you provide.

If you are using MySpeechLab in your communication course, you have access on that site to Outline icons that will allow you to create customized, specific outlines of your presentations.

Try using one or both of these outlining resources to prepare either your preparation outline or your speaking notes for your next presentation. Then evaluate the resource you used. Explain whether it made outlining easier or harder for you than outlining by hand.

      (a) First subdivision of 2
      (b) Second subdivision of 2
II. Second main idea

You will probably not need to subdivide beyond the level of lowercase letters in most presentation outlines.

Use at Least Two Subdivisions, if Any, for Each Point You cannot divide anything into fewer than two parts. On an outline, every I should be followed by a II, every A should be followed by a B, and so on. If you have only one subdivision, fold it into the level above it.

Line Up Your Outline Correctly Main ideas, indicated by Roman numerals, are written closest to the left margin. The *periods* following these Roman numerals line up, so that the first letters of the first words also line up:

I. First main idea
II. Second main idea
III. Third main idea

Letters or numbers of subdivisions begin directly underneath the first letter of the first *word* of the point above:

I. First main idea
   A. First subdivision of I
   B. Second subdivision of I

If a main idea or subdivision takes up more than one line, the second line begins under the first letter of the first word of the preceding line:

I. First main idea
   A. A rather lengthy subdivision that
      runs more than one line
   B. Second subdivision

Within Each Level, Make the Headings Grammatically Parallel Regardless of whether you write your preparation outline in complete sentences or in phrases, be consistent within each level. In other words, if I is a complete sentence, II should also be a complete sentence. If A is an infinitive phrase (one that begins with *to* plus a verb, such as "to guarantee greater security"), B should also be an infinitive phrase.

Following is a sample preparation outline for the presentation we've been watching Maggie Yancey prepare in the Developing Your Presentation Step by Step feature.[21] Your instructor may have additional or alternative requirements for what your preparation outline should include or how it should be formatted.

Chapter 12 Organizing and Outlining Your Presentation 341

Sample Preparation Outline

Writing the purpose statement at the top of the outline helps the speaker keep it in mind. But always follow your instructor's specific requirements for how to format your preparation outline.

Maggie catches her listeners' attention by combining a brief illustration and startling statistics to open her presentation. Other strategies for effectively getting audience attention were discussed earlier in the chapter.

Maggie writes out and labels her central idea and preview. Again, follow your instructor's requirements.

The first main idea of the presentation is indicated by the Roman numeral I. This main idea has three subpoints, indicated by A, B, and C.

Subpoints 1 and 2 provide supporting material for B.

Purpose

At the end of my presentation, the audience will take steps to strengthen the cybersecurity of government servers and communications systems.

Introduction

On March 11, 2007, the Chinese master hacker who goes by the alias Xiao Chen led an unlikely brand of outlaws. According to cnn.com of March 11, 2008, "They are intelligent 20 something year olds who seem harmless," but they claim to have gained access to the world's most sensitive web sites, including the Pentagon, and say they are sometimes paid by the Chinese government. And this band of outlaws is not the only one of its kind. According to Reuters of November 27, 2007, in the fiscal year 2007 alone, there were more than 37,000 breaches of government and private programs; and 80,000 attacks on U.S. military networks were attempted, while other government agencies take great pains to silence reports of their security breaches. The *Washington Times* of November 13, 2007, asserts, "Our technologically based [society] is dependent on our satellites, critical infrastructure computers, the Internet, secure software programming, computer-driven telecommunications, air traffic control centers and other sophisticated sensor systems." It is not just the fact that information is being stolen that is problematic, but as the BBC explained on July 7, 2007, the potential for hackers to use this information to launch a terrorist or cyberterrorist attack upon innocent civilians.

Central Idea

We must take steps to strengthen the cybersecurity of government servers and communications systems.

Preview

In order to establish this security so that we do not fall victim to the dangers posed by unsecured networks, we must first examine why cyberterrorism presents a danger, next delve into what drives cyberterrorism, and finally address and execute some ways to put a stop to these threats to our security.

Body

I. Cyberterrorism occurs because of problems on three levels: unpredictability of targets, insufficiently protected web sites, and obsolete security.
   A. Targets are unpredictable. The *Financial Times* of September 3, 2007, reports that in June of that year the most successful cyber attack on the U.S. defense department occurred when Chinese military hacked into a Pentagon computer network, shutting down Defense Secretary Robert Gates's computer system and foreshadowing cyber warfare.
   B. Web sites are not sufficiently protected.
      1. The vulnerability with which even secure networks can be breached became glaringly evident when, according to CNN on September 27, 2007, the Department of Homeland Security allowed researchers to launch a cyber attack, which caused a generator to self-destruct. This scenario did not require a large-scale terrorist organization, only Internet access and minimal hacking know-how.
      2. In fact, testimony from the House Committee on Cyber Security on April 17, 2007, tells us, "The Departments of Energy and Homeland

(continued)

Sample Preparation Outline (continued)

Maggie's oral citations for this and other web sites are sufficient; she should also have the web address available for her instructor or any other audience member who might want it.

Recognizing that her listeners may not know the term "electronic jihad program," Maggie provides both a definition by classification and an operational definition of the term.

Security have funded 12 separate control system security reviews" which could be "exploited by a low-skill-level attacker," without access to the computers themselves.

C. Security has not been able to keep up with advanced cybertechnology, making it easier for terrorists to cause harm worldwide.
 1. According to Tech Web of July 7, 2007, the "Electronic Jihad Program," available via the jihadi web site Al-jinan.org, is an application that can be used to target specific IP addresses for attack. The application includes a Windows-like interface that lets users choose from a list of target web sites provided via the Al-jinan site, select an attack speed (weak, medium, or strong), and then click on the "attack" button. Attacks take any servers running at those IP addresses offline temporarily.
 2. The previously cited cnn.com reports that a similar web site run by Xiao Chen has 10,000 registered users. It is the simplicity of the thousands of web pages such as this one that is terrifying. This enables terrorists to be virtually invisible and allows them to attack anytime and anywhere.

This signpost summarizes Maggie's first main idea—that cyberterrorism occurs because of problems on three levels—and previews her second main idea—why the identified problems have been allowed to continue.

Signpost: Now that we understand that cyberterrorism occurs because of unpredictability of targets, insufficiently protected web sites, and obsolete security, let's consider why these three problems have not already been solved.

I. The young, tech-savvy cyberterrorists continue to be enabled for two reasons: governmental outsourcing and insufficient resources.
 A. Initially, the government passed the responsibility of ensuring our security to other companies. According to the magazine *Government Security* of December 1, 2007, "85 percent of the Internet infrastructure is in the hands of the private sector" and security is viewed as "a nuisance that hurts profitability."
 B. The government has not devoted sufficient resources to protecting its computer systems.
  1. The 2008 book *Cyber Warfare and Cyber Terrorism* explains, "Experts have said 80 percent of successful intrusion[s] into our government computer systems can be attributed to software errors or poor software quality."
  2. The "air gapped" protection invented by the CIA and FBI is a system ensuring classified information remains classified by isolating networks. The web site of the United States Institute of Peace, last accessed March 1, 2008, noted that as a means of cutting costs, the government does not spread the air gapped protection across all sectors of the government.

Having established the problem and discussed its causes, Maggie turns to solutions.

Signpost: In the wake of September 11, Americans mobilized and created a spirit of camaraderie, after experiencing the largest-ever attack on American soil. Now it is time to do the same against potential cyberterrorist threats.

I. Our security can be restructured in three ways: government regulation, ethical hacking, and citizen involvement.
 A. Initially, identifying steps other countries are taking with technology will help Americans to see how our security should measure up. For example, France has created a defense system to enhance security. According to the BBC on November 28, 2007, "The French government unveiled its high-security intranet baptized ISIS in order to store and transmit classified confidential information inside the state during a crisis period." Our government

Sample Preparation Outline

Maggie uses a literal analogy to argue that a security system implemented in France could also work in the United States.

needs to take similar steps in securing our systems by prioritizing the development of secure servers and the safety of communications devices at every level of development from the factory to the office. And, if they are going to contract networks out, they must be expected to enforce measures.

B. Additionally, reformed hackers are applying their skills for the greater good through ethical hacking. The International Council of Electronic Commerce Consultants, or EC-Council, trains and certifies hackers, then recruits only those who have earned this certification. A government mandate requiring agencies to contract with these Ethical Hackers would enable them to use hacking know-how to their advantage.

Maggie's final solution urges members of her audience to take direct action.

C. Finally, officials will not make changes if they do not hear that, despite their best efforts to keep breaches quiet, the public is aware and concerned. By contacting local newspapers and local representatives, we can finally open this line of communication. By using knowledge that terrorists all have access to, we can all work in unison toward a more secure nation.

In her conclusion, Maggie brings closure to her presentation by restating her central idea and summarizing her main ideas.

Conclusion — Review

Today we have discussed the problems of cyberterrorism, revealed the causes, and finally explored some solutions. We must address those threats to our national security that we can control. Among the most important of these is our cybersecurity, because logging into our computers can change our fate, as well as our country's.

Speaking Notes

As you rehearse your presentation, you will find yourself needing to look at your preparation outline less and less. You have both the structure and the content of your presentation pretty well in mind. At this point, you are ready to develop a shorter outline for your speaking notes.

Your speaking notes should provide all the information you will need to make your presentation as you have planned, without being so detailed that you will be tempted to read rather than speak to your audience. Here are a few suggestions for developing speaking notes.

Use Note Cards They don't rustle as paper does, and they are small enough to hold in one hand. Type or print neatly on one side only, making sure that the letters and words are large enough to be read easily. Plan your note cards according to logical blocks of material, using one note card for your introduction, one or two for the body of your presentation, and one for your conclusion. Number your note cards in case they get out of order while you are speaking.

Include Your Introduction and Conclusion in Abbreviated Form Even if your instructor does not require you to include your introduction and conclusion on your preparation outline, include abbreviated versions of them on your note cards. You might even feel more comfortable delivering the presentation if you have your first and last sentences written out in front of you.

Include Supporting Material and Signposts Write out in full any statistics and direct quotations and their sources. Write your key signposts—your initial preview, for example—to ensure that you will not have to grope awkwardly as you move from one idea to another.

It might have been easier for this student to deliver an effective message if she had prepared concise speaking notes on note cards.

2. Verbal

Figure 12.2
Sample Speaking Notes

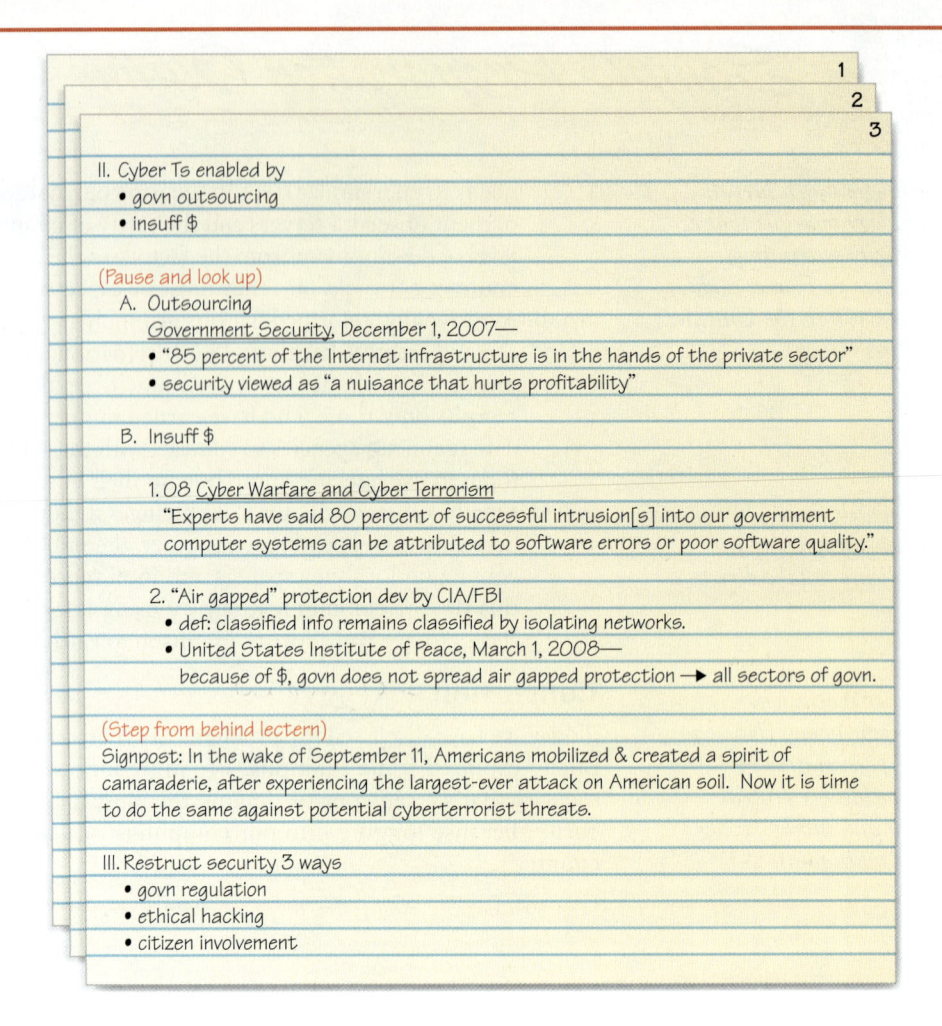

```
                                                              1
                                                              2
                                                              3
  II. Cyber Ts enabled by
    • govn outsourcing
    • insuff $

  (Pause and look up)
    A. Outsourcing
       Government Security, December 1, 2007—
         • "85 percent of the Internet infrastructure is in the hands of the private sector"
         • security viewed as "a nuisance that hurts profitability"

    B. Insuff $

       1. 08 Cyber Warfare and Cyber Terrorism
          "Experts have said 80 percent of successful intrusion[s] into our government
          computer systems can be attributed to software errors or poor software quality."

       2. "Air gapped" protection dev by CIA/FBI
            • def: classified info remains classified by isolating networks.
            • United States Institute of Peace, March 1, 2008—
              because of $, govn does not spread air gapped protection → all sectors of govn.

  (Step from behind lectern)
  Signpost: In the wake of September 11, Americans mobilized & created a spirit of
  camaraderie, after experiencing the largest-ever attack on American soil. Now it is time
  to do the same against potential cyberterrorist threats.

  III. Restruct security 3 ways
    • govn regulation
    • ethical hacking
    • citizen involvement
```

3. Nonverbal

Do Not Include Your Purpose Statement Because you will not actually say your purpose statement during your presentation, do not put it on your speaking notes.

Use Standard Outline Form Standard outline form will help you find your exact place when you glance down at your speaking notes. You will know, for example, that your second main idea is indicated by "II."

Include Delivery Cues Writing on your note cards such cues as "Louder," "Pause," or "Walk two steps left" will remind you to communicate the nonverbal messages you have planned. Write your delivery cues in a different colored ink so that you don't confuse them with your verbal content.

Figure 12.2 illustrates speaking notes for Maggie's presentation on cyberterrorism.

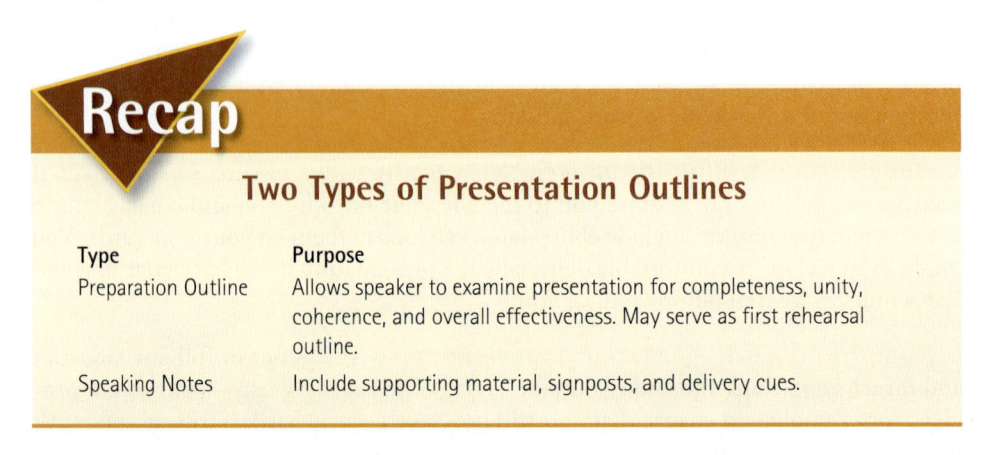

Recap

Two Types of Presentation Outlines

Type	Purpose
Preparation Outline	Allows speaker to examine presentation for completeness, unity, coherence, and overall effectiveness. May serve as first rehearsal outline.
Speaking Notes	Include supporting material, signposts, and delivery cues.

PRINCIPLES FOR A LIFETIME
Enhancing Your Skills

1. Aware

Principle One: Be aware of your communication with yourself and others.
- Use the introduction of your presentation to help establish your own credibility; be aware of the skills, talents, and experiences you have that can enhance your credibility with your listeners.
- Use a preparation outline to demonstrate to yourself that your main ideas are clearly related to your central idea and are logically and adequately supported.

2. Verbal

Principle Two: Effectively use and interpret verbal messages.
- Organize your presentation logically to communicate your verbal message effectively.
- Use verbal transitions to show relationships between ideas in your presentation.
- Introduce your topic and preview your main ideas in your introduction.
- Use stories, examples, illustrations, statistics, a quotation, or other techniques to capture your listeners' attention when you begin your talk.
- In your conclusion, summarize your presentation and reemphasize your main idea in a memorable way.

3. Nonverbal

Principle Three: Effectively use and interpret nonverbal messages.
- Use nonverbal transitions—pauses, facial expression, altered vocal pitch or speaking rate, and movement—to indicate when you are moving from one idea to the next.
- Use nonverbal cues, such as pausing, slowing your rate of speech, and letting your vocal inflection fall, to signal that you are approaching the end of your presentation.
- Add delivery cues and reminders to your final speaking notes.

4. Listen and Respond

Principle Four: Listen and respond thoughtfully to others.
- As you listen to presentations, consider the cultural differences in the organization of speakers from cultures other than your own.

5. Adapt

Principle Five: Appropriately adapt messages to others.
- Investigate and consider using the customary organizational strategy of your audience's culture.
- Discuss last the idea that you most want your audience to remember.
- If you know your audience will be skeptical of some of your ideas, first present ideas on which you can agree.
- Provide signposts as organizational cues for your audience.
- Use your introduction and conclusion to help adapt your presentation to your audience.

Summary

Once you have found supporting material, you are ready to organize your ideas and information. Depending on your topic, purpose, and audience, you can organize the main ideas of your presentation chronologically, topically, spatially, by cause and effect, or by problem and solution. You can sometimes organize supporting material according to one of these same patterns. Topically arranged material is often organized according to the principle of recency, primacy, complexity, or specificity or from soft to hard evidence.

With your presentation organized, you will want to add signposts—previews, transitions, and summaries—to make your organization clearly apparent to your audience. A carefully planned introduction will get your audience's attention, introduce your topic, give the audience a reason to listen, establish your credibility, state your central idea, and preview your main ideas. In an equally carefully planned conclusion, you can summarize your presentation, reemphasize the central idea in a memorable way, motivate your audience to respond, and provide closure.

A final step before beginning to rehearse your presentation is to prepare a detailed preparation outline and speaking notes.

Assessing Your Knowledge

For Discussion and Review

Principle One: Be aware of your communication with yourself and others.

1. Discuss how you might use a preparation outline for your presentation.

Principle Two: Effectively use and interpret verbal messages.

2. List and define three types of verbal signposts.

Principle Three: Effectively use and interpret nonverbal messages.

3. Explain how a speaker can nonverbally signal that he or she is approaching the end of a presentation.

Principle Four: Listen and respond thoughtfully to others.

4. Discuss how a speaker's culture might influence the way in which he or she organizes a presentation.

Principle Five: Appropriately adapt messages to others.

5. Explain what you might do in your introduction to adapt your presentation to your listeners.

Multiple Choice

Choose the *best* answer to each of the following questions.

1. Alexia is giving a presentation utilizing a problem-and-solution organizational pattern. What would Alexia's general purpose be?
   a. to persuade
   b. to inform
   c. to entertain
   d. to coerce

2. When subdividing your standard outline, you should remember to
   a. have only one subdivision per level.
   b. have at least two subdivisions per level.
   c. have at least three subdivisions per level.
   d. keep subdivisions to an absolute minimum.

3. "Now we will turn our attention to the causes of higher tuition rates" is an example of a(n)
   a. preview.
   b. transition.
   c. internal summary.
   d. final summary.

4. In preparing a presentation on golf clubs, Rob came up with four main ideas: "woods," "irons," "specialty clubs," and "putters." Rob used which organizational pattern?
   a. topical
   b. chronological
   c. spatial
   d. problem-and-solution

5. What is the strategy used by a speaker who organizes supporting material so that the most important material is presented last?
   a. complexity
   b. primacy
   c. chronology
   d. recency

6. Melissa is preparing a presentation on Disney World's attractions and their locations. In all likelihood, she will use which organizational pattern for her main ideas?
   a. topical
   b. chronological
   c. spatial
   d. problem-and-solution

7. In your delivery outline, you should remember to
   a. include your purpose statement.
   b. leave out your purpose statement.
   c. include your complete introduction.
   d. leave out your complete introduction.

8. What organizational pattern is the author of this outline using?
   I. Chewing gum dates back to ancient Greek and Mayan cultures.
   II. Modern chewing gum was inspired by General Santa Ana and Thomas Adams.
   III. In the future, chewing gum will be used as a nutraceutical product.
   a. topical
   b. chronological
   c. spatial
   d. problem-and-solution

9. Which of the following topics would be best organized according to a topical organizational pattern?
   a. The Apollo Space Program
   b. How to Bake Banana Bread
   c. The Path of Hurricane Katrina's Destruction
   d. Alternative Energy Options

10. Jesse states the central idea of his speech as follows: "Behavioral problems in public schools can best be solved by requiring that all public school students wear uniforms." Which type of organizational pattern does this central idea suggest?
    a. chronological
    b. topical
    c. cause-and-effect
    d. problem-and-solution

Answers to the questions in this practice test can be found at the end of the book.

Assessing Your Skill

1. Take notes as you listen to a presentation, either live or on audiotape or videotape. Then organize your notes into an outline that you think reflects both the speaker's organization and the intended relationship among ideas and supporting material.

2. Read one of the speeches in Appendix B. Answer the following questions:
   a. How are the main ideas organized?
   b. Look closely at the supporting materials. If two or more are used to support any one main idea, what strategy do you think the speaker used to organize them?
   c. Is there an initial preview statement? If so, what is it?
   d. Is there a final summary? If so, what is it?
   e. Find at least one example of each of the following:
      A transition word or phrase
      An internal preview
      An internal summary

3. Draft an introduction for a presentation on one of the following topics:

   Strategies for surviving a tornado
   Private-school vouchers
   Mars up close
   Celebrities and the press

   In addition to introducing the topic and previewing your main ideas, be sure to plan strategies for getting your audience's attention and giving them a reason to listen. Also devise a way to establish your own credibility as a speaker on that topic.

4. Miguel, who plays guitar in a mariachi band, plans to give an informative presentation on mariachi music. He wants to talk a little about the history of mariachi bands, the kind of music they play, and their role in Mexican and Mexican-American culture. In addition, he plans to introduce the instruments most commonly used in mariachi music: trumpet, guitar, and such percussion instruments as tambourines and maracas.

   Miguel asks you to help him develop a good introduction for the presentation. How do you think he might best introduce his presentation to achieve all six functions of a presentation introduction?

Web Resources to Improve Your Knowledge and Skill

We've emphasized the importance of catching your listeners' attention when you begin your presentation. The Internet can be a good place to find an attention-gaining quote, story, statistic, or illustration. Here are some web addresses that may help you find what you need to begin your presentation in a memorable way:

- Famous quotations:
  <dir.yahoo.com/Reference/quotations>
- Humorous quotations:
  <directory.google.com/Top/Recreation/Humor/Quotations>
- Stories from literature:
  <www.literature.org/Works>
- Statistics from the U.S. Census Bureau:
  <www.census.gov>

Tamayo, Rufino, "The Rock-and-Roll Dancer." © 2008 Museo Tamayo Arte Contemporaneo. Schalkwijk/Art Resource, NY

O the orator's joys! To inflate the chest, to roll the thunder of the voice out from the ribs and throat, to make the people rage, weep, hate, desire. . . .

Walt Whitman

Chapter 13

Delivering Your Presentation

Chapter Outline

- Methods of Delivery
- Effective Verbal Delivery
- Effective Nonverbal Delivery
- Effective Presentation Aids
- Some Final Tips for Rehearsing and Delivering Your Presentation
- Summary

Chapter Objectives

After studying this chapter, you should be able to

1. List and describe the four methods of delivery and provide suggestions for effectively using each one.
2. List and explain five criteria for using words well.
3. List and define three types of figurative language that can be used to make a presentation memorable.
4. Explain ways to create verbal drama and cadence in a presentation.
5. Identify and illustrate characteristics of effective nonverbal delivery.
6. List eleven types of visual aids from which a speaker might select and provide suggestions for using each type effectively.
7. Offer four guidelines for preparing effective presentation aids.
8. List eight suggestions for using presentation aids.

Which is more important: the content of a presentation or the way it is delivered? Speakers and speech teachers have argued about the answer to this question for thousands of years. In the fourth century BC, the Greek rhetorician Aristotle declared delivery "superfluous." On the other hand, when his contemporary and fellow Athenian Demosthenes was asked to name the three most important elements for a speaker to master, he is reported to have replied, "Delivery, delivery, delivery."

The debate continues. Which is more important: content or delivery? It is clear that the way you deliver a speech influences the way listeners respond to you and to your message. In a now-classic study, Alan H. Monroe found that audience members equate effective presentational speaking with such nonverbal factors as direct eye contact, alertness, enthusiasm, a pleasant voice, and animated gestures.[1] Another researcher concluded that delivery was almost twice as important as content when students gave self-introduction presentations, and three times as important when students gave persuasive presentations.[2] Other scholars have found that delivery provides important information about a speaker's feelings and emotions and will in turn affect listeners' emotional responses to the speaker.[3] Most speech teachers today believe that both content and delivery contribute to the effectiveness of a presentation. As a modern speechwriter and communication coach suggests,

> In the real world—the world where you and I do business—content and delivery are always related. And woe be to the communicator who forgets this.[4]

In this chapter, we will discuss how you can apply the five Communication Principles for a Lifetime to delivery. We will talk about both verbal and nonverbal delivery skills. We will consider how important it is to be aware of the words you use and of such nonverbal cues as gestures, eye contact, and facial expression. We will discuss how to determine what presentation aids might be effective for your audience, and we'll offer guidelines for both the preparation and the use of various types of presentation aids.

Methods of Delivery

Audiences today generally expect speakers to use clear, concise, everyday language and conversational delivery style, as opposed to the flowery language and dramatic, choreographed gestures used by speakers a century ago. However, different audiences expect and prefer variations of this delivery style. For example, if you are using a microphone to speak to an audience of 1,000 people, your listeners may expect a relatively formal delivery style. On the other hand, your communication class would probably find it odd if you delivered a formal oration to your twenty-five classmates.

People from different cultures also have different expectations of speakers' delivery. Listeners from Japan and China, for example, prefer subdued gestures to a more flamboyant delivery style. British listeners expect a speaker to stay behind a lectern and use relatively few gestures.

Speakers should consider and adapt to their audience's expectations, their topic, and the speaking situation as they select from four basic methods of delivery: manuscript speaking, memorized speaking, impromptu speaking, and extemporaneous speaking. Each is more appropriate to some speaking contexts and audiences than to others, and each requires a speaker to use a slightly different delivery style. Let's consider each of these four delivery methods in more detail.

Manuscript Speaking

Perhaps you remember the first presentation you ever had to give—maybe as long ago as elementary school. Chances are that you wrote your speech out and read it to your audience.

Unfortunately, **manuscript speaking** is rarely done well enough to be interesting. Most speakers who rely on a manuscript read it in either a monotone or a pattern of

manuscript speaking
Reading a presentation from a written text.

vocal inflection that makes the presentation sound as if it were being read. They are so afraid of losing their place that they keep their eyes glued to the manuscript and seldom look at the audience. These challenges are significant enough that most speakers should avoid reading from a manuscript most of the time.

However, there are some exceptions. Sometimes effective verbal messages depend on careful and exact phrasing. For example, because an awkward statement made by the U.S. secretary of state could cause an international crisis, he or she usually has remarks on critical issues carefully scripted. A company manager or administrator presenting a new, potentially controversial company policy to employees or customers might also deliver that announcement from a manuscript.

If you ever have to speak on a sensitive, critical, or controversial issue, you too might need to deliver a manuscript presentation. If so, consider the following suggestions:[5]

- Type your manuscript in short, easy-to-scan phrases on the upper two-thirds of the paper so that you do not have to look too far down into your notes.
- Use appropriate nonverbal messages. Try to take in an entire sentence at a time so that you can maintain eye contact throughout each sentence.
- Do not read the manuscript too quickly. Use a slash mark (/) or some other symbol to remind you to pause in strategic places.
- Vary the rhythm, inflection, and pace of your delivery so that the presentation does not sound as if it is being read.
- Use gestures and movement to add further nonverbal interest and emphasis to your message.

Memorized Speaking

After that first speech you read in elementary school, you probably became a more savvy speaker, and the next time you had to give a speech, you decided to write it out and memorize it. You thought that no one would be able to tell you had written it out first. What you didn't know then, but probably do now, is that most **memorized speaking** sounds stiff and recited. In addition, you run the risk of forgetting parts of your speech and having to search awkwardly for words in front of your audience. And you forfeit the ability to adapt to your audience while you are speaking.

However, speaking from memory is occasionally justifiable. Memorized speaking might be appropriate in the same instances as manuscript speaking, when exact wording is critical to the success of the message, and when the speaker has time to commit the speech to memory. If you must deliver a short presentation within narrowly proscribed time limits, memorizing and rehearsing it will allow you to time it more accurately. Three guidelines can help you use nonverbal messages effectively when you deliver a presentation from memory:

- Do not deliver your memorized speech too rapidly.
- Avoid patterns of vocal inflection that make the speech sound recited. Focus on what you are saying, and let your voice rise and fall to emphasize key words and phrases and to reflect the structures of your sentences. Consider recording your presentation and listening to it to ensure that your vocal delivery sounds like a conversation rather than a recitation.
- Use gestures and movement to add interest and emphasis to your message.

Impromptu Speaking

In September 1993, then-President Bill Clinton stood before a joint session of Congress to deliver an important speech about health-care reform. What happened during the first nine minutes of that presentation has become what political advisor and commentator Paul Begala calls "part of the Clinton legend":

> The teleprompter screens are whizzing forward and backwards with last year's speech, trying to find it, and finally, they killed it altogether and reloaded it. Nine minutes the guy went without a note, and no one could tell.[6]

2. Verbal

3. Nonverbal

3. Nonverbal

memorized speaking
Delivering a presentation word for word from memory without using notes.

Although you can usually plan your presentations, there are times—as illustrated by Clinton's experience—when the best plans go awry. Another more likely possibility is that you will be asked to answer a question or respond to an argument without advance warning or time to prepare. At such times, you will have to call on your skills in **impromptu speaking**, or speaking "off the cuff."

While having a solid grasp of the topic on which you are asked to speak can help you in such instances, five additional guidelines can also help you avoid fumbling for words or rambling:

- *Consider your audience.* A quick mental check of who your audience members are and what their interests, expectations, and knowledge are can help ensure that your impromptu remarks are audience-centered.
- *Be brief.* As one leadership consultant points out,

    You're not the star—not this time, anyway. If you were the luminary, they would not have asked you to speak without warning. You're merely expected to hit a theme, say a few nice words, and then depart.[7]

    One to three minutes is probably a realistic time frame for most impromptu presentations.
- *Organize.* Think quickly about an introduction, body, and conclusion. If you want to make more than one point, use a simple organizational strategy such as chronological order—past, present, and future. Or construct an alphabetical list, in which your main ideas begin with the letters A, B, and C.[8]
- *Draw on your personal experience and knowledge.* Audiences almost always respond favorably to personal illustrations, so use any appropriate and relevant ones.
- *Use gestures and movement that arise naturally from what you are saying.*
- *Be aware of the potential impact of your communication.* If your subject is at all sensitive or your information is classified, be noncommittal in what you say.

Extemporaneous Speaking

We have saved for last the method of speaking that is the most appropriate choice for most circumstances, preferred by most audiences, and most often taught in public speaking classes: **extemporaneous speaking.** When you speak extemporaneously, you develop your presentation according to the various stages of the audience-centered public speaking model, stopping short of writing it out. Instead, you speak from an outline and rehearse the presentation until you can deliver it fluently. Your audience will know that you have prepared but will also have the sense that the presentation is being created as they listen to it—and to some extent, it is. In short, the extemporaneous presentation is a well-developed and well-organized message delivered in an interesting and vivid manner. It reflects your understanding of how to use both verbal and nonverbal messages effectively and your ability to adapt these messages to your audience.

Although the presentational speaking chapters in this book offer numerous guidelines for extemporaneous speaking, consider these four when you reach the rehearsal and delivery stages:

- Use a full-content preparation outline when you begin to rehearse your extemporaneous presentation. Be aware of your growing confidence in delivering it, and continue to decrease your reliance on your notes.
- Prepare an abbreviated outline in the form of speaking notes. Continue to rehearse, using this new outline.
- Even as you become increasingly familiar with your message, do not try to memorize it word for word. Continue to vary the ways in which you express your ideas and information.
- As you deliver your presentation, adapt it to your audience. Use gestures and movement that arise naturally from what you are saying.

impromptu speaking
Delivering a presentation without advance preparation.

extemporaneous speaking
Speaking from a written or memorized outline without having memorized the exact wording of the presentation.

Recap

Methods of Delivery

Manuscript	Reading a presentation from a written text
Memorized	Giving a presentation word for word from memory without using notes
Impromptu	Delivering a presentation without advance preparation
Extemporaneous	Speaking from a written or memorized outline without having memorized the exact wording of the presentation

Effective Verbal Delivery

In a recent examination of some 125 years' of worth student speeches prepared for intercollegiate competition, researchers Leah White and Lucas Messer found remarkable consistency in students' use of stylized language. White and Messer explain,

> Style and delivery are often tightly connected. Speeches rich in language strategies lend themselves to engaging deliveries.[9]

While you will not write out most presentations word for word, you will want to think about and rehearse words, phrases, and sentences that accurately and effectively communicate your ideas. At the same time, you will want to give your message a distinctive and memorable style. Let's examine some guidelines for effectively using and understanding words and word structures in a presentation.

Using Words Well

The most effective words are specific and concrete, unbiased, vivid, simple, and correct. Building on our discussion in Chapter 3 of the power of verbal messages, we'll examine each of these characteristics in turn.

Specific, Concrete Words

A **specific word** refers to an individual member of a general class—for example, *ammonite* as opposed to the more general term *fossil*, or *sodium* as opposed to *chemical*. Specific words are often **concrete words**, appealing to one of the five senses and clearly communicating an image. For example, which word in each of the following pairs creates a more specific mental picture: *dog* or *poodle*, *utensil* or *spatula*, *toy* or *Lego*? In each case, the second word is more specific and concrete than the first and better communicates the image the speaker intends. For maximum clarity in your communication, use more specific, concrete words than general, abstract ones in your presentations.

Unbiased Words

Unbiased words are those that do not disparage, either intentionally or unintentionally, either gender or any racial, cultural, or religious group or offend any audience member who may belong to one of these groups. Although a speaker can fairly easily avoid overtly offensive language, it is more difficult to avoid language that more subtly stereotypes or discriminates. As we noted in Chapter 3, the once-acceptable use of a masculine noun (*man*, *mankind*) to refer generically to all people may now be offensive to many audience members. Other words that reflect gender bias include *chairman*, *waiter*, and *congressman*. Even if you yourself do not consider these terms offensive, a member of your audience might. When possible, you should adapt to your audience by choosing instead such unbiased gender-neutral alternatives as *chairperson* or *chair*, *server*, and *member of Congress*.

---

specific word
A word that refers to an individual member of a general class.

concrete word
A word that refers to an object or describes an action or characteristic in the most specific way possible.

unbiased word
A word that does not stereotype, discriminate against, or insult either gender or any racial, cultural, or religious group.

Vivid Words **Vivid words** add color and interest to your language. Like concrete words, they help you communicate mental images more accurately and interestingly. Most speakers who try to make their language more vivid think first of adding adjectives to nouns—for example, *distressed oak table* instead of *table*, *scruffy tabby cat* instead of *cat*. And certainly the first phrase of each example is more vivid. However, speakers less frequently consider the potential power of substituting vivid verbs for "blah" verbs—for example, *sprout* instead of *grow*, *devour* instead of *eat*. When searching for a vivid word, you might want to consult a **thesaurus,** or collection of synonyms. But do not assume that the most obscure or unusual synonym you find will necessarily be the most vivid. Sometimes a simple word can evoke a vivid image for your audience.

Simple Words **Simple words** are generally an asset to a speaker. They will be immediately understandable to an audience. In his essay "Politics and the English Language," George Orwell includes this prescription for simplicity:

> Never use a long word where a short one will do. If it is possible to cut a word out, always cut it out. Never use a foreign phrase, a scientific word, or a jargon word if you can think of an everyday English equivalent.[10]

Selected thoughtfully, simple words can communicate with both accuracy and power.

Correct Words Finally, and perhaps most obviously, you should use **correct words** when you speak. Grammatical and usage errors communicate a lack of preparation and can lower your credibility with your audience. Be aware of any errors you make habitually. If you are uncertain of how to use a word, look it up in a dictionary or ask someone who knows. If you are stumped by whether to say "Neither the people nor the president *knows* how to solve the problem" or "Neither the people nor the president *know* how to solve the problem," seek assistance from a good English handbook. (By the way, the first sentence is correct!)

Crafting Memorable Word Structures

We have discussed the importance of using words that are concrete, unbiased, vivid, simple, and correct. Now we will turn our attention to word structures—phrases and sentences that create the figurative language, drama, and cadences needed to provide what one marketing communication specialist calls "ear appeal."[11]

Figurative Language One way to make your presentation memorable is to use **figurative language** or figures of speech, including **metaphors** (implied comparisons), **similes** (overt comparisons using *like* or *as*), and **personification** (the attribution of human qualities to nonhuman things or ideas). Such language is memorable because it is used in a way that is a little different from its ordinary, expected usage. Nineteenth-century Missouri senator George Graham Vest used all three types of figurative lan-

---

2. Verbal

vivid word
A colorful word.

thesaurus
A list of synonyms.

simple word
A short word known to most people who speak the language.

correct word
A word that means what the speaker intends and is grammatically correct in the phrase or sentence in which it appears.

figurative language
Language that deviates from the ordinary, expected meaning of words to make a description or comparison unique, vivid, and memorable.

metaphor
An implied comparison between two things.

simile
An overt comparison between two things that uses the word *like* or *as*.

personification
The attribution of human qualities to inanimate things or ideas.

Recap

Using Words Well

Use specific, concrete words to communicate clearly and specifically.
Use unbiased words to avoid offending people of either gender or from any racial, cultural, or religious group.
Use vivid words to add color and interest to your language.
Use simple words to be understood readily.
Use correct words to enhance your credibility.

guage to good advantage in his short but memorable "Tribute to the Dog" (delivered in Warrensburg, Missouri, in 1870, and nominated by columnist William Safire as one of the greatest speeches of the second millennium).[12] Vest makes the abstract concept of malice more concrete with the metaphor "the stone of malice." He uses a simile to compare the dog's master to a prince: "He guards the sleep of his pauper master as if he were a prince." And he personifies death, which "takes [the dog's] master in its embrace." Vest's speech is memorable at least in part because of the figurative language he employs.

Drama Another way in which you can make your word structures more memorable is to use language to create **drama** in your presentation by phrasing something in an unexpected way. Three specific devices that can help you achieve verbal drama are omission, inversion, and suspension.

When you strip a phrase or sentence of nonessential words that the audience expects or with which they are so familiar that they will mentally fill them in, you are using **omission**. Journalist Bill Moyers described recent modifications in the format of *The New York Times* with the succinct phrase

More money, less news.[13]

Inversion—reversing the normal order of words in a phrase or sentence—can also create drama in a presentation. John F. Kennedy inverted the usual subject–verb–object sentence pattern to object–subject–verb to make this brief declaration memorable:

This much we pledge. . . .[14]

A third way to create drama through sentence structures is to employ verbal **suspension**, saving a key word or phrase for the end of a sentence, rather than placing it at the beginning. Speaking to the Democratic National Convention in July 2004, former U.S. President Jimmy Carter used suspension to dramatize the importance of America's global role:

At stake is nothing less than our nation's soul.[15]

Cadence A final way to create memorable word structures is to create **cadence**, or language rhythm. A speaker does this not by speaking in a singsong pattern, but by using such stylistic devices as parallelism, antithesis, repetition, and alliteration.

Parallelism occurs when two or more clauses or sentences have the same grammatical pattern. Addressing supporters during the 2008 U.S. presidential campaign, Republican candidate John McCain used parallel verb phrases to declare his intent to

deliver health care services, support retirees, fuel our transportation network, stimulate research and development, and harness new technologies.[16]

Antithesis is similar to parallelism, except that the two structures contrast in meaning. Nobel Laureate Elie Wiesel used antithesis in his 1999 Millennium Lecture on "The Perils of Indifference":

Indifference . . . is not only a sin, it is a punishment.[17]

Repetition of a key word or phrase can add emphasis to an important idea and memorability to your message. In her moving convocation address to a grieving Virginia Tech community after the campus shootings of April 2007, poet and Virginia Tech professor Nikki Giovanni repeated five times the stirring affirmation

We are Virginia Tech.[18]

A final strategy for creating cadence is to use **alliteration**, the repetition of an initial consonant sound several times in a phrase, clause, or sentence. In kicking off the "space race" in 1962, John F. Kennedy used this alliterative phrase:

. . . hour of change and challenge.[19]

The repetition of the *ch* sound added cadence—and memorability—to the passage.

Old Drum, the dog made famous by George Graham Vest's use of figurative language.

drama
A characteristic of a speech created when something is phrased in a way that differs from the way the audience expects.

omission
Leaving out a word or phrase the audience expects to hear.

inversion
Reversing the normal word order of a phrase or sentence.

suspension
Withholding a key word or phrase until the end of a sentence.

cadence
The rhythm of language.

parallelism
Using the same grammatical structure for two or more clauses or sentences

antithesis
Contrasting the meanings of the two parts of a parallel structure.

repetition
Emphasizing a key word or phrase by using it more than once.

alliteration
The repetition of a consonant sound (usually the first consonant) several times in a phrase, clause, or sentence.

Recap

Crafting Memorable Word Structures

To make your message memorable, use . . .

Figurative Language

Metaphor	Making an implied comparison
Simile	Making a comparison using *like* or *as*
Personification	Attributing human qualities to nonhuman things or ideas

Drama

Omission	Leaving nonessential words out of a phrase or sentence
Inversion	Reversing the normal order of words in a phrase or sentence
Suspension	Withholding the key words in a phrase or sentence until the end

Cadence

Parallelism	Using two or more clauses or sentences with the same grammatical structure
Antithesis	Using a two-part parallel structure in which the second part contrasts in meaning with the first
Repetition	Using a key word or phrase more than once
Alliteration	Repeating a consonant sound

Poet Nikki Giovanni's words and gestures provided a reaffirming message of community in the wake of the Virginia Tech shootings. How can you listen and respond thoughtfully to others in times of need?

Effective Nonverbal Delivery

At this point, you know how important it is to deliver your presentation effectively and what delivery style most audiences today prefer. You are familiar with the four methods of delivery and know how to maximize the use of each one. And you have some ideas about how to use effective and memorable language. But you may still be wondering, "What do I do with my hands?" "Is it all right to move around while I speak?" "How can I make my voice sound interesting?" To help answer these and similar questions, and to help you use nonverbal messages more effectively, we will examine five major categories of nonverbal delivery: eye contact, physical delivery, facial expression, vocal delivery, and personal appearance. This discussion further develops the fundamental principle of using and interpreting nonverbal messages that we introduced in Chapter 4.

Eye Contact

Of all the nonverbal delivery variables discussed in this chapter, the most important one in a presentational speaking situation for North Americans is **eye contact**. Eye contact with your audience lets them know that you are interested in them and ready to talk to them. It also permits you to determine whether they are responding to you. And most listeners will think that you are more capable and trustworthy if you look them in the eye. Several studies document a relationship between eye contact and speaker credibility, as well as between eye contact and listener learning.[20]

How much eye contact do you need to sustain? One study found that speakers with less than 50 percent eye contact are considered unfriendly, uninformed, inexperienced, and even dishonest by their listeners.[21] Is there such a thing as too much eye contact? Probably not, for North American audiences. Be aware, though, that not all people from all cultures prefer as much eye contact as North Americans do. Asians, for example, generally prefer less.

The following suggestions can help you use eye contact effectively when you speak in public:

- Establish eye contact with your audience before you say anything. Eye contact sends the message "I am interested in you. I have something I want to say to you. Tune me in."
- Maintain eye contact with your audience as you deliver your opening sentence without looking at your notes.
- Try to establish eye contact with people throughout your audience, not just with the front row or only one or two people. Briefly look into the eyes of an individual, then transfer your eye contact to someone else. Do not look over your listeners' heads! They will notice if you do so and may even turn around to try to find out what you are looking at.

Physical Delivery

Gestures, movement, and posture are the three key elements of **physical delivery**. A good speaker knows how to use effective gestures, make meaningful movements, and maintain appropriate posture while speaking to an audience.

Gestures The hand and arm movements you use while speaking are called **gestures**. Nearly all people from all cultures use some gestures when they speak. In fact, research suggests that gesturing is instinctive and that it is intrinsic to speaking and thinking.[22] Yet even if you gesture easily and appropriately in the course of everyday conversation,

5. Adapt

3. Nonverbal

eye contact
Looking at an audience during a presentation.

physical delivery
A person's gestures, movement, and posture, which influence how a message is interpreted.

gestures
Movements of the hands and arms to communicate ideas.

By walking up close to her audience, this speaker establishes a connection with her listeners.

3. Nonverbal

5. Adapt

3. Nonverbal

movement
A change of location during a presentation.

you may feel awkward about what to do with your hands when you are in front of an audience. To minimize this challenge, consider the following guidelines:

- Focus on the message you want to communicate. As in ordinary conversation, when you speak in public, your hands should help to emphasize or reinforce your verbal message. Your gestures should coincide with what you are saying.
- Again, as in conversation, let your gestures flow with your message. They should appear natural, not tense or rigid.
- Be definite. If you want to gesture, go ahead and gesture. Avoid minor hand movements that will be masked by the lectern or that may appear to your audience as accidental brief jerks.
- Vary your gestures. Try not to use the same hand or one all-purpose gesture all the time. Think of the different gestures you can use, depending on whether you want to enumerate, point, describe, or emphasize ideas.
- Don't overdo your gestures. You want your audience to focus not on your gestures, but on your message.
- Make your gestures appropriate to your audience and situation. When you are speaking to a large audience in a relatively formal setting, use bolder, more sweeping, and more dramatic gestures than when you are speaking to a small audience in an informal setting. Consider, too, the culture-based expectations of your audience. Americans in general tend to use more gestures than do speakers from other cultures. If you are speaking to a culturally diverse audience, you might want to tone down your gestures.

Movement Another element of physical delivery is **movement**. You may have wondered, "Should I walk around during my presentation, or should I stay in one place?" "Should I stay behind the lectern, or could I stand beside or in front of it?" "Can I move around among the audience?" The following criteria may help you to determine the answers to these questions:

- Like gestures, any movement should be purposeful. It should be consistent with the verbal content of your message; otherwise it will appear to be aimless wandering. You might signal the beginning of a new idea or major point in your speech with movement. Or you might move to signal a transition from a serious idea to a more humorous one. The bottom line is that your use of movement should make sense to your listeners. No movement at all is better than random, distracting movement.

- If such physical barriers as a lectern, a row of chairs, or an overhead projector make you feel cut off from your audience, move closer to them. Studies suggest that physical proximity enhances learning.[23]
- Adapt to the cultural expectations of your audience. British listeners, for example, have commented to your authors that American lecturers tend to stand too close to an audience when speaking. If you think that movement will make your audience uncomfortable, stay in one carefully chosen spot to deliver your presentation.

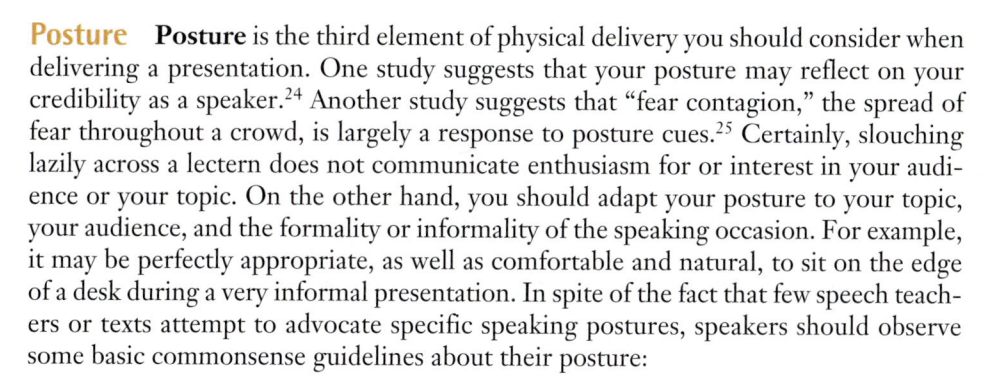

Posture Posture is the third element of physical delivery you should consider when delivering a presentation. One study suggests that your posture may reflect on your credibility as a speaker.[24] Another study suggests that "fear contagion," the spread of fear throughout a crowd, is largely a response to posture cues.[25] Certainly, slouching lazily across a lectern does not communicate enthusiasm for or interest in your audience or your topic. On the other hand, you should adapt your posture to your topic, your audience, and the formality or informality of the speaking occasion. For example, it may be perfectly appropriate, as well as comfortable and natural, to sit on the edge of a desk during a very informal presentation. In spite of the fact that few speech teachers or texts attempt to advocate specific speaking postures, speakers should observe some basic commonsense guidelines about their posture:

- Avoid slouching, shifting from one foot to the other, or drooping your head.
- Unless you are disabled, do not sit while delivering a presentation. The exception might be perching on the edge of a desk or stool (which would still elevate you slightly above your audience) during a very informal presentation.

Like your gestures and movement, your posture should not call attention to itself. It should reflect your interest in and attention to your audience and your presentation.

Facial Expression

Your **facial expression** plays a key role in expressing your thoughts, emotions, and attitudes.[26] Your audience sees your face before they hear what you are going to say, giving you the opportunity to set the tone for your message even before you begin speaking.

Social psychologist Paul Ekman has found that facial expressions of primary emotions are virtually universal, so even a culturally diverse audience will be able to read your facial expressions clearly.[27]

posture
A speaker's stance.

facial expression
An arrangement of the facial muscles to communicate thoughts, emotions, and attitudes.

Communication and Diversity

The Academic Quarter

When speaking at a Polish university a few years ago, one of your authors expected to begin promptly at 11:00 AM, as announced in the program and on posters. By 11:10 it was clear that the speech would not begin on time, and your author began to despair of having any audience at all.

In Poland, it turns out, both students and professors expect to adhere to the "academic quarter." This means that most lectures begin at least 15 minutes, or a quarter of an hour, after the announced starting time.

If your author had asked a Polish professor about the audience's expectations, he would have known about this custom in advance. One way to avoid such misunderstandings is to talk with people you know who are familiar with the cultural expectations. Try to observe other speakers presenting to similar audiences. And ask specific questions, including the following:

1. Where does the audience expect me to stand while speaking?
2. Do listeners expect direct eye contact?
3. When will the audience expect me to start and stop my talk?
4. Will listeners find movement and gestures distracting or welcome?
5. Do listeners expect presentation aids?

Keep cultural differences in mind as you rehearse and deliver presentations to diverse audiences.

Throughout your presentation, your facial expression, like your body language and eye contact, should be appropriate to your message. Present somber news wearing a serious expression. Relate a humorous story with a smile. To communicate interest in your listeners, keep your expression alert and friendly. Consultants criticized both George W. Bush and John Kerry for their inappropriate facial expressions during the 2004 U.S. presidential debates, noting specifically that Bush needed to control his grimaces and smirks, and Kerry needed to develop a more natural, authentic smile.[28]

To ensure that you are maximizing your use of this important nonverbal delivery cue, rehearse your presentation in front of a mirror; or better yet, videotape yourself rehearsing your presentation. Consider as objectively as possible whether your face is reflecting the emotional tone of your ideas.

Vocal Delivery

We have already discussed the importance of selecting words and phrases that will most effectively communicate your ideas, information, and images. We referred to this element of delivery as verbal delivery. **Vocal delivery,** on the other hand, involves nonverbal vocal cues—not the words you say, but the way you say them. Effective vocal delivery requires that you speak so that your audience can understand you and will remain interested in what you are saying. Nonverbal vocal elements include volume, pitch, rate, and articulation.

Volume

Volume is the softness or loudness of your voice. It is the most fundamental determinant of audience understanding. If you do not speak loudly enough, even the most brilliant presentation will be ineffective, because the audience simply will not hear you. In addition, volume can signal important ideas in your presentation; you can deliver a key idea either more loudly or more softly than you have been speaking. Consider these guidelines to help you appropriately adapt the volume of your voice to your audience's needs:

- Speak loudly enough that the members of your audience farthest from you can hear you without straining. This will ensure that everyone else in the room can hear you, too.
- Vary the volume of your voice in a purposeful way. Indicate important ideas by turning your volume up or down.
- Be aware of whether you need a microphone to amplify your volume. If you do and one is available, use it.

There are three kinds of microphones, only one of which demands much technique. The *lavaliere microphone* is the clip-on type often used by news reporters and interviewees. Worn on the front of a shirt or a jacket lapel, it requires no particular care other than not thumping it or accidentally knocking it off.

The *boom microphone* is used by makers of movies and TV shows. It hangs over the heads of the speakers and is remote controlled, so the speakers need not be particularly concerned with it.

The third kind of microphone—which may be attached to a lectern, sitting on a desk, or standing on the floor—is the *stationary microphone.* Generally, the stationary microphones used today are multidirectional. However, you will have to keep your mouth about the same distance from the mike at all times to avoid distracting fluctuations in the volume of sound. You can turn your head from side to side and use gestures, but you will have to limit other movements.

Under ideal circumstances, you will be able to practice before you speak with the type of microphone you will use. If you have the chance, figure out where to stand for the best sound quality and the sensitivity of the mike to extraneous noise. Practice will accustom you to any voice distortion or echo that might occur so that these sound qualities do not surprise you during your presentation.

Pitch

Whereas volume is the loudness or softness of your voice, **pitch** refers to how high or low your voice is. To some extent, pitch is determined by physiology. The

---

3. Nonverbal

5. Adapt

vocal delivery
Nonverbal voice cues, including volume, pitch, rate, and articulation.

volume
The softness or loudness of a speaker's voice.

pitch
How high or low a speaker's voice is.

DEVELOPING YOUR PRESENTATION
Step by Step

Rehearsing Your Presentation

Maggie begins to rehearse her presentation. From the beginning, she stands and speaks aloud, practicing gestures and movement that seem appropriate to her message.

At first, Maggie uses her preparation outline (pp. 341–342). These early rehearsals go pretty well, but the speech runs a little short. Maggie knows that she tends to speak fairly rapidly, and she decides to plan more pauses throughout the speech—some to allow her listeners to think about an important point she has just made, and others to provide nonverbal transitions. When she prepares her speaking notes, Maggie adds the delivery cue "Pause" in several strategic places.

---

faster the folds in your vocal cords vibrate, the higher the habitual pitch of your voice. In general, female vocal folds vibrate much faster than do those of males. However, you can raise or lower your habitual pitch within a certain range. Variation in pitch, called **inflection,** is a key factor in communicating the meaning of your words. You know that a startled "Oh!" in response to something someone has told you communicates something quite different than a lower-pitched, questioning "Oh?" Your vocal inflection indicates your emotional response to what you have heard. Vocal inflection also helps to keep an audience interested in your presentation. If your pitch is a monotone, the audience will probably become bored quickly. To help you monitor and practice your pitch and inflection as you prepare to speak, record and play back your presentation at least once as you rehearse. Listen carefully to your pitch and inflection. If you think you are speaking in too much of a monotone, practice the presentation again with exaggerated variations in pitch.

Rate Another vocal variable is **rate,** or speed. How fast do you talk? Most speakers average between 120 and 180 words per minute but vary their rate to add interest to their delivery and to emphasize key ideas. To determine whether your speaking rate is appropriate and purposeful, become conscious of it. Record your presentation during rehearsal and listen critically to your speech speed. If it seems too fast, make a conscious effort to slow down. Use more **pauses** after questions and before important ideas. If you are speaking too slowly, make a conscious effort to speed up.

Articulation **Articulation** is the enunciation of sounds. As a speaker, you want to articulate distinctly to ensure that your audience can determine what words you are using. Sometimes we fall into the habit of mumbling or slurring—saying *wanna* instead of *want to, chesterdrawers* instead of *chest of drawers.* Some nonstandard articulation may be part of a speaker's **dialect,** a speech style common to an ethnic group or a geographic region. One dialect with which most of us are familiar is the dialect of the southern United States, characterized by a distinctive drawl. Although most native speakers of English can understand English dialects, studies have shown that North American listeners assign more favorable ratings to, and can recall more information presented by, speakers with dialects similar to their own.[29] If your dialect is significantly different from that of your listeners, or if you suspect that it could be potentially distracting, you may want to work to improve or standardize your articulation. To do so, be aware of key words or phrases that you have a tendency to drawl, slur, or chop. Once you have identified them, practice saying them distinctly and correctly.

Appearance

What would you wear to deliver a presentation to your class? To address your city council? The fact that you probably would wear something different for these two occa-

---

inflection
Variation in vocal pitch.

rate
How fast or slowly a speaker speaks.

pause
A few seconds of silence during a presentation, used both to slow a fast pace and to signal a key idea.

articulation
The production of clear and distinct speech sounds.

dialect
A consistent style of pronunciation and articulation that is common to an ethnic group or geographic region.

> ## Recap
> ### Characteristics of Effective Nonverbal Delivery
>
> - **Eye contact** should be established before you say anything and sustained as much as possible throughout your presentation.
> - **Gestures** should be relaxed, definite, varied, and appropriate to your audience and the speaking situation.
> - **Movement** should be purposeful and adapted to the audience's cultural expectations.
> - **Posture** should feel natural and be appropriate to your topic, your audience, and the occasion.
> - **Facial expression** should be alert, friendly, and appropriate to your message.
> - **Volume** should be loud enough that you can be easily heard and should be purposefully varied.
> - **Pitch** should be varied so that the inflection in your voice helps to sustain your audience's interest.
> - **Rate** should be neither too fast nor too slow and can be varied to add interest and emphasize key ideas.
> - **Articulation** should be clear and distinct.
> - **Appearance** should conform to what the audience expects.

1. Aware

3. Nonverbal

5. Adapt

sions suggests that you are already aware of the importance of a speaker's **appearance.** There is considerable evidence that your personal appearance affects how your audience will respond to you and your message. If you violate your audience's expectations, you will be less successful in achieving your purpose. The following guidelines might help make your wardrobe selection a bit easier the next time you are called on to speak:

- Never wear anything that would be potentially distracting—for example, a T-shirt with writing on it. You want your audience to listen to you, not read you.
- Consider wearing appropriate clothing as a presentation aid. For example, if you are a nurse or emergency technician, wear your uniform when you speak about your profession. (We will discuss presentation aids in more detail shortly.)
- Take cues from your audience. If you know that they will be dressed in business attire, dress similarly. If anything, you want to be a bit more dressed up than members of your audience.
- When in doubt about what to wear, select something conservative.

Effective Presentation Aids

We have already discussed two elements of delivery: verbal delivery and nonverbal delivery. A third element used with increasing frequency in this era of sophisticated computer presentation software is the **presentation aid.** The term *presentation aid* refers to anything your audience can listen to or look at to help them understand your ideas. Charts, photographs, posters, drawings, graphs, videos, and CDs are some of the types of presentation aids frequently used by speakers.

As long as they *aid* the speaker, rather than *replace* the speaker, presentation aids can be invaluable. They help you gain and maintain your audience's attention.[30] They communicate your organization of ideas. They illustrate sequences of events or procedures. And they help your audience understand and remember your message. In addition, chances are that for at least one of the assignments in your communication class you will be required to use a presentation aid. Because presentation aids are valuable supplements to your speeches and because students of communication are so often required to use them, let's discuss first the types of presentation aids that are available to you,

appearance
A speaker's dress and grooming.

presentation aid
Any tangible item used to help communicate ideas to an audience.

Communication and Technology

Rehearsing on Videotape

There is no feedback more total or more objective than feedback provided by videotape. First, it reproduces your total image, both visual and aural; and second, it lets you see for yourself. If friends or colleagues tell you that you are a good speaker, you may not respect their judgment, you may think they're being nice rather than honest, or you may think they're biased in your favor. Bruce, a pharmaceutical salesman, simply couldn't believe it when people told him he was a good speaker because an unpleasant high school speaking experience had convinced him he would never be able to speak well. Seeing himself on videotape was a revelation: He saw for himself how good he was. Another person could never have convinced him of it.

By the same token, if someone tells you that your voice is too high, that you slouch, or that you need to loosen up your body, you may not be convinced. A videotape has the inherent reassurance of a machine: It has no ulterior motive, and it lets you see what others see.

People are amazed when they see themselves on videotape—it's as if they were seeing and hearing themselves for the first time. They really see the extra twenty pounds they've been lugging around for ten years; they see the stiff way they stand; they hear the lack of energy in their voices, the *um*'s, the *you see*'s, the *you know*'s, the *like*'s.

Becoming aware of the kind of image you project is the first step toward controlling it or altering it.[31]

---

including computer-generated ones. Then we will discuss guidelines for preparing presentation aids and provide some general suggestions for using your presentation aids effectively.

Types of Presentation Aids

If you are required to use a presentation aid for an assignment or if you think a presentation aid might enhance your message, you have a number of options from which to select. You might decide to use an object or a model; a person; two-dimensional presentation aids such as drawings, photographs, maps, charts, or graphs; or a DVD, CD, or MP3 player.

Objects The first type of presentation aid you ever used—perhaps as long ago as preschool "show and tell"—was probably an object. You took to school your favorite teddy bear or the new remote-control car you got for your birthday. Remember how the kids crowded around to see what you had brought? Objects add interest to a talk because they are real. Whether the members of your audience are in preschool or college, they like tangible, real things. If you use an object as a presentation aid, consider these guidelines:

- Make certain the object can be handled easily. If it is too large, it may be unwieldy; if it is too small, your audience won't be able to see it.
- Don't use dangerous or illegal objects as presentation aids. They may make your audience members uneasy or actually put them at risk.

Models If it is impossible to bring an object to class, you may be able to substitute a model. You cannot bring a 1965 Ford Thunderbird into a classroom, but you may be able to construct and bring a model. You could probably not acquire a dog's heart to bring to class, but you might be able to find a model to use for your explanation of how heartworms damage that vital organ. If you use a model as a presentation aid, be sure that the model is large enough to be seen by all members of your audience.

People You might not think of people as potential presentation aids, but they can be. President George W. Bush has used ordinary people as visual aids for some of his most important speeches, "asking them to stand and then telling stories of their sacrifices or heroism . . . a way of coming down from the stage, as it were, and mingling with the crowd."[32] In other instances, people can model costumes, play a sport with you, or demonstrate a dance. Consider the following guidelines if you are going to ask someone to assist you by acting as a presentation aid for a speech:

- Rehearse with the person who will be helping you.
- Don't have the person stand beside you doing nothing. Wait until you need your presentation aid to have him or her come to the front.
- Don't let your presentation aid steal the show. Make his or her role specific and fairly brief. As the speaker, you should remain the "person of the hour."

Drawings   You can use simple drawings to help illustrate or explain ideas that you are talking about. For example, you could sketch the tunnels of a fire ant mound to show your audience why it is so difficult to eradicate an entire colony. You could sketch the plants and animals crucial to the life cycle of the Florida Everglades. If you use a drawing as a visual aid, consider these suggestions:

- Keep your drawings large and simple. Line drawings are often more effective than more detailed ones.
- Consider drawing or photocopying your drawing on a sheet of overhead transparency film and using an overhead projector to show the drawing to your audience.
- Your drawing does not have to be original artwork. You could ask a friend to help you prepare a drawing, or you could utilize computer software to generate a simple image. Just be sure to credit your source if you use someone else's sketch.

Photographs   If you are giving a speech on urban forestry, you might want to show your audience good color pictures of trees appropriate for urban sites in your area. In this case, photographs would show color and detail that would be nearly impossible to achieve with drawings. The biggest challenge to using photographs as presentation aids is size; most photos are simply too small to be seen clearly from a distance. If you want to use a photograph, you will usually have to enlarge it. Consider the following options for making photographs into viable presentation aids:

- Have a copy center or photo shop produce a poster-size color photocopy.
- Transfer your photograph to a slide and project it onto a screen.
- Store digital photos on a computer disk. Then, when you want the photos, you can bring them up on your computer screen and use a video projection system to enlarge them for your audience.

Maps   Like photographs, most maps are too small to be useful as presentation aids; you must enlarge them in some way. Consider these suggestions for using maps effectively in a presentation:

- Enlarge your map by photocopying it or by transferring it to a slide. An outline map with few details can be copied or drawn on overhead transparency film.
- Highlight on your map the areas or routes you are going to talk about in your presentation.

Charts   Charts can summarize and organize a great deal of information in a small space. Consider using a chart any time you need to present information that could be organized under several headings or in several columns. The chart in Figure 13.1 displays projected growth in the U.S. population age 65 and over.[33] You can prepare charts quite easily by using the Table feature in your word-processing program. Keep in mind these guidelines:

- Whether you use a large flip chart, transfer your chart to an overhead transparency, or use a computer presentation program, be certain your chart is big enough to be seen easily.
- Keep your chart simple. Do not try to put too much information on one chart. Eliminate any unnecessary words.
- Print or type any lettering on a chart, instead of writing in script.

Projected Growth in U.S. Population Aged 65 and Over

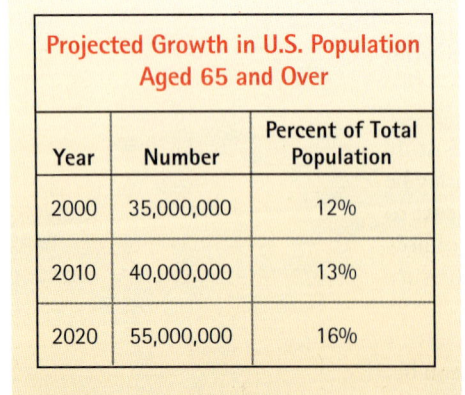

Year	Number	Percent of Total Population
2000	35,000,000	12%
2010	40,000,000	13%
2020	55,000,000	16%

Figure 13.1   Chart

Graphs Graphs are effective ways to present statistical relationships to your audience. They help to make data more concrete. You are probably already familiar with the three main types of graphs. A **bar graph** consists of bars of various lengths that represent percentages or numbers. It is useful for making comparisons. A round **pie graph** shows how data are divided proportionately. And a **line graph** can show both trends over a period of time and relationships among variables. Figure 13.2 illustrates all three types of graphs, displaying the statistics from the chart in Figure 13.1. All three graphs were generated by Microsoft Excel. The following guidelines will help you use graphs more effectively in your presentations:

- Make your graphs big by drawing them on a large piece of paper, drawing or copying them on an overhead transparency, or putting them on a computer disk for projection.
- Keep your graphs simple and uncluttered.
- Remember that many computer programs will generate graphs from statistics. You don't usually need to draw your own.

DVDs, Videotapes, and Streaming Video Both DVDs and videotapes will allow you to show scenes from a movie, an excerpt from a training film, or a brief original video to an audience. Modern players have good picture and sound quality and permit freeze-frame viewing. They also allow you to replay a scene several times if you want your audience to watch different specific elements.

Streaming video, the technology used by YouTube, is another option for a video presentation aid if you will have a computer and projection equipment available in the room where you will speak.

If you plan to use a video presentation aid, consider these suggestions:

- Be certain that the equipment you need will be available in the room in which you are going to speak.

bar graph
A graph consisting of bars of various lengths that represent numbers or percentages.

pie graph
A circular graph that shows how a set of data is divided proportionately.

line graph
A graph that shows trends over a period of time and relationships among variables.

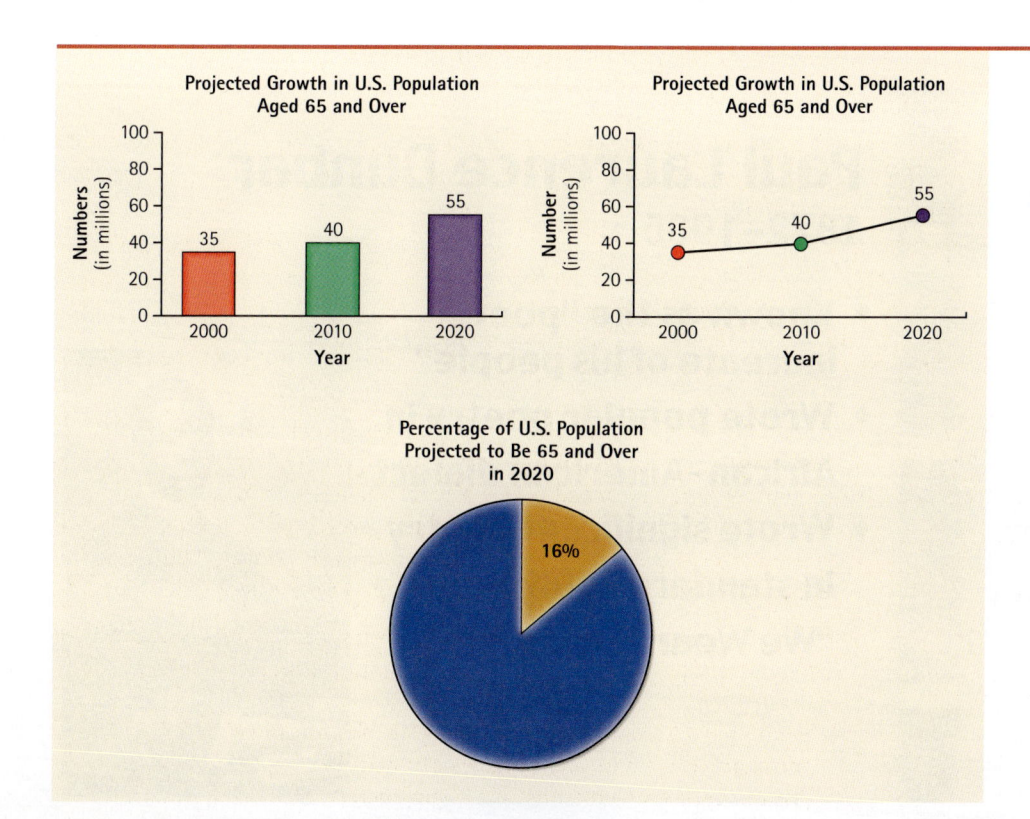

Figure 13.2
Three Types of Graphs: Bar Graph, Line Graph, and Pie Graph

- If you have an audience of twenty-five to thirty people, you can use a twenty-five-inch television screen for a videotape or DVD. For larger audiences, you will need several television monitors or projection technology.
- Have the equipment set up and ready to go before you speak.
- Use only brief clips and excerpts. Video should always supplement, rather than supplant, your speech.

CDs and MP3 Files If you want to supplement your speech with audio presentation aids—say, music or excerpts from speeches or interviews—you might want to play a CD or MP3 file. Both are readily available, and their sound can be amplified to fill various size rooms. If you use one of these audio presentation aids, consider these suggestions:

- Be certain that your CD or MP3 player is amplified so that your audience can hear it without straining.
- Use audio presentation aids sparingly. You do not want them to engage the audience's attention to the point that they interfere with the speech.

Computer-Generated Presentation Aids Not too many years ago, if you wanted to use a drawing or graph as a visual aid, you had to draw it by hand on a chalkboard, flip chart, or overhead transparency. If you wanted to use a photograph or map, you had to have it professionally enlarged. While speakers still use overheads, chalkboards, flip charts, and posters, today they also have another option: computer graphics programs.

Using such software as PowerPoint, you can develop a list of your main points that audience members can refer to as you speak, as illustrated in Figure 13.3. You can present graphs and charts. You can use clip art, or you can scan in or electronically cut-and-paste photographs, maps, or drawings. You can even incorporate video and audio clips. If computer-projection equipment is available in the room in which you will speak, you can display your presentation by connecting a computer to a special large-screen projector or an LCD panel that fits on top of an overhead projector. You can then run your program with a keyboard or mouse, or even set it to run automatically.

Computer graphics programs are an important way to adapt your message to audiences who increasingly expect sophisticated technical support. You will undoubtedly

Figure 13.3
PowerPoint Slide

Source: Photo of Paul Laurence Dunbar from the Ohio Historical Society, Dunbar House Web page, January 14, 2002, <www.ohiohistory.org/places/dunbar>, retrieved July 9, 2002.

Paul Laurence Dunbar
1872–1906

- Known as the "poet laureate of his people"
- Wrote popular poetry in African-American dialect
- Wrote significant poetry in standard English: "We Wear the Mask"

encounter and be expected to use these programs again in the business world. Gaining experience with them now can give you an edge in seeking employment and in making your earliest business presentations more effective.

However, such programs also have inherent risks. As one management professor points out,

> Untrained speakers use the projection equipment as a teleprompter, project the speech outline as bullet points, or dim the lights as though they were showing 35mm slides. Technical difficulties and apprehension can create additional barriers between audience and speaker.[34]

The solution? As with other presentation aids we have discussed, don't let your PowerPoint slides become your presentation—use them to supplement it. Don't use too many slides. Make certain that the ones you do use contain significant information in a simple, uncluttered style. Don't overuse bulleted text. Instead, take advantage of the ease with which you can create and show such visual elements as graphs, charts, and photos on PowerPoint slides. Finally, practice with your PowerPoint slides so that you can time them to coincide with your oral presentation.

Guidelines for Preparing Presentation Aids

In addition to the specific guidelines for preparing and using various types of presentation aids that we have just discussed, four general guidelines can help you prepare all types of presentation aids more effectively.

Select the Right Presentation Aids   As is evident from the above discussion, you have a number of options for presentation aids. If you are trying to decide which to use, consider these suggestions:

1. Adapt to your audience. Let their interests, experiences, and knowledge guide your selection of presentation aids. For example, an audience of accountants would readily understand arbitrage charts that might be incomprehensible to a more general audience. If you will be speaking to a large audience, be certain that everyone will be able to see or hear your presentation aid.

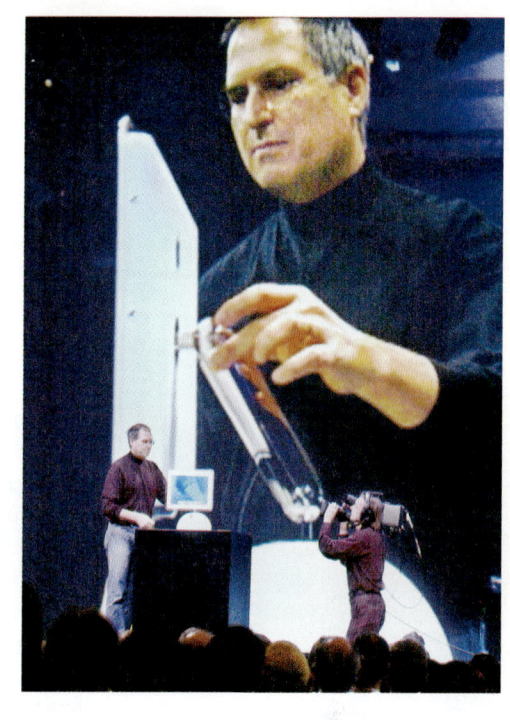

Steve Jobs, chief executive officer of Apple Computer, uses a large-screen projector to make sure his audience can see his PowerPoint presentation and the product he used to create it.

5. Adapt

"I need someone well versed in the art of torture—do you know PowerPoint?"

Communication and Ethics

Profanity in an Audio Presentation Aid

Matt wants to talk to his college classmates about the use of profanity in rap music. He plans to play sound clips of several profane lyrics from current hits to illustrate his point. Should Matt play these songs, even though doing so might offend several members of his audience?

---

2. Be constantly aware of your specific purpose. Be certain that your presentation aid contributes to its achievement.
3. Consider your own skill and experience. Use equipment with which you have had experience, or allow yourself ample time to practice. It may be better to make an overhead transparency of your PowerPoint image if the alternative is to fumble with an unfamiliar computer and LCD projector.
4. Take into account the room in which you will speak. If it has large windows and no shades, for example, do not plan to use a visual presentation aid that will require a darkened room. If you plan to run a PowerPoint presentation, be sure that both hardware and software are available and in good working order.

Make Your Presentation Aids Easy to See You have probably experienced the frustration of squinting and straining to read a speaker's too-small presentation aid. If you are going to remember only one thing about using a presentation aid, remember this: Make it big!

Keep Your Presentation Aids Simple Don't cram too much information on any single presentation aid. Limit text to key words or phrases. Leave plenty of white space.

Polish Your Presentation Aids Especially in this day of readily available, professional-looking computer graphics, audiences have high expectations for the appearance of presentation aids. A sloppy, hand-drawn visual will detract from even the best verbal message. Prepare your presentation aids well in advance of your speaking date and make them as attractive and professional as possible. Even if you can't run a PowerPoint presentation in the room in which you are speaking, consider using such a program to produce your presentation aids.

Guidelines for Using Presentation Aids

5. Adapt

Once you have prepared potentially effective presentation aids, you will want to utilize them effectively as well. In addition to the guidelines offered earlier in this chapter for using specific types of presentation aids, the following general suggestions will help you more effectively adapt various types of presentation aids to your audience.

Rehearse with Your Presentation Aids The day of your speech should not be the first time you deliver your presentation while holding up your chart, turning on your projector, or cueing your CD. Practice setting up and using your presentation aids until you feel at ease with them. Consider during rehearsal what you would do at various stages of the speech if you had to carry on without your presentation aid. Electricity fails, equipment fails to show up, and bulbs burn out. Have contingency plans.

Maintain Eye Contact with Your Audience, Not with Your Presentation Aids You can glance at your presentation aids during your talk, but do not talk to them. Keep looking at your audience.

Chapter 13 Delivering Your Presentation 369

In what ways did Tim Russert's use of a simple whiteboard on Election Night 2000 adapt to needs of the setting? What about the needs of his audience? How can you adapt when speaking impromptu?

Explain Your Presentation Aids Always talk about and explain your presentation aids. Do not assume that the audience will understand their relevance and how to interpret them.

Time the Display of Your Presentation Aids to Coincide with Your Discussion of Them Don't put a presentation aid in front of your audience until you are ready to use it. Likewise, remove your presentation aid after you are finished with it. Keeping presentation aids in front of an audience before or after you use them will only serve to distract from your message.

Do Not Pass Objects, Pictures, or Other Small Items Among Audience Members Passing things around distracts audience members. Either people are focused on whatever they are looking at, or they are counting the number of people who will handle the object before it reaches them. If the item is too small for everyone to see it when you hold it up, it is not a good presentation aid.

Use Handouts Effectively Handing out papers during your presentation can also distract audience members. If possible, wait to distribute handouts until after you have spoken. If your audience needs to refer to the material while you're talking about it, go ahead and pass out the handouts; then, at various points in your presentation, tell audience members where in the handout they should focus.

Use Small Children and Animals with Caution Small children and even the best-trained animals are unpredictable. In a strange environment, in front of an audience, they may not behave in their usual way. The risk of having a child or animal detract from your presentation may be too great to justify using either as a presentation aid.

Use Technology Thoughtfully Computer-generated graphics, LCDs, and DVDs have become increasingly common components of presentations; more and more classrooms and seminar rooms are equipped for them. However, resist the temptation to use

> ### Recap
> **Preparing and Using Presentation Aids**
>
> **Tips for Preparing and Using Specific Types of Presentation Aids**
> - Use **objects** that you can handle easily and that are safe and legal.
> - Be sure that any **models** you use are large enough to be seen easily.
> - Rehearse with **people** who will serve as presentation aids, and don't let them steal the show.
> - Keep **drawings** simple and large.
> - Be sure **photographs** are large enough to be seen easily.
> - Highlight on a **map** the geographic areas you will discuss.
> - Limit the amount of information you put on any single **chart**.
> - Keep **graphs** simple and uncluttered.
> - Use only brief excerpts and clips from **DVDs**, **videotapes**, or **streaming video**, and have equipment set up and ready to go before you speak.
> - Amplify any **CD** and **MP3** players so that they can be heard easily.
>
> **General Tips for Preparing and Using Presentation Aids**
>
> *Preparing Presentation Aids*
> - Select the right presentation aids.
> - Make your presentation aids easy to see.
> - Keep your presentation aids simple.
> - Polish your presentation aids.
>
> *Using Presentation Aids*
> - Rehearse with your presentation aids.
> - Maintain eye contact with your audience, not with your presentation aids.
> - Explain your presentation aids.
> - Time the display of your presentation aids to coincide with your discussion of them.
> - Do not pass objects, pictures, or other small items among your audience.
> - Use handouts effectively.
> - Use small children and animals with caution.
> - Use technology thoughtfully.

them just because they are glitzy. One speechwriter and presentation coach warns against this bleak but all-too-common scenario:

> The presenter says, "And now, I'd like to talk about quality." And lo and behold . . . the word *quality* flashes on a screen. Now, folks, does this slide offer any new information? Does it clarify a complex point? Does it strengthen the bond between presenter and audience? You know the answer: a resounding "no."[35]

Sometimes the simplest visual aids can still be the most effective. For example, the Smithsonian Institute now houses the dry-erase whiteboard on which the late NBC political analyst Tim Russert wrote, "Florida! Florida! Florida!" late on election night 2000.

Be sure that the technology you use helps you communicate your message. And be sure that you know how to operate the hardware and that you rehearse with it.

Some Final Tips for Rehearsing and Delivering Your Presentation

Throughout this chapter, we have described and offered suggestions for effective verbal and nonverbal delivery and use of presentation aids. In addition to the tips offered throughout the chapter, the following suggestions will help you make the most of your rehearsal time and ultimately deliver your presentation successfully:

- Finish your preparation outline several days before you must deliver the presentation. Begin to rehearse from the preparation outline. Revise the presentation as necessary so that you can deliver it within your given time limits. Outline your speaking notes. Continue to rehearse and to modify your speaking notes as necessary.
- Practice, practice, practice. Rehearse aloud as often as possible. Only by rehearsing will you gain confidence in both the content of the presentation and your delivery.
- Use good delivery skills while rehearsing. Rehearse your presentation standing up. Pay attention to your gestures, posture, eye contact, facial expression, and vocal delivery, as well as the verbal message. Rehearse with your presentation aids.
- If possible, practice your presentation for someone. Researchers in one study found that students who practice their speeches before an audience score higher on evaluation instruments than do students who practice without an audience.[36]
- Tape record or videotape your presentation. But try not to be overly critical when you listen to or watch yourself, as many of us tend to be. Note whether you use too many filler sounds or words, such as "uh," "er," "okay," "you know," and "like." But realize that you're developing a delivery style unique to you, so don't try to change too much.
- Re-create the speaking situation in your final rehearsals. Try to rehearse in a room similar to the one in which you will deliver the presentation. Use the speaking notes you will use the day you deliver the presentation. Give the presentation without stopping. The more realistic the rehearsal, the more confidence you will gain.
- Get plenty of rest the night before you speak. Being well rested is more valuable than squeezing in a frantic, last-minute rehearsal.
- Arrive early. If you don't know for certain the location of the room in which you'll make your presentation, give yourself plenty of time to find it. Rearrange any furniture or equipment, and set up and check your presentation aids.
- Review and apply the suggestions offered in Chapter 11 for becoming a more confident speaker. As the moment for delivering your presentation nears, remind yourself of the effort you have spent preparing it. Visualize yourself delivering the presentation effectively. Silently practice your opening lines. Think about your audience. Breathe deeply, and consciously relax.
- After you have delivered your presentation, seek feedback from members of your audience. Use the information you gain to improve your next presentation.

2. Verbal
3. Nonverbal

1. Aware

DEVELOPING YOUR PRESENTATION
Step by Step

Delivering Your Presentation

The long-awaited day of Maggie's presentation has arrived at last. She got a full night's sleep last night and ate a light breakfast before setting out for class.

As she waits to speak, Maggie visualizes herself delivering her speech calmly and confidently. When her name is called, she rises, walks to the front of the room, and establishes eye contact with her audience before she begins to speak.

During her speech, Maggie focuses on adapting her message to her listeners. She looks at individual members of her audience, uses purposeful and well-timed gestures, and speaks loudly and clearly.

Even before she hears her classmates' applause, Maggie knows that her presentation has gone well.

PRINCIPLES FOR A LIFETIME
Enhancing Your Skills

1. Aware

Principle One: Be aware of your communication with yourself and others.
- If your subject is sensitive or your information classified, be cautious and noncommittal in any impromptu remarks you make.
- As you become increasingly comfortable rehearsing an extemporaneous presentation, you can decrease your reliance on your notes.
- Grammatical and usage errors communicate a lack of preparation. If you are uncertain of how to use a word or phrase, look it up or ask someone.
- Use a microphone if you need one and one is available. Be sure to rehearse with it.
- Be aware of your speaking rate, and adjust it if necessary.
- Identify key words or phrases that you have a tendency to drawl, slur, or chop. Practice saying them distinctly and clearly.
- Be certain that your presentation aids, including those that utilize technology, contribute to your specific purpose.
- Pay attention to your nonverbal delivery when you rehearse your presentation.
- During rehearsal, tape record or videotape your presentation; objectively and critically observe your gestures, posture, eye contact, facial expression, and vocal delivery, as well as your verbal message; and make necessary adjustments.
- When you deliver your presentation, apply the suggestions offered in Chapter 11 for becoming a more confident speaker.

2. Verbal

Principle Two: Effectively use and interpret verbal messages.
- Give a manuscript or memorized speech when exact wording is critical.
- Phrase your ideas so that they will be clear, accurate, and memorable.
- Do not try to memorize an extemporaneous presentation word for word; vary the ways in which you express ideas and information.
- Use words that are concrete, unbiased, vivid, simple, and correct.
- Make your presentation memorable with figurative images, drama, and cadence.

3. Nonverbal

Principle Three: Effectively use and interpret nonverbal messages.
- When you deliver a manuscript speech, try to look at an entire sentence at a time so that you can maintain eye contact as you say the sentence.
- Do not read a manuscript speech too rapidly; vary the rhythm, inflection, and pace of delivery so that the speech does not sound as though it is being read.
- Do not deliver a memorized speech too rapidly, and avoid patterns of vocal inflection that make the speech sound recited.
- Use gestures and movement to add interest and emphasis to both manuscript and memorized speeches.
- Use gestures to reinforce your verbal message.
- Move during your presentation to signal the beginning of a new idea or major point or to signal a transition between a serious idea and a humorous one.
- To heighten your credibility and to increase listener learning, use eye contact to let your audience know that you are interested in them and ready to talk to them.
- Speak loudly enough to be heard easily by all members of your audience.
- Vary the volume of your voice to emphasize ideas and sustain the audience's interest.
- Vary your speaking rate to add interest to your delivery and to emphasize key ideas.
- Articulate your words clearly.

4. Listen and Respond

Principle Four: Listen and respond thoughtfully to others.
- Use eye contact to help you determine how your audience members are responding to you.
- If possible, rehearse your presentation for someone and seek feedback about both your content and your delivery.

Principle Five: Appropriately adapt messages to others.

5. Adapt

- Although audiences today generally expect speakers to use everyday language and a conversational delivery style, you will need to adapt your delivery to audiences of different sizes and from different cultures.
- Consider your audience and speaking context when you select a method of delivery.
- Consider your audience's interests, expectations, and knowledge to ensure that your impromptu presentation is audience-centered.
- As you deliver an extemporaneous presentation, adapt it to your audience.
- Avoid any language that might be offensive to a member of your audience.
- Adapt your gestures to your audience. Use bolder, more sweeping, and more dramatic gestures with large audiences. Tone down gestures if you are speaking to a culturally diverse audience who might prefer a more subdued style.
- Adapt your movement during a presentation to the cultural expectations of your audience. Better to stay in one carefully chosen spot than to make your audience uncomfortable.
- Assume a posture that seems natural to you in light of your topic, your audience, and the formality of the occasion.
- Adapt the amount of eye contact you use to the expectations of your audience. North Americans prefer as much eye contact as possible; Asians generally prefer less.
- To communicate your interest in your listeners, keep your facial expression alert and friendly.
- Adapt the volume of your voice to your audience's needs.
- Adapt your appearance to meet your audience's expectations.
- Let your audience's interests, experiences, and knowledge guide your preparation and selection of presentation aids.

Summary

Once you have developed, supported, and organized your presentation, you are ready to begin to rehearse aloud in preparation for delivering it. The way in which you deliver your presentation will in large part determine your success as a speaker.

As you begin to consider how you will deliver your presentation, you will select from four methods of delivery: manuscript speaking, memorized speaking, impromptu speaking, and extemporaneous speaking. Extemporaneous speaking is the style taught today in most presentational speaking classes and preferred by most audiences.

Once you know what method of delivery you will use, you should begin to think about and rehearse words, phrases, and sentences that will best communicate your intended message and give it a distinct and memorable style. The most effective language is concrete, unbiased, vivid, simple, and correct. You can also make your presentation memorable by using figurative language and language that creates drama and cadence.

Nonverbal variables are also critical to effective delivery. Physical delivery includes a speaker's gestures, movement, and posture. Eye contact is perhaps the most important delivery variable, determining to a large extent your credibility with your audience. Facial expression plays a key role in expressing thoughts, emotions, and attitudes. Vocal delivery includes such elements as volume, pitch, rate, and articulation. And finally, your personal appearance can also affect how your audience responds to you and your message.

Presentation aids may not always be necessary, but they are used with increasing frequency. Presentation aids may include objects or models, people, drawings, photographs, maps, charts, graphs, videotapes, DVDs, streaming video, MP3 files, and CDs. Today, many presentation aids can be created and displayed by computer graphics programs such as PowerPoint. Guidelines for using any type of presentation aid include selecting the right one for the audience, occasion, and room and making the presentation aid simple, easy to see or hear, and polished. Be sure to rehearse with your presentation aid, maintain eye contact with your audience, explain your presentation aid, time your use of your presentation aid, refrain from passing things around or using handouts indiscriminately, remember that small children and animals are unpredictable presentation aids, and use technology thoughtfully.

Final suggestions for rehearsing your presentation include allowing ample time to conduct realistic rehearsals, audiotaping or videotaping your presentation, and practicing your presentation for someone who will offer feedback. Final tips for delivering your presentation include getting plenty of rest the night before you speak, arriving early, and applying the suggestions offered in Chapter 11 for becoming a more confident speaker.

Assessing Your Knowledge

For Discussion and Review

Principle One: Be aware of your communication with yourself and others.

1. Discuss how you might use a videotape of a rehearsal to improve your final delivery of a presentation.

Principle Two: Effectively use and interpret verbal messages.

2. List and explain five characteristics of effective words.

Principle Three: Effectively use and interpret nonverbal messages.

3. What can facial expression communicate during a presentation?

Principle Four: Listen and respond thoughtfully to others.

4. Explain how eye contact can help a speaker respond to his or her audience.

Principle Five: Appropriately adapt messages to others.

5. Provide examples of how a speaker might adapt gestures to his or her audience.

Multiple Choice

Choose the *best* answer to each of the following questions.

1. In selecting presentation aids, it is important to
    a. adapt the aids to your audience.
    b. use aids that are just slightly beyond your skill and experience.
    c. use the most current technology possible.
    d. use the type of aid with which you are most familiar, regardless of the way your room is set up.

2. Which of the following presentation styles do North American public speaking classes teach most often?
    a. manuscript   c. impromptu
    b. memorized   d. extemporaneous

3. A speaker's pitch, rate, volume, and articulation are referred to as vocal
    a. delivery.   c. credibility.
    b. pronunciation.   d. diction.

4. When using visual aids in a speech, a speaker should
    a. display the visual aids only when discussing them.
    b. maintain eye contact with the audience.
    c. avoid passing handouts to the audience during the speech, if possible.
    d. all of the above

5. Which of the following will help you establish effective eye contact with an audience?
    a. Scan your audience without sustaining eye contact with any one individual for too long.
    b. Read from your notes during your opening to make sure you get it right.
    c. Focus most of your eye contact on people in the first few rows.
    d. Establish eye contact with the audience only after you have started your presentation.

6. When rehearsing an extemporaneous presentation, you should
    a. memorize your message word for word.
    b. rehearse only with your full-content preparation outline.
    c. vary the ways you express your ideas and information.
    d. keep gestures and movement to a minimum.

7. The rhythm with which you speak is your
    a. drama.   c. parallelism.
    b. omission.   d. cadence.

8. If you are giving a presentation in a room that has a large desk between you and the audience, it would probably be best to
    a. leave the desk where it is and speak from behind it.
    b. incorporate the desk into your visual aids.
    c. move in front of the desk to be closer to the audience.
    d. postpone your presentation until you can find a more suitable room.

9. Tabitha naturally speaks at a rate of 185 words per minute. The average speaker delivers a presentation at a rate of 120–180 words per minute. Tabitha should
    a. stand still so as not to overstimulate the audience when speaking fast.
    b. pause after questions and important ideas.

c. use more visual aids than normal so that her audience can keep up.
   d. all of the above
10. At the beginning of Diego's presentation about how to choose a diamond, the overhead projector he is using dies. Diego should
   a. postpone the speech until the projector can be fixed or replaced.
   b. continue with the speech, but pass pictures around instead.
   c. continue with the speech, but use concrete language to describe the images instead.
   d. tape the transparencies to white paper and have a classmate hold them up for the audience.

Answers to the questions in this practice test can be found at the end of the book.

Assessing Your Skill

1. Consult either a print thesaurus or the electronic thesaurus that is part of your word-processing program to find a more concrete or specific word to express each of the following:

   go   happy
   say   green
   big   cat
   dark   street
   good   car

2. Listen to a political campaign speech in person or on television. Pay particular attention to the politician's delivery. Critique his or her use of gestures, movement, posture, eye contact, facial expression, vocal delivery, and appearance. What advice would you give this politician?

3. Videotape one of your presentations, either during rehearsal or as you deliver it to your class. Analyze your strengths and weaknesses based on the principles and suggestions offered in this chapter.

4. You are a speech consultant to the superintendent of your local school district. She is about to begin working on her annual "State of the District" address, which she gives to an audience of about 250 teachers, parents, and community members. This year, she wants to enliven her presentation of enrollment statistics, student achievement facts, and the state of the physical plant with some presentation aids. Write an advisory memo to the superintendent in which you suggest types of presentation aids she might employ and ways of using each one effectively.

5. You will need the following materials to complete this assignment:
   - One or two pieces of paper or poster board measuring at least 15 × 20 inches
   - Felt-tipped markers or a set of marking pens in at least two different colors
   - A ruler or straightedge
   - A pencil with an eraser

   Three speech topics are listed below, each with a brief description and information that could be communicated with the help of a presentation aid. Design one or more presentation aids for one of the three speeches.
   a. A speech about personal information management tools that college students can use to keep track of assignments and projects. These tools include computer software, e-mail, paper calendars and organizers, and instant messaging.[37]
   b. A speech about the spread of AIDS. The numbers of new cases of HIV infection in 2007 on various continents are listed below.[38]
      - North America, Western and Central Europe: 81,000
      - Caribbean: 20,000
      - Latin America: 140,000
      - Eastern Europe and Central Asia: 110,000
      - North Africa and Middle East: 40,000
      - Sub-Saharan Africa: 1,900,000
      - Asia: 380,000
      - Oceania: 13,000
   c. A speech that discusses web sites offering useful information about nutrition and diet. Sites might include the following:
      - <www.mypyramid.gov/tips_resources/index.html>, which provides tips and resources from the USDA to help you choose healthful food and physical activity
      - <www.dietsite.com>, which allows users to enter recipes to obtain a calorie count
      - <www.mealsforyou.com>, which offers thousands of healthful recipes

Web Resources to Improve Your Knowledge and Skill

There are several sites on the web where you can both see and hear famous speeches from the past and today.

C-SPAN Online: <www.c-span.org/watch>
History Channel Archive of Speeches: <www.historychannel.com/speeches/index.html>
U.S. Presidential Inaugural Speeches: <www.bartleby.com/inaugural>
Michigan State University Vincent Voice Library: <vvl.lib.msu.edu/index.cfm>

Diana Ong. "The Defense." © Diana Ong/SuperStock, Inc.

If you think knowledge is expensive, try ignorance.

Derek Bok

Chapter 14

Speaking to Inform

Chapter Outline

- Types of Informative Presentations
- Strategies for Organizing Your Informative Presentation
- Strategies for Making Your Informative Presentation Clear
- Strategies for Making Your Informative Presentation Interesting
- Strategies for Making Your Informative Presentation Memorable
- Summary

Chapter Objectives

After studying this chapter, you should be able to

1. Explain the purpose of speaking to inform.
2. Describe and illustrate five types of informative presentations.
3. Identify and use appropriate strategies for organizing informative presentations.
4. Identify and use strategies for making informative presentations clear.
5. Identify and use strategies for making informative presentations interesting.
6. Identify and use strategies for making informative presentations memorable.

This is the information age. With the help of today's technology, we are immersed in facts, data, and words. The Internet is an overflowing fount of information on every conceivable topic. Information is a good thing; it is necessary to help us live our lives. But the volume of information may create a problem. There is often too much of a good thing. Trying to use and interpret all the information we encounter can be like trying to take a drink from a fire hose; the volume of information makes this nearly an overwhelming task.

Countless times each day, you are called on to share information with others. Whether it's directions to your house, the answer to a question from a teacher, or an update on a project at work, your competence as a communicator is often based on how clearly you can present information to others. One survey of both speech teachers and students who had taken a communication course found that the single most important skill taught in a presentational speaking class is how to give an informative presentation.[1] This is not surprising, given the importance in our lives of sending and receiving information.

The purpose of a message to **inform** is to share information with others to enhance their knowledge or understanding of the information, concepts, and ideas you present. When you inform someone, you assume the role of a teacher by defining, illustrating, clarifying, or elaborating on a topic.

Speaking to inform others can be a challenging task. The information you communicate to someone else is rarely, if ever, understood exactly as you intend it. As we have noted, we're all different. We literally experience the world in different ways. As a student, you have firsthand experience that just because a teacher presents information, you don't always soak up knowledge like a sponge. Informing or teaching others is a challenge because of a simple fact: *Presenting information does not mean that communication has occurred.* Communication happens when listeners make sense of the information.

Another challenge of speaking to inform is to keep your informative message from becoming a persuasive one. It cannot be denied that informing and persuading are interrelated. Information alone may persuade someone to think or do something in a different way. However, if you intentionally try to change or reinforce your listeners' feelings, ideas, or behavior, your speech may become more persuasive than informative.

In this chapter, we will suggest ways to build on your experience and enhance your skill in informing others. We will examine different types of informative tasks and identify specific strategies to help you organize your messages and make them clear, interesting, and memorable. Throughout our discussion, we will remind you of the five Communication Principles for a Lifetime.

1. Aware
2. Verbal
3. Nonverbal
4. Listen and Respond
5. Adapt

Types of Informative Presentations

When preparing an informative presentation, your first task, after considering the needs and backgrounds of your audience, is to select a topic. Although you may be assigned a topic based on your job, experience, or expertise, there are times (such as in a communication class) when you are given a free hand in determining what you will talk about. Identifying the type of informative presentation you will deliver can help you select and narrow your topic, organize your message, and select appropriate supporting material.

Presentations About Objects

A speech about an object might be about anything tangible—anything you can see or touch. You may or may not show the actual object to your audience while you are talking about it. Objects that could form the basis of an interesting presentation might include the following:

> Objects from your own collection (antiques, compact discs, baseball cards)
> The Eiffel Tower

inform
To share information with others to enhance their knowledge or understanding of the information, concepts, and ideas you present.

Communication and Ethics

Confidential or Potentially Dangerous Information

Mike, a computer engineering major, understands how a computer hacker recently accessed confidential personal information files on faculty members at his university. The procedure is actually simple enough that even people without sophisticated technical ability could understand and replicate it. Mike thinks the procedure might be a good topic for an interesting informative presentation.

Meanwhile Mike's classmate Paul, a chemistry major, considers whether to give an informative presentation on how to create homemade explosives. If you are privy to confidential or potentially dangerous information, is it ethical to share it with others in an informative presentation?

>   Cellos
>   Digital cameras
>   The Roosevelt Memorial
>   Toys

The time limit for your speech will determine the amount of detail you can share with your listeners. Even in a thirty- to forty-five-minute presentation, you cannot talk about every aspect of any of the objects listed. So you will need to focus on a specific purpose.

Presentations About Procedures

A presentation about a procedure discusses how something works (for example, how blood travels through the human circulatory system) or describes a process that produces a particular outcome (such as how grapes become wine). At the close of such a presentation, your audience should be able to describe, understand, or perform the procedure you have described. Here are some examples of procedures that could be the topics of effective informative presentations:

>   How to upload a video on YouTube
>   How state laws are made
>   How to refinish furniture
>   How to select a personal digital assistant (PDA)
>   How to plant an organic garden
>   How to select and purchase stock

Notice that all of these examples start with the word *how*. A presentation about a procedure usually focuses on how a process is completed or how something can be accomplished. Presentations about procedures are often presented in workshops or other training situations in which people learn skills. One good way to teach people a skill is to follow the acronym T-E-A-C-H, which stands for Tell-Example-Apply-Coach-Help.[2]

- *Tell:* Describe what you want your listeners to know.
- *Example:* Show them an example of how to perform the skill.
- *Apply:* Give them an opportunity to apply the knowledge by performing the skill.
- *Coach:* Provide positive coaching to encourage them.
- *Help:* Help them learn by correcting mistakes.

Many presentations about procedures include visual aids. Whether you are teaching people how to install a computer modem or how to give a presentation, showing them how to do something—the *Example* step of the T-E-A-C-H acronym—is almost always more effective than just telling them how to do it.

Presentations About People

A biographical presentation could be about someone famous or about someone you know personally. Most of us enjoy hearing about the lives of real people, whether famous or not, living or dead, who have some special quality. The key to making an effective biographical presentation is to be selective. Don't try to cover every detail of your subject's life. Relate the key elements in the person's career, personality, or other significant life features so that you build to a particular point, rather than just recite facts about the individual. Perhaps your grandfather was known for his generosity, for example. Mention some notable examples of his philanthropy. If you are talking about a well-known personality, pick information or a period that is not widely known, such as the person's private hobby or childhood. One speaker gave a memorable presentation about his friend:

> To enter Charlie's home was to enter a world of order and efficiency. His den reflected his many years as an Air Force officer; it was orderly and neat. He always knew exactly where everything was. When he finished reading the morning paper, he folded it so neatly by his favorite chair that you would hardly know that it had been read. Yet for all of his efficiency, you knew the minute you walked into his home that he cared for others, that he cared for you. His jokes, his stories, his skill in listening to others drew people to him. He never met a stranger. He looked for opportunities to help others.

Note how these details capture Charlie's personality and charm. Presentations about people should give your listeners the feeling that the person is a unique, authentic individual.

One specific type of presentation about a person is an introduction of another speaker and his or her topic. There are two cardinal rules for introducing another speaker: Be brief, and be accurate. Remember that the audience has come to hear the main speaker, not to listen to you. And be certain that you know how to pronounce the speaker's name and that you have accurate information about him or her.

Presentations About Events

Where were you on September 11, 2001, the day terrorists attacked the World Trade Center and the Pentagon? Chances are that you clearly remember where you were and what you were doing on that and other similarly fateful days. Major events punctuate our lives and mark the passage of time.

A major event can form the basis of a fascinating informative presentation. You can choose to talk about an event that you have either witnessed or researched. Your goal is to describe the event in concrete, tangible terms and to bring the experience to life for your audience. Have you experienced a major disaster such as a hurricane or a tornado? Have you witnessed the inauguration of a president, governor, or senator? Or you may want to re-create an event that your parents or grandparents lived through. What was it like to be at Pearl Harbor on December 7, 1941? How did people react when Neil Armstrong took his first steps on the moon on July 20, 1969?

You may have heard a recording of the famous radio broadcast of the explosion and crash of the dirigible *Hindenburg*. The announcer's ability to describe both the scene and the incredible emotion of the moment has made that broadcast a classic. As that broadcaster was able to do, your purpose as an informative speaker describing an event is to make that event come alive for your listeners and to help them visualize the scene.

Presentations About Ideas

Presentations about ideas are by nature more abstract than the other types of presentations. The following principles, concepts, and theories might be topics of idea presentations:

> Principles of time management
> Freedom of speech
> Evolution
> Theories of communication
> Buddhism
> Animal rights

As you look at this list, you may think, "Those topics sure look boring." The key to gaining and maintaining interest in your presentation about an idea lies in your selection of supporting material. A good speaker selects illustrations, examples, and anecdotes that make an otherwise abstract idea seem both exciting and relevant to the audience.

2. Verbal

Strategies for Organizing Your Informative Presentation

As with any presentation, your audience will more readily understand your informative presentation if you organize your ideas logically. Regardless of the length or complexity of your message, you must follow a logical pattern in order to be understood.

Organizing Presentations About Objects

Presentations about objects may be organized topically; a topical pattern is structured around the logical divisions of the object you're describing. Here's a sample topical outline for a speech about an object—a nuclear power plant:

I. The reactor core
   A. The nuclear fuel in the core
   B. The placement of the fuel in the core
II. The reactor vessel
   A. The walls of a reactor vessel
   B. The function of the coolant in the reactor vessel
III. The reactor control rods
   A. The description of the control rods
   B. The function of the control rods

Presentations about objects may also be organized chronologically. A speaker might, for example, focus on the history and development of nuclear power plants; such a presentation would probably be organized chronologically. Or, depending on the speaker's specific purpose, the presentation could be organized spatially, describing the physical layout of a nuclear power plant.

Organizing Presentations About Procedures

Speeches about procedures are usually organized chronologically, according to the steps involved in the process. Anita chose a chronological organization for her explanation of how to develop a new training curriculum in teamwork skills:

I. Conduct a needs assessment of your department.
   A. Identify the method of assessing department needs.

B. Implement the needs assessment.
II. Identify the topics that should be presented in the training.
　　A. Specify topics that all members of the department need.
　　B. Specify topics that only some members of the department need.
III. Write training objectives.
　　A. Write objectives that are measurable.
　　B. Write objectives that are specific.
　　C. Write objectives that are attainable.
IV. Develop lesson plans for the training.
　　A. Identify the training methods you will use.
　　B. Identify the materials you will need.

Note that Anita grouped the tasks into steps. Her audience will remember the four general steps much more easily than they could have hoped to recall the curriculum development process if each individual task were listed as a separate step.

Organizing Presentations About People

One way to talk about a person's life is in chronological order—birth, school, career, family, professional achievements, death. However, if you are interested in presenting a specific theme, such as "Winston Churchill, master of English prose," you may decide instead to organize Churchill's experiences topically. You could first discuss Churchill's achievements as a brilliant orator whose words defied the German military machine in 1940 and then trace the origins of his skill to his work as a cub reporter in South Africa during the Boer War of 1899 to 1902.

When speaking about Native American rock art in Texas, this speaker may find it helpful to organize her speech either topically, spatially, or chronologically.

Organizing Presentations About Events

Most speeches about an event follow a chronological arrangement. But a presentation about an event might also describe the complex issues or causes behind the event and be organized topically. For example, if you were to talk about the Civil War, you might choose to focus on three causes of the war:

I. Political
II. Economic
III. Social

Although these main points are topical, specific subpoints may be organized chronologically. However you choose to organize your speech about an event, your goal should be to ensure that your audience is enthralled by your vivid description.

5. Adapt

Organizing Presentations About Ideas

Most presentations about ideas are organized topically (by logical subdivisions of the central idea) or according to complexity (from simple ideas to more complex ones). The following example illustrates how Thompson organized a presentation about philosophy into an informative speech:

I. Definition of philosophy
　　A. Philosophy as viewed in ancient times
　　B. Philosophy as viewed today
II. Three branches of the study of philosophy

Recap

Organizing Informative Presentations

Presentation Type	Description	Typical Organizational Patterns	Sample Topics
Objects	Present information about tangible things	Topical Spatial Chronological	The Rosetta Stone MP3 players Space shuttle The U.S. Capitol

Procedures	Review how something works or describe a process	Chronological
		Topical
		Complexity
			How to . . .
			  Clone an animal
			  Operate a nuclear power plant
			  Use a computer
			  Trap lobsters

People	Describe either a famous person or a personal acquaintance	Chronological Topical	Rosa Parks Nelson Mandela Indira Gandhi Your grandmother Your favorite teacher
Events	Describe an actual event	Chronological Topical Complexity Spatial	Chinese New Year Inauguration Day Cinco de Mayo
Ideas	Present abstract information or information about principles, concepts, theories, or issues	Topical Complexity	Communism Economic theory Tao Te Ching

  A. Metaphysics
    1. The study of ontology
    2. The study of cosmology
  B. Epistemology
    1. Knowledge derived from thinking
    2. Knowledge derived from experiencing
  C. Logic
    1. Types of reasoning
    2. Types of proof

Thompson decided that the most logical way to give an introductory talk about philosophy was first to define it and then to describe three branches of philosophy. Because of time limits, he chose only to describe three branches or types of philosophy. He used a topical organizational pattern to organize his message.

Strategies for Making Your Informative Presentation Clear

Think of the best teacher you ever had. He or she was probably a great lecturer with a special talent for making information clear, interesting, and memorable. Like teachers, some speakers are better than others at presenting information clearly. In this section, we will review some of the principles that can help you become the kind of speaker whose presentations are memorable.[3]

A message is clear when the listener understands it in the way the speaker intended. Phrased in baseball terminology, a message is clear when what I threw is what you caught. How do you make your messages clear to others? First, be aware (mindful) of what you intend to communicate. Is the message clear to you? Say to yourself, "If I heard this message for the first time, would it make sense to me?"

If the message makes sense to you, select appropriate words, reinforced with appropriate nonverbal cues, to express your ideas. If you detect that your listeners are puzzled by what you say, stop and try another way to express your ideas.

Adapt your message to your audience. Be audience-centered. Keep your listeners in mind as you select and narrow a topic, fine-tune your purpose, and complete each preparation and presentation task. Here are several additional specific strategies to make your message clear.

Simplify Ideas

Your job as a presentational speaker is to get your ideas through to your audience, not to see how much information you can cram into your speech. The simpler your ideas and phrases, the greater the chance that your audience will remember them.

Let's say you decide to talk about state-of-the-art personal computer hardware. Fine—but don't try to make your audience as sophisticated as you are about computers in a five-minute presentation. Discuss only major features and name one or two leaders in the field. Don't load your presentation with details. Edit ruthlessly.

Pace Your Information Flow

Arrange your supporting material so that you present an even flow of information, rather than bunch up a number of significant details around one point. If you present too much new information too quickly, you may overwhelm your audience. Their ability to understand may falter.

You should be especially sensitive to the flow of information if your topic is new or unfamiliar to your listeners. Make sure that your audience has time to process any new information you present. Use supporting material to regulate the pace of your presentation.

Again, do not try to see how much detail and content you can cram into a presentation. Your job is to present information so that the audience can grasp it, not to show off how much you know.

Relate New Information to Old

Most of us learn by building on what we already know. We try to make sense out of our world by associating the new with the old. When you meet someone for the first time, you may be reminded of someone you already know. Your understanding of calculus is based on your knowledge of algebra.

When presenting new information to a group, help your audience associate your new idea with something that is familiar to them. Use an analogy. Tell bewildered college freshmen how their new academic life will be similar to high school and how it will be different. Describe how your raising cattle over the summer was similar to taking care of any animal; they all need food, water, and shelter. By building on the familiar, you help your listeners understand how your new concept or information relates to their experience.

Strategies for Making Your Informative Presentation Interesting

He had them. Every audience member's eyes were riveted on the speaker. It was as quiet as midnight in a funeral home. Audience members were leaning forward ever so slightly, not wanting to miss a single idea or brilliant illustration. No one moved. They hung on every word. How can you create such interest when *you* speak? Here are several strategies that can help you keep your audiences listening for more.

Relate to Your Listeners' Interests

Your listeners may be interested in your topic for a variety of reasons. It may affect them directly, it may add to their knowledge, it may satisfy their curiosity, or it may entertain them. These reasons are not mutually exclusive. For example, if you were talking to a group of businesspeople about the latest changes in local tax policies, you would be discussing something that would affect them directly, add to their knowledge, and satisfy their curiosity. But your listeners' primary interest would be in how the taxes would affect them. By contrast, if you were giving a lecture on fifteenth-century Benin sculpture to a middle-class audience at a public library, your listeners would be interested because your talk would add to their knowledge, satisfy their curiosity, and entertain them. Such a talk can also affect your listeners directly by making them more interesting to others. If your audience feels that they will benefit from your presentation in some way, your presentation will interest them.

Throughout this book, we have encouraged you to adapt to your communication partners—to develop an audience-centered approach to presentational speaking. Being an audience-centered informative speaker means that you are aware of information that your audience can use. Specifically, what factors help maintain audience interest? Consider the following strategies.[4]

- *Activity and movement.* We are more likely to listen to a story that is action-packed than to one that listlessly lingers on an idea too long.
- *Issues and events close to an audience.* To capture your listeners' attention, relate your information to what is happening in your school, community, or state. Not

1. Aware
5. Adapt

Before delivering your presentation to a given audience, consider taking the time to talk and listen to audience members, which will help you customize your message to them.

Communication and Diversity

Using an Interpreter

It is quite possible that you may at some time be asked to speak to an audience of people who do not understand English or who cannot hear. In such a situation, you will need an interpreter to translate your message so that your audience can understand you. When using an interpreter, consider the following tips:

1. Realize that a presentation that may take you thirty minutes to deliver without an interpreter will take at least an hour to present with an interpreter. Edit your message to make sure it fits within the time limit.
2. Even with an experienced interpreter, you'll need to slow your speaking rate a bit. Also, be sure to pause after every two or three sentences to give the interpreter time to translate your message.
3. Don't assume that your audience doesn't understand you just because you are using an interpreter. Don't say anything that you don't want your audience to hear.
4. If you have many facts, figures, or other detailed data, write this information down before you speak, and give it to your interpreter.
5. Humor often doesn't translate well. Be cautious of using a joke that was a real knee-slapper when you told it to your colleagues in your office; it may not have the same effect on people with a different cultural background and different language. Also, even a very skilled interpreter may have difficulty communicating the intended meaning of your humor.
6. Avoid using slang, jargon, or any terms that will be unfamiliar to your listeners or the interpreter.
7. When possible, talk with your interpreter before you deliver your presentation. Tell him or her the general points you will present. If possible, give the interpreter an outline or a transcript if you are using a manuscript.

---

surprisingly, most people are interested in themselves. Therefore, one of the secrets to making a presentation interesting is to use examples to which your audience can relate. Make it personal. When appropriate, mention specific audience members' names.

- *Conflict.* Clashes of ideas, stories that pit one side against another, or opposing forces in government, religion, or interpersonal relationships grab attention. The Greeks learned long ago that the essential ingredient of any play, be it comedy or tragedy, is conflict.

Another way you can make your message interesting is to think about why you are interested in the topic. Once you are aware of your own interests and background, you can often find ways to establish common bonds with your audience.

Use Attention-Catching Supporting Material

Supporting material is effective if it both clarifies your ideas and keeps your listeners' attention. One classic type of supporting material often used in informative speaking is definition. But if you are trying to tell your listeners about a complex or abstract process, you will need more than definitions to explain what you mean. When describing abstract ideas or processes, it's usually more difficult to hold listeners' attention. Research suggests that you can demystify a complex process and increase audience interest if you first provide a simple overview of the process with an analogy, model, picture, or vivid description.[5]

Before going into great detail, first give listeners the "big picture" or convey the gist of the process. Analogies (comparisons) are often a good way to do this. For example, if you were describing how a personal computer works, you could say that it stores information the way a filing cabinet does or that computer software works like a piano roll on an old-fashioned player piano. In addition to using an analogy, consider using a model or other visual aid to show relationships among the steps of a complex process.

You can also describe the process, providing more detail than you do when you just define something. Descriptions answer questions about the *who, what, where, why*, and *when* of the process. Who is involved in the process? What is the process, idea, or event that you want to describe? Where and when does the process take place? Why does it occur, or why is it important to the audience? (Of course, not all of these questions apply to every description.)

Establish a Motive for Your Audience to Listen to You

Most audiences will probably not be waiting breathlessly for you to talk to them. You will need to motivate them to listen to you.

Some situations have built-in motivations for listeners. A teacher can say, "There will be a test covering my lecture tomorrow. It will count as 50 percent of your semester grade." Such threatening methods may not make the teacher popular, but they certainly will motivate the class to listen. Similarly, a boss might say, "Your ability to use these sales principles will determine whether you keep your job." Your boss's statement will probably motivate you to learn the company's sales principles. However, unlike a teacher or a boss, you will rarely have the power to motivate your listeners with such strong-arm tactics, and you will therefore need to find more creative ways to get your audience to listen to you.

One way to arouse the interest of your listeners is to ask them a question. Speaking on the high cost of tuition, you might ask, "How many of you are interested in saving tuition dollars this year?" You'll probably have their attention. Then proceed to tell them that you will talk about several approaches to seeking low-cost loans and grants. "Who would like to save money on their income taxes?" "How many of you would like to have a happier home life?" "How many of you would like to learn an effective way of preparing your next speech?" These are other examples of questions that could stimulate your listeners' interest and motivate them to give you their attention. Besides using rhetorical questions, you can begin with an anecdote, a startling statistic, or some other attention-grabbing device.

Don't assume that your listeners will be automatically interested in what you have to say. Pique their interest with a question. Capture their attention. Motivate them to listen to you. Tell them how the information you present will be of value to them. As the British writer G. K. Chesterton once said, "There is no such thing as an uninteresting topic; there are only uninterested people."

Use Word Pictures

Words have the ability to create powerful images that can gain and hold an audience's attention. A **word picture** is a lively description that helps your listeners form a mental image by appealing to one or more of their senses of sight, sound, smell, touch, and taste. Consider using a word picture to make your message vivid and interesting.

Once you yourself have a clear mental image of the person, place, or object you want to describe, use the following suggestions to construct an effective word picture:

- *Sight.* Use lively language to describe the flaws and foibles, bumps and beauties of the people, places, and things you want your audience to see.
- *Sound.* Describe what your listeners would hear. Use colorful, onomatopoetic words, such as *buzz, snort, hum, crackle,* or *hiss,* to imitate the sound you want your listeners to hear with their "mental ear." For example, instead of saying, "When I walked in the woods, I heard the sound of twigs breaking beneath my feet and wind moving the leaves above me in the trees," you might say, "As I walked in the woods, I heard the *crackle* of twigs underfoot and the *rustle* of leaves overhead."
- *Smell.* What fragrance or aroma do you want your audience to recall? Such diverse subjects as nighttime in the tropics and the first day of school lend themselves to olfactory imagery. A warm, humid evening in Miami smells of salt air and gardenia blossoms. The first day of school evokes for many the scents of new shoe leather, unused crayons, and freshly painted classrooms. In each case, the associated smells greatly enhance the overall word picture.
- *Touch.* Describe how an object feels when touched. Rather than saying that something is rough or smooth, use a simile, such as "the rock was rough as sandpaper" or "the pebble was as smooth as a baby's skin." These descriptions appeal to both visual and tactile senses.
- *Taste.* Thinking about your grandmother may evoke for you memories of her rich, homemade noodles; her sweet, fudgy, nut brownies; and her light, flaky, buttery pie crust. Descriptions of these taste sensations would be welcomed by almost any audience, particularly your fellow college students subsisting mainly on dormitory food or their own cooking! More important, such description can help you paint an accurate, vivid image of your grandmother.

In addition to describing sensory images, you can enhance a word picture by describing the emotion that a listener might feel if he or she were to experience the situation you relate. Use specific adjectives rather than general terms such as *happy* or *sad*. One speaker, talking about receiving her first speech assignment, described her reaction with these words:

> My heart stopped. Panic began to rise up inside. Me? . . . For the next five days I lived in dreaded anticipation of the forthcoming event.[6]

Note how effectively such words and phrases as "my heart stopped," "panic," and "dreaded anticipation" invoke the speaker's terror at the prospect of giving a speech—much more so than if she had said simply "I was scared." The more vividly and accurately you can describe emotion, the more intimately involved in your description the audience will become. One word of caution, however: Don't describe horrific events too explicitly. You will risk alienating your audience, rather than engaging them.

Create Interesting Presentation Aids

Research about learning styles suggests that many of your listeners are more likely to remember your ideas if you can reinforce them with presentation aids. Pictures, graphs, posters, and computer-generated graphics can help you gain and maintain audience members' attention, as well as increase their retention of the information you present.

2. Verbal

1. Aware

word picture
Vivid words that invite listeners to draw on their senses.

Communication and Technology

Using an Electronic Thesaurus

Most word-processing programs include an electronic thesaurus. To use this tool in Microsoft Word, highlight a word in your text for which you would like to find a synonym. Then click on "Thesaurus" under the "Tools" menu. You will get a pop-up box with several alternatives for your highlighted word. If one of these synonyms creates a better word picture, you might want to replace your original word with the new one.

A word of caution, however, about using any thesaurus, whether electronic or traditional: Be sure that you know the alternative word well enough to understand its connotations and how to use it in a grammatically correct way. A thesaurus should remind you of a word with which you are already familiar, not launch you into an uncharted adventure in diction!

Today's audiences are exposed daily to a barrage of messages conveyed through such highly visual electronic media as DVDs and streaming video. They have grown to depend on more than words alone to help them remember ideas and information. When you present summaries of data, a well-crafted line graph or colorful pie chart can quickly and memorably reinforce the words and numbers you cite.

3. Nonverbal

Use Humor

"Humor is the spice of speeches," says comedian Michael Klepper. "Too little and your message may be bland or lifeless, too much and it can burn the mouth."[7] The challenge is to use just the right kind of humor in the right amounts. Use humor wisely by considering the following ideas:"[8]

- *Use humor to make a point.* Don't tell jokes just for the sake of getting a laugh. Make sure your story or punch line relates to your message. Here's an example of how a brief joke was used to make a point about the value of teamwork:

  I read recently about a veterinarian and a taxidermist who decided to share a shop in a small town in Ohio. The sign in the front window read: "Either way, you get your dog back."

  There is an important lesson there. We need to work together to solve our problems. People from marketing need to work with operations people. Designers need to work with engineers. Then, when we find a problem that one part of the organization can't solve, someone else may suggest a solution. It doesn't matter who comes up with the solution. The important thing is to "get your dog back."[9]

- *Make yourself the butt of the joke.* Audiences love it when you tell a funny or embarrassing story about yourself. And if the joke's on you, you don't have to worry about whether you will offend someone else.
- *Use humorous quotations.* You don't have to be a comedy writer to be funny. Quote humorous lines of proverbs, poetry, or sayings from others. But remember, what may be funny to you may not be funny to your audience. Some people love the humor of George Carlin; some don't. Try out your quotes and jokes on others before you present them from behind the lectern. Also, don't try to pass off a quotation from someone else as one of your own; always give credit for quotations you use.
- *Use cartoons.* Using an overhead projector to display a cartoon or scanning a cartoon into your computer presentation may be just the right way to make your point. Make sure your cartoon is large enough to be seen by everyone in the audience. As with any humor, don't overdo your use of cartoons.

How can you use humor to gain and maintain the attention of your audience? What kinds of nonverbal cues can you use to reinforce your ideas and make your message as memorable as possible?

Strategies for Making Your Informative Presentation Memorable

If you've made your message clear and interesting, you're well on your way to ensuring that your audience members remember what you say. The goal is for your ideas to stick in your listeners' minds as if they were made of Velcro, rather than slide off as if they were made of Teflon. When you inform or teach, your job is to ensure as much retention of what you have conveyed as possible, by presenting the information as effectively as you can. People remember what is important to them. So one of the keys to making a message memorable is, again, to adapt your message to your listeners. Presenting a well-organized message will also go a long way toward helping your listeners remember what you say. Here are several strategies for making your presentation memorable.

Build in Redundancy

It is seldom necessary for writers to repeat themselves. If readers don't quite understand a passage, they can go back and read it again. When you speak, however, it is useful to repeat key points. As we have noted before, audience members generally cannot stop you if a point in your presentation is unclear or if their minds wander; you need to build in redundancy to make sure that the information you want to communicate will get across. Most speech teachers advise their students to structure their presentations as follows:

1. *Tell them what you're going to tell them.* In the introduction of your presentation, provide a broad overview of the purpose of your message. Identify the major points you will present.
2. *Tell them.* In the body of your presentation, develop each of the main points mentioned during your introduction.
3. *Tell them what you've told them.* Finally, in your conclusion, summarize the key ideas discussed in the body.

Use Adult Learning Principles

If your audience consists of adult listeners, you will need to ensure that you deliver your message in the way that adults learn best. **Adult learning principles** suggest that adults prefer the following.[10]

- To be given information they can use immediately
- To be involved actively in the learning process
- To connect their life experiences with the new information they learn
- To know how the new information is relevant to their busy lives
- To receive information that is relevant to their needs

Most people who have office jobs have in-baskets (or simply "in-piles") on their desks, where they place work that needs to be done. Similarly, adult learners tend to have "mental in-baskets"; as audience members, they have mental agendas of what they want or need to gain from listening to a presentation. Remember the characteristics of adult learners, as well as the important principle of adapting your message to others. You will make your message memorable and also have more success in informing your audience if you tailor your information to address *their* agenda.

Reinforce Key Ideas Verbally

You can reinforce an idea by using a phrase such as "This is the most important point" or "Be sure to remember this next point; it's the most compelling one." Suppose you

adult learning principles
Adults prefer practical, useful information that is relevant to their busy lives; they seek information that connects with their life experiences.

have four suggestions for helping your listeners chair a meeting, and your last suggestion is the most important. How can you make sure your audience knows that? Just tell them: "Of all the suggestions I've given you, this last tip is the most important one. Here it is: Never fail to distribute an agenda before you chair any meeting." Be careful not to overuse this technique. If you claim that every other point is a key point, soon your audience will not believe you.

Reinforce Key Ideas Nonverbally

You can also signal the importance of a point with nonverbal emphasis. Gestures serve the purpose of accenting or emphasizing key phrases, as italics do in written communication.

A well-placed pause can provide emphasis and reinforcement for a point. Pausing just before or just after you make an important point will focus attention on your thought. Raising or lowering your voice can also reinforce a key idea.

Movement can help emphasize major ideas. Moving from behind the lectern to tell a personal anecdote can signal that something special and more intimate is about to be said. Remember that your movement and gestures should be meaningful and natural, rather than seeming arbitrary or forced. Your need to emphasize an idea can provide the motivation to make a meaningful movement.

In the sample informative presentation on the universal power of music that follows, student Alton Tisino applies most of the strategies for making an informative presentation clear, interesting, and memorable. The speech can be categorized as an informative speech about an idea, organized topically. Alton makes his presentation clear by simplifying information where necessary—for example, by illustrating statistical data with a personal anecdote. He makes his presentation interesting by explicitly relating both his introduction and his conclusion to his listeners' interests and experiences and by offering an auditory word picture created by poet Langston Hughes. And he makes his presentation memorable by building in redundancy with previews, summaries, and signposts. Finally, Alton draws on the principles of adult learning by explaining how the elements of music apply to everyone's life.

Recap

Strategies for Making an Informative Presentation Clear, Interesting, and Memorable

Make Your Presentation Clear

Simplify ideas.
Pace the information flow.
Relate new information to old.

Make Your Presentation Interesting

Relate to your listeners' interests.
Use attention-catching supporting material.
Establish a motive for your audience to listen to you.
Use word pictures.
Create interesting presentation aids.
Use humor.

Make Your Presentation Memorable

Build in redundancy.
Use adult learning principles.
Reinforce key ideas verbally.
Reinforce key ideas nonverbally.

---

2. Verbal

3. Nonverbal

Sample Informative Presentation

The Power of Music[11]

Alton Tisino
Texas State University–San Marcos

Alton establishes a motive for his audience to listen by referring to music experiences common to all people.

When I woke up this morning, one thing on my mind was music. I'm sure everyone wakes up with a certain tune or a favorite song in their head. Music is a treasured art form that we all share. Sometimes we can hear a song, and it will take us back to a significant time in our lives; or other times, a song can give us inspiration or motivate us to continue whatever it is we are doing. Whether it is in a car or at home, or at a restaurant or even in an elevator, music plays a big part in our daily lives and can bring us together like no other art form.

Alton further arouses the interest of his listeners by asking two rhetorical questions.

Alton previews the two main ideas of his presentation.

So why is music so powerful? What are the elements that make music so special? Some people say they like the beat of a song, some people say they like the melody in a song, while others simply enjoy the lyrics in a song. Well, according to world-famous composer Duke Ellington, there are three major elements in music: rhythm, melody, and harmony. In order for us to discover what makes music so special, we must first understand these terms, and then see how music itself is beneficial to us in our daily lives.

Alton uses both a definition and an explanation to clarify the role of rhythm in music.

The *Dictionary of Music* defines *rhythm* as "the division of impulses, sound, and accents or movement in musical time." There are many theories on how rhythm was transformed into music. But, I'd like to cite poet Langston Hughes and his explanation on how rhythm was transformed into music:

> The rhythm of the heart is the first and most important rhythm in human life. Thousands of years ago men transformed the rhythm of the heartbeat into a drumbeat. And the rhythm of music began. They made a slow steady drumbeat to walk to or march to, a faster beat to sing to, and a changing beat to dance to. Rhythm is something we share in common. You and I, with all the plants and animals and people in the world and with all the stars and moon and sun and all the vast universe beyond this wonderful earth which is our home.[12]

Alton provides a signpost to summarize his first subpoint and preview the next one.

Now that we have found our rhythm, we must look further into the foundation of music and discover melody.

Melody is defined as "an arrangement of single tones in a meaningful sequence." A melody gives life to a song and is the root for every tune you will ever hear. We have now found our melody and now we're only missing one piece to the puzzle of music.

Harmony is defined as "the sound resulting from the simultaneous sounding of two or more tones consonant with each other." Rhythm and melody would not be complete without harmony.

This signpost signals Alton's move from his first main idea to his second main idea.

Now that we have discovered the foundations of music, let me now explain to you how music is beneficial to us.

Many health experts believe music is good for the digestive system. According to researchers at the *Continuous Music Network*, slow music is better for your digestive system than no music at all. Clinical studies show that people take on average three mouthfuls when there's soothing music in the background, versus four mouthfuls when no tunes are played at all.

While music can help us relax at the dinner table, it can also help us go that extra mile when exercising. The music network *Galaxie* program director Mike Guinta stated that "Studies show men increase their workout time by 30 percent

Sample Informative Presentation

Having offered statistical evidence that music is beneficial to exercise, Alton relates a brief personal anecdote.

and women by 25 percent. . . ." Scientific studies have shown that music keeps your mind off the physical discomfort of a straining activity. I can personally recall a time I felt I could no longer go on with the strenuous activity of a workout. But somehow by listening to music on my headphones, it gave me an extra boost of energy.

Studies also have shown that unborn babies who listen to classical music in the mother's womb become smarter. Many therapists and psychiatrists have their patients listen to music to help them relax and deal with stress and depression. These are just a few of the many benefits that music has for us.

As part of the necessary built-in redundancy of informative presentations, Alton briefly summarizes his main ideas.

We have discovered the three major elements in music: rhythm, melody, and harmony. Whether it be the hard-hitting drums of rock, the melodic tunes of our favorite pop songs, or the harmonic, complex style of jazz, music is the universal language of the world because it can generate the feelings of human emotions—joy, sorrow, love, and pain—thus making it beneficial in our daily lives.

By explaining how the elements of music apply to everyone's life, Alton draws on the principles that adult learners prefer to connect their life experiences with the new information they have learned and that they prefer relevant information. Alton closes his presentation with a reference to George Gershwin's famous song "I Got Rhythm."

The fact of the matter is we make our own music all the time. Now let me explain to you how we do this. Just by being alive, our heartbeat makes its own rhythm. We make melody by arranging our thoughts in a meaningful sequence. And we make the final stage of music, harmony, simply by interacting with each other. We all have rhythm, and we all have music, and with music we have good times.

PRINCIPLES FOR A LIFETIME
Enhancing Your Skills

1. Aware

Principle One: Be aware of your communication with yourself and others.

- Be conscious of the type of informative message you are developing (presentation about an object, a procedure, a person, an event, or an idea), to help you determine how best to organize your message.
- Be consciously aware of using strategies that will make your informative messages clear, interesting, and memorable.

Principle Two: Effectively use and interpret verbal messages.

- Use supporting material such as stories, examples, and illustrations to gain and maintain attention.
- Use word pictures to make images and stories interesting and memorable.
- Pace the flow of the information you present to enhance message clarity.
- Relate new information to old information to increase clarity and retention.
- Verbally reinforce ideas to help make your message memorable.
- Use simple ideas rather than complex ideas to make your message clear.
- Build in message redundancy to enhance message retention.

Principle Three: Effectively use and interpret nonverbal messages.

- Use presentation aids to make messages clear, interesting, and memorable.
- Observe the nonverbal behavior of your audience to help you determine whether your message has been communicated clearly.
- Nonverbally reinforce ideas to make your message memorable.

Principle Four: Listen and respond thoughtfully to others.

- Before you deliver your presentation to an audience, talk and listen to audience members to help you customize your message for them.

Principle Five: Appropriately adapt messages to others.

- Adapt the structure and flow of your presentation to your listeners to enhance message clarity.
- Adapt your examples and illustrations to your listeners to help gain and maintain interest and attention.
- Develop a motivation for your audience to listen to you.

Summary

To inform is to teach someone something you know. In this chapter, you have studied the goals, principles, and strategies that presentational speakers use to inform others.

There are five basic types of informative presentations. Messages about objects discuss tangible things. Messages about procedures explain a process or describe how something works. Messages about people can be about either the famous or the little known. Messages about events describe major occurrences or personal experiences. Messages about ideas are often abstract and generally discuss principles, concepts, or theories.

Strategies for organizing your informative presentation will vary according to the type of informative presentation and your specific purpose. A presentation about an object may be organized topically, chronologically, or spatially. A presentation about a procedure will usually be organized chronologically. Presentations about either people or events are also usually organized chronologically but can be organized topically. And a presentation about an idea will probably be organized topically.

To make your message clear, use simple rather than complex ideas, pace the flow of your information, and relate new information to old ideas. In order to increase interest in your presentation, relate information to your listeners' interests, find and use attention-catching supporting material, establish a motive for your audience to listen to you, use vivid word pictures, create intriguing and clear presentation aids, and use humor appropriately. Finally, to make messages memorable, build in some redundancy (tell them what you're going to tell them; tell them; tell them what you've told them), use principles of adult learning, and reinforce key ideas both verbally and nonverbally.

Assessing Your Knowledge

For Discussion and Review

Principle One: Be aware of your communication with yourself and others.

1. Discuss what a speaker must do before he or she can create a word picture for an audience.

Principle Two: Effectively use and interpret verbal messages.

2. Explain how to reinforce key ideas verbally.

Principle Three: Effectively use and interpret nonverbal messages.

3. Explain how presentation aids can enhance an informative presentation.

Principle Four: Listen and respond thoughtfully to others.

4. How can listening and responding to others help you decide whether to use a humorous quotation?

Principle Five: Appropriately adapt messages to others.

5. List and explain five characteristics of adult learners that can help you adapt your presentation to an adult audience.

Multiple Choice

Choose the *best* answer to each of the following questions.

1. When using humor in a presentation, you should do all of the following *except*
    a. use jokes to relax the audience, without worrying about making a point with them.
    b. make yourself the butt of your own jokes.
    c. quote others' humorous sayings.
    d. use visuals such as cartoons.

2. Asking your audience "How many of you are interested in doubling your income in one year?" helps to
    a. build redundancy into your message.
    b. reinforce your key ideas.
    c. establish a motive for the audience to listen to you.
    d. alienate a number of audience members.

3. Presentations about ideas are usually arranged in a _____ pattern.
    a. causal
    b. topical
    c. chronological
    d. spatial

4. Which of the following is a good strategy for explaining something unfamiliar to your listeners?
    a. Give them plenty of details about the new idea.
    b. Challenge them to find out more information about the new idea.
    c. Relate the new information to something they already know.
    d. Gloss over the new information quickly to get back to more familiar territory.

5. Christie gave a presentation on the Gateway Arch in St. Louis. Christie's presentation was about
    a. an object.
    b. a procedure.
    c. an event.
    d. an idea.

6. Creating a word picture will do all of the following *except*
    a. be too abstract for most audiences.
    b. help to gain the audience's attention.
    c. appeal to the audience's senses.
    d. help the audience remember your message.

7. If you are speaking on a topic that is new or unfamiliar to your audience, you should
    a. put as much information as you can at the beginning of the presentation.
    b. maximize the amount of information throughout the presentation.
    c. use supporting material to control the flow of information throughout the presentation.
    d. wait until the end of the speech to give the audience as much information as you can.

8. According to the T-E-A-C-H acronym, the first step in teaching people a skill is to
    a. describe what it is you want them to know.
    b. give them an opportunity to perform the skill.
    c. provide positive encouragement.
    d. show them an example of how to perform the skill.

9. A presentation about the day John F. Kennedy was assassinated would likely be organized
    a. spatially.
    b. topically.
    c. according to cause and effect.
    d. chronologically.

10. Seonaid is giving a presentation on nanotechnology. Based on the principles of adult learning, she should
    a. focus on how nanotechnology will revolutionize medicine in the future.
    b. explain how nanotechnology is affecting the audience members' lives today.
    c. discuss the theories behind nanotechnology.
    d. review the key pioneers in the field of nanotechnology.

Answers to the questions in this practice test can be found at the end of the book.

Assessing Your Skill

When you deliver a presentation in class, your instructor may provide written feedback on an evaluation form that lists specific criteria. You may find it useful to refer to a similar list of criteria while you are developing your presentation and perhaps even when you are asked to offer feedback on a classmate's presentation. Following is a checklist for an effective informative presentation.

Checklist for an Effective Informative Presentation

Element	Criteria	Additional Comments
Audience	_____ Adapted to needs, interests, and background of audience.	
Topic	_____ Appropriate to audience, occasion, and speaker. _____ Focused on objects, procedures, people, events, or ideas. _____ Narrowed to fit the time limits.	
Purpose	_____ Informative general purpose—to share information by teaching, defining, illustrating, describing, or explaining. _____ Audience-centered specific purpose. _____ General and specific purposes achieved.	
Central Idea	_____ Clear one-sentence declarative summary of the presentation.	
Main Ideas	_____ Related to central idea as natural divisions, reasons, or chronological steps. _____ Previewed in introduction of presentation. _____ Developed in body of presentation. _____ Summarized in conclusion of presentation.	
Supporting Material	_____ Ideas simplified. _____ Information flow appropriately paced. _____ New information related to old. _____ Use of attention-catching supporting material. _____ Use of word pictures. _____ Appropriate use of humor.	
Organization	_____ Introduction caught attention, established motive for audience to listen, stated central idea, previewed main ideas. _____ Body organized in a logical way. _____ Redundancy and reinforcement of key ideas evident. _____ Conclusion restated central idea, summarized main ideas, and provided closure.	

Element	Criteria	Additional Comments
Delivery	_____ Nonverbal reinforcement of key ideas. _____ Eye contact with listeners. _____ Appropriate volume and vocal inflection. _____ Appropriate gestures, movement, and posture. _____ Interesting and effectively prepared presentation aids, if any.	

Web Resources to Improve Your Knowledge and Skill

The Internet is a vast resource of material for informative speeches. In addition to using search engines to perform keyword searches, you may want to take advantage of such resources as web-based encyclopedias, almanacs, and statistical databases. Take a look at the following:

Infoplease provides access to a number of informative resources, including *The Columbia Electronic Encyclopedia*, 6th edition, and the *Information Please Almanac*:

<www.infoplease.com>

Factfinder is a user-friendly site that offers population, housing, economic, and geographic data from the U.S. Census Bureau:

<factfinder.census.gov>

FedStats offers official statistical information from more than one hundred federal government agencies:

<www.fedstats.gov>

Appendix B

Sample Speeches for Discussion and Evaluation

Informative Speech

Advertising and Reptilian Codes — Mary Kate Raffetto [1]

In the late 1990's, sales of the Chrysler Jeep Wrangler were plummeting. Unable to keep up with the fancier sleeker cars that appeared on the market, the company spent hundreds of thousands of dollars on market research and discovered the problem: The Jeep didn't look enough like a horse. Clotaire Rapaille, a cultural anthropologist and marketing guru, advised Chrysler to shape the hood of the Jeep like a horse's snout, and to change the square headlights into round ones, to mimic nostrils. According to the September 11, 2007, *Business Weekly*, after Rapaille's help, sales of the Jeep began to skyrocket. Rapaille had discovered that what he calls the "reptilian code" for Jeep was *horse*.

Clotaire Rapaille has pioneered the search for "reptilian codes," one-word symbols that subconsciously represent our earliest associations with products. Rapaille believes that every product has a unique reptilian code, which once unlocked can literally sell people anything. While his ideas may seem off the beaten path, the January 4, 2008, *Milwaukee Journal Sentinel* explains that Chrysler isn't the only company turning to Rapaille for help. In fact, Rapaille's firm, Archetype Discoveries, is on the payroll of 50 of the Fortune 100 companies, including Procter and Gamble, AT&T, General Motors, Loreal Cosmetics, and Exxon. As the documentary "The Persuaders" points out,

> If corporations really can reduce us to our "reptilian mind," a brain state which represents our most animalistic and childlike desires, we have to wonder whether or not [these techniques] will have dangerous impacts on our lives.

So, to better understand Clotaire Rapaille's methods, let us first understand the psychoanalytical process he uses to unlock reptilian codes, next discover how the codes are used in marketing strategies, and finally develop some implications for one man's eccentric research, which has drastically changed the landscape of consumerism over the last twenty years, without our ever knowing it.

It probably doesn't help that Rapaille is incredibly secretive about his research. In fact, his privacy agreements with companies often keep their names and the codes he finds from being released until they are no longer in use. But how does Rapaille uncover these peculiar but powerful codes? As the July 10, 2007, *Financial Post* states, in order to unlock a reptilian code, Rapaille takes a group of 25 subjects through a three-step psychological journey which unearths their earliest associations with a product. Each step represents a different part of the brain: the cortex, the limbic, and the reptilian.

First, Rapaille appeals to the subject's cortex region. The cortex is the most advanced part of the brain, but as Rapaille explains, the least important, because it reveals little about a consumer's true desires. He allows the subjects an hour to write all of their thoughts and emotions about a specific product. But then he ignores their responses. Rapaille's dismissal of his subjects' responses usually ignites some sort of frustration on their part. This allows Rapaille to appeal to the limbic region, which is the emotional part of the brain. He asks the respondents to pretend that they're an alien telling a story about the product to a child. But once again, Rapaille ignores the responses. As he explains in a May 20, 2006, interview with salon.com, the subjects need to "examine their rational and emotional thoughts" before he can unlock the final stage of the brain—the reptilian, or instinctual section.

In his 2004 book *The Culture Code*, Rapaille explains that the reptilian stage is the most important, because

> while we may offer excuses from the cortex—like "I want great safety features"—what really motivates us are the primitive thoughts of the reptilian—like "I want freedom and strength."

He asks each subject to lie on the floor of a dark room with blankets and a pillow, making them feel like they're back in the womb. Then they are asked to share their first experience with the product. This first experience, which is usually an early childhood memory, is called an "imprint." When Rapaille examines a set of subjects' imprints, he can usually find one underlying symbol behind all of them. This symbol becomes the reptilian code for the product.

In the United States, the code for cheese is *dead*. That's why, in the 1990's, cheese companies like Kraft began keeping our cheese singles tightly packaged in plastic—or, as Rapaille calls it, their own individual body bags. But he hasn't just changed how cheese is packaged. To understand the scope of Rapaille's research, we have to examine how companies use existing reptilian codes and also how cultures can be coded.

First, Rapaille sells the reptilian codes to companies and helps them alter their products' features and advertising to fit the code. For example, the January 16, 2006, *Adweek* explains that Brown-Forman, who makes Jack Daniel's, hired Rapaille, who found that the code for whiskey was *rebel*. He advised the company to focus their advertising around the fictional life story of Jack Daniel, a free spirit of the American West, so they unveiled billboards that read, "Mr. Jack Daniel was no saint. But he did start something of a religion." Since, Brown-Forman has seen consistent growth in revenue.

But Rapaille doesn't just crack codes, he also creates them. By manipulating the experiences we have in childhood, Rapaille claims that he can "code" a culture to have a reptilian desire for certain products. The March 10, 2007, *Toronto Star* explains how, after years of failing to sell coffee in Japan, Nestlé hired Rapaille, who discovered that the Japanese had no reptilian code for coffee, because they had no childhood imprint for it. Rapaille advised Nestlé to develop a line of coffee-flavored desserts for children, who would then mature to desire coffee. Doing this would create an imprint for coffee in Japanese culture. Nestlé could later use this imprint to discover coffee's reptilian code. As the August 10, 2006, *Business Line* explains, Nestlé went from selling almost zero pounds of coffee to now anticipating annual sales of half a billion pounds.

Three years ago, an American cosmetics company hired Rapaille. He discovered that the code for seduction was *manipulation*. Since the company didn't want consumers to feel manipulated by seductive images, they changed their approach. Nowadays we can't escape the easy, breezy, beautiful . . . Covergirls. But Rapaille's research does more than provide Queen Latifah with a paycheck; it has implications for cultural diversity and psychoanalytical ethics.

First, despite his incredible influence, Rapaille and his methods are a bit shady, to say the least. We have to weary of any theory that claims social and cultural homogeny. Rapaille uses the word *culture* almost interchangeably with *country*, not really accounting for the incredible diversity present within nations. So we have to ask whose experiences get to determine the American imprint for Folgers coffee? Probably not the poor or working class.

Next, the use of psychology or psychoanalysis to manipulate, rather than aid, the general population creates a scary precedent for the mental health field. According to the previously cited *Toronto Star*, the American reptilian code for sex is *violence*. Instead of using culture coding to decode Americans' psyche and help improve mental health issues surrounding sex and violence, the code was sold to an anonymous corporation and used for profit. Rapaille and other psychoanalysts have to have an ethical responsibility to improve the mental health of society, and not profit from its manipulation.

So today, we've examined Clotaire Rapaille's research methods, discovered how reptilian codes are used, and, finally, developed several critical implications. While not all companies are utilizing Rapaille and his codes, the need for his help is continually increasing—proving that even in today's rational world, we might still be driven by the most basic instinct.

Persuasive Speech

Untitled — Amy Solomito [2]

Thirty-eight-year-old cystic fibrosis sufferer Charlie Stockley was admitted to the hospital on December 12, 2006, for lung failure. At that time, he was at the top of a national lung transplant waiting list. For two weeks, his family and friends held a vigil by his bedside, anxiously waiting for a single compatible donor organ to become available. Charlie grew weaker by the day, and soon he could only breathe with the help of a ventilator. His family could do nothing but helplessly wait. On Christmas Eve Charlie ran out of time, leaving behind his mother, two sisters, and his fiancée, Margie Roper. The lifegiving organs Charlie needed to stay alive never materialized. Sadly, this scene is playing out over and over again in hospitals across the nation. According to the April 4, 2007, *Washington Post*, one American—like Charlie—dies every hour while waiting for healthy organs. Furthermore, the December 7, 2006, *Baltimore Sun* points out that "Most of these deaths are needless. Americans bury or cremate about 20,000 organs which are in transplantable condition every year." We are squandering the opportunity to save thousands of lives every year. I'm not saying anything new here. We all know that organ donation is important. What I am suggesting is that we fix the system once and for all so there are no more excuses. It is imperative that we first pinpoint why our country's organ donor system fails. Next, we need to examine a simple and viable alternative called presumed consent. Finally we must implement this change that can—and will—save thousands of lives every year.

Our current organ donor system does not meet our nation's medical needs. We must first examine our current organ deficit, second uncover why this deficit is perpetuated. The National Center for Policy Analysis's web site, last updated April 2, 2007, explains the current organ deficit by stating, "At present the number of people needing organ transplants far exceeds the available supply." The United Network for Organ Sharing's web site *unos.org* reports that as of this morning, 96,201 Americans are waiting for healthy organs. Waiting time varies depending on a number of factors including age, blood type, and organ needed. Only 15 percent of those people can expect the organs they need. In 2006, according to the UNOS web site, updated daily, only 28,931 organs made it to people on the waiting list. Thousands of others had nothing to do but wait. Every second, every minute, every hour was a little more time—and with it a little more hope—that slipped away.

The process by which an individual becomes an organ donor varies in every state. Generally, according to the December 16, 2006, *St. Louis Post-Dispatch*, individuals can agree to donate their organs either by joining a statewide organ donor registry or by checking a box when they receive their driver's license. This process is known as informed consent or "opting in." Conversely, those people who do not take the time or effort to fill out the required paperwork are not registered as organ donors. Why don't people fill out this paperwork? It seems largely due to confusion or bureaucratic reasons. In fact, most people are in favor of organ donation. The January 2, 2007, edition of the *Copley News Service* states that in a national survey, 90 percent of Americans are in favor of being involved with organ donation. The June 28, 2006, *Daily News* confirms these sentiments when it argues "75 percent of Americans would be willing to donate their organs, but don't make their preferences known." As a result, only 30 percent of Americans are registered organ donors. Clearly, our current system isn't working. More needs to be done to provide patients with the organs they need for life-saving transplant.

The American Medical Association fully supports the development of a presumed consent organ donor system. So we must first understand how presumed consent works, and second show that presumed consent will not lead to organ harvesting. The November 2006 edition of *Bioethics* explains that presumed consent is an opt-out system of organ donation where every citizen is automatically considered an organ donor unless they specify otherwise. The Summer 2006 *Law, Medicine, & Ethics* notes that presumed consent shifts the default from an opt-in system to an opt-out system. This means that if someone wants to become an organ donor, they do not need to fill out any forms or go through any bureaucratic red tape—they already are a registered organ donor. However, it is important to note that whether we operate under an opt-in or an opt-out system of organ donation, those few Americans who do not wish to participate still have that choice. Under presumed consent, an individual just has to make known their preference not to participate rather than to participate. However, because of the organ shortage, there is concern that doctors will let some patients die in order to procure their organs. The *Daily Princetonian's* web site, last accessed January 31, 2007, notes that presumed consent could eliminate America's organ shortage. Since there would be a greater supply of organs, doctors would have no need to let their patients die just to harvest their organs. Risky decisions would not be necessary, since a doctor would not have to work under the burden of an organ shortage. The Mayo Clinic web site, updated daily, states that organ farming is just a myth, and that "When you go to the hospital for treatment, doctors focus on saving your life—not somebody else's." Regardless of whether or not this myth is true, an opt-out system of organ donation eliminates the need and temptation to farm organs. Now that we have examined one way to increase the number of donor organs and thus save lives, we can look at some ways to get this system implemented in America.

According to the May 16, 2006, *New York Times*, presumed consent is both popular and effective in Europe. The February 22, 2006, *CBC News* notes that European countries that practice presumed consent have no waiting lists for organs. So, taking a cue from Europe, solutions to this problem can be considered on one level: governmental. Since states are currently responsible for creating organ donor laws, we need to push our state legislatures to adopt a presumed consent policy. The December 9, 2006, *Buffalo News* reports that former New York Governor George Pataki signed into law a bill requiring New York's Organ Transplant Council to bring the state in line with international presumed consent standards. More states need to follow New York's lead and implement an opt-out policy. Unfortunately, short of these steps, there is no viable personal solution to this problem. While we could individually become organ donors, we need to think much bigger. Personal solutions are not the answer; for change, we must come together. Legislation is the key. Optimally, the federal government will hear our cries for action, and will implement presumed consent into blanket, nationwide law. More realistically, we can push for the other 49 states to follow New York's lead by donating our time and money to organizations like the Presumed Consent Foundation. Through them, we can push for change on both a state and federal level. The longer we wait, the more the clock keeps on ticking. In another hour, one more person will have died while waiting for donor organs.

Today, we have examined the shortcomings of America's current organ donor laws, studied presumed consent as a viable alternative, and explored what can be done in order to implement presumed consent in the United States. Through implementing presumed consent, America's organ donor system will get the reform it desperately needs. In the December 26, 2006, *San Francisco Chronicle*, Dr. David Weill explains that he "thought a lot about Charlie Stockley. It is far more disappointing when a patient dies before we transplant. I feel like we never gave them the opportunity." If America operated under the presumed consent system of organ donation, Charlie Stockley would have had that opportunity, and his family, like thousands of others, would not have had to watch their loved one die while they needlessly wait for donor organs. At this moment, thousands of people, like Charlie, are clinging to hope on an organ transplant waiting list. If we operated under presumed consent, that list would not exist, and those people would already have their second chance at life.

Endnotes

CHAPTER 1

1. E. T. Klemmer and F. W. Snyder, "Measurement of Time Spent Communicating," *Journal of Communication 20* (1972): 142.
2. We thank Tom Burkholder, University of Nevada, Las Vegas, for this idea.
3. D. Quinn, *My Ishmael* (New York: Bantam Books, 1996).
4. V. Marchant, "Listen Up!" *Time* (June 28, 1999): 72.
5. A. Vangelisti and J. Daly, "Correlates of Speaking Skills in the United States: A National Assessment," *Communication Education 38* (1989): 132–143.
6. M. Cronin, ed., "The Need for Required Oral Communication Education in the Undergraduate General Education Curriculum," unpublished paper, 1993, available from the National Communication Association, Washington, D.C.
7. J. Ayres and T. S. Hopf, "The Long-Term Effect of Visualization in the Classroom: A Brief Research Report," *Communication Education 39* (1990): 75–78.
8. See J. C. McCroskey and M. Beatty, "The Communibiological Perspective: Implications for Communication in Instruction," *Communication Education 49* (2000): 1; also see J. C. McCroskey, J. A. Daly, M. M. Martin, and M. J. Beatty, eds., *Communication and Personality: Trait Perspectives* (Cresskill, NJ: Hampton Press, 1998).
9. J. H. McConnell, *Are You Communicating? You Can't Manage without It* (New York: McGraw-Hill, 1995).
10. J. L. Winsor, D. Curtis, and R. D. Stephens, "National Preferences in Business and Communication Education: A Survey Update," *Journal of the Association of Communication Administration 3* (1997): 170–179.
11. The University of Wisconsin–River Falls, Career Services, "What Skills and Attributes Employers Seek When Hiring Students," <http://www.uwrf.edu/ccs/skills/htm>, retrieved June 4, 2007; C. Luckenbaugh and K. Gray, "Employers Describe Perfect Job Candidate," National Association of Colleges and Employers Survey, <http://www.naceweb.org/press/display.asp?year=2003&prid=169>, retrieved June 4, 2007; R. S. Hansen and K. Handson, "What Do Employers Really Want? Top Skills and Values Employers Seek from Job-Seekers," <http://www.quintcareers.com/job_skills_values.html>, retrieved June 4, 2007.
12. K. E. Davis and M. Todd, "Assessing Friendship: Prototypes, Paradigm Cases, and Relationship Description," in *Understanding Personal Relationships*, edited by S. W. Duck and D. Perlman (London: Sage, 1985); B. Wellman, "From Social Support to Social Network," in *Social Support: Theory, Research and Applications*, edited by I. G. Sarason and B. R. Sarason (Dordrecht, Netherlands: Nijhoff, 1985); R. Hopper, M. L. Knapp, and L. Scott, "Couples' Personal Idioms: Exploring Intimate Talk," *Journal of Communication 31* (1981): 23–33.
13. M. Argyle and M. Hendershot, *The Anatomy of Relationships* (London: Penguin Books, 1985), 14.
14. D. Goleman, "Emotional Intelligence: Issues in Paradigms Building," in *The Emotionally Intelligent Workplace*, edited by C. Cherniss and D. Goleman (San Francisco: Jossey Bass, 2001), 13.
15. V. Satir, *Peoplemaking* (Palo Alto, CA: Science and Behavior Books, 1972).
16. M. Argyle, *The Psychology of Happiness* (London: Routledge, 2001).
17. J. J. Lynch, *The Broken Heart: The Medical Consequences of Loneliness* (New York: Basic Books, 1977).
18. D. P. Phillips, "Deathday and Birthday: An Unexpected Connection," in *Statistics: A Guide to the Unknown*, edited by J. M. Tanur (San Francisco: Holden Day, 1972); also see F. Korbin and G. Hendershot, "Do Family Ties Reduce Mortality? Evidence from the United States 1968," *Journal of Marriage and the Family 39* (1977): 737–746; K. Heller and K. S. Rook, "Distinguishing the Theoretical Functions of Social Ties: Implications of Support Interventions," in *Handbook of Personal Relationships* 2e, edited by S. W. Duck, K. Dindia, W. Ickes, R. Milardo, R. S. L. Mills, and B. R. Sarason (Chichester: Wiley, 1997); B. R. Sarason, I. G. Sarason, and R. A. R. Gurung, "Close Personal Relationships and Health Outcomes: A Key to the Role of Social Support," in *Handbook of Personal Relationships*, Duck et al., eds.; also see S. Duck, *Relating to Others* (Buckingham, England: Open University Press, 1999), 1.
19. F. E. X. Dance and C. Larson, *Speech Communication: Concepts and Behavior* (New York: Holt, Rinehart and Winston, 1972).
20. Dance and Larson, *Speech Communication*.
21. J. T. Masterson, S. A. Beebe, and N. H. Watson, *Invitation to Effective Speech Communication* (Glenview, IL: Scott, Foresman, 1989).
22. M. Gladwell, *Blink: The Power of Thinking without Thinking* (New York: Little Brown and Company, 2005).
23. This section is based on Masterson, Beebe, and Watson. We are especially indebted to J. T. Masterson for this discussion.
24. See R. P. Wolff, *About Philosophy* (Upper Saddle River, NJ: Prentice Hall, 2000), 308–335.
25. C. S. Lewis, *The Abolition of Man* (New York: Macmillan, 1947); also see A. M. Nicholi, Jr., *The Question of God: C. S. Lewis and Sigmund Freud Debate God, Love, Sex, and the Meaning of Life* (New York: The Free Press, 2002).
26. C. Christians and M. Traber, *Communication Ethics and Universal Values* (Beverly Hills, CA: Sage, 1997); also see S. Bok, *Common Values* (Columbia, MO: University of Missouri Press, 2002).
27. Christians and Traber, *Communication Ethics and Universal Values*.
28. For an excellent discussion of comparative religions and the common principle of being other-oriented, see W. Ham, *Man's Living Religions* (Independence, MO: Herald Publishing House, 1966), 39–40.
29. For additional discussion of the ethical values taught in the world's religions, see H. Smith, *The World's Religions* (San Francisco: HarperSanFrancisco, 1991).
30. National Communication Association, "NCA Credo for Communication Ethics," 1999 (June 27, 2001) <http://www.natcom.org/conferences/Ethics/ethicsconfcredo99.htm>.
31. H. Lasswell, "The Structure and Function of Communication in Society," in *The Communication of Ideas*, edited by L. Bryson (New York: Institute for Religious and Social Studies, 1948), 37.
32. See V. E. Cronen, W. B. Pearce, and L. M. Harris, "The Coordinated Management of Meaning: A Theory of Communication," in *Human Communication Theory: Comparative Essays*, edited by F. E. X. Dance (New York: Harper & Row, 1982), 61–89.
33. Y. Amichai-Hamburger, *The Social Net: Human Behavior in Cyberspace* (Oxford, England: Oxford University Press, 2005), v; K. Y. A. McKenna and J. A. Bargh, "Plan 9 from Cyberspace: The Implications of the Internet for Personality and Social Psychology," *Personality and Social Psychology Review 4* (2000): 57–75.
34. R. Kraut, M. Patterson, V. Lundmark, S. Kiesler, M. Tridas, and W. Scherlis, "Internet Paradox: A Social Technology That Reduces Social Involvement and Psychological Well-Being?" *American Psychologist 53* (1998): 1017–1031.
35. R. Kraut, S. Kiesler, B. Boneva, J. Cummings, V. Helgeson, and A.

Crawford, "Internet Paradox Revisited," *Journal of Social Issues* 58 (2002): 49–74; P. E. N. Howard, L. Raine, and S. Jones, "Days and Nights on the Internet: The Impact of a Diffusing Technology," *American Behavioral Scientist* 45 (2001): 383–404; M. A. Mazur and R. J. Burns, "Perceptions of Relational Interdependence in Online Relationships: The Effects of Communication Apprehension and Introversion," *Communication Research Reports* 17 (4) (2000): 397–406.

36. L. Barker, R. Edwards, C. Gaines, K. Gladney, and F. Holley, "An Investigation of Proportional Time Spent in Various Communication Activities of College Students," *Journal of Applied Communication Research* 8 (1981): 101–109.
37. See D. Barnlund, *Interpersonal Communication: Survey and Studies* (Boston: Houghton Mifflin Company, 1968).
38. See C. R. Berger and J. J. Bradac, *Language and Social Knowledge: Uncertainty in Interpersonal Relations* (London: Arnold, 1982).
39. O. Wiio, *Wiio's Laws—and Some Others* (Espoo, Finland: Welin-Goos, 1978).
40. T. Watzlawick, J. B. Bavelas, and D. Jackson, *The Pragmatics of Human Communication* (New York: W. W. Norton, 1967).
41. S. B. Shimanoff, *Communication Rules: Theory and Research* (Beverly Hills: Sage, 1980).
42. For an excellent review of intrapersonal communication theory and research, see D. Voate, *Intrapersonal Communication: Different Voices, Different Minds* (Hillsdale, NJ: Lawrence Erlbaum, 1994).
43. Quinn, *My Ishmael*.
44. Barker et al., "An Investigation of Proportional Time Spent in Various Communication Activities of College Students."
45. We appreciate and acknowledge our friend and colleague M. Redmond for his contributions to our understanding of interpersonal communication. For more information, see S. A. Beebe, S. J. Beebe, and M. V. Redmond, *Interpersonal Communication: Relating to Others* 4e (Boston: Allyn & Bacon, 2005).
46. For an excellent discussion of the power of dialogue to enrich the quality of communication, see D. Yankelovich, *The Magic of Dialogue: Transforming Conflict into Cooperation* (New York: Simon & Schuster, 1999).
47. S. A. Beebe and J. T. Masterson, *Communicating in Small Groups: Principles and Practices* 8e (Boston: Allyn & Bacon, 2006).
48. For a discussion of group size, see Beebe and Masterson, *Communicating in Small Groups*.

CHAPTER 2

1. S. R. Covey, *The Seven Habits of Highly Effective People* (New York: Simon & Schuster, 1989), 67.
2. D. W. Johnson, *Reaching Out: Interpersonal Effectiveness and Self-Actualization* (Boston: Allyn & Bacon, 2006), 51.
3. S. E. Wood, E. Green Wood, and D. Boyd, *Mastering the World of Psychology* 3e (Boston: Allyn & Bacon, 2008), 115.
4. R. A. Baron, N. R. Branscombe, and D. R. Byrne, *Social Psychology* 12e (Boston: Allyn & Bacon, 2009).
5. D. Layder, *Social and Personal Identity: Understanding YourSelf* (London: Sage, 2004), 7–19.
6. K. Horney, *Neurosis and Human Growth* (New York: W. W. Norton & Co., 1950), 17.
7. A. Elliott, *Concepts of the Self* 2e (Cambridge, UK: Polity Press, 2007); K. J. Gergen, *The Saturated Self: Dilemmas of Identity in Contemporary Life* (New York: Basic Books, 2000); B. Goss, *Processing Communication: Information Processing in Intrapersonal Communication* (Belmont, CA: Wadsworth, 1982), 72.
8. J. T. Masterson, S. A. Beebe, and N. H. Watson, *Invitation to Effective Speech Communication* (Glenview, IL: Scott, Foresman, 1989).
9. G. Bukobza, "The Epistemological Basis of Selfhood," *New Ideas in Psychology* 25 (2007): 37–65.
10. Bukobza, "The Epistemological Basis of Selfhood," 39.
11. Bukobza, "The Epistemological Basis of Selfhood," 40.
12. W. James, *Principles of Psychology* (New York: Henry Holt and Company, 1890).
13. M. Krcmar, S. Giles, and D. Helme, "Understanding the Process: How Mediated and Peer Norms Affect Young Women's Body Esteem," *Communication Quarterly* 56 (2008): 111–130; C. Heldman, "Out-of-Body Image," *Ms.* (Spring 2008), 52–55; H. Dohnt and M. Tiggemann, "The Contribution of Peer and Media Influences to the Development of Body Satisfaction and Self-Esteem in Young Girls: A Prospective Study," *Developmental Psychology* 42 (2006): 929–936; S. Steese, M. Dollette, W. Phillips, E. Hossfeld, G. Matthews, and G. Taormina, "Understanding Girls' Circle as an Intervention on Perceived Social Support, Body Image, Self-Efficacy, Locus of Control, and Self-Esteem," *Adolescence* 41 (2006): 55–74; P. Koch, P. Mansfield, D. Thurau, and M. Carey, "'Feeling Frumpy': The Relationships between Body Image and Sexual Response Changes in Midlife Women," *Journal of Sex Research* 42 (2005): 215–223; A. Botta, "Television Images and Adolescent Girls' Body Image Disturbance," *Journal of Communication* 49 (1999): 22–37; M. Wiederman and S. R. Hurst, "Body Size, Physical Attractiveness, and Body Image among Young Adult Women: Relationships to Sexual Experience and Sexual Esteem," *Journal of Sex Research* 35 (1998): 272–281.
14. S. Mulkens and A. Jansen, "Changing Appearances: Cosmetic Surgery and Body Dysmorphic Disorder," *Netherlands Journal of Psychology* 62 (2006): 34–41; K. Harrison, L. Taylor, and A. Marske, "Women's and Men's Eating Behavior Following Exposure to Ideal-Body Images and Text," *Communication Research* 33 (2006): 507–529; Women's Sports Foundation, "O-zone," *O: The Oprah Winfrey Magazine* (June 2006): 39.
15. S. Grogan, *Body Image: Understanding Body Dissatisfaction in Men, Women, and Children* (New York: Psychology Press, 2007); S. Cahill and A. Mussap, "Emotional Reactions Following Exposure to Idealized Bodies Predict Unhealthy Body Change Attitudes and Behaviors in Women and Men," *Journal of Psychosomatic Research* 62 (2007): 631–639; M. Flocker, *The Metrosexual Guide to Style: A Handbook for the Modern Man* (Cambridge, MA: DeCapo Press, 2003); L. Luciano, *Looking Good: Male Body Image in Modern America* (New York: Hill and Wang, 2002); T. Spiker, "How Men Really Feel about Their Bodies," *O: The Oprah Winfrey Magazine* (August, 2003): 150–151, 181–182; G. B. Forbes, L. E. Adams-Curtis, B. Rade, and P. Jaberg, "Body Dissatisfaction in Women and Men: The Role of Gender-Typing and Self-Esteem," *Sex Roles* 44 (2001): 461–484.
16. C. H. Cooley, *Human Nature and the Social Order* (New York: Scribner's, 1912).
17. G. H. Mead, *Mind, Self, and Society* (Chicago: University of Chicago Press, 1934).
18. J. Stewart, K. E. Zediker, and S. Witteborn, *Together: Communicating Interpersonally* 6e (Los Angeles: Roxbury, 2005).
19. M. L. Hecht, M. J. Collier, and S. A. Ribeau, *African American Communication: Ethnic Identity and Cultural Interpretation* (Newbury Park, CA: Sage, 1993).
20. J. N. Martin and T. K. Nakayama, *Experiencing Intercultural Communication* 3e (New York: McGraw-Hill, 2007).
21. D. K. Ivy and P. Backlund, *GenderSpeak: Personal Effectiveness in Gender Communication* 4e (Boston: Allyn & Bacon, 2008); J. E. O. Blakemore and R. E. Centers, "Characteristics of Boys' and Girls' Toys," *Sex Roles* 53 (2005): 619–634; T. L. Kuther and E. McDonald, "Early Adolescents' Experiences with and Views of Barbie," *Adolescence* 39 (2004): 39–51; M. A. Messner, "Barbie Girls versus Sea Monsters: Children Constructing Gender," *Gender and Society* 14 (2000): 765–784.
22. Martin and Nakayama, *Experiencing Intercultural Communication*.
23. J. E. Stake, "Gender Differences and Similarities in Self-Concept within Everyday Life Contexts," *Psychology of Women Quarterly* 16 (1992): 349–363.
24. G. Steinem, *Revolution from Within: A Book of Self-Esteem* (Boston: Little, Brown and Company, 1993), 26.
25. J. D. Campbell, P. D. Trapnell, S. J. Heine, I. M. Katz, L. F. Lavallee, and D. R. Lehman, "Self-Concept Clarity: Measurement, Personality Correlates, and Cultural Boundaries," *Journal of Personality and Social Psychology* 70 (1996): 141–156.
26. For more information on self-concept clarity, see J. D. Campbell, "Self-Esteem and Clarity of the Self-Concept," *Journal of Personality and Social Psychology* 59 (1990): 538–549; J. D. Campbell and L. F. Lavallee, "Who Am I? The Role of Self-Concept Confusion in Understanding the Behavior of People with Low Self-Esteem," in *Self-Esteem: The Puzzle of Low Self-Regard*, edited by R. F. Baumeister (New York: Plenum Press, 1993), 3–20; C. Leite and N. A. Kuiper, "Client Uncertainty and the Process of Change in Psychotherapy: The Impact of Individ-

ual Differences in Self-Concept Clarity and Intolerance of Uncertainty," *Journal of Contemporary Psychotherapy* 38 (2008): 55–64; T. English and S. Chen, "Culture and Self-Concept Stability: Consistency across and within Contexts among Asian Americans and European Americans," *Journal of Personality and Social Psychology* 93 (2007): 478–490.

27. T. DeHart and B. W. Pelham, "Fluctuations in State Implicit Self-Esteem in Response to Daily Negative Events," *Journal of Experimental Social Psychology* 43 (2007): 157–165.

28. Ivy and Backlund, *GenderSpeak*.

29. G. D. Webster, L. A. Kirkpatrick, J. B. Neziek, C. V. Smith, and E. L. Paddock, "Different Slopes for Different Folks: Self-Esteem Instability and Gender as Moderators of the Relationship between Self-Esteem and Attitudinal Aggression," *Self and Identity* 6 (2007): 74–94; B. W. Pelham, S. L. Koole, C. D. Hardin, J. J. Hetts, E. Seah, and T. DeHart, "Gender Moderates the Relation between Implicit and Explicit Self-Esteem," *Journal of Experimental Social Psychology* 41 (2005): 84–89; B. J. Meyers, M. Polce-Lynch, W. Kliewer, and C. Kilmartin, "Adolescent Self-Esteem and Gender: Exploring Relations to Sexual Harassment, Body Image, Media Influence, and Emotional Expression," *Journal of Youth and Adolescence* 30 (2001): 225–244; C. Gilligan, *In a Different Voice: Psychological Theory and Women's Development* (Cambridge, MA: Harvard University Press, 1982); P. Orenstein, *Schoolgirls: Young Women, Self-Esteem, and the Confidence Gap* (New York: Doubleday, 1994); R. A. Josephs, H. R. Markus, and R. W. Tafarodi, "Gender and Self-Esteem," *Journal of Personality and Social Psychology* 63 (1991): 391–402.

30. American Association of University Women, *Shortchanging Girls, Shortchanging America* (Washington, DC: AAUW Educational Foundation, 1991).

31. M. Sadker and D. Sadker, *Failing at Fairness: How America's Schools Cheat Girls* (New York: Charles Scribner's Sons, 1994), 77.

32. E. Daniels and C. Leaper, "A Longitudinal Investigation of Sport Participation, Peer Acceptance, and Self-Esteem among Adolescent Girls and Boys," *Sex Roles* 55 (2006): 875–880; J. A. Clark, "Retirement from Competitive Athletics: Key Predictors of Post-Collegiate Self-Esteem in Former Division I Athletes," *Dissertation Abstracts International* 68 (2008): 5562; J. Sandoz, "Victory? New Language for Sportswomen," *Women and Language* 23 (2000): 33–36.

33. L. Smith LeBeau and J. T. Buckingham, "Relationship between Social Comparison Tendencies, Insecurity, and Perceived Relationship Quality," *Journal of Social and Personal Relationships* 25 (2008): 71–86; C. McFarland, R. Beuhler, R. von Ruti, L. Nguyen, and C. Alvaro, "The Impact of Negative Moods on Self-Enhancing Cognitions: The Role of Reflective versus Ruminative Mood Orientations," *Journal of Personality and Social Psychology* 93 (2007): 728–750; A. M. Guest, "Cultures of Childhood and Psychosocial Characteristics: Self-Esteem and Social Comparison in Two Distinct Communities," *Ethos* 35 (2007): 1–32; B. Butzer and N. A. Kuiper, "Relationships between the Frequency of Social Comparisons and Self-Concept Clarity, Intolerance of Uncertainty, Anxiety, and Depression," *Personality and Individual Differences* 41 (2006): 167–176; L. Festinger, "A Theory of Social Comparison Processes," *Human Relations* 2 (1954): 117–140.

34. K. N. Kubic and R. M. Chory, "Exposure to Television Makeover Programs and Perceptions of Self," *Communication Research Reports* 24 (2007): 283–291.

35. M. M. Martin and J. W. Gentry, "Stuck in the Model Trap," in *Taking Sides: Clashing Views on Controversial Issues in Mass Media and Society* 8e, edited by A. Alexander and J. Hanson (Dubuque, IA: McGraw-Hill/Dushkin, 2005), 52–61.

36. M. Cottle, "Turning Boys into Girls," in *Taking Sides*.

37. M. K. Matsuba, "Searching for Self and Relationships Online," *CyberPsychology & Behavior* 3 (2006): 275–284.

38. Matsuba, "Searching for Self and Relationships Online," 283.

39. L. Jussim and K. D. Harber, "Teacher Expectations and Self-Fulfilling Prophecies: Knowns and Unknowns, Resolved and Unresolved Controversies," *Personality and Social Psychology Review* 9 (2005): 131–155; L. Jussim, K. D. Harber, J. T. Crawford, T. R. Cain, and F. Cohen, "Social Reality Makes the Social Mind: Self-Fulfilling Prophecy, Stereotypes, Bias, and Accuracy," *Interaction Studies* 6 (2005): 85–102; S. Madon, M. Guyll, R. Spoth, and J. Willard, "Self-Fulfilling Prophecies," *Psychological Science* 15 (2004): 837–845.

40. J. Hattie, *Self-Concept* (Hillsdale, NJ: Lawrence Erlbaum, 1992).

41. S. Zhang and L. Stafford, "Perceived Face Threat of Honest but Hurtful Evaluative Messages in Romantic Relationships," *Western Journal of Communication* 72 (2008): 19–39; M. H. Kernis, C. E. Lakey, and W. L. Heppner, "Secure versus Fragile High Self-Esteem as a Predictor of Verbal Defensiveness: Converging Findings across Three Different Markers," *Journal of Personality* 76 (2008): 477–512; R. W. Robins and K. H. Trzesniewski, "Self-Esteem Development across the Lifespan," *Current Directions in Psychological Science* 14 (2005): 158–162; A. Chatham-Carpenter and V. DeFrancisco, "Pulling Yourself Up Again: Women's Choices and Strategies for Recovering and Maintaining Self-Esteem," *Western Journal of Communication* 61 (1997): 164–187.

42. Goss, *Processing Communication*, 72.

43. L. C. Lederman, "The Impact of Gender on the Self and Self-Talk," in *Women and Men Communicating: Challenges and Changes* 2e, edited by L. P. Arliss and D. J. Borisoff (Prospect Heights, IL: Waveland, 2001), 78–89; J. R. Johnson, "The Role of Inner Speech in Human Communication," *Communication Education* 33 (1984): 211–222; C. R. Streff, "The Concept of Inner Speech and Its Implications for an Integrated Language Arts Curriculum," *Communication Education* 33 (1984): 223–230; J. L. McFarland, "The Role of Speech in Self-Development, Self-Concept, and Decentration," *Communication Education* 33 (1984): 231–236; J. Ayres, "The Power of Positive Thinking," *Communication Education* 37 (1988): 289–296.

44. C. J. Mruk, *Self-Esteem: Research, Theory, and Practice* 3e (New York: Springer, 2006).

45. B. R. Schlenkere, S. A. Wowra, R. M. Johnson, and M. L. Miller, "The Impact of Imagined Audiences on Self-Appraisals," *Personal Relationships* 15 (2008): 247–260; see J. Ayres and T. S. Hopf, "The Long-Term Effect of Visualization in the Classroom: A Brief Research Report," *Communication Education* 39 (1990): 75–78; J. Ayres and T. S. Hopf, "Visualization: Is It More Than Extra-Attention?" *Communication Education* 38 (1989): 1–5.

46. J. Ayres, T. S. Hopf, and D. M. Ayres, "An Examination of Whether Imaging Ability Enhances the Effectiveness of an Intervention Designed to Reduce Speech Anxiety," *Communication Education* 43 (1994): 252–258.

47. J. M. Twenge, *Generation Me: Why Today's Young Americans Are More Confident, Assertive, Entitled—and More Miserable than Ever Before* (New York: Free Press, 2006), 2.

48. J. M. Twenge, S. Konrath, J. D. Foster, W. K. Campbell, and B. J. Bushman, "Egos Inflating over Time: A Cross-Temporal Meta-Analysis of the Narcissistic Personality Inventory," *Journal of Personality* 76 (2008): 875–901; S. Konrath, J. M. Twenge, W. K. Campbell, J. D. Foster, and B. J. Bushman, "This Generation Is More Special than the Others: A Cross-Temporal Meta-Analysis of the Narcissistic Personality Inventory," paper presented at the conference on Educating the Next Generation of College Students, University of San Diego, February 27, 2007.

49. For other research as well as popular literature on narcissism and self-esteem, see J. K. Bosson, C. E. Lakey, W. K. Campbell, V. Zeigler-Hill, C. H. Jordan, and M. H. Kernis, "Untangling the Links between Narcissism and Self-Esteem: A Theoretical and Empirical Review," *Social and Personality Psychology Compass* 2 (2008): 1415–1439; V. Zeigler-Hill, "Discrepancies between Implicit and Explicit Self-Esteem: Implications for Narcissism and Self-Esteem Instability," *Journal of Personality* 74 (2006): 119–144; E. Hoover, "Here's You Looking at You, Kid: Study Says Many Students Are Narcissists," *The Chronicle of Higher Education* (March 9, 2007); A. L. Ball, "The New and Improved Self-Esteem," *O: The Oprah Winfrey Magazine* (January 2008): 164–265, 217–219; P. Marx, "Can You Have Too Much Self-Esteem?" *O: The Oprah Winfrey Magazine* (May 2004): 249; C. Sedikides, E. A. Rudich, A. P. Gregg, M. Kumashiro, and C. Rusbult, "Are Normal Narcissists Psychologically Healthy?: Self-Esteem Matters," *Journal of Personality and Social Psychology* 87 (2004): 400–416; R. F. Baumeister, B. J. Bushman, and W. K. Campbell, "Self-Esteem, Narcissism, and Aggression: Does Violence Result from Low Self-Esteem or from Threatened Egotism?" *Current Directions in Psychological Science* 9 (2000): 26–29.

50. Covey, *The Seven Habits of Highly Effective People*, 105.

51. P. R. Hinton, *The Psychology of Interpersonal Perception* (New York: Routledge, 1993).
52. A. S. Rancer, F. F. Jordan-Jackson, and D. A. Infante, "Observers' Perceptions of an Interpersonal Dispute as a Function of Mode of Presentation," *Communication Reports 16* (2003): 35–48; D. A. Kenny, *Interpersonal Perception: A Social Relations Analysis* (New York: Guilford Press, 1994); U. Neisser, *Cognition and Reality: Principles and Implications of Cognitive Psychology* (San Francisco: W. H. Freeman and Company, 1976).
53. D. Kimura, "Sex and Cognition," in *Taking Sides: Clashing Views on Controversial Issues in Sex and Gender* 2e, edited by E. L. Paul (New York: McGraw-Hill/Dushkin, 2002), 94–96; D. Halpern, *Sex Differences in Cognitive Abilities* 3e (Mahwah, NJ: Lawrence Erlbaum, 2000).
54. L. Kohlberg, "A Cognitive-Developmental Analysis of Children's Sex-Role Concepts and Attitudes," in *The Development of Sex Differences*, edited by E. E. Maccoby (Stanford, CA: Stanford University Press, 1966), 82–173; A. Bandura, "Social-Learning Theory of Identificatory Processes," in *Handbook of Socialization Theory and Research*, edited by D. A. Goslin (Chicago: Rand McNally, 1971); R. A. Lippa, *Gender, Nature, and Nurture* 2e (Mahwah, NJ: Lawrence Erlbaum, 2006); J. A. Hall, "Women's and Men's Nonverbal Communication: Similarities, Differences, Stereotypes, and Origins," in *The Sage Handbook of Nonverbal Communication*, edited by V. Manusov and M. L. Patterson (Thousand Oaks, CA: Sage, 2006), 201–218; D. Vogt and C. R. Colvin, "Interpersonal Orientation and the Accuracy of Personality Judgments," *Journal of Personality 71* (2003): 267–295.
55. M. Schmid Mast and J. A. Hall, "Women's Advantage at Remembering Others' Appearance: A Systematic Look at the Why and When of a Gender Difference," *Personality and Social Psychology Bulletin 32* (2006): 353–364; E. C. Dickey and F. H. Knower, "A Note on Some Ethnological Differences in Recognition of Simulated Expressions of Emotions," *American Journal of Sociology 47* (1941): 190–193; R. Rosenthal, J. A. Hall, M. R. DiMatteo, P. L. Rogers, and D. Archer, *Sensitivity to Nonverbal Communication: The PONS Test* (Baltimore: Johns Hopkins University Press, 1979).
56. D. J. Schneider, A. H. Hastorf, and P. C. Ellsworth, *Person Perception* 2e (Reading, MA: Addison-Wesley, 1979).
57. Baron, Branscombe, and Byrne, *Social Psychology*; D. T. Kenrick, S. L. Neuberg, and R. B. Cialdini, *Social Psychology: Goals in Interaction* 4e (Boston: Allyn & Bacon, 2006).
58. D. L. Oswald, "Gender Stereotypes and Women's Reports of Liking and Ability in Traditionally Masculine and Feminine Occupations," *Psychology of Women Quarterly 32* (2008): 196–203; C. Hoessler and A. L. Chasteen, "Does Aging Affect the Use of Shifting Standards?" *Experimental Aging Research 34* (2008): 1–12; A. C. Pseekos, E. R. Dahlen, and J. J. Levy, "Development of the Academic Stereotype Threat Inventory," *Measurement and Evaluation in Counseling and Development 41* (2008): 2–12; A. Maass, C. D'Ettole, and M. Cadinu, "Checkmate? The Role of Gender Stereotypes in the Ultimate Intellectual Sport," *European Journal of Social Psychology 38* (2008): 231–245.
59. C. N. Macrae, G. V. Bodenhausen, A. B. Milne, and J. Jetten, "Out of Mind but Back in Sight: Stereotypes on the Rebound," *Journal of Personality and Social Psychology 67* (1994): 808–817.
60. Macrae et al., "Out of Mind," 808.
61. This chapter benefited from the fine scholarship and work of M. V. Redmond, coauthor of *Interpersonal Communication: Relating to Others* 4e (Boston: Allyn & Bacon, 2005).

CHAPTER 3

1. "World Briefing, Australia: And It Came 2 Pass," *New York Times* (October 7, 2005): 8.
2. R. Rettie, "Texters Not Talkers: Phone Call Aversion among Mobile Phone Users," *Psychology Journal 5* (2007): 33–57; D. Harley, S. Winn, S. P. Pemberton, and P. Wilcox, "Using Texting to Support Students' Transition to University," *Innovations in Education and Teaching International 44* (2007): 229–241; T. Igarashi, J. Takai, and T. Yoshida, "Gender Differences in Social Network Development via Mobile Phone Text Messages: A Longitudinal Study," *Journal of Social and Personal Relationships 22* (2005): 691–713; C. Thurlow, "Generation Txt? The Sociolinguistics of Young People's Text Messaging," *Discourse Analysis Online 1* (2003): 1.
3. L. Thompson and J. Cupples, "Seen and Not Heard? Text Messaging and Digital Sociality," *Social and Cultural Geography 9* (2008): 95–108; S. Friess, "Yo, can u plz help me write English?: Parents Fear Online Chatting Ruins Kids' Language Skills," *USA Today* (April 1, 2003).
4. J. Scott, "I Feel," *Bitch: Feminist Response to Pop Culture* (Spring 2003): 25.
5. "College Graduates Aren't Ready for the Real World," *The Chronicle of Higher Education* (February 18, 2005): B11.
6. B. Spitzberg and J. P. Dillard, "Social Skills and Communication," in *Interpersonal Communication Research: Advances Through Meta-Analysis*, edited by M. Allen, R. W. Preiss, B. M. Gayle, and N. Burrell (Mahwah, NJ: Lawrence Erlbaum, 2002), 89–107.
7. D. Spender, *Man Made Language* 2e (London: Routledge & Kegan Paul, 1985).
8. B. L. Whorf, "Science and Linguistics," in *Language, Thought, and Reality*, edited by J. B. Carroll (Cambridge: Massachusetts Institute of Technology Press, 1956).
9. R. F. Verderber and K. S. Verderber, "Elements of Language," in *Making Connections: Readings in Relational Communication* 4e, edited by K. M. Galvin and P. J. Cooper (Los Angeles, CA: Roxbury, 2006), 37–45.
10. *Oxford Desk Dictionary and Thesaurus, American Edition* (New York: Oxford University Press, 2007).
11. D. A. Stapel and G. R. Semin, "The Magic Spell of Language: Linguistics Categories and Their Perceptual Consequences," *Journal of Personality and Social Psychology 93* (2007): 23–33; A. M. Glenberg, M. Sato, L. Cattaneo, L. Riggio, D. Palumbo, and G. Buccino, "Processing Abstract Language Modulates Motor System Activity," *Quarterly Journal of Experimental Psychology 61* (2008): 905–919; K. M. Douglas and R. M. Sutton, "When What You Say about Others Says Something about You: Language Abstraction and Inferences about Describers' Attitudes and Goals," *Journal of Experimental Social Psychology 42* (2006): 500–508.
12. C. Condon, M. Perry, and R. O'Keefe, "Denotation and Connotation in the Human-Computer Interface: The 'Save As . . .' Command," *Behaviour & Information Technology 23* (2004): 21–31.
13. Condon et al., "Denotation and Connotation in the Human-Computer Interface," 21.
14. A. G. Smith, ed., *Communication and Culture* (New York: Holt, Rinehart, & Winston, 1966).
15. A. De Fina, "Code-Switching and the Construction of Ethnic Identity in a Community of Practice," *Language in Society 36* (2007): 371–392; E. Richardson, "'She Was Workin Like Foreal': Critical Literacy and the Discourse Practices of African American Females in the Age of Hip Hop," *Discourse & Society 18* (2007): 789–809.
16. T. L. Weldon, "Reflections on the Ebonics Controversy," *American Speech 75* (2000): 275–277.
17. R. R. Heredia and J. Altarriba, "Bilingual Language Mixing: Why Do Bilinguals Code-Switch?" *Current Directions in Psychological Science 10* (2001): 164–168; F. Grosjean and J. L. Miller, "Going In and Out of Languages: An Example of Bilingual Flexibility," *Psychological Science 5* (1994): 201–206.
18. E. E. Davies and A. Bentahila, "Code Switching as a Poetic Device: Examples from Rai Lyrics," *Language and Communication 28* (2008): 1–20; K. Emmorey, H. B. Borinstein, R. Thompson, and T. H. Gollan, "Bimodal Bilingualism," *Bilingualism: Language and Cognition 11* (2008): 43–61.
19. Y. Osward, *Every Word Has Power: Switch on Your Language and Turn on Your Life* (New York: Atria Books/Simon & Schuster, 2008); P. Denton, *The Power of Our Words: Teacher Language That Helps Children Learn* (Turners Falls, MA: Northwest Foundation for Children, 2007).
20. D. K. Ivy and P. Backlund, *GenderSpeak: Personal Effectiveness in Gender Communication* 4e (Boston: Allyn & Bacon, 2008).
21. A. Ellis, *A New Guide to Rational Living* (North Hollywood, CA: Wilshire Books, 1977).
22. C. Peterson, M. E. P. Seligman, and G. E. Vaillant, "Pessimistic Explanatory Style Is a Risk Factor for Physical Illness: A 35-Year Longitudinal Study," *Journal of Personality and Social Psychology 55* (1988): 23–27.
23. M. A. Overland, "Suggesting the Impossible," *The Chronicle of Higher Education* (June 13, 2008): A6.

24. S. Dunn, "Standing Up for 'Bad' Words," *The Chronicle of Higher Education: The Chronicle Review* (March 14, 2008): B28.
25. L. Pitts, "African-American? Hispanic? Indian? Does It Really Matter What We Call Ourselves?" *Corpus Christi Caller Times* (May 25, 2003): A15.
26. M. P. Orbe and T. M. Harris, *Interracial Communication: Theory into Practice* 2e (Thousand Oaks, CA: Sage, 2008); B. J. Allen, *Differences Matter: Communicating Social Identity* (Long Grove, IL: Waveland Press, 2004); D. J. Napoli, *Language Matters: A Guide to Everyday Questions about Language* (New York: Oxford University Press, 2003); D. I. Kertzer and D. Arel, *Census and Identity: The Politics of Race, Ethnicity, and Language in National Censuses* (New York: Cambridge University Press, 2002); R. Harris, *The Language, Ethnicity, and Race Reader* (New York: Routledge, 2003); J. K. Swim, R. Mallett, and C. Stangor, "Understanding Subtle Sexism: Detection and Use of Sexist Language," *Sex Roles* 51 (2004): 117–128; J. Briere and C. Lanktree, "Sex-Role Related Effects of Sex Bias in Language," *Sex Roles* 9 (1983): 625–632; L. Brooks, "Sexist Language in Occupational Information: Does It Make a Difference?" *Journal of Vocational Behavior* 23 (1983): 227–232; A. Stericker, "Does This 'He or She' Business Really Make a Difference? The Effect of Masculine Pronouns as Generics on Job Attitudes," *Sex Roles* 7 (1981): 637–641.
27. S. Ardener, "Muted Groups: The Genesis of an Idea and Its Praxis," *Women and Language* 28 (2005): 50–54; C. Kramarae, "Muted Group Theory and Communication: Asking Dangerous Questions," *Women and Language* 28 (2005): 55–61.
28. H. S. O'Donnell, "Sexism in Language," *Elementary English* 50 (1973): 1067–1072, as cited by J. C. Pearson, L. Turner, and W. Todd Mancillas, *Gender & Communication* 3e (Dubuque, IA: William C. Brown, 1995).
29. J. L. Stinger and R. Hopper, "Generic He in Conversation?" *Quarterly Journal of Speech* 84 (1998): 209–221; J. Gastil, "Generic Pronouns and Sexist Language: The Oxymoronic Character of Masculine Generics," *Sex Roles* 23 (1990): 629–641; D. K. Ivy, L. Bullis-Moore, K. Norvell, P. Backlund, and M. Javidi, "The Lawyer, the Babysitter, and the Student: Inclusive Language Usage and Instruction," *Women and Language* 18 (1994): 13–21; W. Martyna, "What Does 'He' Mean? Use of the Generic Masculine," *Journal of Communication* 28 (1978): 131–138.
30. APA Style.org, "Removing Bias in Language," March 2006, <www.apastyle.org/sexuality.html>.
31. L. Madson and R. M. Hessling, "Does Alternating between Masculine and Feminine Pronouns Eliminate Perceived Gender Bias in a Text?" *Sex Roles* 41 (1999): 559–576; D. Kennedy, "Review Essay: She or He in Textbooks," *Women & Language* 15 (1992): 46–49.
32. See R. Maggio, *The Nonsexist Word Finder: A Dictionary of Gender-Free Usage* (Boston: Beacon, 1988); C. Miller, K. Swift, and R. Maggio, "Liberating Language," *Ms.* (September/October, 1997): 50–54.
33. Ivy and Backlund, *GenderSpeak*; C. H. Palczewski, "'Tak[e] the Helm,' Man the Ship ... and I Forgot My Bikini! Unraveling Why Woman Is Not Considered a Verb," *Women and Language* 21 (1998): 1–8; Maggio, *The Nonsexist Word Finder*.
34. A. Walker, as cited in A. Bilger, "The Common *Guy*: One Seemingly Benign Phrase Makes a Man Out of All of Us," *Bitch: Feminist Response to Pop Culture* (Fall 2002): 87.
35. Ivy and Backlund, *GenderSpeak*.
36. Ivy and Backlund, *GenderSpeak*.
37. N. Updike, "That's So Gay!" September 14, 2000, <salon.com>; Associated Press, "'That's So Gay' Prompts a Lawsuit: Student Sent to Principal's Office Insists It Was Not a Homophobic Putdown," February 28, 2007, <msnbc.com>.
38. A. Williams and J. F. Nussbaum, *Intergenerational Communication across the Life Span* (Mahwah, NJ: Lawrence Erlbaum, 2000); E. O'Reilly, *Decoding the Cultural Stereotypes about Aging: New Perspectives on Aging Talk and Aging Issues* (New York: Routledge, 1997).
39. R. K. S. Macaulay, *Talk That Counts: Age, Gender, and Social Class Differences in Discourse* (New York: Oxford University Press, 2005); M. Argyle, *The Psychology of Social Class* (New York: Routledge, 1993).
40. J. S. Seiter, J. Larsen, and J. Skinner, "'Handicapped' or 'Handicapable'? The Effects of Language about Persons with Disabilities on Perceptions of Source Credibility and Persuasiveness," *Communication Reports* 11 (1998): 21–31.
41. D. O. Braithwaite and C. A. Braithwaite, "Understanding Communication of Persons with Disabilities as Cultural Communication," in *Intercultural Communication: A Reader* 10e, edited by L. A. Samovar and R. E. Porter (Belmont, CA: Wadsworth, 2002), 136–145; D. O. Braithwaite and T. L. Thompson, *Handbook of Communication and People with Disabilities: Research and Application* (Mahwah, NJ: Lawrence Erlbaum, 2000).
42. E. T. Booth, "Assign This: Trigger Words," *Spectra* (Washington, DC: National Communication Association, June/July 2007).
43. J. R. Gibb, "Defensive Communication," *Journal of Communication* 11 (1961): 141–148; J. A. H. Becker, B. Ellevold, and G. H. Stamp, "The Creation of Defensiveness in Social Interaction II: A Model of Defensive Communication among Romantic Couples," *Communication Monographs* 75 (2008): 86–110; L. Cairns, "Reinforcement," in *The Handbook of Communication Skills* 3e, edited by O. Hargie (London: Routledge, 2006), 147–164; J. A. H. Becker, J. R. B. Halbesleben, and H. D. O'Hair, "Defensive Communication and Burnout in the Workplace: The Mediating Role of Leader-Member Exchange," *Communication Research Reports* 22 (2005): 143–150.
44. M. B. Rosenberg, *Nonviolent Communication: A Language of Life* (Encinitas, CA: PuddleDancer Press, 2005); L. A. Moore, "Empathy: A Clinician's Perspective," *The ASHA Leader* (August 15, 2006): 16–35; L. K. Thaler, "The Power of Nice," *O: The Oprah Winfrey Magazine* (September 2006): 143–145; M. Beck, "Have a Heart: The Empathy Workout," *O: The Oprah Winfrey Magazine* (March 2006): 77–82; M. V. Redmond, "The Functions of Empathy (Decentering) in Human Relations," *Human Relations* 42 (1993): 593–606.

CHAPTER 4

1. M. Fox, *Talking Hands: What Sign Language Reveals about the Mind* (New York: Simon & Schuster, 2007); R. B. Grossman and J. Kegl, "Moving Faces: Categorization of Dynamic Facial Expressions in American Sign Language by Deaf and Hearing Participants," *Journal of Nonverbal Behavior* 31 (2007): 23–38.
2. A. Mehrabian, *Nonverbal Communication* (Chicago: Aldine-Atherton, 1972).
3. L. E. Boone and D. L. Kurtz, *Contemporary Business* 12e (Belmont, CA: South-Western Publishing, 2009); V. Quercia, *Internet in a Nutshell* (Cambridge, MA: O'Reilly, 1997).
4. R. Bringhurst, *The Elements of Typographic Style* 3e (New York: Harts and Marks, 2004).
5. R. L. Birdwhistell, *Kinesics and Context* (Philadelphia: University of Pennsylvania Press, 1970).
6. F. J. Bernieri, "The Expression of Rapport," in *The Sourcebook of Nonverbal Measures: Going beyond Words*, edited by V. Manusov (Mahwah, NJ: Lawrence Erlbaum, 2005), 347–359; F. J. Bernieri, "Toward a Taxonomy of Interpersonal Sensitivity," in *Interpersonal Sensitivity: Theory and Measurement*, edited by J. A. Hall and F. J. Bernieri (Mahwah, NJ: Lawrence Erlbaum, 2001), 3–20.
7. W. E. Chaplin, J. B. Phillips, J. D. Brown, N. R. Clanton, and J. L. Stein, "Handshaking, Gender, Personality, and First Impressions," *Journal of Personality and Social Psychology* 79 (2000): 110–117.
8. J. K. Burgoon, L. A. Stern, and L. Dillman, *Interpersonal Adaptation: Dyadic Interaction Patterns* (Cambridge, England: Cambridge University Press, 1995).
9. P. Ekman, "Communication through Nonverbal Behavior: A Source of Information about an Interpersonal Relationship," in *Affect, Cognition, and Personality*, edited by S. S. Tomkins and C. E. Izard (New York: Springer, 1965).
10. M. Argyle, *Bodily Communication* (New York: Methuen & Company, 1988).
11. H. A. Elfenbein, "Learning in Emotion Judgments: Training and the Cross-Cultural Understanding of Facial Expressions," *Journal of Nonverbal Behavior* 30 (2006): 21–36; D. Matsumoto and S. H. Yoo, "Culture and Applied Nonverbal Communication," in *Applications of Nonverbal Communication*, edited by R. E. Riggio and R. S. Feldman (Mahwah, NJ: Lawrence Erlbaum, 2005), 255–277; D. Matsumoto, "American-Japanese Cultural Differences in the Recognition of Universal Facial Expressions," *Journal of Cross-Cultural Psychology* 23 (1992): 72–84; D. Matsumoto, "Face, Culture, and Judgments of Anger and Fear: Do the Eyes Have It?" *Journal of Nonverbal Behavior* 13 (1989):

171–188; D. Matsumoto and P. Ekman, "American-Japanese Cultural Differences in Intensity Ratings of Facial Expressions of Emotion," *Motivation and Emotion* 13 (1989): 143–157; P. Collett, "History and Study of Expressive Action," in *Historical Social Psychology*, edited by K. Gergen and M. Gergen (Hillsdale, NJ: Erlbaum, 1984); I. Eibl-Eibesfeldt, "Similarities and Differences between Cultures in Expressive Movements," in *Nonverbal Communication*, edited by R. A. Hinde (Cambridge, England: Royal Society and Cambridge University Press, 1972); P. Ekman and W. V. Friesen, "Constants across Cultures in the Face and Emotion," *Journal of Personality and Social Psychology* 17 (1971): 124–129.

12. L. A. Samovar, R. E. Porter, and E. R. McDaniel, "An Introduction to Intercultural Communication," in *Intercultural Communication: A Reader* 12e, edited by L. A. Samovar, R. E. Porter, and E. R. McDaniel (Belmont, CA: Wadsworth, 2008).

13. J. Douglas, Jr., "Outside Texas, 'Hook 'em Horns' Gesture Has Different and Unflattering Meanings," *Fort Worth Star Telegram* (January 23, 2005): 2A.

14. "Watch Your Tongue; This Isn't Tibet," *Fort Worth Star Telegram* (October 10, 2004): 2A; E. Adams, "Manners Can Sink International Business Dealings," *Corpus Christi Caller Times* (November 2, 2003): K2.

15. See J. K. Burgoon and S. B. Jones, "Toward a Theory of Personal Space Expectations and Their Violations," *Human Communication Research* 2 (1976): 131–146. For discussions and applications of expectancy violations theory, see J. K. Burgoon and N. E. Dunbar, "Nonverbal Expressions of Dominance and Power in Human Relationships," in *The Sage Handbook of Nonverbal Communication*, edited by V. Manusov and M. L. Patterson (Thousand Oaks, CA: Sage, 2006), 279–297; S. Campo, K. A. Cameron, D. Brossard, and M. S. Frazer, "Social Norms and Expectancy Violation Theories: Assessing the Effectiveness of Health Communication Campaigns," *Communication Monographs* 71 (2004): 448–470; L. A. Erbert and K. Floyd, "Affectionate Expression as Face-Threatening Acts: Receiver Assessments," *Communication Studies* 55 (2004): 254–270; J. L. Bevan, "General Partner and Relational Uncertainty as Consequences of Another Person's Jealousy Expression," *Western Journal of Communication* 68 (2004): 195–218; J. L. Bevan, "Expectancy Violation Theory and Sexual Resistance in Close, Cross-Sex Relationships." *Communication Monographs* 70 (2003): 68–82; W. A. Afifi and J. K. Burgoon, "The Impact of Violations on Uncertainty and the Consequences for Attractiveness," *Human Communication Research* 26 (2000): 203–233.

16. J. Fast, *Body Language* (New York: M. Evans, 1970).

17. P. Ekman and W. V. Friesen, "The Repertoire of Nonverbal Behavior: Categories, Origins, Usage, and Coding," *Semiotica* 1 (1969): 49–98.

18. E. Tenner, "Political Timber: Glitter, Froth, and Measuring Tape," *The Chronicle of Higher Education* (October 1, 2004): B12–B13.

19. C. Edwards, A. Edwards, Q. Qing, and S. T. Wahl, "The Influence of Computer-Mediated Word-of-Mouth Communication on Student Perceptions of Instructors and Attitudes toward Learning Course Content," *Communication Education* 56 (2007): 255–277; A. Edwards and C. Edwards, "The Impact of Instructor Verbal and Nonverbal Immediacy on Student Perceptions of Attractiveness and Homophily," *Journal on Excellence in College Teaching* 12 (2001): 5–16; K. A. Rocca and J. C. McCroskey, "The Interrelationship of Student Ratings of Instructors' Immediacy, Verbal Aggressiveness, Homophily, and Interpersonal Attraction," *Communication Education* 48 (1999): 308–316; G. Montell, "Do Good Looks Equal Good Evaluations?" *The Chronicle of Higher Education: Career Network*, October 15, 2003, <http://chronicle.com>.

20. B. Ackerman, "The Dangers of Body Dysmorphic Disorder: Discover the Dangers Associated with This Unhealthy Behavior," *American Fitness* (2006): 24–26; M. M. Martin and J. W. Gentry, "Stuck in the Model Trap," in *Taking Sides: Clashing Views on Controversial Issues in Mass Media and Society* 8e, edited by A. Alexander and J. Hanson (Dubuque, IA: McGraw-Hill/Dushkin, 2005), 52–61; G. B. Forbes, L. E. Adams-Curtis, B. Rade, and P. Jaberg, "Body Dissatisfaction in Women and Men: The Role of Gender-Typing and Self-Esteem," *Sex Roles* 44 (2001): 461–484; R. A. Botta, "Television Images and Adolescent Girls' Body Image Disturbance," *Journal of Communication* 49 (1999): 22–37; M. Wiederman and S. Hurst, "Body Size, Physical Attractiveness, and Body Image among Young Adult Women: Relationships to Sexual Experience and Sexual Esteem," *Journal of Sex Research* 35 (1998): 272–281.

21. E. Hatfield and S. Sprecher, *Mirror, Mirror...: The Importance of Looks in Everyday Life* (Albany: SUNY Press, 1986); C. M. Marlowe, S. L. Schneider, and C. E. Nelson, "Gender and Attractiveness Biases in Hiring Decisions: Are More Experienced Managers Less Biased?" *Journal of Applied Psychology* 81 (1998): 11–21; W. R. Zakahi, R. L. Duran, and M. Adkins, "Social Anxiety, Only Skin Deep? The Relationships between Ratings of Physical Attractiveness and Social Anxiety," *Communication Research Reports* 11 (1994): 23–31; L. A. Zebrowitz, *Reading Faces: Window to the Soul?* (Boulder, CO: Westview, 1997).

22. R. Pante, "Image Builds Business," *Today's Chiropractic* 34 (2006): 73–75; A. Rainey, "Tress for Success," *The Chronicle of Higher Education* 52 (2006): A6; G. Thornbory and C. White, "How to Project a Professional Image," *Occupational Health* 58 (2006): 24; J. Gorham, S. H. Cohen, and T. L. Morris, "Fashion in the Classroom III: Effects of Instructor Attire and Immediacy in Natural Classroom Interactions," *Communication Quarterly* 47 (1999): 281–299; K. D. Roach, "Effects of Graduate Teaching Assistant Attire on Student Learning, Misbehaviors, and Ratings of Instruction," *Communication Quarterly* 45 (1997): 125–141.

23. J. T. Molloy, *New Dress for Success* (New York: Warner Books, 1988); J. T. Molloy, *New Woman's Dress for Success Book* (New York: Warner, 1996).

24. L. Averyt, "Casual-Attire Fridays Are Spreading to Rest of Week in Many Companies," *Corpus Christi Caller Times* (August 31, 1997): A1, A6; M. G. Frank and T. Gilovich, "The Dark Side of Self- and Social Perception: Black Uniforms and Aggression in Professional Sports," *Journal of Personality and Social Psychology* 54 (1988): 74–85; P. A. Andersen, *Nonverbal Communication: Forms and Functions* (Mountain View, CA: Mayfield, 1999); V. Santos-Garza, "School Code Is Dressed in Stress," *Corpus Christi Caller Times* (August 1, 2004): C1; O. Garcia Hunter, "Goodbye Grunge," *Corpus Christi Caller Times* (July 18, 2004): A1, A8.

25. N. Armstrong and M. Wagner, *Field Guide to Gestures: How to Identify and Interpret Virtually Every Gesture Known to Man* (Philadelphia: Quirk Books, 2003).

26. Birdwhistell, *Kinesics and Context*; D. G. Leathers, *Successful Nonverbal Communication: Principles and Applications* 3e (Boston: Allyn & Bacon, 1997).

27. Ekman and Friesen, "The Repertoire of Nonverbal Behavior."

28. R. E. Axtell, *Gestures: Do's and Taboos of Body Language around the World* (New York: John Wiley & Sons, 1998).

29. E. Stevanoni and K. Salmon, "Giving Memory a Hand: Instructing Children to Gesture Enhances Their Event Recall," *Journal of Nonverbal Behavior* 29 (2005): 217–233; G. Beattie and H. Shovelton, "Mapping the Range of Information Contained in the Iconic Hand Gestures That Accompany Spontaneous Speech," *Journal of Language & Social Psychology* 18 (1999): 438–462; J. Streeck, "Gesture as Communication I: Its Coordination with Gaze and Speech," *Communication Monographs* 60 (1993): 275–299.

30. W. G. Woodall and J. P. Folger, "Nonverbal Cue Context and Episodic Memory: On the Availability and Endurance of Nonverbal Behaviors as Retrieval Cues," *Communication Monographs* 52 (1985): 320–333; A. A. Cohen and R. P. Harrison, "Intentionality in the Use of Hand Illustrators in Face-to-Face Communication Situations," *Journal of Personality and Social Psychology* 28 (1973): 276–279.

31. C. Darwin, *Expression of Emotions in Man and Animals* (London: Appleton; reprinted University of Chicago Press, 1965).

32. J. Beavin Bavelas and N. Chovil, "Nonverbal and Verbal Communication: Hand Gestures and Facial Displays as Part of Language Use in Face-to-Face Dialogue," in Manusov and Patterson, *The Sage Handbook of Nonverbal Communication*, 97–115; M. Coulson, "Attributing Emotion to Static Body Postures: Recognition Accuracy, Confusions, and Viewpoint Dependence," *Journal of Nonverbal Behavior* 28 (2004): 117–139; E. McClure and K. Pope, "Facial Expression Recognition in Adolescents with Mood and Anxiety Disorders," *Journal of Psychology* 160 (2003): 1172–1175; V. Lee and H. Wagner, "The Effect of Social Presence on the Facial and Verbal Expression of Emotion and the

Interrelationships among Emotion Components," *Journal of Nonverbal Behavior* 26 (2002): 3–23.

33. P. Collett, *The Book of Tells* (London: Bantam, 2004); L. A. Renninger, T. J. Wade, and K. Grammer, "Getting That Female Glance: Patterns and Consequences of Male Nonverbal Behavior in Courtship Contexts," *Evolution and Human Behavior* 25 (2004): 416–431; D. Singh, "Mating Strategies of Young Women: Role of Physical Attractiveness," *Journal of Sex Research* 41 (2004): 43–54; K. Grammer, K. Kruck, A. Juette, and B. Fink, "Nonverbal Behavior as Courtship Signals: The Role of Control and Choice in Selecting Partners," *Evolution and Human Behavior* 21 (2000): 371–390.

34. M. M. Moore, "Nonverbal Courtship Patterns in Women: Context and Consequences," *Ethology and Sociobiology* 6 (1985): 237–247; D. Knox and K. Wilson, "Dating Behaviors of University Students," *Family Relations* 30 (1981): 255–258.

35. D. D. Henningsen, "Flirting with Meaning: An Examination of Miscommunication in Flirting Interactions," *Sex Roles* 50 (2004): 481–489; M. M. Moore, "Courtship Communication and Perception," *Perceptual and Motor Skills* 94 (2002): 97–105; E. Koukounas and N. M. Letch, "Psychological Correlates of Perception of Sexual Intent in Women," *Journal of Social Psychology* 141 (2001): 443–456; A. Abbey, "Sex Differences in Attributions for Friendly Behavior: Do Males Misperceive Females' Friendliness?" *Journal of Personality and Social Psychology* 42 (1982): 830–838; L. B. Koeppel, Y. Montagne, D. O'Hair, and M. J. Cody, "Friendly? Flirting? Wrong?" *The Nonverbal Communication Reader: Classic and Contemporary Reading.* 2e, edited by L. K. Guerrero, J. DeVito, and M. L. Hecht (Prospect Heights, IL: Waveland, 1999), 290–297.

36. A. Abbey, T. Zawacki, and P. O. Buck, "The Effects of Past Sexual Assault Perpetration and Alcohol Consumption on Reactions to Women's Mixed Signals," *Journal of Social and Clinical Psychology* 24 (2005): 129–157; H. J. Delaney and B. A. Gluade, "Gender Differences in Perception of Attractiveness of Men and Women in Bars," *Journal of Personality and Social Psychology* 16 (1990): 378–391.

37. A. E. Scheflen, "Quasi-Courtship Behavior in Psychotherapy," *Psychiatry* 28 (1965): 245–257; K. Grammer, K. B. Kruck, and M. S. Magnusson, "The Courtship Dance: Patterns of Nonverbal Synchronization in Opposite Sex Encounters," *Journal of Nonverbal Behavior* 22 (1998): 3–25.

38. J. A. Daly, E. Hogg, D. Sacks, M. Smith, and L. Zimring, "Sex and Relationship Affect Social Self-Grooming," *Journal of Nonverbal Behavior* 7 (1983): 183–189.

39. J. Knight, "The Truth about Lying," *Nature* 428 (2004): 692–694; J. Ruscio, "Exploring Controversies in the Art and Science of Polygraph Testing," *The Skeptical Inquirer* 29 (2005): 34–39.

40. D. K. Ivy and S. T. Wahl, *The Nonverbal Self: Communication for a Lifetime* (Boston: Allyn & Bacon, 2009); A. Vrij, "Nonverbal Communication and Deception," in Manusov and Patterson, *The Sage Handbook of Nonverbal Communication*, 341–359; P. A. Andersen, *The Complete Idiot's Guide to Body Language* (New York: Alpha, 2004); L. Anolli and R. Ciceri, "The Voice of Deception: Vocal Strategies of Naive and Able Liars," *Journal of Nonverbal Behavior* 21 (1997): 259–284; P. Ekman, W. V. Friesen, and K. R. Scherer, "Body Movement and Voice Pitch in Deceptive Interaction," *Semiotica* 16 (1976): 23–27; P. Ekman, M. O'Sullivan, W. V. Friesen, and K. R. Scherer, "Face, Voice, and Body in Detecting Deceit," *Journal of Nonverbal Behavior* 15 (1991): 125–135; M. O'Sullivan, "Emotional Intelligence and Deception Detection: Why Most People Can't 'Read' Others, but a Few Can," in Riggio and Feldman, *Applications of Nonverbal Communication*, 215–253.

41. L. K. Guerrero and K. Floyd, *Nonverbal Communication in Close Relationships* (Mahwah, NJ: Lawrence Erlbaum, 2006); C. S. Rhys, "Gaze and Turn: A Nonverbal Solution to an Interactive Problem," *Clinical Linguistics and Phonetics* 19 (2005): 419–431; Collett, *The Book of Tells*; Renninger, Wade, and Grammer, "Getting That Female Glance"; Grammer, Kruck, Juette, and Fink, "Nonverbal Behavior as Courtship Signals".

42. M. L. Knapp and J. A. Hall, *Nonverbal Communication in Human Interaction* 6e (Belmont, CA: Thomson/Wadsworth, 2006).

43. S. A. Beebe, "Eye Contact: A Nonverbal Determinant of Speaker Credibility," *Speech Teacher* 23 (1974): 21–25.

44. M. L. Jensen and J. K. Burgoon, "Interpersonal Deception Theory," in *The Nonverbal Communication Reader* 3e, edited by L. K. Guerrero and M. L. Hecht (Long Grove, IL: Waveland, 2008), 421–431; M. L. Knapp, *Lying and Deception in Human Interaction* (Boston: Pearson/Allyn & Bacon, 2008); L. A. Stromwall, M. Hartwig, and P. A. Granhag, "To Act Truthfully: Nonverbal Behavior and Strategies during a Police Interrogation," *Psychology, Crime, and Law* 12 (2006): 207–219; Vrij, "Nonverbal Communication and Deception."

45. B. M. DePaulo, J. L. Lindsay, B. E. Malone, L. Muhlenbruck, K. Charlton, and H. Cooper, "Cues to Deception," *Psychological Bulletin* 129 (2003): 74–118; M. Zuckerman and R. E. Driver, "Telling Lies: Verbal and Nonverbal Correlates of Deception, in *Multichannel Integrations of Nonverbal Behavior*, edited by A. W. Siegman and S. Feldstein (Hillsdale, NJ: Lawrence Erlbaum, 1985), 129–148.

46. P. Ekman and W. Friesen, *Unmasking the Face* (Englewood Cliffs, NJ: Prentice-Hall, 1975); R. L. Birdwhistell, "The Language of the Body: The Natural Environment of Words," in *Human Communication: Theoretical Explorations*, edited by A. Silverstein (New York: John Wiley & Sons, 1974), 203–220.

47. E. Krumhuber, A. S. Manstead, and A. Kappas, "Temporal Aspects of Facial Displays in Person and Expression Perception: The Effects of Smile Dynamics, Head-Tilt, and Gender," *Journal of Nonverbal Behavior* 31 (2007): 39–56; W. Sato and S. Yoshikawa, "Enhanced Experience of Emotional Arousal in Response to Dynamic Facial Expressions," *Journal of Nonverbal Behavior* 31 (2007): 119–135; K. Domenici and S. W. Littlejohn, *Facework: Bridging Theory and Practice* (Thousand Oaks, CA: Sage, 2006); H. A. Elfenbein, "Learning in Emotion Judgments: Training and the Cross-Cultural Understanding of Facial Expressions," *Journal of Nonverbal Behavior* 30 (2006): 21–36; A. J. Fridlund and J. A. Russell, "The Functions of Facial Expressions," in Manusov and Patterson, *The Sage Handbook of Nonverbal Communication*, 299–319.

48. M. Mendolia, "Explicit Use of Categorical and Dimensional Strategies to Decode Facial Expressions of Emotion," *Journal of Nonverbal Behavior* 31 (2007): 57–75; A. P. Atkinson, J. Tipples, D. M. Burt, and A. W. Young, "Asymmetric Interference between Sex and Emotion in Face Perception," *Perception and Psychophysics* 67 (2005): 1199–1213.

49. Ekman and Friesen, *Unmasking the Face*.

50. P. M. Cole, "Children's Spontaneous Control of Facial Expression," *Child Development* 57 (1986): 1309–1321.

51. S. Dang, "Abused Kids More Sensitive to Anger: Study Shows Victims Identify More Faces as 'Angry' than Non-Abused," *Corpus Christi Caller Times* (June 23, 2002): A26.

52. T. Field, "Touch Deprivation and Aggression against Self among Adolescents," in *Developmental Psychobiology of Aggression*, edited by D. M. Stoff and E. J. Susman (New York: Cambridge University Press, 2005), 117–140; S. Trenholm, *Thinking through Communication* (Boston: Allyn & Bacon, 2001); M. Turp, "Touch, Enjoyment and Health: In Adult Life," *European Journal of Psychotherapy, Counseling and Health* 3 (2000): 61–76; S. E. Jones and A. E. Yarbrough, "A Naturalistic Study of the Meanings of Touch," *Communication Monographs* 52 (1985): 19–56.

53. G. Lappin, "Using Infant Massage Following a Mother's Unfavorable Neonatal Intensive Care Unit Experiences: A Case Study," *RE:view* 37 (2005): 87–95; R. Feldman, A. L. Eidelman, L. Sirota, and A. Weller, "Comparison of Skin-to-Skin (Kangaroo) and Traditional Care: Parenting Outcomes and Preterm Infant Development," *Pediatrics* 110 (2002): 16–26; K. Onzawa, V. Glover, D. Adam, N. Modi, and R. C. Kumar, "Infant Massage Improves Mother-Infant Interaction for Mothers with Postnatal Depression," *Journal of Affective Disorders* 63 (2001): 201–207; C. Cullen, T. Field, A. Escalona, and K. Hartshom, "Father-Infant Interactions Are Enhanced by Massage Therapy," *Early Childhood Development and Care* 164 (2000): 41–47; T. Field, "Infant Massage Therapy," in *Handbook of Infant Mental Health* 2e, edited by C. H. Zeanah (New York: Guilford, 2000), 494–500; A. Montague, *Touching: The Human Significance of the Skin* (New York: Harper & Row, 1978).

54. Ivy and Wahl, *The Nonverbal Self*.

55. R. DiBiase and J. Gunnoe, "Gender and Culture Differences in Touching Behavior," *Journal of Social Psychology* 144 (2004): 49–62; M. Hickson, III, D. W. Stacks, and N.-J. Moore, *Nonverbal Communication: Studies and Applications* 4e (Los Angeles: Roxbury, 2004); E. T. Hall, *The Hidden Dimension* 2e (Garden City, NY: Anchor/Doubleday, 1966);

E. T. Hall, *Beyond Culture* (New York: Doubleday, 1981); M. S. Remland, T. S. Jones, and H. Brinkman, "Proxemic and Haptic Behavior in Three European Countries," *Journal of Nonverbal Behavior 15* (1991): 215–231; M. S. Remland, T. S. Jones, and H. Brinkman, "Interpersonal Distance, Body Orientation and Touch: Effect of Culture, Gender, and Age," *Journal of Social Psychology 135* (1995): 281–295.

56. B. McEwan and S. L. Johnson, "Relational Violence: The Darkest Side of Haptic Communication," in Guerrero and Hecht, *The Nonverbal Communication Reader* 3e, 421–431; M. A. Beres, E. Herold, and S. B. Maitland, "Sexual Consent Behaviors in Same-Sex Relationships," *Archives of Sexual Behavior 33* (2004): 475–486; J. W. Lee and L. K. Guerrero, "Types of Touch in Cross-Sex Relationships between Coworkers: Perceptions of Relational and Emotional Messages, Inappropriateness, and Sexual Harassment," *Journal of Applied Communication Research 29* (2001): 197–220; M. S. Remland, *Nonverbal Communication in Everyday Life* 3e (Boston: Allyn & Bacon, 2008); J. D. Murphy, D. M. Driscoll, and J. R. Kelly, "Differences in the Nonverbal Behavior of Men Who Vary in the Likelihood to Sexually Harass," *Journal of Social Behavior and Personality 14* (1999): 113–128; D. K. Ivy and S. Hamlet, "College Students and Sexual Dynamics: Two Studies of Peer Sexual Harassment," *Communication Education 45* (1996): 149–166.

57. P. A. Andersen, *Nonverbal Communication: Forms and Functions* 2e (Long Grove, IL: Waveland, 2008); P. A. Andersen, L. K. Guerrero, and S. M. Jones, "Nonverbal Behavior in Intimate Interactions and Intimate Relationships," in Manusov and Patterson, *The Sage Handbook of Nonverbal Communication*, 259–277; J. A. Hall, "Women's and Men's Nonverbal Communication: Similarities, Differences, Stereotypes, and Origins," in Manusov and Patterson, *The Sage Handbook of Nonverbal Communication*, 201–218; L. M. Kneidinger, T. L. Maple, and S. A. Tross, "Touching Behavior in Sport: Functional Components, Analysis of Sex Differences, and Ethological Considerations," *Journal of Nonverbal Behavior 25* (2001): 43–62; L. K. Guerrero and P. A. Andersen, "Public Touch Behavior in Romantic Relationships between Men and Women," in Guerrero, DeVito, and Hecht, *The Nonverbal Communication Reader* 2e, 202–210.

58. C. A. Braithwaite, "Cultural Uses and Interpretations of Silence." In Guerrero, DeVito, and Hecht, *The Nonverbal Communication Reader*, 163–172.

59. A. Karpf, *The Human Voice: How This Extraordinary Instrument Reveals Essential Clues about Who We Are* (New York: Bloomsbury, 2006); A. Nelson and S. K. Golant, *You Don't Say: Navigating Nonverbal Communication between the Sexes* (New York: Prentice Hall, 2004); L. K. Wells, *The Articulate Voice: An Introduction to Voice and Diction* 4e (Boston: Allyn & Bacon, 2004); S. Feldstein, F. A. Dohm, and C. L. Crown, "Gender and Speech Rate in the Perception of Competence and Social Attractiveness," *Journal of Social Psychology 141* (2001): 785–808.

60. F. Roberts, A. L. Francis, and M. Morgan, "The Interaction of Inter-Turn Silence with Prosodic Cues in Listener Perceptions of 'Trouble' in Conversation," *Speech Communication 48* (2006): 1079–1093; S. Feldstein, F. A. Dohm, and C. L. Crown, "Gender and Speech Rate in the Perception of Competence and Social Attractiveness," *Journal of Social Psychology 141* (2001): 785–808; T. DeGroot and S. J. Motowidlo, "Why Visual and Vocal Interview Cues Can Affect Interviewers' Judgments and Predict Job Performance," *Journal of Applied Psychology 84* (1999): 986–993; N. Christenfeld, "Does It Hurt to Say Um?" *Journal of Nonverbal Behavior 19* (1995): 171–186; J. K. Burgoon, T. Birk, and M. Pfau, "Nonverbal Behaviors, Persuasion, and Credibility," *Human Communication Research 17* (1990): 140–169.

61. Guerrero and Floyd, *Nonverbal Communication in Close Relationships*; K. Tracy, *Everyday Talk: Building and Reflecting Identities* (New York: Guilford Press, 2002).

62. A. Georgakopoulos, "The Role of Silence and Avoidance in Interpersonal Conflict," *Peace and Conflict Studies 11* (2004): 85–95; M. L. Knapp and A. L. Vangelisti, *Interpersonal Communication and Human Relationships* 5e (Boston: Allyn & Bacon, 2005); A. Jaworski, "The Power of Silence in Communication." In Guerrero, DeVito, and Hecht, *The Nonverbal Communication Reader*, 156–162.

63. D. D. Henningsen, D. Dryden, M. G. Cruz, and M. C. Morr, "Pattern Violations and Perceptions of Deception," *Communication Reports 13* (2000): 1–10; M. A. deTurck, T. H. Feeley, and L. A. Roman, "Vocal and Visual Cue Training in Behavioral Lie Detection," *Communication Research Reports 14* (1997): 249–259; T. H. Feeley and M. A. deTurck, "Global Cue Usage in Behavioral Lie Detection," *Communication Quarterly 43* (1995): 420–430.

64. S. J. Baker, "The Theory of Silence," *Journal of General Psychology 53* (1955): 145–167.

65. A. Vogler and J. Jorgensen, "Windows to the World, Doors to Space: The Psychology of Space Architecture," *Leonardo 38* (2005): 390–399; P. Harris and D. Sachau, "Is Cleanliness Next to Godliness? The Role of Housekeeping in Impression Formation," *Environment and Behavior 37* (2005): 81–99.

66. I. Vilnai-Yavetz, A. Rafaeli, and C. Schneider-Yaacov, "Instrumentality, Aesthetics, and Symbolism of Office Design," *Environment and Behavior 37* (2005): 533–551; J. Sandberg, "Want to Know Someone's Job Status? Look at Desk Location," *Corpus Christi Caller Times* (March 2, 2003): D4.

67. D. R. Peterson, "Interpersonal Relationships as a Link between Person and Environment," in *Person–Environment Psychology*, edited by W. B. Walsh, K. H. Craig, and R. H. Price (Hillsdale, NJ: Lawrence Erlbaum, 1991), 154.

68. A. Rapoport, *The Meaning of the Built Environment: A Nonverbal Communication Approach* (Beverly Hills: Sage, 1982).

69. S. D. Gosling, S. J. Ko, T. Mannarelli, and M. E. Morris, "A Room with a Cue: Personality Judgments Based on Offices and Bedrooms," *Journal of Personality and Social Psychology 82* (2002): 379–398; A. Lohmann, X. B. Arriaga, and W. Goodfriend, "Close Relationships and Placemaking: Do Objects in a Couple's Home Reflect Couplehood?" *Personal Relationships 10* (2003): 437–449.

70. J. F. Sallis and J. Kerr, "Physical Activity and the Built Environment," in Guerrero and Hecht, *The Nonverbal Communication Reader* 3e, 270–286; A. H. Maslow and N. L. Mintz, "Effects of Esthetic Surroundings: I," *Journal of Psychology 41* (1956): 247–254.

71. M. M. Aslam, "Are You Selling the Right Color? A Cross-Cultural Review of Color as a Marketing Cue," *Journal of Marketing Communications 12* (2006): 15–30; C. Jansson, N. Marlow, and M. Bristow, "The Influence of Color on Visual Search Times in Cluttered Environments," *Journal of Marketing Communications 10* (2004): 183–193; J. A. Bellizzi and R. E. Hite, "Environmental Color, Consumer Feelings, and Purchase Likelihood," *Psychology and Marketing 9* (1992): 347–363.

72. Hall, *The Hidden Dimension*.

73. S. Li and Y. Li, "How Far Is Far Enough? A Measure of Information Privacy in Terms of Interpersonal Distance," *Environment and Behavior 39* (2007): 317–331; D. Matsumoto, "Culture and Nonverbal Behavior," in Manusov and Patterson, *The Sage Handbook of Nonverbal Communication*, 219–235; C. M. J. Beaulieu, "Intercultural Study of Personal Space: A Case Study," *Journal of Applied Social Psychology 34* (2004): 794–805; S. Li, "How Close Is Too Close? A Comparison of Proxemic Reactions of Singaporean Chinese to Male Intruders of Four Ethnicities," *Perceptual and Motor Skills 93* (2001): 124–126.

74. Burgoon and Dunbar, "Nonverbal Expressions of Dominance and Power in Human Relationships"; D. R. Carney, J. A. Hall, and L. Smith LeBeau, "Beliefs about the Nonverbal Expression of Social Power," *Journal of Nonverbal Behavior 29* (2005): 105–123; J. A. Hall, E. J. Coats, and L. Smith LeBeau, "Nonverbal Behavior and the Vertical Dimension of Social Relations: A Meta-Analysis," *Psychological Bulletin 131* (2005): 898–924; R. Sommer, "Studies in Personal Space," *Sociometry 22* (1959): 247–260.

75. J. A. Hall, "Women's and Men's Nonverbal Communication: Similarities, Differences, Stereotypes, and Origins," in Manusov and Patterson, *The Sage Handbook of Nonverbal Communication*, 201–218; N. M. Henley, "Body Politics," in *Self and Society: Blackwell Readers in Sociology*, edited by A. Branaman (Malden, MA: Blackwell, 2001), 288–297; J. A. Hall, *Nonverbal Sex Differences: Communication Accuracy and Expressive Style* (Baltimore: Johns Hopkins University Press, 1984).

76. S. M. Lyman and M. B. Scott, "Territoriality: A Neglected Sociological Dimension," in Guerrero, DeVito, and Hecht, *The Nonverbal Communication Reader*, 175–183.

77. A. L. S. Buslig, "'Stop' Signs: Regulating Privacy with Environmental Features," in Guerrero, DeVito, and Hecht, *The Nonverbal Communication Reader*, 241–249.

78. Ivy and Wahl, *The Nonverbal Self*; Knapp and Hall, *Nonverbal Communication in Human Interaction*.
79. Mehrabian, *Nonverbal Communication*. For applications of Mehrabian's immediacy principle to the instructional context, see N. F. Burroughs, "A Reinvestigation of the Relationship of Teacher Nonverbal Immediacy and Student Compliance-Resistance with Learning," *Communication Education 56* (2007): 453–475; Q. Zhang, "Teacher Immediacy and Classroom Communication Apprehension: A Cross-Cultural Investigation," *Journal of Intercultural Communication Research 34* (2005): 50–64; M.-J. Smythe and J. A. Hess, "Are Student Self-Reports a Valid Method for Measuring Teacher Nonverbal Immediacy?" *Communication Education 54* (2005): 170–179; S. D. Johnson and A. N. Miller, "A Cross-Cultural Study of Immediacy, Credibility, and Learning in the U.S. and Kenya," *Communication Education 51* (2002): 280–292; M. A. Jaasma and R. J. Koper, "Out-of-Class Communication between Female and Male Students and Faculty: The Relationship to Student Perceptions of Instructor Immediacy," *Women's Studies in Communication 25* (2002): 119–137; J. L. Chesebro and J. C. McCroskey, "The Relationship of Teacher Clarity and Immediacy with Student State Receiver Apprehension, Affect, and Cognitive Learning," *Communication Education 50* (2001): 59–68; P. L. Witt and L. R. Wheeless, "An Experimental Study of Teachers' Verbal and Nonverbal Immediacy and Students' Affective and Cognitive Learning," *Communication Education 50* (2001): 327–342.
80. Argyle, *Bodily Communication*.
81. Andersen, *Nonverbal Communication*.
82. K. McGinty, D. Knox, and M. E. Zusman, "Nonverbal and Verbal Communication in 'Involved' and 'Casual' Relationships among College Students," *College Student Journal 37* (2003): 68–71; C. C. Weisfeld and M. A. Stack, "When I Look into Your Eyes: An Ethological Analysis of Gender Differences in Married Couples' Nonverbal Behaviors," *Psychology, Evolution, and Gender 4* (2002): 125–147; B. Le Poire, A. Duggan, C. Shepard, and J. Burgoon, "Relational Messages Associated with Nonverbal Involvement, Pleasantness, and Expressiveness in Romantic Couples," *Communication Research Reports 19* (2002): 195–206.
83. M. Schmid Mast and J. A. Hall, "Who Is the Boss and Who Is Not? Accuracy of Judging Status," *Journal of Nonverbal Behavior 28* (2004): 145–165; M. Helweg-Larsen, S. J. Cunningham, A. Carrico, and A. M. Pergram, "To Nod or Not to Nod: An Observational Study of Nonverbal Communication and Status in Female and Male College Students," *Psychology of Women Quarterly 28* (2004): 358–361; L. Z. Tiedens and A. R. Fragale, "Power Moves: Complementarity in Dominant and Submissive Nonverbal Behavior," *Journal of Personality and Social Psychology 84* (2003): 558–568; H. Aguinis and C. A. Henle, "Effects of Nonverbal Behavior on Perceptions of a Female Employee's Power Bases." *Journal of Social Psychology 141* (2001): 537–549; J. A. Hall, L. S. LeBeau, J. G. Reinoso, and F. Thayer, "Status, Gender, and Nonverbal Behavior in Candid and Posed Photographs: A Study of Conversations between University Employees." *Sex Roles 44* (2001): 677–692; Mehrabian, *Nonverbal Communication*.

CHAPTER 5

1. L. Barker et al., "An Investigation of Proportional Time Spent in Various Communication Activities of College Students," *Journal of Applied Communication Research 8* (1981): 101–109.
2. J. Brownell, "Perceptions of Effective Listeners: A Management Study," *Journal of Business Communication* (Fall 1990): 401–415; D. A. Romig, *Side by Side Leadership* (Austin, TX: Bard, 2001).
3. For additional support for the importance of listening in interpersonal relationships, see L. Sparks, S. S. Travis, and S. R. Thompson, "Listening for the Communication Signals of Humor, Narratives, and Self-Disclosure in the Family Caregiver Interview," *Health & Social Work 30 (4)* (2005): 340–343; S. Wright, "The Beauty of Silence: Deep Listening Is a Key Nursing Skill That Can Be Learned with Practice," *Nursing Standard 20 (50)* (2006): 18–20.
4. P. Skaldeman, "Converging or Diverging Views of Self and Other: Judgment of Relationship Quality in Married and Divorced Couples," *Journal of Divorce & Remarriage 44* (2006): 145–160.
5. C. Jacobs and D. Coghlan, "Sound from Silence: On Listening in Organizational Learning," *Human Relations 58 (1)* (2005): 115–138.
6. Adapted from the International Listening Association's definition of *listening*, which may be found on their web site <http://www.listen.org>.
7. S. C. Bentley, "Listening in the 21st Century," *International Journal of Listening 14* (2000): 129–142; also see A. D. Wovin and C. G. Coakley, "Listening Education in the 21st Century," *International Journal of Listening 14* (2001): 143–152. For an excellent literature review of definitions and perspectives on defining listening, see S. Bentley, "Benchmarking Listening Behaviors: Is Effective Listening What the Speaker Says It Is?" *International Journal of Listening 11 (1)* (2008): 51–68.
8. D. Mount and A. Mattila, "Last Chance to Listen: Listening Behaviors and Their Effect on Call Center Satisfaction," *Journal of Hospitality & Tourism Research 26 (2)* (2002): 124–137.
9. Bentley, "Listening in the 21st Century"; also see Wovin and Coakley, "Listening Education in the 21st Century."
10. D. A. Schwartz, "Review Essay Listening Out of the Box: New Perspectives for the Workplace," *International Journal of Listening 18* (2004): 47–55.
11. A. Mulanx and W. G. Powers, "Listening Fidelity Development and Relationship to Receiver Apprehension and Locus of Control," *International Journal of Listening 17* (2003): 69–78.
12. W. L. Randall, S. M. Prior, and M. Skarborn, "How Listeners Shape What Tellers Tell: Patterns of Interaction in Lifestory Interviews and Their Impact on Reminiscence by Elderly Interviewees," *Journal of Aging Studies 20 (4)* (2006): 381–396.
13. K. W. Watson, L. L. Barker, and J. B. Weaver, *The Listener Style Inventory* (New Orleans: SPECTRA, 1995).
14. D. L. Worthington, "Exploring the Relationship between Listening Style Preference and Personality," *International Journal of Listening 17* (2003): 68–87; D. L. Worthington, "Exploring Juror's Listening Processes: The Effect of Listening Style Preference on Juror Decision Making, " *International Journal of Listening 17* (2003): 20–37.
15. M. D. Kirtley and J. M. Honeycutt, "Listening Styles and Their Correspondence with Second Guessing," *Communication Research Reports 13* (1996): 174–182.
16. J. B. Weaver III and M. Kirtley, "Listening Styles and Empathy," *Southern Communication Journal 60 (2)* (1995): 131–141.
17. G. D. Bodie and W. A. Villaume, "Aspects of Receiving Information: The Relationship between Listening Preferences, Communication Apprehension, Receiver Apprehension, and Communicator Style," *International Journal of Listening 17* (2003): 48–67.
18. Worthington, "Exploring the Relationship between Listening Style Preference and Personality."
19. Worthington, "Exploring Juror's Listening Processes."
20. S. L. Sargent and J. B. Weaver, "Correlates between Communication Apprehension and Listening Style Preferences," *Communication Research Reports 14* (1997): 74–78.
21. Sargent and Weaver, "Correlates between Communication Apprehension and Listening Style Preferences."
22. Bodie and Villaume, "Aspects of Receiving Information."
23. L. L. Barker and K. W. Watson, *Listen Up* (New York: St. Martin's Press: 2000); also see M. Imhof, "Who Are We as We Listen? Individual Listening Profiles in Varying Contexts," *International Journal of Listening 18* (2004): 36–45.
24. Imhof, "Who Are We as We Listen?"
25. C. Y. Cheng, "Chinese Philosophy and Contemporary Communication Theory," in *Communication Theory: Eastern and Western Perspectives*, edited by D. L. Kincaid (New York: Academic Press, 1987).
26. T. S. Lebra, *Japanese Patterns of Behavior* (Honolulu: University Press of Hawaii, 1976).
27. A. Yugi (trans. N. Chung), *Ilbon-in ye usik koo-jo (Japanese Thought Patterns)* (Seoul: Baik Yang Publishing Co. [in Korean], 1984).
28. J. O. Yum, "The Impact of Confucianism on Interpersonal Relationships and Communication Patterns in East Asia," in *Intercultural Communication: A Reader*, edited by L. A. Samovar and R. E. Porter (Belmont, CA: Wadsworth, 2000), 86.
29. W. Winter, A. J. Ferreira, and N. Bowers, "Decision-Making in Married and Unrelated Couples," *Family Process 12* (1973): 83–94.
30. R. Montgomery, *Listening Made Easy* (New York: AMACOM, 1981); also see O. Hargie, C. Sanders, and D. Dickson, *Social Skills in Interpersonal Communication* (London: Routledge, 1994); O. Hargie, ed., *The Handbook of Communication Skills* (London: Routledge, 1997).

31. R. G. Owens, "Handling Strong Emotions," in *The Handbook of Communication Skills*, edited by O. Hargie (London: Croom Helm/New York University Press, 1986).
32. D. Goleman, *Emotional Intelligence: Why It Can Matter More than IQ* (New York: Bantam Books, 1995); also see D. Goleman, "Emotional Intelligence: Issues in Paradigm Building," in *The Emotionally Intelligent Workplace*, edited by C. Cherniss and D. Goleman (San Francisco: Jossey Bass, 2001), 13.
33. J. L. Gonzalez-Balado, ed., *Mother Teresa: In My Own Words* (New York: Gramercy Books, 1997).
34. R. G. Nichols, "Factors in Listening Comprehension," *Speech Monographs* 15 (1948): 154–163; G. M. Goldhaber and C. H. Weaver, "Listener Comprehension of Compressed Speech When the Difficulty, Rate of Presentation, and Sex of the Listener Are Varied," *Speech Monographs* 35 (1968): 20–25.
35. M. Fitch-Hauser, D. A. Barker, and A. Hughes, "Receiver Apprehension and Listening Comprehension: A Linear or Curvilinear Relationship?" *Southern Communication Journal* (1988): 62–71; P. E. King and R. R. Behnke, "Patterns of State Anxiety in Listening Performance," *Southern Communication Journal* 70 (1) (2004): 72–81.
36. Fitch-Hauser et al., "Receiver Apprehension and Listening Comprehension."
37. K. Watson, L. Barker, and J. Weaver, "The Listening Styles Profile (LPP16): Development and Validation of an Instrument to Assess Four Listening Styles," *Journal of the International Listening Association* (1995), research cited on *20/20*, ABC television network, September 1998.
38. Imhof, "Who Are We as We Listen?"
39. A. Carruthers, "Listening, Hearing and Changing," *Business Communicator* 5 (2004): 3.
40. K. K. Halone and L. L. Pecchioni, "Relational Listening: A Grounded Theoretical Model," *Communication Reports* 14 (2001): 59–71.
41. I. W. Johnson, C. G. Pearce, T. L. Tuten, and L. Sinclair, "Self-Imposed Silence and Perceived Listening Effectiveness," *Business Communication Quarterly* 66 (2003): 23–45.
42. M. V. Redmond, "The Functions of Empathy (Decentering) in Human Relations," *Human Relations* 42 (1993): 593–606.
43. A. Mehrabian, *Nonverbal Communication* (Chicago: Aldine Atherton, 1970); A. Mehrabian, *Silent Messages* (Belmont, CA: Wadsworth, 1981); also see D. Lapakko, "Three Cheers for Language: A Closer Examination of a Widely Cited Study of Nonverbal Communication," *Communication Education* 46 (1997): 63–67.
44. M. Argyle and M. Cook, *Gaze and Mutual Gaze* (Cambridge, MA: Cambridge University Press, 1976).
45. Hargie et al., *Social Skills in Interpersonal Communication*; Hargie, *The Handbook of Communication Skills*.
46. For a review of the literature on gender, listening, and communication, see D. K. Ivy and P. Backlund, *GenderSpeak* (New York: McGraw-Hill, 2005).
47. S. L. Sargent and J. B. Weaver, "Listening Styles," *International Journal of Listening* 17 (2003): 5–18.
48. C. G. Pearce, I. W. Johnson, and R. T. Barker, "Assessment of the Listening Styles Inventory," *Journal of Business & Technical Communication* 17 (2003): 84–113.
49. M. K. Johnston, J. B. Weaver, K. W. Watson, and L. L. Barker, "Listening Styles: Biological or Psychological Differences?" *International Journal of Listening* 14 (2000): 32–46.
50. J. Silverman, "Attentional Styles and the Study of Sex Differences," in *Attention: Contemporary Theory and Analysis*, edited by D. I. Mostofsky (New York: Appleton-Century-Crofts, 1970), 61–79.
51. See R. G. Nichols and L. A. Stevens, "Listening to People," *Harvard Business Review* 35 (September–October 1957): 85–92.
52. K. McComb and F. M. Jablin, "Verbal Correlates of Interviewer Empathic Listening and Employment Interview Outcomes," *Communication Monographs* 51 (1984): 353–371.
53. A. Clark, "Communication Confidence and Listening Competence: An Investigation of the Relationships of Willingness to Communicate, Communication Apprehension, and Receiver Apprehension to Comprehension of Content and Emotional Meaning in Spoken Messages," *Communication Education* 38 (1989): 237–248.
54. Halone and Pecchioni, "Relational Listening: A Grounded Theoretical Model."
55. Pearce et al., "Assessment of the Listening Styles Inventory."
56. Pearce et al., "Assessment of the Listening Styles Inventory."
57. Jacobs and Coghlan, "Sound From Silence."
58. E.-A. Doohan, "Listening Behaviors of Married Couples: An Exploration of Nonverbal Presentation to a Relational Insider," *International Journal of Listening* 21 (1) (2007): 24–41.
59. For a classic discussion of empathy and interpretive listening, see J. Stewart, "Interpretive Listening: An Alternative to Empathy," *Communication Education* 32 (1983): 379–391; R. Bommelje, J. M. Houston, and R. Smither, "Personality Characteristics of Effective Listeners: A Five Factor Perspective," *International Journal of Listening* 17 (2003): 32–46; J. Hakansson and H. Montomery, "Empathy as an Interpersonal Phenomenon," *Journal of Social and Personal Relationships* 20 (2003): 267–284.
60. Weaver and Kirtley, "Listening Styles and Empathy."
61. P. Toller, "Learning to Listen, Learning to Hear: A Training Approach," *Time to Listen to Children: Personal and Professional Communication*, edited by C. Birgit (Florence, KY: Taylor, Frances/Routledge, 1999), pp. 48–61; T. Drollinger, L. B. Comer, and P. T. Warrington, "Development and Validation of the Active Empathetic Listening Scale," *Psychology & Marketing* 23 (2) (2006): 161–180; S. L. Do and D. L. Schallert, "Emotions and Classroom Talk: Toward a Model of the Role of Affect in Students' Experiences of Classroom Discussions," *Journal of Educational Psychology* 96 (4) (2004): 619–634.
62. Goleman, "Emotional Intelligence."
63. A. De Saint-Exupery, as quoted in Goleman, "Emotional Intelligence."
64. C. R. Rogers, "Empathic: An Unappreciated Way of Being," in *A Way of Being* (Boston: Houghton Mifflin, 1980), 137–163.
65. H. J. M. Nouwen, "Listening as Spiritual Hospitality," in *Bread for the Journey* (New York: HarperCollins, 1997).
66. J. C. McCroskey and M. J. Beatty, "The Communibiological Perspective: Implications for Communication in Instruction," *Communication Education* 49 (2000): 1–6; M. J. Beatty and J. C. McCroskey, "Theory, Scientific Evidence and the Communibiological Paradigm: Reflections on Misguided Criticism," *Communication Education* 49 (2001): 36–44.
67. D. F. Barone, P. S. Hutchings, H. J. Kimmel, H. L. Traub, J. T. Cooper, and C. M. Marshall, "Increasing Empathic Accuracy through Practice and Feedback in a Clinical Interviewing Course," *Journal of Social and Clinical Psychology* 24 (2005): 156–171.
68. Goleman, "Emotional Intelligence."
69. Hargie et al., *Social Skills in Interpersonal Communication*; R. Boulton, *People Skills* (New York: 1981). We also acknowledge others who have presented excellent applications of listening and responding skills in interpersonal and group contexts: D. A. Romig and L. J. Romig, *Structured Teamwork* (D Guide) (Austin, TX: Performance Resources, 1990); S. Deep and L. Sussman, *Smart Moves* (Reading, MA: Addison-Wesley, 1990); P. R. Scholtes, *The Team Handbook* (Madison, WI: Joiner Associates, 1988); Hargie, *The Handbook of Communication Skills*.
70. R. Lemieux and M. R. Tighe, "Attachment Styles and the Evaluation of Comforting Responses: A Receiver Perspective," *Communication Research Reports* 21 (2004): 144–153; also see W. Samter, "How Gender and Cognitive Complexity Influence the Provision of Emotional Support: A Study of Indirect Effects," *Communication Reports* 15 (2002): 5–16.
71. Our discussion of appropriate and inappropriate social support responses is taken from B. D. Burleson, "Emotional Support Skill," in *Handbook of Communication and Social Interaction Skills*, edited by J. O. Greene and B. R. Burleson (Mahwah, NJ: Lawrence Erlbaum, 2003), 566–568.
72. L. B. Comer and T. Drollinger, "Active Empathic Listening and Selling Success: A Conceptual Framework," *Journal of Personal Selling & Sales Management* 19 (1999): 15–29; S. B. Castleberry, C. D. Shepherd, and R. Ridnour, "Effective Interpersonal Listening in the Personal Selling Environment: Conceptualization, Measurement, and Nomological Validity," *Journal of Marketing Theory and Practice* (Winter 1999): 30–38.
73. F. C. B. Hansen, H. Resnick, and J. Galea, "Better Listening: Paraphrasing and Perception Checking—A Study of the Effectiveness of a Multimedia Skills Training Program," *Journal of Technology in Human Services* 20 (2002): 317–331.

CHAPTER 6

1. Research documents several culture-based differences in communication, including approaches to leadership, deception, and conflict management styles. See N. Ensari and S. E. Murphy, "Cross-Cultural Variations in Leadership Perceptions and Attribution of Charisma to the Leader," *Organizational Behavior and Human Decision Processes 92* (2003): 52–66; M. K. Lapinski and T. R. Levine, "Culture and Information Manipulation Theory: The Effects of Self-Construal and Locus of Benefit on Information Manipulation," *Communication Studies 5* (2000): 55–73; D. Cai and E. L. Fink, "Conflict Style Differences between Individualists and Collectivists," *Communication Monographs 69* (2002): 67–87.
2. M.-S. Kim and A. S. Ebesu Hubbard, "Intercultural Communication in the Global Village: How to Understand 'The Other,'" *Journal of Intercultural Communication Research 36* (3) (2007): 223–235.
3. J. Gray, *Men Are from Mars, Women Are from Venus* (New York: HarperCollins, 1992).
4. D. K. Ivy and P. Backlund, *GenderSpeak: Personal Effectiveness in Gender Communication* 3e (New York: McGraw Hill, 2004); D. J. Canary and T. R. Emmers-Sommer, *Sex and Gender Differences in Personal Relationships* (New York: Guilford, 1997).
5. D. Tannen, *You Just Don't Understand* (New York: William Morrow, 1990).
6. A. C. Selbe, *Are You from Another Planet or What?* Workshop presented at the Joint Service Family Readiness Matters Conference, Phoenix, AZ, July 1999.
7. R. B. Rubin, E. M. Perse, and C. A. Barbato, "Conceptualization and Measurement of Interpersonal Communication Motives," *Human Communication Research 14* (1988): 602–628; D. Tannen, *That's Not What I Meant!* (London: Dent, 1986).
8. T. Mottet, "The Role of Sexual Orientation in Predicting Outcome Value and Anticipated Communication Behaviors," *Communication Quarterly 43* (Summer 2000): 223–239.
9. G. M. Herek, "Heterosexuals' Attitudes toward Lesbian and Gay Men; Correlates and Gender Differences," *Journal of Sex Research 25* (1988): 451–477.
10. G. M. Herek, "Heterosexuals' Attitudes toward Lesbian and Gay Men"; M. S. Weinberg and C. J. Williams, *Male Homosexuals: Their Problems and Adaptations* (New York: Free Press, 1974); Mottet, "The Role of Sexual Orientation in Predicting Outcome Value and Anticipated Communication Behaviors."
11. APAStyle.org, "Removing Bias in Language; Sexuality," March 2006, <www.apastyle.org/sexuality.html>.
12. *Random House Webster's Unabridged Dictionary* (New York: Random House, 1998), 1590.
13. R. Lewontin, "The Apportionment of Human Diversity," *Evolutionary Biology 6* (1973): 381–397.
14. D. Matsumoto and L. Juang, *Culture and Psychology* (Belmont, CA: Wadsworth/Thomson, 2004), 16.; also see H. A. Yee, H. H. Fairchild, F. Weizmann, and E. G. Wyatt, "Addressing Psychology's Problems with Race," *American Psychologist 48* (1994): 1132–1140.
15. B. J. Allen, *Differences Matter: Communicating Social Identity* (Long Grove, IL: Waveland Press, 2004).
16. Allen, *Differences Matter*.
17. Matsumoto and Juang, *Culture and Psychology*, 80–81.
18. A. Williams and P. Garrett, "Communication Evaluations across the Life Span: From Adolescent Storm and Stress to Elder Aches and Pains," *Journal of Language and Social Psychology 21* (June 2002): 101–126; also see D. Cai, H. Giles, and K. Noels, "Elderly Perceptions of Communication with Older and Younger Adults in China: Implications for Mental Health," *Journal of Applied Communication Research 26* (1998): 32–51.
19. J. Montepare, E. Koff, D. Zaitchik, and M. Albert, "The Use of Body Movements and Gestures as Cues to Emotions in Younger and Older Adults," *Journal of Nonverbal Behavior 23* (Summer 1999): 133–152.
20. J. Harwood, E. B. Ryan, H. Giles, and S. Tysoski, "Evaluations of Patronizing Speech and Three Response Styles in a Non-Service-Providing Context," *Journal of Applied Communication Research 25* (1997): 170–195.
21. C. Segrin, "Age Moderates the Relationship between Social Support and Psychosocial Problems," paper presented at the International Communication Association, San Diego, California (2003).
22. N. Howe and W. Strauss, *Millennials Rising: The Next Great Generation* (New York: Vintage Books, 2000).
23. Howe and Strauss, *Millennials Rising*.
24. Information summarized from Howe and Strauss, *Millennials Rising*.
25. Our discussion of generational differences and communication is also based on J. Smith, "The Millennials Are Coming," workshop presented at Texas State University, San Marcos, TX (2006).
26. Howe and Strauss, *Millennials Rising*; H. Karp, C. Fuller, and D. Sirias, *Bridging the Boomer–Xer Gap: Creating Authentic Teams for High Performance at Work* (Palo Alto, CA: Davies-Black Publishing, 2002).
27. A. Molinsky, "Cross-Cultural Code-Switching: The Psychological Challenges of Adapting Behavior in Foreign Cultural Interactions," *Academy of Management Review 32* (2) (2007): 622–640.
28. S. Roberts, *Who We Are Now: The Changing Face of America in the Twenty-First Century* (New York: Henry Holt, 2004).
29. Adapted from *Information Please Almanac* (Boston: Houghton Mifflin, 1990) and *World Almanac and Book of Facts* (New York: World Almanac, 1991), as cited by Lustig and Koester, *Intercultural Competence*, 11.
30. M. E. Ryan, "Another Way to Teach Migrant Students," *Los Angeles Times* (March 31, 1991): B20, as cited by M. W. Lustig and J. Koester, *Intercultural Competence: Interpersonal Communication across Cultures* (New York: HarperCollins, 1999), 11.
31. Robert Bernstein, press release, Public Information Office, U.S. Census Bureau, <http://www.census.gov/Press-Release/www/releases/archives/population/010048.html>, retrieved May 26, 2008.
32. G. Chen and W. J. Starosta, "A Review of the Concept of Intercultural Sensitivity," *Human Communication 1* (1997): 7.
33. Lustig and Koester, *Intercultural Competence*.
34. *Newsweek* (July 12, 1999): 51.
35. Bernstein, press release.
36. U.S. Census Bureau Report 1999, as reported in R. E. Schmid, *Austin-American Statesman* (September 17, 1999): A20.
37. "One Nation, One Language?" *U.S. News & World Report* (September 25, 1995): 40, as cited by Lustig and Koester, *Intercultural Competence*, 10.
38. Bernstein, press release.
39. Roberts, *Who We Are Now*, 122; A. Caldwell, "Census: More than Half of Texans Are Minorities," *Austin-American Statesman* (August 11, 2005): 1B.
40. Roberts, *Who We Are Now*, 126.
41. Bernstein, press release.
42. Los Angeles Almanac, <http://www.laalmanac.com/population/po55.htm>, retrieved May 26, 2008.
43. Yankelovich, Inc., 2003, "Beyond the Boomers: Millennials and Generation X," <http://resources.ketchum.com/web/boomers.pdf>, retrieved May 26, 2008.
44. T. Friedman, *The World Is Flat: A Brief History of the Twenty-First Century* (New York: Farrar, Straus and Giroux, 2005).
45. A. G. Smith, ed., *Communication and Culture* (New York: Holt, Rinehart & Winston, 1966).
46. E. T. Hall, *Beyond Culture* (Garden City, NY: Doubleday, 1976).
47. For example, see A. V. Matveeve and P. E. Nelson, "Cross Cultural Competence and Multicultural Team Performance: Perceptions of American and Russian Managers," *International Journal of Cross Cultural Management 4* (2004): 253–270.
48. G. Hofstede, *Culture's Consequences: International Differences in Work-Related Values* (Beverly Hills: Sage, 1980); G. Hofstede, *Cultures and Organizations: Software of the Mind* (London: McGraw-Hill, 1991).
49. H. J. Ladegaard, "Global Culture—Myth or Reality? Perceptions of 'National Cultures' in Global Corporation," *Journal of Intercultural Communication Research 36* (2) (2007): 139–163; also see T. R. Levine, H. S. Park, and R. K. Kim, "Some Conceptual and Theoretical Challenges for Cross-Cultural Communication Research in the 21st Century," *Journal of Intercultural Communication Research 36* (3) (2007): 205–221.
50. See J. B. Walther, "Interpersonal Effects in Computer-Mediated Interaction: A Relational Perspective," *Communication Research 19* (1992): 52–90; J. B. Walther, "Relational Aspects of Computer-Mediated Communication: Experimental and Longitudinal Observations," *Organizational Science 6* (1995): 186–203; J. B. Walther, J. F. Ander-

son, and D. Park, "Interpersonal Effects in Computer-Mediated Interaction: A Meta-Analysis of Social and Anti-Social Communication," *Communication Research 21* (1994): 460–487.

51. For an excellent overview of issues in teaching intercultural communication, see Levine, Park, and Kim, "Some Conceptual and Theoretical Challenges for Cross-Cultural Communication Research in the 21st Century."

52. C. Ward, S. Bochner, and A. Furnham, *The Psychology of Culture Shock* (Hove, England: Routledge, 2001).

53. For an excellent discussion of worldview and its implications for intercultural communication, see C. H. Dodd, *Dynamics of Intercultural Communication* (New York: McGraw Hill, 1998).

54. Hall, *Beyond Culture*.

55. L. A. Samovar, R. E. Porter, and L. A. Stefani, *Communication between Cultures* (Belmont, CA: Wadsworth, 1998).

56. Hofstede, *Culture's Consequences*; G. Hofstede and G. J. Hofstede, *Cultures and Organizations: Software of the Mind* 2e (New York: McGraw-Hill, 2005).

57. For research about the impact of individualistic and collectivistic cultural values on communication and conflict management, see R. Kaushal and C. T. Kwantes, "The Role of Culture and Personality in Choice of Conflict Management Strategy," *International Journal of Intercultural Relations 30* (2006): 579–603.

58. H. C. Triandis, "The Many Dimensions of Culture," *Academy of Management Executive 18* (2004): 88–93.

59. M. Voronov and J. A. Singer, "The Myth of Individualism-Collectivism: A Critical Review," *Journal of Social Psychology 142* (2002): 461–480.

60. For an excellent review of Hofstede's work, see J. W. Bing, "Hofstede's Consequences: The Impact of His Work on Consulting and Business Practices," *Academy of Management Executive 18* (2004): 80–87.

61. Hofstede, *Culture's Consequences*; Hofstede, *Cultures and Organizations*.

62. W. B. Gudykunst, *Bridging Differences: Effective Intergroup Communication* (Newbury Park, CA: Sage, 1998).

63. Hofstede, *Culture's Consequences*; Hofstede, *Cultures and Organizations*.

64. Hofstede, *Culture's Consequences*; Hofstede, *Cultures and Organizations*.

65. Hofstede, *Culture's Consequences*; Hofstede, *Cultures and Organizations*.

66. G. Hofstede, "Cultural Dimensions in Management and Planning," *Asia Pacific Journal of Management* (January 1984): 81–98; Hofstede, *Cultures and Organizations*.

67. For a discussion of long- and short-term oriented national cultures, see Hofstede and Hofstede, *Cultures and Organizations*, 210–238.

68. Hofstede and Hofstede, *Cultures and Organizations*.

69. See L. Davis, "Domestic Violence," in *Encyclopedia of Social Work*, vol. 1 (Washington, DC: National Association of Social Work, 2008): 780–789; Federal Bureau of Investigation, *Violence against Women: Estimates from the Redesigned Survey*, August 1995 <http://www.ojp.usdoj.gov>; L. K. Hamberger, D. G. Saunders, and M. Hovey, "The Prevalence of Domestic Violence in Community Practice and Rate of Physician Inquiry," *Family Medicine 24* (1992): 283–287; Women's Action Coalition, *WAC Stats: The Facts about Women* (New York: The New Press, 1993).

70. J. W. Neuliep, "Assessing the Reliability and Validity of the Generalized Ethnocentrism Scale," *Journal of Intercultural Communication Research 31* (2002): 201–215. For additional research on the role of ethnocentrism in communication, see Y. Lin, A. Rancer, and A. Sunhee Lim, "Ethnocentrism and Intercultural Willingness to Communicate: A Cross-Cultural Comparison between Korean and American College Students," *Journal of Intercultural Communication Research 32* (2003).

71. See Ensari and Murphy, "Cross-Cultural Variations in Leadership Perceptions and Attribution of Charisma to the Leader"; Lapinski and Levine, "Culture and Information Manipulation Theory"; Cai and Fink, "Conflict Style Differences between Individualists and Collectivists."

72. C. Kluckhohn and S. Murray, 1953, as quoted by J. S. Caputo, H. C. Hazel, and C. McMahon, *Interpersonal Communication* (Boston: Allyn & Bacon, 1994), 304.

73. Y. Kashima, E. S. Kashima, U. Kim, and M. Gelfand, "Describing the Social World: How Is a Person, a Group, and a Relationship Described in the East and in the West?" *Journal of Experimental Social Psychology 42* (2006): 388–396.

74. D. E. Brown, "Human Universals and Their Implications," in *Being Humans: Anthropological Universality and Particularity in Transdisciplinary Perspectives*, edited by N. Roughley (New York: Walter de Gruyter, 2000). For an applied discussion of these universals, see S. Pinker, *The Blank Slate: The Modern Denial of Human Nature* (London: Penguin Books, 2002).

75. D. W. Kale, "Ethics in Intercultural Communication," in *Intercultural Communication: A Reader* 6e, edited by L. A. Samovar and R. E. Porter (Belmont, CA: Wadsworth, 1991).

76. L. A. Samovar and R. E. Porter, *Communication between Cultures* (Stamford, CT: Wadsworth and Thomson Learning, 2001), 29.

77. C. S. Lewis, *The Abolition of Man* (New York: Macmillan Publishing Company, 1944).

78. M. Gladwell, *Blink: The Power of Thinking without Thinking* (New York: Little Brown, 2005).

79. S. Kamekar, M. B. Kolsawalla, and T. Mazareth, "Occupational Prestige as a Function of Occupant's Gender," *Journal of Applied Social Psychology 19* (1988): 681–688.

80. Eleanor Roosevelt, as cited by Lustig and Koester, *Intercultural Competence*.

81. S. Ting-Toomey, "Intercultural Conflict Training: Theory-Practice Approaches and Research Challenges," *Journal of Intercultural Communication Research 36* (3) (2007): 255–271.

82. M. R. Hammer, M. J. Bennett, and R. Wiseman, "Measuring Intercultural Sensitivity: The Intercultural Development Inventory," *International Journal of Intercultural Relations 27* (2003): 422.

83. Hammer, Bennett, and Wiseman, "Measuring Intercultural Sensitivity," 421–443.

84. For additional research about the validity of measuring intercultural adaptation, see J. F. Greenholtz, "Does Intercultural Sensitivity Cross Cultures? Validity Issues in Porting Instruments across Languages and Cultures," *International Journal of Intercultural Relations 29* (2005): 73–89.

85. A. N. Miller and J. A. Samp, "Planning Intercultural Interaction: Extending Anxiety/Uncertainty Management Theory," *Communication Research Reports 24* (2) (2007): 87–95.

86. W. B. Gudykunst and Y. Kim, *Communicating with Strangers* (New York: Random House, 1984); Gudykunst, *Bridging Differences*.

87. Miller and Samp, "Planning Intercultural Interaction."

88. For a classic discussion of egocentrism and ethnocentrism, see T. W. Adorno, E. Frenkel-Brunswik, D. J. Levinson, and R. N. Sanford, *The Authoritarian Personality* (New York: Harper & Brothers, 1950).

89. Neuliep, "Assessing the Reliability and Validity of the Generalized Ethnocentrism Scale"; Lin, "Ethnocentrism and Intercultural Willingness to Communicate."

90. S. DeTurk, "Intercultural Empathy: Myth, Competency, or Possibility for Alliance Building?" *Communication Education 50* (2001): 374–384.

91. S. Glazer, "Social Support across Cultures," *International Journal of Intercultural Relations 30* (2006): 605–622.

92. M. V. Redmond, "The Functions of Empathy (Decentering) in Human Relations," *Human Relations 42* (1993): 593–606; also see M. V. Redmond, "A Multidimensional Theory and Measure of Social Decentering," *Journal of Research in Personality* (1995); for an excellent discussion of the role of emotions in establishing empathy, see D. Goleman, *Emotional Intelligence* (New York: Bantam, 1995).

93. See B. J. Broome, "Building Shared Meaning: Implications of a Relational Approach to Empathy for Teaching Intercultural Communication," *Communication Education 40* (1991): 235–249. Much of this discussion is based on the treatment of social decentering and empathy in S. A. Beebe, S. J. Beebe, and M. V. Redmond, *Interpersonal Communication: Relating to Others* 4e (Boston: Allyn & Bacon, 2005).

94. For an excellent discussion of empathy as it relates to intercultural communication, see D. W. Augsburger, *Pastoral Counseling Across Cultures* (Philadelphia: The Westminster Press, 1986), 28–30.

95. H. J. M. Nouwen, *Bread for the Journey* (New York: HarperCollins, 1997).

96. Molinsky, "Cross-Cultural Code-Switching."

97. S. M. Fowler, "Training across Cultures: What Intercultural Trainers Bring to Diversity Training," *International Journal of Intercultural Relations 30* (2006): 401–411.

98. L. J. Carrell, "Diversity in the Communication Curriculum: Impact on Student Empathy," *Communication Education 46* (1997): 234–244.

99. Ting-Toomey, "Intercultural Conflict Training"; D. F. Barone, P. S.

Hutchings, H. J. Kimmel, H. L. Traub, J. T. Cooper, and C. M. Marshall, "Increasing Empathic Accuracy through Practice and Feedback in a Clinical Interviewing Course," *Journal of Social and Clinical Psychology* 24 (2005): 156–171.
100. R. H. Farrell, ed., *Off the Record: The Private Papers of Harry S Truman* (New York: Harper & Row, 1980), 310.

CHAPTER 7

1. E. A. Konijn, S. Utz, M. Tanis, and S. B. Barnes, *Mediated Interpersonal Communication* (New York: Routledge, 2008); S. B. Barnes, *Computer-Mediated Communication: Human-to-Human Communication across the Internet* (Boston: Pearson, 2003); L. C. Tidwell and J. B. Walther, "Computer-Mediated Communication Effects on Disclosure, Impressions, and Interpersonal Evaluations: Getting to Know One Another a Bit at a Time," *Human Communication Research* 28 (2002): 317–348; J. B. Walther, C. L. Slovacek, and L. C. Tidwell, "Is a Picture Worth a Thousand Words? Photographic Images in Long-Term and Short-Term Computer-Mediated Communication," *Communication Research* 28 (2001): 105–134; J. T. Hancock and P. J. Dunham, "Impression Formation in Computer-Mediated Communication Revisited: An Analysis of the Breadth and Intensity of Impressions," *Communication Research* 28 (2001): 325–347.
2. K. M. Galvin and C. Wilkinson, "The Communication Process: Impersonal and Interpersonal," in *Making Connections: Readings in Relational Communication* 4e, edited by K. M. Galvin and P. Cooper (Los Angeles, CA: Roxbury, 2006): 4–10.
3. Y. Abraham, "Aspiring Doctors Have a New Exam to Pass: Bedside Manner 101," *Corpus Christi Caller Times* (July 20, 2003): A14; J. Small and J. Mulry, *Improving Your Bedside Manner: A Handbook for Physicians to Develop Therapeutic Conversations with Their Patients* (Austin, TX: Eupsychian Press, 2008).
4. E. Berscheid, "Interpersonal Attraction," in *The Handbook of Social Psychology*, edited by G. Lindzey and E. Aronson (New York: Random House, 1985), 413–484, as reported in J. A. Simpson and B. A. Harris, "Interpersonal Attraction," in *Perspectives on Close Relationships*, edited by A. L. Weber and J. H. Harvey (Boston: Allyn & Bacon, 1994), 45–66.
5. W. Stoebe, "Self-Esteem and Interpersonal Attraction," in *Theory and Practice in Interpersonal Attraction*, edited by S. Duck (London: Academic Press, 1977).
6. D. M. Amodio and C. J. Showers, "'Similarity Breeds Liking' Revisited: The Moderating Role of Commitment," *Journal of Social and Personal Relationships* 22 (2005): 817–836.
7. L. K. Guerrero, P. A. Andersen, and W. A. Afifi, *Close Encounters: Communicating in Relationships* 2e (Thousand Oaks, CA: Sage, 2007); D. Byrne, "An Overview (and Underview) of Research and Theory within the Attraction Paradigm," in *Understanding Research in Personal Relationships: A Text with Readings*, edited by W. Dragon and S. Duck (Thousand Oaks, CA: Sage, 2005), 14–26; S. Sprecher and S. Duck, "Sweet Talk: The Importance of Perceived Communication for Romantic and Friendship Attraction Experienced during a Get-Acquainted Date," in Dragon and Duck, *Understanding Research in Personal Relationships*, 26–36; A. Feingold, "Sex Differences in the Effects of Similarity and Physical Attractiveness on Opposite-Sex Attraction," *Basic and Applied Social Psychology* 12 (1991): 357–367; V. Sharma and T. Kaur, "Interpersonal Attraction in Relation to Similarity and Help," *Psychological Studies* 39 (1995): 84–87; T. Shaikh and S. Kanakar, "Attitudinal Similarity and Affiliation Need as Determinants of Interpersonal Attraction," *Journal of Social Psychology* 134 (1994): 257–259; R. Miller, D. Perlman, and S.S. Brehm, *Intimate Relationships* 4e (New York: McGraw-Hill, 2006); M. Sunnafrank, "Interpersonal Attraction and Attitude Similarity: A Communication-Based Assessment," in *Communication Yearbook 14*, edited by J. A. Andersen (Newbury Park, CA: Sage, 1991): 451–483; J. E. Lydon, D. W. Jamieson, and M. Zanna, "Interpersonal Similarity and the Social and Intellectual Dimensions of First Impressions," *Social Cognition* 6 (1988): 269–286.
8. K. Y. A. McKenna, A. S. Green, and M. E. J. Gleason, "Relationship Formation on the Internet: What's the Big Attraction?" *Journal of Social Issues* 58 (2002): 9–31.
9. B. R. Burleson, A. W. Kunkel, and J. D. Birch, "Thoughts about Talk in Romantic Relationships: Similarity Makes for Attraction (and Happiness, Too)," *Communication Quarterly* 42 (1994): 259–273.
10. M. T. Whitty and J. K. Gavin, "Age/Sex/Location: Uncovering the Social Cues in the Development of On-Line Relationships," *Cyberpsychology and Behavior* 4 (2001): 623–630.
11. D. K. Ivy and S. T. Wahl, *The Nonverbal Self: Communication for a Lifetime* (Boston: Allyn & Bacon, 2009); L. K. Guerrero and K. Floyd, *Nonverbal Communication in Close Relationships* (Mahwah, NJ: Lawrence Erlbaum, 2006); J. H. Harvey and A. L. Weber, *Odyssey of the Heart: Close Relationships in the 21st Century* 2e (Mahwah, NJ: Lawrence Erlbaum, 2002).
12. M. T. Whitty, "Cyber-Flirting: An Examination of Men's and Women's Flirting Behavior Both Offline and on the Internet," *Behavior Change* 21 (2004): 115–126; M. T. Whitty, "Cyber-Flirting: Playing at Love on the Internet," *Theory & Psychology* 13 (2003): 339–357; M. T. Whitty and A. N. Carr, "Cyberspace as Potential Space: Considering the Web as a Playground to Cyber-Flirt," *Human Relations* 56 (2003): 861–891; J. A. McCown, D. Fisher, R. Page, and M. Homant, "Internet Relationships: People Who Meet People," *Cyberpsychology & Behavior 4* (2001): 593–596; A. Cooper and L. Sportolari, "Romance in Cyberspace: Understanding Online Attraction," *Journal of Sex Education and Therapy* 22 (1997): 7–14; McKenna, "Relationship Formation on the Internet."
13. A. Cooper, I. P. McLoughlin, and K. M. Campbell, "Sexuality in Cyberspace: Update for the 21st Century," *Cyberpsychology & Behavior* 32 (2000): 521–536.
14. Guerrero et al., *Close Encounters*, 44.
15. D. Singh, "Mating Strategies of Young Women: Role of Physical Attractiveness," *Journal of Sex Research* 41 (2004): 43–54; A. Furnham, A. McClelland, and L. Omer, "A Cross-Cultural Comparison of Ratings of Perceived Fecundity and Sexual Attractiveness as a Function of Body Weight and Waist-to-Hip Ratio," *Psychology, Health & Medicine* 8 (2003): 219–230; M. R. Cunningham, A. R. Roberts, A. P. Barbee, P. B. Druen, and C. Wu, "'Their Ideas of Beauty Are, on the Whole, the Same as Ours': Consistency and Variability in the Cross-Cultural Perception of Female Physical Attractiveness," *Journal of Personality and Social Psychology* 68 (1995): 261–279.
16. M. Krcmar, S. Giles, and D. Helme, "Understanding the Process: How Mediated and Peer Norms Affect Young Women's Body Esteem," *Communication Quarterly* 56 (2008): 111–130; C. Heldman, "Out-of-Body Image," *Ms.* (Spring, 2008), 52–55; H. Dohnt and M. Tiggemann, "The Contribution of Peer and Media Influences to the Development of Body Satisfaction and Self-Esteem in Young Girls: A Prospective Study," *Developmental Psychology* 42 (2006): 929–936; S. Steese, M. Dollette, W. Phillips, E. Hossfeld, G. Matthews, and G. Taormina, "Understanding Girls' Circle as an Intervention on Perceived Social Support, Body Image, Self-Efficacy, Locus of Control, and Self-Esteem," *Adolescence* 41 (2006): 55–74; P. Koch, P. Mansfield, D. Thurau, and M. Carey, "'Feeling Frumpy': The Relationships between Body Image and Sexual Response Changes in Midlife Women," *Journal of Sex Research* 42 (2005): 215–223; A. Botta, "Television Images and Adolescent Girls' Body Image Disturbance," *Journal of Communication* 49 (1999): 22–37; M. Wiederman and S. R. Hurst, "Body Size, Physical Attractiveness, and Body Image among Young Adult Women: Relationships to Sexual Experience and Sexual Esteem," *Journal of Sex Research* 35 (1998): 272–281.
17. D. Crary, "40 Years after Ruling, Interracial Marriage Growing," *Corpus Christi Caller Times* (April 15, 2007): 21A.
18. A. K. Foeman and T. Nance, "From Miscegenation to Multiculturism: Perceptions and Stages of Interracial Relationship Development," in Galvin, *Making Connections*, 140–144.
19. M. P. Orbe and T. M. Harris, *Interracial Communication: Theory into Practice* 2e (Thousand Oaks, CA: Sage, 2008).
20. Orbe and Harris, *Interracial Communication*, 141–142.
21. S. W. Duck, *Personal Relationships and Personal Constructs: A Study of Friendship Formation* (New York: John Wiley & Sons, 1973).
22. G. B. Forbes, L. E. Adams-Curtis, B. Rade, and P. Jaberg, "Body Dissatisfaction in Women and Men: The Role of Gender-Typing and Self-Esteem," *Sex Roles* 44 (2001): 461–484; D. Bar-Tal and L. Saxe, "Perceptions of Similarity and Dissimilarity of Attractive Couples and Individuals," *Journal of Personality and Social Psychology* 33 (1976):

772–781; V. B. Hinsz, "Facial Resemblance in Engaged and Married Couples," *Journal of Social and Personal Relationships* 6 (1989): 223–229.
23. Guerrero et al., *Close Encounters*; Ivy and Wahl, *The Nonverbal Self*.
24. E. Sahlstein, "Making Plans: Praxia Strategies for Negotiating Uncertainty-Certainty in Long-Distance Relationships," *Western Journal of Communication* 70 (2006): 147–165; L. Stafford, *Maintaining Long-Distance and Cross-Residential Relationships* (Mahwah, NJ: Lawrence Erlbaum, 2005); A. R. Rhodes, "Long-Distance Relationships in Dual-Career Commuter Couples: A Review of Counseling Issues," *The Family Journal: Counseling and Therapy for Couples and Families* 10 (2002): 398–404; M. Dainton and B. Aylor, "A Relational Uncertainty Analysis of Jealousy, Trust, and Maintenance in Long-Distance versus Geographically Close Relationships," *Communication Quarterly* 49 (2001): 172–188; S. Blake, *Loving Your Long-Distance Relationship* (New York: Anton Publishing, 1996); K. R. Van Horn, A. Arnone, K. Nesbitt, L. Desilets, T. Sears, M. Giffin, and R. Brudi, "Physical Distance and Interpersonal Characteristics in College Students' Romantic Relationships," *Personal Relationships* 4 (1997): 15–24; M. E. Rohlfing, "'Doesn't Anybody Stay in One Place Anymore?' An Exploration of the Understudied Phenomenon of Long-Distance Relationships," in *Understudied Relationships: Off the Beaten Track*, edited by J. T. Wood and S. Duck (Thousand Oaks, CA: Sage, 1995), 173–196.
25. Miller et al., *Intimate Relationships*.
26. K. Shonbeck, "Thoughts on CMC by an E-mailer, IMer, Blog Reader, and Facebooker," in Galvin, *Making Connections*, 372–378; S. B. Barnes, "Internet Interpersonal Relationships," in Galvin, *Making Connections*, 347–354; Konijn, *Mediated Interpersonal Communication*; M. K. Rabby and J. B. Walther, "Computer-Mediated Communication Effects on Relationship Formation and Maintenance," in *Maintaining Relationships through Communication: Relational, Contextual, and Cultural Variations*, edited by D. J. Canary and M. Dainton (Mahwah, NJ: Lawrence Erlbaum, 2003), 141–184; E. R. Merkle and R. A. Richardson, "Digital Dating and Virtual Relating: Conceptualizing Computer-Mediated Relationships," *Family Relations* 49 (2000): 187–196.
27. Shonbeck, "Thoughts on CMC by an E-mailer, IMer, Blog Reader, and Facebooker."
28. Guerrero et al., *Close Encounters*; Miller et al., *Intimate Relationships*.
29. W. Schutz, *FIRO: A Three-Dimensional Theory of Interpersonal Behavior* (New York: Holt, Rinehart, and Winston, 1960).
30. A. Mehrabian, *Nonverbal Communication* (Chicago: Aldine-Atherton, 1972).
31. P. Collett, *The Book of Tells* (London: Bantam, 2004); J. A. Daly, E. Hogg, D. Sacks, M. Smith, and L. Zimring, "Sex and Relationship Affect Social Self-Grooming," in *The Nonverbal Communication Reader: Classic and Contemporary Readings* 2e, edited by L. K. Guerrero, J. DeVito, and M. L. Hecht (Prospect Heights, IL: Waveland, 1999), 56–61.
32. M. T. Whitty, "Cyber-Flirting: An Examination of Men's and Women's Flirting Behaviour Both Offline and on the Internet," *Behaviour Change* 21 (2004): 115–126.
33. Merkel and Richardson, "Digital Dating and Virtual Relating," 190; for research on initial interaction in online relationships, see A. Ramirez, Jr. and J. K. Burgoon, "The Effect of Interactivity on Initial Interactions: The Influence of Information Valence and Modality and Information Richness on Computer-Mediated Interaction," *Communication Monographs* 71 (2004): 422–447; J. B. Walther and M. R. Parks, "Cues Filtered out, Cues Filtered in: Computer-Mediated Communication and Relationships," in *Handbook of Interpersonal Communication* 3e, edited by M. L. Knapp and J. A. Daly (Thousand Oaks, CA: Sage, 2002): 529–563; J. A. McCown, D. Fischer, R. Page, and M. Homant, "Internet Relationships: People Who Meet People," *Cyberpsychology & Behavior* 4 (2001): 593–596; McKenna et al., "Relationship Formation on the Internet."
34. M. Sunnafrank and A. Ramirez, "At First Sight: Persistent Relational Effects of Get-Acquainted Conversations," *Journal of Social and Personal Relationships* 21 (2004): 361–379.
35. C. R. Berger and R. J. Calabrese, "Some Explorations in Initial Interaction and Beyond: Toward a Developmental Theory of Interpersonal Communication," *Human Communication Research* 1 (1975): 99–112; C. R. Berger and J. J. Bradac, *Language and Social Knowledge: Uncertainty in Interpersonal Relations* (Baltimore: Edward Arnold, 1982).
36. A. Lenhart, O. Lewis, and L. Rainie, "Teenage Life Online: The Rise of the Instant Message Generation and the Internet's Impact on Friendships and Family Relationships," in Galvin, *Making Connections*, 355–362; M. White, "On the Internet, Everybody Worries That You're a Dog: The Gender Expectations and Beauty Ideals of Online Personals and Text-Based Chat," in *Readings in Gender Communication*, edited by P. M. Backlund and M. R. Williams (Belmont, CA: Thomson/Wadsworth, 2004), 284–298; McCown, "Internet Relationships"; Whitty, "Cyberspace as Potential Space"; A. N. Joinson and B. Dietz-Uhler, "Explanations for the Perpetration of and Reactions to Deception in a Virtual Community," *Social Science Computer Review* 20 (2002): 275–289; D. Knox, V. Daniels, L. Sturdivant, and M. E. Zusman, "College Student Use of the Internet for Mate Selection," *College Student Journal* 35 (2001): 158–160; McCown et al., "Internet Relationships."
37. C. L. Kleinke, F. B. Meeker, and R. A. Staneski, "Preference for Opening Lines: Comparing Ratings by Men and Women," *Sex Roles* 15 (1986): 585–600.
38. E. Weber, *How to Pick Up Girls!* (New York: Bantam Books, 1970).
39. P. W. Eastwick and E. J. Finkel, "Sex Differences in Mate Preferences Revisited: Do People Know What They Initially Desire in a Romantic Partner?" *Journal of Personality and Social Psychology* 94 (2008): 245–264; E. J. Finkel, P. W. Eastwick, and J. Matthews, "Speed-Dating as an Invaluable Tool for Studying Romantic Attraction: A Methodological Primer," *Personal Relationships* 14 (2007): 149–166; R. Kurzbon and J. Weeden, "Do Advertised Preferences Predict the Behavior of Speed Daters?" *Personal Relationships* 14 (2007): 923–932.
40. M. C. Morr Serewicz and E. Gale, "First-Date Scripts: Gender Roles, Context, and Relationship," *Sex Roles* 58 (2008): 149–164; P. A. Mongeau, J. Jacobsen, and C. Donnerstein, "Defining Dates and First Date Goals: Generalizing from Undergraduates to Single Adults," *Communication Research* 34 (2007): 526–547; C. A. Sanderson, E. J. Keiter, M. G. Miles, and D. J. A. Yopyk, "The Association between Intimacy Goals and Plans for Initiating Dating Relationships," *Personal Relationships* 14 (2007): 225–243.
41. D. Dickson and O. Hargie, "Questioning," in *The Handbook of Communication Skills* 3e, edited by O. Hargie (London: Routledge, 2006), 121–145.
42. L. Whitworth, K. Kimsey-House, H. Kimsey-House, and P. Sandahl, *Co-Active Coaching: New Skills for Coaching People toward Success in Work and Life* 2e (Mountain View, CA: Davies-Black Publishing, 2007), xxi.
43. Whitworth et al., *Co-Active Coaching*, 77.
44. A. L. Vangelisti, M. L. Knapp, and J. A. Daly, "Conversational Narcissism," *Communication Monographs* 57 (1990): 251–274.
45. J. M. Twenge, S. Konrath, J. D. Foster, W. K. Campbell, and B. J. Bushman, "Egos Inflating over Time: A Cross-Temporal Meta-Analysis of the Narcissistic Personality Inventory," *Journal of Personality* 76 (2008): 875–901; J. M. Twenge, *Generation Me: Why Today's Young Americans Are More Confident, Assertive, Entitled—and More Miserable than Ever Before* (New York: Free Press, 2006).
46. C. Derber, *The Pursuit of Attention: Power and Ego in Everyday Life* (New York: Oxford University Press, 2000).
47. J. Holmes, "Complimenting—A Positive Politeness Strategy," in *Language and Gender: A Reader*, edited by J. Coates (Malden, MA: Blackwell, 1998), 100–120.
48. D. C. Marigold, J. G. Holmes, and M. Ross, "More than Words: Compliments from Romantic Partners Foster Security in Low Self-Esteem Individuals," *Journal of Personality and Social Psychology* 92 (2007): 232–248; E. M. Doohan and V. Manusov, "The Communication of Compliments in Romantic Relationships: An Investigation of Relational Satisfaction and Sex Differences and Similarities in Compliment Behavior," *Western Journal of Communication* 68 (2004): 170–194.
49. C. Parisi and P. Wogan, "Compliment Topics and Gender," *Women and Language* 29 (2006): 21–28.
50. M. Beck, "Why It's Harder to Receive than to Give," *O: The Oprah Winfrey Magazine* (September 2006): 81–83.
51. S. Jourard, *The Transparent Self* (Princeton, NJ: Van Nostrand, 1971); J. C. Pearson, *Interpersonal Communication: Concepts, Components, and Contexts* 2e (New York: McGraw-Hill, 1990).
52. D. W. Johnson, *Reaching Out: Interpersonal Effectiveness and Self-Actualization* 9e (Boston: Allyn & Bacon, 2006), 48–49.
53. Harvey and Weber, *Odyssey of the Heart*, 105–106.
54. J. H. Harvey and J. Omarzu, *Minding the Close Relationship: A Theory*

of Relationship Enhancement (New York: Cambridge University Press, 2006).

55. For more information on blogging, see M. A. Stefanone and C.-Y. Jang, "Writing for Friends and Family: The Interpersonal Nature of Blogs," *Journal of Computer-Mediated Communication* 13 (2007): 123–140; J. R. Baker and S. M. Moore, "Distress, Coping, and Blogging: Comparing New MySpace Users by Their Intention to Blog," *Cyberpsychology & Behavior* 11 (2008): 81–85; K. M. Dawson, "Blog Overload," *The Chronicle of Higher Education* (February 2, 2007): C2–C3; S. Reistad-Long, "Losing It on the Web," *O: The Oprah Winfrey Magazine* (March 2007): 183–186; "Can Blogging Derail Your Career? 7 Bloggers Discuss the Case of Juan Cole," *The Chronicle of Higher Education* (July 28, 2006): B6–B9; H. Farrell, "The Blogosphere as a Carnival of Ideas," *The Chronicle of Higher Education* (October 7, 2005): B14, B15.
56. Shonbeck, "Thoughts on CMC by an E-mailer, IMer, Blog Reader, and Facebooker," 377.
57. Shonbeck, "Thoughts on CMC by an E-mailer, IMer, Blog Reader, and Facebooker," 376.
58. J. P. Mazer, R. E. Murphy, and C. J. Simonds, "I'll See You on 'Facebook': The Effects of Computer-Mediated Teacher Self-Disclosure on Student Motivation, Affective Learning, and Classroom Climate," *Communication Education* 56 (2007): 1–17; S. Lipka, "For Professors, 'Friending' Can Be Fraught," *The Chronicle of Higher Education* (December 7, 2007): A1, A8; K. Mangan, "Etiquette for the Bar: First-Year Students at Drake U.'s Law School Learn the Value of Online Discretion," *The Chronicle of Higher Education* (January 12, 2007): A31.
59. R. Stross, "How to Lose Your Job on Your Own Time: Your Employer Can Learn Far Too Much about You on the Internet," *Corpus Christi Caller Times* (January 6, 2008): 1D, 3D.
60. S. Petronio, "Translational Research Endeavors and the Practices of Communication Privacy Management," *Journal of Applied Communication Research* 35 (2007): 218–222; S. Petronio, "The Boundaries of Privacy: Praxis of Everyday Life," in *Balancing Secrets of Private Disclosure*, edited by S. Petronio (Mahwah, NJ: Lawrence Erlbaum, 2000), 37–49; L. B. Rosenfeld, "Overview of the Ways Privacy, Secrecy, and Disclosure Are Balanced in Today's Society," in Petronio, *Balancing Secrets of Private Disclosure*, 3–17.
61. L. Heatherington and J. A. Lavner, "Coming to Terms with Coming Out: Review and Recommendations for Family Systems-Focused Research," *Journal of Family Psychology* 22 (2008): 329–343; M. L. Rasmussen, "The Problem of Coming Out," *Theory into Practice* 43 (2004): 144–151.
62. L. H. Turner and R. West, "Theories of Relational Communication," in Galvin, *Making Connections*, 20–34; C. A. Vanlear, Jr., "The Formation of Social Relationships: A Longitudinal Study of Social Penetration," *Human Communication Research* 13 (1987): 299–322.
63. Harvey and Weber, *Odyssey of the Heart*.
64. J. Fine, "Intimacy," *O: The Oprah Winfrey Magazine* (October 2001): 225.
65. M. Kito, "Self-Disclosure in Romantic Relationships and Friendships among American and Japanese College Students," *Journal of Social Psychology* 145 (2005): 127–140; M. Knapp and A. L. Vangelisti, *Interpersonal Communication and Human Relationships* 6e (Boston: Allyn & Bacon, 2008).
66. C. H. Tardy and K. Dindia, "Self-Disclosure: Strategic Revelation of Information in Personal and Professional Relationships," in Hargie, *The Handbook of Communication Skills*, 229–266; D. Borisoff, "The Effect of Gender on Establishing and Maintaining Intimate Relationships," in *Women and Men Communicating: Challenges and Changes* 2e, edited by L. P. Arliss and D. J. Borisoff (Prospect Heights, IL: Waveland, 2001), 15–31; K. Galvin and C. Bylund, "First Marriage Families: Gender and Communication," in Arliss and Borisoff, *Women and Men Communicating*, 132–148; J. T. Wood and C. C. Inman, "In a Different Mode: Masculine Styles of Communicating Closeness," *Journal of Applied Communication Research* 21 (1993): 279–295.
67. P. Dobransky and L. A. Stamford, *The Power of Female Friendship: How Your Circle of Friends Shapes Your Life* (New York: Plume, 2008); B. Fehr, "Intimacy Expectations in Same-Sex Friendships: A Prototype Interaction-Pattern Model," *Journal of Personality and Social Psychology* 86 (2004): 265–284; P. H. Wright, "Toward an Expanded Orientation to the Study of Sex Differences in Friendship," in *Sex Differences and Similarities in Communication*, edited by D. J. Canary and K. Dindia (Mahwah, NJ: Lawrence Erlbaum, 1998), 41–63.
68. B. Fehr, "Intimacy Expectations in Same-Sex Friendships"; T. J. Peterson, "Another Level: Friendships Transcending Geography and Race," *Journal of Men's Studies* 15 (2007): 71–82.
69. W. K. Rawlins, "Times, Places, and Social Spaces for Cross-Sex Friendship," in Arliss and Borisoff, *Women and Men Communicating*, 93–114.
70. Wood and Inman, "In a Different Mode."
71. I. Altman and D. Taylor, *Social Penetration: The Development of Relationships* (New York: Holt, Rinehart and Winston, 1973); Miller et al., *Intimate Relationships*; B. M. Montgomery, "Communication in Close Relationships," in Weber, *Perspectives on Close Relationships*, 67–87.
72. J. Luft, *Group Process: An Introduction to Group Dynamics* (Palo Alto, CA: Mayfield, 1970).
73. P. Mehta and M. S. Clark, "Toward Understanding Emotions in Intimate Relationships," in Weber, *Perspectives on Close Relationships*, 88–109.
74. M.-S. Kim and A. S. Ebesu Hubbard, "Intercultural Communication in the Global Village: How to Understand 'The Other,'" *Journal of Intercultural Communication Research* 36 (2007): 223–235; A. Molinsky, "Cross-Cultural Code-Switching: The Psychological Challenges of Adapting Behavior in Foreign Cultural Interactions," *Academy of Management Review* 32 (2007): 622–640; S. Glazer, "Social Support across Cultures," *International Journal of Intercultural Relations* 30 (2006): 605–622; A. Hochschild, "The Economy of Gratitude," in *The Sociology of Emotions: Original Essays and Research Papers*, edited by D. Franks and E. D. McCarthy (Greenwich, CT: JAI Press, 1989), 95–113.
75. E. R. McDaniel, "Nonverbal Communication: A Reflection of Cultural Themes," in *Intercultural Communication: A Reader* 8e, edited by L. A. Samovar and R. E. Porter (Belmont, CA: Wadsworth, 1997), 256–265.
76. P. M. Cole, "Children's Spontaneous Control of Facial Expression," *Child Development* 57 (1986): 1309–1321.
77. R. W. Simon and L. E. Nath, "Gender and Emotion in the United States: Do Men and Women Differ in Self-Reports of Feelings and Expressive Behavior?" *American Journal of Sociology* 109 (2004): 1137–1176; L. K. Guerrero and R. L. Reiter, "Expressing Emotion: Sex Differences in Social Skills and Communicative Responses to Anger, Sadness, and Jealousy," in Canary, *Sex Differences and Similarities in Communication*, 321–350.
78. Jourard, *The Transparent Self*.
79. F. Warren, *PostSecret* (New York: William Morrow, 2005), 2.
80. E. Aries, "Sex Differences in Interaction: A Re-Examination," in Canary, *Sex Differences and Similarities in Communication*, 21–37; B. B. Burleson, "Introduction to the Special Issue: Psychological Mediators of Sex Differences in Emotional Support," *Communication Reports* 15 (2002): 1–4.
81. W. Pollack, *Real Boys: Rescuing Our Sons from the Myths of Boyhood* (New York: Owl Books, 1999); O. Silverstein and B. Rashbaum, *The Courage to Raise Good Men* (New York: Penguin, 1995); V. Monroe, "How to Raise the Men We'd Want to Marry," *O: The Oprah Winfrey Magazine* (June 2003): 163, 203; P. C. McGraw, "Dr. Phil's MANual," *O: The Oprah Winfrey Magazine* (June 2003): 46–50; P. C. McGraw, "Dr. Phil: Who *Is* That Masked Man?" *O: The Oprah Winfrey Magazine* (March 2005): 52, 56.
82. This chapter benefited from the fine scholarship and work of M. Redmond, coauthor of *Interpersonal Communication: Relating to Others* 4e (Boston: Allyn & Bacon, 2005).
83. <www.wildxangel.com>; <www.bol.ucia.edu>; <www.thirdage.com>; <www.onlinedatingmagazine.com>, retrieved October 15, 2008.
84. D. Scott, "Marriage Online: Saying 'I Do' by a Virtual Waterfall, Moving into a Virtual House," *Corpus Christi Caller Times* (March 7, 1999): H1, H3.
85. S. Winston, "Cyberlove: Florida Man Gives On-Line Advice for the Lovelorn," *Corpus Christi Caller Times* (May 28, 1995): G1, G7.

CHAPTER 8

1. M. Paul, *The Friendship Crisis: Finding, Making, and Keeping Friends When You're Not a Kid Anymore* (New York: Rodale Books, 2004); B. Fehr, *Friendship Processes* (Thousand Oaks, CA: Sage, 1996); W. Rawlins, *Friendship Matters: Communication, Dialectics, and the Life Course*

(Hawthorne, NY: Aldine de Gruyter, 1992); W. J. Dickens and D. Perlman, "Friendship over the Life-Cycle," in *Personal Relationships 2: Developing Personal Relationships*, edited by S. W. Duck and R. Gilmour (London: Academic Press, 1981).

2. R. Blieszner, "Close Relationships over Time," as reported in J. A. Simpson and B. A. Harris, "Interpersonal Attraction," in *Perspectives on Close Relationships*, edited by A. L. Weber and J. H. Harvey (Boston: Allyn & Bacon, 1994), 1–18.

3. J. Yager, *Friendshifts: The Power of Friendship and How It Shapes Our Lives* (Stamford, CT: Hannacrois Creek Books, 1999); W. Rawlins, "Being There for Friends," in *Making Connections: Readings in Relational Communication* 4e, edited by K. M. Galvin and P. Cooper (Los Angeles: Roxbury, 2006), 329–332; R. Blieszner and R. Adams, *Adult Friendships* (Newbury Park, CA: Sage, 1992).

4. A. J. Johnson, E. Wittenberg, M. M. Villagran, M. Mazur, and P. Villagran, "Relational Progression as a Dialectic: Examining Turning Points in Communication among Friends," *Communication Monographs* 70 (2003): 230–249.

5. P. M. Sias and D. J. Cahill, "From Coworkers to Friends: The Development of Peer Friendships in the Workplace," *Western Journal of Communication* 62 (1998): 273–299; G. A. Fine, "Friendships in the Workplace," in Galvin and Cooper, *Making Connections*, 270–277.

6. M. Hughes, K. Morrison, and K. J. K. Asada, "What's Love Got to Do with It? Exploring the Impact of Maintenance Rules, Love Attitudes, and Network Support on Friends with Benefits Relationships," *Western Journal of Communication* 69 (2005): 49–66.

7. K. Bogle, *Hooking Up: Sex, Dating, and Relationships on Campus* (New York: New York University Press, 2008); D. Freitas, *Sex and the Soul: Juggling Sexuality, Spirituality, Romance, and Religion on America's College Campuses* (New York: Oxford University Press, 2008); E. M. Eshbaugh and G. Gute, "Hookups and Sexual Regret among College Women," *Journal of Social Psychology* 148 (2008): 77–89; J. Weeden and J. Sabini, "Subjective and Objective Measures of Attractiveness and Their Relation to Sexual Behavior and Sexual Attitudes in University Students," *Archives of Sexual Behavior* 36 (2007): 79–88; W. F. Flack, Jr., K. A. Daubman, M. L. Caron, J. A. Asadorian, N. R. D'Aureli, S. N. Gigliotti, A. T. Hall, S. Kiser, and E. R. Stine, "Risk Factors and Consequences of Unwanted Sex among University Students: Hooking Up, Alcohol, and Stress Response," *Journal of Interpersonal Violence* 22 (2007): 139–157; T. A. Lambert, A. S. Kahn, and K. J. Apple, "Pluralistic Ignorance and Hooking Up," *Journal of Sex Research* 40 (2003): 129–133; E. L. Paul and K. A. Hayes, "The Casualties of 'Casual' Sex: A Qualitative Exploration of the Phenomenology of College Students' Hookups," *Journal of Social and Personal Relationships* 29 (2002): 639–661; E. L. Paul, B. McManus, and K. A. Hayes, "'Hookups': Characteristics and Correlates of College Students' Spontaneous and Anonymous Sexual Experiences," *Journal of Sex Research* 37 (2000): 76–88; W. A. Afifi and S. L. Faulkner, "On Being 'Just Friends': The Frequency and Impact of Sexual Activity in Cross-Sex Friendships," *Journal of Social and Personal Relationships* 17 (2000): 205–222.

8. Hughes et al., "What's Love Got to Do with It?"

9. L. Gee, *Friends: Why Men and Women Are from the Same Planet* (New York: Bloomsbury, 2004); M. Monsour, *Women and Men as Friends: Relationships across the Life Span in the 21st Century* (Mahwah, NJ: Lawrence Erlbaum, 2002).

10. D. Carnegie, *How to Win Friends and Influence People* (New York: Simon & Schuster, 1937).

11. K. Galvin and C. Bylund, "First Marriage Families: Gender and Communication," in *Women and Men Communicating: Challenges and Changes* 2e, edited by L. P. Arliss and D. J. Borisoff (Prospect Heights, IL: Waveland, 2001), 132–148; V. Satir, "The Rules You Live By," in Galvin and Cooper, *Making Connections*, 168–174; S. S. Brehm, R. Miller, D. Perlman, and S. M. Campbell, *Intimate Relationships* 4e (New York: McGraw-Hill, 2006).

12. *The Miami Herald* (July 9, 1982): 12A.

13. D. O. Braithwaite, P. W. Toller, K. L. Daas, W. T. Durham, and A. C. Jones, "Centered but Not Caught in the Middle: Stepchildren's Perceptions of Dialectical Contradictions in the Communication of Co-Parents," *Journal of Applied Communication Research* 36 (2008): 33–55; R. L. Deal, *The Smart Stepfamily: Seven Steps to a Healthy Family* (New York: Bethany House, 2006); M. K. DeGenova and F. P. Rice, "Why Examine Family Background?" in Galvin and Cooper, *Making Connections*, 104–107; M. Coleman, M.A. Fine, L. H. Ganong, K. J. M. Downs, and N. Pauk, "When You're Not the Brady Bunch: Identifying Perceived Conflicts and Resolution Strategies in Stepfamilies," *Personal Relationships* 8 (2001): 55–73; D. O. Braithwaite, L. N. Olson, T. D. Golish, C. Soukup, and P. Turman, "'Becoming a Family': Developmental Processes Represented in Blended Family Discourse," *Journal of Applied Communication Research* 29 (2001): 221–247; J. D. Teachman, L. M. Tedrow, and K. D. Crowder, "The Changing Demography of America's Families," *Journal of Marriage and the Family* 62 (2000): 1234–1246.

14. V. Satir, *The New Peoplemaking* (Mountain View, CA: Science & Behavior Books, 1988), 4.

15. Work and Family Facts & Stats, <www.aflcio.org>, retrieved June 26, 2008; *Contexts: A Publication of the American Sociological Association* 3, 2004, <www.contextsmagazine.org>; AFL-CIO, *National Study of the Changing Workforce* (2002), <www.aflcio.org>.

16. National Association of Colleges and Employers, "Job Outlook 2008," 2008, <http://www.jobweb.com>; M. S. Peterson, "Personnel Interviewers' Perceptions of the Importance and Adequacy of Applicants' Communication Skills," *Communication Education* 46 (1997): 287–291.

17. M. L. Knapp and A. Vangelisti, "Relationship Stages: A Communication Perspective," in Galvin and Cooper, *Making Connections*, 132–139; M. L. Knapp and A. L. Vangelisti, *Interpersonal Communication and Human Relationships* 6e (Boston: Allyn & Bacon, 2008); S. A. Welch and R. B. Rubin, "Development of Relationship Stage Measures," *Communication Quarterly* 50 (2002): 24–40; J. H. Harvey and A. L. Weber, *Odyssey of the Heart: Close Relationships in the 21st Century* 2e (Mahwah, NJ: Lawrence Erlbaum, 2002); L. K. Guerrero, P. A. Andersen, and W. A. Afifi, *Close Encounters: Communicating in Relationships* 2e (Thousand Oaks, CA: Sage, 2007).

18. S. W. Duck, "A Topography of Relationship Disengagement and Dissolution," in *Personal Relationships 4: Dissolving Relationships*, edited by S. W. Duck (New York: Academic Press, 1982); Guerrero et al., *Close Encounters*.

19. M. L. Knapp, *Social Intercourse: From Greeting to Goodbye* (Boston: Allyn & Bacon, 1978).

20. Duck, "A Topography of Relationship Disengagement and Dissolution."

21. For research on relationship termination, see J. K. Kellas, D. Bean, C. Cunningham, and K. Y. Cheng, "The Ex-Files: Trajectories, Turning Points, and Adjustment in the Development of Post-Dissolutional Relationships," *Journal of Social and Personal Relationships* 25 (2008): 23–50; P. W. Eastwick, E. J. Finkel, T. Krishnamurti, and G. Loewenstein, "Mispredicting Distress Following Romantic Breakup: Revealing the Time Course of the Affective Forecasting Error," *Journal of Experimental Social Psychology* 44 (2008): 800–807; G. W. Lewandowski, Jr., and N. M. Bizzoco, "Addition through Subtraction: Growth Following the Dissolution of a Low Quality Relationship," *Journal of Positive Psychology* 2 (2007): 40–54; M. L. Knapp and A. L. Vangelisti, "Relational Decline," in Galvin and Cooper, *Making Connections*, 269–273; W. R. Cupach, "Dialectical Process in the Disengagement of Interpersonal Relationships," in Galvin and Cooper, *Making Connections*, 274–280; K. Koenig Kellas, "'The Worst Part Is, We Don't Even Talk Anymore': Post-Dissolutional Communication in Break Up Stories," in Galvin and Cooper, *Making Connections*, 281–290.

22. L. Stafford, S. L. Kline, and J. Dimmick, "Home E-Mail: Relational Maintenance and Gratification Opportunities," *Journal of Broadcasting & Electronic Media* 43 (1999): 659–669.

23. V. S. Millner, "Internet Infidelity: A Case of Intimacy with Detachment," *The Family Journal* 16 (2008): 78–82; B. H. Henline, L. K. Lamke, and M. D. Howard, "Exploring Perceptions of Online Infidelity," *Personal Relationships* 14 (2007): 113–128; B. L. Avila Mileham, "Online Infidelity in Internet Chat Rooms: An Ethnographic Exploration," *Computers in Human Behavior* 23 (2007): 11–31; K. M. Hertlein and F. P. Piercy, "Internet Infidelity: A Critical Review of the Literature," *The Family Journal* 14 (2006): 366–371.

24. F. S. Christopher and S. Sprecher, "Sexuality in Marriage, Dating, and Other Relationships: A Decade Review," in *Speaking of Sexuality: Interdisciplinary Readings*, edited by J. K. Davidson, Sr., and N. B. Moore (Los Angeles: Roxbury, 2005): 54–71.

25. K. Y. A. McKenna, A. S. Green, and P. K. Smith, "Demarginalizing the Sexual Self," *Journal of Sex Research* 38 (2001): 302–316; A. Cooper, I. P. McLoughlin, and K. M. Campbell, "Sexuality in Cyberspace: Update for the 21st Century," *Cyberpsychology & Behavior* 3 (2000): 521–536.

26. McKenna et al., "Demarginalizing the Sexual Self."

27. L. A. Baxter and B. M. Montgomery, *Relating: Dialogues and Dialectics* (New York: Guilford, 1996); L. A. Baxter and B. M. Montgomery, "Rethinking Communication in Personal Relationships from a Dialectical Perspective," in *Communication and Personal Relationships*, edited by K. Dindia and S. Duck (New York: John Wiley, 2000), 31–53; D. Goldsmith, "A Dialectic Perspective on the Expression of Autonomy and Connection in Romantic Relationships," *Western Journal of Speech Communication* 54 (1990): 537–556; R. A. Bell and N. L. Buerkel-Rothfuss, "S(he) Loves Me, S(he) Loves Me Not: Predictors of Relational Information-Seeking in Courtship and Beyond," *Communication Quarterly* 38 (1990): 64–82; R. Nozick, "Love's Bond," in *Gender Basics: Feminist Perspectives on Women and Men*, edited by A. Minas (Belmont, CA: Wadsworth, 1993), 152–159; L. A. Peplau, "Men and Women in Love," in *Gender, Families, and Close Relationships*, edited by D. L. Sollie and L. A. Leslie (Newbury Park, CA: Sage, 1994), 19–49; Galvin and Bylund, "First Marriage Families."

28. L. H. Turner and R. West, "Theories of Relational Communication," in Galvin and Cooper, *Making Connections*, 20–34.

29. J. G. Oetzel and S. Ting-Toomey (eds.), *The Sage Handbook of Conflict Communication* (Thousand Oaks, CA: Sage, 2006).

30. P. M. Kellett, *Conflict Dialogue: Working with Layers of Meaning for Productive Relationships* (Thousand Oaks, CA: Sage, 2007), xi–xii.

31. M. Deutsch, *The Resolution of Conflict* (New Haven: Yale University Press, 1973).

32. W. W. Wilmot and J. L. Hocker, *Interpersonal Conflict* 7e (New York: McGraw-Hill, 2005).

33. G. R. Miller and M. Steinberg, *Between People: A New Analysis of Interpersonal Communication* (Chicago: Science Research Associates, 1975).

34. Kellett, *Conflict Dialogue*, 147.

35. M. E. Roloff and K. L. Johnson, "Serial Arguing over the Relational Life Course: Antecedents and Consequences," in *Stability and Change in Relationships* (Cambridge, UK: Cambridge University Press, 2002), 107–128, as cited in M. E. Roloff and R. M. Reznik, "Communication during Serial Arguments," in *Studies in Applied Interpersonal Communication*, edited by M. T. Motley (Thousand Oaks, CA: Sage, 2008), 97–119.

36. C. Waite Miller, "Irresolvable Interpersonal Conflicts," in Galvin and Cooper, *Making Connections*, 253–259.

37. S. Ting-Toomey and L. Chung, *Understanding Intercultural Communication* (New York: Oxford University Press, 2004); S. Ting-Toomey and J. G. Oetzel, *Managing Intercultural Conflict Effectively* 2e (Newbury Park, CA: Sage, 2001); S. Ting-Toomey, "Managing Intercultural Conflicts Effectively," in *Intercultural Communication: A Reader* 9e, edited by L. A. Samovar and R. E. Porter (Belmont, CA: Wadsworth, 1999), 388–399.

38. C. R. Berger, "Social Power and Interpersonal Communication," in *Explorations in Interpersonal Communication*, edited by G. R. Miller (Newbury Park, CA: Sage, 1976).

39. Brehm et al., *Intimate Relationships*.

40. P. J. Kalbfleisch and M. J. Cody, eds., *Gender, Power, and Communication in Human Relationships* (Hillsdale, NJ: Lawrence Erlbaum, 1995); L. P. Arliss, "When Myths Endure and Realities Change: Communication in Romantic Relationships," in Arliss and Borisoff, *Women and Men Communicating*, 115–131; F. E. Millar and L. E. Rogers, "Relational Dimensions of Interpersonal Dynamics," in *Interpersonal Process: New Directions in Communication Research*, edited by M. E. Roloff and G. R. Miller (Newbury Park, CA: Sage, 1987), 117–139.

41. M. Schuessler Harper, *Keeping Quiet: Self-Silencing and Its Association with Relational and Individual Functioning among Adolescent Romantic Couples*, unpublished doctoral dissertation, University of Tennessee, Knoxville, 2004; "Unhealthy for Women Not to Speak Up during Marital Spats," *Harvard Women's Health Watch* (January 2008): 6–7; T. Parker-Pope, "Marital Spats, Taken to Heart," *New York Times*, October 7, 2007, <nytimes.com>.

42. A. S. Rancer and T. A. Avtgis, *Argumentative and Aggressive Communication: Theory, Research, and Application* (Thousand Oaks, CA: Sage, 2006); D. A. Infante, A. S. Rancer, and D. F. Womack, *Building Communication Theory* 4e (Prospect Heights, IL: Waveland, 2003); D. A. Infante and A. S. Rancer, "Argumentativeness and Verbal Aggressiveness: A Review of Recent Theory and Research," *Communication Yearbook* 19 (1996): 319–351.

43. Wilmot and Hocker, *Interpersonal Conflict*.

44. A. L. Vangelisti, S. L. Young, K. E. Carpenter-Theune, and A. L. Alexander, "Why Does It Hurt? The Perceived Causes of Hurt Feelings," *Communication Research* 32 (2005): 443–477; C. M. Carey and P. A. Mongeau, "Communication and Violence in Courtship Relationships," in *Family Violence from a Communication Perspective*, edited by D. D. Cahn and S. A. Lloyd (Hillsdale, NJ: Lawrence Erlbaum, 1996), 127–150.

45. P. Yelsma, "Couples' Affective Orientations and Their Verbal Aggressiveness," *Communication Quarterly* 43 (1995): 100–114.

46. T. C. Sabourin, "The Role of Negative Reciprocity in Spousal Abuse: A Relational Control Analysis," *Journal of Applied Communication Research* 23 (1995): 271–283.

47. A. L. Vangelisti, K. C. Maguire, A. L. Alexander, and G. Clark, "Hurtful Family Environments: Links with Individual, Relationship, and Perceptual Variables," *Communication Monographs* 74 (2007): 357–385; M. S. McCloskey, R. Lee, M. E. Berman, K. L. Noblett, and E. F. Coccaro, "The Relationship between Impulsive Verbal Aggression and Intermittent Explosive Disorder," *Aggressive Behavior* 34 (2008): 51–60; L. N. Olson, "Exploring 'Common Couple Violence' in Heterosexual Romantic Relationships," *Western Journal of Communication* 66 (2002): 104–128; T. C. Sabourin and G. H. Stamp, "Communication and the Experience of Dialectical Tensions in Family Life: An Examination of Abusive and Nonabusive Families," *Communication Monographs* 62 (1995): 213–242.

48. Infante et al., *Building Communication Theory*; A. S. Rancer, "Argumentativeness, Verbal Aggressiveness, and Persuasion," in J. S. Seiter and R. H. Gass, *Perspectives on Persuasion, Social Influence, and Compliance-Gaining* (Boston: Allyn & Bacon, 2004), 113–131; M. M. Martin, C. M. Anderson, and C. L. Horvath, "Feelings about Verbal Aggression: Justifications for Sending, and Hurt from Receiving, Verbally Aggressive Messages," *Communication Research Reports* 13 (1996): 19–26; D. Cloven and M. E. Roloff, "The Chilling Effect of Aggressive Potential on the Expression of Complaints in Intimate Relationships," *Communication Monographs* 60 (1993): 199–219.

49. Satir, *The New Peoplemaking*; Wilmot and Hocker, *Interpersonal Conflict*.

50. L. L. Putnam and C. E. Wilson, "Communicative Strategies in Organizational Conflicts: Reliability and Validity of a Measurement Scale," in *Communication Yearbook 6*, edited by M. Burgoon (Beverly Hills: Sage, 1982).

51. Cloven and Roloff, "The Chilling Effect of Aggressive Potential on the Expression of Complaints in Intimate Relationships"; Wilmot and Hocker, *Interpersonal Conflict*.

52. M. A. Gross, L. K. Guerrero, and J. K. Alberts, "Perceptions of Conflict Strategies and Communication Competence in Task-Oriented Dyads," *Journal of Applied Communication Research* 32 (2004): 249–270.

53. R. Fisher, W. Ury, and B. Patton, *Getting to Yes: Negotiating Agreement without Giving In* 2e (New York: Penguin Books, 1991).

54. This information is based on several excellent discussions of conflict management skills. We acknowledge W. R. Cupach and D. J. Canary, *Competence in Interpersonal Conflict* (Long Grove, IL: Waveland, 2000); D. Borisoff and D. A. Victor, *Conflict Management: A Communication Skills Approach* 2e (Boston: Allyn & Bacon, 1999); D. Yankelovich, *The Magic of Dialogue: Transforming Conflict into Cooperation* (New York: Simon & Schuster, 1999); Wilmot and Hocker, *Interpersonal Conflict*; O. Hargie, ed., *The Handbook of Communication Skills* 3e (London: Routledge, 2006); O. Hargie, C. Saunders, and D. Dickson, *Social Skills in Interpersonal Communication* 3e (London: Routledge, 1994); W. A. Donohue, with R. Holt, *Managing Interpersonal Conflict* (Newbury Park, CA: Sage, 1992); D. A. Romig and L. J. Romig, *Structured Teamwork© Guide* (Austin: Performance Resources, 1990); S. Deep and L. Sussman, *Smart Moves* (Reading, MA: Addison-Wesley, 1990); Fisher et al., *Getting to Yes*; M. D. Davis, E. L. Eshelman, and M. McKay, *The Relaxation and Stress Reduction Workbook* (Oakland, CA: New Har-

binger, 1982); R. Boulton, *People Skills* (New York: Simon & Schuster, 1979).
55. J. B. Rubin, "Stand Back from the Rope!" *O: The Oprah Winfrey Magazine* (March 2005): 193–194, 197.
56. B. M. Gayle and R. W. Preiss, "Language Intensity Plus: A Methodological Approach to Validate Emotions in Conflicts," *Communication Reports 12* (1999): 43–50; Wilmot and Hocker, *Interpersonal Conflict*.
57. C. R. Knee, C. Lonsbary, A. Canevello, and H. Patrick, "Self-Determination and Conflict in Romantic Relationships," *Journal of Personality and Social Psychology 89* (2005): 997–1009; M. Mongrain, "Conflict over Emotional Expression: Implications for Interpersonal Communication," *Personality and Social Psychology Bulletin 29* (2003): 545–555.
58. A. Ellis, *A New Guide to Rational Living* (North Hollywood, CA: Wilshire Books, 1977).
59. L. C. Lederman, "The Impact of Gender on the Self and Self-Talk," in Arliss and Borisoff, *Women and Men Communicating*, 78–89; Ellis, *A New Guide to Rational Living*.
60. H. Gardner, as cited in D. Raffel, "Brain to Brain: How to Get Anyone to Agree with You," *O: The Oprah Winfrey Magazine* (May 2005): 201–202.
61. Fisher, *Getting to Yes*.

CHAPTER 9

1. R. K. Mosvick and R. B. Nelson, *We've Got to Start Meeting Like This!* (Glenview, IL: Scott, Foresman, 1987).
2. Mosvick and Nelson, *We've Got to Start Meeting Like This!*
3. K. W. Hawkins and B. P. Fillion, "Perceived Communication Skill Needs for Work Groups," *Communication Research Reports 16* (1999): 167–174; also see S. Burkhalter, J. Gastil, and T. Kelshaw, "A Conceptual Definition and Theoretical Model of Public Deliberation in Small Face-to-Face Groups," *Communication Theory 12* (2002): 398–422.
4. S.A. Beebe and J.T. Masterson, *Communicating in Small Groups: Principles and Practices* 9e (Boston: Allyn and Bacon, 2009).
5. N. Katz and G. Koenig, "Sports Teams as a Model for Workplace Teams: Lessons and Liabilities," *Academy of Management Executive 15* (2001): 56–67.
6. Our discussion of teams and teamwork is from Beebe and Masterson, *Communicating in Small Groups*; for an excellent review of teamwork theoretical models, see V. Rousseau, C. Aube, and A. Savoie, "Teamwork Behaviors: A Review and an Integration of Frameworks," *Small Group Research 27 (5)* (2006): 540–570.
7. A. G. Sheard and A. P. Kakabadse, "From Loose Groups to Effective Teams: The Nine Key Factors of the Team Landscape," *Journal of Management Development 21* (2002): 133–151.
8. See F. C. Broadbeck and T. Breitermeyer, "Effects of Individual versus Mixed Individual and Group Experience in Rule Induction on Group Member Learning and Group Performance," *Journal of Experimental Social Psychology 36* (2002): 621–648.
9. S. B. Shimanoff, *Communication Rules: Theory and Research* (Beverly Hills: Sage, 1980).
10. M. Hoegl, "Goal Setting and Team Performance in Innovative Projects: On the Moderating Role of Teamwork Quality," *Small Group Research 34* (2003): 3–19.
11. F. LaFasto and C. Larson, *Teamwork* (Thousand Oaks, CA: Sage, 2001); A. T. Pescosolido, "Group Efficacy and Group Effectiveness: The Effects of Group Efficacy over Time on Group Performance and Development," *Small Group Research 34* (2003): 20–43.
12. E. Salas, D. R. Nichols, and J. E. Driskell, "Testing Three Team Training Strategies in Intact Teams: A Meta Analysis," *Small Group Research 38 (4)* (2007): 471–488.
13. Beebe and Masterson, *Communicating in Small Groups*.
14. B. Bell and S. W. J. Kozlowski, "A Typology of Virtual Teams: Implications for Effective Leadership," *Group & Organization Management 27* (2002): 14–49; A. Thatcher, "Small Group Decision-Making in Face-to-Face and Computer-Mediated Environments: The Role of Personality," *Behavior & Information Technology 22* (2003): 203–218; D. R. Lemus, D. R. Seibold, A. J. Flanagin, and M. J. Metzger, "Argument and Decision Making in Computer-Mediated Groups," *Journal of Communication 54* (2004): 302–320; E. V. Hobman, P. Bordia, B. Irmer, and A. Chang, "The Expression of Conflict in Computer-Mediated and Face-to-Face Groups," *Small Group Research 33* (2002): 439–464; R. Benbunan-Fich, S. R. Hiltz, and M. Turoff, "A Comparative Content Analysis of Face-to-Face vs. Asynchronous Group Decision Making," *Decision Support Systems 34* (2002): 457–469; D. S. Staples and J. Webster, "Exploring Traditional and Virtual Team Members' 'Best Practices,'" *Small Group Research 38 (1)* (2007): 60–97; S. Z. Schiller and M. Mandviwalla, "Virtual Team Research: An Analysis of Theory Use and a Framework for Theory Appropriation," *Small Group Research 38 (1)* (2007): 12–59; J. T. Polzer, C. B. Crisp, S. L. Jarvenpaa, and J. W. Kim, "Extending the Faultline Model to Geographically Dispersed Teams: How Colocated Subgroups Can Impair Group Functioning," *Academy of Management Journal 49 (4)* (2006): 679–692.
15. C. E. Timmerman and C. R. Scott, "Virtually Working: Communicative and Structural Predictors of Media Use and Key Outcomes in Virtual Work Teams," *Communication Monographs 73 (1)* (2006): 108–136.
16. J. M. Wilson, S. G. Straus, and B. McEvily, "All in Due Time: The Development of Trust in Computer-Mediated and Face-to-Face Teams," *Organizational Behavior and Human Decision Processes 99* (2006): 16–33.
17. K. D. Benne and Paul Sheats, "Functional Roles of Group Members," *Journal of Social Issues 4* (1948): 41–49. For a good review of role development in groups, see A. P. Hare, "Types of Roles in Small Groups: A Bit of History and a Current Perspective," *Small Group Research 25* (1994): 433–438; A. J. Salazar, "An Analysis of the Development and Evolution of Roles in the Small Group," *Small Group Research 27* (1996): 475–503.
18. T. Halfhill, E. Sundstrom, J. Lahner, W. Calderone, and T. M. Nielsen, "Group Personality Composition and Group Effectiveness: An Integrative Review of Empirical Research," *Small Group Research 36 (1)* (2005): 83–105.
19. R. F. Bales, *Interaction Process Analysis* (Chicago: University of Chicago Press, 1976).
20. Shimanoff, *Communication Rules*.
21. M. Shaw, *Group Dynamics: The Psychology of Small Group Behavior* (New York: McGraw-Hill, 1981), 281.
22. J. I. Hurwitz, A. F. Zander, and B. Hymovitch, "Some Effects of Power on the Relations among Group Members," in *Group Dynamics: Research and Theory*, edited by D. Cartwright and A. Zander (New York: Harper & Row, 1953), 483–492; D. C. Barnlund and C. Harland, "Propinquity and Prestige as Determinants of Communication Networks," *Sociometry 26* (1963): 467–479; G. C. Homans, *The Human Group* (New York: Harcourt Brace and World, 1992); H. H. Kelly, "Communication in Experimentally Created Hierarchies," *Human Relations 4* (1951): 36–56.
23. C. Anderson, J. S. Beer, S. Chatman, S. Srivastava, and S. E. Spataro, "Knowing Your Place: Self-Perceptions of Status in Face-to-Face Groups," *Journal of Personality and Social Psychology 91 (6)* (2006): 1094–1110.
24. M. R. Singer, *Intercultural Communication: A Perceptual Approach* (Englewood Cliffs, NJ: Prentice-Hall, 1987), 118.
25. J. R. P. French and B. H. Raven, "The Bases of Social Power," in Cartwright and Zander, *Group Dynamics*, 607–623.
26. D. Neumann, "Small Group Cohesion and Frequency of Idiom Use," paper presented at the annual meeting of the National Communication Association, Chicago, IL, November 2004.
27. M. R. Barrick, B. H. Bradley, A. L. Kristof-Brown, and A. E. Colbert, "The Moderating Role of Top Management Team Interdependence: Implications for Real Teams and Working Groups," *Academy of Management Journal 50 (3)* (2007): 544–557.
28. Adapted from E. G. Bormann and N. C. Bormann, *Effective Small Group Communication* (Minneapolis: Burgess, 1980), 70–72.
29. N. Katz, D. Lazer, H. Arrow, and N. Contractor, "Network Theory and Small Groups," *Small Group Research 35* (2004): 307–332.
30. S. Wheelan, B. Davidson, and F. Tilin, "Group Development across Time: Reality or Illusion?" *Small Group Research 34* (2003): 223–245; S. Furst, M. Reeves, B. Rosen, and R. S. Blackburn, "Managing the Life Cycle of Virtual Teams," *Academy of Management Executive 18* (2004): 6–22.
31. B. A. Fisher, "Decision Emergence: Phases in Group Decision-Making," *Speech Monographs 37* (1970): 60.

32. For a discussion of primary tension and group phases, see E. Bormann, *Discussion and Group Methods* (New York: Harper & Row, 1975).
33. M. A. Von Glinow, D. Shapiro, and J. Brett, "Can We Talk, and Should We? Managing Emotional Conflict in Multicultural Teams," *Academy of Management Review* 29 (2004): 578–592.
34. M. Janssens and J. M. Brett, "Cultural Intelligence in Global Teams: A Fusion Model of Collaboration," *Group & Organization Management* 31 (1) (2006): 124–153.
35. S. A. Wheelan and T. Williams, "Mapping Dynamic Interaction Patterns in Work Groups," *Small Group Research* 34 (2003): 433–467; Wheelan et al., "Group Development across Time."
36. M. S. Poole, "Decision Development in Small Groups III: A Multiple Sequence Model of Group Decision Development," *Communication Monographs* 50 (1983): 321–341; also see C. Pavitt and K. Kline Johnson, "Scheidel and Crowell Revisited: A Descriptive Study of Group Proposal Sequencing," *Communication Monographs* 69 (2002): 19–32.
37. G. Hofstede, *Culture's Consequences: International Differences in Work-Related Values* (Beverly Hills: Sage, 1980): G. Hofstede, *Cultures and Organizations: Software of the Mind* (London: McGraw-Hill, 1991).
38. Adapted from J. Mole, *Mind Your Manners: Managing Business Cultures in Europe* (New York: Nicholas Brealey Publishing, 1995).
39. For a comprehensive discussion of bona fide groups, see L. L. Putnam, "Rethinking the Nature of Groups: A Bona Fide Group Perspective," in *Small Group Communication Theory and Practice: An Anthology*, edited by R. Y. Hirokawa, R. S. Cathcart, L. A. Samovar, and L. D. Hennman (Los Angeles: Roxbury Publishing Company, 2003).
40. Beebe and Masterson, *Communicating in Small Groups*.

CHAPTER 10

1. See N. R. F. Maier, "Assets and Liabilities in Group Problem Solving: The Need for an Integrative Function," *Psychological Review* 74 (1967): 239–249; M. Argyle, *Cooperation: The Basis of Sociability* (London: Routledge, 1991); H. A. M. Wilke and R. W. Meertens, *Group Performance* (London: Routledge, 1994).
2. Maier, "Assets and Liabilities in Group Problem Solving"; Argyle, *Cooperation*; Wilke and Meertens, *Group Performance*.
3. R. Y. Hirokawa, "Discussion Procedures and Decision-Making Performance: A Test of a Functional Perspective," *Human Communication Research* 12 (1985): 203–224.
4. R. Y. Hirokawa, "Why Informed Groups Make Faulty Decisions: An Investigation of Possible Interaction-Based Explanations," *Small Group Behavior* 18 (1987): 3–29.
5. R. Y. Hirokawa and K. Rost, "Effective Group Decision-Making in Organizations: Field Test of the Vigilant Interaction Theory," *Management Communication Quarterly* 5 (1992): 267–288; Hirokawa, "Why Informed Groups Make Faulty Decisions"; R. Y. Hirokawa, "Group Communication and Decision-Making Performance: A Continued Test of the Functional Perspective," *Human Communication Research* 14 (1988): 487–515; M. O. Orlitzky and R. Y. Hirokawa, "To Err Is Human, to Correct for It Divine: A Meta-Analysis of Research Testing the Functional Theory of Group Decision-Making Effectiveness," paper presented at the meeting of the National Communication Association, Chicago, IL, November, 1997.
6. Hirokawa, "Discussion Procedures and Decision-Making Performance."
7. C. E. Larson and F. M. J. LaFasto, *Teamwork: What Must Go Right/What Can Go Wrong* (Beverly Hills: Sage, 1989); also see D. D. Chrislip and C. E. Larson, *Collaborative Leadership* (San Francisco: Jossey-Bass, 1994); D. A. Romig, *Breakthrough Teamwork: Outstanding Results Using Structured Teamwork* (Chicago: Irwin, 1996); M. A. Marks, J. E. Mathieu, and S. J. Zaccaro, "A Temporally Based Framework and Taxonomy of Team Processes," *Academy of Management Review* 26 (2001): 356–376; N. Katz, "Sports Teams as a Model for Workplace Teams: Lessons and Liabilities," *Academy of Management Executive* 15 (2001): 56–67.
8. Larson and LaFasto, *Teamwork*; Chrislip and Larson, *Collaborative Leadership*; Romig, *Breakthrough Teamwork*.
9. Larson and LaFasto, *Teamwork*.
10. O. S. Chernyshenko, A. G. Miner, M. R. Baumann, and J. A. Sniezek, "The Impact of Information Distribution, Ownership, and Discussion on Group Member Judgment: The Differential Cue Weighting Model," *Organizational Behavior and Human Decision Processes* 91 (2003): 12–25.
11. Orlitzky and Hirokawa, "To Err Is Human, to Correct for It Divine."
12. Orlitzky and Hirokawa, "To Err Is Human, to Correct for It Divine"; B. L. Smith, "Interpersonal Behaviors That Damage the Productivity of Creative Problem Solving Groups," *Journal of Creative Behavior* 27 (1993): 171–187.
13. A. B. Henley and K. H. Price, "Want a Better Team? Foster a Climate of Fairness," *Academy of Management Executive* 16 (2002): 153–155.
14. See A. B. VanGundy, *Techniques of Structured Problem Solving* (New York: Van Nostrand Reinhold Company, 1981), 4; Romig, *Breakthrough Teamwork*.
15. S. A. Beebe and J. T. Masterson, *Communicating in Small Groups: Principles and Practices* 4e (Boston: Allyn & Bacon, 2009); VanGundy, *Techniques of Structured Problem Solving*.
16. J. K. Brilhart and L. M. Jochem, "Effects of Different Patterns on Outcomes of Problem-Solving Discussion," *Journal of Applied Psychology* 48 (1964): 174–179; W. E. Jurma, "Effects of Leader Structuring Style and Task Orientation Characteristics of Group Members," *Communication Monographs* 49 (1979): 282–295; S. Jarboe, "A Comparison of Input–Output, Process–Output, and Input–Process–Output Models of Small Group Problem-Solving Effectiveness," *Communication Monographs* 55 (1988): 121–142; VanGundy, *Techniques of Structured Problem Solving*.
17. D. M. Berg, "A Descriptive Analysis of the Distribution and Duration of Themes Discussed by Task-Oriented Small Groups," *Speech Monographs* 34 (1967): 172–175; E. G. Bormann and N. C. Bormann, *Effective Small Group Communication* 2e (Minneapolis: Burgess, 1976), 132; M. S. Poole, "Decision Development in Small Groups III: A Multiple Sequence Model of Group Decision Development," *Communication Monographs* 50 (1983): 321–341.
18. J. Dewey, *How We Think* (Boston: D. C. Heath, 1910).
19. This explanation of the Journalist's Six Questions method is based on a discussion by J. E. Eitington, *The Winning Trainer* (Houston: Gulf Publishing, 1989), 157.
20. Based on the research of K. Lewin, "Frontiers in Group Dynamics," *Human Relations* 1 (1947): 5–42.
21. M. Gladwell, *Blink: The Power of Thinking without Thinking* (New York: Little, Brown and Company, 2005).
22. See S. Taggar, "Individual Creativity and Group Ability to Utilize Individual Creative Resources: A Multilevel Model," *Academy of Management Journal* 45 (2002): 315–330; C. E. Johnson and M. A. Hackman, *Creative Communication: Principles and Applications* (Prospect Heights, IL: Waveland Press, 1995).
23. A. F. Osborn, *Applied Imagination* (New York: Scribner's, 1962).
24. A. L. Delberg, A. H. Van de Ven, and D. H. Gustason, *Group Techniques for Program Planning: A Guide to Nominal Group and Delphi Processes* (Glenview, IL: Scott, Foresman, 1975), 7–16.
25. D. Straker, *Rapid Problem Solving with Post-it® Notes* (Tucson: Fisher Books, 1997).
26. M. A. Roberto, "Strategic Decision-Making Processes: Beyond the Efficiency–Consensus Trade-Off," *Group & Organizational Management* 29 (2004): 625–658.
27. Adapted from Beebe and Masterson, *Communicating in Small Groups*.
28. R. Y. Hirokawa, D. S. Gouran, and A. Martz, "Understanding the Sources of Faulty Group Decision Making: A Lesson from the Challenger Disaster," *Small Group Behavior* 19 (1988): 411–433.
29. R. K. M. Haurwitz, "Faculty Doubted Bonfire's Stability," *Austin-American Statesman* (December 10, 1999), A1, A2.
30. D. Jehl, "Panel Unanimous: 'Groupthink' Backed Prewar Assumptions, Report Concludes," *New York Times* (July 10, 2004), 1; also see *The 9/11 Commission Report: Final Report of the National Commission on Terrorist Attacks upon the United States* (Washington, DC: National Commission on Terrorist Attacks, 2004).
31. J. F. Veiga, "The Frequency of Self-Limiting Behavior in Groups: A Measure and an Explanation," *Human Relations* 44 (1991): 877–895.
32. I. L. Janis, *Victims of Groupthink* (Boston: Houghton Mifflin, 1973).
33. C. M. Mason and M. R. Griffin, "Group Task Satisfaction: The Group's Attitude to Its Task and Work Environment," *Group & Organization Management* 30 (6) (2005): 625–652.
34. M. S. Limon and B. H. La France, "Communication Traits and Lead-

ership Emergence: Examining the Impact of Argumentativeness, Communication Apprehension, and Verbal Aggressiveness in Work Groups," *Southern Communication Journal* 70 (2) (2005): 123–133; also see A. M. L. Raes, U. Glunk, M. G. Heijltjes, and R. A. Roe, "Top Management Team and Middle Managers: Making Sense of Leadership," *Small Group Research* 38 (3) (2007): 360–386.

35. See B. M. Bass, *Stodgill's Handbook of Leadership* (New York: The Free Press, 1981).

36. A. Srivastava, K. M. Bartol, and E. A. Locke, "Empowering Leadership in Management Teams: Effects of Knowledge Sharing, Efficacy, and Performance," *Academy of Management Journal* 49 (6) (2006): 1239–1251.

37. G. J. Galanes, "In Their Own Words: An Exploratory Study of Bona Fide Group Leaders," *Small Group Research* 34 (2003): 741–770.

38. P. Balkundi and D. Harrison, "Ties, Leaders, and Time in Teams: Strong Inference about Network Structure's Effects on Team Viability and Performance," *Academy of Management Journal* 49 (1) (2006): 49–68.

39. R. White and R. Lippitt, "Leader Behavior and Member Reaction in Three 'Social Climates,'" in *Group Dynamics* 3e, edited by D. Cartwright and A. Zander (New York: Harper & Row, 1968), 319.

40. M. Van Vugt, S. F. Jepson, C. M. Hart, and D. De Cremer, "Autocratic Leadership in Social Dilemmas: A Threat to Group Stability," *Journal of Experimental and Social Psychology* 40 (2004): 1–13.

41. S. Halverson, S. E. Murphy, and R. E. Riggio, "Charismatic Leadership in Crisis Situations: A Laboratory Investigation of Stress and Crisis," *Small Group Research* 35 (2004): 495–514.

42. S. S. K. Lam, X. P. Chen, and J. Schaubroeck, "Participative Decision Making and Employee Performance in Different Cultures: The Moderating Effects of Allocentrism/Idiocentrism and Efficacy," *Academy of Management Journal* 45 (2002): 905–914.

43. David C. Korten, "Situational Determinants of Leadership Structure," *Journal of Conflict Resolution* 6 (1962): 222–235.

44. F. Fiedler, *A Theory of Leadership Effectiveness* (New York: McGraw-Hill, 1967), 144.

45. A. Malhotra, A. Majchrzak, and B. Rosen, "Leading Virtual Teams," *Academy of Management Perspectives* (February 2007): 60–70.

46. B.M. Bass and M.J. Avolio, "Transformational Leadership and Organizational Culture," *International Journal of Public Administration* 17 (1994): 541–554; also see F. J. Yammarino and A. J. Dubinsky, "Transformational Leadership Theory: Using Levels of Analysis to Determine Boundary Conditions," *Personnel Psychology* 47 (1994): 787–809.

47. For additional research about the efficacy of transformational leadership, see J. McCann, P. Langford, and R. M. Rawlings, "Testing Behling and McFillen's Syncretical Model of Charismatic Transformational Leadership," *Group & Organization Management* 31 (2) (2006): 237–263; R. F. Piccolo and J. Colquitt, "Transformational Leadership and Job Behaviors: The Mediating Role of Core Job Characteristics," *Academy of Management Journal* 49 (2) (2006): 327–340; R. S. Rubin, D. C. Muniz, and W. H. Bommer, "Leading from Within: The Effects of Emotion Recognition and Personality on Transformational Leadership Behavior," *Academy of Management Journal* 48 (5) (2005): 845–858; A. Ergeneli, R. Gohar, and Z. Temirbekova, "Transformational Leadership: Its Relationship to Culture Value Dimensions," *International Journal of Intercultural Relations* 31 (2007): 703–724.

48. P. M. Senge, "The Leader's New Role: Building Learning Organizations," *Sloan Management Review* 32 (1) (1990).

49. D. I. Jung and J. J. Sosik, "Transformational Leadership in Work Groups: The Role of Empowerment, Cohesiveness, and Collective Efficacy on Perceived Group Performance," *Small Group Research* 33 (2002): 313–336; also see T. Dvir, D. Eden, B. J. Avolio, and B. Shamir, "Impact of Transformational Leadership on Follower Development and Performance: A Field Experiment," *Academy of Management Journal* 45 (2002): 735–744; C. L. Hoyt and J. Blascovich, "Transformational and Transactional Leadership in Virtual and Physical Environments," *Small Group Research* 34 (2003): 678–715.

50. V. U. Druskat and J. V. Wheeler, "Managing from the Boundary: The Effective Leadership of Self-Managing Work Teams," *Academy of Management Journal* 46 (2003): 435–457.

51. M. Zellmer-Bruhn and C. Gibson, "Multinational Organization Context: Implications for Team Learning and Performance," *Academy of Management Journal* 49 (3) (2006): 501–518.

52. For an excellent discussion of transformational leadership applied to teams, see S. D. Dionne, F. J. Yammarino, L. E. Atwater, and W. D. Spangler, "Transformational Leadership and Team Performance," *Journal of Organizational Change Management* 17 (2004): 177–193.

53. J. A. Raelin, "Don't Bother Putting Leadership into People," *Academy of Management Executive* 18 (2004): 131–135; M. W. McCall, "Leadership Development through Experience," *Academy of Management Executive* 18 (2004): 127–130; J. Conger, "Developing Leadership Capability: What's inside the Black Box?" *Academy of Management Executive* 18 (2004): 136–139; D. Vera and M. Crossan, "Strategic Leadership and Organizational Learning," *Academy of Management Review* 29 (2004): 222–239.

54. D. Barry, *Dave Barry Turns 50* (New York: Ballantine Books, 1998), 182.

55. For a discussion of monochronic and polychronic time, see E. T. Hall, *The Silent Language* (New York: Doubleday, 1959).

56. Hall, *The Silent Language*.

57. Hall, *The Silent Language*.

58. M. J. Waller, M. E. Zellmer-Bruhn, and R. C. Giambatista, "Watching the Clock: Group Pacing Behavior under Dynamic Deadlines," *Academy of Management Journal* 45 (2002): 1046–1055.

59. R. K. Mosvick and R. B. Nelson, *We've Got to Start Meeting Like This!* (Glenview, IL: Scott, Foresman, 1987).

60. Suggestions about organizing meeting agendas are based on M. Doyle and D. Straus, *How to Make Meetings Work* (New York: Playboy Press, 1976); Mosvick and Nelson, *We've Got to Start Meeting Like This!*; G. Lumsden and D. Lumsden, *Communicating in Groups and Teams: Sharing Leadership* (Belmont, CA: Wadsworth, 1993); D. B. Curtis, J. J. Floyd, and J. L. Winsor, *Business and Professional Communication* (New York: HarperCollins, 1992); Romig, *Breakthrough Teamwork*; T. A. Kayser, *Mining Group Gold* (El Segundo, CA: Serif Publishing, 1990); J. E. Tropman and G. Clark Morningstar, *Meetings: How to Make Them Work for You* (New York: Van Nostrand Reinhold, 1985): 56; Beebe and Masterson, *Communicating in Small Groups*.

61. J. E. Tropman, *Making Meetings Work* (Thousand Oaks, CA: Sage, 1996).

62. See D. S. Gouran, "Variables Related to Consensus in Group Discussions of Questions of Policy," *Speech Monographs* 36 (1969): 385–391; T. J. Knutsun, "An Experimental Study of the Effects of Orientation Behavior on Small Group Consensus," *Speech Monographs* 39 (1972): 159–165; J. A. Kline, "Orientation and Group Consensus," *Central States Speech Journal* 23 (1972): 44–47.

63. Mosvick and Nelson, *We've Got to Start Meeting Like This!*

64. J. B. Walther and U. Bunz, "The Rules of Virtual Groups: Trust, Liking, and Performance in Computer-Mediated Communication," *Journal of Communication* (December 2005): 828–846.

65. S. A. Beebe and J. K. Barge, "Evaluating Group Discussion," in *Small Group Communication: Theory & Practice*, edited by R. Y. Hirokawa, R. S. Cathcart, L. A. Samovar, and L. D. Henman (Los Angeles, CA: Roxbury, 2003).

CHAPTER 11

1. J. Fitzgerald, "Metcalfe to MIT Geeks: Get to Writin'," *The Boston Herald* (April 28, 2005).

2. The sample presentation developed in this chapter is adapted from M. Yancey, "Cyberterrorism," prepared for Individual Events/Persuasive Speaking competition, The University of Texas, Spring 2008.

3. S. Booth-Butterfield, "Instructional Interventions for Situational Anxiety and Avoidance," *Communication Education* 37 (1988): 214–223.

4. Survey conducted by R. H. Bruskin and Associates, *Spectra* 9 (December 1973): 4.

5. J. K. Rowling, "The Fringe Benefits of Failure, and the Importance of Imagination," Harvard University commencement address, June 5, 2008, <www.news.harvard.edu/gazette/2008/06.05/99-rowlingspeech.html>.

6. K. Savitsky and T. Gilovich, "The Illusion of Transparency and the Alleviation of Speech Anxiety," *Journal of Experimental Social Psychology* 39 (2003): 618–625.

7. K. Dwyer and D. Fus, "Perceptions of Communication Competence,

Self-Efficacy, and Trait Communication Apprehension: Is There an Impact on Basic Course Success?" *Communication Research Reports 19* (2002): 29–37.

8. M. Booth-Butterfield, "Stifle or Stimulate? The Effects of Communication Task Structure on Apprehensive and Non-Apprehensive Students," *Communication Education* 35 (1986): 337–348; Charles R. Berger, "Speechlessness: Causal Attributions, Emotional Features, and Social Consequences," *Journal of Language and Social Psychology* 23 (June 2004): 147–179.

9. J. Ayres, "Speech Preparation Processes and Speech Apprehension," *Communication Education* 45 (1996): 228–235.

10. P. Addison, E. Clay, S. Xie, C. R. Sawyer, and R. R. Behnke, "Worry as a Function of Public Speaking State Anxiety Type," *Communication Research Reports 16* (Summer 2003): 125–131.

11. Addison, Clay, Xie, Sawyer, and Behnke, "Worry as a Function of Public Speaking State Anxiety Type."

12. S. C. McCullough, S. G. Russell, R. R. Behnke, C. R. Sawyer, and P. L. Witt, "Anticipatory Public Speaking State Anxiety as a Function of Body Sensations and State of Mind," *Communication Quarterly* 54(*1*) (February 1, 2006): 101–109; P. L. Witt, K. C. Brown, J. B. Roberts, J. Weisel, C. R. Sawyer, and R. R. Behnke, "Somatic Anxiety Patterns before, during, and after Giving a Public Speech," *Southern Communication Journal* 71(*1*) (March 2006): 87–100.

13. Critics of systematic desensitization argue that there may be a placebo effect: Just thinking that a treatment will reduce apprehension may contribute to reduced apprehension. See D. C. Duff, T. R. Levine, M. J. Beatty, J. Woolbright, and H. S. Park, "Testing Public Anxiety Treatments against a Credible Placebo Control," *Communication Education* 56 (January 2007): 72–88.

14. J. Ayres and B. Huett, "An Examination of the Impact of Performance Visualization," *Communication Research Reports 16* (1999): 29–39; J. Ayres and B. Huett, "An Examination of the Long-Term Effect of Performance Visualization," *Communication Research Reports 17* (2000): 229–236.

15. L. Tracy, "Taming Hostile Audiences," *Vital Speeches of the Day* 71(*10*) (March 1, 2005).

16. J. Humphrey, "Taking the Stage: How Women Can Achieve a Leadership Presence," *Vital Speeches of the Day* (May 1, 2001): 437.

17. Data provided by Center for Defense Information, "Chronology of Major Terrorist Attacks against U.S. Targets," *CDI Terrorism Project*, June 27, 2002, <www.cdi.org/terrorism/chronology-pr.html>; "September 11 Fatalities Make 2001 the Worst Year," *Airwise News*, January 4, 2002 <news.airwise.com/stories/2002/01/1010177858.html>, retrieved June 27, 2002.

18. D. Sullivan, "Google 2.0: Google Universal Search," *Search Engine Land*, May 16, 2007, <searchengineland.com/070516-143312.php>.

19. W. Mossberg, "Product Review: Vertical Search Sites Promising," *Tucson Citizen*, April 6, 2005, <www.tucsoncitizen.com/index.php?page=business&story_id=040605d1_vertical&toolbar=print_story>, retrieved May 24, 2005.

20. B. Hartzer, "A New Search Engine for Surgeons Launches," *WebProNews*, June 4, 2008, <www.webpronews.com/blogtalk/2008/06/04/a-new-search-engine-for-surgeons-launches> retrieved June 11, 2008; "New Web Company BizAg.com Launches," *PRWeb*, June 4, 2008 <news.yahoo.com/s/prweb/20080604/bs_prweb/prweb995854_1>, retrieved June 11, 2008.

21. These criteria for evaluating web resources are adapted from E. Kirk, "Practical Steps in Evaluating Internet Resources," May 7, 2001, <Milton.mse.jhu.edu:8001/research/education/practical.html>, retrieved May 22, 2001.

22. J. Heffernan et al., *Writing: A College Handbook* 5e (New York: Norton, 2001), 53–54.

23. P. Gorski, "A Multicultural Model for Evaluating Educational Web Sites," December 1999, <curry.edschool.Virginia.edu/go/multicultural/net/comps/model.html>, retrieved May 22, 2001; "Section 508," August 15, 2002, <www.section.508.gov/index.cfm?FuseAction=Content&ID=11>, retrieved May 26, 2005.

24. "Section 508."

25. M. Mirapaul, "Making Federal Web Sites Friendly to Disabled Users," *New York Times* (June 11, 2001): B2.

26. U.S. Government Printing Office, "National Bibliography Program," *GPO Access*. May 8, 2007, <www.access.gpo.gov/su_docs/fdlp/cip/index.html>, retrieved June 11, 2008.

27. George W. Bush, State of the Union address, January 28, 2008, *Vital Speeches of the Day* 74(*3*) (March 2008): 98–103.

28. B. Moyers, "What Adam Said to Eve," prepared remarks for the annual conference of the Association for Education in Journalism and Mass Communication, Washington, D.C., August 8, 2007, <www.pbs.org/moyers/journal/blog/2007/08/what_adam_said_to_eve.html>.

29. M. Sanchez, "Diplomatic Immunity Unjustified," in *Winning Orations 1996* (Mankato, MN: Interstate Oratorical Association, 1996), 66.

30. M. Limon and D. Kazoleas, "A Comparison of Exemplar and Statistical Evidence in Reducing Counter-Arguments and Responses to a Message," *Communication Research Reports* 21 (2004): 291–298.

31. D. Lessing, "On Not Winning the Nobel Prize," *Vital Speeches of the Day* 74(*2*) (February 2008), Academic Search Complete, Texas State U–San Marcos Lib., San Marcos, TX, <web.ebscohost.com>, retrieved June 7, 2008.

32. R. B. Ginsburg, "The Role of Dissenting Opinions," *Vital Speeches of the Day* 74(*4*) (April 2008): 157–160. Academic Search Complete, Texas State U–San Marcos Lib., San Marcos, TX, <web.ebscohost.com>, retrieved June 7, 2008.

33. S. Horton, "How Hollywood Learned to Stop Worrying and Love the (Ticking) Bomb," *Vital Speeches of the Day* 74(*4*) (April 2008): 181–185, Academic Search Complete, Texas State U–San Marcos Lib., San Marcos, TX, <web.ebscohost.com>, retrieved June 7, 2008.

34. K. Gunderson, "Following Fiscal Footsteps: Can European Tax Trends Work for America?" *Winning Orations 2006* (Mankato, MN: Interstate Oratorical Association, 2006), 28.

35. R. Pausch, "Really Achieving Your Childhood Dreams," lecture given at Carnegie Mellon University, September 18, 2007, <download.srv.cs.cmu.edu/~pausch/>.

36. J. Celoria, "The Counterfeiting of Airline Safety: An Examination of the Dangers of Bogus Airline Parts," *Winning Orations 1997* (Mankato, MN: Interstate Oratorical Association, 1997), 79.

37. J. T. Masterson and N. Watson, "The Effects of Culture on Preferred Speaking Style," paper presented at the meeting of the Speech Communication Association, November, 1979.

38. See D. A. Lieberman, *Public Speaking in the Multicultural Environment* 2e (Boston: Allyn & Bacon, 1997).

39. J. Sweeney, "Fairness and Economic Equality," *Vital Speeches of the Day* 74(*5*) (May 2008): 226–228, Academic Search Complete. Texas State U–San Marcos Lib., San Marcos, TX, <web.ebscohost.com>, retrieved June 7, 2008.

40. S. Brunner, "Advanced Technology: Solving the DUI Dilemma," *Winning Orations 2007* (Mankato, MN: Interstate Oratorical Association, 2007), 77.

41. J. Pruitt, "College Credit Card Crisis," *Winning Orations 1996* (Mankato, MN: Interstate Oratorical Association, 1996), 26.

42. J. Zucker, "A Time for Change," *Vital Speeches of the Day* 74(*5*) (May 2008): 204–208, Academic Search Complete, Texas State U–San Marcos Lib., San Marcos, TX, <web.ebscohost.com>, retrieved June 7, 2008.

43. Adapted from Austin Wright, "Superbug," prepared for Individual Events/Persuasive Speaking competition, The University of Texas, Spring 2008.

CHAPTER 12

1. L. Tracy, "Taming Hostile Audiences," *Vital Speeches of the Day* 71(*10*) (March 1, 2005).

2. K. Aristilde, "Ignorance and Poverty," *Winning Orations 2006* (Mankato, MN: Interstate Oratorical Association, 2006), 33.

3. D. A. Lieberman, *Public Speaking in the Multicultural Environment* 2e (Boston: Allyn & Bacon, 1997), 23.

4. Lieberman, *Public Speaking in the Multicultural Environment*.

5. C. Vian, "The Continued Segregation of American Schools," *Winning Orations 2006* (Mankato, MN: Interstate Oratorical Association, 2006), 62.

6. A. Norman, untitled speech, *Winning Orations 2006* (Mankato, MN: Interstate Oratorical Association, 2006), 17.

7. M. Erikson, "See Jane, See Jane's Dilemma," *Winning Orations 1997* (Mankato, MN: Interstate Oratorical Association, 1997), 63.

8. R. Pausch, "Really Achieving Your Childhood Dreams," lecture given at Carnegie Mellon University, September 18, 2007, <download.srv.cs.cmu.edu/~pausch/>.
9. S. Hamilton, "Cruise Ship Violence," *Winning Orations 2000* (Mankato, MN: Interstate Oratorical Association, 2000), 95.
10. B. Ruet, "Sudan's Forgotten War," *Winning Orations 2006* (Mankato, MN: Interstate Oratorical Association, 2006), 49.
11. B. Collins, commencement address delivered at Rollins College, May 11, 2008, quoted in "Remembering Commencement 2008," <news.rollins.edu/08commencements.shtml>.
12. B. Obama, "A More Perfect Union," *Vital Speeches of the Day 74(5)* (May 2008): 194–199, Academic Search Complete, Texas State U–San Marcos Lib., San Marcos, TX, <web.ebscohost.com>, retrieved June 9, 2008.
13. C. Reed, "Decreasing Red Meat in Your Diet," speech delivered at Texas State University–San Marcos, 2005.
14. A. Watson, "Post-Traumatic Stress Disorder: Our Soldiers' Next War," *Winning Orations 2007* (Mankato, MN: Interstate Oratorical Association, 2007), 81.
15. Watson, "Post-Traumatic Stress Disorder: Our Soldiers' Next War," 81.
16. A. Lincoln, "Gettysburg Address," delivered at Gettysburg, PA, November 19, 1863, Douglass Archives of American Public Address, August 19, 1998, <douglass.speech.nwu.edu/linc_b33.htm>, retrieved July 12, 1999.
17. D. MacArthur, "Farewell to the Cadets," address delivered at West Point, May 12, 1962, in *Contemporary American Speeches* 7e, edited by R. L. Johannesen, R. R. Allen, and W. A. Linkugel (Dubuque, IA: Kendall/Hunt, 1992), 393.
18. M. L. King Jr., "I Have a Dream," delivered in Washington, DC, August 28, 1963, in *Contemporary American Speeches*, 369.
19. T. Kirchhefer, "The Deprived," *Winning Orations 2000* (Mankato, MN: Interstate Oratorical Association, 2000), 151.
20. S. Brunner, "Advanced Technology: Solving the DUI Dilemma," *Winning Orations 2007* (Mankato, MN: Interstate Oratorical Association, 2007), 78.
21. The preparation outline on pages 341–343 and the speaking notes that appear on page 344 are adapted from a speech by M. Yancey, "Cyberterrorism," prepared for Individual Events/Persuasive Speaking Competition, The University of Texas, Spring 2008.

CHAPTER 13

1. A. H. Monroe, "Measurement and Analysis of Audience Reaction to Student Speakers' Studies in Attitude Changes," *Bulletin of Purdue University Studies in Higher Education 22* (1937).
2. P. Heinbert, "Relationship of Content and Delivery to General Effectiveness," *Speech Monographs 30* (1963): 105–107.
3. A. Mehrabian, *Nonverbal Communication* (Hawthorne, NY: Aldine, 1972).
4. J. Detz, "Delivery plus Content Equals Successful Presentation," *Communication World 15* (1998): 34.
5. Adapted from R. Ailes, *You Are the Message* (New York: Doubleday, 1989), 37–38.
6. P. Begala, "Flying Solo," PBS, *The Clinton Years: Anecdotes*, 2000 <http://www.pbs.org/wgbh/pages/frontline/shows/clinton/anecdotes/#5>, retrieved July 14, 2002.
7. J. Wareham, "Doing It off-the-Cuff," *Across the Board 35* (1998): 49–50.
8. Wareham, "Doing It off-the-Cuff."
9. L. White and L. Messer, "An Analysis of Interstate Speeches: Are They Structurally Different?" *National Forensic Journal 21(2)* (Fall 2003): 15, <cas.bethel.edu/dept/comm/nfa/nfj.html>.
10. G. Orwell, "Politics and the English Language," in *About Language*, edited by W. H. Roberts and G. Turgeson (Boston: Houghton Mifflin, 1986), 282.
11. M. Klepper, *I'd Rather Die than Give a Speech* (New York: Carol Publishing Group, 1994), 45.
12. W. Safire, "Faithful, Even in Death," *New York Times Magazine* (April 18, 1999): 72–74. Quotes from Vest's speech are from the text reprinted in this article.
13. B. Moyers, "What Adam Said to Eve," prepared remarks for the annual conference of the Association for Education in Journalism and Mass Communication, Washington, DC, August 8, 2007, <www.pbs.org/moyers/journal/blog/2007/08/what_adam_said_to_eve.html>.
14. J. F. Kennedy, inaugural address, January 20, 1961, in *Speeches in English*, edited by B. Aly and L. F. Aly (New York: Random House, 1968), 272.
15. J. Carter, address to the Democratic National Convention, July 2004, <www.dems2004.org/site/pp.asp?c=1u12LAPYG&b=92959>, retrieved August 1, 2004.
16. J. McCain, "A Leader We Can Believe In," address delivered June 3, 2008, in Kenner, LA, <www.americanrhetoric.com/speeches/johnmccainrepublicannominationspeech.htm>.
17. E. Wiesel, "The Perils of Indifference," delivered at the White House, April 12, 1999 <http://www.historyplace.com/speeches/wiesel.htm>, retrieved July 1, 1999.
18. N. Giovanni, convocation address at Virginia Tech, April 17, 2007, <www.vt.edu/remember/archive/Giovanni_transcript.php>, retrieved June 25, 2007.
19. J. F. Kennedy, "Address at Rice University on the Space Effort," delivered at Rice University, September 12, 1962, <http://riceinfo.rice.edu/Fondren/Woodson/speech.html>, retrieved July 1, 1999.
20. S. A. Beebe, "Eye Contact: A Nonverbal Determinant of Speaker Credibility," *Speech Teacher 23* (1974): 21–25; S.A. Beebe, "Effects of Eye Contact, Posture and Vocal Inflection upon Credibility and Comprehension," *Australian Scan Journal of Nonverbal Communication 7–8* (1979–1980): 57–70; M. Cobin, "Response to Eye Contact," *Quarterly Journal of Speech 48* (1963): 415–419.
21. Beebe, "Eye Contact."
22. E. Adler, "Gestures May Give You a Hand with Speaking," *Austin American-Statesman* (November 25, 1998): E6.
23. J. C. McCroskey, V. P. Richmond, A. Sallinen, J. M. Fayer, and R. A. Barraclough, "A Cross-Cultural and Multi-Behavioral Analysis of the Relationship between Nonverbal Immediacy and Teacher Evaluation," *Communication Education 44* (1995): 281–290.
24. M.J. Beatty, "Some Effects of Posture on Speaker Credibility," library paper, Central Missouri State University, 1973.
25. R. Schmid, "Study: Posture Able to Communicate Fear," The Associated Press, November 16, 2004, <news.yahoo.com>.
26. P. Ekman, W. V. Friesen, and S. S. Tomkins, "Facial Affect Scoring Technique: A First Validity Study," *Semiotica 3* (1971).
27. P. Ekman and W. Friesen, *Unmasking the Face* (Englewood Cliffs, NJ: Prentice-Hall, 1975).
28. "Bush's Smirk and Kerry's Smile Send the Wrong Message, Say Experts," The Associated Press, October 1, 2004, <news.yahoo.com>.
29. M. M. Gill, "Accents and Stereotypes: Their Effect on Perceptions of Teachers and Lecture Comprehension," *Journal of Applied Communication Research 22* (1994): 348–361.
30. E. Bohn and D. Jabusch, "The Effect of Four Methods of Instruction on the Use of Visual Aids in Speeches," *Western Journal of Speech Communication 46* (1982): 253–265.
31. Adapted from S. Linver, *Speak Easy: How to Talk Your Way to the Top* (New York: Summit Books, 1978), 204–205.
32. A. Wilson, "In Defense of Rhetoric," *The Toastmaster 70(2)* (2004): 11.
33. U.S. Department of Health and Human Services, Administration on Aging, "Older Population by Age: 1900 to 2050," June 2005, <www.aoa.gov/prof/Statistics/online_stat_data/AgePop2050.asp>, retrieved June 17, 2008.
34. D. Cyphert, "Presentation Technology in the Age of Electronic Eloquence: From Visual Aid to Visual Rhetoric," *Communication Education 56(2)* (April 2007): 168–192, Communication and Mass Media Complete, Texas State U–San Marcos Lib., San Marcos, TX, June 11, 2008.
35. Detz, "Delivery plus Content Equals Successful Presentation."
36. T. Smith and A. B. Frymier, "Get 'Real': Does Practicing Speeches before an Audience Improve Performance?" *Communication Quarterly 54(1)* (February 2006): 111–125.
37. Review of *Personal Information Management*, edited by W. Jones and J. Teevan (Seattle: University of Washington Press, 2007), June 13, 2008, <www.washington.edu/uwpress/search/books/JONPEP.html>, retrieved June 17, 2008.
38. UNAIDS, "2008 Report on the Global AIDS Epidemic," July 2008,

CHAPTER 14

1. J. R. Johnson and N. Szczupakiewicz, "The Public Speaking Course: Is It Preparing Students with Work-Related Public Speaking Skills?" *Communication Education* 36 (1987): 131–137.
2. For an excellent discussion of teaching someone to perform a skill, especially a social skill, see M. Argyle, *The Psychology of Interpersonal Behavior* (London: Penguin, 1990).
3. For an excellent discussion of strategies for informing others, see K. E. Rowan, "A New Pedagogy for Explanatory Public Speaking: Why Arrangement Should Not Substitute for Invention," *Communication Education* 44 (1995): 236–250.
4. For an excellent discussion of factors affecting audience attention in public speaking, see D. Ehninger, B. E. Gronbeck, R. E. McKerrow, and A. H. Monroe, *Principles and Types of Speech Communication* (Glenview, IL: Scott, Foresman, 1986), 43.
5. This suggestion is based on an excellent review of the literature found in Rowan, "A New Pedagogy for Explanatory Public Speaking."
6. M. Groover, "Learning to Communicate: The Importance of Speech Education in Public Schools," in *Winning Orations 1984* (Mankato, MN: Interstate Oratorical Association, 1984), 7.
7. M. Klepper and R. Gunther, *I'd Rather Die than Give a Speech* (New York: Carol Publishing Group, 1995).
8. Our discussion of using humor is adapted from Klepper and Gunther, *I'd Rather Die than Give a Speech*.
9. Klepper and Gunther, *I'd Rather Die than Give a Speech*.
10. M. Knowles, *The Adult Learner: A Neglected Species* 3e (Houston: Gulf Publishing Co., 1990).
11. A. Tisino, "The Power of Music," Texas State University–San Marcos, 2005.
12. L. Hughes, *The First Book of Rhythms* (New York: Franklin Watts, 1954).

APPENDIX B

1. M. K. Raffetto, "Advertising and Reptilian Codes," prepared for Individual Events/Informative Speaking Competition, The University of Texas, Spring 2008.
2. A Solomito, untitled speech, in *Winning Orations 2007* (Mankato, MN: Interstate Oratorical Association, 2007), 72–74.

Practice Test Answer Key

CHAPTER 1
1. b
2. b
3. b
4. d
5. a
6. b
7. c
8. b
9. b
10. c

CHAPTER 2
1. a
2. d
3. b
4. a
5. c
6. b
7. d
8. b
9. c
10. c

CHAPTER 3
1. b
2. b
3. b
4. a
5. b
6. a
7. c
8. d
9. b
10. d

CHAPTER 4
1. d
2. d
3. b
4. d
5. c
6. a
7. a
8. b
9. d
10. c

CHAPTER 5
1. b
2. b
3. c
4. d
5. a
6. d
7. b
8. d
9. b
10. d

CHAPTER 6
1. d
2. c
3. c
4. a
5. a
6. d
7. d
8. c
9. a
10. b

CHAPTER 7
1. d
2. d
3. c
4. d
5. c
6. d
7. a
8. b
9. c
10. a

CHAPTER 8
1. a
2. c
3. a
4. b
5. c
6. a
7. d
8. a
9. a
10. d

CHAPTER 9
1. c
2. b
3. c
4. c
5. a
6. c
7. d
8. b
9. d
10. a

CHAPTER 10
1. d
2. d
3. b
4. c
5. b
6. a
7. c
8. b
9. d
10. c

CHAPTER 11
1. b
2. a
3. c
4. d
5. a
6. c
7. c
8. b
9. c
10. b

CHAPTER 12
1. a
2. b
3. b
4. a
5. d
6. c
7. b
8. b
9. d
10. d

CHAPTER 13
1. a
2. d
3. a
4. d
5. a
6. c
7. d
8. c
9. b
10. c

CHAPTER 14
1. a
2. c
3. b
4. c
5. a
6. a
7. c
8. d
9. d
10. b

Index

A.Word.A.Day, 83
ABI/Inform Global, 314
Abolition of Man, The (Lewis), 159
Abstract meaning, 63–65
Abuse, verbal, 218
Academic quarter, 359
Academic Search Complete, 314
Acronyms, online use of, 181
Action
 communication as, 10–12
 in motivated sequence, 417
Action-oriented listener, 118
Active listening, 131
Active strategy, for reducing uncertainty, 182–183
Acton, Lord, 157
Ad hominem argument, 412
Adaptation, 22, 142, 166–167
 to age, 146–148
 barriers to, 157–160
 culture and, 148–156, 161–167, 318
 ethical, 148, 167
 to ethnicity, 146
 to gender, 143–145
 to interviewee's behavior, 445
 persuasive speeches and, 419–421
 presentation aids and, 367
 to sexual orientation, 145
Adaptor behaviors, 97
Adult learning principles, 390
Advertising, TV, 400, 418
"Advertising and Reptilian Codes" (Raffetto), 448–450
Affect displays, 97
Affection, 180
African Americans
 language bias and, 71
 in U.S. population, 149
Age
 adapting to, 146–148
 biased language and, 74–75
Agenda, meeting, 281–282
Aggressive communication, 218–219
Aggressor (group role), 243
All-channel network pattern of small group communication, 247, 248, 249
Alliteration, 355
Allness, 69
Altman, Irwin, 191, 192
Ambiguity, 163–164
American Association of University Women, 41
American Sign language, 66, 86
Amish community, as co-culture, 150
Analogy
 figurative, 318
 literal, 317

reasoning by, 411
Andersen, Peter, 106
Androgynous, 143
Anticipatory communication, 120
Antithesis, 355
Appeal(s)
 to fear, 403–404
 to invitation, 97–98
 to misplaced authority, 413
Appearance
 of job interviewee, 439–440
 nonverbal messages and, 95
 of speaker, 361–362
Appraisal interview, 430–431
Appropriateness, in self-disclosure, 188–189
Arguments, serial, 216
Aristilde, Kerlin, 331
Aristotle, 25, 202, 350, 400, 408
Armstrong, Nancy, 96
Arousal cues, 106–107
Articulation, 361
Artifacts, 95
Asada, Kelli Jean, 203
ASCII file, 443
Ascribed identity, 38
Asian Americans, 149
Assertive communication, 218–220
Asynchronous communication, 15, 116
Attending, 115–116
Attention
 in motivated sequence, 416
 perception and, 50–51
 shifting, 124
Attitudes, 34, 87–88, 406
Attraction, 177–182
Audience, 295–296
 adapting to. *See* Adaptation
 central idea and, 306
 conclusion and, 338
 introduction and, 337
 motivations of, 387–388, 402–405, 416–419
 organizing for, 333–335
 purpose and, 303–305, 405–406
 speaker anxiety and, 298–299
 topic and, 300, 385–386
 types of, 419–421
Audience-centered presentational speakers, 296
Authoritarian leaders, 275–276
Autonomy vs. connection, 212–213
Avowed identity, 38
Awesome Library, 171
Axtell, Roger, 96

Baby boomers, 147, 148, 149
Back-channel cues, 102
Bafflegab, 79, 83
Baker, Sidney, 102

Bandwagon fallacy, 412
Bar graph, 365
Barker, Larry, 118, 119
Barnlund, Dean, 17
Barry, Dave, 279
Barton, Nicholas, 415
Baxter, Leslie, 211, 212
Bedside manner, 175
Begala, Paul, 351
Beliefs, 34, 406
Benne, Kenneth, 240
Bentley, Sheila, 116
Berger, Charles, 182
Bias
 of interviewer, 445
 in language, 69–75
 on web sites, 312
Bible Society, 60
BizAg (search engine), 311
Black English, 66
Blink: The Power of Thinking Without Thinking (Gladwell), 160
Blocker (group role), 243
Blog, 189
Bodenhausen, Galen, 57
Body Language (Fast), 93
Body movement, 95–98
Bok, Derek, 376
Bona fide perspective, 252–253
Boolean search, 311
Boom microphone, 360
Bradac, James, 182
Brainstorming, 268–270, 301–302
Braithwaite, Charles, 100
Breakups, 209–210
BreakUpService.com, 210
Brothers, Joyce, 112
Brown, Donald, 159
Bryant, Donald C., 419
Buddhism, moral code of, 9
Bukobza, Gabriel, 35
Burgoon, Judee, 92
Bush, George W., 69, 91, 315, 360, 363, 400
Bypassing, 63

C-SPAN Online, 375
Cadence, in delivery, 355
Calabrese, Richard, 182
Call number, 312–313
Campbell, Jennifer, 40
Card catalog, 313
CareerBuilder.com, 436, 440
Carell, Steve, 99
Carnegie, Dale, 204
Carrell, Lori, 167
Carter, Jimmy, 355
Cartoons, in informative presentation, 389

Index

"Caucasian," language bias and, 71
Causal fallacy, 412
Causal reasoning, 412
Cause-and-effect organization
  of main ideas, 330
  of persuasive speech, 415–416
CDs, as presentation aids, 366
Central idea
  developing, 305–307
  conclusion and, 337–338
  main ideas and, 308–309
  as persuasive proposition, 406–408
Centralized power, 155
Certainty, and culture, 154, 155
Chain network pattern of small group
  comunication, 248–249
Challenger space shuttle, 271
Channel, 11
Chaplin, William, 89
Charisma, 409
Charts
  as presentation aids, 364
  T-, 272–273
Cheng, C. Y., 120
Choice, relationships of, 176
Christianity, moral code of, 9
Christians, Clifford, 8
Chronological organization, 329
Churchill, Winston, 77, 296
Circumstance, relationships of, 176
Classification
  definition by, 317
  library system of, 312–313
Clinton, Bill, 75, 351
Clique, 247–248
"Close talker," 92, 93
Closed questions, 433
Closure, 51, 338
CMC (computer-mediated communication),
  88, 189
Coaching, life, 185–186
Co-cultures, 68, 150
Code switching, 60, 66
Coercion, 400
Coercive power, 245–246
Cognitive dissonance, 402
Cohesiveness, of groups/teams, 246–247,
  256–257
Collaborative learning, 237
Collectivistic cultures, 153–156, 163
  conflict and, 217
  groups/teams and, 252
Collins, Billy, 336
Columbia space shuttle, 271
Come here gesture, 96
Communication, 5–7. *See also* Conflict,
    interpersonal; Messages
  of attraction, 180–181
  characteristics of, 16–18
  competent, 7–9
  defensive, 76–77
  group, 23–25
  health and, 4–5, 26
  impersonal, 23, 175
  interpersonal, 3–4, 23, 144, 174, 194,
    206–207
  intrapersonal, 19–20. *See also* Self-talk
  mediated, 13–16, 25, 43, 88, 151, 189
  meta-, 127
  models of, 9–16, 17

organizational, 25–26
presentational, 25–26
principles of, 18–22
rules of, 18, 92–93
small group, 24, 233–234, 236–237
supportive, 76, 77–80, 135. *See also* Other-oriented communication
work and, 3
Communication Ethics and Universal Values
  (Christians and Traber), 8
Communication interaction pattern, 247–249
Communication Principles for a Lifetime,
  18–22. *See also* Adaptation; Listening;
  Responding; Self-awareness
  family relationships and, 204–205
  friendships and, 204
  nonverbal communication as, 20–21,
    105–108
  verbal communication as, 21
  workplace relationships and, 205–206
Communication triage, 123
Compacting, of statistics, 319
Comparisons, social, 41–42
Competence, 7–9
  intercultural communication, 161–162
  and self-awareness, 33
  of speaker, 409
Complementary relationship, 180, 218
Complexity principle, 329
Compliments, 187
Compromiser (group role), 242
Computer-generated presentation aids,
  366–367
Computer-mediated communication (CMC),
  88, 189
Computer terms, 64
Computing style, of conflict management, 220
Conclusions, 337–338, 343
Concrete meaning, 63–65
Concrete words, 353
Conditional language, 78
Condon, C., 64
Conflict, interpersonal
  assertive/aggressive communication and,
    218–220
  functions of, 217–218
  managing, 220–225, 272
  in groups/teams, 236–237
  types of, 214–216
Conflict phase, of group development,
  249–250, 251
Confrontational style, 221
Connection versus autonomy, 212–213
Connotative meaning, 63, 64
Conrad, Joseph, 398
Conscious competence/incompetence, 33
Consensus, in groups/teams, 270–273
Constructive conflict, 215–216
Contemporary English Version Bible, 60
Content, of communication, 18, 133–134
Content-oriented listener, 118, 119
Context(s), 12, 102–103
  and barriers to listening, 124–125
  cultural, 151–152
  meanings and, 65
Control, in relationships, 180, 217–218
Conversational narcissism, 186–187
Cooley, Charles Horton, 37
Cooperative style, 221
Coordinator (group role), 242

Correct words, 354
Cottle, Michelle, 41
Courtship readiness, 97
Covey, Stephen, 32, 48
Creativity, in problem solving, 268
Credibility, of speaker, 337, 408–410
Credo for Communication Ethics, 9
Criteria
  for evaluating web sites, 311–312
  in problem solving, 267
Criticism, 122–123
"Cultural Uses and Interpretations of Silence"
  (Braithwaite), 100
Culture(s), 91, 148–151
  communication principles and, 24
  conflict and, 217
  contexts of, 151–152, 153
  emotions and, 193
  ethnocentrism and, 157–158
  expectations of, 22
  and groups/teams, 252
  humor and, 386
  language and, 68
  listening styles and, 120
  meanings and, 65
  movement during speech delivery and, 359
  organizational patterns and, 332
  prejudice and, 160
  self-concepts in diverse, 35
  similarities/differences among, 158–159,
    161–167
  touch and, 100
  use of time and, 154, 156, 279
  values of, 152–156, 217, 252
Culture shock, 151
Cybersex, 211

Darwin, Charles, 96
Databases
  full-text, 313–314
  newspaper, 314
Dating, virtual, 198–199
"Death of Reading, The" (Barton), 415
Decentering, social, 126–127, 165
Decentralized power, 155
Declarative sentence, 306–307
Decoding, 11
Deductive reasoning, 412–413
Deep-breathing techniques, 299
"Deep Throat," 320
Defensive communication, 76–77
Definition, of terms, 317
De-intensification stage, of relational de-
  escalation, 207, 209
Delivery, speech
  methods of, 350–352
  nonverbal, 357–362
  presentation aids and, 362–370
  tips for, 296–300, 371
  verbal, 353–355
Delivery cues, 344
Democratic leaders, 276
Demosthenes, 350
Denotative meaning, 63, 64
Derived credibility, 410
de Saint-Exupéry, Antoine, 132
Description(s)
  versus evaluation, 77
  responding with, 131–132
  as supporting material, 316, 317

Desensitization, systematic, 299
Destructive conflict, 215
Deviate, group, 247
Dewey, John, 266
Dialect, 361
Dialectical perspective, 211–213
Diana, Princess of Wales, 409
Direct perception checking, 54–55
Directories, web, 302, 310
Dissonance, cognitive, 402
Distracting style, of conflict management, 220
Dodd, Carley, 151
Dominance cues, 107–108
Dominator (group role), 243
Doohan, Eve-Anne, 131
Drama, in delivery, 355
Drawings, as presentation aids, 364
Duck, Steve, 209
DVDs, as presentation aids, 365–366
Dyad, 24
Dynamism, of speaker, 409

E-resumés, 443
Ear appeal, 354
Ebonics, 66
Education Research Complete, 314
Ego conflict, 216
Ego identity, 43
Egocentric, 164
Either-or fallacy, 412
Ekman, Paul, 94, 99, 359
Elaboration likelihood model (ELM), 404–405
Elaborator (group role), 242
Electronic communication. *See* Mediated communication
ELM, 404–405
Emblems, 96
Emergence phase, of group development, 250, 251
Emerson, Ralph Waldo, 172
Emoticons, 88, 181
Emotion expresser (group role), 243
Emotional Intelligence (Goleman), 122
Emotional noise, 121–122
Emotions
    conflict and, 222–223
    culture and, 193
    gender and, 193–194
    masking of, 99–100
    nonverbal messages and, 87–88
    paraphrasing of, 134–136
Empathy, 78, 165–166. *See also* Other-oriented communication
    listening and, 129
    responding with, 132–136
Employability, and communication, 3
Encoding, 11
Encourager (group role), 242
English language learners, 149
Entertaining purpose, 304
Environment, physical, 102–103
Ethic(s), 8–9
    adaptation and, 148, 167
    sources of, 10
    touch, 100
Ethnicity
    adapting to, 146
    biased language and, 69–71
    friendships and, 179
Ethnocentric cultural perspective, 162

Ethnocentrism, 157–158
Ethnorelative cultural perspective, 162
Ethos, 408–410
European Americans, and language bias, 70–71
Evaluation, 242
    versus description, 77
    of ideas, 263
    of web sites, 311–312
Evaluator/critic (group role), 242
Evidence, 331, 411. *See also* Supporting material
Exclusive language, 72
Expectancy violations model, 92
Expert power, 245
Expert testimony, 319
Explanations, as supporting material, 316–317
Exploration stage, of relationship, 207, 209
Expression–privacy dialectic, 213
Extelligence Creative Word Dictionary, 83
Extemporaneous speaking, 352
External noise, 124–125
Eye contact, 90–91, 98–99, 127, 357, 368

Face-and-emotion.com, 111
Face-to-face (FtF) encounters, 174–175, 178
    communicating attraction in, 181–182
    first conversation and, 183–185
    self-absorption and, 186
    uncertainty and, 182–183
Facebook, 180, 189, 440
Facial expressions, 96–97, 99–100, 111, 359–360
Fact, propositions of, 407
Factfinder, 397
Failing at Fairness: How America's Schools Cheat Girls (Sadker & Sadker), 41
Fallacies, 412–413, 428
Family
    communication in, 4
    importance of, 204–205
Fast, Julius, 93
Faulty consensus, 270
Fear appeals, 403–404
Fear contagion, 359
FedStats, 397
Feedback, 12, 131–132. *See also* Responding
Felt, Mark, 320
Feminine cultures, 155–156
Feminine listening style, 128
Field Guide to Gestures (Armstrong & Wagner), 96
Figurative analogy, 318
Figurative language, 354–355
Fillion, Bryant, 257
Final summary, 335
Fine, Jeffrey, 190
Fisher, Aubrey, 249
Flirting cues, 97
Focus groups, 238–239
Follower (group role), 243
Fonts, in computer-mediated communication, 88
Force field analysis technique, 267, 268
Formatting, of computer-mediated communication, 88
Foxworthy, Jeff, 53
Friedman, Thomas, 150
Friends, 75
Friends with benefits relationship (FWBR), 203

Friendships
    ethnicity and, 179
    gender and, 190–191
    importance of, 202–204
Friesen, Wallace, 94, 99
Frost, Robert, 105
FtF encounters. *See* Face-to-face encounters
Full-text database, 313–314
Functional approach
    to group communication, 261
    to leadership, 274–275
Funnel (questioning) sequence, 433–435
FWBR, 203

Gardner, Howard, 224
Gatekeeper (group role), 243, 283–284
Gay community, 149
    bias and, 145
    as co-culture, 150
Gender
    adapting to, 143–145
    bias and, 72–73, 353
    emotions and, 193–194
    friendships and, 190–191
    listening and, 128
    perception and, 52
    self-concept and, 39
    self-esteem and, 40–41
Gender-neutral language, 73
General purpose, 304
Generalization, hasty, 412
Generation, 147–148, 149
Generation Me: Why Today's Young Americans Are More Confident, Assertive, Entitled—and More Miserable than Ever Before (Twenge), 46
Generation X, 147, 148, 149
Generic term, 72–73
Gestures, 90–91, 95–98, 357–358
Gestures: Do's and Taboos of Body Language Around the World (Axtell), 96
Gibb, Jack, 76
Gide, André, 162
GIGO, 262
Ginsberg, Ruth Bader, 316
Giovanni, Nikki, 355
Giving-in style, 220
Gladwell, Malcolm, 160, 268
Globalization, 150
Goals
    of conflict, managing, 224
    of meetings, 281
    of small groups/teams, 233, 234, 237, 261–262
Golden Rule, 9
Goleman, Daniel, 122, 132
Google Alert, 440
Google Scholar, 310
Government documents, 314–315
Grammar, 60, 62
Graphs, as presentation aids, 365
Grave-dressing, 209–210
Gray, John, 143
Group deviate, 247
Group observer role, 243
Groups, 232–234. *See also* Small groups
    communication in, 23–25
    conflict in, 236–237
    identity within, 39
    leadership of, 273–279

roles in, 239–241, 242–243
types of, 237–239
use of time by, 280
U.S. minority, 149. *See also specific groups*
Groupthink, 270–273
Gudykunst, William, 164
Gunny-sacking, 79–80

Habituation, 299
Hall, Edward T., 103–104, 150, 152
Handouts, 369
Handshake index, 89
Haptics, 100
Hard evidence, 331
Harmonizer (group role) 242
Harris, Tina, 179
Harvey, John, 188
Hasty generalization, 412
Hawking, Stephen, 123
Hawkins, Katherine, 257
Health communication, 4–5, 26
Hearing, 115
Helical model of communication, 17
Help seeker (group role), 243
Heterosexist language, 72, 74
Hierarchy of needs, 403
High-context cultures, 152, 153
Hindenburg, 380
Hinduism, moral code of, 9
Hirokawa, Randy, 261
Hispanic Americans, 149
History Channel Archive of of Speeches, 375
Hocker, Joyce, 215
Hofstede, Geert, 150, 153, 154
Holmes, Janet, 187
Homophobia, 72, 74, 75, 145
Honesty
    nonverbal messages and, 88–89
    relationships and, 78, 135
    self-esteem and, 47
Hookup, versus FWBR, 203
Hoover, J. Edgar, 68
Horney, Karen, 34
Horton, Scott, 317
How We Think (Dewey), 266
Howe, Neil, 147
HTML format, 443
Huddleston, Angela, 194
Hughes, Mikayla, 203
Human communication, 6–7. *See also* Communication
Humor, 386, 389
Hyperlink, 311, 443
Hypothetical illustration, 316
Hypothetical questions, 433

"I" statements, 77, 223–224, 284
Identity. *See* Self-concept
If-then statement, 404
Illusion of transparency, 297
Illustrations, 315–316
Illustrators, 96–97
Immediacy, 106, 181
Impersonal communication, 23, 175
Impromptu speaking, 351–352
Imus, Don, 69–70
Inclusion, 180
Inclusive language, 73–74
Incompetence, and self-awareness, 33
Indeed (search engine), 310

Indexes
    newspaper, 314
    periodical, 313
Indirect perception checking, 54
Indirect persuasive factors, 404–405
Individual roles within groups, 240, 243
Individualistic cultures, 153–154
    conflict and, 217
    groups/teams and, 252
Individualization stage of relational de-escalation, 207, 209
Inductive reasoning, 411
Infante, Dominic, 219
Infinite interpretation, 120
Inflection, 361
Infoplease, 397
Information-gathering interview, 430, 443–444
Information giver/seeker (group roles), 242
Information management, 223–224
Information overload, 123
Information-processing barriers to listening, 123–124
Informative purpose, 304
Informative speech(es)
    audience interest in, 385–389
    checklist for, 396–397
    clarity of, 383–384
    memorable, 390–391
    organizational strategies for, 381–383
    sample, 392–393, 448–450
    types of, 378–381
Ingham, Harry, 192
Initial credibility, 409–410
Initial preview, 333
Initiation stage, of relationship, 207–208
Initiator/contributor (group role), 242
Inner speech, 4, 44–45, 122, 164, 223
Integration–separation dialectic, 212–213
Intensification stage, of relationship, 207, 208
Interaction
    communication as, 12
    of group/team, 247–249, 265, 283–284
Interactive strategy, 183
Intercultural communication, 151, 171. *See also* Culture(s)
Intercultural communication competence, 161–162
Interlibrary loan, 315
Internal previews, 333
Internal summaries, 334–335
International Communication Association, 29
International Listening Association, 139
Internet, 13–16. *See also* Web sites
    communication organizations on, 29
    cybersex and, 211
    identity and, 43
    meetings and, 238, 277, 278, 286, 289
    relationships on. *See* Online relationships
    as source of speech topics, 325
    speech mills on, 314
    supporting material on, 310–312
Internet-speak, 60
Interpersonal attraction, 177–182
Interpersonal communication, 3–4, 23, 44
    and de-escalation of relationships, 208–211
    definition of, 174–176
    and initiation of relationships, 176–187, 206–208
    and maintenance of relationships, 187–194
Interpersonal power, 180, 217–218

Interpretation
    infinite, 120
    perception and, 51
Interpreter, 386
Interracial Communication (Orbe & Harris), 179
Interrupting, 130
Interviewer, responsibilities of, 444–446
Interviews
    conducting, 444–446
    preparing for, 436–444
    structure of, 432–435
    types of, 430–432
Intimacy
    relationship escalation and, 207, 208
    self-disclosure and, 190
Intimacy stage of relationship, 208
Intimate space, 103
Intrapersonal communication, 19–20. *See also* Self-talk
Introductions, 335–337, 343
Inversion, in delivery, 355
Inverted funnel (questioning) sequence, 434–435
Invitation, appeals to, 97–98
Irresolvable conflict, 216
Islam, moral code of, 9

James, William, 36
Job interview, 431–432, 436–443
Johari window, 192–193
Johnson, David, 32, 188
Joker (group role), 243
Jones, Paula, 75
Jourard, Sidney, 188, 193
Journalists' Six Questions method, 266
Journals, professional, 313
Judaism, moral code of, 9
Just-in-time (JIT) approach, 132

Kale, David, 159
Keenan, Mabel A., 30
Keillor, Garrison, 438
Keller, Helen, 75
Kellett, Peter, 214, 216
Kennedy, Florynce R., 326
Kennedy, John F., 99, 101, 296, 355
Kenrick, Douglas, 53
Kerry, John, 360
Kiesler, Sara, 16
Killer inch problem, 267
Kincannon, Louis, 149
Kinesics, 95–98
King, Larry, 446
King, Martin Luther Jr., 101
Klepper, Michael, 389
Kluckhohn, Clyde, 158
Knapp, Mark, 209
Kraut, Robert, 16

Labels
    self-, 39–40
    words as, 66–67
LaFasto, Frank, 235
Laissez-faire leaders, 276
Language, 20, 60–62. *See also* Grammar; Symbols; Words
    bias in, 69–75
    central idea and specific, 307
    figurative, 354–355
    nature of, 62–65

Language *(Cont.)*
  and paralanguage, 101
  power of, 65–69
  sign, 66, 86
  supportive relationships and, 76–79
Lao Tsu, 279
Larson, Carl, 235
Lasswell, Harold, 10, 12
"Last Lecture" (Pausch), 318, 334–335
Lavaliere microphone, 360
Lay testimony, 319
Layder, Derek, 33
Leadership, group/team, 273–279
Learning
  collaborative, 237
  principles of adult, 390
Learnthenet.com, 289
Lebra, T. S., 120
Legitimate power, 245
Lesbian community, 149
  bias and, 145
  as co-culture, 150
Lessing, Doris, 316
"Lethal Aspects of the Male Role, The" (Jourard), 193
Lewis, C. S., 8, 140, 142, 159
Library, supporting material in, 312–315
Library of Congress classification system, 313
Lie detectors, 98
Life coaching, 185–186
Lindbergh, Anne Morrow, xxviii
Line graph, 365
Lippman, Walter, 250
"Listen" (Anonymous), 135–136
Listening, 21–22, 125–131
  barriers to, 120–125, 130
  as communication principle, 21–22
  conflict and, 224
  elements of, 115–117
  importance of, 114–115, 204, 445
  improving, 125–131
  questioning and, 133, 163, 185
  self-absorption and, 186–187
  styles of, 117–119, 120, 128
  for topic ideas, 302–303
  as work skill, 3
Literal analogy, 317
Literary quotations, 319
Logical fallacy, 412
Logos, 408, 411–413
Long-term maintenance attraction, 177
Long-term time orientation, 156
Love.com, 199
Luft, Joe, 192
Luvcoach, 199
Lying, detecting, 98, 102

Magazines, 313
Main ideas, 307–309
  in introduction, 337
  organizing, 328–330
  reinforcing, 390–391
Manuscript speaking, 350–351
Maps, as presentation aids, 364
Markers, territorial, 104
Masculine-as-generic language, 72–73
Masculine cultures, 154, 155–156
Masculine listening style, 128
Maslow, Abraham, 33, 403

Mass communication, 25
Matching hypothesis, 179
Material self, 36
Matsuba, M. Kyle, 43
Matures (generation), 147
McCain, John, 65, 355
McConnell, John H., 3
McCroskey, James C., 324
Mead, George Herbert, 37–38
Mead, Margaret, 234, 258
Meanings, 6, 63
  concrete versus abstract, 63–65
  denotative versus connotative, 63, 64
Mediated communication, 13–16, 25, 43, 88, 151, 189
Mediation services, 229
Meetings, 279–281
  interaction in, 283–285
  structure of, 281–283
  virtual, 286, 289
Mehrabian, Albert, 87, 88, 105–107
Memorized speaking, 351
Men Are from Mars, Women Are from Venus (Gray), 143
Men's Health, 41–42
Mental summaries, 123, 129
Messages, 11
  creation of, 13
  exchange of, 12
  recorded, 116
  transfer of, 10–12
Messer, Lucas, 353
Meta-communication, 127
Metadiscussion, 284
Meta-message, 127
Metaphors, 64, 354
Metcalf, Bob, 294
Michigan State University Vincent Voice Library, 375
Microphones, 360
Microsoft Office, 64
Microsoft Word, 64
  outlining in, 340
  thesaurus in, 389
Millennials, 147, 149
Miller, Courtney Waite, 216
Miller, Gerald, 216
Mind, Self, and Society (Mead), 37
Mindfulness, 164
Minority groups, U.S., 149. *See also specific groups*
Minto, Mary, 441
Misplaced authority, appeal to, 413
Model trap, 36, 41–42
Monochronic, 280
Monroe, Alan, 350, 416
Montgomery, Barbara, 211, 212
Monthly Catalog of U.S. Government Publications, 315
Moral code, religious, 9
Morrison, Kelly, 203
Mosvick, Roger, 285
Mother Teresa, 122, 123
Motivated sequence, 416–419
Motivation, audience, 387–388, 402–405, 416–419
Movement
  as nonverbal communication, 95–98
  in speech delivery, 358–359
Moyers Bill, 315, 355

MP3 files, as presentation aids, 366
Murrah Federal Building memorial, 79
Murray, Henry, 158
MySpace, 189, 440

Narcissism, 46, 186–187
Narcissistic Personality Inventory, 46
National Association for Self-Esteem, 57
National Bibliography of U.S. Government Publications, 315
National Board of Medical Examiners, 175
National Communication Association, 9, 29
National Forum on People's Differences, 83
Native Americans, 149
Nay, Sherry, 416, 417
Needs
  of audience, 403, 416–417
  of potential employer, 439
Negative visualization, 417
Nelson, Robert, 285
Network patterns, of small group communication, 247–249
Neutral audience, 419–420
New York Supreme Court, 204
Newspaper index, 314
Newspaper Source, 314
9/11 commission, 271
Nixon, Richard, 99
Noise, 11–12, 21
  emotional, 121–122
  external, 124–125
Nominal group technique, 269
Non sequitur, 413
Nonconfrontational style, 220–221
Nonverbal communication, 6–7, 86–87, 91
  attitudes and, 87–88
  codes of, 94–105
  conflict and, 223
  functions of, 89–91
  perception checking and, 93
  relationships and, 89
  rules of, 92–93
  using and interpreting, 21, 105–108
  verbal communication and, 88–89, 90
Nonverbal transition, 334
Norms, 241, 244
Notes, speaking, 343–344
Nouwen, Henri, 132, 165–166
Novelty versus predictability, 213

O'Keefe, R., 64
Obama, Barack, 65, 336, 400
Omission, in delivery, 355
Online relationships, 175, 176, 178, 198–199
  communicating attraction in, 181–182
  first conversation and, 183–185
  proximity and, 180
  self-absorption in, 186
  uncertainty and, 182–183
Open-ended questions, 77, 433
Openness
  versus closedness, 213
  in teams, 235
Operational definition, 317
Opinion giver/seeker (group role), 242
Opinions, as supporting material, 319
Oral citation, 320
Orbe, Mark, 179
Organization
  audience and, 333–335

of informative speech, 381–383
of main ideas, 328–330
perception and, 51
of persuasive speech, 414–419
of supporting material, 330–332, 343
Organizational communication, 25–26
Orientation phase, of group development, 249, 251
Orienter (group role), 242
Orwell, George, 354
Other-oriented communication, 6–7, 21–22, 78, 164–167, 263–264. *See also* Adaptation; Listening; Responding
Outline, 339–344
Oxford English Dictionary, 72

Pacific Islanders, 149
Paralanguage, 101
Parallel relationship, 218
Parallelism, 355
Paraphrasing
of content, 133–134
of emotions, 134–136
Passive strategies, for reducing uncertainty, 182
Pathological Internet usage (PIU), 43
Pathos, 408, 413–414
Pauling, Linus, 230
Pausch, Randy, 318, 334–335
Pauses, in speech, 361
People-oriented listener, 118
Pep talk, mental, 299
Perception, 48–52
Perception checking, 93
conflict and, 224
direct/indirect, 54–55
in workplace, 205–206
Performance interview, 430–431
Performance visualization, 299–300
Periodical indexes, 313
Periodicals, 313–314
Peripheral persuasive factors, 405
Perry, M., 64
Personal attack, 412
Personal coaching, 185–186
Personal Report of Communication Apprehension (PRCA-24), 324
Personal space, 103
Persuasion, 400–401
Persuasion interview, 431
Persuasive purpose, 304, 405–406
Persuasive speech(es)
adaptation and, 419–421
audience motivation and, 402–405
central idea of, 406–408
checklist for, 427–428
organizing, 414–419
purpose of, 405–406
sample, 421–424, 450–451
supporting, 408–414
topic of, 405
Philosophypages.com, 428
Photographs, as presentation aids, 364
Physical attraction, 178–179
Physical attractiveness
self-concept and, 36
self-esteem and, 41–42
Physical delivery, 357–359
Physical environment, 102–103

Pie graph, 365
Pitch, of voice, 360–361
Pitts, Leonard, 71
Placating style, of conflict management, 220
Plain text file, 443
Platinum Rule, 133
Polarization, 69, 73
Policy, propositions of, 407–408
Policy question, 266
"Politics and the English Language" (Orwell), 354
Polychronic, 280
Porter, Richard, 91, 159
Positional cues, 97
Positive appeals, 404
Positive silence, 102
Positive visualization, 417
Positivity, and self-esteem, 47
Post-American World, The (Zakaria), 302
Post hoc, ergo propter hoc, 412
Post-interaction stage, of relational de-escalation, 207, 209–210
PostSecret (Warren), 194
Posture, 95–98, 359
Power
culture and distribution of, 154, 155
types of, 180, 217–218, 245–246
"Power of Music, The" (Tisino), 392
PowerPoint, 366–367
Predictability versus novelty, 213
Preening behaviors, 97
Pre-interaction awareness stage, of relationship, 207
Pre-interaction phase, of listening, 126
Prejudice, 160. *See also* Bias
Preparation outline, 339–343
Presentation, 295–296
central idea of, 305–307
conclusion of, 337–338, 343
delivery of. *See* Delivery, speech
introduction of, 335–337, 343
main ideas of, 307–309, 390–391
organizing, 328–335, 343, 381–383, 414–419
outlining, 339–344
purpose of, 303–305
speaker anxiety and, 296–300
supporting material for. *See* Supporting material
topic of. *See* Topic
Presentation aids, 362–363
guidelines for, 368–370
for informative speech, 388–389
types of, 363–367
Presentational communication, 25–26
Preview, 333
Primacy principle, 329, 333, 421
Primary group, 237
Primary tension, 249
Probing questions, 433
Problem solving
in groups/teams, 235, 238, 264–273
orientation toward, 224–225
Problem-and-solution organization, 330, 415
Problem-solving groups, 238
Problem-solving interview, 431
Procedural technician (group role), 242
Process functions, of leaders, 274, 275
Processing rate, 123
Professional job skills, 436–437

Project911.com, 139
Proof, 411
Prophecy, self-fulfilling, 43, 45
Propositions, 406–408
Proxemics, 103–104
Proximity, in relationships, 179–180
Pseudoconflict, 216
Public space, 103
Purposes, of presentations, 303–305. *See also* Goals
general, 303–304
persuasive, 405–406
specific, 303, 304–305
Putnam, Linda, 252
Puzzability.com, 83

Quasi-courtship behavior, 97
Questions
communication barriers and, 163
interview, 433–435, 440–441, 442, 445–446
listening and, 133, 163, 185
policy, 266
relationship development and, 185–186
Quinn, Daniel, 2, 20
Quintilian, 409
Quorum, 283
Quotations
humorous, 389
on Internet, 347
literary, 319

Race
biased language and, 69–71
U.S. census categories for, 71
Raffetto, Mary Kate, 448–450
Rancer, Andrew, 219
Rate
processing, 123
speaking, 361, 386
Reader's Guide to Periodical Literature, The, 313–314
Reading, for topic ideas, 302–303
Reasoning, 411–413
by analogy, 411
Rebound effect, 54
Receiver, of message, 11
Receiver apprehension, 124
Recency principle, 329, 333
Receptive audience, 419
Reciprocal borrowing privileges, 315
Reciprocity, in self-disclosure, 188
Recognition seeker (group role), 243
Recorded messages, 116
Recorder (group role), 242
Red herring, 413
Redmond, Mark, 165
Redundancy, in informative presentation, 390
Reference resources, library, 314
Referent power, 245
Reflective thinking, 266–273
Reframing, 45–47
Refutation, 416
Regulators, 97
Rehearsal
with presentation aids, 368
speaker anxiety and, 298
tips for, 361, 371
on videotape, 363
Reinforcement phase, of group development, 250–251

Index

Relational dialectics, 211–213
Relationship Coaching chatroom, 199
Relationship dimension, of communication, 18
Relationships, 174–176
  of choice, 176
  of circumstance, 176
  conflict in. *See* Conflict, interpersonal
  development of, 206–210
  escalation/de-escalation of, 207–210
  importance of, 202–206
  initiating, 176–187, 206–208
  language and, 68–69, 76–77
  maintaining, 187–194
  nonverbal communication and, 89
  online. *See* Online relationships
  self-esteem and, 47
  symmetrical, 218
  tensions in, 211–213
  in workplace, 205–206
Religions
  biased language and, 69–71
  ethics and, 9
Remembering, 116–117
Repetition, in delivery, 355
Responding to communication, 12, 21–22, 117
  with description, 131–132
  with empathy, 132–136. *See also* Other-oriented communication
  friendship and, 204
  importance of, 114–115
Response latency, 102
Results-driven structure, of groups, 262
Resumé, 437–439, 443
Retail environments, 102–103
Revolution from Within: A Book of Self-Esteem (Steinem), 40
Reward power, 245
Rewarding communicator, 92
Rhetoric, 25, 419
Rhetoric, The (Aristotle), 25, 400
Rogers, Carl, 132
Roles
  identity and, 39
  in groups/teams, 239–241, 242–243
Roosevelt, Eleanor, 161
Roosevelt, Franklin D., 292, 409
Rowling, J. K., 296
Rubin, Jeffrey, 222
Ruet, Buey, 336
Rules
  of communication, 18, 92–93
  for groups/teams, 234, 241
  versus norms, 244
Russert, Tim, 370

Sadker, David, 41
Sadker, Myra, 41
Safire, William, 355
Samovar, Larry, 91, 159
Sapir, Edward, 62, 84
Sapir–Whorf Hypothesis, 62
Sargent, Stephanie, 128
Satir, Virginia, 4, 204–205
Save as command, 64
Schutz, Will, 180
Search engine, 310–311
Seashore Index of Group Cohesiveness, 256–257
Second guessing, 118
Secondary tension, 250

Secret Lives of Men and Women (Warren), 194
Seinfeld, 92
Seinfeld, Jerry, 45
Selecting, in listening, 115
Selection, and perception, 50–51
Self, 33
Self-absorbed communicator style, 186–187
Self-awareness, 19–20, 32–34
  perception and, 48–55
  self-concept and, 34–40
  self-esteem and, 40–48
Self barriers, to listening, 121–123
Self-centeredness, 46
Self-concept, 34–40
  confirmation of, 208
  Internet use and, 43
Self-concept clarity, 40
Self-confessor (group role), 243
Self-disclosure, 187–193, 199
Self-esteem, 40–48, 57
Self-expectations, 42
Self-focus, 121
Self-fulfilling prophecy, 43, 45
Self-image. *See* Self-concept
Self-labels, 39–40
Self-reflexiveness, 39
Self-silencing, 219
Self-talk, 4, 44–45, 122, 164, 223
Senge, Peter, 277
Sentence, declarative, 306–307
Separation stage, of relational de-escalation, 207, 209
Serial arguments, 216
Seven Habits of Highly Effective People, The (Covey), 32
Sex, versus gender, 40
Sex and the City, 210
Sexist language, 72
Sexual attraction, 178
Sexual orientation
  adapting to, 145
  biased language and, 72, 74
Shannon, Claude, 10, 12
Sheats, Paul, 240
Shimanoff, Susan, 18
Shonbeck, Katrina, 180, 189
Short-term initial attraction, 177
Short-term time orientation, 156
Sign language, 66, 86
Signposts, 333, 338, 343
Silence, 101–102
Silent brainstorming, 269–270, 301–302
Similarity, and attraction, 177–178
Similes, 354
Simmons, Andy, 440
Simple conflict, 216
Simple words, 354
Situational approach to leadership, 277
Slanguage, 60, 66
Small group communication, 24, 233–234, 236–237
Small groups, 233–234
  conflict in, 236–237
  development of, 249–253
  dynamics of, 239–249
  enhancing meetings of, 279–286
  functions of, 260–264
  leadership of, 273–279
  problem solving in, 235, 238, 264–273
  versus teams, 232

Social Cognition Laboratory, 57
Social comparison, 41–42
Social decentering, 126–127, 165
Social groups, 239
Social networking sites, 180. *See also specific sites*
Social penetration model, 191–192
Social roles, 239–240, 242–243
Social self, 36–37
Social space, 103
Social support
  expressing, 135
  health and, 4–5
Socioeconomic class, and biased language, 75
Soft evidence, 331
Solomito, Amy, 450–451
Solution orientation, 220, 221
Source, of communication, 10–11
Southern Methodist University, 91
Space, 102, 103–104
Spatial organization, 329–330
Speaker anxiety, 296–300
Speaking notes, 343–344
Special-interest pleader (group role), 243
Specific purpose, 304–305
Specific words, 353
Specificity principle, 331
Speech. *See* Presentation
Spender, Dale, 62
Spiritual self, 37
Springer, Jerry, 121
Stability, of relationship, 207
Stability–change dialectic, 213
Stacks, 312
Stagnation stage, of relational de-escalation, 207, 209
Standard outline format, 339, 344
Stanford University, 229
Starr, Robert Bruce, 199
Stationary microphone, 360
Statistics, as supporting material, 318–319, 347
Status, in group, 244
Steinberg, Mark, 216
Steinem, Gloria, 40
Stereotypes, 53–54, 160
Stewart, John, 38
Stories, from literature, on Internet, 347
Strauss, William, 147
Streaming video, as presentation aid, 365
Structure
  of interview, 432–435
  of group/team, 265
  of meetings, 281–283
  of words, 354–355
Structured problem, 265
Study groups, 237
Styles approach to leadership, 275–277
Summaries, 123, 129, 334–335
"Superbugs" (Wright), 421–424
Supporting material
  acknowledging, 320–321
  in informative speech, 386–387
  organizing, 330–332, 343
  sources of, 310–315
  types of, 315–319
Supportive communication, 76, 77–80, 135. *See also* Other-oriented communication
Surgeryfindit (search engine), 311
Suspension, in delivery, 355
Sweeney, John J., 319
Swingers, 51

Syllogism, 411
Symbolic displacement, 216
Symbolic interactionism theory, 37–38
Symbolic self-awareness, 32–33
Symbols, 6, 20–21, 62–63
Symmetrical relationships, 218
Synchronous communication, 15
Syntax, 60, 62
Systematic desensitization, 299

T-chart, 272–273
Taking It Global, 171
Tannen, Deborah, 143
Task functions, of leaders, 274, 275
Task roles, 239, 242
Taylor, Dalmas, 191, 192
T-E-A-C-H, 379
Teams, 24–25, 234
    communicating in, 234–237
    development of, 249–253
    dynamics of, 239–249
    enhancing meetings of, 279–286
    ethics of, 237
    functions of, 260–264
    ground rules for, 241
    leadership of, 273–279
    problem solving in, 235, 238, 264–273
    versus small groups, 232
    use of time by, 280
    types of, 237–239
Television advertising, 400, 418
Tension
    primary/secondary, 249–250
    in relationships, 211–213
Tension reliever (group role), 243
Terminal credibility, 410
Terms
    computer, 64
    defining little-known, 317
    generic, 72–73
Territorial markers, 104
Territoriality, 102, 104–105
Testimony, expert/lay, 319
Texas A&M University, 271
Texas State University, 229
Text messaging, 60, 210
Therapy groups, 238
Thesaurus, 354, 389
Thoreau, Henry David, 319
3-1-2 drafting strategy, 328
Time
    as listening barrier, 124
    use of in groups/teams, 280
Time orientation
    of culture, 154, 156, 279
    of listener, 118
Timeliness, of response, 132
Ting-Toomey, Stella, 217
Tisino, Alton, 391
Tolstoy, Leo, 202
Topic
    central idea and, 306
    introducing, 336–337
    selecting/narrowing, 300–303, 385–386, 405
Topical organization, 329
Totalnews.com, 325
Touch, 100–101
Touch ethic, 100
Traber, Michael, 8

Tracy, Larry, 328
Trait approach to leadership, 274
Transaction, communication as, 13
Transformational approach to leadership, 277–279
Transition, 333–334
Transparency, illusion of, 297
"Tribute to the Dog" (Vest), 355
Trigger words, 76
Truman, Harry, 167
Trustworthiness, of speaker, 409
Tunnel (questioning) sequence, 435
Turmoil stage, of relational de-escalation, 207, 209
Turner, Lynne, 213
Twain, Mark, 160
Twenge, Jean, 46

Unbiased words, 353
Uncertainty avoidance, and culture, 154, 155
Uncertainty-reduction theory, 182–183, 189
Unconscious competence/incompetence, 33
Understanding, 116
University of Virginia, 229
Unreceptive audience, 420–421
Unstructured problem, 265
URL, domain in, 311
U.S. Census Bureau, 71, 179
U.S. Presidential inaugural speeches, 375

Value(s), 34, 406
    cultural, 152–156, 217, 252
    generational, 148
    propositions of, 407
Van Gundy, Arthur, 265
Verbal abuse/aggression, 219
Verbal communication, 6–7. *See also* Language; Words
    nonverbal communication and, 88–89, 90
    using and interpreting, 20–21
Verbal transitions, 333–334
Vertical search engine, 310–311
Vest, George Graham, 354–355
Videotape(s)
    as presentation aids, 365–366
    rehearsing on, 363
Vigilant thinkers, 261
Virtual dating, 198–199. *See also* Online relationships
Virtual group/team, 238, 277, 278
Virtual Meeting Assistant, The, 289
Virtual meetings, 286
Visualization, 45, 417
Vivid words, 354
Vocal cues
    emotional meaning and, 87
    in lying, 98
Vocal delivery, 360–361
Vocalics, 101
Voice, 101–102
Volume, 360

Wagner, Melissa, 96
Walker, Alice, 73
Warren, Frank, 194
Watson, Kitty, 118, 119
We've Got to Start Meeting Like This! (Mosvick and Nelson), 285

"We" language, 78
Weaver, James, 118
Weaver, Warren, 10, 12
Web directories, 302, 310
Web log, 189
Web pages, 302
Web site(s)
    to answer embarrassing questions, 83
    evaluating, 311–312
    on facial expressions, 111
    on facilitating meetings, 289
    on fallacies, 428
    on famous speeches, 375
    for groups/teams, 257
    on informative resources, 397
    on intercultural communication, 171
    on listening skills, 139
    on literary stories, 347
    on mediation services, 229
    on quotations, 347
    on seldom-used words, 83
    on self-esteem, 57
    on statistics, 347, 397
    on stereotyping, 57
    on topic ideas, 325
    on virtual dating, 198–199
    on word games, 83
Weber, Ann, 188
Welty, Eudora, 200
West, Richard, 213
Wheel network pattern of small group communication, 248–249
White, Leah, 353
Whitman, Walt, 348
Whitworth, Laura, 185–186
Whorf, Benjamin Lee, 62
Wiesel, Elie, 355, 412
Wiio, Osmo, 17
Wikipedia, 311
Wilmot, William, 215
Withdrawing style, of conflict management, 220
Women's Sports Foundation, 36
Word pictures, 388
Words
    meanings of, 63–65
    pictures with, 388
    power of, 20–21, 65–69
    structure of, 354–355
    supportive relationships and, 76–77
    as symbols, 62–63
    types of, 353–354
Workplace relationships, 205–206
World Communication Association, 29
Worldview, 151, 158
Wright, Austin, 421–424

Yahoo!, 310, 325
Yancey, Maggie, 296, 304, 309, 316, 340–343, 361, 371
"You" statements, 77, 284
YouTube, 365

Zakaria, Fareed, 302
Ziggs (search engine), 311
Ziglar, Zig, 441
Zucker, Jeff, 319

Credits

Page 4, top: © Ryanstock/Getty Images; bottom: © Stuart Pearce/AGE Fotostock; 8, © AlisonWright/Stock Boston; 18, Skjold/The Image Works; 23, © Jeff Greenberg/PhotoEdit; 36, © Michael Newman/PhotoEdit; 38, © John Giustina/Getty Images; 41, © David Grossman/The Image Works; 42, © Mary Kate Denny/PhotoEdit; 60, © Kevin Dodge/CORBIS; 67, © Stockbyte; 70, © James Marshall/The Image Works; 72, © Kathy Ferguson/PhotoEdit; 79, © Chris Hamilton/Aurora & Quanta Productions, Inc.; 87, © G & M David de Lossy/Getty Images; 91, © Stuart Ramson/AP Images; 96, © Bill Bachman/The Image Works; 101, © Gary Wagner/Stock Boston; 117, Image Source/Getty Images; 122, © Bruce Miller/Alamy; 123, © Santoni Sasak/Liaison/Getty Images; 129, © Supernova/Getty Images; 130, © Michael Newman/PhotoEdit; 144, © BananaStock/SuperStock; 152, © Ali Yussef/AFP/Getty Images; 159, © AlisonWright/Stock Boston; 166, © Eastcott Momatiuk/The Image Works; 177, © PhotoDisc/Getty Images; 182, © Deborah Jaffe/Getty Images; 184, © Photos.com/JupiterImages; 188, Bill Aron/PhotoEdit; 193, © Jon Feingersh/AGE Fotostock; 203, © Jack Kurtz/The Image Works; 206, © Blend Images/JupiterImages; 208, © Jon Riley/Getty Images; 220, © Michael Newman/PhotoEdit; 233, © Corbis RF/JupiterImages; 240, © Bob Daemmrich/Stock Boston; 245, © Bonnie Kamin/PhotoEdit; 250, © Andrew Wakeford/Getty Images; 261, © Sean Cayton/The Image Works; 263, © Goodshoot RF/JupiterImages; 269, © Spencer Grant/PhotoEdit; 280, © Bill Aron/PhotoEdit; 297, © Robert Spencer/Getty Images; 301, © BananaStock/JupiterImages; 306, © Bob McLaughlin/The Image Works; 317, © David Young-Wolff/PhotoEdit; 318, © Bob Daemmrich/The Image Works; 334, © Daily Progress, Kaylin Bowers/AP Images; 336, © John Sommers/Reuters/CORBIS; 338, © Ron Chapple Stock/Photolibrary; 343, © Bob Daemmrich/Stock Boston; 355, Courtesy of the Greater Warrensburg Area Chamber of Commerce & Visitors Center; 356, © Steve Helber/AP Images; 358, © Michael Newman/PhotoEdit; 366, Photo of Paul Laurence Dunbar from Ohio Historical Society, Dunbar House Web page is used with permission of the Ohio Historical Society; 367, © Paul Sakuma/AP Images; 369, © Alex Wong/Getty Images for Meet the Press; 382, © Bob Daemmrich/Stock Boston; 385, © David Paul Morris/Getty Images; 386, © Bob Daemmrich/The Image Works; 389, © BananaStock/SuperStock.